# Human biology

# Human biology

## AN INTRODUCTION TO HUMAN EVOLUTION, VARIATION, GROWTH AND ECOLOGY

### Second edition

BY

G. A. HARRISON
*Department of Biological Anthropology, University of Oxford*

J. S. WEINER
*M.R.C. Environmental Physiology Unit, London School of Hygiene and Tropical Medicine, University of London*

J. M. TANNER
*Department of Growth and Development, Institute of Child Health, University of London*

N. A. BARNICOT
*late of the Department of Anthropology, University College, University of London*

WITH A CHAPTER ON 'THE EVOLUTION OF HUMAN SOCIETY'
BY

V. REYNOLDS
*Department of Biological Anthropology, University of Oxford*

OXFORD UNIVERSITY PRESS · 1977

*Oxford University Press, Walton Street, Oxford* OX2 6DP

OXFORD  LONDON  GLASGOW  NEW YORK
TORONTO  MELBOURNE  WELLINGTON  CAPE TOWN
IBADAN  NAIROBI  DAR ES SALAAM  LUSAKA  ADDIS ABABA
KUALA LUMPUR  SINGAPORE  JAKARTA  HONG KONG  TOKYO
DELHI  BOMBAY  CALCUTTA  MADRAS  KARACHI

FIRST EDITION 1964
SECOND EDITION 1977

Human Biology.—2nd ed.
Index.
ISBN 0-19-857164-X
ISBN 0-19-857165-8  Pbk.
1. Harrison, Geoffrey Ainsworth
573.2          GN281
Human evolution
Physiology

PRINTED IN GREAT BRITAIN
BY BUTLER & TANNER LTD
FROME AND LONDON

# Foreword

P. B. MEDAWAR

WHAT is 'human biology'? Is it just an attempt to market old and familiar goods under a new name or does it indeed stand for a new conception of the natural history of mankind?

'Conception' is, I think, the right word; for human biology is not so much a discipline as a certain attitude of mind towards the most interesting and important of animals. Human biology portrays mankind on the canvas that serves also for other living things. It is about men rather than man: about their origin, evolution, and geographical deployment; about the growth of human populations and their structure in space and time; about human development and all that it entails of change of size and shape. Human biology deals with human heredity, the human genetical system, and the nature and import of the inborn differences between individuals; with human ecology and physiology, and with the devices by which men have met the challenges of enemies and of hostile environments. Human biology deals also with human behaviour—not with its wayward variations from one individual to another, but rather with the history and significance of, for example, family life; or of love, play, showing off, and real or sham aggression. Finally, and most important—because most distinctively human—it must expound and explain the nature, origin, and development of communication between human beings and the non-genetical system of heredity founded upon it.

Man (if I may relapse into universals) is a very proper study for biologists, particularly for beginners in biology. Many of the so-called 'principles' of biology can be taught as well upon a human text as upon any other, and some can be taught better. Man is the great amateur among animals. Where other animals have specialized in ways that commit them to one or another particular and restricted way of life, human beings have retained their amateur status. As nearly as any animals can be, they are biologically uncommitted, disengaged. As mammals go we are quite simple creatures, without any very noteworthy anatomical (or genetical or developmental) singularity not already foreshadowed by lower primates. Binocular vision and the crossing-over of the optic tracts, the enlargement of the cerebral cortex, the liberation of the forelimbs for manipulation, the prolongation of childhood—these are not innovations of mankind, but exaggerations of tendencies already to be seen in apes. As it happens human beings, considered as a biological enterprise, succeeded—but only just, and only quite recently. People forget or do not realize how precarious was the hold of human beings upon the earth for their first many tens of thousands of years. One way or another the biologist has much to learn from human biology, and chiefly this lesson: that the distinction he has been wont to draw between Nature, on the one hand, remote and wild, and, on the other hand, Man and his works, is one that damages his understanding of both.

Human biology is also a very proper study for medical students and for those who practise medicine. The 'biological principles' bandied about by an earlier or older generation of physicians are, most of them, nonsense—among them the deep-seated and all but ineradicable belief that natural dispositions and adaptations are well-nigh perfect, and that sickness and other disabilities are part of a long-drawn-out expiation for leaving nature and leading unnatural lives. A case can be made for thinking out medical education anew and rebuilding it upon a foundation of human biology. Certainly medical education has defects, of both a medical and an educational character, that cannot be made good by mere juggling with syllabuses. How much of what is to be read in the following pages can be found in a medical syllabus today? A good deal, somewhere or other, as it happens, but not where it ought to be, at the *beginning* of the medical course, where plenty of room could be found for it if only the dogfish and the earthworm could be given their *congé* after so many years of undistinguished service to the medical profession. As matters stand, human genetics makes its appearance, if at all, as a supernumerary course fitted somewhere into the clinical years; demography is mixed up with sanitation, and human ecology is treated as something which, though it may help us to understand the medical predicaments of foreigners, is barely relevant to our own cosy domestic medical scene.

For all these various reasons I believe that this excellent text, by four authors who are pioneers of human biology and who have made distinguished contributions to the subjects they expound, will have an important influence on the development of all the individual sciences that deal with mankind.

# Preface to the second edition

SINCE the publication of the first edition of this book in 1964 there have been many advances in our understanding of the biological organization of past and present human populations, and although the book is essentially an introductory one, concentrating more on principle than on factual detail, many sections had become out of date. In this revised edition, we have remedied this generally and particularly by extensive rewriting of the sections on Primate and human evolution, genetic variation at the molecular and biochemical level, and the nature of growth and adaptation processes. There is also a completely new chapter on Primate behaviour and the origins of human society, written by Dr. V. Reynolds. We have, however, preserved the original structure and tried to avoid much expansion in length.

We wish again to record our thanks to the staff of the Oxford University Press for their continued help and forbearance in the production of the book.

We should like to acknowledge the help of the following colleagues of the late Professor Barnicot who assisted him in the revision of his chapters for this new edition. Dr. J. Beard, Professor and Mrs. Walter Bodmer, Mr. David Coleman, Dr. Irvine Johnson, Dr. A. E. Mourant, Dr. M. F. Perutz, Dr. D. A. Price Evans, Dr. J. H. Renwick, Professor A. G. Steinberg, Mr. A. Stevens, Mr. D. Tills, and Mrs. H. Weymes. All the diagrams for Professor Barnicot's section were drawn by Mr. Tony Lee, and Miss Mary Tinegate deserves special thanks for doing the typing and helping with various other aspects of the work. Acknowledgement is also due to the various authors and publishers (mentioned individually in the text) who kindly allowed reproduction of figures.

Professor N. A. Barnicot completed the revision of his section of this book only a few weeks before his death after a long illness in the spring of 1975. We wish here to pay tribute to our former colleague whose scholarship and courage were our inspiration. His loss is irreplaceable not only to the continuance of this book but also to the whole of biological anthropology in Great Britain.

*Oxford*                                                                      G.A.H.
*1976*                                                                         J.S.W.
                                                                               J.M.T.

# Contents

x   **Contents**

## Part III: Biological variation in modern populations
N. A. BARNICOT

# Part IV: Human growth and constitution

J. M. TANNER

# Part V: Human ecology

J. S. WEINER

xiv    **Contents**

# Part I: Human evolution

G. A. HARRISON

J. S. WEINER

AND

V. REYNOLDS

# 1. Patterns of evolution

## Evolutionary principles

THE evolutionary theory, to all intents and purposes now completely verified, means that all organisms are related to one another and have shared a common ancestry at some time since the origin of life. However heterogeneous the organic world, past and present, may appear to be, in the final analysis it is solely the product of a single evolutionary process. Charles Darwin and Alfred Russel Wallace were the first to appreciate fully the nature of this process.

The essence of the 'Darwinian' argument can be expressed in the following way. All organisms possess a reproductive capacity to increase their numbers progressively; yet the size of populations at least for long periods of time typically remains more or less constant. More young are produced than survive and reproduce, and in the sense that many of those born do not themselves contribute offspring to the next generation, there is a 'struggle for existence'. No two individuals are ever absolutely identical, and in every population there is considerable variation. It may, therefore, be expected that the distinctive characteristics of some individuals will increase their chances of leaving offspring. If these characteristics are inherited it follows that they will appear more frequently in the next generation and that the differential survival and fertility has produced a genetic change in the population. This is the process of evolution by 'natural selection'. Although change from one generation to the next is usually very slight, it is now held that the whole of evolution can be explained by the action of natural selection on the fresh variability that is constantly arising in populations, since the time available is so long. The origin of life took place at least 1000 million years ago.

The study of natural populations of plants and animals, in conjunction with theoretical advances, has illuminated the dynamics of selection; and the nature of the heritable variation that characterizes all populations is also now well understood. It is the mode of origin of this variation about which least is known. As will become evident later, part of it arises by the recombination of hereditary factors already present in a population, but the ultimate source of all new variation is the relatively rare phenomenon of gene and chromosomal mutation, and the causes of this process are still obscure. It can, however, be said with certainty that exposure to a given environment does not elicit mutations which confer an advantage in that environment. Indeed, most mutant genes and chromosomes are disadvantageous in the struggle for existence and are, therefore, eliminated by natural selection; only rarely does one arise which fortuitously produces an advantageous effect and by being favoured becomes established in a population. Those that are thus favoured are likely to produce only small alterations in the development of the individual, and this is why evolutionary change tends to be gradual. It is true that polyploidy has been responsible for the abrupt origin of new plant forms largely because in them the unique genetic constitution can be transmitted to a number of individuals by vegetative reproduction. However, macro-changes of this kind have probably played less of a part in the evolution of animals. The rarity of mutation gives stability to the genetic structure of populations and imposes an inertia on evolutionary change.

## Evolution and ecology

However, when it is found that, in any given time, one form has evolved more slowly than another, it must not be automatically assumed that it has been restricted by the supply of new variation, i.e. by genetic inertia. The factor that controls the rate of evolutionary change in populations over any fairly long period of time is more likely to be the nature of the selective forces operating. The reason that Protozoa have not evolved into men is not because their genetic potentialities were more limited than man's protozoan ancestor but because selection has not operated to change them in this direction. There exist a whole host of ecological niches for which the protozoan grade of organization is the best, and in these niches selection has operated to maintain and improve this organization. It is evident, then, that while the origin of variation is not environmentally orientated, the consequence of the whole evolutionary process is that organisms are fitted for the exploitation of the multiplicity of environments available to them.

The requirements for different environments are often mutually exclusive. Thus, for instance, a form perfectly adapted to an arboreal existence cannot at the same time be the fastest runner, the best burrower, and the strongest swimmer, though in some particular habitat advantage may be gained if a creature can perform all these activities reasonably well. The exclusiveness of adaptations has far-reaching evolutionary consequences. When natural selection has adapted an organism to some particular niche, it can only be displaced by another under special circumstances, since the necessary adaptations can only be evolved in the niche, and a form which has never occupied it cannot have them, and is unlikely to succeed in competition with one that has. Looked at in a different way, this also means that forms which have become adapted to one mode of life tend to be committed to it. When this happens, extinction will follow the disappearance of the habitat. However, sometimes an adaptation which is acquired for a particular niche at the same time facilitates survival in many others, and makes possible their colonization. This will happen if the overall advantage gained by a form with a 'general adaptation' is greater than the disadvantage of not having 'special adaptations'. The ability of the Eutheria to displace earlier mammals from their niches is probably directly attributable to their greater reproductive efficiency. Only in Australia, and to a lesser extent in South America, have marsupials persisted. Australia was separated from the main landmass of Eurasia before the origin of placental mammals; it had no eutherian fauna until discovered by man. The evolution of the human brain, as will be seen, had its origin as an arboreal adaptation, but it also opened many other evolutionary opportunities and is largely responsible for man's unique ability to alter the environment to suit his needs.

It is important at this stage to stress the differences between structures which are 'specialities' for particular modes of life and those which are in varying degrees evolutionary 'specializations'. The long neck of the giraffe, the single-toed condition of the horse, the structure of the limbs of crossopterygian fish, and the brain of man are all specialities in that they are distinctive features of the forms concerned, but whereas the first two seem to have restricted the evolutionary potentialities of their possessors and may be termed 'specializations', the last two opened immense evolutionary opportunities. The difficulty in recognizing specializations is that the judgements must be *post hoc*. In the Devonian the crossopterygian fish might have been regarded as very highly specialized, but in fact the group gave rise to the tetrapods.

The quality of specialization resides not so much in the genetic potentialities of an organism as in the ecological circumstances in which it exists. At the beginning of the Tertiary, when there were no large fast-moving predatory land animals, an arboreal form might very easily colonize a terrestrial habitat. In the mid-Tertiary it would have little chance of adopting such a mode of life without some attribute to compensate for its lack of speed, since by this time the constant struggle for existence in the terrestrial fauna had led to the evolution of fast-moving carnivores. One of the principal reasons why evolutionary trends are typically irreversible is because evolution itself produces constant changes in the environments of organisms. Another is that every stage in an evolutionary sequence must confer a greater survival value than the preceding one. This is an important corollary of the evolutionary mechanism, since it means that if there exist a number of possible ways of meeting an environmental demand, and one of these is 'chosen' by an organism because the appropriate

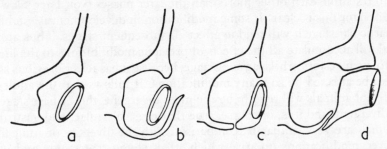

FIG. 1.1. Diagram illustrating the various relations of tympanic ring (os ectotympanicum) to the tympanic bulla. (a) Primitive mammalian condition in which the ring is exposed and the floor of the tympanic cavity is unossified: (b) the Lemuriform type in which the ring is enclosed within an osseous bulla; (c) the Lorisiform and Platyrrhine type in which the ring is placed at the surface and contributes to the formation of the outer wall of the bulla; (d) the Catarrhine type (also seen in the modern Tarsius) in which the ring is produced outwards to form a tubular auditory meatus. (From Le Gros Clark, *The antecedents of man*, Edinburgh University Press, 1959.)

variation for it arose first, the evolutionary destiny of that form is committed to the amplification of this way, even though its evolutionary potentialities both in the short and the long term are more limited than those of some other way. Organisms cannot 'await' the most appropriate variation to become available; selection operates on the variation that arises as it arises. In the lemurs the tympanum is suspended within the auditory bulla in the ectotympanic ring. In the higher Anthropoidea it is placed at the end of an external auditory meatus which is formed by the ectotympanic being placed superficially to the bulla and drawn out to form a tube. If the contrast solely represents two different ways of protecting the tympanum it is difficult to envisage how one state could be transformed to the other, since gradual change would produce intermediate stages, such as still exist in lorises and New World monkeys, in which the tympanum was more exposed to damage (Fig. 1.1).

## Evolution and development of the individual

The characteristics of an individual which confer an evolutionary advantage on him compared with others have clearly come into being during his growth and development. It may, therefore, be said that evolutionary change takes place through the modification of life-histories. A similarity in the development of the individual (ontogeny) and its evolutionary history (phylogeny) was recognized by early comparative anatomists and led Haeckel to propound his famous law that 'ontogeny recapitulates phylogeny'. If this law were strictly true it would mean that the evolutionary modification of life-histories has progressed solely by the addition of developmental stages to the end of ancestral life-histories. Such hypermorphosis does occur but it is by no means the only way by which development is modified in evolution. Any stage in development will be changed if the consequence is to produce a better-adapted individual. It is true, however, that the early phases in the life-histories of different animals tend to resemble each other more than the later phases (von Baer's law) and the reason for this is clear. If some modification in development is established at a particular stage it will tend to affect all subsequent stages. Thus an adult animal will accumulate all the effects of previous modifications to the life-histories of its ancestors, whilst a young stage, because it has fewer previous stages, will not be affected by so many modifications. It follows that the adult form of different animals will tend to be the most divergent, the earliest stages the least divergent, and it is, of course, true that eggs, blastulae, and gastrulae of all animals are very similar by comparison with the diversity of adult forms. However, modifications do arise which affect young stages only and which, instead of being carried on to affect the adult, are subsequently lost. They come into being solely to increase the chances of survival of the individual during its development. The evolutionary modification of life-histories to produce such larval or embryonic adaptations is termed 'caenogenesis'. It has played a particularly important role in the evolution of insects, where early development in many forms takes a course without relevance to the differentiation of the imago, but it has also occurred in other groups. The evolution of foetal membranes and their modification to form a placenta in mammals was a caeno-genetic adaptation of far-reaching consequence. The head shape of most adult mammals is long and narrow, and not very different from that of reptiles. But to facilitate passage through the birth canal the mammalian foetal head is globular.

It is now recognized that the evolutionary modification of ontogeny can occur in a completely contrary direction to that envisaged by Haeckel; that instead of changes occurring by the addition of stages to a life-history, they may be effected by the abbreviation of development. All that is necessary before such abbreviation can happen is for sexual maturity to occur at progressively younger morphological stages; and selection would favour variations that caused this, if it meant that an organism could escape adult specializations which, as a result of environmental change, had begun to limit its chances of survival. Evolutionary modification involving the retention of infantile stages, is known as neoteny. The very origin of the chordates probably resulted from a combination of caenogenic and neotenous processes, since it is believed that they arose from a larval Echinoderm, and it is likely that human head-shape originated by retention of the foetal shape. There are in fact many characteristics about the

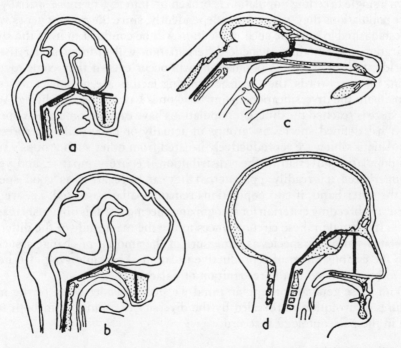

FIG. 1.2. A series of sections showing the angle which the head makes with the trunk in: (a) embryo dog; (b) embryo human being; (c) adult dog; (d) adult human being. The embryonic curvature is preserved in adult man (after Bolk). (From De Beer, *Embryos and ancestors*, Clarendon Press, 1958.)

structure of man which are 'infantile' and may well have arisen by neoteny as, for example, the retention of cranial flexure, the forward position of the foramen magnum, the flatness of the face, the small face as compared with the braincase, and the hairlessness of the body (Fig. 1.2).

## Types of evolutionary change

Evolutionary change can be considered as involving two processes, though both are occurring simultaneously. First, there is change in a single lineage, as one generation replaces another. This type of change may be termed 'phylal'. (Anagenesis (Rensch) has a similar meaning but also implies that there is evolutionary progress along the lineage.) Secondly, there is the break-up of lineages so that a diversity of contemporaneous forms is evolved. Such change has been termed 'diversification' or 'kladogenesis'.

It is evident that differentiation of populations can only occur if they are isolated from one another, otherwise the mutant genes which arise within one population will spread to the others. In phylal change time alone separates descendant populations from their ancestors, but for diversification to occur other isolating factors must come into play. At first the important one is spatial separation. This may come about in a variety of ways, but, whatever the cause, when a single breeding population is broken up into two or more spatially discrete populations they will evolve independently, since the mutant genes which are established in any one such population will be confined to it. If the spatial separation is maintained, genetic differentiation will proceed so far that no hybridization between the populations will occur even if they come together again. In other words, the extrinsic isolating factors are no longer necessary to maintain the diversification, as intrinsic ones have come into being. When this stage is reached the different populations have each become a new species. Mayr has defined species as 'groups of actually or potentially interbreeding populations which are reproductively isolated from other such groups'. When two populations overlap in their distribution, i.e. are sympatric, and yet do not interbreed, it is readily apparent that they can be regarded as 'good' species. On the other hand, if two populations remain spatially isolated, i.e. are allopatric, the breeding criterion for recognizing specific status is obviously inapplicable. It is usual in these circumstances to use the magnitude of the difference in related sympatric species as a measure of the amount of change associated with the establishment of reproductive isolation. The same type of criterion has to be employed in the recognition of palaeospecies.

With these general concepts in mind we shall consider some of the major features of evolution as revealed by the diversity of animal form both today and in the palaeontological record.

## Adaptive radiation

The continual changes both inorganic or organic that occur in natural environments have constantly offered animals a series of new evolutionary opportunities. The colonization of the land by plants made possible the evolution of land animals. The decline of the reptiles at the end of the Mesozoic, probably caused by climatic changes, offered innumerable ecological niches to the early mammals who, because of their homeothermy, were able to withstand these changes. The re-establishment of a land bridge between North and South America at the end of the Tertiary offered opportunities for northern forms to exploit the southern ecologies. (The opportunities for movement in the opposite direction were, of course, also offered by these geological changes, but only a few forms such as the opossum were biologically equipped for seizing them.) Further, as already mentioned, a particular adaptation occasionally turns out to be of general value and opens up many ecological niches to its possessor. When a group of animals is presented with such a multiplicity of opportunities, it undergoes rapid diversification. All the available niches are colonized and the occupants of each of them acquire, through natural selection, the particular adaptations demanded. This is the phenomenon of adaptive radiation. The reptiles were the first vertebrates to become fully independent of an aquatic existence, and during the Mesozoic they adaptively radiated into the innumerable habitats available on land. This radiation produced not only a diversity of herbivorous and carnivorous dinosaurs varying in size from many small thecodonts to the enormous *Brontosaurus* and *Tyrannosaurus*, but also the lizards and snakes, the crocodiles, the pterodactyls and even groups such as the turtles, ichthyosaurs and plesiosaurs which re-colonized the sea. Indeed, the very origins of the birds and the mammals must be regarded as part of this enormous reptilian radiation.

In the Tertiary, the radiation of the reptiles was replaced by that of the mammals. On a smaller scale, fine examples of adaptive radiation are offered by the marsupial mammals in Australia, by the lemurs in Madagascar, and by a small group of birds, Darwin's finches, on the Galapagos Islands. In Australia the basic marsupial stock not only gave rise to a variety of terrestrial herbivores and carnivores but also to arboreal, gliding, burrowing, and aquatic forms. The radiation in Madagascar resulted in the evolution of such aberrant lemurs as *Megaladapis* and *Daubentonia* and in the Galapagos a number of different species of finch, each adapted to some particular food supply available on the islands, was produced by natural selection acting on one ancestral stock. Singling out such cases of adaptive radiation is not meant to imply that the phenomenon is a restricted one. All diversification in the broadest sense is adaptive radiation, but it is usual to restrict the term to those cases where a single stock of animals has given rise, more or less contemporaneously, to a variety of different forms each very obviously adapted to its ecological niche.

## Convergence and parallelism
The adoption of some particular way of life imposes upon an animal a very specific structure. A permanently burrowing animal, for instance, cannot be

large, it must possess a streamlined body-form with no weak segments, and if it cannot move round earth particles or eat its way through soil, it needs mechanically strong limbs for excavation. Eyes are valueless and may be positively disadvantageous; they are typically lost or greatly reduced in burrowing animals. These are but a few of the requirements and consequences of a burrowing mode of life, and if other aspects of a subterranean ecological niche were specified, such as climatic conditions and available food supply, they would impose yet further limitations. Indeed, it is felt by some evolutionists that if all the aspects of an environment are specified, then one has also specified in detail all the attributes of animals that have become adapted to it. This could not be the case only if there exist more than one way of exploiting the niche or if inertia, either selective or genetic, has delayed the acquisition of the most efficient adaptations. In any case, it is evident that if the same ecological niche exists in two or more places, animals that occupy it will come to be similar, irrespective of whether or not they are closely related. When two forms are more alike than their ancestors, their evolution is said to be convergent. When they acquire the same characteristics independently, but these make them no more like each other than their ancestors were alike, their evolution has been in parallel. The distinction is only one of degree and parallelism is merely the limiting case of convergence. One of the first recognized examples of convergence was the similarity in the body-form of whales and fish, which results from the demands of a fast-moving aquatic existence. These characteristics are also now known to have been shared by the ichthyosaurs. The marsupial carnivores possess many characteristics in common with the placental carnivores as a consequence of their similar habits. Mammalian 'moles' have been evolved on at least three occasions, twice in the Insectivora and once in the marsupials. The evolution of the New World monkeys has been largely if not completely independent from that of the Old World monkeys and affords an example of parallelism, since the 'non-monkey' ancestors of both were also very much alike.

These examples could be multiplied many times over, for convergence is widespread in evolution. It is the cause of most of the difficulties in trying to determine the evolutionary history of a group whose fossil record is poor, since it obviously cannot be automatically assumed that a similarity between forms indicates a close evolutionary relationship. The convergence of the whales on fish is easily detected because despite it, whales still possess many more mammalian characteristics than fish ones, but if one knew nothing of amphibia and reptiles it might well have been concluded that whales were the most primitive mammals. Further, the reason that whales and fish are distinguishable is not merely that the amount of change needed to make them identical would be enormous (after all, whales like all mammals did have a fish ancestry), but because there are ecological niches in the sea which can be better exploited by marine mammals than by fish. When there is little difference in the ancestors of convergent forms it is often completely impossible to detect the convergence. In the case of the geographical variation within the human species, for instance, it may well be that the dark-skinned peoples of Melanesia and Africa acquired their many similarities from a common ancestor, but it is equally likely that they were convergently evolved as a result of similar selective forces in the two regions.

## Evolutionary trends
In general, interspecific competition increasingly particularizes ecological niches and intraspecific competition perfects their exploitation. Phylal change, therefore, characteristically involves the continual elaboration of the adaptations demanded by an ever more restricted mode of life, and lineages display quite distinct trends. These are very well evidenced in horse evolution, which is characterized by progressive increase in body-size, reduction in the number of digits, molarification of the premolar teeth, elaboration of the molar-tooth pattern, and increase in the height of the molar teeth. Similar trends occur in every other group of animals where the fossil record is good enough for them to be identified. The existence of the trends helps in the unravelling of the course of evolution. If, for instance, the origin of some lineage is obscure but among a possible group of ancestors, one displays incipiently characteristics which are amplified in the lineage, it is most likely to be the ancestral form.

It has been maintained that the existence of evolutionary trends indicated that organisms were 'driven from within' along certain evolutionary pathways. Indeed, the extinction of such forms as the sabre-tooth tiger and the Irish elk has been attributed to these inner drives taking the trend beyond the stage where it was adaptive. It was supposed that the canine teeth of sabre-tooths eventually became so long that animals could not bite effectively. However, it has been pointed out that the canines of the Oligocene sabre-tooth *Eusmilus* were relatively just as long as the Pleistocene *Smilodon*. As Simpson says, 'To characterize as finally ineffective a mechanism that persisted without essential change in a group abundant and obviously highly successful for some 40 000 000 years seems quaintly illogical.'

In discussing evolutionary trends it is worth while pointing out that there exist between different parts of an organism definite growth relationships, known as allometric relationships, and if one structure changes, others will also automatically change, by amounts depending upon the nature of the relationship. Of course, if a particular environment demands a change in a growth relationship, it will be produced. Much of the evolutionary change in horse dentition can be directly attributed to change in body-size, but in those horses that turned from a browsing to a grazing habit, a new relationship between tooth-height and -size was established since the great tooth wear that grass-chewing causes demanded the evolution of hypsodont teeth.

Whilst there is no unequivocal evidence favouring orthogenesis, i.e. intrinsic evolutionary drives, it is true, as already indicated, that evolutionary trends often lead organisms into specialization. All the stages in the evolution of the Irish elk were, in their overall effect, adaptive, but the great antlers, probably principally evolved by intraspecific reproductive competition, no doubt contributed to the animal's extinction. With such specialities a quite small change of conditions might tend to make them disadvantageous.

## Pre-adaptation

The evolution of a group of organisms is not only restricted by the opportunities that are offered by the environment but also by the capacity of the group to seize these opportunities before others do. It is not surprising that shore-living forms gave rise to the first land animals since they were in the habitat most favourably placed to colonize the land. But not all shore-living forms were able to seize this opportunity. The lamellibranch molluscs, for instance, have never given rise to any land animals, though they were apparently presented with much the same ecological opportunities as groups that did. It must not be concluded from this that there exist inherent limitations in the organization of animals which under all circumstances exclude them from certain ways of life. The reason that lamellibranchs never evolved land representatives is probably because other forms could more easily be modified by natural selection to occupy the land niches and having done so tended to exclude further colonization. Nevertheless, it may be said that the lamellibranchs were poorly pre-adapted to a land existence as compared with the gastropods or the crossopterygian fish, for example, which require relatively little modification of their organization to develop appropriate adaptations. There is nothing mystical about pre-adaptation. It is to be expected that some modes of life and the organizations they produce better fit an animal for seizing particular evolutionary opportunities than others, and the degree of their pre-adaptations has very much determined which of a group of animals has taken up a specific habit. As we shall see, the evolutionary success of man as a terrestrial animal owed much to arboreal adaptations, which turned out to be pre-adaptations for a certain type of terrestrial existence.

The phenomenon of pre-adaptation helps one to determine the evolutionary relationships between animals. If two forms adopt similar modes of life, such as, for instance, the lemurs and the lorises, it is likely that they were able to do this because they possessed similar pre-adaptations. These they may have acquired convergently but are more likely to have come from a common ancestry. Further, even forms with different modes of life probably had the same pre-adaptations if the demands of these different modes of life are met by the evolution of similar characteristics. It will be seen that many of the similarities between apes and man were evolved in parallel for different purposes. The mere fact that such similar changes occurred suggests common pre-adaptations.

One of the most general pre-adaptations seems to be small size, since most of the great radiations appear to have started from relatively small animals. This may well be because such animals typically have a short generation time which will tend to offset the limitations of genetic inertia and facilitate rapid evolutionary change.

## Rates of evolution

It is evident from the study of living forms and from the palaeontological record that there is no constancy in both the rate of phylal change or the rate of diversification. Some forms have persisted more or less unchanged over vast aeons of time, whilst others have evolved very rapidly. Further, a single lineage may change hardly at all during one period and then exhibit a burst of evolution. The present-day brachiopod *Lingula* is practically indistinguishable in its hard parts from the Cambrian *Lingulella*. In 80 million years the skeleton of the opossum has remained almost entirely unchanged whilst in the last 60 million of these years *Eohippus* has given rise to *Equus*. The Artiodactyles evolved much more slowly from the Eocene to the Miocene, than they did subsequently.

The rate of evolutionary change in a group is often expressed as the number of new genera which appear in unit time, e.g. per million years. This is a somewhat crude measure as, unlike the species, the taxonomic category 'genus' is largely an arbitrary one and differences which are regarded as of generic magnitude in one group may not be in another. However, this approach does afford estimates of comparative evolutionary rates which are not inconsistent with those obtained by more objective methods.

New genera arise both by phylal change and diversification, but if one considers only the former, it has been found that the rate of change in hoofed mammals during the Tertiary is of the order of one genus per 8 million years. For instance, in the horse lineage leading to *Equus*, eight genera have been recognized prior to the origin of *Equus*, which works out at one genus per 7·5 million years. The rate in many other groups of mammals including Primates is probably similar. On the other hand, forms like the hedgehog and tree-shrews are still very like the basic stock from which all eutherian mammals are descended.

As already indicated, these differential rates do not mean that the slowly evolving forms have been restricted by genetic inertia. Once an animal has become as perfectly adapted as possible to some particular ecological niche, natural selection will operate to maintain it unchanged as long as the niche remains unchanged. Rapid evolution occurs when many constantly changing habitats become available. It may therefore be presumed that the niches occupied by the opossum and the hedgehog have not changed radically since these forms first arose.

So far consideration has only been given to the rates of evolution of different animals, but different parts of an animal can also evolve at different rates. Thus, for instance, the foot of the horse *Hipparion* is very similar to that of its Miocene ancestor, but the teeth are strikingly different. (It is worth noting here that in other early Pliocene horses different stages have been reached. In *Hypohippus* neither foot nor teeth have changed much, whilst *Pliohippus* is advanced in both these structures.) Another example of differential rates of somatic evolution is found in *Necrolemur*, most of whose characters are those of a primitive tarsier but whose teeth have departed more from the ancestral type than any other tarsiiform. As will later be seen, human evolution can broadly be divided into three stages, first the assumption of bipedalism, secondly the reduction of the jaws, and finally the expansion of the brain. Admittedly there is considerable overlap, but one does find forms with perfect bipedal adaptations but with skull characteristics relatively unchanged from the ancestral anthropoid type. Even extant man combines many advanced features such as his brain, with some primitive ones like the general morphology of his forelimb. On the other hand, whilst different organ systems can evolve at different rates, at all times an animal must be adequately adapted to its way of life. This necessarily limits the amount of independent change that can occur. In particular, parts of a single functional unit must evolve together, and one does not find, for instance, mammalian upper jaws evolving at completely different rates from lower jaws. One of the facts that drew attention to the fraudulent nature of the Piltdown remains was the functional incompatibility of the jaws.

## Taxonomy

The function of the taxonomist is to identify, describe, name, and classify organisms. Every animal, when it is first discovered, is referred to a particular species, this to a particular genus, family, order, class, and phylum. These are the obligatory ranks; others such as suborder, infraorder, superfamily, subfamily, etc., may be used if the taxonomist finds that not all the information he wishes to convey about a group can be expressed in the obligatory categories (see, e.g. the classification of the Primates, p. 22).

There are three basic types of classification: (1) the key, (2) the phenetic or natural, (3) the phyletic (phylogenetic). The key classification is devised solely for identification purposes and in it very different forms might be grouped together just because they have one striking character in common. Examples of key classifications are the various *Faunas* and *Floras* which have been devised for identifying the animals and plants which inhabit a particular region or country. In contrast, the phenetic classification arranges organisms according to their degree of *overall* resemblance and hence was said to be a natural classification by the pre-Darwinians. In a phenetic classification the most similar forms are most closely grouped together and the most different are most widely separated. The difficulties involved in determining phenetic affinities are mainly technical. Methods are required for combining the differences in a large number of characters into a single expression of overall difference and only in the last 10–20 years or so have advances in statistics, such as the methods of multivariate analysis, made this objectively possible. Another difficulty is that not all characters are measurable in the same units so that transformations to some abstract scale are required. Further, with complicated 'geometries' like the structure, physiology, behaviour, and genetics of organisms, it is often difficult to recognize what in different forms is in fact comparable, and it has been known for characters which are merely mathematical correlates of each other to be treated as though they gave independent information about phenetic relationships. Nevertheless, one can set about establishing a phenetic classification of a group of animals in the same sort of way as one would compare a series of inanimate objects. No concern is given to how resemblances came into being. On the other hand, a phyletic classification attempts to group organisms according to their evolutionary relationships. If during the evolutionary process all lineages diverged from each other at the same rate, measures of overall similarities would also be measures of evolutionary relationship, and a phenetic classification would be the same as a phyletic one. However, whilst it is often true that the degree of similarity between forms indicates the closeness of their phyletic relationship, we have already seen that evolution produces the convergence of lineages as well as their divergence and that rates of change in different lineages and in the same lineage at different times are rarely constant. This means that forms may be similar, not because they have a recent common ancestor, but because they are convergent upon each other, and that large differences may indicate either slow divergence from a remote common ancestor or rapid divergence from a recent one.

Because evolutionary rates of divergence are not constant, there are two distinct types of evolutionary relationship, and failure to recognize this has frequently caused confusion in the past. All the similarities between organisms that are not due to convergence are due to their inheritance from a common ancestor, and one aspect of phyletic relationship is, therefore, the extent to which forms possess the same characters as a result of their ancestry. This type of relationship has been called 'patristic affinity'. However, forms may have little patristic affinity but still be closely related in the sense that they share a recent common ancestor. This situation arises when there is rapid evolutionary diversification. The genealogical relationship between forms has been referred to as 'cladistic affinity'. Fig. 1.3 indicates the difference between the two types of evolutionary relationship.

It is evident that unless the fossil record of a group of animals is to all intents and purposes complete, the taxonomist who wishes to establish the phyletic relationships in it has to make judgements about the likelihood of convergence

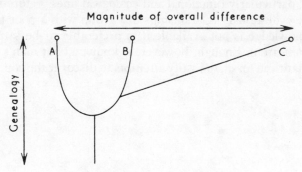

FIG. 1.3. Forms of phyletic affinity.

having occurred, probable rates of evolutionary change, and also whether certain changes are likely to have occurred at all. A number of general principles help in the making of these judgements, the more important of which are summarized as follows.

1. If a form appears late in the fossil record it is unlikely to be the ancestor of one that appears early. There is, however, the possibility that the apparently late form had long existed before its appearance in the fossil record in some region where conditions for fossilization were poor or which has not been explored. (The principal value of knowing the time of occurrence of different forms is to give direction to an evolutionary sequence.)

2. If two similar forms occur in regions that have long been geographically separated, the possibility of their being convergent is greater than if they occur in geographically contiguous areas.

3. If two similar forms inhabit the same type of ecological niche, there is a strong possibility that they are convergent.

4. If, on the other hand, the differences between two forms can be directly attributed to particular requirements for their different ecologies, it is likely that these differences would be evolved rapidly.

5. If some character is of value for many modes of life, i.e. is a general improvement, it is unlikely to be lost, and therefore a form with it is probably not ancestral to one without it.

6. If a progressive functional trend is recognizable in a series of forms, they are likely to be stages of the same lineage or of closely related lineages.

7. If two forms have evolved different ways of performing the same function, it is unlikely that one was derived from the other, particularly if it seems probable that the intermediate stages had lower adaptive values.

8. If the performance of some particular function necessarily determines the nature of a number of characters, forms which have one of these characters are as likely to have acquired the others by convergence as from a common ancestor. Such characters are necessary functional correlates and give no phyletic information at all.

These considerations show how necessary is a knowledge of all attributes of organisms, particularly functional and ecological ones, before it is possible to unravel the evolutionary relationships in a group with a poor fossil record. When this knowledge is not available it is preferable to be satisfied with a phenetic classification. Enough, however, is known about man's closest relatives, both extant and fossil, to justify attempts to discover the course of human evolution.

# 2. The primates

## Characteristics of Primates

WITH the cataclysmic decline of the reptiles at the end of the Mesozoic period, the early mammals, till then an inconspicuous group, were provided with a variety of evolutionary opportunities. Into the vacant ecological niches they adaptively radiated during the Tertiary (Table 2.1) making yet further opportunities for themselves as they evolved. The basic eutherian stock is the Insectivora, an order which is represented today by such forms as the hedgehog, shrew, and mole. All other placental mammals can be considered to have descended from the Insectivora (cf. p. 32), and most of those which colonized exclusively arboreal habitats acquired the same sort of adaptations for a tree-living existence and are known as the Primates. The similarity in these adaptations is no doubt largely due to the fact that they are all needed for one type of arboreal life. But those animals that seized the opportunity must have had the same potentialities and it can be reasonably assumed that they inherited these from a common ancestor. This, anyway, is the justification for regarding the Primates as a single phyletic as well as a phenetic group.

The order is comprised of the lemurs, now confined to Madagascar, the lorises with a distribution today in tropical Africa and Asia, the tarsiers represented by a single extant genus in the East Indies, the New World monkeys, the Old World monkeys, the anthropoid apes (including the gibbon and the three great apes—the orang-utan, the chimpanzee, and the gorilla), and man (Fig. 2.1(a) and (b)). Until recently most Primate taxonomists also included the tree-shrews of India and South East Asia in the order. They show many morphological similarities with the lemurs such as the bony conformation of the medial wall of the orbit and the general organization of the middle ear region. However, a number of characteristics have been found with appear to indicate an early separation in the phylogeny of tree-shrews and Primates, as, for example, the fact that the middle-ear conformation, although it superficially resembles the Lemuriform one, is composed of different bones. Nevertheless, tree-shrews seem to represent a level of organization very similar to that through which primates must have passed.

Many different classifications have been proposed. One of the most recent and authorative is that of E. L. Simons and the following scheme, in which many of the better-known genera, extant and fossil, are included, is based on it (Table 2.2).

The classical definition of the Primates is that of Mivart (1836) who specified the order as:

Unguiculate, claviculate, placental mammals with orbits encircled by bone; three kinds of teeth at least at one time of life; brain always with a posterior lobe and cal-

TABLE 2.1

## GEOLOGICAL TIME SCALE

| MILLIONS OF YEARS SINCE BEGINNING | ERAS | PERIODS | EPOCHS |
|---|---|---|---|
| 0·01 | CENOZOIC | QUATERNARY | RECENT |
| C.A. 2 | | | PLEISTOCENE |
| 5 | | TERTIARY | PLIOCENE |
| 23 | | | MIOCENE |
| 36 | | | OLIGOCENE |
| 54 | | | EOCENE |
| 65 | | | PALAEOCENE |
| 135 | MESOZOIC | CRETACEOUS | |
| 165 | | JURASSIC | |
| 205 | | TRIASSIC | |
| 230 | PALAEOZOIC | PERMIAN | |
| 280 | | CARBONIFEROUS | |
| 325 | | DEVONIAN | |
| 360 | | SILURIAN | |
| 425 | | ORDOVICIAN | |
| 505 | | CAMBRIAN | |
| | ARCHAEOZOIC | | |
| 2000 | PROTEROZOIC | | |

VERTEBRATE EVOLUTION:

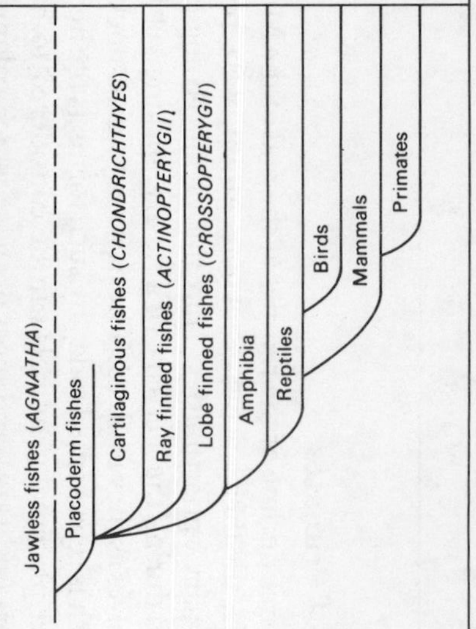

Primates
Mammals
Birds
Reptiles
Amphibia
Lobe finned fishes (CROSSOPTERYGII)
Ray finned fishes (ACTINOPTERYGII)
Cartilaginous fishes (CHONDRICHTHYES)
Placoderm fishes
Jawless fishes (AGNATHA)

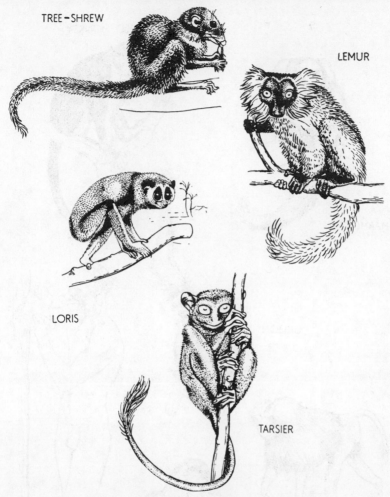

TREE-SHREW

LEMUR

LORIS

TARSIER

FIG. 2.1(a). The prosimian Primates.

carine fissure; the innermost digits of at least one pair of extremities opposable, hallux with a flat nail or none; a well marked caecum, penis pendulous, testes scrotal; always two pectoral mammae.

Not one of these characteristics is diagnostic. Most occurred in the basal mammalian stock and hence can be regarded as primitive; all are shared to some extent with a number of other mammalian forms, particularly some of the arboreal marsupials and the Insectivora. Moreover, not all forms which are usually classified as Primates have every one of these characters. *Daubentonia* in particular is highly anomalous, yet current opinion regards it only as a fairly recent specialization of the Lemuriform radiation in Madagascar. Further, if the family Tupaiidae (the tree-shrews) were included within the

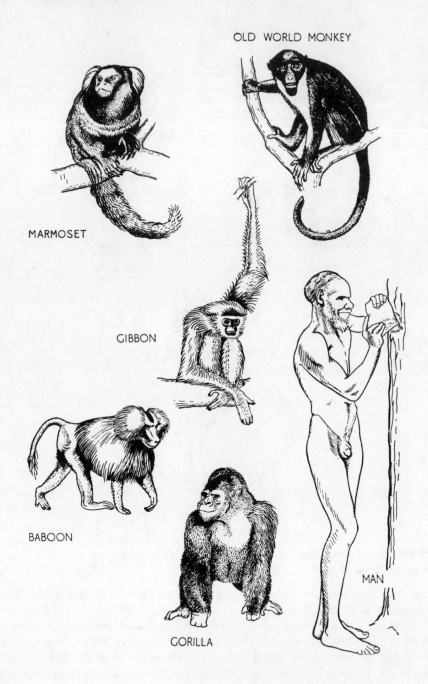

OLD WORLD MONKEY

MARMOSET

GIBBON

BABOON

GORILLA

MAN

FIG. 2.1(b). The anthropoid Primates.

order Mivart's criteria become even less discriminating. It is clear then that only in combination do Mivart's criteria define a Primate and that any one Primate may lack some of them.

From the general biological point of view it is more meaningful to consider the Primates in terms of their evolutionary trends. Those which characterize the group as a whole are almost solely determined by the arboreal mode of life. Even the forms which are now completely terrestrial show striking evidence of the arboreal period in their history. It is therefore of prime importance in understanding the biology of man to appreciate the effects of his arboreal ancestry.

The tendencies that are displayed to at least some extent in all Primates and which result from the arboreal heritage are as follows.

1. *Development of limbs as grasping organs.* Tree-living animals obviously require some special means of maintaining themselves in their precarious habitat. Some, like the squirrel, employ sharp claws for the purpose, but Primates have evolved prehensile hands and feet. These have arisen through increasing the independent mobility of the digits and in particular of the pollex and the hallux, which to varying degrees in different forms are opposable to the other digits. A truly opposable digit is one which can be completely turned on its axis so that its palmar surface lies against the palmar surface of the other digits. In New World monkeys the pollex has little opposability and in man, associated with his bipedalism, there is now none in the hallux. But in all Primates there is evidence that the limbs have or have had a greater branch-grasping ability than is found in other placental mammals. This ability is most developed in the extant lemurs and lorises in which the fourth digit rather than the third is the longest. A wider grip is thereby provided. In the Lorisinae, indeed, the second and third digits are markedly reduced so as not to interfere with this grip.

Another striking feature of Primates due to the grasping habit is the replacement of claws by flattened nails (unguiculate). Again there is considerable variation. In the living tree-shrews, and in the fossil Plesiadapids all the digits are clawed; in *Daubentonia* a nail occurs only on the hallux; in other lemurs the second pedal digit possesses a claw for toilet purposes and the nails of New World monkeys, particularly the marmosets, are sharply compressed. Nevertheless, there is a marked trend in Primates for the evolution of nails, and this results from the particular way they have adapted to the arboreal environment (Fig. 2.1).

Associated also with grasping is the expansion of the plantar pads which become covered with roughened skin. The primitive mammalian pattern is one of separate and well-defined pads, and this is preserved in most plantigrade forms. In Primates the pads have progressively merged to provide a large frictional surface and which gain support from the flattened nails. A prehensile tail has been evolved in some New World monkeys to afford yet another means of hanging on to the branches of trees.

TABLE 2.2

*A classification of the primates*

Order: PRIMATES
 Suborder: PROSIMI
  Infraorder: PLESIADAPIFORMES*
   Family: PLESIADAPIDAE* (Pal-Eoc)
    Subfamily: PLESIADAPINAE*                    *Plesiadapis**
    Subfamily: SAXONELLINAE*                     *Saxonella**
   Family: CARPOLESTIDAE* (Pal-Eoc)             *Carpolestes**
   Family: PAROMOMYIIDAE* (Cret-Eoc.)
    Subfamily: PAROMOMYINAE*                     *Paromomys*, Purgatorius**
    Subfamily: PHENACOLEUMURINAE*                *Phenacolemur**
   Family: PICRODONTIDAE?* (Pal)                *Pierodus**
  Infraorder: LEMURIFORMES
   Superfamily: ADAPOIDEA
    Family: ADIPIDAE* (Eoc)
     Subfamily: ADAPINAE*                        *Adapis*, Pronycticebus**
     Subfamily: NOTHARCTINAE*                    *Notharctus*, Pelycodus**
   Superfamily: LEMUROIDEA
    Family: LEMURIDAE (Rec)
     Subfamily: LEMURINAE                        *Lemur, Hapalemur*
     Subfamily: CHEIROGALEINAE                   *Cheirogaleus Microcebus*
    Family: INDRIIDAE (Pleist-Rec)
     Subfamily: INDRIINAE                        *Propithecus, Indri*
     Subfamily: HADROPITHECINAE*                 *Hadropithecus**
     Subfamily: ARCHAEOLEMURINAE*                *Archaeolemur**
    Family: DAUBENTONIIDAE (Rec)                 *Daubentonia*
    Family: MEGALADAPIDAE (Pleist)              *Megaladapis**
  Infraorder: LORISIFORMES
   Family: LORISIDAE (Mio-Rec)
    Subfamily: LORISINAE                         *Loris, Nycticebus, Arctocebus,*
                                                 *Perodicticus*
    Subfamily: GALAGINAE                         *Galago*
  Infraorder: TARSIIFORMES
   Family: TARSIIDAE (M.Eoc-Rec)
    Subfamily: TARSIINAE                         *Tarsius*
    Subfamily: MICROCHOERINAE*                   *Necrolemur*, Pseudoloris**
   Family: ANAPTOMORPHIDAE* (Eoc-Olig)
    Subfamily: ANAPTOMORPHINAE*                  *Tetonius*, Anaptomorphus**
    Subfamily: OMOMYINAE*                        *Omomys*, Hemiacodon*,*
                                                 *Rooneyia*, Teilhardina**

 Suborder: ANTHROPOIDEA
  Superfamily: CEBOIDEA
   Family: CEBIDAE (Olig-Rec)
    Subfamily: AOTINAE                           *Homunculus*, Aotus, Callicebus*
    Subfamily: PITHECINAE                        *Cacajao, Pithecia*
    Subfamily: ALOUATTINAE                       *Alouatta*
    Subfamily: CEBINAE                           *Cebus, Neosaimiri**
    Subfamily: CEBUPITHECINAE*                   *Cebupithecia**
    Subfamily: ATELINAE                          *Ateles, Lagothrix*
    Subfamily: CALLIMICONINAE                    *Callimieo*
   Family: CALLITHRICIDAE (Rec)                  *Callithrix*
   Family: XENOTHRICIDAE* (Pleist)              *Xenothrix**
  Superfamily: CERCOPITHECOIDEA
   Family: CERCOPITHECIDAE (Olig-Rec)
    Subfamily: CERCOPITHECINAE                   *Macaca, Papio, Cercopithecus,*
                                                 *Libypithecus**
    Subfamily: PARAPITHECINAE*                   *Parapithecus*, Apidium**
    Subfamily: COLOBINAE                         *Presbytis, Colobus, Mesopithecus**
  Superfamily: OREOPITHECOIDEA*
   Family: OREOPITHECIDAE* (Mio-L Plio)         *Oreopithecus*, Mobokopithecus**

Superfamily: HOMINOIDEA
Family: HYLOBATIDAE (Olig-Rec)
  Subfamily: PLIOPITHECINAE*                     *Pliopithecus**, *Limnopithecus**,
                                                    *Aeolopithecus**
  Subfamily: HYLOBATINAE                        *Hylobates, Symphalangus*
Family: PONGIDAE (Olig-Rec)
  Subfamily: DRYOPITHECINAE*                *Dryopithecus**, *Aegyptopithecus**,
                                                  *Propliopithecus**
    (uncertain status)                         *Oligopithecus**
  Subfamily: PONGINAE                           *Pongo, Pan, Gorilla*
  Subfamily: GIGANTOPITHECINAE*           *Gigantopithecus**
Family: HOMINIDAE (Mio-Rec)                    *Ramapithecus**, *Australopithecus**
                                                  *Homo*

\* Represents fossil forms.

(After E. L. Simons 1972.)

A variety of different means of locomotion are found among primates. These have been classified into (a) quadrupedalism as found in many monkeys; (b) bipedal walking as in man; (c) slow climbing as in lorises; (d) brachiation or arm-swinging, particularly evidenced in the gibbons, who move for about 80 per cent of their time in this fashion, but also displayed by the orang-utan, spider monkey, and to some extent by the chimpanzee; and (e) vertical clinging and leaping, which characterizes the locomotion of many prosimians and is defined by Napier and Walker as 'an arboreal leaping mode of progression during which the two hind limbs, used together provide the propulsive forces in locomotion. The trunk is held in vertical position before and after each leap; vertical supports are preferred.' Many living Primates, including prosimians, spend much of their time on the ground and some, like man, the gorilla, and the baboons, and their relatives have become essentially, but secondarily, terrestrial. This is usually associated with quadrupedalism, but man, of course, is an erect biped and 'vertical clingers and leapers' also tend to be erect when on the ground as they proceed by bipedal hopping. It may be noted here that when the African apes are being terrestrial they usually walk quadrupedally but use the knuckles of their forelimbs rather than the plantar surface of the hand—a form of locomotion known as 'knuckle walking'.

2. *Development of the forelimb as an exploratory organ.* The arboreal environment is complicated and irregular. Merely as a consequence of this, agile tree-living animals will tend to be capable of a wider range of limb movements than most mammals. The retention of a clavicle by Primates and the increased ability to pronate and supinate the forearm are partly to be explained in these terms alone. But because the arboreal environment is also precarious, awareness of

its irregularity will have very great survival value. Primates, therefore, have typically emancipated the forelimb from functioning solely for locomotion and support and have incorporated it into the exteroceptive sense-organ system as an exploratory device. This emancipation of the forelimb in conjunction with its ability to grasp also means that it can be used for gathering food and transferring it to the mouth and that a long snout is no longer necessary for feeding. It may be seen then that the human hand with its great dexterity and tactile sensitivity had its origin as an arboreal adaptation.

3. *Development of herbivorous digestive systems*. The environmental factors that most persistently direct the course of animal evolution are nutritional, and the very origin of the Primates can be attributed, in the final analysis, to the presence of an arboreal food supply. Most of the group are in fact either herbivorous, frugiverous, or omniverous, though a few such as *Daubentonia* seem to be nearly exclusively insectivorous. Apart from the Old World monkeys, in which either cheek pouches or sacculated stomachs are developed, the structure of the alimentary canal of all Primates departs little from that found in the Insectivora. A well-developed caecum presumably persists because of the essentially vegetarian diet. On the other hand, this diet has clearly determined the form of primate teeth which, while not the highly specialized structures found in such orders as the Artiodactyla and Perissodactyla, are both elaborated in structure and reduced in number from the condition in Insectivora. The basic eutherian dental formula is $I\frac{3}{3}:C\frac{1}{1}:PM\frac{4}{4}:M\frac{3}{3}$, a condition found in the Oligocene Anagale once thought to be a Primate. In all Primates there has been some reduction which particularly affects the incisors and premolars. In the extant tree-shrews there are only two upper incisors, whilst in *Notharctus* and *Adapis* a lower incisor has been lost as well. The most common formula among living prosimians is $\frac{2}{2}:\frac{1}{1}:\frac{3}{3}:\frac{3}{3}$ and this is likewise the case in the New World monkeys, except for the marmosets in which the last molar also typically fails to erupt. In the Old World monkeys, apes, and man, the reduction of premolar number has gone a stage further and the dental formula is typically $\frac{2}{2}:\frac{1}{1}:\frac{2}{2}:\frac{3}{3}$.

There is a corresponding tendency to increase the morphological complexity of the teeth, affecting particularly the premolars and molars. In the basic mammalian stock, the premolars are unicuspid and the molars tritubercular. In occlusion the lower teeth fit into the spaces between the upper teeth and therefore in biting offer a cutting surface along their anterior and posterior borders. In other words, the premolars and molars are sectorial teeth suitable for breaking up insects. For the chewing necessary in dealing with vegetable matter, the whole of the occlusal surfaces of the teeth need to be brought into contact. This is effected by the evolution of a posterior lingual cusp on the upper molars, the hypocone, and a heel or talonid to the lower molars. The latter is raised eventually to the level of the trigonid and from it develop an entoconid, hypoconid, and often a hypoconulid. The heel thus opposes with the posterior part

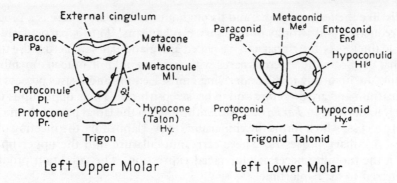

F I G. 2.2. Diagrams of the occlusal surfaces of the crowns of generalized Primate check-teeth. (From Simpson, *Biol. Rev.*, 1937.)

of the upper molar. However, the paraconid is progressively lost, since it is not involved in occlusion anteriorly. The upper teeth are, therefore, quadritubercular, whilst the lower ones possess either 4 or 5 main cusps (Fig. 2.2). All the different stages in this change are represented in Primates, but in general it can be said that a tritubercular pattern is most evident in the prosimians and a quadritubercular one in the anthropoids.

The premolars undergo similar functional changes. In the basal Insectivora they possess a single cusp and this state, particularly in the more anterior teeth, is to be found in many lemurs and *Tarsius*. In the Anthropoidea the premolars have typically become bicuspid except for the anterior lower one, which, because it functions with the upper canine in cutting, is usually a sectorial unicuspid tooth. The tendency to molarize the premolars has progressed even further in some of the lorises, particularly the Galaginae, in which the posterior premolars may possess 3 or even 4 cusps.

While considering teeth it may be mentioned that most Primates, especially the Anthropoidea, tend to have long sectorial canines for defence and aggression. Modern man is therefore exceptional. However, there is developmental and palaeontological evidence that the human canine was more strongly developed in man's ancestors. The lower canine of living lemurs and lorises, but not of the early fossil forms, is also inconspicuous since it has been incorporated into the strikingly characteristic tooth–comb formed mainly by the procumbent lower incisors. As a consequence of this non-biting function of these teeth, the upper incisors are greatly reduced and in some forms may be completely absent. A feature found in many of the earliest prosimians, as, for example, in the presiadapids is marked enlargement of the central incisors in both the upper and lower jaws, with the lower ones tending to be procumbent. Typically associated with this enlargement goes reduction in the lateral incisors, canines, and anterior premolars which may be completely lost.

4. *Reduction in the olfactory sense.* The arboreal habitat is not a 'world of

smells' like the terrestrial one, and throughout the Primates there is a progressive reduction and atrophy of olfactory mechanisms. This is particularly evident in the loss of the rhinarium—a naked and glandular skin across the upper lip that connects the external nares with a strong fold of mucous membrane binding the lip firmly to the underlying gums. Lemurs and lorises possess such a rhinarium and are therefore said to be 'strepsirhine'. Their upper lip is completely immobile. In *Tarsius* and the Anthropoidea the labial part of the median nasal process, which forms the rhinarium, is overlapped by the meeting of the lateral maxillary processes. These carry musculature into the upper lip and give it the mobility necessary for facial expression. The condition produced is referred to as 'haplorhine'.

The strepsirhine–haplorhine distinction is paralleled by changes in the conformation of the nasal cavities. In lemurs and lorises these cavities, in association with the prominent snout, are relatively large and are complicated by the elaborate projecting system of well-developed turbinate bones. In *Tarsius* and the Anthropoidea the cavities and the turbinals, with their covering of nasal-epithelium, are greatly reduced.

5. *Development of great visual acuity.* It is apparent that natural selection will strongly favour the better sighted among arboreal animals; consequently vision has become the dominant exteroceptive sense in all Primates. This is clearly evidenced in the size of the eye, its position, and the differentiation of the retina.

Two types of photoreceptor characterize the vertebrate retina: rods and cones. Rods are sensitive to low luminosity and are important in 'twilight' or scotopic vision. They are probably mainly concerned in detecting the movement of objects. Cones, on the other hand, are stimulated by bright light and function in the appreciation of fine details of form. This is indicated by the fact that each cone has its own optic nerve-fibre, in contrast with rods, many of which are served by a single fibre. Cones are also concerned in colour vision. Rods predominate in the retina of all Primates, particularly in the peripheral regions; but whenever cones occur they are practically the only element at the centre of the retina. This region of concentrated cones, the point of greatest visual acuity, is known as the macula lutea or yellow spot. There is typically a small depression or fovea here, caused by the absence of those superficial elements in the retinal epithelium which elsewhere cover the photoreceptors.

The retina of Primates vary in their photoreceptor composition and in construction. The lemurs, lorises, and *Tarsius*, along with the New World monkey *Aotes*, possess only rods. In consequence in these forms there is no macula and fovea, though in *Tarsius* the layer of rods is thrown into convoluted folds in the central region. On the other hand, in all the Anthropoidea (except the night monkey) cones also occur and macula and fovea are in varying degrees differentiated (Fig. 2.3). A step in this differentiation is evidenced in *Callithrix*, where, since the macula is not completely exposed, the fovea is only incipient. It is not to be concluded from this distinction between the prosimians and

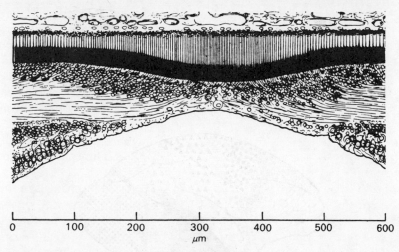

| | | | | | | |
|0|100|200|300|400|500|600|

*μm*

F I G. 2.3. Central fovea of human retina—note that only cones are present in the foveal pit and that these are very close to the surface as the overlying layers are spread aside; a few rod nuclei (shaded) begin to appear outside the outer fovea, amongst the cone nuclei (circles). (After Polyak, *The vertebrate visual system*, Chicago University Press, 1957.)

anthropoids that the earliest Primates had solely a rod retina and that cones have been re-evolved in the order. All the extant prosimians and *Aotes* are essentially nocturnal animals and their absence of cones is related to this mode of life. The anthropoids presumably arose from the prosimians before the latter assumed the nocturnal habit and have preserved and further elaborated the diurnal type of retina. The tree-shrew has in fact a diurnal type of retina.

The eyes are relatively large in the Primates, particularly in *Tarsius*. This form represents the culmination of a very striking trend within the Tarsiiformes generally and is probably related to their saltatorial habit. Great visual acuity is obviously necessary in jumping from tree to tree. Even some of the Eocene forms such as *Hemiacodon* had enormous orbits. But quite apart from this group, there is a general trend throughout the Primates for the eyes to become larger. More striking, however, is the tendency for the orbits to migrate from a position on the side of the face on to the front. In primitive mammals the eyes are completely lateral and there is no overlap of visual fields. The situation in lemurs is similar, though some forward movement has occurred. In the Anthropoidea the optical axes are more or less parallel. This overlapping of the visual fields makes stereoscopy possible: an obvious advantage in tree-living animals. That stereoscopy has been achieved in the Anthropoidea is indicated by the fact that in them about half of the optic tract fibres decussate. In the lemurs there is no crossing and only a little occurs in *Tarsius*, whose eyes are completely immobile. Because of the decussation the lateral geniculate body of the midbrain has six laminae rather than the three found in prosimians (it has been demonstrated in man and the macaque monkey that alternate layers

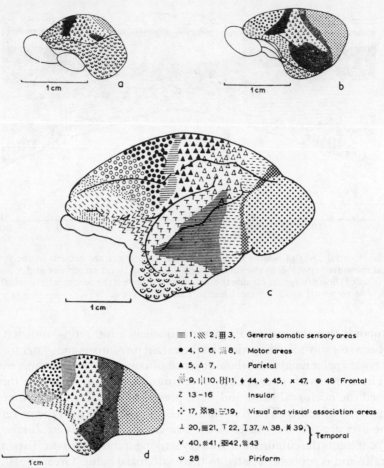

FIG. 2.4(a). Cyto-architectonic charts of the cortical areas of (a) Hedgehog; (b) *Tupaia*; (c) *Lemur*; (d) *Tarsius*. ((a), (b), from Le Gros Clark, *The antecedents of man*; (c), after Brodmann; (d) from Woollard, *J. Anat.* **60**, 1952.)

of the lateral geniculate body receive crossed and uncrossed optic fibres respectively).

6. *Development of the brain.* As already stressed, an awareness of many facets of the environment is necessary for survival in the trees and concomitantly with the increased elaboration of sense organs, both extero- and proprioceptive, there occurs throughout the Primates progressive development of those parts of the cerebral cortex concerned with sensory representation. In addition, since in such a precarious habitat fine control of movement and balance is needed, the cortical areas of motor control and the cerebellum are elaborated. The net effect is for the development of relatively large brains. This is evident even in the most primitive Primates such as *Adapis*, as compared with Insectivores,

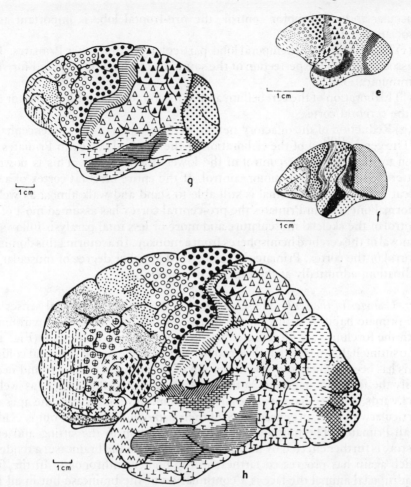

FIG. 2.4(b). Cyto-architectonic charts of the cortical areas of (e) *Callithrix*, (f) *Cercopithecus*, (g) chimpanzee, (h) man. ((e), (f), (h), after Brodmann (for Key, see Fig. 2.4(b); (g) after Walker, *J. Anat.* 13, 1938).

and is progressive throughout the order culminating in man. The morphological changes can be summarized as follows (Fig. 2.4):

(a) Expansion of the forebrain and especially the neopallium.

(b) Increasing fissuration of the neopallial cortex with the appearance, in particular, of a true Sylvian fissure.

(c) Expansion of the occipital lobe which increasingly projects posteriorly and becomes distinct from the adjoining parietal area by the formation of a calcarine sulcus (cf. Mivart's definition). This lobe is concerned with visual interpretation and association.

(d) Elaboration of the pre-central cortex. The frontal lobe is concerned with muscular and vocal motor control; the pre-frontal lobe is important as an association region.

(e) Elaboration of the temporal lobe, particularly in the higher Primates. This is associated with the perfection of the sound discrimination required for vocal communication.

(f) Elaboration of the cerebellum and of its connections with the motor area of the cerebral cortex.

(g) Reduction of the olfactory neural mechanisms, i.e. the rhinencephalon.

The general effect of the elaboration of the cerebral cortex in Primates has been to subordinate the control of the lower brain centres. This is nowhere better evidenced than in motor control. If the entire cerebral cortex of a dog or cat is removed the animal is still able to stand and walk almost as well as a normal one. But in Primates the pre-central cortex has assumed most of the control of the skeletal musculature and more or less total paralysis follows the removal of the cerebral hemispheres from a monkey. In acquiring this dominant control of the cortex, Primates have obtained a higher degree of muscular co-ordination, admittedly at the expense of vulnerability.

7. *Changes in the skull.* These changes in the brain and special senses and the primate habit of sitting on the haunches and exploring the environment with the forelimbs are all reflected in the conformation of the skull (Fig. 2.5). The sitting habit means that the head is set at an angle to the vertebral column. This has been facilitated by the migration of the occipital condyles (and necessarily the foramen magnum) so that they are directed downwards as well as backwards. The tendency reaches its maximum development in the apes and particularly in man, in consequence of their orthograde posture, but is evident in all Primates. The morphological accommodation to the sitting and erect posture is further effected by the flexion of the face on the braincase; a tendency which again has progressed farthest in the higher anthropoids. In the fully quadrupedal animal the face is a continuation of the braincase but in all Primates it tends to be placed partly underneath the braincase with the production of a distinct basi-cranial angle (Fig. 1.2). The reduction of the snout due to diminished importance of olfaction and the evolution of the hand has permitted this flexion and accounts for the relative smallness of the primate face. It is significant that when Primates become mainly quadrupedal on the ground, as has happened secondarily in the baboons and related genera, a long snout is re-evolved but the basi-cranial flexion remains.

The enlargement of the eyes and their migration on to the front of the face is obviously reflected in the size and position of the orbits. It may be mentioned here that in all but some of the very earliest forms a post-orbital bar is developed so that the orbits become completely surrounded by bone. Whilst a post-orbital bar is not confined to Primates a completely distinctive condition characterizes the Tarsiiformes and Anthropoidea. In these groups, particularly the Anthropoidea, the orbit is more or less completely separated from the temporal fossa

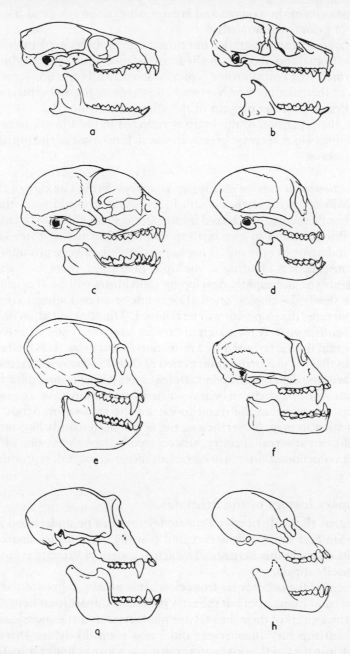

FIG. 2.5. Primate skulls: (a) *Ptilocercus*; (b) *Galago*; (c) *Tarsius*; (d) *Cebus*; (e) *Presbytis*; (f) gibbon; (g) chimpanzee; (h) *Proconsul*. ((a), (b), (d), (e), from Le Gros Clark, *The antecedents of man*, Edinburgh University Press, 1959.)

by the expansion of the zygoma and greater wing of the sphenoid (i.e. the alisphenoid of primitive mammals).

The enlargement and migration of Primate eyes probably explains why bones besides the frontal and maxilla usually form the medial wall of the orbit behind the lachrymal. In Lemuriformes typically these two bones are separated by a process of the palatine, which extends forwards to the lachrymal, while in all other Primates the os planum of the ethmoid is involved.

Finally, the expansion of the brain is reflected in the frontal, parietal, and occipital bones which increase greatly in size to form most of the top and sides of the braincase.

8. *Reduction in the number of offspring at any one birth.* The care of the newborn is obviously particularly difficult in trees and it would seem that more offspring can be successfully reared if litter size is small rather than large. Certainly all Primates tend to give birth to no more than two or three offspring at a time and many to only one. This has probably had very profound evolutionary consequences. During a multiple pregnancy there is competition between embryos and rapidly developing individuals will be at an advantage over more slowly developing ones. If only one or a few foetuses are carried, selection for rapid development will be reduced. The same situation holds after birth while offspring rely on maternal care for survival. Thus an extension of developmental time is favoured by a reduction in litter size. It is characteristic of Primates that the pre-maturation period of their life-history is extended and that they are long dependent upon maternal care. These factors offer the ideal prerequisites for a plasticity in behaviour based on learning. As a consequence of his social organization the trend to extend the maturation period reaches its culmination in man. Nevertheless, the origin of human behaviour can be attributed to an arboreal ancestry, since a tree-living habit is one of the few in which a reduction of litter size carries an increased overall reproductive fitness.

### Evolutionary history of the Primates

It is clear that all the distinctive Primate features can be understood in terms of the demands of arboreal existence and that the evolutionary dominance of man has its origin in this heritage. The actual course of Primate evolution can now be briefly considered.

The origin of the order is far from clear. It is usually supposed that it took place from basal Insectivora but the early prosimians, apart from being generalized in many aspects of their skeletal morphology, show little specific similarity with the contemporary Insectivores and it now seems likely that there was an early division in the Cretaceous pantothere stock, with one line eventually giving rise to the Primates along with the ungulates, condylarths, and hedgehogs and the other line to the 'true' insectivores and tree-shrews as well as the creodonts and some other major eutherian groups. The earliest form assigned, and that

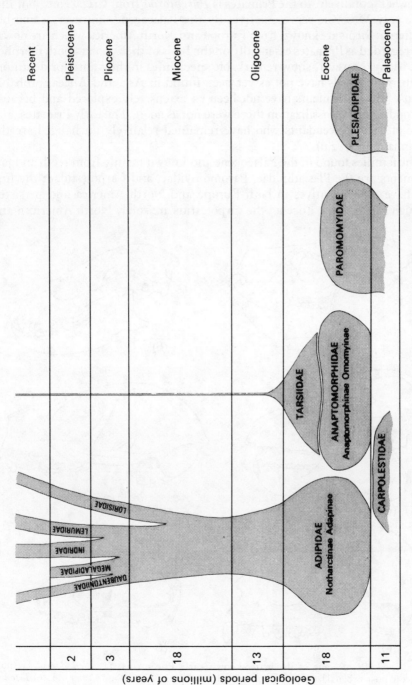

FIG. 2.6. Genealogical plan of the relationships of the Prosimii.

somewhat tentatively, to the Primates is *Purgatorius* from Cretaceous, but this is the only Mesozoic representative. By the Palaeocene, however, a number of different forms are known from Europe and North America which are nowadays regarded as Primates essentially on the basis of their molar-tooth morphology. Many, however, show remarkable specialities in their anterior dentition. Comparable fossils have not as yet been found in Asia and Africa, probably because these continents have not been as extensively explored and because the conditions for fossilization there were not as good. The early Primates, and those of their descendants who have remained relatively unchanged are the prosimians (Fig. 2.6).

The families found in the Palaeocene and known mainly from teeth and jaw fragments are the Plesiadipidae, Paromomyidae, and Carpolestidae; the first two have representatives in both Europe and North America and persisted through much of the Eocene: the carpolestids are solely North American and

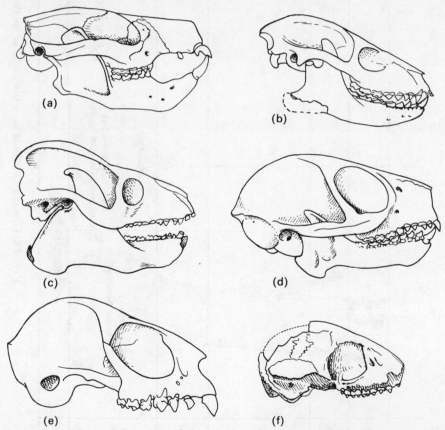

FIG. 2.7. Skulls of some of the better-known early Prosimians: (a) *Plesiadapis* ×1 (note absence of post-orbiatal bar). (b) *Notharctus* ×1. (c) *Adapis* ×1. (d) *Necrolemur* ×1. (e) *Tetonius* ×3. (f) *Rooneyia* ×1.

became extinct shortly after the beginning of this epoch. The early Eocene saw the rise of the two important families, the Adapidae and the Anaptomorphidae. The adapids, consist of an Old World subfamily and a New World subfamily, and it seems very likely that among the former the ancestors of modern lemurs are to be found. The anaptomorphids are the first tarsiers; they are known mainly from North American deposits, but the anaptomorphine *Berruvius* and the omomyne *Teilhardina* are of Old World provenance. This family persisted throughout the Eocene and probably into the Miocene. In the middle Eocene it is joined by the Old World Microchoerinae, which Simons includes in the family Tarsiidae and from which modern Tarsius is probably descended. The cranial features of some of these early prosimians for comparison with recent forms are illustrated in Fig. 2.7.

Although the Eocene was the time of the greatest faunal interchange between Eurasia and North America, there is little evidence of an interchange of particular genera of prosimians. Nevertheless, the similarities between the Old and New World forms were very great.

There is a sharp decline in the number of prosimian fossils at the end of the Eocene, and they are completely absent from the subsequent deposits of North America and Europe. In part this decline is only apparent since pre-Pleistocene fossils from tropical Africa and Asia are poorly or not at all known. However, it is likely that the radiations of the Eocene represent the heyday of the prosimians and that they have been on the decline ever since. This decline was probably in part brought about by competition with evolving Rodents, but also no doubt by the success of their own descendants—the Anthropoidea (Fig. 2.8). These Primates are on a higher plane of organization and it is significant that it is only in Madagascar, cut off from the mainland of Africa before 'monkeys' were able to colonize it, that the prosimians are still prevalent. It was here that they underwent a secondary radiation with the production of such exceptional forms as *Daubentonia* and *Megaladapis*.

The monkey grade of organization exists in both the New World and Old World and very nearly came into being in Madagascar too, for the Pleistocene lemuroid, Archaeolemur shows many monkey-like characteristics. Some Oligocene representatives of New World monkeys, *Branisella* and *Dolichopithecus*, are known but they are rather fragmentary and of uncertain evolutionary status. It has usually been concluded that Old World monkeys and New World ones have had independent prosimian ancestries. In part this conclusion was based on the belief that the earliest Old World monkeys possessed such advanced features as an external auditory meatus and reduction of the premolar number to two. This is now known not to be the case, and by invoking continental-drift theory, it is possible to envisage an anthropoid stock ancestry to both the Old and New World forms. However, whether the common ancestry was prosimian or anthropoid, there can be little doubt that there has been much parallel evolution in the two faunistic zones.

There are grounds for supposing that the Old World Anthropoidea were

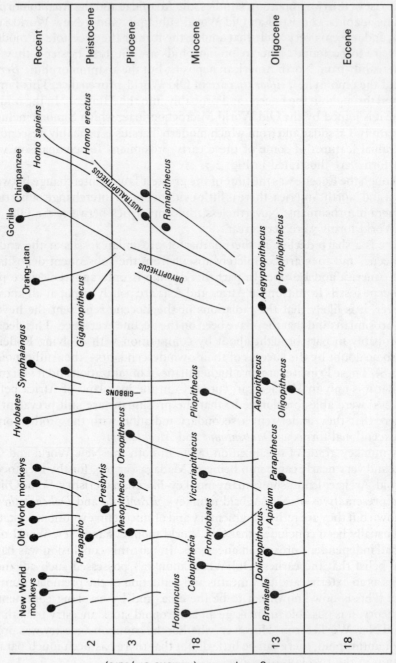

FIG. 2.8. Genealogical plan of the relationships of the Anthropoidea.

derived from a generalized prototarsioid, possibly like *Teilhardina*. Their earliest remains are from the Fayuum region of Egypt where a series of Oligocene deposits were laid down when the area was covered with swampy rain forest. A large number of Primate remains have now been recovered from these deposits representing a number of genera including the early 'monkeys' *Apidium* and *Parapithecus*, and the primitive 'apes' *Oligopithecus*, *Aeolopithecus*, *Propliopithecus*, and *Aegyptopithecus*. For many years the amount of fossil material from the Fayuum was small and fragmentary and there was much speculation concerning its phylogenetic status. However, as a result of recent excavations some of the above genera are now known from extensive material. *Apidium* and *Parapithecus* are remarkable among Old World anthropoids in having three premolars in both the upper and lower jaws, but the cranial remains of *Apidium* and the molar tooth morphology in both show them to be quite definitely Anthropoidea. Further the incipient bilophodonty (tendency for the anterior cusps to be joined transversely to form a bar, and the posterior cusps likewise) of the molars, so characteristic of *Cercopithecoidea* identifies them with this group. It has been noted, however, that there are indications in these teeth of affinity also with the *Oreopithecidae* (cf. p. 39).

The status of *Oligopithecus* is particularly uncertain. It is known solely from part of a lower jaw, which displays a number of primitive features and has been likened to that of an Omomyinae. On the other hand, it possesses only two premolars, and though the lower canine is quite small the morphology of the teeth is clearly anthropoid. The molars show some tendency to bilophodonty but the general concensus of opinion is that *Oligopithecus* should be regarded as a small ape, albeit one which is very generalized and possibly with pleuripotential evolutionary opportunities.

*Aelopithecus* is also only known from a single lower jaw with a dental formula of 2 : 1 : 2 : 3. It too was a small animal but the canine tooth is large for an animal of this size, and the anterior lower premolar is distinctly sectorial. Atypically for Old World anthropoids the third molar is reduced in size, a condition often found in gibbons (and generally in man), and Simons, its discoverer, regards *Aelopithecus* as probably an ancestral hylobatid. There exists, in fact, a morphological series of forms of appropriate geological age connecting *Aelopithecus* with modern gibbons. The main features of this series are that the canines become longer, the anterior lower premolars more sectorial, and a V-shaped jaw is transformed into a U-shaped jaw. As Le Gros Clark has emphasized, the existence of such a series does not necessarily mean that the true phylogeny of the gibbons is known, but one can be reasonably sure that, whatever the lineage, it must have passed through stages similar to those represented by *Aelopithecus–Limnopithecus–Pliopithecus* (which still possessed a tail)–*Hylobates* and *Symphalangus*. The early separation of the gibbon line from that of the rest of the Hominoidea is interesting, for gibbons share many peculiar characteristics particularly in limb structure with the great apes. Since these did not occur in the early forms of either group, obviously they must have arisen in parallel; as they also did to a lesser extent in the evolution of the spider monkey in South America.

*Propliopithecus*—represented by a long-known lower jaw and possibly by a recently discovered molar tooth—has been a subject of much debate. It possesses a number of primitive dental characteristics, and before the discovery of *Aelopithecus* was generally viewed as an ancestral gibbon. It has also been regarded, however, as a possible hominid ancestor. On the basis of the very fragmentary evidence it would seem best not to place it in any very specific phylogenetic position, particularly one with profound evolutionary implications: after all many genera of fossil Primates gave rise to no new ones. Although the evolutionary opportunities offered to the Oligocene anthropoids were immense, *Propliopithecus* might well have become extinct without descendants. It is best regarded as a generalized ape. The situation with respect to *Aegyptopithecus* is much clearer, since it is not only known from a number of jaws and teeth but also from a quite well-preserved cranium, and some probably associated post-cranial bones. It shows just the sort of combination of primitive and advanced characters that one would expect in the transition from prosimian to anthropoid status. It was somewhat larger than *Propliopithecus* but smaller than later apes. Unlike these latter it had a markedly projecting snout with very well-developed premaxillary bones and the brain case is relatively small. The orbits are separated from the temporal fossae to the degree usually found in New World monkeys and as in them there is no well-defined external auditory meatus. The upper canines are large but the lower ones small; the molar tooth morphology is essentially of ape-like form. So far as can be judged from the post-cranial material, *Aegyptopithecus* was probably an active runner and perhaps leaper in the canopy of the forests which covered the Fayuum in Oligocene times.

By the Miocene the adaptive radiation of the Anthropoidea was well under way. A number of genera of ceboids are known from this epoch from jaws and teeth: *Homunculus* from Argentina and *Cebupithecia*, *Neosaimiri* and *Strirtonia* from Colombia and Miocene cereopithecoids, e.g. *Prohylobates* and *Victoriapithecus* have been found in Africa. *Limnopithecus* is known from lower Miocene deposits in East Africa and *Pliopithecus*, which also extended into the Pliocene, from various Old World sites, mainly European. In addition, a number of ape remains have been discovered in Europe, India, and East Africa of Miocene provenance, which, although varying considerably in size, are now referred to a single genus *Dryopithecus*, but with a number of species. The more particular characteristics of this genus will be discussed later but it can be said now that these dryopithecines are rather generalized anthropoids without the extensive limb specialities found in the present-day gorilla, chimpanzee, and orang-utan. Many of their features are, indeed, like Old World monkeys and must be regarded as primitive. They were, no doubt, ancestral as a group to the present-day great apes, but what is more significant some of these dryopithecines, and in particular the lower Miocene forms from East Africa, formerly attributed to the genus *Proconsul* could have been very close to the ancestors of the first hominids.

By the Pliocene, the cercopithecoid and hominoid distribution was if anything wider than that of today. Many Old World monkey genera are known from this epoch and *Dryopithecus* continued into it. From this time comes *Oreopithecus* recovered from lignite coal deposits in north Italy. This genus known from a practically complete skeleton shows a number of unusual features in its molar-tooth morphology, which almost certainly separate it from other lines of hominoid phylogeny, but there are characteristics of its pelvis and limb structure which suggest it might have been incipiently bipedal. Also from the Pliocene and late Miocene comes *Ramapithecus*, so important in considering the bifurcation in hominid and pongid phylogeny and the first Australopithecines.

# 3. Apes and man

THE modern apes, to varying degrees, are arboreal brachiators; man is a terrestrial biped. Both modes of locomotion involve the orthograde posture, and those similarities between apes and man which are due to this posture are as likely to have resulted from parallelism as from a common ancestry.

In the pronograde animal, the abdominal viscera are slung in the main from the dorsal body-wall. It is obvious that this would not serve as an adequate supporting system in the orthograde posture. In both apes and man mesenteric attachments have been added superiorly. Visceral support has also been added below by the incorporation of the tail musculature into a pelvic diaphragm: a change made possible by the fact that the tail itself, being of no consequence as a balancing structure, has been lost.

The thoracic cage of a quadruped is typically 'heart-shaped' in cross-section, being deep dorso-ventrally but flattened laterally. This not only provides a low centre of gravity with consequent stability, but helps in bringing the forelimbs underneath the body for mechanically efficient support, and permits their fore-and-aft movement in the same plane as the hind limbs. These limitations on thoracic shape are removed in the orthograde posture. In both apes and man this posture is associated with an increased range of movement of the forelimb, and while this occurs for different reasons, it imposes a new set of restrictions on thoracic shape which becomes compressed antero-posteriorly and expanded laterally.

When the forelimbs are planted firmly on either the ground or the boughs of trees, the shoulder girdle muscles can be used for performing respiratory movements of the rib-cage as well as locomotor movements. The respiratory role of these muscles is inevitably much smaller when the limb is free and in apes and man the intercostals and particularly the diaphragm are much more important as respiratory muscles.

In association with the freedom of movement of the forelimb, the pectoralis musculature of apes and man is well developed. This is reflected in the fusion of sternebrae to form a more-or-less unified sternum. Because of their brachiating habits it is much more marked in the great apes than in man, but it occurs in both groups and for essentially the same reasons. This would seem to be a good example of evolution by hypermorphosis, since the sternebrae arise as discrete bones in development and are largely unfused in the monkeys.

The vertebral column of the pronograde animal is basically an arch with a mid-thoracic anticlinal vertebra and long spring-like lumbar region. With the assumption of the erect posture, however, a multiplicity of modifications are required. Important among these is the need to balance the head on the column and this is facilitated by the formation of an anteriorly convex cervical curve. It occurs in conjunction with a forward displacement of the foramen magnum on the base of the skull and as the balance of the head becomes more perfect there is less need for a heavy nuchal musculature and therefore prominent cervical spines and occipital crests. Concomitantly, as the stabilizing role of the sterno-mastoid muscle increases, mastoid processes are developed. These changes in the support of the head have progressed much farther in any known hominid than in any ape, but all show the same tendencies over the pronograde animal.

The lumbar region is one of weakness in the orthograde posture and it is, therefore, not surprising that it is reduced in relative length in both apes and man. The reduction has progressed farther in the former since the brachiating habits of apes do not necessitate the existence of a marked lumbar curve for bringing the legs in line with the axis of the spine. The shortening of the lumbar region has in a sense been accomplished by the incorporation of lumbar vertebrae into the sacrum.

The sacrum of the pronograde monkeys contains on the average 3 vertebrae, in that of the gibbon there are usually 4, whilst in man and the great apes between 5 and 6 are the typical number. In part this sacralization of lumbar vertebrae may be due to the increase in body-size which has occurred in pongid and hominid evolution, but there can be no doubt that it is also associated with the adoption of the orthograde posture which throws the whole weight of the trunk on to the pelvis. The support that the pelvis must give is effected by its vertical 'compression', lateral widening, and the antero-posterior extension of the iliac blades. These pelvic characters, however, are only incipiently developed in apes and it is evident that the many distinctive features of the human pelvis are principally determined by bipedalism (Fig. 3.1).

It may be mentioned that the acetabulum in pongids, as in lower Primates, is at the level of the lower border of the sacrum whereas in man it is relatively higher being opposite the sacro-iliac articulation. This makes for greater stability at the hip-joint. Further, in man the ischial tuberosity is approximated to the acetabulum: a condition which enhances the action of the hamstring muscles. Both these distinctive features of man result from his bipedalism.

As many of the similarities between apes and man can be seen to be due to their common posture, so many of the differences between them can be ascribed, either directly or indirectly, to their different modes of locomotion (Fig. 2.1). To generalize it may be said that it is the forelimbs of apes which have departed most from the primitive anthropoid condition, whilst changes in limb structure have principally involved the legs of hominids. In association with their brachiation, the arms of apes are greatly elongated, particularly the forearms and the development of the hand as a hook involves the abbreviation of the thumb. This reduction is reflected in its musculature, for a flexor pollicis longus is not a constant feature of the three great apes, and the short intrinsic volar muscles of the pollex, apart from the adductor pollicis, are also weakly developed or even lacking. It is interesting that these changes in musculature

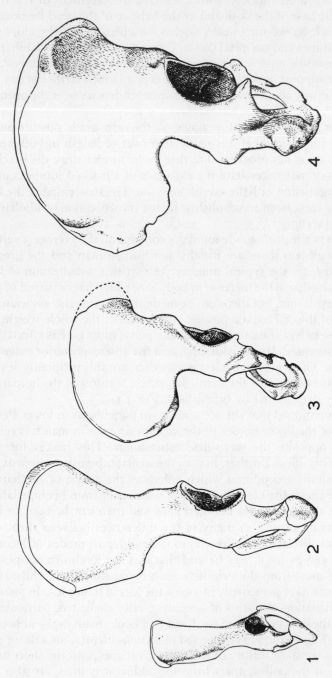

FIG. 3.1. Innominate bones of (1) monkey, (2) chimpanzee, (3) *Australopithecus* (Sterkfontein), and (4) *Homo sapiens*. (The iliac blades are all orientated parallel to the plane of the paper.)

have also occurred in the brachiating *Ateles* and some Colobinae but not in
the Hylobatinae. The anomalous situation in the gibbons is attributed by Straus
to the difference in their way of adapting to the brachiating mode of progression.

Many of the diagnostic features of man occur in the structure of the hind
limb. The characteristics of the pelvis have already been mentioned; also as
a consequence of the bipedalism there is a relative lengthening of the whole
of the pre-tarsal leg skeleton and numerous modifications of the foot skeleton

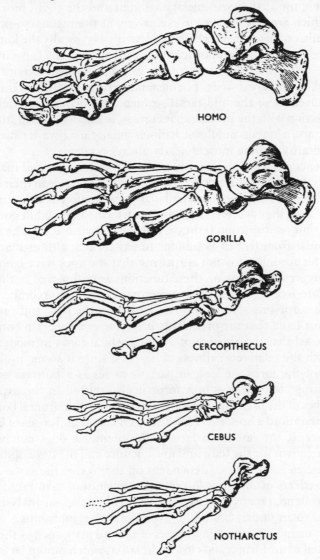

HOMO

GORILLA

CERCOPITHECUS

CEBUS

NOTHARCTUS

F IG. 3.2. Foot skeleton of a series of Primates. (After Gregory, *Mem. Am. Mus. nat. Hist.*,
1920)

for carrying the whole weight of the body (Fig. 3.2). The latter involve the development of a 'heel', longitudinal as well as transverse arching of the tarso-metatarsal region, and a hallux which is in line with the other digits, incorporated into the general mass of the foot and with a plantar surface. These characteristics exclude the possibility of the hallux retaining its primitive independence of movement and the pre-axial metatarsal articulates with the entocuneiform by means of a flat surface. There is, in fact, little independent movement of the big toe at the tarso-metatarsal joint and the slight movements of abduction which are possible occur exclusively at the metatarso-phalalangial joint. The hallux of man, then, which incidentally is typically the longest pedal digit, is entirely part of the supporting unit, with no grasping capacity. Despite these unique features of the human foot, in some ways it is more primitive than the foot of the great apes. For instance, it has not undergone antero-posterior shortening of the mid-tarsal segment, the plantaris muscle, even if it lacks connection with the plantar aponeurosis, is usually present, the tendons of flexor digitarum longus and flexor hallucis longus are always closely united, and the quadratus plantae muscle nearly always occurs.

The difference in the mode of locomotion of modern apes and man has also been in part responsible for a second type of major difference in their structure. When apes are arboreal, their forelimbs are pre-occupied with support and progression; when they are terrestrial (and such forms as the adult gorilla spend most of their time on the ground) they are usually quadrupedal. The forelimbs, therefore, are far from free of locomotor functions and, although at rest they can be used for feeding, it is not surprising that the apes have large jaws for defence and aggression. In man, these functions are subserved in the main by the hand, made free by the small locomotor role of the forelimb. It is consequently not surprising that in contrast with apes the jaws and canine teeth of man are small and that the premaxilla is no longer a separate bone. It may also be surmised that the absence of a supra-orbital torus in modern man is associated with the relative smallness of his jaws, since it seems probable that the function of the torus, at least in part, is to act as a buttress against the stresses of biting; but the loss of a torus is also related to the expansion of the frontal lobes of the brain, demanding, as it does, vertical frontal bones which themselves then afford a buttress. The characteristic sagittal crests of large adult apes arise because the lateral surface of the braincase does not provide an adequate attachment for the temporal musculature and the development of the temporal muscles is, of course, dependent on the size of the jaws. It can be seen that the effects of different locomotor mechanisms have ramifying consequences throughout many systems, and it is evident that an analysis of function is critical to an understanding of evolutionary relationships.

There exist many differences in the jaws of ape and man, such as the presence of a simian shelf in the former and chin in the latter, which cannot be so convincingly related to changes in the forelimb. Other factors, such as differences in diet (which are but remotely related to locomotor habit) and use of the tongue are without doubt very important. Nevertheless, it is surely apparent that structural characteristics must always be thought of in terms of interacting functional effects.

The principal differences between apes and man are found in the limbs, jaws, and brain. The further evolution of the brain will be discussed later. But there are other differences to which considerable phyletic significance has been attributed, particularly by Wood Jones. He points out that in man the lachrymal bone meets the ethmoid on the medial wall of the orbit whilst in apes the two bones are typically separated by a fronto-maxillary junction. Similarly, in man the ethmoid sutures with the sphenoid in the anterior cranial fossa, but in apes the characteristic condition is for the frontals to intervene. The human condition at the pterion is to have a meeting of the alisphenoid with the parietals, while in apes the frontals suture with the squamo-temporal. Wood Jones also draws attention to the fact that ischial callosities do not occur in man, that the human kidney is multi-pyramidal, and that man's aortic arch gives rise to innominate, left common carotid, and left subclavian arteries, whilst in apes the left common carotid comes off the innominate artery. In all these features man is more primitive than the great apes and the cercopithecoid monkeys, and this led Wood Jones to believe that man was directly descended from a tarsier and had no common ancestor with the Old World monkeys and apes at the anthropoid level.

However, as Schultz has pointed out, many of these differences are not absolute and insufficient account was taken of the individual variability to be found in the different species. Many apes retain the primitive disposition of the cranial bones, particularly the orang-utan, and some human skulls possess the so-called 'cercopithecoid' condition. Ischial callosities are also very small in the gibbon. In fact, the apes stand intermediate in position between the Old World monkey and man in these characters. This variability suggests either that these differences are of little phyletic consequence or that the deviation has arisen relatively recently.

Further, the very characteristics which Wood Jones believed excluded an ape ancestry to man do not exist in some of the fossil ape genera. Thus, so far as is ascertainable, *Dryopithecus* (Fig. 2.5) possessed the primitive arrangement of cranial bones as found in the tarsiers and man. There seems to be, in fact, no characteristic of this early Miocene anthropoid which excludes it from hominid ancestry. The limb proportions show none of the extreme brachiating specializations found in present-day apes. It seems probable that progression intermittently involved brachiation as in some present-day monkeys, but the limbs were sufficiently generalized to allow for subsequent development of the typical pongid and hominid pattern. The skull of *Dryopithecus africanus* was delicately built and lacked a supra-orbital torus, and the conformation of the nasal aperture was primitive as in monkeys. No simian shelf was developed and the incisors were small and the symphysial region of the jaw narrow. In present-day apes the incisors are large and spatulate and the dental arcade

U-shaped whilst in man the incisors are small and the dental arcade is parabolic in shape. Apart from some small features in the molar teeth, the dental morphology of *Dryopithecus* is primitive in anthropoid terms. For instance, the molar teeth lack the bilophodonty so characteristic of Old World monkeys. Admittedly the canine is a large tooth and, in consequence, the anterior lower premolar is sectorial. But this is the primitive state in the Anthropoidea and, as already mentioned, there is evidence that the canine was a large tooth in man's ancestors. In extant man the newly erupted canine, particularly the deciduous one, is often projecting, and the permanent tooth characteristically has a long root and erupts late. More telling is the fact that the canines in some undoubted fossil hominids were large and a definite diastema is occasionally found.

The features that distinguish pongids and hominids are summarized by the following taxonomic definitions of the two families drawn up by Le Gros Clark.

*Family Pongidae*—a subsidiary radiation of the Hominoidea distinguished from the Hominidae by the following evolutionary trends: progressive skeletal modifications in adaptation to arboreal brachiation shown particularly in a proportionate lengthening of the upper extremity as a whole and of its different segments; acquisition of a strong opposable hallux and modification of morphological details of limb bones for increased mobility and for the muscular developments related to brachiation; tendency to relative reduction of pollex; pelvis retaining the main proportions characteristic of quadrupedal mammals; in the skull [Fig. 3.3] the following features: marked prognathism, with late retention of facial component of premaxilla and sloping symphysis; development (in larger species) of massive jaws associated with strong

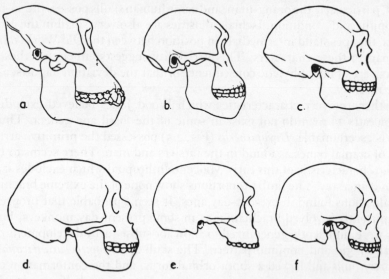

F IG. 3.3. Lateral views of the skull: (a) gorilla; and the hominids: (b) *Australopithecus*; (c) *Homo erectus*; (d) Neanderthal man (La Chapelle); (e) Steinheim man; (f) modern man.

muscular ridges on the skull; nuchal area of occiput becoming extensive, with relatively high position of the inion; occipital condyles retaining a backward position well behind the level of the auditory apertures; only a limited degree of flexion of basicranial axis associated with maintenance of low cranial height; cranial capacity showing no marked tendency to expansion; progressive hypertrophy of incisors with widening of symphysial region of mandible and ultimate formation of 'simian shelf'; enlargement of strong conical canines interlocking in diastemata and showing distinct sexual dimorphism; accentuated sectorialization of first lower premolar with development of strong anterior root; post-canine teeth preserving a parallel or slightly divergent alignment in relatively straight rows; first deciduous molar retaining a predominantly unicuspid form; no acceleration in eruption of permanent canine.

*Family Hominidae* [Fig. 3.3]—a subsidiary radiation of the Hominoidea, distinguished from the Pongidae by the following evolutionary trends: progressive skeletal modifications in adaptation to erect bipedalism, shown particularly in a proportionate lengthening of the lower extremity, and changes in the proportions and morphological details of the pelvis, femur, and pedal skeleton related to mechanical requirements of erect posture and gait and to the muscular development associated therewith; preservation of well-developed pollex; ultimate loss of opposability of hallux; increasing flexion of basi-cranial axis associated with increasing cranial height; relative displacement forward of the occipital condyles; restriction of nuchal area of occipital squama, associated with low position of inion; consistent and early ontogenetic development of a pyramidal mastoid process; reduction of subnasal prognathism, with ultimate early disappearance (by fusion) of facial component of premaxilla; diminution of canines to a spatulate form, interlocking slightly or not at all, and showing no pronounced sexual dimorphism; disappearance of diastemata; replacement of sectorial first lower premolars by bicuspid teeth (with later secondary reduction of lingual cusp); alteration in occlusal relationships, so that all the teeth tend to become worn down to a relatively flat even surface at an early stage of attrition; development of an evenly rounded dental arcade; marked tendency in later stages of evolution to a reduction in size of the molar teeth; progressive acceleration in the replacement of deciduous teeth in relation to the eruption of permanent molars; progressive 'molarization' of first deciduous molar; marked and rapid expansion (in some of the terminal products of the hominid sequence of evolution) of the cranial capacity, associated with reduction in size of jaws and area of attachment of masticatory muscles and the development of a mental eminence.

Some remains of upper and lower jaw fragments of the Siwalik Hills in India, which were for many years referred to Dryopithecine apes, are now regarded as being of critical significance in the early differentiation of hominids. They belong to a form known as *Ramapithecus brevirostis* which in its jaw structure and tooth morphology shows many similarities with undoubted later hominids. It is now known that *Ramapithecus* also existed in East Africa from remains initially attributed to '*Kenyapithecus*' but which are very similar to the Indian fossils. The hominid features include a short face, small incisor and canine teeth, and the shape, comparative size, enamel thickness and overall morphology and type of wear of the molar teeth. The tooth row is also parabolic in shape and the anterior lower premolar is only semi-sectorial in form. It appears that the jaw movement was a rotatory grinding one, rather than strictly up and down as in apes. The geological date of these forms is upper Miocene and Pliocene. It has been hypothesized by Jolly that the distinctive condition of the dentition found in hominids is related to a change from a frugiverous type of diet to a graminiferous one, based on the hard and coarse seeds of plants like grasses. This presupposes the occupation of savanna kinds of ecological niche. The fauna found associated with *Ramapithecus* both in India and East Africa primarily indicates fairly heavy forest but it is not inconceivable that it occurred in a mixed forest–savanna type of environment.

## Molecular relationships

In recent years a number of techniques have been developed for determining the molecular affinities of Primates. The first to be used, and now refined in various elegant ways, involves the making by immunization, of an antibody to some particular protein, e.g. albumin found in one species and then determining the extent to which this antibody cross-reacts with the same type of protein found in other presumably closely related species. More penetrating as a technique, since it is concerned with the whole chemistry rather than just those parts which determine antigenicity, is amino-acid sequencing of proteins from different species. Here, by such combined techniques as controlled hydrolysis and chromatography, not only are the amino acids which compose a protein identified but their order in the polypeptide chain is also established. The degree of similarity between the amino-acid sequences of the proteins from different species can thus be assessed. The principle is to align the sequences for a protein in a pair of species so as to maximize the similarities and then simply to count the number of amino-acid differences. The procedure can be refined by calculating the minimum mutation distance, which involves estimating the minimum number of nucleotides that would need to be changed in order to convert a codon for one amino acid into a codon for the other wherever a difference in amino-acid sequence occurs (cf. p. 136). This sort of work has been done for a number of proteins in Primates as, for example, haemoglobin, cytochrome C, and fibrinopeptides. A third method involves direct investigation of the complementarity of the DNA from different species. The method is based on the principle that if single-strand DNA from one species is chemically presented with single-strand DNA from another they will only re-associate into two-strand DNA in those segments which are homologous. To the immunological and biochemical findings can be added the evidence of cytogenetics which demonstrates the similarities between the chromosomal composition and structure of different species.

The application of these molecular approaches to Primate taxonomy produces a pattern of phenetic affinities which is broadly comparable with the morphological evidence, and confirm the distinctiveness of the tree-shrews. They do, however, suggest a closer similarity between the lemurs and the lorises than is recognized in the formal taxonomy (p. 22) and indicate affinity of the tarsier with the Anthropoidea. Further, all the molecular evidence points to a greater difference between the orang-utan and the gorilla and chimpanzee than between the latter two forms and man.

Various attempts have been made to reconstruct the phylogeny of the primates on the basis of protein structure. Without direct fossil evidence there are, however, great difficulties primarily arising from the necessary assumption that the rates of molecular evolutionary change for any one group of proteins is constant. Over extended periods of geological time this assumption, when checked against chronometric dating of known phylal divergence, would seem to be more or less true, but at the moment it would seem unwise to accept it generally, especially as it implies that molecular evolution has not been profoundly determined by natural selection.

# 4. The hominid progression

## The Pleistocene

MOST of the evidence for hominid evolution comes from geological deposits which are attributed to the Pleistocene. The forms from the earliest part of this epoch still possessed many patristic affinities with fossil apes; by the end of it, man, in much the same anatomical form as he is today had arisen. The lapse of time is put at about 2–3 million years and during this relatively short period extensive changes in climate, terrain, flora, and fauna occurred with marked effects on the hominid populations and their way of life (Table 4.1).

By the close of the Pliocene the greater part of the Tertiary phase of mountain-building had ended and events of the Pleistocene are dominated by a sequence of climatic fluctuations, probably due to changes in the sun's radiation. Whatever the cause, the whole earth was periodically subjected to cooling and warming. This was particularly reflected in the size of the Arctic ice-cap and the mountain glaciations of the Northern Hemisphere. Though glacial activity in New Zealand, for example, also fluctuated intermittently, the Antarctic ice-cap was much more constant throughout the Pleistocene and never had anything like the same influence on the Southern Hemisphere.

In all, there were four Ice Ages in the Northern Hemisphere separated by three interglacial periods, when the climate ameliorated. Of these the middle or Great Interglacial was the longest. The names given to the successive advances of the Alpine glaciers in order of decreasing antiquity are Günz, Mindel, Riss, and Würm. Each of these was itself interrupted by at least one interstadial when conditions ameliorated and in the case of the Würm glaciation two such interstadial periods occurred. Contemporaneous with these advances of the Alpine glaciers, the ice-sheets centred on Scandinavia likewise spread, so that in fact there was but a narrow corridor between the two. The periods of greatest glacial activity in North America correspond with the cold periods of Europe.

Although the Pleistocene is popularly regarded as the 'Ice Age', the Pliocene–Pleistocene boundary is now taken as being much earlier than the beginning of the glacial phases. It is defined in fact as the time when *Elephas, Bos, Equus*, and *Camelus* first appear in the fossil record. At the beginning of the epoch, in the so-called Lower Pleistocene, these mammals are found in association with a number of Tertiary species now extinct, to form a faunal complex known as the Villafranchian. This term has been used to distinguish the pre-glacial period of the Pleistocene, but it now appears that a Villafranchian-type fauna persisted in Europe throughout the first advances of the ice. The Lower Pleistocene is, therefore, considered as extending up to the end of the Günz glacial phase.

During the glacial periods immense amounts of water were 'locked up' in

TABLE 4.1

| PROVISIONAL TIME SCALE (YEARS) | GEOLOGICAL PERIODS | | | CULTURAL PERIODS | | | | |
|---|---|---|---|---|---|---|---|---|
| | EUROPE | | Africa | EUROPE, SOUTH EAST ASIA, AFRICA | | | | |
| | POSTGLACIAL | | | METAL AGES NEOLITHIC MESOLITHIC | | | | |
| 10 000 | | | | | | | | |
| 50 000 | Fourth glaciation Würm | D W | | Magdalenian Aurignacian | | | | Classic Neanderthals |
| | | W | | Mousterian | | | HOMO SAPIENS | |
| 115 000 | Last interglacial | Drier | | | | Lavalloisian techniques spreading | | Progressive Neanderthals   Modern man |
| | Third glaciation Riss | Wetter | | Acheulian | | | | |
| 250 000 | Middle interglacial period | Drier | | | | | | |
| | Second glaciation Mindel | Wetter | | | Clactonian | | | |
| 500 000 | First interglacial period | Drier | | Abbevillian | | | HOMO ERECTUS | |
| | First glaciation Günz | Wetter | | | | | | |
| | | Dry | | | | Oldaway Africa | | |
| 1 000 000 | Villafranchian | | | | | | | |
| 2 000 000 | PLIOCENE | | | | | | AUSTRALOPITHECUS | |

(left vertical labels for EUROPE geological column: PLEISTOCENE)

(left vertical label for cultural period: PALAEOLITHIC)

the ice-sheets, with a consequent lowering of sea-level. The effect of this was to rejuvenate river systems which in their lower reaches cut through the alluvial deposits previously laid down. The remains of the old deposits persist as a terrace on either side of the river. The repeated advances and retreats of the ice in fact led to the formation of a series of such terraces, which are characteristic features of Pleistocene geology. Raised shore-lines around coasts and lakes were often formed in a similar way.

Much can be deduced about the climatic conditions prevailing in particular localities at particular times from other geological sources. Tundra conditions are evidenced by fossil frost soils whilst horizons of buried soils formed by chemical weathering testify to mild climatic phases. One of the most characteristic Pleistocene deposits of Euro-Asia is loess, wind-blown dust derived from periglacial rock waste, which, in suitable places, accumulated in enormous quantities very quickly and is indicative of steppe conditions where wind erosion is an important land-forming agent.

Climatic conditions can also be determined from the nature of the fossil fauna and flora. Pollen analysis has proved particularly fruitful, since each species of plant has a distinctive form of pollen grain, and one knows from present-day observations the climatic preferences of the species recognized. Molluscan shells have been used in much the same way, and a number of mammalian species are quite diagnostic of particular ecological conditions. At the beginning of the Pleistocene, the southern elephant, *Elephas meridionalis*, roamed Europe. It appears that during the Pleistocene this form gave rise to *E. antiquus* and *E. primigenius*. These two species are easily identified particularly by the structure of their molar teeth. The mammoth was an animal of the steppe and tundra, whilst *E. antiquus* is a form of woodland and semi-open country; it only occurs in interglacial deposits. Similarly, the woolly rhinoceros *(Tichorhinus antiquitatis)* was adapted to the same biome as the mammoth, whilst *Dicerorhinus etruscus* and *D. merkii* were warm climate forms. As today, the presence of the wild horse was indicative of open grasslands and the reindeer of tundra conditions.

During the Pleistocene the tropical zone was subjected to a series of pluvial periods (wet phases) and inter-pluvials (dry phases) but the correlation of these successions with the glacial ones to the north is not yet certainly known. There is no necessary reason why the tropical pluvials should have any correspondence at all with the glacial periods of Europe, nor even with the pluvial phases that also occurred around the Mediterranean. This is unfortunate, since all the evidence, palaeontological, archaeological, and even physiological, indicates that hominid evolution began in tropical zones, well outside the regions directly subject to periglacial influence. There is no evidence that hominids existed in Europe and the main Asiatic land mass early in the Pleistocene; when these regions were colonized it was, at first, only during the interglacial and inter-stadial phases. Apparently man was not able to adapt to cold biomes until almost the end of the Pleistocene. It is by reference to the succession of glacial and interglacial phases and pluvials and interpluvial periods that hominid remains and stone implements are dated.

## Geological dating

It is obvious that the dating of fossil remains is necessary if one is to ascertain the most probable evolutionary relationships. Even when no absolute time scale is available, it is often possible to say that one form was earlier than another but later than a third. But if one wants information on rates of evolutionary change it is evident that absolute dating is necessary.

There are a number of methods for both relative and absolute dating. We shall briefly review some of these here, but refer the reader to special works on geochronology for a full discussion.

The most important problem in dating is to establish the sequence of events and to cross-correlate the ages of different deposits. It frequently happens also that within the same horizons at a single site, remains occur of at least two different ages. Some are contemporaneous with the deposits whilst others are merely intrusions. In the case of man these may take the form of deliberate interments. An important problem of dating then is to recognize such heterogeneity.

When the climatic conditions characteristic of a particular deposit have been ascertained (from the fauna, flora, or soil structure) this greatly narrows the probable age within the Pleistocene succession. Sometimes, however, much more precise information can be obtained, particularly when the stratigraphy contains undoubted post-Pleistocene remains. A most revealing example is provided by the succession of strata in cave deposits at Sante Fé and Albuquerque in America. The uppermost layer in these caves is composed of loose dust in which is to be found pottery of recent Pueblo Indians. Beneath this there exists a consolidated layer of calcium carbonate which could only have been formed during a pluvial period. The third layer is a bone breccia containing remains of extinct horses, camels, and ground sloths, and also implements of the Folsom type. This stratum is separated below from another containing fossil animal remains in association with Sandia implements, by a yellow ochrous band containing no animal or plant remains. It is this latter layer which is so important, since such deposits are characteristically laid down from percolating waters containing 'humic acids'—the product of slowly decaying coniferous leaves. The only time that one would expect to find a coniferous forest vegetation in this south-west part of the USA would be during a glacial period to the north. It may therefore be concluded that the ochrous band was formed at the time of the last advance of the last ice sheets and the Sandia culture was of final interstadial age.

Remains found in river terrace gravels can be dated in much the same way. It is apparent from what has been said earlier that not only do the terraces represent interglacial periods, but also that the highest terrace is the oldest and the lowest the youngest. Much use of this correlation between climate and terrace formation has been made in Europe in dating skeletal and archaeological remains.

Another valuable source of evidence about the age of fossil hominid remains comes from their frequent association with animal and plant remains. The general proposition is that deposits containing a similar assemblage of fossil remains are of the same age and, therefore, one deposit can serve to date the others. It is obvious that this procedure cannot be used uncritically since forms which become extinct in one area at some particular time can persist for a long time elsewhere. It is also worth while remembering that, conversely, after a new form has arisen in some zoo-geographical area, it may take thousands of years to spread into other areas, if it spreads at all.

Despite these reservations it does appear that at least within certain geographical zones, various animal forms, including some mammals, can be used as age-indicators. Thus the sabre-tooth tiger (*Machairodus*), the southern elephant (*E. meridionalis*), and the Etruscan rhinoceros (*D. etruscus*) are in evidence in Europe only in the Lower Pleistocene; the mammoth (*E. primigenius*) is an example of a species restricted to the Upper Pleistocene.

A number of ways are available for determining the homogeneity of specimens occurring in single deposits and were extensively used by Weiner, Oakley, and Le Gros Clark for demonstrating the fraudulent nature of the Piltdown remains. One of the most widely used methods is the 'fluorine test'. As bones lie in earth deposits, their main mineral salt hydroxyapatite $Ca_5(PO_4)_3OH$ is slowly converted to fluorapatite $Ca_5(PO_4)_3F$ by the uptake of 'fluorine' from the percolating waters. Naturally, the rate depends upon the concentration of fluorine present in the water, but in any single deposit the fluorine content of the bone is a function of geological age. If, then, it is found that such bones contain different amounts of fluorine, those with the greatest amount have been there longest or have come from elsewhere.

Relative dating can also be carried out by comparing the organic nitrogen, or organic carbon content of bones in the same deposit. The older bones will contain less of these substances due to a greater degree of decomposition.

Many early attempts to determine the minimum absolute age of a deposit were based on estimates of the length of time required for subsequent deposits to be laid down. Since so many continually varying factors determine the rate of sedimentation, such estimates were inevitably crude. Recently the formation rates of some particular deposits, such as stalagmites and stalagtites, have been more precisely determined, and in the case of glacio-fluvial deposits the sediments themselves are represented as annual formations. During the winter there is little melting at the ice front of a glacier and the sediment laid down at this time of year is small both in amount and in particle size. In contrast the summer deposition is large and consists of coarse gravels as well as finer till. Each annual deposit is, therefore, distinguishable from those of preceding and subsequent years and constitutes a varve. The counting of varves then at the present glacial front and over the area which has been previously glaciated can establish an absolute date for any particular formation. This method was first employed by the Swede, Baron de Geer, and has been widely used both in Europe and America for dating purposes.

Somewhat similar in general principle is the method of dendrochronology. In seasonal climates the nature of the new wood formed by trees varies with the seasons. In cross-section, therefore, the tree trunk can be seen to be made up of concentrically arranged annual rings, which at the base indicate the age of the tree. The thickness of any particular ring depends on how favourable to growth the year was in which it was formed and such an event as a series of severe years is represented by a close disposition of the annual rings formed at that time. A distinctive landmark like this may occur near the centre of a living tree but at the periphery of a fossil piece of wood. The records of these two specimens can be then associated to give an annual ring-count which is greater than either of the individual specimens alone. By tying in a series of samples of different age like this, it is sometimes possible to date quite accurately an archaeological site containing pieces of fossil wood. The varve-counting method and dendrochronology have enabled us to date the more recent archaeological stages—those within the last 5000 years.

There are a number of 'radioactivity' methods for determining absolute geological time. For relatively short-range dating of organic material the radioactive carbon method developed particularly by Libby has proved of immense value. It provides dates going back some 50 000–60 000 years. Carbon-14 is continually being formed in the upper atmosphere by the reaction of cosmic radiation on nitrogen. Chemically it behaves like ordinary $^{12}$C and is therefore incorporated, according to its concentration, in the substance of living matter. At death, there is no further turnover and the $^{14}$C slowly breaks down. It has a half-life of $5568 \pm 30$ years. The $^{14}$C content, therefore, of organic matter is a function of its age: the smaller the content the greater the age. There is an error of between $\pm 100$ years and $\pm 1200$ years in dates established by this method (the particular magnitude of the error increasing with increasing age) and the reliable range is only back to about 20 000–30 000 years. Nevertheless, it has been widely and most profitably used, particularly for chronometric dating of remains from Upper Pleistocene and subsequent deposits.

For deposits older than half a million years other radioactive methods are available based on the accumulation of lead isotopes from radioactive minerals containing uranium and thorium, and on the decay rate of radioactive potassium into argon. This latter method depends upon the presence in naturally occurring potassium of a minute content of the isotope potassium-40, which decays to calcium-40 and argon-40 with a half-life of $1 \cdot 3 \times 10^9$ years. It has provided strong confirmation of the dates of the various Tertiary epochs (Table 2.1) and indicates that the Pliocene-Villafranchian boundary well exceeds a million years, as once thought, and is probably 2–3 million years old.

An important site where radiometric methods have been invaluable is Olduvai Gorge in Tanzania. Here a series of deposits lying on top of each other have been exposed in a canyon by river erosion in the late Pleistocene. The base of the sequence is a layer of basalt produced by volcanic action and dated by the potassium–argon method at around 2 million years. On this rest a series of beds—Beds I–V. Bed I, the earliest and containing a number of important hominid fossils, is also mainly volcanic in origin and a particular zone about half-way up in it, known as Marker Bed A is potassium–argon dated at 1·75 million years. Bed II also contains hominid remains but has been formed mainly of water lain stream and lake deposits and thus cannot be dated radiometrically. In places it is as thick as Bed I, but probably took much longer to form. Olduvai Gorge forms part of the Great East African Rift Valley system which extends northward through Kenya and Ethiopia. In southern Ethiopia it is represented by the valley of the Omo river which drains into Lake Rudolf in Kenya. These are also important fossil sites which have been dated radiometrically.

A new chronometric method of promise for bones which still contain protein material is known as the amino-acid racemization technique. In living material the 20 amino acids exist in one geometric configuration; that which in crystallized form rotates polarized light to the left, i.e. they are laevo-rotary. After death, however, a gradual change occurs with increasing amounts of the dextrorotary form appearing. The ratio of laevo- to dextro-rotary forms is therefore related to the time since death. The method has so far been mainly used for the amino acid isoleucine and has provided, as at Olduvai Gorge, dates which are comparable with those obtained by radioactive techniques. One important factor, however, which has to be taken into account is the temperature history of the specimen since heat increases the rate of racemization.

## Australopithecus

Extensive excavations of travertine cave deposits in Botswana and the Transvaal of South Africa led to the discovery by Dart, Broom, and Robinson, mainly in the 1930s and 1940s, of a great wealth of fossil material attributable to an early hominid form. That extracted from the different caves was given different generic or specific status: *Australopithecus africanus* from Taungs, *A. prometheus* from Makapansgat, *Plesianthropus transvaalensis* from Sterkfontein, *Paranthropus robustus* from Kromdrai, *Paranthropus crassidens*, and, at a higher level, *Telanthropus capensis* from Swartkrans.

There are certain differences between these forms, but those between the Taungs, Makapansgat, and Sterkfontein remains are very small and do not justify specific, let alone generic, distinction. Most authorities now refer them to the single genus *Australopithecus*. On the other hand, the contrast between this group and that referred to as '*Paranthropus*' is considerable. In particular, '*Paranthropus*' has a much more massive and robust skull, typically with a distinct sagittal crest, a completely flat or even 'dish-shaped' face, and very receding frontal bones. Further, the relative size of the teeth contrast with all other hominids, for, whereas the molars and premolars are enormous, the incisors and canines are quite small. Robinson interprets this dental difference as indicating that *'Paranthropus'* was more or less exclusively a herbivorous animal whilst all other known hominids were omnivorous. However, the differences between all these South African remains seem to be no greater than those which occur within other accepted genera of mammals and only the single genus *Australopithecus* is here recognized, albeit with two species *A. africanus* and *A. robustus ('Paranthropus')*.

More recently attention has moved to East Africa where in Kenya, Tanzania, and Ethiopia a number of workers, and especially L. S. B. Leakey and his family, have recovered a variety of fossil forms, which, whatever their exact taxonomic status, can probably be broadly referred to as Australopithecine. One of the first to be discovered was a nearly complete cranium from near the base of Bed I at Olduvai Gorge, Tanzania. This was first designated *Zinjanthropus boisei*, but it is generally agreed today to be a local variant of *Australopithecus robustus*. Other East-African representatives of this species have also been recovered from deposits at Peninj, the Omo Valley, and to the east of Lake Rudolf. Contemporaneous with the 'robustus' remains at Olduvai and extending through Bed I and into Bed II was another form which was initially regarded as belonging to the genus *Homo* and called *H. habilis*. It is known from a number of specimens including much of a skull, referred to colloquially as 'Twiggy' or specimen OH24. This has an overall general resemblance to one of the better-preserved *A. africanus* skulls (Sterkfontein 5) from South Africa, but compared with this it has a shorter jaw and molar teeth and thus a less projecting mouth. The occipital region is more rounded and the foramen magnum is also further forward on the base of the skull. Other Australopithecine remains include a mandible from Lothagam and a humeral fragment from Kanopoi, both in northern Kenya. And from the east-Rudolf site comes much of the braincase and face of an individual, referred to as ER1470 which has recently attracted much attention and whose status will be discussed shortly. Another recent find of some importance is the almost complete skeleton discovered by Johanson from Afar in the Haggar region of Ethiopia. This, known as 'Lucy', has not yet been described but is said to be Australopithecine.

Le Gros Clark has formally defined *Australopithecus* as a genus of the Hominidae distinguished by the following characters:

Relatively small cranial capacity, ranging from about 450 to about 700 cc; strongly built supra-orbital ridges; a tendency in individuals of larger varieties for the formation of a low sagittal crest in the fronto-parietal region of the vertex of the skull (but not associated with a high nuchal crest); occipital condyles well behind the mid-point of the cranial length but on a transverse level with the auditory apertures; nuchal area of occiput restricted, as in *Homo*; consistent development (in immature as well as mature skulls) of a pyramidal mastoid process of typical hominid form and relationships; mandibular fossa constructed on the hominid pattern but in some individuals showing a pronounced development of the postglenoid process; massive jaws, showing considerable individual variation in respect of absolute size; mental eminence absent or slightly indicated; symphysial surface relatively straight and approaching the vertical; dental arcade parabolic in form with no diastema; spatulate canines wearing down flat from the tip only; relatively large premolars and molars, anterior lower premolar bicuspid with subequal cusps; pronounced molarization of the first deciduous molar; progressive increase in size of permanent lower molars from first to third; the limb skeleton (so far as it is known) conforming in its main features to the hominid type but differing from *Homo* in a number of details [Fig. 3.1], such as the forward prolongation of the region of the anterior superior spine of the ilium and a relatively small sacro-iliac surface, the relatively low position (in some individuals) of the ischial tuberosity, the marked forward prolongation of the intercondylar notch of the femur, and the medial extension of the head of the talus.

When Dart in 1925 described the first find of *Australopithecus*—part of the skull and an endocranial cast of an immature individual from Taungs—the consensus of opinion was that it was no more than the remains of another fossil pongid. However, with the discovery of much more material, most authorities are now convinced that *Australopithecus* is a hominid. The reason for this change of view is that although the skull has an overall ape-like appearance and the cranial capacity is low, it does show many hominid features. Further, it has now become evident from the anatomy of the post-cranial skeleton that *Australopithecus* was a terrestrial biped. It will be noted in the preceding definition of the genus that the conformation of the pelvis, the position of the occipital condyles and nuchal line, and the development of mastoid processes, all indicate hominid posture and gait. The jaws and teeth likewise display an overall morphological pattern which is hominid. This is particularly evident in the form of both the permanent and deciduous canine and lower anterior premolar teeth and the shape of the whole dental arcade. The structure of the articulation of the mandible with the cranium and the wear on the molar teeth show that *Australopithecus*, like other hominids, performed rotatory chewing movements whilst in the apes, as a result of their large interlocking canines only vertical jaw movement is possible. Admittedly, in extant man in contrast with *Australopithecus* the post-glenoid process is represented merely by a small tubercle, and the molar teeth decrease in size backwards, but intermediate conditions are found in other hominids. As already seen, the absence of a chin is primitive in the hominoids and no particular significance can therefore be attributed to this condition. In *Australopithecus* it is, however, phyletically important that there is no simian shelf and that the symphysis is more vertical than in pongids. The development of a supra-orbital torus is found in other hominids and, as already mentioned, is to be expected in forms with large jaws and low frontal bones, irrespective of their relationships. *Australopithecus*, however, is unique among hominids in that some individuals possess a sagittal crest. Whilst this differs from the crest in apes in that it does not join up with an occipital crest, some palaeontologists have held that its presence in *Australopithecus* excludes the form from subsequent hominid evolution. But such a crest is solely a function of the small braincase and large jaws and one would expect it to disappear if further evolution involved either increasing braincase size or decreasing jaw size. Trends in both these directions characterize hominid phylogeny.

That the braincase should be small in *Australopithecus* is not surprising, for this is the ancestral hominoid condition—at some time in hominid evolution the brain must have been small. It is this character which at first sight gives *Australopithecus* its ape-like appearance, but even in it there are indications of a hominid trend, for Le Gros Clark has shown that the proportion of the braincase which rises above the level of the orbits is greater in *Australopithecus* than in great apes. In this connection it is of considerable consequence that at least some of the Australopithecines made simple stone tools. Such artifacts have been found associated with skeletal remains at Olduvai Gorge and Swartkrans. There is also some evidence that animal bones, horns, and teeth were used as tools by the South-African group.

The preceding definition of *Australopithecus* provided by Le Gros Clark was drawn up before most of the East-African material had been recovered and it is appropriate to ask whether these recently discovered remains fall within it, require a re-definition, or need some additional taxonomic category. All authorities appear to be agreed that the remains which have been attributed to '*Homo habilis*' at Olduvai Gorge, and especially those from Bed II, are morphologically advanced as compared with most of the material from South Africa. This is evidenced in tooth-shape and size and in the indications of greater cranial capacity. On the basis of this L. S. B. Leakey and his colleagues recognized the new species '*habilis*' and referred it to the genus *Homo*. And now there is the remarkable cranium ER1470 from east Rudolf which has a cranial capacity of at least 800 cm$^3$, overlapping the range for *Homo erectus* and showing a number of other advanced characteristics including a rounded cranium [Fig. 4.1]. It may be noted here that re-evaluation of the '*Telanthropus capensis*' remains from Swartkrans, which include part of a cranium as well as a lower jaw, also indicates a more advanced hominid than the rest of the South-African Australopithecines which shares many features with the succeeding *Homo erectus*. '*Telanthropus*' was probably the maker of the Swartkrans tools.

The situation well illustrates the problems of attempting to impose a discrete taxonomy of qualitative classes on what is a quantitative evolutionary continuum. When the fossils known are separated by morphological 'gaps' it is possible to use the 'gaps' as divisions between taxa, but as the fossil record becomes more complete the divisions become increasingly arbitrary. Eventually taxonomic decisions in palaeoanthropology are dependent upon one's largely subjective judgement of the amount of morphological variation found in a temporal sequence which is compatible with identification of a single species. Many authorities take the view that there is insufficient difference between *Australopithecus africanus* as represented by the original South African remains and the earliest *Homo erectus* representatives from Java to permit the recognition

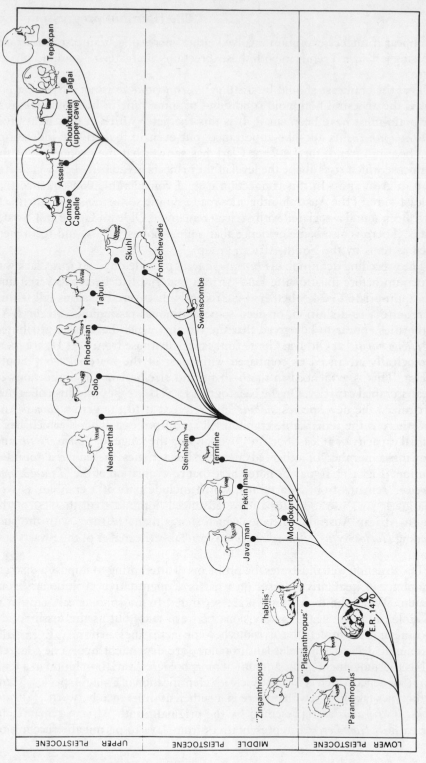

FIG. 4.1. Genealogical plan to indicate the relationships of the Hominidae.

of a new species between them. On this view the new finds have to be placed in either one taxa or the other and those who take it usually attribute them to *A. africanus*. On the other hand, the taxonomists who recognize the species category 'habilis' nowadays tend to refer it to *Australopithecus*, i.e. *A. habilis* rather than *Homo* on the grounds of greater similarity to other Australopithecine material than *Homo erectus* fossils. In either procedure, forms like E.R. 1470 are difficult to deal with, though in considering individual fossils one is apt to fail to allow adequately for population variability. E.R. 1470 could well be those of a particularly large male individual. Certainly, however, if attributed to *Australopithecus* its discovery does necessitate some revision of the definition of the genus to embrace at least occasional forms with such a large cranial capacity. And there are those who consider that E.R. 1470, 'Telanthropus' and some other as yet undescribed discoveries from East Africa should definitely be referred to *Homo* (and possibly to *Homo erectus* which would greatly increase the antiquity of this species.)

Of course what matters is not so much the taxonomy but the course of the phylogeny. Understanding of this has been greatly increased by the East-African discoveries mainly because it has been possible to establish the absolute date of the deposits from which they were recovered. The South-African remains coming as they do from deposits of non-igneous origin have always presented dating problems. Bed I and the lower parts of Bed II at Olduvai Gorge were laid down between 1·9 and 1·6 million years ago. The dates for the East-Rudolf deposits, containing E.R. 1470 as well as *A. robustus* remains are between 2·6 and 2 million years old. The Kanopoi humerus, probably Australopithecine, has a date of more than 4 million years and the Lothagam mandible of more than 5 million. Into this considerable time span come the estimates for the South-African material, mainly based on analyses of associated fauna, of 3–2·5 million years for the '*africanus*' remains and later, but not later than Olduvai Gorge Bed I for the '*robustus*' representatives at Kromdrai and Swartkrans—both considerably older than was for long supposed.

A conservative interpretation of the evidence is of a long extant genus, which for much of its known history was represented by two often sympatric species, *A. africanus* and *A. robustus* with the latter eventually becoming extinct but the former gradually changing, through habiline forms, towards *Homo* and, on the assumption that it was the tool-maker, progressively adopting a hunting form of existence. It is, however, possible that the origin of *Homo* predated any of the better known Australopithecines and that there were in the Lower Pleistocene three contemporary lineages rather than two. Even if this turns out to be the case one can feel confident in the view that the ancestry of man passed through a general Australopithecine phase much resembling *A. africanus*. More uncertain is the phylal relationship between *A. africanus* and *A. robustus*. The separation of the pongid and hominid lines must have occurred well before 5 million years B.P. and it seems quite likely that *Australopithecus* itself was descended from some form like *Ramapithecus*.

## Homo

All the other fossil hominids known are nowadays usually attributed to the single genus *Homo*, but two species are recognized *H. erectus* (formerly included in the genus *Pithecanthropus*), now extinct, and *H. sapiens* which contains all present-day populations and a number of fossil forebearers. The following is a formal definition of the genus based on those provided by Le Gros Clark and Leakey, Tobias, and Napier.

A genus of the Hominidae characterised by relatively large cranial capacity, typically greater than 800 cm$^3$ and ranging up to more than 1600 cm$^3$; the muscular ridges on the cranium vary from being strongly marked to virtually imperceptible, but the temporal crests or lines never reach the midline; although a post-orbital constriction may be present it is never as marked as in *Australopithecus*; the supra-orbital region of the frontal bone is very variable ranging from a massive and very salient supra-orbital torus to a complete lack of any supra-orbital projection and a high smooth brow region; the facial skeleton varies from moderately prognathous to orthognathous but it is not concave (or dished); the anterior symphyseal contour varies from a marked retreat to a forward slope while the bony chin may be entirely lacking, or may vary from a slight to a very strongly developed mental trigone; the dental arcade is evenly rounded with no diastema in most members of the genus; the first lower premolar is clearly bicuspid; the molar teeth, though variable in size are smaller than in *Australopithecus*; the canines and incisors are also small. The structure of the pelvic girdle and hind-limb skeleton is fully adapted to habitual erect posture and bipedal gait; the hand capable of a complete precision grip.

### Homo erectus

The fossils which are usually attributed to this species are tabulated according to geographical locality in Table 4.2.

The first remains of *Homo erectus* were discovered in Java in 1891 by Dubois, who referred them to the genus *Pithecanthropus*. Since that time more material has intermittently been found by Von Koenigswald, Jacob and Sartone, mainly in the region of Sangiran. The fossils have come from two geological horizons (cf. Table 4.2) the Middle Pleistocene Trinil zone, which has been absolutely dated at 700 000 years at its base and 500 000 years near the top and the older Lower Pleistocene Djetis zone which at its base, but near the site from which the 'Djetis' child cranium was recovered, has yielded a date of $1.9 \times 10^6$ years. This, however, is probably a considerable overestimate. The Trinil-zone forms are quite homogeneous, and an estimated mean cranial capacity of 5 crania yields a value of 860 cm$^3$. This, however, does include a well-preserved recently discovered specimen (VIII) which had a cranial volume of 1029 cm$^3$. The Djetis-zone forms are in a number of respects more primitive, with evidence, for instance, of a small diastema in the upper dentition. The one skull provides an estimated brain size of 750 cm$^3$. Included in the Djetis fossils are some fragmentary jaw fragments, formerly known as *Meganthropus palaeojavanicus*. They show similarities with *Australopithecus*, particularly *A. robustus*, and have been included in this genus by a number of workers. However, because of the frag-

TABLE 4.2

| Country | Place | Remains | Frequently referred to as | Age or geological horizon (years) |
|---|---|---|---|---|
| Java | Trinil | Calvaria and femur | *Pithecanthropus* I <br> *P. erectus* | |
| Java | Sangiran | Calvaria | *Pithecanthropus* II <br> *P. erectus* | Trinil |
| Java | Sangiran | Parietal | *Pithecanthropus* III <br> *P. erectus* | 500 000–700 000 |
| Java | Sangiran | Parts of 4 crania | *Pithecanthropus* V– <br> VIII | |
| Java | Sangiran | Post part calvaria + maxilla | *Pithecanthropus* IV <br> *P. robustus* | |
| Java | Modjokerto | Immature skull | *Homo modjokertensis* | Djetis |
| Java | Sangiran | Mandibular fragment | *Pithecanthropus* IV | lower levels $1 \cdot 9 \times 10^6$ |
| Java | Sangiran | Mandibular fragment | *P. dubius* | |
| Java | Sangiran | Mandibular fragment | *Meganthropus palaeojavanicus* | |
| China | Choukoutien | About 14 individuals (mainly skulls and teeth) | *Sinanthropus pekinensis* | 300 000 |
| China | Lantian | Skull and jaw | Lantian man | early Middle Pleistocene |
| Algeria | Ternefine | Three mandibles and small piece of parietal | *Atlanthropus mauritanicus* | |
| Morocco | Sidi Abder Rahman | Mandible | *A. mauritanicus* | |
| Tanzania | Olduvai Gorge | Calvaria skull fragments, teeth and some post-cranial bones | | Upper Bed II  700 000—Bed IV |
| Germany | Heidelberg | Mandible | *Homo heidelbergensis* | Günz–Mindel interglacial |
| Greece | Petralona | Skull | | Middle Pleistocene |
| Hungary | Vërtesszöllös | Occipital bone | | Mindel interstadial |

mentary nature of the remains it is not possible to be sure of their taxonomic status, though it would be very important if one had clear evidence of *Australopithecus* in Asia. The remaining Djetis fossils, however, show close affinity with the Trinil ones, and though, as one would expect, there is evolutionary progression in time, they clearly all belong to a single species.

The fossils from the lower cave at Choukoutien near Peking (and formerly referred to the genus *Sinanthropus*) are more advanced than any of the Javanese remains, with cranial capacities that range from 915 cm³ to 1225 cm³, and they are also later in time. A character-by-character comparison between the Javanese and the Peking remains was made in exemplary fashion by Weidenreich. Of some 120 morphological features studied by him in the Peking remains 74 could be used for direct comparison. In 57 of these the agreement was very close and in only 4 were there very striking differences. The main differences are itemized in the following table, and at most would only warrant subspecific taxonomic recognition.

The *H. erectus* fossils from Europe and Africa are scanty. They are more-or-less contemporaneous with either the Trinil-zone Javanese specimens or the Peking ones, and bear many likenesses to them. The occipital bone found at Vertesszöllös shows some particularly advanced features, and from it an esti-

TABLE 4.3

*Contrasts between Java man and Peking man*

|                          | Java man                                     | Peking man                                     |
| ------------------------ | -------------------------------------------- | ---------------------------------------------- |
| Cranial capacity         | Around 900 cm³                               | 1075 cm³                                       |
| Maximum cranial length   | 190 mm                                       | 194 mm                                         |
| Cranial height           | 105 mm                                       | 115 mm                                         |
| Frontal bones            | Very receding                                | Not so receding                                |
| Frontal sinus            | Moderately developed                         | Poorly developed                               |
| Supra-orbital torus      | Not separated from curvature of frontals     | Separated by a furrow from curvature of frontals |
| Palate                   | Smooth                                       | Rough                                          |
| Body of mandible         | Massive                                      | Not so massive                                 |
| Mental eminence          | Absent                                       | Incipiently developed                          |
| Molar teeth              | Large                                        | Not so large                                   |

mated cranial capacity of between 1350 cm³ and 1400 cm³ has been obtained. This is well into the range of modern crania, and Vertesszöllös man has been viewed as representing a transition between *H. erectus* and *H. sapiens*. The much better-preserved skull from Petralona, however, yields a cranial capacity of only 1120 cm³. Although so little is known of these western forms, it can be concluded on the present evidence that they broadly correspond to the Javanese and Peking fossils and belong to the same species. This is not to deny that there was probably considerable geographical variation between *H. erectus* populations. A definition of the species, based on that provided by Le Gros Clark for *Pithecanthropus* when the forms were recognized at generic level, is as follows:

A species of the genus Homo characterized by a cranial capacity with a mean value of about 1000 cm³; marked platycephaly, with little frontal convexity; massive supra-orbital tori; pronounced postorbital construction; opisthocranion coincident with the inion; vertex of skull marked by sagittal ridge; mastoid process variable, but usually small; thick cranial wall; tympanic plate thickened and tending towards a horizontal disposition; broad, flat nasal bones; heavily constructed mandible, lacking a mental eminence; teeth large, with well-developed basal cingulum; canines sometimes projecting and slightly interlocking, with small diastema in upper dentition; first lower premolar bicuspid with subequal cusps; molars with well-differentiated cusps complicated by secondary wrinkling of the enamel; second upper molar may be larger than the first, and the third lower molar may exceed the second in length; limb bones not distinguishable from those of *H. sapiens*.

*Homo erectus* clearly displays 'primitive' and 'advanced' features and may be considered in its morphological status to be intermediate between *Australopithecus* on the one hand and *H. sapiens* on the other. The following are the principal primitive features of *H. erectus*:

(1) bones of the cranial vault very thick;
(2) strongly developed supra-orbital torus extending above the orbits as an uninterrupted bar of bone;

(3) receding frontal bones;
(4) well-developed occipital ridge which extends into the supra-mastoid region and produces an angular contour to the occipital bone;
(5) small mastoid processes;
(6) greatest breadth of the cranium at the level of the ear-holes;
(7) Disposition of the tympanic plate;
(8) broad nasal bones;
(9) pronounced sub-nasal prognathism;
(10) massive body of the mandible;
(11) absence of a projecting chin;
(12) frequent occurrence of multiple mental foramina;
(13) large upper incisors.

The advanced features include the following:

(1) cranial capacity overlaps the lower range found in *H. sapiens* and the cranial vault is 'inflated';
(2) compared with *Australopithecus*, increased flexion of the face on the braincase so that the anterior cranial fossa extends well over the orbits;
(3) relative size of the face reduced more than in *Australopithecus*;
(4) foramen magnum is positioned more anteriorly than in *Australopithecus*;
(5) conformation of the tempero-mandibular joint as in *H. sapiens*;
(6) dental arcade parabolic in shape;
(7) dental morphology more like *H. sapiens* than is that of *Australopithecus*;
(8) incipient development of a chin in Peking man;
(9) limb bones in size and proportions indistinguishable from those of *H. sapiens*.

The overall impression gained from the crania of *H. erectus* is of form considerably different from *Australopithecus*, including even the most advanced 'habiline' material from Olduvai Gorge. This comes about from a flattening as well as an expansion of the braincase and relative reduction in jaw size. On the basis of this difference L. S. B. Leakey was led to exclude *H. erectus* from the direct lineage of *H. sapiens*, but there seems no justification for such a view. It may be emphasized that in overall morphology there are no differences in the post-cranial anatomy of *H. erectus* as it is known and modern man. *H. erectus* was fully adapted to bipedal walking.

Not only is *H. erectus* morphologically 'intermediate' between *Australopithecus* and *H. sapiens* but chronologically it is intermediate too. Admittedly if the absolute dating for the base of the Djetis zone were correct it would indicate near synchrony of the Olduvai sequence and the Javanese one, but as has already been mentioned the Djetis dates are probably gross overestimates. It seems quite likely that the earliest *H. erectus* remains are not more than a million years old.

It is not possible to say where the transition from *Australopithecus* to *H.*

*erectus* occurred, especially if it is accepted that '*Meganthropus*' was in fact an Australopithecine, and it would probably be naive anyway to think of this transition occurring among just a few populations in some restricted and isolated geographical area. Since the Australopithecine sequence is known mainly from Africa, and man's closest living relatives are the African apes, it is usually concluded that hominids had an African ancestry and underwent most of their early evolution in that continent. However, it needs to be remembered that *Ramapithecus* also existed in Asia, and it is possible that parallel evolution towards *Homo* occurred there. Nevertheless, a concensus would favour a spread of late Australopithecines or early *H. erectus* forms from Africa to Asia. Whatever the case, it seems clear that with the advent of *H. erectus*, the hominids came to spread much more widely over the Old World and began to occupy higher latitudes and more temperate zones. And there is some evidence that Peking man made fire.

### Homo sapiens

Many (Fig. 4.1) fossil hominids have been found other than the ones we have referred to *Australopithecus* and *H. erectus*, and almost every one of them has been given a distinctive specific, if not generic, name by some 'authority' or other. Hominid taxonomists, impressed by what in general zoological practice would be regarded as trivial differences, have constructed a multitude of intricate phylogenetic interpretations of the later phases of human evolution. For example, some French anthropologists recognized in the European human remains dating from the end of the first advance of the Würm glaciations to the termination of the Pleistocene, some four or five distinct races. But Morant showed that the total variability of this sample was no greater than that of a single population of Eskimos and was actually less than that of seventeenth-century Londoners. It cannot be emphasized too strongly that in all taxonomic and therefore evolutionary assessment, consideration must be given to the variation which is such an integral feature of all natural populations.

The differences between the various Pleistocene hominid remains that have not been attributed to *H. erectus* are greater than the differences within this species, but a number of distinctive characters are common to them all and there seems little justification for recognizing more than the single further species *H. sapiens*. The following is a slightly abbreviated form of Le Gros Clark's formal definition:

*Homo sapiens*—A species of Homo, distinguished mainly by a large cranial capacity with a mean value of more than 1100 cm$^3$; supra-orbital ridges variably developed; facial skeleton orthognathous or moderately prognathous; occipital condyles situated approximately at the middle of the cranial length; temporal ridges variable in their height on the cranial wall but never reaching the midline; mental eminence variably developed; dental arcade evenly rounded, with no diastema, first lower premolar bicuspid with much reduced lingual cusp; molar teeth rather variable in size, with a relative reduction of the last molar; canines relatively small, with no overlapping after the initial stages of wear; limb skeleton adapted for fully erect posture and gait.

In considering the fossil remains of *H. sapiens* (Fig. 4.1) it is convenient to distinguish, in the first place, those which are essentially like extant man, and those which differ more from any form of present-day man than any of the living races differ from each other. Table 4.4 is a list of the former from the Pleistocene referred to by the locality at which it was found. No claim to completeness is made, but the list includes the best-known remains whose geological date is reasonably certain. The earliest of these remains is datable to the lower part of the Upper Pleistocene. So far as western Europe is concerned where, as we have seen, the geochronology is most firmly established, representatives of completely modern man first appeared at the end of the Würm I glacial period. The $^{14}$C method has provided a date of about 30 000 years for the Combe-Capelle remains and associated Lower-Aurignacian industry. It has indicated somewhat greater ages for the first modern-type man in other regions. Charcoal associated with the Niah skull from Borneo has yielded a date of about 40 000 years, and the peat in which the Florisbad skull from South Africa was found has been estimated to be between 35 000 years and at least 47 000 years old. The dates for the Omo skulls is probably well over 37 000 years and other modern-type remains in South Africa may be as much as 60 000 years old. Knowledge of the dating of the African archaeological sequences is very much in a state of flux at the moment and it may be that they are much older than was formerly supposed.

In western Europe modern man was preceded by Neanderthal man, who alone occupied the region during the Würm I glaciations (70 000–40 000 years ago).

The neanderthaloid remains of this time and place are very homogeneous and distinctive (Table 4.5). They differ from those of modern man particularly in that the skull is low, the frontal bone receding, and there is a heavy supraorbital torus extending as a single uninterrupted bar of bone across the orbits. Characteristically, the occipital bone is 'bun-shaped' when viewed from the side and associated with the strongly developed neck musculature, the foramen magnum is farther back, and the mastoid processes are smaller than in modern man. The facial skeleton is less flexed on the cranial base and is long, prognathous, and narrow: the zygomatic arches are not strongly angulated. A canine fossa is also absent. The mandibular symphysis slopes backwards, for a mental eminence is not developed but the genioglossal muscles arose from genial tubercles as in modern man. The post-cranial skeleton in most features is likewise essentially similar to that of modern man, and despite the difference in the shape of the skull the cranial capacity of these so-called 'classical neanderthalers' was also large, with a volume of between 1300 cm$^3$ and 1600 cm$^3$.

TABLE 4.4

*Remains of modern man of probable Upper Pleistocene age*

| Country | Locality | Nature of remains | Archaeological association | Comment |
|---------|----------|-------------------|---------------------------|---------|
| *Europe* | | | | |
| Britain | Paviland, nr. Swansea | Post-cranial male skeleton | 'Aurignacian' Late Creswellian | — |
| Czecho-slovakia | Brünn | Brünn I, part of young male skull+post-cranial skeleton | Aurignacian | — |
| | Predmost, N.E. Moravia | Parts of some 20 individuals | — | — |
| France | Chancelade, Commune de Chancelade, Dordogne | Male skull+part of post-cranial skeleton, age 35–40 | Magdalenian | Supposed Eskimo affinities no longer accepted |
| | Combe-Capelle, Commune de Montferrand, Dordogne | Male skull+part of post-cranial skeleton, age 40–50 | Aurignacian (Chatell-perronian) | — |
| | Cro-Magnon, Commune de Tayac, Dordogne | Part of 5 adults+ debris of children's bones | Aurignacian | Old man=type specimen of so-called Cro-Magnon race |
| | Laugerie-Basse, Commune de Tayac, Dordogne | Parts of 4 individuals | Magdalenian | — |
| | Solutré, Commune de Mâcon, Saône-et-Loire | Parts of some 60 individuals | Aurignacian and Solutréan | — |
| Germany | Oberkassel, nr. Bonn | Parts of 2 individuals | Magdalenian | |
| Italy | Grottes des Enfants, Grimaldi, Riviera | Remains of various U. Pleistocene and recent age. Oldest, those of adult female and young male | Aurignacian | Supposed Negroid affinities no longer accepted |
| *Africa* | | | | |
| N. Africa | Afalou-bou-Rhummel, nr. Bougie, Algeria | Parts of some 50 individuals | Ibéro-Maurusian 'Oranian' | — |
| | Mechta-el-Arbi, nr. Constantine, Algeria | Parts of some 30 individuals | Ibéro-Maurusian Capsian | — |
| W. Africa | Asselar, north of Timbuktu | Skull and post-cranial skeleton | — | Considered to be Negro |
| E. Africa | Bromhead's Site, Elmenteita, Kenya | Parts of 30 individuals | — | Considered not to be Negro |
| | Gamble's Cave, Elmenteita, Kenya | Parts of 5 individuals | Kenya Capsian | Considered not to be Negro |
| | Kanam, Kavirondo Gulf, Kenya | Anterior part of mandible | Kafuan? | Considered not to be Negro |
| | Kanjera, Kavirondo Gulf, Kenya | Parts of 4 crania | Late Acheulian | Considered not to be Negro |

| Country | Locality | Nature of remains | Archaeological association | Comment |
|---|---|---|---|---|
| | Omo, S.W. Ethiopia | Parts of 2 skulls + limb bone fragments | — | 1 skull completely modern other showing primitive features >37 000 years old |
| | Olduvai, S.E. Serengeti Plains, Tanzania | Complete skeleton | Mesolithic? | Considered not to be Negro |
| S. Africa | Boskop, Potchefstroom District, Transvaal | Skull and post-cranial skeleton | — | Type specimen of so-called Boskopoid race reputedly with close affinities to Bushmen and Hottentots |
| | Cape Flats, nr. Cape Town | Parts of 3 individuals | Stillbay? | Boskopoid |
| | Fish Hoek, nr. Cape Town | Skull and post-cranial skeleton | Stillbay | Boskopoid |
| | Florisbad, nr. Bloemfontein | Calvarium | African Early Middle Stone Age | Supposedly with Australoid affinity |
| | Matjes River, west of Port Elizabeth | Parts of 26 individuals | African Middle and Late Stone Age | Boskopoid |
| | Springbok Flats, north of Pretoria | Skull and post-cranial skeleton | African Middle Stone Age | Boskopoid |
| *Asia* China | Choukoutien, nr. Peking | Parts of 7 individuals in upper cave | Upper Palaeolithic | — |
| Java | Wadjak, nr. Trinil | 2 crania | — | Very like Keilor skull |
| Borneo | Niah cave | Skull | — | $^{14}C+40\,000$ Melanesian–Tasmanian affinities |
| *Australasia* Australia | Keilor, nr. Melbourne | Calvarium and parts of femora | Quartzite flake | $^{14}C+6546\pm250$ |
| | Kow Swamp, N. Victoria | A number of burials | | 8000 B.C. some resemblance to Solo man |
| | Lake Mungo, N.S.W. | Skeleton | — | Date 23 500 B.C. |
| New Guinea | Aitape | Parts of Calvarium | — | — |
| *America* USA | Natchez, Mississippi | Pelvis | — | $^{14}C+11\,003$ $\pm500$ |
| Mexico | Tepexpan, nr. Mexico City | Skull and parts of post-cranial skeleton | — | — |

## TABLE 4.5

### *Better-known classical Neanderthal remains*

| Country | Locality | Remains | Archaeological association |
|---|---|---|---|
| Belgium | Engis I, Commune d'Engis, Province de Liège | Part of infant skull | Mousterian |
| | La Naulette, Commune d'Ulsonniaux, Namur | Part of mandible+post-cranial fragments | — |
| | Spy, Commune de Spy, Province de Namur | Parts of 2† male skulls and tibial fragment | Mousterian |
| Britain | St. Brelade's Bay, Jersey | Teeth and tibial fragments+ fragment of child's skull | Late Levalloiso–Mousterian |
| France | La Chapelle-aux-Saints, Corrèze | Male skull and nearly complete post-cranial skeleton | Mousterian |
| | La Ferrassie, Savignac du Bugue, Dordogne | Parts of 6 individuals 1 nearly complete (male) | Mousterian |
| | Le Moustier, Commune de Peyzac, Dordogne | Part of 1 male skull | Mousterian |
| | La Quina, Commune de Gardes–Le-Pontaroux (Charente) | Parts of female skull+post-cranial fragments | Mousterian |
| Germany | Neanderthal, nr. Düsseldorf | Parts of male skull and post-cranial skeleton | — |
| Gibraltar | Forbes' Quarry | Calvarium of female | — |
| | Devil's Tower | Fragment of child's skull | Upper Mousterian |
| Italy | Monte Circeo, Provincia de Latina, south of Rome | Calvarium of 1 male individual+ part of mandible of another | Mousterian |
| Iraq | Shanidar, northern Iraq | Parts of 3 adult individuals and 1 child | Mousterian |
| Israel | Mt. Carmel, Cave of Mugharet Tabün | 1 adult female well-preserved+1 male mandible and many fragments | Levalloiso–Mousterian |
| | Amud Cave | Much of skull and skeleton | — |
| USSR | Teshik Tash, Uzbekistan | Parts of skull of 8–10-year-old child | — |

† The diagnosis of sex in both this table and in Table 4.6 is, of course, extremely tentative.

Remains in many ways similar to the classical Neanderthals and of similar date have also been found in the Middle East, at Shanidar in Iraq, and the Tabun Cave at Mount Carmel, and the Amud Cave in Israel and at Teshik Tash in Uzbekistan. There may be some systematic geographical heterogeneity, since none of these Middle-East forms show a typical 'bun-shaped' occiput, and Amud man had large mastoid processes. However, there can be no doubt of their general affinity with the western Neanderthals.

Most of the other remains of *Homo sapiens* from Europe and neighbouring regions, datable to the same period or earlier, show, in varying degrees, some of these neanderthaloid characters. But in many of the features which distinguish classical Neanderthal from modern man, the majority of these remains are more neanthropic. There is considerable heterogeneity but, in contrast with the classical neanderthalers, they typically have braincases which are shorter, narrower, but with laterally expanded walls and more highly arched foreheads. There is a tendency to separate medial and lateral supra-orbital toral elements and the expanded occipital bones tend to possess an external protuberance associated with an ill-developed occipital torus. Flexion of the cranial base is greater and the facial skeleton is smaller. The jugals have a more antero-lateral orientation and are clearly demarcated from the maxillae, while the latter show a tendency for the formation of a canine fossa. In all these features these often-called 'progressive neanderthalers' are more like modern man than are the classical forms. A list of the localities at which they were found is given in Table 4.6.

A clear exception to this general statement are the fossils discovered by the Lumleys in the south of France which belong to the Riss glacial phase: the Suard and Arago remains. These retain many paleonthropic features and indeed in some respects appear even more primitive than Vertesszöllös man. It

## TABLE 4.6

*Homo sapiens remains from Europe, North Africa and the Middle East of Middle and Lower Upper Pleistocene age*

| Country | Locality | Remains | Geological horizon | Archaeological association |
|---|---|---|---|---|
| Morocco | Jebel Ighoud | Two skulls | Würm ?45 000 B.C. | Levalloiso–Mousterian |
| Palestine | Jebel Quafza | Complete cranium and parts of other individuals | Würm | Levalloiso–Mousterian |
| Israel | Cave of Mugharet es-Skhūl | Parts of at least 10 individuals | Würm 36 000 B.C. | Levalloiso–Mousterian |
| Yugoslavia | Krapina, nr. Zagreb | Fragmentary remains of some 13 individuals | ?Early Würm | Mousterian |
| Germany | Ehringsdorf, nr. Weimar | Parts of female cranium (Ehringsdorf I) and 2 mandibles + remains of child's skeleton (Ehringsdorf II) | Riss–Würm interglacial | 'Pre-Mousterian' |
| Italy | Saccopastore, nr. Rome | Female cranium (Saccopastore I) and parts of male skull (Saccopastore II) | Riss–Würm interglacial | Mousterian |
| Czecho-slovakia | Ganovce | Endocranial cast | Riss–Würm interglacial | |
| France | Fontéchevade, Commune de Charente | Frontal bone of 1 individual (I) Calotte of second (II) | Riss–Würm interglacial | Tayacian |
| France | Abri Suard la Chaise, Commune de Charante | Occipital, parietal, and temporal bones | Late Riss | |
| France | Lazaret, nr. Nice | Parietal bone | Riss | |
| France | Arago Cave, Tautanel | Cranial front and face and 2 mandibles | Early Riss | |
| France | Montmaurin, Haute-Garonne | Mandible and teeth | ?Mindel–Riss interglacial | Pre-Mousterian |
| Germany | Steinheim, nr. Stuttgart | Female cranium | Mindel–Riss interglacial | |
| England | Swanscombe, Kent | Occipital and parietal bones | Mindel–Riss interglacial | Middle Acheulian hand-axe industry |

is perhaps significant that like classical Neanderthal man they come from a glacial phase. That more neanthropic forms were already in existence is demonstrated by the Steinheim and Swanscombe remains which come from Great-Interglacial deposits. The occipital and parietal bones which make up Swanscombe man and which were found in the 100 ft terrace of the River Thames in association with Acheulian hand-axes, are indistinguishable from those of modern man except for being unusually thick. The Steinheim cranium, though possessing a heavy supra-orbital torus also appears to show many progressive features. Some of the forms from the last interglacial period, e.g. the Ehringsdorf and Saccopastore crania, show clear neanderthaloid affinities, but it would appear that Fontéchevade man did not possess a heavy supra-orbital torus. On the other hand, the later fossils from the Skūhl Cave at Mount Carmel in Israel and from Jebel Quafza in Palestine, although very modernistic in many features, do retain this structure. It is usually concluded nowadays that these latter forms represent the penultimate stage in the skeletal differentiation of man as we now know him.

But before considering in detail the relevance of this whole assemblage of European and Near-Eastern fossils to the ultimate phase of human evolution it is as well to mention first the hominid remains of Pleistocene date found in other parts of the world. Africa has proved to be a particularly rich source. From it have been obtained not only the already discussed Australopithecine fossils, but also remains of the quite distinctive 'Rhodesian' man, which gets its name from the single cranium found at Broken Hill, Northern Rhodesia. This fossil has been said to be about 30 000 years old but may be much older. The facial skeleton, though very large and lacking a canine fossa, is not radically different in its conformation from that of modern man. The braincase, however, is extremely low and the frontal bones strongly recede. The brow ridges are massive and extend as a continuous bony bar above the orbits. All the bones are excessively thick, so much so in fact that the internal length of the braincase is only 81 per cent of the skull length. Despite these palaeanthropic features, the foramen magnum is almost as far forward as in modern man, and although the occipital attachments of the nuchal musculature were higher than in present-day forms, the occiput was not buried in the neck as in classical neanderthalers. This in itself suggests that the modern-type limb bones also found in the same cave probably belonged to the same individual as the cranium. As long as only a single representative of Rhodesian man was known, it could reasonably be suspected that it was a pathological form, but the discovery of another skull at Saldanha Bay, almost indistinguishable from the original one at Broken Hill, makes this hypothesis extremely unlikely.

Reference must also be made to the so-called *Africanthropus*. This form is probably non-*sapiens*, but the remains, found in Tanzania, are too ill preserved to allow proper taxonomic assessment.

Many other fossil hominids have been found in Africa, but all are very like modern man. Considerable evolutionary significance has been attached to the remains discovered at Kanam and Kanjera because it was thought originally that they were of great antiquity. However, all the evidence now indicates that they and all the other undoubted *sapiens* material are no older than the Upper Pleistocene. Many of the forms are probably even more recent than this.

A number of hominid remains of probable Pleistocene age have also been found in eastern and South-East Asia, and in Australia, but with the exception of the discoveries made at Ngandong, Java, in the terraces of the Solo river, all are essentially modern in their morphology. 'Solo' man, represented by 11 skulls, all lacking a facial skeleton, and two incomplete tibiae, is according to von Koenigswald, of Upper-Pleistocene date. The skulls are platycephalic, with unusually thick cranial walls, and each has a strongly developed supra-orbital torus. The disposition of the foramen magnum shows a number of distinctive features, but, apart from the low cranial capacity ($1150–1300\,cm^3$) and the fact that the tibiae are slender and straight-shafted, the general conformation is neanderthaloid.

During the early decades of this century a number of human remains found in the Americas were claimed to be of considerable antiquity. All, however, are certainly of *sapiens* form and many are in all probability quite recent. Nevertheless, it does appear from archaeological evidence that man was present in the Americas at least from the middle of the last glacial period and the skeletal remains found at Tepexpan in Mexico have been fairly certainly determined to be at least 10 000 years old.

The evolutionary relationships between the various forms of *Homo* have been the subject of great speculation and controversy. On one point, however, most authorities now agree, namely that all forms of *Homo sapiens* are descended from *H. erectus*. The principal change that has occurred in this descent is enlargement of the brain and concomitantly of the cranium. In addition, the general hominid trend towards jaw reduction and perfection of the balance of the head on the vertebral column has been carried further.

In considering the terminal phases of hominid evolution, it is important to realize that there has probably been widespread gene flow between populations, which by offsetting the tendencies to diverge has produced a reticulate type of evolution. However, it seems most likely that in relative isolation in Africa, *H. erectus* evolved into Rhodesian man, and that Solo man was the direct descendant of the eastern representatives of this species. The situation in Euro-Asia is more complicated. The three most reasonable interpretations of the evidence are presented in diagrammatic form in Fig. 4.2. Fig. 4.2(a) indicates an early origin for modern man and completely independent evolution of the neanderthalers. This view rests upon the undoubted similarity of Swanscombe and Fontéchevade man with present-day man. It was much favoured before the exposure of the Piltdown fraud when even an '*erectus*' stage in the differentiation of *H. sapiens* was considered unlikely.

The scheme, however, ignores the great likeness between the Swanscombe remains and the corresponding bones of Steinheim man. In fact, many authori-

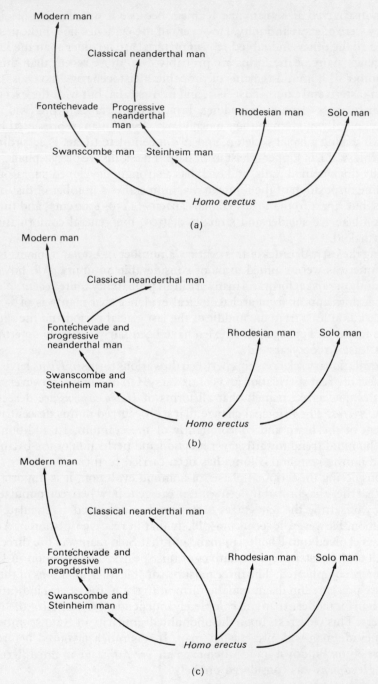

Modern man

Classical neanderthal man

Fontéchevade    Progressive
neanderthal
man    Rhodesian man    Solo man

Swanscombe man    Steinheim man

*Homo erectus*

(a)

Modern man

Classical neanderthal man

Fontéchevade and
progressive
neanderthal man    Rhodesian man    Solo man

Swanscombe and
Steinheim man

*Homo erectus*

(b)

Modern man

Classical neanderthal man

Fontéchevade and
progressive
neanderthal man    Rhodesian man    Solo man

Swanscombe and
Steinheim man

*Homo erectus*

(c)

FIG. 4.2. Three alternative phylogenetic schemes to show the evolution and differentiation of *Homo* (see text for explanation of (a), (b), and (c)).

ties now believe that Swanscombe man was also a progressive neanderthaler, albeit representing the most neanthropic range of the variation. If this is the case, then there is no evidence for modern man before the last interglacial, and a progressive neanderthaloid ancestry for him must be presumed, with the Skūhl, Jebel Quafza, and Fontéchevade remains representing the final stages in the differentiation. This view, which would now seem to be the most widely accepted, is represented in Fig. 4.2(b). However, the last scheme, in contrast with the preceding ones, indicates a quite separate ancestry for the progressive and classical neanderthalers. The principal reason for recognizing an ancestor–descendant relationship between these two groups is their temporal continuity in the same geographical region, but it is difficult to account for the apparent reversal of the main evolutionary trend of the hominids which such a relationship involves. Admittedly it is possible that the palaeanthropic features of the classical neanderthalers represent adaptations to a cold biome, since most of the remains have been recovered from the part of Europe isolated from Asia by the expansion of the Alpine and Scandinavian ice sheets. However, it seems at least as likely that the palaeanthropic characters are primitive. If this is the case, there exists both a temporal as well as a morphological gap between classical neanderthalers and *H. erectus*, but if classical Neanderthal man was a northern form it is not surprising that his earlier remains have not been found; the northern parts of the Euro-Asian land-mass are poorly explored. The palaeanthropic features of the Suard and Arago remains are here relevant.

One cannot, of course, fully know the means by which modern man replaced classical neanderthalers when he was able to enter western Europe at the end of the Würm I Ice Age. However, it is no doubt very significant that the Upper-Palaeolithic knives, burins, and spear- and arrow-heads made by the invaders were vastly superior implements to the mousterian flint industry which characterizes classical Neanderthal culture. Further, this advanced material culture is also likely to reflect a superior social organization.

It is impossible to say which of the present-day races is most similar to the first fully differentiated populations of modern man, but the widespread distribution of the Australoid form in both fossil and living populations, and its greater morphological affinity with ancestral stages, suggest that it most closely resembles primitive modern-type man. However, at least in Europe, this type has not been recognized, though at one time or another various ancestors to the extant races have been distinguished, almost certainly falsely, in the Upper-Palaeolithic populations of the area. It is also noteworthy that the earliest remains found in Australia, i.e. at Lake Mungo, appear to be of a more gracile form than such later groups as those represented at Kow Swamp.

The division of such evolutionary dendrites as are represented in Fig. 4.2 into discrete taxa must obviously be largely arbitrary. In the past, classical Neanderthal man, Rhodesian man, Solo man, and even some of the progressive neanderthalers were accorded their own specific status. But such a practice leads to many difficulties and nowadays it is customary to include all these forms in a single species *H. sapiens* albeit with a number of subspecies, i.e. *neanderthalensis*, *rhodesiensis*, *soloensis*, and, perhaps, the major geographical races of upper palaeolithic and present-day man.

# 5. The evolution of human society

## Introduction

DISCUSSION of the origins and evolution of human society must necessarily be largely speculative. Speculation is not necessarily idle, however; it can be informed. The problem then becomes: which information is most relevant to the discussion? Two kinds of information seem most pertinent to this enquiry: the social behaviour of other Primates and the actual data, mainly in the form of fossil remains, of *Australopithecus* and other forms of early man. The former can give us ideas about the nature of Primate social organization other than that of man himself in his modern form; the latter can tell us something about the ecological and physical conditions of pre-human existence. The advantage of studying Primate species other than modern man is that these give us a variety of possibilities of social organization which can then be compared on the basis of the Primates themselves and their ecological circumstances with what is known of the conditions in which our ancestors lived. It is probably better to look at the societies of other Primates rather than those of living hunter–gatherers for models of the social organization of the pre-hominids because it is clear that during human evolution a major change has occurred in relation to society—namely the social re-organization achieved by man with the increasing complexity of his brain and the evolution of language. In other words, non-human Primates give us examples of social organizations based on social signals and learning processes which are not dependent on the learning of symbolic language. With regard to the use of fossil data and information about the ecological circumstances of our ancestors, this can tell us very little about the actual nature of social life in pre-hominid or early hominid times; however, what little it can tell us is of a hard and factual kind and is therefore of great significance.

The present chapter adopts the following method. Initially some baseline data concerning the social organization of a few Primate species are given. Second, we look at some general ideas that have emerged from these and other studies of social organization in Primates. Third, we briefly examine the environment and fossil data relating to the early hominids. Finally, we shall attempt to integrate the data from non-human Primates with the data from pre-hominids into a coherent argument concerning the society of early man.

## Primate societies

### Common baboons (Papio anubis) *and rhesus monkeys* (Macaca mulatta)

The social life of these Old World species has been extensively studied over a prolonged period of time. The baboon is a successful species of Primate which is widespread on the African savannahs at the present time. Rhesus monkeys occur in India, in forests and inhabited areas.

Baboons are terrestrial vegetarians. This does not mean they never climb trees or cliffs, nor does it mean they do not eat meat and insects—occasionally they do both. However, they are not primarily meat-eaters and they have left the typical Primate habitat which is trees and forest.

Baboons live in large groups ranging in size from 8 to 185; the average for different areas is 30–50 animals. In most areas studied the groups are somewhat closed to outsiders; however, in an area of forest studied by Rowell (1966) it was found that groups were more open to members of other nearby groups, and males in particular tended to move from one group of baboons to another. More typically the baboon group keeps largely to itself and avoids contact and mixing with other groups, except occasionally at water-holes, when groups may meet and mix but generally leave without exchanging members. During the normal day a baboon group moves in a loose assemblage over its range, returning to a particular grove of sleeping trees in what has been called its 'core area' at night. The ranges of a number of baboon groups may overlap; however, the groups themselves do not approach very close but tend to avoid each other. The average distance travelled is 3 miles per day. Groups consist of males and females in equal numbers, but females mature faster than males, attaining maturity by $3\frac{1}{2}$–5 years of age, whereas males are not fully mature until 7–10 years old. Thus the sex ratio of mature adults is 1 male to 2 or even 3 females.

Baboons show considerable sexual dimorphism. Males are twice or 3 times as big as females. The explanation for this phenomenon is probably to be found in predator pressure. It is advantageous for males to be large in order to protect the group against leopards, hyenas, cheetahs, lions, and other predators; on the other hand, the large size of the males increases the food needs of the group and therefore it is advantageous for protective actions and aggressiveness to be focused on one sex only, namely males, while females can remain small and survive by means of the protection offered by the males. This reduces the bio-mass of the group and therefore its food needs and increases its survival potential. Selection for aggressiveness on the part of males may have had important effects on the social organization of the species.

This brings us into the field of dominance relationships. The aggressive nature of adult male baboons, together with the fact that they form close-knit social groups, has led to the formation of dominance hierarchies in this species. Dominance is expressed in a number of ways. To understand the meaning of the concept we can document the success of the dominant male of a baboon group in a number of contexts. We can see to what extent he has preferential selection of mates; we can observe other monkeys in his group giving him submission signals; we can observe to what extent he engages in aggressive acts against other members of the group; we can see to what extent he acts as a leader in threatening other Primates or other species which come close to the group, and finally we can see that he is a protector in so far that mothers cluster close to him at times of danger. Where there are several adult males in a group a linear order of dominance may not necessarily occur. The reason for this is that certain males act together as a unit. Chance (1967) has drawn attention to the cohort of adult males which forms the dominant core of groups of rhesus macaques. In such a group individuals are all adult males and they pay close attention to each others' movements, stay together, and between them control the movements and social behaviour of other members of the group. The dominance of these animals is largely dependent on their relations with each other. De Vore and Hall (1965) have shown how, when one of a dominant pair of baboons disappears, the other falls below a baboon previously inferior to it. The rank order of males is constantly reinforced and occasionally changed by the occurrence of quarrels in the group. Threats and counter-threats, re-directed threats, and protected threats (in which an animal simultaneously threatens a subordinate and signals its own submissiveness to a more dominant group member) are certain of the complex mechanisms of social behaviour by which social status is achieved and maintained.

Females also have a rank order; they also engage in quarrels, but in the case of females rank appears to be related to oestrus condition and their association with particular males, especially the most dominant male. In addition the rank order of females, and indirectly that of males, in macaques is affected by their relative position in the hierarchy of matriarchies or lineages of which they form part. Thus it is clear from studies of Japanese and rhesus macaques that besides the status achieved by competition there is a social status which is acquired by virtue of being born into a lineage, the dominant members of which are already of high status.

The spatial relations of animals in a macaque or baboon group are such that the dominant animals tend to be centrally located with the less dominant animals on the periphery of the group. Thus sub-adult males tend to be found further from the centre of the group than other members, and in some species of macaques they leave the group altogether and return to it, if at all, after a number of years. In the case of baboons, young males do not appear to leave the group but stay around its periphery where they are functional as 'sentinels' giving warning of approaching predators or other hazards.

Like dominance behaviour, sexual behaviour and relationships are important aspects of social organization. Female baboons have oestrus cycles of 35 days. They show a pronounced sexual swelling at the time of ovulation; this then declines after ovulation. In a typical *Papio anubis* group the dominant male copulates with a female at the peak of her oestrus cycle over a period of 3–4 days. After mating the pair breaks up and there is no evidence that they continue to associate with each other for a prolonged period, in contrast with the situation in Hamadryas baboons (see below) in which individual males and females form long-lasting bonds, and macaques, in which such bonds not infrequently occur. Mating is seasonal in some areas (Kenya) and not in others (South Africa).

Mother–infant relations constitute another set of social bonds. The new-born infant is dark coloured and clings tightly by a series of reflex actions to its mother underneath her belly. The mother moves to the social centre of the group on childbirth and stays there in the protection of the dominant caucus of adult males and with other females who may or may not have infants. The infant is investigated by the other females during the first few days of life but it clings tightly to its mother. During the first few months the infant begins to move into the dorsal position, riding on the mother's back, tasting the food she eats, leaving her for brief exploratory ventures. Later at the age of 6 months it loses its dark colour, begins to eat solids, and to play with its peers. It is protected by the mother and by adult males until weaning at 11–15 months. From weaning the infant engages in play which becomes progressively rougher and youngsters may incur the displeasure of adults. The tolerance of adult males towards the growing young male is progressively reduced, and eventually the sub-adult males are not able to interact with adult males without incurring their displeasure. Mothers go back to cycling when lactation is finished and no longer protect their youngsters after weaning.

Friendly relationships between animals are frequently observed and are characterized by mutual grooming behaviour. There are particular postures which stimulate grooming by a partner. Most grooming is of females by females and females spend longer grooming than males. Females very frequently groom an adult male especially the dominant male. They also groom a female in œstrus and the mother with a new infant. Low-status animals tend to groom high-status animals more than the reverse. Grooming is thus seen to create and reinforce social bonds.

A variety of vocalizations is emitted by baboons in communicating with each other. These can be categorized according to the situation and supposed underlying motivation. For instance, one can distinguish attack calls (barks, grunts, and roars); escape calls (screeching); sexual calls (growling); and friendly calls (chattering and grunting). The naming and categorizing of calls is a difficult procedure because of (a) the fact that calls form a graded system in most cases, running into each other, and (b) there are problems of observer description. These latter are to some extent overcome by the use of sonograms.

With these calls goes a wide variety of visual signals given primarily by facial expressions but also by the body and limbs. For example, in the range of attack signals, there are yawning, jerking the head, raising the hair, slapping, and chasing. Expressions of fear include baring of the teeth and cowering on the ground; friendly postures include lip-smacking and presenting. Finally there are tactile signals such as biting, mounting, and grooming.

### Hamadryas baboons (Papio hamadryas)

The social organization of Hamadryas baboons has been studied over a number of years by Hans Kummer and his co-workers in Ethiopia (Kummer 1968). The Hamadryas baboon is specialized for open and semi-arid areas, living in more barren environments than the common baboon. This species lives in large groups ranging from 12 to 750 members with an average of 136. These large groups, however, are found only during the night at sleeping sites. During the daytime they split up into a large number of smaller foraging units. These foraging units are based on a one-male group organization consisting of a single adult male together with one or more adult females and their young, plus a few older animals accompanying the group. These one-male groups are the basic units of Hamadryas baboon society and serve to distinguish the social organization of this species from that of common baboons, which lack this subgrouping tendency. The Hamadryas one-male group is a spatially coherent unit and stays together during the lifetime of the individuals concerned. The male threatens his females if they lag behind or if they consort with other males. He does this by raising his brows and staring at them, lunging at them, or chasing and neck-biting them. Females respond by keeping close to their male and uttering a staccato cough if his threat is mild or a scream if he bites them. Bloodshed is rare. Average frequency of male–female agonistic encounters is one bite per male per day. Males are possessive over their females as is seen from the fact that they position themselves in front of the female with respect to other males. If other males approach a one-male group the females in the group will run towards their overlord. If a male loses one of his females he will search for her persistently; Kummer reports a search lasting 12 minutes. If a unit member is sick or delayed it is not abandoned by the unit, in contrast with the situation in common baboons where animals that are delayed or sick are generally left behind.

Copulation is limited to members of one-male groups. There are a number of males in Hamadryas society which do not possess females. These form bachelor bands, and males in bachelor bands never copulate. If a male has one female only in his one-male group copulation is limited to periods when she is in œstrus and does not occur when she is pregnant or nursing. The rules about copulation apply to adult males only; sub-adult and juvenile males copulate with any females. This action by the females, however, may anger their unit leaders. In such cases the offending females are attacked by their males, and such a male does not attack another male engaging in copulation with one of his females. As a result such copulations usually occur out of sight of the leader male. Precocious copulation is practised by both juvenile females and juvenile males.

As in common baboons, grooming is a frequent form of friendly social activity. Both sexes groom, females rather more than males. Females spend up to 28 per cent of their time at their sleeping rock, grooming. Certain postures are associated with grooming, e.g. presentation. Grooming is focused on the leader, and leaders themselves often ignore the posture of sub-adult females inviting them to groom. Instead they have preferred grooming partners with whom they spend most of their time.

In their aggressive relations females quarrel, e.g. over grooming access to

a male. If this quarrelling is protracted males may intervene and end it with
a bite. Between males avoidance occurs; leaders do not groom each other but
keep at a distance at least 1·5 m apart. Occasionally they fight, their fights taking
the form of ritualized 'fencing' with bites and hits, facing each other. Such
fights last up to 10 s, when one animal flees. There is a well-developed submission signal in Hamadryas baboons which consists of exposure of neck or throat,
as seen in dogs. Of 13 fights observed by Kummer, 10 were over females, 3
were 'mistakes'. Such mistakes occur if a threat intended for another animal
is misinterpreted by a male. The fights between males over females are not
always caused by illicit copulation but result from attacks by a male on
another male's female; her leader then retaliates on the male. The fights do
not concern œstrus females, only anœstrus ones. Thus *possession* is the issue,
not sex.

The origins of one-male groups are extremely interesting. Kummer has
observed that sub-adult males tend to snatch and keep black infants for periods
of up to 30 minutes, and he calls this behaviour 'kidnapping'. This kidnapping
turns into 'adoption' when the sub-adult male obtains an infantile or juvenile
female aged between 1 and $1\frac{1}{2}$ years old and holds on to her, carrying her around
with him and staying close to her all the time. These small units, consisting
of one young adult leader male and one infantile or juvenile female are very
cohesive units with much grooming by the female of the male. Sexual relations
are absent because the female is at this point too immature. There is no neck-
bite by the male. The female at times clings to the male as if he were a mother,
and males carry their infant like a mother. It appears that the motivation underlying this activity of the male is not sexual but is of a pseudo-maternal kind,
and it is this small unit which forms the 'pair bond' which lies at the basis
of the one-male group found in adult Hamadryas baboons. Although there is
no neck-bite at the early stages males do retrieve their females with their hands
if they wander off. How do the males initially separate a juvenile female from
her natal unit? This is not clearly understood. But we should note (a) the loss
of the mother's protection for the infant at 6 months and (b) the fact that adult
male leaders do not cling to young females in their group. Females are thus
available for adoption in this species. A selective advantage to the system is
that it releases young animals for interaction with other groups, thus avoiding
the genetic results of inbreeding by providing for an outmating system. These
young females who are adopted do not have young until they are 4 years of
age, although copulation begins well in advance of this.

There is another way in which one-male units may be formed. Males in their
prime occasionally take over females from older leaders. In the case of old
leaders there is no retaliation to such events and the prior leader allows his
female to transfer from himself to a younger male. In the case of females, the
transfer from one male to another appears to be a relatively straightforward
matter, i.e. females have learnt following behaviour rather than devotion to
a particular male.

The wider unit of Hamadryas society, i.e. the large group of animals that sleep together at night, breaks down, as already stated, into one-male groups during the daytime, but it also breaks down into bands of intermediate size which tend to keep together. These bands can be distinguished from each other by putting out experimental food samples, when 'battles' develop between the bands, the winning band taking all the food and the losing band retreating. One such battle occurred naturally over a sleeping rock. Kummer suggests that the friendly relations between males in these bands may be based on friendly peer-group relationships between males established during their early years before they become unit leaders.

A feature of the movement of groups during the daytime when they are foraging is the occurrence of two-male teams. These consist of the senior and a junior male in a one-male unit that move and march together. Eight such teams were observed by Kummer. Each had one young leader and one old leader. One of these went in front of the group and the other took the rear, with the females in between. The direction of movement of the groups was a compromise of the two males' actions, but the older male had more decisive power than the younger. Kummer therefore suggests that this system of co-ordination of travel be called the ID system in which the letter I stands for the initiative role of the younger male and the letter D stands for the decision-making role of the senior male.

## Chimpanzees (Pan troglodytes)

Wild chimpanzees have been studied in a number of forest areas and groups of provisionized chimpanzees have also been studied for a long period at the Gombe National Park and in other areas of western Tanzania. In this section I shall focus mainly on the forest-living chimpanzees, in particular those of the Budongo forest in Uganda.

These chimpanzees differ in their social organization from the baboon and macaque species described above in that they do not form closed groups either of the large size found in common baboons and rhesus monkeys, or of the one-male group type found in Hamadryas baboons. Instead the distinctive feature of their society is the flexible nature of their groups which is such that members come together, stay together for a few hours or days or perhaps longer, and then part to meet again later on. This at any rate is the kind of social organization found in wild chimpanzees in the tropical rain forest. In other areas, such as the woodland areas of Tanzania, it seems that chimpanzees do form more exclusive communities. However, reports by various Japanese workers have indicated movement of females from group to group in woodland areas (Kawanaka and Nishida 1974). The process of fission and fusion seen in Budongo forest chimpanzees was analysed to determine whether there were any principles of social organization or whether groups formed and re-formed at random. This analysis indicated that four types of grouping occurred with a high degree of frequency. These were groups of adult males excluding females and younger animals; groups of mothers consisting of females with their young, but no childless females or adolescents and only the occasional older male; groups of adults consisting of adult members of both sexes and often including females in œstrus but no youngsters; and mixed groups which consisted of all sex and age classes together.

Functionally these groups could be differentiated from each other in the following way. Groups of adult males tended to be very mobile, rather vociferous, and to be the first to locate new food sources as they travelled round the forest. By contrast, groups of mothers were relatively immobile, did not make much noise, and tended to stay in one spot before moving to a particular new area which they had located as a result of hearing the calls of other animals. When they moved they moved fairly rapidly in a straight line and did not roam around the forest. Mothers often had a pair of offspring or even occasionally 3 offspring. The youngest was carried under the belly, older offspring were carried on the back, and relatively independent offspring trotted along beside or behind the mother. It is known that in chimpanzees the young remain with the mother up to 5 years of age. Adult groups were those in which sexual activity was most often seen, often resulting from the tendency of a female in œstrus displaying a vivid sexual swelling to attract a number of adult males. One of these would copulate with the female while others waited nearby; these took over the copulation when the first male had finished. Mixed groups were mostly seen on trees containing a large amount of food, e.g. fig trees. They were mostly aggregations resulting from the coming together of a large number of animals for purposes of feeding.

The types of groups described above should not be taken as absolutes but as highly probable kinds of social organization of chimpanzees in rain-forest conditions such as those encountered in Budongo. Quite possibly social organization is different in other areas and studies currently under way in Tanzania and elsewhere are helping to throw light on this problem. The total population size of a region of rain forest was estimated as 70–80 chimpanzees by Reynolds and Reynolds for a 'community' living in a given region of forest. Other regions studied were thought to have populations of similar size. However, owing to the high frequency of visits between one community and others, it was difficult to delimit either the area of exclusive use or the exact population size. In the Budongo forest the density appears to be approximately 10 chimpanzees to the square mile, which is the highest density so far recorded for a chimpanzee population.

There do now appear to be real differences between the type of social organization described above and the kind found in the woodland–savannah zone described by Kawanaka and Nishida (1974). In the latter case, chimpanzees form groups which are clearly distinct from each other, although by no means 'closed' (see below). These groups occupy ranges which overlap extensively. Nevertheless, dominance relations appear to exist between the groups, so that the subordinate group moves away from the overlap zone on the approach of the dominant group. It appears that the chorusing vocalizations of the dominant group are sufficient to cause anxiety and eventually flight in the subordinate group, a very different situation from that found in forest-living chimpanzees, where chorusing appears to be an attractive force.

Most interestingly, the antagonism between woodland–savannah-dwelling chimpanzee groups seems to reside in antagonism between the adult males that make up the core of such groups. The males in two groups studied were not seen to change groups for over 8 years; females by contrast frequently moved from one group to the other, nearly always at times of sexual receptivity. The implications of such an arrangement for the study of early hominid social organization are considerable, and are discussed below (pp. 89–90).

Chimpanzee social behaviour has been described by Goodall and others, and it is clear that the variety and complexity of facial and body movements, of tactile signals and vocalizations, is very great. Important categories of behaviour in these animals include, as usual, aggressive, maternal, and sexual signals. A further important category encountered in chimpanzees is commonly called greeting behaviour. This consists of a variety of facial expressions, body movements, and tactile gestures, given mainly with the hands, which are seen when chimpanzees meet each other. There is also a series of display movements, mainly by dominant adult males, which appears to focus the attention of other animals in the group on the central and largest males present. A further interesting characteristic is the phenomenon described in the early literature as 'carnivals' (Garner 1896). These prolonged outbursts of noisy calling and drumming, dancing around, and branch-shaking by large numbers of chimpanzees gathered together appear to be expressions of excitement engendered by the meeting of groups of chimpanzees. The reference to drumming perhaps calls for explanation: chimpanzees produce a loud drumming sound by beating on the buttresses of trees such as ironwood trees with the palms of their hands and occasionally the soles of their feet. These calls carry long distances and appear to function in communicating the whereabouts of chimpanzees to others in the vicinity, in conditions where visibility is severely limited. The loud and noisy outbursts of calling and drumming by numbers of chimpanzees in the forest is thought by Reynolds and Reynolds (1965) to serve as a long-distance communication system informing other chimpanzees of the whereabouts of good food sources. This suggestion arises from the observed fact that when fruit is scarce chimpanzees are quiet whereas when fruit is abundant they make a large amount of noise, attracting other chimpanzees from the surrounding forest to the fruiting trees.

## Ecological and phylogenetic determinants of social organization

A number of authors have sought to make generalizations concerning Primate social organizations. Some have tended to emphasize ecological determinants, others phylogenetic ones. DeVore (1963) drew up a demographic table of the then-studied primate species, ranging them from the most arboreal to the most terrestrial, and concluded (a) that the more terrestrial primates had a larger home range than the more arboreal species, and (b) that the more terrestrial Primates lived in larger organized groups than the more arboreal ones. Crook and Gartlan (1966) have drawn up a table of 'adaptive grades' of Primates, representing adaptations to forest, tree savannah, grassland, and arid environments. In general, forest species were found to live in small groups and to hold territories, as conditions became more open species became more territorial and lived in larger, multi-male groups, but in the poorer environment of arid savannah there was a tendency to form one-male groups. Sexual dimorphism and role differentiation increased with the extent of territoriality and extent of food dispersion.

In contrast with the view that ecological factors largely determine Primate social organizations is the view that social behaviour and social structure are largely delimited by phylogenetic factors. Struhsaker (1969) has studied a number of West-African forest-living monkeys, mainly species of *Cercopithecus* but also drills, mangabeys, and colobus. He found that most of the arboreal forest monkeys and all the *Cercopithecus* species lived in one-male groups. He concluded that 'in considering the relation between ecology and society it must be emphasized that each species brings a different phylogenetic heritage into a particular ecological scene. Consequently one must consider not only ecology but also phylogeny in attempting to understand the evolution of primate social organisation.'

As we shall see, the question of how much weight to place on ecological and phylogenetic determinants of social structures plays an important part in the selection of species to serve as models for generating ideas about the social life of early man. Clearly, both are important. On the ecological side the most convincing data are those showing that a particular species of primate can show different patterns of social organization in different environments—as is the case in langurs *(Presbytis entellus)*, for example, and also in common baboons *(Papio anubis)* when comparisons are made between forest and savannah or open woodland groups. In other cases, however, social organization seems less variable. *Cercopithecus* species seem to be largely restricted to one-male groups whether in forest or savannah. Hamadryas baboons seem relatively inflexible with regard to their social arrangements, for although they do not occur in a forest habitat they maintain their one-male group system in captivity. Clutton-Brock has re-emphasized the need for caution in construing social organizations as outcomes of ecological pressures. In a comparison of two colobus species he has stressed that different species may approach the exploitation of any given habitat type in different ways based on their phylogenetic predispositions (feeding habits in particular). Second, he has pointed out that we need to be cautious in assuming that habitat categories such as 'forest', 'woodland', and 'savannah', and dietetic categories such as 'Insectivore', 'Frugivore', 'Folivore', and 'Omnivore' do in fact specify particular ecological conditions. They may tend to disguise important nutritional differences of detail between particular kinds and distributions of food and between particular species' feeding habits.

In conclusion, then, it seems that existing generalizations attempting to relate Primate social organizations to phylogenetic or ecological factors in any relatively straightforward way have met with difficulties and we are thrown back on the closer study of the precise adaptations of particular groups to their particular environmental situations.

## Ecology and social organization of early hominids

The morphology of *Australopithecus* was described on pp. 56–62. Functionally, we can conclude from the skeletal evidence that this was an erect, bipedal hominid whose arms and hands were freed from locomotion and were more likely used for carrying, manipulating, and perhaps also throwing objects. Brain-size was akin to that of modern apes, and thus small compared with subsequent forms of *Homo*, but as Holloway (1974) has argued (on the basis of endocasts) *Australopithecus* already had a brain of characteristically human proportions, so that we are perhaps justified in treating this as a species whose intelligence exceeded that of present-day apes. The probable existence of a degree of sexual dimorphism may perhaps be taken as evidence of a division of labour of some kind.

Efforts to reconstruct the natural environment of *Australopithecus* have been made from time to time, including artists' impressions based on faunal and vegetative data (Howell). The terrain is variously described as 'savannah', 'open country', 'open woodland', and 'parkland'. It seems clear that *Australopithecus* was not a forest-living species, though it is arguable that remains do not preserve well in forest conditions and so the only Australopithecine remains are those from non-forest areas. (In this connection, common baboons, often characterized as a savannah-living species, do also inhabit forest areas.) An increased need for a large daily water intake in early hominids, perhaps resulting from loss of coat and development of sweating as a heat-loss mechanism, may have necessitated living near water. The two main East-African sites where remains have been found, Olduvai Gorge and Lake Rudolf, appear to indicate preference for a waterside zone. Such a zone would attract many species of animals and would provide ample opportunities for scavenging and catching live game.

Glynn Isaac (1970) has discussed the archaeological and palaeontological evidence of Australopithecine sites in South and East Africa. At Makapansgat in South Africa there is ample evidence of both Australopithecine material and material from a wide spectrum of other animal species, but owing to problems of stratigraphy it is not wholly clear whether *Australopithecus* brought in other species to its living sites or whether all the material has accumulated there as a result of other factors. The former is, however, very arguably the case. In East Africa the associations are better. At Olduvai Gorge we find hominid bones, bones of other animal species, and artificially introduced stones. Isaac distinguishes three types of site: kill/butchery sites, occupation sites, and workshop sites. The first contain many animal bones but few artifacts, the second a mixture of bones and artifacts, the latter mainly artifacts. Some sites are very rich in artifacts. For example, site FLK 1, the *Zinjanthropus* site, has yielded 2659 artifacts, and site BK II has yielded 7223 artifacts. Types of animal species found with *Australopithecus* include mainly *Dinotherium*, antelopes, and pigs, with in addition smaller creatures such as reptiles, frogs, birds, and rodents. How much actual hunting was done by *Australopithecus* cannot be established from the remains; it is conceivable that actual hunting did not occur at all, but from the fact that present-day chimpanzees can in certain circumstances co-ordinate their behaviour sufficiently to catch, share out, and eat monkeys, bush pig, and bushbuck (Teleki 1973) it seems probable that *Australopithecus* could do likewise.

We now come to the final challenge, how best to put together the data and theories arising from studies of living non-human Primates and the data relating to *Australopithecus* itself to form a picture of the social life of early man.

Basically, what we have to deal with is a species arising from pongid (Dryopithecine) origins, and thus phylogenetically pongid rather than cercopithecid. *Australopithecus*, and its successor *Homo*, are aberrant apes not abberant monkeys. The essential nature of the hominid divergence is the adoption of terrestrial bipedalism, as an adaptation to waterside, open-country conditions. If we were dealing with an aberrant monkey  then we could fairly confidently use living savannah-adapted monkeys as models. We could look at species such as patas monkeys, common baboons, Hamadryas baboons, or geladas, and make inferences from them. But these would necessarily be uncertain, for a wide variety of social organizations has been reported both within and between particular species. However, for the sake of simplicity, we could think in terms of 'ideal types'.

On a common baboon/macaque model, the early hominids on the open savannahs lived in large groups which were rather closed to outsiders. Sexual dimorphism was marked and went with sexual division of labour, males protecting the females and young from predators. Between adult males there were well-established status differentials, sexually attractive females and other scarce resources, such as sharp stone tools or preferred sleeping sites, being objects of inter-male competition. Rank was not, however, solely an outcome of competition, for there existed marked matrilineages that to some extent determined the ranks of individuals. The group gathered and scavenged for food as it moved around its range, sub-adults acting as scouts or sentinels, while the big males functioned internally as agents of social control and externally as protection from predators.

On a Hamadryas baboon (or gelada or patas monkey) model, the chief difference from the above would relate to the existence within the group of smaller subgroups consisting of an adult male with one or more mature females and their young. (In the case of the patas model this one-male–multi-female group becomes the actual maximal unit of social organization.) We can now begin to think in terms of a 'pair-bond' or some such tendency for the sexes to form relationships lasting well beyond the immediate period of sexual arousal and even beyond the period of infantile dependence. With such a system go rules of sexual exclusiveness and rules governing copulation, and the formation of 'bachelor bands' consisting of males without sexual partners.

Many more such 'monkey models' can be, and have been, postulated. In so far as phylogenetic factors are important, however, we should consider carefully the evidence of studies of living pongids as models. On a chimpanzee model we can see yet a third possibility of adaptation to savannah conditions. This is based on an 'open-society' idea, namely a form of social organization in which individuals are much freer to change membership from group to group than in the models described above, and as a result groups themselves are not likely to maintain a permanent membership over prolonged periods of time. Males in such a system join forces to find food and stay together for a while, then split up to join or are joined by sexually active females for a time. Mothers with infants stay together, but as their infants mature they become more mobile and drift apart. Kinship is a principle of social organization and offspring maintain contacts with their matrilineal kin into maturity. The gathering and dispersion of groups is primarily related to food supply, but is secondarily related to what may be termed a 'sense of community', and in areas where owing to food shortages the population density is low (say 1 or 2 per square mile) these communities emerge as separate groups or 'tribes'. In such a system neither dominance hierarchies nor sexual exclusiveness are important elements in the organization of social relations. In answer to the question of how the 'nuclear family' is supposed to have arisen in such a system it can be argued that it arose with the formation of an evolved pair-bonding tendency out of a state of sexual promiscuity, or that it arose for primarily economic reasons and has never been anything more than a socially sanctioned economic arrangement, cutting across rather than falling in line with the natural inclinations of adult hominids.

Particular reference needs to be made in this connection to the findings of the Japanese workers referred to above (pp. 84–5). If we use a woodland–savannah, rather than a forest, chimpanzee model for our early hominids (and this does indeed seem the most appropriate model from both the phylogenetic and ecological standpoints) then we can introduce the most remarkable feature of such groups, namely the tendency for a semi-closed organization to exist, with a series of groups based on mutually antagonistic adult males, but based also on a complete freedom of movement of sexually receptive adult females between groups. Such a model, for the reasons stated, it is to be preferred to all other models, and in addition it seems to provide a much-needed link between the non-human primate material and one of the characteristics stressed by anthropologists such as Lévi-Strauss as being unique to early man, namely the invention of the idea of exchanging women between groups. Perhaps, instead of inventing such a system, man merely took an existing tendency and codified it, making it subject to social rules, as seems to have been the case with incest taboos and kinship systems.

We have looked at four kinds of non-human Primate society, selected because each provides a working model for informed speculation about the society of early man. The basic outlines of these four models are shown in Fig. 5.1. Other species could have been selected—e.g. the small family-unit system of gibbons

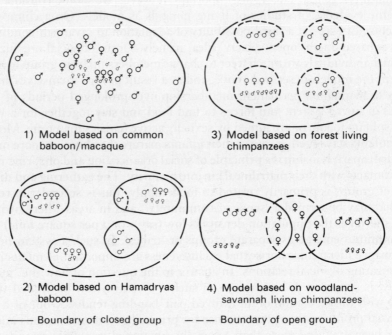

1) Model based on common baboon/macaque

3) Model based on forest living chimpanzees

2) Model based on Hamadryas baboon

4) Model based on woodland-savannah living chimpanzees

—— Boundary of closed group　　――― Boundary of open group

FIG. 5.1. Models of early man's social organization.

and siamangs, with its high degree of territorial exclusiveness. The ones we have chosen, however, do provide marked contrasts and have all (except the last, which has only recently been described) been used by a number of authors over the years as bases for envisaging the social organization of early man. Whether it will ever be possible to eliminate any of the possible models as being completely unworkable, or find actual fossil evidence or evidence of living sites complete enough to allow of direct inferences about social organization we do not know; at present it is not possible to do either of these.

Finally, a word on language. The development of symbolic category systems encoded in words has led to the kind of society found in modern man. One assumption behind the use of non-human Primate models is that they are not based on symbolic category structures, and are thus useful for envisaging pre-hominid society. When, however, did language and the consequent possibilities for re-modelling society arise? It is impossible to be certain that *Australopith-*

*ecus* lacked symbolic language. Brain-size, or relative brain-size, are an in-adequate source of information on this point, since brain organization, structure, and complexity are the issues at stake, and in so far as we are able to determine these from the fossil material with the use of endocranial casts they do seem to indicate a man-like kind of brain. In recent years chimpanzees, given intensive training, have been found to be capable of making signs with their hands or of manipulating plastic discs or push-buttons of different shapes or colours in ways that amount to low-level symbolic communication (Gardner and Gardner 1969; Premack and Premack 1972). Perhaps *Australopithecus* was already ahead of this in its abilities; we do not know.

It seems inherently more likely, however, that *Homo erectus*, the first hominid to show a major surge forward in brain-*size*, would have been the first linguist. Indeed it can be argued that it was the development of linguistic ability and the new kind of selection pressures this introduced that led to the brain-size increase seen in *H. erectus* and the further increase seen in *H. sapiens*. Whether language was originally gestural and later oral, as argued by Hewes (1973) and others, or did not pass through a gestural stage but began as an oral technique in conjunction with special brain 'speech areas' (Broca's area and Wernicke's area) is a matter of debate. Again, whether all hominids since *H. erectus* have had the full linguistic abilities of modern man is uncertain; Lieberman *et al.* (1972) have argued that Neanderthal man possessed a supra-laryngeal vocal tract that was inadequate for full articulation and suited 'at best' only 'for communication at slow rates'. Falk (1975) has, however, questioned this conclusion, arguing that the above authors placed the reconstructed hyoid bone too high, and the question remains open for further study.

## Suggestions for further reading (Part I)

BARTHOLOMEW, G. A. and BIRDSELL, J. B. (1953). Ecology and proto-hominids. *Am. Anthrop.* **55**, 481–98.

BEACH, F. A. (1947). Evolutionary changes in the physiological control of mating behaviour in mammals. *Psychol. Rev.* **54**, 297–315.

BIRDSELL, J. B. (1972). *Human evolution*. Rand McNally and Co., Chicago.

CAIN, A. J. (1954). *Animal species and their evolution*. Hutchinson's University Library, London.

—— HARRISON, G. A. (1960). Phyletic weighting. *Proc. zool. Soc. Lond.* **135**, 1–31.

CAMPBELL, B. G. (1966). *Human evolution*. Heinemann Educational Books, London.

—— (1967). *Human evolution: an introduction to man's adaptations*. Heinemann, London.

CHANCE, M. R. A. (1967). Attention structure as the basis of primate rank orders. *Man* **2**, 503–18.

CLUTTON-BROCK, T. (1974). Primate social organisation and ecology. *Nature, Lond.* **250**, 539–42.

*Cold Spring Harb. Symp. quant. Biol.* (1950). **11**, *Origin and evolution of man*.

COON, C. S. (1963). *The origin of races*. Jonathan Cape, London.

CROOK, J. H. and GARTLAN, J. S. (1966). Evolution of primate societies. *Nature, Lond.* **210**, 1200–3.

DAY, M. H. (1965). *Guide to fossil man*. World Publication Co., Cleveland.

DE BEER, G. R. (1951). *Embryos and ancestors* (revised edn). Oxford University Press, London.

DE VORE, I. (1963). A comparison of the ecology and behaviour of monkeys and apes. In *Classification and human evolution* (ed. S. L. Washburn). Viking Fund Publ. Anth. Volume 37, pp. 301–19.

—— and HALL, K. R. L. (1965). Baboon ecology. In *Primate behavior* (ed. I. DeVore), pp. 20–25. Holt, Rinehart and Winston, New York.

DOLHINOW, P. and SARICH, V. M. (eds) (1971). *Background for man: readings in physical anthropology*. Little, Brown and Co., Boston.

FALK, D. (1975). Comparative anatomy of the larynx in man and the chimpanzee: implications for language in Neanderthal. *Am. J. Phys. Anth.* 43, 123–32.

FOX, R. (1967). In the beginning: aspects of hominid behavioural evolution. *Man* 2, 415–433.

GARNER, R. L. (1896). *Gorillas and chimpanzees*. Osgood, London.

GARDNER, R. A. and GARDNER, B. T. (1969). Teaching sign language to a chimpanzee. *Science, N.Y.* 165, 664–72.

GOODALL, J. (1965). Chimpanzees of the Gombe Stream Reserve. In *Primate behavior* (ed. I. DeVore), pp. 425–73. Holt, Rinehart and Winston, New York.

GOODALL, J. VAN LAWICK (1968). The behaviour of free-living chimpanzees in the Gombe Stream Reserve. *Anim. Behav. Monogr.* 1.

HEWES, G. (1973). Primate communication and the gestural origin of language. *Current Anthrop.* 14, 5–12.

HOLLOWAY, R. L. (1974). The casts of fossil hominid brains. *Sci. Am.*, July.

HOWELL, F. C. (1966). *Early man*. Time–Life, New York.

HOWELLS, W. W. (1967). *Mankind in the making*. Pelican, London.

—— (1973). *Evolution of the genus Homo*. Addison-Wesley. Reading, Mass.

HULSE, F. S. (1971). *The human species* (2nd edn). Random House, New York.

HUXLEY, J. S. (1942). *Evolution, the modern synthesis*. Allen and Unwin, London.

ISAAC, G. (1970). The diet of early man: aspects of archaeological evidence from lower and middle Pleistocene sites in Africa. *Wld Arch.* 2, 278–99.

JOLLY, C. J. (1970). The seed eaters: a new model of hominid differentiation based on a baboon analogy. *Man* 5, 5–26.

JOLLY, A. (1972). *The evolution of primate behavior*. Macmillan, New York.

KAWANAKA, K. and NISHIDA, T. (1974). Recent advances in the study of inter-unit-group relationships and social structure of wild chimpanzees of the Mahali Mountains. *Symp. 5th Cong. Int. Primat. Soc.*, 173–86.

KUMMER, H. (1968). *Social organisation of hamadryas baboons*, p. 189. University of Chicago Press.

LE GROS CLARK, W. E. (1948). *Observations on certain rates of somatic evolution in the Primates*, pp. 171–80. Robert Broom Commemorative Volume of the Royal Society of South Africa.

—— (1955). *The fossil evidence for human evolution*. Chicago University Press.

—— (1967). *Man-apes or ape-men?* Holt, Rinehart and Winston, New York.

—— (1971). *The antecedents of man* (3rd edn). Edinburgh University Press.

—— (1973). *History of the Primates* (10th edn). British Museum (Nat. Hist.), London.

LIEBERMAN, P., CRELIN, E. S. and KLATT, D. H. (1972). Phonetic ability and related anatomy of the newborn and adult human, Neanderthal man and the chimpanzee. *Am. Anthrop.* 74, 287–307.

MAYR, E. (1963). *Animal species and evolution*. Harvard University Press.

NAPIER, J. (1971). *The roots of mankind*. Allen and Unwin, London.

OAKLEY, K. P. (1969). *Frameworks for dating fossil man* (3rd edn). Weidenfeld and Nicolson, New York.

—— (1973). *Man the tool-maker* (5th edn). British Museum (Nat. Hist.), London.

PFEIFFER, J. E. (1969). *The emergence of man*. Harper, New York.

PILBEAM, D. (1972). *The ascent of man: an introduction to human evolution.* Macmillan, New York.

PREMACK, A. J. and PREMACK, D. (1972). Teaching language to an ape. *Scient. Am.*, October, 92–9.

REYNOLDS, V. (1966). Open groups in hominid evolution. *Man* 1, 441–52.

—— and REYNOLDS, F. (1965). Chimpanzees of the Budongo Forest. In *Primate behavior* (ed. I. DeVore), pp. 368–424. Holt, Rinehart and Winston, New York.

ROWELL, T. E. (1966). Forest living baboons in Uganda. *J. Zool.* 147, 344–64.

SANDERSON, I. T. (1950). The physical distinctions of man. *Proc. Am. phil. Soc.* 94, 428–449.

—— (1957). *The monkey kingdom.* Hamish Hamilton, London.

SIMONS, E. L. (1972). *Primate evolution: an introduction to man's place in nature.* Macmillan, New York.

SIMPSON, G. G. (1950). *The meaning of evolution.* Oxford University Press, London.

—— (1953). *The major features of evolution.* Columbia University Press, New York.

—— (1961). *Principles of animal taxonomy.* Columbia University Press, New York, and Oxford University Press, London.

SNEATH, P. H. A. and SOKAL, R. R. (1973). *Numerical taxonomy. The principles and practice of numerical classification.* Freeman, San Francisco.

SPUHLER, J. N. (ed.) (1959). Evolution of man's capacity for culture. *Human Biol.* 31, 1–54. (Papers by Hackett, Harlow, Sahlins).

STRUHSAKER, R. T. (1969). Correlates of ecology and social organisation among African Cercopithecines. *Folia Primat.* 11, 80–118.

TELEKI, G. (1973). *The predatory behavior of wild chimpanzees.* Bucknell University Press, Lewisburg.

WASHBURN, S. L. and DEVORE, I. (1961). Social behaviour of baboons and early man. In *Social life of early man.* Viking Fund Publications, Anthropology, Volume 31, pp. 91–104.

WASHBURN, S. L. (1963). *Classification and human evolution.* Aldine, Chicago.

WEINER, J. S. (1956). The evolutionary taxonomy of the Hominidae in the light of the Piltdown investigation. *Selected papers of the Fifth International Congress of Anthropological and Ethnological Sciences*, pp. 741–52.

—— (1971). *Man's natural history.* Weidenfeld and Nicolson, London.

—— (1958). The pattern of evolutionary development of the genus *Homo. S. Afr. J. med. Sci.* 23, 111–20.

# Part II: Human genetics

G. A. HARRISON

# 6. Mendelism in man

## Introduction

IN THE 70 years that have elapsed since the re-discovery of Mendel's laws, genetics has become not only a most important discipline in itself but also an integral part of every biological science. In particular, it is a keystone in human biology, for in the ultimate analysis the interaction between inherited constitutions and the environment are the sole biological determinants of all the characteristics of an individual and therefore of the population variability which is the prime concern of the human biologist. Most of the early advances in genetics came from work with plants and 'lower' animals whose generation time is short and whose mating can be arranged. Discovering the laws of heredity from the study of man would have been extremely difficult. But once it was demonstrated that Mendelism was the mode of human inheritance, it became possible for the human biologist to contribute in a fundamental way to the general advance of genetics. In no other organism is the biology of the individual, and, more important, the structure and history of population, better known. Since the first edition of this book advances in human genetics have been dramatic, especially in the areas of molecular, biochemical, cellular, and medical genetics. Much, however, remains to be discovered, particularly in developmental and population genetics. On the other hand, the basic laws have continued to stand the test of time, and at this elementary level a great deal of what was written in the earlier edition is still valid.

## Particulate inheritance

Mendel's First Law—the Law of Segregation—states that inherited characters are controlled by pairs of discrete factors. Members of a pair separate (or segregate) from one another during the formation of the germ cells and pass into different gametes. The pairs are restored at fertilization which allows their combining together in definite proportions. In consequence the characters which they determine may also segregate for they will appear in subsequent generations with definite numerical frequencies.

The working of the law can be exemplified by reference to the discovery, nature and inheritance of a human blood-group system—the MN system. Blood groups are complex substances in the membranes of red blood corpuscles. The MN system was discovered by Landsteiner and Levine in 1927. These workers injected rabbits with human blood and subsequently tested the ability of the rabbit's sera to agglutinate various human red cells. Although there are certain technical difficulties, the nature of the MN blood-group system is conveniently revealed in the following way. If an anti-human blood immune serum from rabbits was exhausted with one sample of human blood, it sometimes still contained antibodies, specifically termed 'agglutinins', which would agglutinate the red blood-cells of some other people. If the blood from one of these people is used to exhaust the anti-human serum, this serum will still contain an agglutinin capable of reacting with the first type of blood.

These results are explicable on the basis that human red cells carry one or both of two antigens or haemagglutinogens, M and N. The corresponding antibodies do not occur in human sera but are manufactured by the rabbit when injected with human blood of the appropriate type. Thus if blood carrying both M and N antigens is administered, antibodies to both are produced. When added to an excess of blood carrying only the N antigen the anti-N will be used in agglutinating the red cells, but the anti-M is not involved and will subsequently react with people whose blood contains the M antigen. Conversely, if M-blood is used to exhaust the anti-human serum, this will still contain its anti-N.

So far as this blood-group system is concerned, there are, then, 3 types of people: those whose red cells carry the antigen M, those whose red cells carry the antigen N, and those whose red cells carry both antigens. When there are 3 types of people in a population there are 6 possible sorts of mating. These and the types of children they beget are presented in Table 6.1.

TABLE 6.1

| Types of mating | Children | | |
|---|---|---|---|
| M · M | M | | |
| N · N | | | N |
| M · N | | MN | |
| MN · M | $\frac{1}{2}$M | $\frac{1}{2}$MN | |
| MN · N | | $\frac{1}{2}$MN | $\frac{1}{2}$N |
| MN · MN | $\frac{1}{4}$M | $\frac{1}{2}$MN | $\frac{1}{4}$N |

When different types of child are produced they occur in definite proportions. In single small families these proportions will often not be recognizable, but if families were very large close agreement to the proportions given would be found. The children from many marriages of the same type is the genetical equivalent of a single large family and if data from such marriages are combined the expected ratios are also evident.

The mode of inheritance of the MN antigens can be explained on the basis

TABLE 6.2

| Hereditary constitution of parents | Hereditary constitution of children | | |
|---|---|---|---|
| $Ag^M Ag^M \times Ag^M Ag^M$ | $Ag^M Ag^M$ | | |
| $Ag^N Ag^N \times Ag^N Ag^N$ | | | $Ag^N Ag^N$ |
| $Ag^M Ag^M \times Ag^N Ag^N$ | | $Ag^M Ag^N$ | |
| $Ag^M Ag^M \times Ag^M Ag^N$ | $\frac{1}{2}Ag^M Ag^M$ | $\frac{1}{2}Ag^M Ag^N$ | |
| $Ag^N Ag^N \times Ag^N Ag^N$ | | $\frac{1}{2}Ag^M Ag^N$ | $\frac{1}{2}Ag^N Ag^N$ |
| $Ag^M Ag^N \times Ag^M Ag^N$ | $\frac{1}{4}Ag^M Ag^M$ | $\frac{1}{2}Ag^M Ag^N$ | $\frac{1}{4}Ag^N Ag^N$ |

that their presence in an individual is determined by unit factors which maintain their identity from generation to generation. Any individual has two such factors, one derived from each parent; they may be the same or they may differ. If the factors are represented by the symbols $Ag^M$ and $Ag^N$ the hereditary basis for the results presented in Table 6.1 can be represented as in Table 6.2.

The behaviour of these factors in heredity is consistent with the view that they are carried in the cell nucleus on the chromosomes. Their intranuclear position is indicated by the fact that it is of no consequence whether a factor is transmitted by a male or a female: the result is the same. But the ovum contains very much more cytoplasm than the sperm. The chromosomal association is indicated by the complete correspondence of the behaviour of the chromosomes during the formation of the sex cells or gametes, as witnessed by microscopic examination, and the behaviour of the factors as demonstrated in inheritance. With certain exceptions, in every somatic nucleus there are the same number of chromosomes, and this number, the so-called diploid number, is constant for a species. Because it has been difficult to prepare good cytological preparations of human chromosomes, there has been in the past some dispute as to how many chromosomes occur in the nuclei of man. But it is now certain that there are 46 (Plate I).

The chromosomes that pair together throughout their length, during the formation of the gametes, are said to be homologous and typically each member of a pair is seen to be structurally identical. Apart from the possibility of minor differences in such characteristics as the arrangement of parts, this is certainly true of the female, in which, therefore, every type of chromosome is represented twice in all somatic nuclei. In the male there are 22 identical pairs and 2 other chromosomes which possess, at most, only a small homologous section. One of these is identical with the 23rd pair of the female and is known as an X-chromosome; the other is much smaller, exclusive to males, and referred to as the Y-chromosome. X- and Y-chromosomes are known as the sex chromosomes, the rest of the chromosomes as the autosomes.

The gametes, as a result of meiosis, contain representatives of only one member of each homologous pair and, therefore, half the number of chromosomes of a somatic cell. This is the haploid number. The diploid number is restored at fertilization.

Now it can be seen that the inheritance of the MN blood-group system can be completely explained if the responsible hereditary factors are carried by a pair of chromosomes. In an $Ag^M Ag^N$ type one member of a chromosomal pair carries the factor $Ag^M$ and its homologue carries $Ag^N$. Members of a pair have an equal chance of being represented in a gamete, so half the gametes formed by the $Ag^M Ag^N$ type carry only $Ag^M$ and the other half only $Ag^N$. If mating takes place between such a type and another which possesses only one of the factors $Ag^M Ag^M$ (or $Ag^N Ag^N$), and whose gametes are therefore obviously all alike, $Ag^M$ (or $Ag^N$), it is equally probable that union will occur between unlike gametes as between like gametes. From such a mating the chance of a child being like one parent is equal to its chance of being like the other; in other words, half the children will be expected to be like one parent and half the children like the other.

|  |  | Parent $Ag^M Ag^N$ | |
|---|---|---|---|
| Gametic ratio | | $\frac{1}{2}Ag^M$ | $\frac{1}{2}Ag^N$ |
| | | Zygotic ratio | |
| Parent $Ag^M Ag^M$ | $Ag^M$ | $\frac{1}{2}Ag^M Ag^M$ | $\frac{1}{2}Ag^M Ag^N$ |

(The 'bars' can be considered as representing the chromosomes which carry the factors.)

If two $Ag^M Ag^N$ types mate together, both will form two types of gamete in equal frequency and three types of child will be produced of which a half will be like their parents. The other half will possess only $Ag^M$ or $Ag^N$.

|  |  | Parent $Ag^M Ag^N$ | |
|---|---|---|---|
| Gametic ratio | | $\frac{1}{2}Ag^M$ | $\frac{1}{2}Ag^N$ |
| | | Zygotic ratio | |
| Parent $Ag^M Ag^N$ | $\frac{1}{2}Ag^M$ | $\frac{1}{4}Ag^M Ag^M$ | $\frac{1}{4}Ag^M Ag^N$ |
| | $\frac{1}{2}Ag^N$ | $\frac{1}{4}Ag^M Ag^N$ | $\frac{1}{4}Ag^N Ag^N$ |

## Definitions

It is convenient at this stage to define a number of genetical terms. The factors $Ag^M$ and $Ag^N$ are termed 'genes' because they are heritable factors which determine the characteristics of an organism. The particular site they occupy on a chromosome is their 'locus'. Because these two genes occupy homologous loci and can therefore replace one another in any individual they are said to be 'alleles' or 'allelomorphs'. When the genes at homologous loci are the same, e.g. $Ag^M Ag^M$ or $Ag^N Ag^N$, the individual is termed a 'homozygote', for which ever gene is present; when the genes differ, e.g. $Ag^M Ag^N$, the individual is a 'heterozygote'. A mating between a homozygote and a heterozygote is referred to as a 'backcross', one between two heterozygotes as an 'intercross'. The characteristics of the individual—e.g. whether its red cells carry the agglutinogens M, N, or MN—constitute its 'phenotype'. The genetic composition of the individual, e.g. whether it is $Ag^M Ag^M$, $Ag^N Ag^N$, or $Ag^M Ag^N$, is its 'genotype'.

In the case of the MN blood-group system each of the three genotypes is phenotypically distinct. In many other comparably inherited characters, however, individuals of the same phenotype are genetically different. Some people can taste very dilute solutions of phenylthiocarbamide (PTC) and related substances, whilst others are incapable of doing so (see p. 284). The former are referred to as 'tasters', the latter as 'non-tasters'. The capacity to taste PTC is inherited in a similar way to the MN blood-group system, with two responsible alleles $T$ and $t$. The reason that there are only two types of people and not three is because the heterozygote $Tt$ can taste PTC as well as the homozygote $TT$ (Table 6.3). In other words, these two genotypes are phenotypically indistinguishable. The ability to taste is therefore said to be 'dominant' to non-tasting, or contrariwise, non-tasting is 'recessive' to tasting. Another example of dominance and recessiveness is to be found in the secretor status of man. Some people secrete large quantities of the ABH blood-group substances in their body-fluids including saliva, whilst others do not secrete them or do so only in small amounts. In this case the secretor condition is dominant to the non-secretor one (see p. 252). It is desirable to use the terms 'dominant' and 'recessive' to refer to characters rather than to genes, since some effects of a gene may be dominant whilst other effects of the same gene are recessive. However, it is frequently convenient to use these terms for describing genes themselves, but when this is done it must be remembered that it is only a form of shorthand.

## TABLE 6.3

| Phenotypes of parents | Genotypes of parents | Phenotypes of children | | Genotypes of children | | |
|---|---|---|---|---|---|---|
| Taster × taster | $TT \times TT$ | Taster | | $TT$ | | |
| | $TT \times Tt$ | Taster | | $\frac{1}{2}TT$ | $\frac{1}{2}Tt$ | |
| | $Tt \times Tt$ | $\frac{3}{4}$ Taster | $\frac{1}{4}$ Non-taster | $\frac{1}{4}TT$ | $\frac{1}{2}Tt$ | $\frac{1}{4}tt$ |
| Taster × non-taster | $TT \times tt$ | Taster | | $Tt$ | | |
| | $Tt \times tt$ | $\frac{1}{2}$ Taster | $\frac{1}{2}$ Non-taster | $\frac{1}{2}Tt$ | $\frac{1}{2}tt$ | |
| Non-taster × non-taster | $tt \times tt$ | Non-taster | | $tt$ | | |

## Allelism

It will be evident that one can only study the genetic determination of characters which occur in two or more alternative forms. If all people were of blood-group M one could not discover how the character was inherited: the contrast with blood of group N is necessary for this. There are many human characteristics in which only one form is ever found; every individual being homozygous for the responsible genes. On the other hand, more than two alleles may exist, determining the form of some particular character, though, of course, only two of them can normally be present in any one individual. Thus the ABO blood-group system is controlled by four common alleles plus a number of rare ones (p. 251).

When only one gene occurs there can obviously be only one genotype; with 2 alleles there are 3 genotypes—the 2 homozygotes and a heterozygote; with 3 alleles the number of possible genotypes rises to 6—the 3 homozygotes and

3 heterozygotes:

e.g.    $A^1A^1$        $A^2A^2$        $A^3A^3$
                        $A^1A^2$        $A^1A^3$
                                        $A^2A^3$

With $n$ alleles there are:

$$n+(n-1)+(n-2)+(n-3) \ldots +\{n(n-1)\}$$

possible genotypes. The number of phenotypes obviously depends upon the existence of dominance. If in the above theoretical example the effects of $A^1$ are dominant to $A^2$ and the effects of $A^2$ dominant to $A^3$ there will be only 3 phenotypes, since all the heterozygotes will appear either like $A^1A^1$ or $A^2A^2$.

## The chromosome complement

The 23 pairs of human chromosomes have been classified into groups on the basis of variations in size and position of centromeres. In Plate I the karyotype of a normal human male is shown in which homologous chromosomes have been paired together and the autosomes arranged in seven classes A–G. Within each class it is often difficult in ordinary cytological preparations to distinguish some of the chromosome pairs from one another and indeed to be sure that homologous chromosomes have been accurately paired in drawing up the karyotype, but identification of most of the pairs is usually possible. Group A consist of 3 chromosome pairs which are relatively large, and the centromere is in a median position making the two arms of the chromosomes of approximately equal length. In Group B the 2 pairs are also large but the centromere is placed much nearer one end than the other (referred to as being distal) so that the arms are of unequal length. The 7 pairs of Group C are of medium size, and the centromere to varying degrees slightly off-centre (submedian). The X-chromosome is also assigned to this group. Group D consists of 2 pairs also of medium size but with the centromere very close to one end. This situation is referred to as being 'acrocentric', though it should be noted that a short arm as well as a long arm exists. Three pairs of chromosomes are assigned to Group E, though in one pair the centromere is strictly median, while in the other 2 it is submedian. They are, however, all designated small. Even smaller with shorter arms are the 2 pairs in Group F and in them the centromere is in a median position. Finally, Group G consists of 2 autosomal pairs of very small size with the centromere acrocentrically placed though again short arms exist. To this group the Y-chromosome is also assigned. Sometimes all the chromosomes with median, submedian, and distal centromeres are referred to together as being 'metacentric' to distinguish them from the acrocentrics.

The identification of particular chromosomes is facilitated by the fact that some show characteristic constrictions along their lengths or possess minute terminal structures known as satellites. Recently it has been shown that when

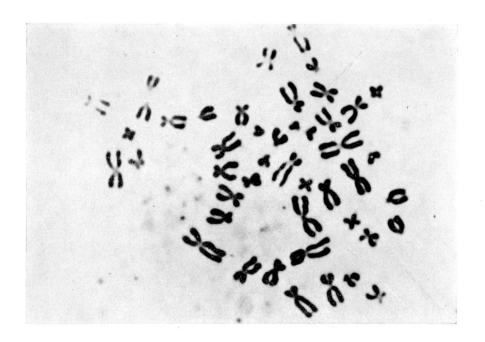

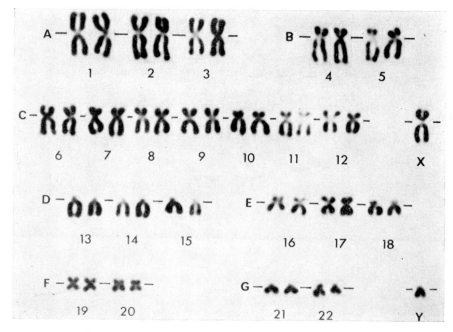

PLATE I. Mitosis in a leucocyte of a human male after colchicine treatment, and karyotype.

treated under appropriate conditions with certain fluorescent dyes such as quinacrine hydrochloride the chromosomes stain differentially along their lengths with the production of fluorescent bands. These bands are distinctive from one chromosomal pair to another and the technique has greatly facilitated the precise identification of particular chromosomes.

## Pedigree analysis

Apart from systems in blood, most is known about the genetics of human characters which are of rare occurrence in a population, since such characters are usually inherited in a simple way. Many of these characters are of medical importance because their rarity is largely due to the fact that individuals possessing them are not as fit as those who have the alternative form of character. It is usual, therefore, to refer to the type of individual displaying the abnormal condition as 'affected' and to their normal relatives as 'non-affected'. The gene determining a particular abnormal condition is represented by some diagnostic symbol, but the normal allele may be represented by a $+$ irrespective of the condition.

The mode of inheritance of a character is established from an analysis of families in which the 2 or more forms of the character occur. A convenient way of representing such family histories is by means of diagrammatic pedigrees such as is exemplified in Fig. 6.1. There are a number of different ways of presenting pedigrees, but the system used in the example is as good as any and others can easily be understood from it.

## Dominant inheritance

Whether the hair of a person is woolly or non-woolly would not seem to be of great biological consequence, but for a number of possible reasons, woolly hair, of the sort considered in the pedigree, is of very rare occurrence in any population. It is obvious from a glance at the pedigree, however, that in certain families it can occur very frequently. This is typical of many inherited conditions of greater medical importance but for which family histories are rarely so complete.

In the pedigree of woolly as opposed to non-woolly hair it will be seen that all affected individuals had one parent with similar hair and the character therefore never skips a generation. The same phenomenon, looked at in a different way, is that two non-affected parents never have affected children however closely they may be related to affected persons. It will also be seen that the 20 marriages between affected and non-affected people produced 38 affected and 43 non-affected children. This ratio does not differ significantly from 1 : 1. Finally, it may be noted that woolly hair occurs approximately as frequently in females as in males and is transmitted in the same way by mothers as by fathers. These last phenomena indicate that the character is neither sex-limited nor sex-linked (see pp. 117 and 113).

A 1 : 1 ratio is characteristic of a backcross mating to the recessive homozy-

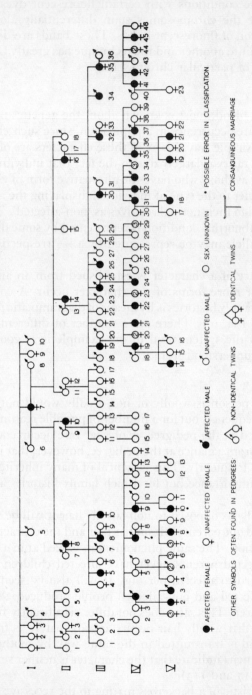

FIG. 6.1. Pedigree illustrating dominant inheritance in man. 'Woolly hair' in a Norwegian family with no Negro ancestry. (From Mohr, *J. Hered*, 1932.)

gote. If woolly hair were recessive to non-woolly the type of marriage which would produce this ratio would be $+w \times ww$, where $w$ represents the gene for woolly hair and $+$ its allele for non-woolly. But if woolly hair were recessive one would also expect marriages in the pedigree of the type $++\times ww$ and incidentally of the type $+w \times +w$. No woolly-haired children would be produced from the first of these even though one of the parents is affected. Only once in the illustrated pedigree does a woolly-haired parent fail to have an affected child and this does not disturb the $1:1$ ratio. From the second type of marriage a quarter of the children would be woolly haired although their parents were non-affected. Yet, as has been noted, woolly-haired children always have an affected parent.

Now, if the woolly-hair gene expresses itself in single dosage, i.e. in heterozygotes, the backcross mating is of the type $W+\times ++$. Again half the children will be affected and the other half non-affected, though in any particular small family one or other type by chance might not occur. In this explanation it is obvious that woolly-haired children must always have a woolly-haired parent, since the $W$ gene which expresses itself in the child, and which it obtains from a parent, will also express itself in that parent. Conversely, two non-woolly-haired parents cannot have a woolly-haired child because neither of them possesses a $W$ gene. This explanation, then, fits all the facts of the pedigree and it can be concluded that woolly hair is determined by a gene which expresses itself in heterozygotes.

In medical genetics it would frequently be said that woolly hair is dominant to non-woolly hair, or conversely that the latter is recessive to the former. This is not strictly true. Before one can conclude that woolly hair is a dominant trait one must know that the heterozygote $W+$ is indistinguishable from the homozygote $WW$. Since woolly hair is a very rare condition it is unlikely that two heterozygotes will marry, and this is the only way that the homozygote $WW$ can first be produced. There are no marriages between two woolly-haired individuals in the pedigree and so far as is known none has ever occurred. One therefore does not know what the homozygote $WW$ looks like. It may well be indistinguishable from the heterozygote, but it is just as likely that it will be different. Inheritance may, then, be dominant versus recessive like tasting capacity or it may be intermediate and somewhat like the MN blood-group system. The MN blood-group system does not show strict intermediate inheritance. Since both antigens are produced by the heterozygote they are preferably referred to as being 'co-dominant'.

Other examples of human traits which are inherited in a similar way to woolly hair are anonychia, achondroplasia, congenital stationary night blindness, Huntington's chorea, and elliptocytosis. Anonychia is a condition in which some or all of the fingers and toes fail to develop nails. Often there is, in addition, deformity in the hands and feet such as the absence of one or more digits. Achondroplasics are dwarfs in which the head and trunk are of normal dimensions but the limbs are stunted as a result of faulty growth in the epiphyseal cartilages of the long bones. The skull base, because it also is preformed in cartilage is likewise deformed. Congenital stationary night blindness is a condition in which 'twilight' (scotopic) vision is grossly defective. It is present at birth and becomes no worse with age. On the other hand, Huntington's chorea is a progressive degeneration of the nervous system which eventually leads to death. Typically, though not invariably, the age of onset of the disease is between 30 years and 40 years. In people with elliptocytosis, also known as ovalocytosis, at least 20 per cent and frequently as many as 50 per cent of the red blood-cells are elongated and elliptical and there may be also a mild anaemia.

It will be apparent from these few examples that diseases of simple genetic origin occur in every system of the body and are of varying severity. In two further conditions, brachydactyly and multiple telangiectasia, individuals probably homozygous for the abnormal gene have been reported. Brachydactyly is a condition in which to varying degrees the fingers and toes are shortened, but in a marriage between an affected man and his cousin, who was probably also affected, a child was produced whose entire skeletal system was abnormal and who died early in life. Similarly, two people suffering from multiple telangiectasia, a disease of the vascular capillary system, married and had a child who died when only $2\frac{1}{2}$ months old with multiple superficial and internal haemorrhages. This suggests that these conditions are not strictly dominant and that the disease is much more severe in the homozygous state than in the heterozygous one. On the other hand, achondroplasic dwarfs have married one another and produced children no more severely affected than themselves. The same is true, on the few occasions that two individuals suffering from congenital cataract, a disease of the lens of the eye, have married. This suggests that these conditions are truly dominant, but the numbers are small and it may have chanced that the homozygote has never been formed. It is also possible that the homozygote is so inviable that it aborts very early in pregnancy. Only a statistical analysis of the concordance between expected and observed ratios of affected and non-affected children, when many more data have been collected, will reveal which of these explanations is correct.

In all, well over a hundred rare human traits are known which are inherited as simple dominants, or, at least, in which the responsible gene expresses itself in the heterozygote. There are admittedly some genetic complications to many of these, but there are also many conditions known which are probably determined in a comparable way, but, for one reason or another, have not or cannot be studied genetically. In the latter category are conditions which are lethal before the age of reproduction and which are, therefore, never inherited.

## Recessive inheritance

In considering the pedigree of woolly versus non-woolly hair attention was focused on the genetics of the woolly condition which demonstrated the characteristics of dominant inheritance. As was pointed out, however, the non-woolly

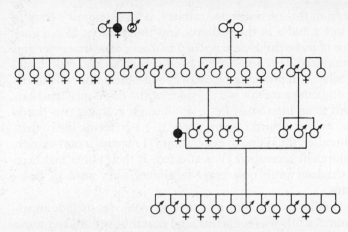

F I G . 6.2. Pedigree illustrating recessive inheritance in man. Albinism. (From Pearson, Nettleship, and Usher, *A Monograph on albinism in man*, Cambridge University Press, 1911–13.)

condition is contrariwise inherited as a recessive. But this is the normal form, and to demonstrate in a comparable way the features of recessive inheritance it is necessary to consider a rare condition such as albinism. There is great variation in the skin, hair, and eye colour of people not only from one population to another but within a single population. This variation is inherited in a complex way, but occasional individuals produce no, or very little, melanin. Their skin and hair are therefore very pale, and their eyes are red, because the blood-supply to the retina is not masked by pigment. A pedigree for albinism is represented in Fig. 6.2. It contrasts strikingly with the woolly-hair pedigree particularly in the frequency of affected individuals. Note also that the children of an affected person may all be unaffected and yet the trait appears in a subsequent generation. In other words, non-affected parents can have albino children. But when this happens, some of the other children in the family will almost invariably be non-affected, since the marriages are of the type $+a \times +a$ and, on average, only a quarter of the children will be albino. If families are small it is quite likely that two heterozygotes on marrying will have no affected children and they will, therefore, fail to be recognized in collecting data. Such cases will tend to disturb the expected $3:1$ ratio. There are ways of compensating for this, the most usual being to exclude the propositus from the analysis. A propositus is an affected individual who first draws attention to a family in which the abnormality is occurring.

Other types of marriage which can produce albino children are $aa \times aa$ and $aa \times +a$. From the first of these it is obvious that all the children must be albino, while from the second, a backcross mating to the homozygote recessive, a half of the children, on average, will be albino and the other half will be unaffected heterozygotes. Unaffected heterozygotes are referred to as 'carriers'. The most common type of marriage involving an albino person is of the type $++ \times aa$

and all the children from this marriage are carriers. This is almost certainly what has happened in I 1 and 2 in the pedigree and the children II 1–12 are all heterozygotes. One of these children happened to marry another carrier and an albino child was produced, II 1. Some of her brothers and sisters, collectively termed 'siblings' or 'sibs', will probably be carriers and others not. The likelihood in favour of a sib being a carrier is 2 : 1, since of the three-quarters non-affected children born to an intercross, i.e. $+a \times +a$, on average, two-thirds will be heterozygotes and one-third homozygotes $++$. It seems likely that, like her albino grandmother, the albino in generation III married a non-carrier, since none of the children in generation IV is affected. If their father had been a carrier, half of the children would on average be albino. They must all, however, be heterozygotes.

Examples of other conditions which are inherited as recessives include alkaptonuria, phenylketonuria, ichthyosis congenita, and deaf mutism. Alkaptonuria and phenylketonuria are both 'inborn errors of metabolism' which have received considerable biochemical and genetical attention. Alkaptonurics are characterized by the presence of alkapton, also known as homogentisic acid, in their urine. In consequence, this urine rapidly darkens on exposure to the air as the homogentisic acid is oxidized and the condition is frequently recognized in early infancy by a characteristic staining of napkins. Homogentisic acid appears to be an intermediate in the normal katabolism of the amino acids phenylalanine and tyrosine and it is now known that in alkaptonurics the enzyme homogentisic acid oxidase, responsible for the converson of homogentisic acid to maleylacetoacetate, is either absent or present only in very minute amounts. A similar situation exists in phenylketonurics, who, because the enzyme phenylalanine hydroxylase is absent, cannot convert phenylalanine into tyrosine. Phenylalanine therefore accumulates in the blood and is converted among other things into phenylpyruvic acid, phenyllactic acid, and phenylacetylglutamine, which are excreted in the urine. However, unlike homogentisic acid, which has little deleterious effect, one or more of these substances when in abnormal concentration are toxic and cause cerebral damage, and phenylketonurics are typically also mentally deficient. The condition has recently achieved some renown because it has been shown that if children suffering from phenylketonuria are put on a diet containing only the basic requirements for phenylalanine véry early in life, this cerebral damage can be avoided. It would obviously be of great medical value if carrier parents could be recognized, so that children could be tested and, if need be, put on a suitable diet. This has now to some extent been achieved, since it has been shown that the plasma concentration of phenylalanine in heterozygotes is often about twice as great as that of non-carriers after both have been fed with a standard dose of phenylalanine. However, not all heterozygotes can as yet be identified.

Ichthyosis congenita is an extremely rare condition and is often so severe that the child is born dead or dies shortly after birth. In the most severe form huge horny plates cover the entire skin surface with deep fissuring between them, and respiration is impossible. By contrast with ichthyosis, genetically determined deaf mutism is relatively common and, at least in modern society carries no very severe biological disability. This is unusual for a recessive trait in which a fertility as high as a third of that of unaffected individuals is probably exceptional. The deafness results from a disorder of the inner ear, and its presence from birth determines the mutism. Of very great interest, from the genetical point of view, is the very high proportion of deaf mutes who marry other deaf mutes.

It must be pointed out now that even a condition which is recognizable as a single medical entity is not necessarily determined by the same gene in all cases. Thus, for instance, while albinism is usually inherited as a recessive condition in man, in occasional families it is dominant. Alkaptonuria and deaf mutism sometimes behave in a similar way. Further, the frequent marriages between deaf mutes have shown that, even the recessive form of the condition is determined by different genes, since the children of such marriages can occasionally be normal.

# 7. Genetics of sex

## Sex determination

BEFORE going on to consider the mode of inheritance of characters whose determining genes are located on the sex chromosomes, it is convenient to discuss briefly the sex-determining mechanism in man. The genetic basis of sex depends upon the chromosomal constitution of the zygote; if this contains two X-chromosomes it is female, if it contains one X-chromosome and one Y-chromosome it is male. Of course, as with other genetically determined conditions, the two phenotypes only become a final reality after a period of developmental differentiation and, in the case of sex, this is long and the process complex. Anatomically the embryo is at first neuter, the gonads consist of both a cortex and a medulla, mullerian and wolffian ducts are laid down, and the external genitalia are not distinctive. If, however, the embryo is of an XX constitution, the cortical region of the gonad proliferates, the mullerian ducts become differentiated into vagina, uterus, and oviducts, while the wolffian ducts degenerate, and the external genitalia develop into the characteristic form of a female. Conversely, if the embryo is of an XY constitution, the medullary region of the gonad alone persists and differentiates, the wolffian ducts develop into the elaborate system of sperm ducts while the mullerian ducts become vestigial, and a penis and a scrotum, into which the testes descend, are formed. Finally, at adolescence, the gonads and accessory reproductive systems complete their maturation and differential growth, affecting particularly the mammary glands, the pelvis, and hair, produces the distinctive appearance of the sexes.

Experiments involving the administration of sex hormones, castration, and the transplantation of gonads have all conclusively demonstrated the importance of the endocrine system in determining the secondary sexual characteristics of mammals. The differentiation of these somatic tissues is not irrevocably determined by their genetic constitution. Somewhere, however, in the course of development the genotype is decisive; it would seem to control whether the cortical or medullary layers of the developing gonad proliferate.

From the point of view of sex determination, a female produces only one type of egg, namely one which contains a single X-chromosome, whereas a male produces two types of sperm, one containing an X-chromosome and the other containing a Y-chromosome. If an X-bearing sperm fertilizes an egg the child is a girl, and if a Y-bearing sperm effects fertilization the child is a boy. In man, then, as in other mammals, the male is the heterogametic sex and a father, in a sense, is responsible for the sex of his children. It is worth noting that in some animals, e.g. birds and Lepidoptera, the female is heterogametic and the male homogametic.

It was once thought that in man, as in *Drosophila* and some other animals, the Y-chromosome as such was of no importance in sex determination; that what really mattered was the balance between the number of X-chromosomes and the number of autosomes. In *Drosophila* it seems that most, if not all, of the male-determining genes are located on the autosomes and the female-determing genes occur mainly on the X-chromosome. When there is only one X-chromosome present in a zygote, the effects of the male-determining genes are preponderant, whereas when two X-chromosomes are present there are twice as many female-determining genes and this swings the balance in favour of femaleness. Certainly a *Drosophila* lacking a Y-chromosome and with only one X-chromosome is morphologically a perfectly normal male. In man, however, it has been shown that the Y-chromosome has an effect on sex determination. A condition of intersexuality exists, known as Turner's syndrome, in which the external genitalia and accessory reproductive system are feminine in form but remain immature. The gonads are undifferentiated. The number of chromosomes in Turner subjects is 45, and chromosome analysis shows that they are of an XO composition, the Y-chromosome being absent. The general femaleness of a Turner subject indicates very clearly that the Y-chromosome is strongly male-determining. This view is reinforced by the existence of another type of human intersex, the Klinefelter's syndrome. Those affected are outwardly nearly normal males but have small testes with azoospermia. The majority of Klinefelter subjects have 47 chromosomes instead of 46 and are of the genetic composition XXY. Others are XXXY, XXXXY, and XXXXXY. This indicates that the Y-chromosome is so strongly male-determining that even in the presence of two or more X-chromosomes it channels development in an essentially male direction.

Such intersexes result from the non-disjunction of the sex chromosomes at meiosis. Thus, if the X-chromosomes in a female fail to separate, ova are produced which contain either two X-chromosomes or no X-chromosomes: while if non-disjunction occurs in the male XY and OO sperm are formed. It is worth noting here that other abnormal sex genotypes are known to occur, as, for example, XXX, XXXX, XXYY, and XYY. XXX individuals are morphologically normal female, and, though some are mentally subnormal, they are fertile. Those with a greater number of X chromosomes suffer severe mental deficiency. XXYY subjects display Klinefelter characteristics, and there is some suggestion, by no means yet proven, that XYY, who tend to be unusually tall, are predisposed to anti-social behaviour.

## The sex ratio

The number of males to every 100 females in a population is the most commonly used way of expressing the sex ratio. The sex ratios at conception, birth, and maturity are known respectively as primary, secondary, and tertiary. Since normal meiosis leads to the production of X-bearing and Y-bearing sperm in equal numbers one would expect that the chances are equal that any particular child conceived will be a girl or a boy. Yet the secondary sex ratio is invariably high, i.e. there is an excess of male births. In the white American population the ratio is 106:100 and in the American Negro population nearly 103:100. In Greece the ratio rises to 113:100, and even in Cuba, one of the places where it is lowest, it is still over 101:100. Populations at high altitude seem to have particularly high sex ratios. It might at first be thought that this inequality in favour of males results from a greater mortality of female embryos. But in fact, the very opposite seems to be the case, for at least in the later stages of pregnancy male foetuses are more likely to be lost than female ones. There is no reason to suppose that it is different earlier in development, since at every other stage of life, males are less viable than females. The presumption must, indeed, be that the primary sex ratio is in favour of even a greater proportion of males than the secondary one. The ultimate explanation for this phenomenon would seem to be that natural selection is operating on the sex ratio, in a rather interesting way, to produce an equality of the sexes at maturity.

R. A. Fisher pointed out that the production of offspring involves an expenditure on the part of the parents of material, energy, and time. This expenditure is wasted if the offspring do not survive to maturity and reproduce; the biological value of the expenditure can be expressed in terms of the number of offspring produced who become parents themselves. More boys than girls die during the period when the parents are expending themselves on their children, so the average expenditure is greater for each boy reared and less for each boy born than it is for girls at the corresponding stages. Now, consider a monogamous population in which the primary sex ratio is equality. The capital that is expended on the boys who die during the time of parental influence is wasted, but even more is wasted on those females who survive but cannot mate because the death of the boys means there are not mates available for them. They have received the full quota of capital but have no reproductive value. Under these circumstances it is an advantage for parents to have a higher frequency of male births, for the average cost to the parents in producing a son *who will be a father* is less than that involved in producing a daughter *who will be a mother*. In perhaps more realistic terms, more fathers than mothers can be produced for the same expenditure. There is, then, a selective advantage in a greater than equality sex ratio and any genetic mechanism which produces it will spread in the population. The ratio will in this way increase until the parental expenditure on females is of equivalent biological value to the expenditure on males. And this equilibrium point in white Americans gives a secondary sex ratio, as mentioned, of 106:100. The reason that the ratio is lower in American Negroes and Cubans is probably because the total child mortality is greater or, at least, has been greater, in these populations, for this will tend to mask the differential mortality of males and females.

Just how the primary sex ratio is disturbed from equality is not known. It could well be that Y-bearing sperm have a greater mobility, a greater viability, or greater capacity to fertilize an egg than X-bearing sperm, and it is known in some mammals that there is a relationship between the blood pH of fathers and the sex ratio: a low pH favouring the production of daughters. All such characters can, of course, be under genetic control, and, indeed, genes are known to occur, in wild populations of animals, that control the frequency of the two types of sperm. In *Drosophila pseudo-obscura*, for instance, there is a gene which eliminates nearly all Y-bearing sperms, and it occurs quite commonly in nature.

## Sex-linked inheritance

Other genes than sex-determining ones are located on the sex chromosomes, and the characters whose development they control are obviously linked in inheritance with sex. Such genes may either be on the X-chromosome, in which case one speaks of X-linked inheritance, or on the Y-chromosome: Y-linked inheritance. The former is by far the more common, no doubt because the X-chromosome is quite a large chromosome, and its distinctive characteristics can easily be understood by remembering first that every man receives his X-chromosome from his mother and transmits it to all his daughters and none of his sons, and secondly that every woman receives an X-chromosome from each of her parents and transmits either one or other of them to her sons and her daughters.

Red-green colour blindness affords an example (see p. 285). It is recessive in the female to normal colour vision; females only being colour blind if they are homozygous for the colour-blind gene. The terms 'dominant' and 'recessive' can have no meaning in the male, since he has only one X-chromosome and, therefore, only one colour-vision gene. Males are consequently said to be hemizygous. The 6 possible matings between the 3 possible female genotypes and the 2 possible male genotypes, and the types of sons and daughters they produce, are represented in Table 7.1. $C$ represents the gene for normal colour vision; $c$ the allele for colour blindness.

Two important points, characteristic of recessive X-linkage, emerge from an examination of Table 7.1. First, colour-blind men are much commoner than colour-blind women, since whenever a gene for colour blindness occurs in a man it will express itself, whereas a woman must possess two colour-blind genes before she is colour blind. It follows that a colour-blind daughter can only be produced by a marriage in which the father is colour blind, since she inherits one of her X-chromosomes from him and this must carry a colour-blind gene if she is going to be a homozygote. Whether or not she actually is colour blind depends on the genotype of her mother. Secondly, and very important from the medical viewpoint, is that the colour vision of a son depends only on the genotype of his mother, since he derives his sole X-chromosome from her. Thus, for instance, half the sons of a carrier woman will be colour blind irrespective of the genetic constitution of her husband. The typical pattern of recessive sex-linked inheritance through a number of generations, for a condition such as colour blindness, which is relatively rare, is one of alternating generations of affected men and carrier women, since, if a colour-blind man marries a homozygous normal woman, all his daughters will be carriers, but, while none of his sons will be affected, half of his grandsons will be colour blind, inheriting their grandfather's colour-blind gene from their mothers. Such a pattern is frequently referred to as 'crisscross' inheritance.

TABLE 7.1

| Genotypes of parents | | Genotypes of children | | | |
|---|---|---|---|---|---|
| Mothers | Fathers | Sons | | Daughters | |
| $CC$ | $C$ | $C$ | | $CC$ | |
| $CC$ | $c$ | $C$ | | $Cc$ | |
| $Cc$ | $C$ | $\frac{1}{2}C$ | $\frac{1}{2}c$ | $\frac{1}{2}CC$ | $\frac{1}{2}Cc$ |
| $Cc$ | $c$ | $\frac{1}{2}C$ | $\frac{1}{2}c$ | $\frac{1}{2}Cc$ | $\frac{1}{2}cc$ |
| $cc$ | $C$ | $c$ | | $Cc$ | |
| $cc$ | $c$ | $c$ | | | $cc$ |

The individuals who are actually colour blind are underlined.

Another condition which is usually inherited as a sex-linked recessive is haemophilia: a disorder in which the blood fails to clot. Two forms of sex-linked haemophilia are now known: haemophilia A, the classic variety, in which 'anti-haemophilic globulin' is deficient, and the rarer haemophilia B or Christmas disease, where the 'plasma thromboplastin component' is lacking. Haemophilia is a much more severe affliction than colour blindness and consequently is much rarer in the population, only about 1 in 10 000 males being affected. Haemophiliac women are very rare, and one of the reasons is that they would only be expected to occur with a frequency of $(1/10\,000)^2$, i.e. $1/100\,000\,000$. The explanation for this relationship between the frequency of affected males and females will become evident when the behaviour of genes in populations is described. Haemophilia has achieved some general notoriety because Queen Victoria was a carrier of the condition and from her the gene was introduced into two of the royal houses of Europe (Fig. 7.1).

If an X-linked condition is expressed in the heterozygote, then, in contrast with a recessive, it will be more common in females than in males, since two-thirds of the X-chromosomes in the population occur in females. Not many conditions are known which are inherited in this way, and those that do exist are very rare. One that often seems to meet the requirements is brown tooth enamel and another a form of phosphataemia resulting in Vitamin-D-resistant rickets. With such rare conditions most matings will be either between a heterozygous woman and an unaffected man, or between an affected man and an unaffected woman. Since a heterozygous woman transmits her X-chromosome carrying the responsible gene equally to her sons and to her daughters, half the sons and half the daughters from the first type of marriage will be affected and the other half of the sons and daughters will be unaffected. In other words, the condition behaves genetically in this type of mating like an autosomal gene

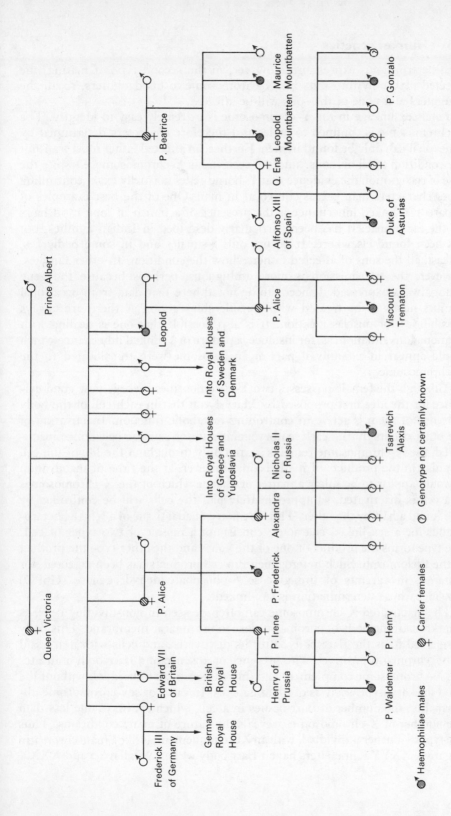

FIG. 7.1. Pedigree of Haemophilia in descendents of Queen Victoria.

Queen Victoria

Prince Albert

Frederick III of Germany

Edward VII of Britain

P. Alice

Leopold

P. Beatrice

German Royal House

British Royal House

Into Royal Houses of Greece and Yugoslavia

Into Royal Houses of Sweden and Denmark

P. Irene

Henry of Prussia

Alexandra

Nicholas II of Russia

P. Alice

Alfonso XIII of Spain

Q. Ena

Leopold Mountbatten

Maurice Mountbatten

P. Frederick

P. Waldemar

P. Henry

Tsarevich Alexis

Viscount Trematon

Duke of Asturias

P. Gonzalo

Haemophiliac males

Carrier females

Genotype not certainly known

with heterozygous expression. However, in the second type of mating, the affected man only transmits his X-chromosome to his daughters, so all the daughters and none of the sons will be affected.

Total sex linkage in the Y-chromosome is extremely easy to identify. The Y-chromosome is confined to males and therefore characters determined by genes on it can only be found in men. Further, an affected father must transmit the condition to all his sons, since all receive his Y-chromosome. Despite the ease of recognition the evidence that Y-borne genes normally exist, controlling other characters than sex, is equivocal in man. One of the best examples of apparent Y-linked inheritance is the presence of a bunch of long rigid hairs on the ear pinnae. It has been particularly described in Indian families, but has been found elsewhere. It occurs only in males and in some pedigrees, at least, all the sons of affected fathers show the condition. In other families, however, the transmission is more ambiguous, perhaps because the gene is not always expressed. It needs to be noted here that data from occasional families needs to be treated with considerable caution as there are always possibilities for misclassification. It is also possible that one is dealing with an anomalous situation, as, for instance, a pattern of Y-linked inheritance which would appear in a family if part of an autosome were translocated to the Y-chromosome.

Although the female possesses two X-chromosomes there is now good evidence for the idea first proposed by Mary Lyon that in each cell of the body only one of them is active in controlling metabolic function. Inactivation of the other occurs during early embryogenis and for somatic cells, once inactivated, the X-chromosome remains so, not only throughout the life of the cell but also in the products of its division. However, at the time of inactivation it would appear to be solely a matter of chance which of the X-chromosomes in a cell is inactivated, so approximately half the cells will be controlled by one X and a half by the other. Thus the non-gonadal tissue of a female, heterozygous for a sex-linked character, consists of a mosaic of two types of cell: one type forms the product of one of the genes and the other type the product of the allelomorph. Such heterogeneity in cell products has been detected, for instance, in variants of the glucose 6-phosphate dehydrogenase (G6PD) enzyme, whose determination is sex-linked.

The inactivated X-chromosome can often be seen in non-dividing cells, as a darkly staining body of chromatin close to the nuclear membrane. This body is referred to as the Barr body, after its discoverer, and cells with it are said to be 'chromatin positive'. The presence or absence of a Barr body indicates the X-chromosome complement and thus the sex of an individual, without the need for karyotype analysis of dividing cells. In cases of sex-chromosome abnormality, the number of Barr bodies in a cell, which is always one less than the number of X-chromosomes, reveals the nature of many conditions. Thus the typical Turner individual, with an XO complement, is like a male chromatin negative. XXYY Klinefelters have 1 Barr body while XXX have 2 and XXXX

3. Among the British population about 0·2 per cent of males and 0·08 per cent of females show abnormal numbers of Barr bodies.

### Sex-limited inheritance

It does not follow that if some character occurs more frequently in one sex than another that its inheritance is sex-linked. Premature baldness is a dominant condition which is limited to males, and the Laurence–Moon–Biedle syndrome and one form of oligophrenia (imbecility) are recessive conditions which occur more frequently in males than females. But the responsible genes are located on the autosomes, as is indicated in their mode of transmission. The preferential sex distribution arises from the fact that the female genotype produces an environment which inhibits or reduces the expression of these genes. Such characters are said to display sex-limited or sex-controlled inheritance.

# 8. Independent assortment and linkage

## Independent assortment

THE mode of inheritance of characters considered singly having been described, it is possible to discuss the inheritance of two characters considered together. Mendel's second law states that characters assort themselves independently of one another. So far as the genes responsible are concerned this means that when two or more pairs of genes segregate simultaneously, the members of any one pair are distributed in the gametes independently of the distribution of any other pair.

This is conveniently demonstrated by considering the gametes formed by an individual heterozygous for taster versus non-taster and secretor versus non-secretor genes, namely *TtSese*. With independent segregation, such an individual will form 4 types of gamete in equal frequency, namely *TSe*, *tSe*, *Tse*, *tse*. In other words, the gene *T* is as likely to be associated with the *Se* gene as is *t*, and they are both equally likely to be associated with the *se* gene. If this double heterozygote mates with a double recessive homozygote *ttsese* (a backcross mating) 4 types of children can be produced and will appear in equal frequency, if the family is large enough to obviate sampling errors.

| | Gametic ratio | *TtSese* (taster secretor) | | | |
|---|---|---|---|---|---|
| | | $\frac{1}{4}TSe$ | $\frac{1}{4}tSe$ | $\frac{1}{4}Tse$ | $\frac{1}{4}tse$ |
| | | | Zygotic ratio | | |
| *ttsese* (non-taster non-secretor) | *tse* | $\frac{1}{4}TtSese$ (taster secretor) | $\frac{1}{4}ttSese$ (non-taster secretor) | $\frac{1}{4}Ttsese$ (taster non-secretor) | $\frac{1}{4}ttsese$ (non-taster non-secretor) |

If two double heterozygotes mate together then both will form all 4 types of gamete in equal frequency and, as can be worked out in the same way as in the above example, the 4 types of children will be produced in the well-known Mendelian ratio of 9 taster secretor: 3 non-taster secretor: 3 taster non-secretor: 1 non-taster non-secretor. This ratio, of course, depends upon the existence of dominance in both characters, so that the genotypes *TTSeSe*, *TtSeSe*, *TTSese*, and *TtSese* are all of the taster-secretor phenotype; *TTsese* and *Ttsese* are both taster non-secretors, *ttSeSe* and *ttSese* are both non-taster secretors, and only the genotype *ttsese*, being non-taster non-secretor, has a phenotype unique to it. However, if the heterozygote for both characters were distinguishable from the homozygotes, each of the 9 different genotypes would be phenotypically distinctive.

The 1 : 1 : 1 : 1 ratio found in the backcross to the double recessive is the multiplicative extension of the 1 : 1 ratio found when only 1 character is considered, and the 9 : 3 : 3 : 1 ratio is an extension for 2 characters of the 3 : 1 ratio. If 3 characters in each of which dominance exists, are considered together, the phenotype classes from an intercross occur in the frequency of 9 : 3 : 3 : 1 × 3 : 1 = 27 : 9 : 9 : 9 : 3 : 3 : 3 : 1. And so the situation for any number of characters considered together can be worked out.

The reason that characters assort independently of one another is that their determining genes are located on different chromosomes. The distribution of members of a pair of chromosomes into the gametes is, in most circumstances, in no way dependent upon the distribution of members of another pair. The genes for tasting and non-tasting, for instance, are on a different pair of chromosomes from the secretor non-secretor genes. Thus, it is solely a matter of chance whether a chromosome carrying an $Se$ gene finds itself in association in a gamete with a chromosome carrying $T$ or $t$. And similarly for the $se$ gene.

## Linkage

Now, while Mendel's first law stands without qualification, exceptions to the second are continually being discovered. The reason is obvious, for chromosomes carry many genes, and genes which are located on the same chromosome will not assort independently of one another, but, being bound as it were in a common vehicle of hereditary transmission, will tend to be inherited together. Consider, as a theoretical example, a mating of the type $AABB \times aabb$, in which the two loci concerned are on the same chromosome. If there is no exchange between homologous chromosomes, the first generation hybrid produced by such a mating, namely $AaBb$ can itself only form 2 types of gamete, namely the two parental types $AB$ and $ab$, instead of the 4 possible under independent assortment, since the chromosome which carries gene $A$ into a gamete will inevitably also carry gene $B$, and the chromosome which carries gene $a$ will also carry gene $b$. The situation can be represented diagrammatically as follows.

Parents

$$P_1 \qquad\qquad P_2$$

$$\frac{A \quad B}{A \quad B} \quad \times \quad \frac{a \quad b}{a \quad b}$$

Gametes

$$\frac{A \quad B}{} \qquad\qquad \frac{a \quad b}{}$$

$F_1$ Hybrid

$$\frac{A \quad B}{a \quad b}$$

Gametes

$$\tfrac{1}{2}\frac{A \quad B}{} \\ + \\ \tfrac{1}{2}\frac{}{a \quad b}$$

Conversely, if the parental mating is of the type $AAbb \times aaBB$, the first-generation hybrid, genetically of course $AaBb$ as in the previous example, but in which the genes are arranged

$$\frac{A \quad b}{a \quad B},$$

can only form gametes like those of its own parents, namely $Ab$ and $aB$. Genes which occur on the same chromosome are referred to as being linked. When, as in the first example above, the genes whose effects are dominant are on the same chromosome, they are said to be in 'coupling' or the 'cis phase'. When, as in the second example, they are on different chromosomes of a pair, they are said to be in 'repulsion' or the 'trans phase'. The situation is made somewhat more complicated by the fact that linkage is rarely complete. In most organisms an interchange of chromosomal material between homologous chromosomes takes place during the prophase of the first meiotic division, as can be seen microscopically by the formation of chiasmata between pairs of chromatids. A particular chromosome, therefore, does not remain constitutionally identical from generation to generation. Because of this phenomenon of 'crossing-over', a double heterozygote can form all 4 possible types of gametes, instead of just the two parental types, even when genes occur on the same chromosome. In simplified form the way in which this happens can be illustrated as follows.

Each of the 4 products eventually passes into a gamete. In this case, the gametes $Ab$ and $aB$ are termed 'recombinants', because they have been formed by the recombination of chromatids, whereas the gametes $AB$ and $ab$ are 'non-recombinants'.

Although crossing-over leads to the production of all 4 types of gamete, linkage between genes can be recognized because the gametes belonging to the recombinant classes usually are formed in lower frequency than the non-recombinant gametes. This follows first from the fact that a cross-over must occur *between* two pairs of linked genes if there is to be any recombination of them. In the above diagram the two loci have been placed at opposite ends of a chromosome, but if the $B$ locus were nearer to the $A$ locus than the crossing-over point, no recombinant-type gametes would have been produced, so far as these particular genes are concerned.

e.g.

$$\begin{array}{cc}
\underline{A \qquad B} & \underline{A \qquad B} \\
\underline{A \qquad B} \qquad \rightarrow & \underline{A \qquad B} \quad \cdots\cdots \\
a \quad\cdots\cdots\cdots b \;\times\; \cdots & a \quad\cdots\cdots\cdots b \quad\cdots\cdots\cdots \\
a \quad\cdots\cdots\cdots b \quad\cdots\cdots\cdots & a \quad\cdots\cdots\cdots b \quad\cdots\cdots\cdots
\end{array}$$

The second reason is that since typically more than one cross-over will be formed between chromatids, if two loci are so widely separated, that any cross-over will separate them, a second will also often form between them and restore their original association on the same chromosome.

$$\begin{array}{cc}
\underline{A \qquad\qquad B} & \underline{A \qquad\qquad B} \\
\underline{A \qquad\qquad B} & \underline{A \quad\cdots\cdots\cdots B} \\
a \;\times\; \cdots\cdots \times\cdots b & a \cdots\cdots\cdots\cdots b \\
a \cdots\cdots\cdots\cdots b & a \cdots\cdots\cdots\cdots b
\end{array}$$

An odd number of cross-overs between two genes will obviously separate them; an even number will maintain their original association. Linkage between genes which are so far apart that they assort apparently independently can only be discovered by reference to intermediate genes with which both are detectably linked.

Evidence is accruing that, in man, crossing-over is more frequent in females than in males but under standardized conditions the amount of crossing-over between two linked genes is constant. With certain reservations, which need not be discussed here, a cross-over is equally likely to occur at any place along the length of the chromatids, and it is evident therefore that the frequency with which linked genes are separated by crossing-over is principally a function of their distance apart on the chromosome. The closer they are together, the less likely it is that a cross-over will form between them and the less frequent the recombinant types of gametes will be. Here, then, is a basis for mapping the distribution of genes along chromosomes and this has progressed far in some animals and plants.

Genes which are near together on the chromosome, and therefore rarely separated by crossing-over, are said to be closely linked; those which are far apart, and separated so frequently by crossing-over that they seem to assort almost independently, are loosely linked.

In plant and animal genetics, the simplest way of demonstrating linkage and determining the cross-over value between two genes is to backcross the double heterozygote to the double recessive homozygote. With independent assortment, as already mentioned, the 4 possible genotypes, each phenotypically distinct, are produced in equal frequency. If linkage exists, then the 2 phenotypes of the double heterozygote's parents, though themselves produced in equal frequency, will be more numerous than the 2 non-parental phenotypes. The frequency of the latter combined is, of course, the total frequency of recombinants and, therefore, the cross-over value.

Linkage between human genes is more difficult to demonstrate, since it is not possible to arrange the appropriate breeding tests. It is apparent that no information can be obtained about linkage from an examination of correlations between characters in a population, since, unless two genes are so closely linked that to all intents and purposes they are never separated, crossing-over will cause the genes to be as frequently in coupling as in repulsion. For instance, even if tasting capacity and secretor status were linked, the ratio in a population of taster secretors to non-tasters secretors would be the same as if they were unlinked. On the other hand, the genetic composition of individuals whose marriages are suitable for detecting linkage is often determinable and pedigree analysis is a standard way of studying human linkage. However, difficulties arise because human families are typically small so that data from different families must be combined. Also, even when suitable matings occur, information on a number of generations is needed and this is often not available. This latter difficulty has been overcome in varying degrees by the devising of indirect methods, of which Penrose's sib-pair comparison is the most easy to apply, since it requires only information about siblings.

Consider again a mating of the type $AaBb \times aabb$ in which the two loci concerned are linked and dominance exists in both characters. The double heterozygote may be of the chromosomal constitution $AB/ab$ or $Ab/aB$. In the first of these cases, if no crossing-over occurs, the children will either be $AB/ab$ or $ab/ab$. If the character determined by $A$ versus $a$ is referred to as the 'first character' and that determined by $B$ versus $b$ as the 'second character', all those who are $AB/ab$ will obviously be like each other for both the first and second character. So will those who are $ab/ab$. But an $AB/ab$ child when compared with an $ab/ab$ one, is dissimilar in both characters. Similarly, in the second case where the parent is $Ab/aB$, the children, either $Ab/ab$ or $aB/ab$, will be either like one another in both characters, if they are of the same genotype, or unlike in both characters, if they are of different genotype. In both cases, only by crossing-over can children be produced which are alike in one character, but unlike in the other. The recombinant children from the mating $AB/ab \times ab/ab$ are either $Ab/ab$ or $aB/ab$. Compared with each other, the two types are dissimilar in both characters but if the $Ab/ab$ type is compared with the non-recombinant $AB/ab$ it is like it in the first character but not in the second. If it is compared with $ab/ab$ it is unlike in the first and alike in the second. The same is true with the recombinant type $aB/ab$. It is like $AB/ab$ only in the second character and like $ab/ab$ only in the first. Similarly, the recombinant children from the mating $Ab/aB \times ab/ab$, namely $AB/ab$ and $ab/ab$, when compared with the non-recombinants are like them only in one character and unlike them in the other.

It is evident now that if in any sibship from a backcross mating to the double recessive, one compares each sib with every other sib for likeness and unlikeness in the characters considered, it will be found, if linkage exists, that the joint frequency of comparisons in which sibs are alike in both characters and unlike in both characters is greater than the frequency of comparisons in which sibs are alike in one character but unlike in the other, since only crossing-over will produce the latter class. And this is true whether the mating is of the type $AB/ab \times ab/ab$ or $Ab/aB \times ab/ab$ so the data from different sibships can easily be combined.

Other sorts of mating produce similar results to those of the backcross to the double recessive. For revealing linkage, the double heterozygote is obviously always necessary as at least one parent. It is the only genotype in which crossing-over produces different sorts of gamete from those formed if recombination does not occur. Should one of the alleles at each locus be rare in the population, as is often the case, the double recessive will be produced very infrequently. If, for instance, the genes $a$ and $B$ are common in the population and their alleles $A$ and $b$ rare, sibships which show, phenotypically, segregation for both pairs of alleles will, in general, be the result of matings of the type $AaBb \times aaBb$. It will again be found, however, if linkage exists, that the ratio of the comparisons of sibs who are either alike in both characters or unlike in both characters to the comparisons of sibs who are alike in one and not the other is greater than would be expected under independent assortment, although in this case some non-recombinant children are produced, which, on comparison with other non-recombinants, are alike in one character and not in the other. If then a table such as Table 8.1 of all possible sib comparisons is drawn up it will be found, if linkage exists, there are preferential entries in panels 1 and 4. The extent by which these entries depart from those expected under independent assortment can be used for calculating the cross-over values. Under independent assortment it is to be expected that, apart from chance differences, those sibs who are alike in one character should be alike and unlike in the other in the proportion with which likeness and unlikeness occurs in this character as a whole. Similarly, sibs who are unlike in this character will be alike and unlike in the other in the same proportion. In terms of the panel numbers in the table, under independent assortment, $1:2$ will equal $1+3:2+4$ and $3:4$ will also equal $1+3:2+4$. The expected values, of course, can also be obtained as $1:3$   $1+2:3+4$ and $2:4$   $1+2:3+4$. This is not a very efficient way of detecting linkage, and has been considerably modified by Penrose, but it does demonstrate the nature of the problem and the ways it can be tackled.

TABLE 8.1

|  |  | First character | |
|  |  | Like | Unlike |
| --- | --- | --- | --- |
| Second | Like | 1 | 2 |
| character | Unlike | 3 | 4 |

Another method, known as the 'method of likelihood ratio', can be exemplified in principle in the following way. Consider the simple pedigree

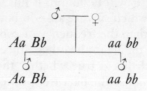

In the doubly heterozygous father the two loci if linked could be in coupling $AB/ab$ or in repulsion $Ab/aB$. The first son clearly received the alleles $AB$ from his father and the second son $ab$. In other words if the genes were in coupling neither son received a recombinant arrangement from his father; if they were in repulsion, both sons were derived from recombinant gametes. Let $x$ equal the recombination value. The probability of obtaining the first son by recombination is $\frac{1}{2}x$ and likewise the second son by recombination also $\frac{1}{2}x$. So the combined probability of obtaining the offspring in this pedigree, when the genes in the father are in repulsion is $(\frac{1}{2}x)^2$. On the other hand if the genes are in coupling, and no recombination has occurred, the probability of obtaining the first son's genotype is $\frac{1}{2}(1-x)$ and likewise for the second son $\frac{1}{2}(1-x)$, so the total probability is $\{\frac{1}{2}(1-x)\}^2$. The combined probability, therefore, of obtaining the results in the pedigree, whether under repulsion or coupling, is

$$(\tfrac{1}{2}x)^2 + \{\tfrac{1}{2}(1-x)\}^2 = \tfrac{1}{4}(1 - 2x + x^2).$$

Substituting in this, if $x$ is given a value of 0·5, which represents independent assortment, the probability is 1/16; if it is given a value of 0, which represents total linkage, the probability is 2/16. In other words it is twice as likely that the observed results represent total linkage as independent assortment. Much more extensive pedigrees can be approached in the same way and the formulae for each observed pattern of inheritance worked out. It is then possible by substituting different values of $x$ between 0·5 and 0 to find out which value best fits the overall data, and thus the degree of linkage.

Despite these and other elegant techniques now available the number of known examples of human autosomal linkage is as yet small, though growing. Very close linkage exists in a number of serological systems, e.g. within the rhesus and MNS blood-group systems Gm immunoglobulin variants, the HL-A system of tissue antigens and for the genes responsible for $\beta$- and $\delta$-polypeptide chains of the haemoglobin molecule, and recombination within these systems is rare. In some families elliptocytosis is linked to the rhesus blood-group system with a cross-over value of about 3 per cent, but in other families the two characters seem to be segregating independently indicating, of course, that genes at two loci at least can produce elliptocytosis. The nail-patella syndrome, a pathological condition in which among other things a nail dystrophy is associated with rudimentary patellae and the development of 'horns' on the iliac bones, is linked to the ABO blood-group system with a cross-over value of just over 10 per cent. The Lutheran blood-group system is linked with the locus concerned with the secretion of ABH substances with about 15 per cent crossing over and the transferrin system with serum cholinesterase variants with 16 per cent crossing over. Most of the autosomal linkages so far detected concern only two loci, but there is evidence that the so called uncoiler chromosome locus is linked with the Duffy blood-group system and the latter is very closely linked with a type of congenital eye cataract.

A few other cases of autosomal linkage are known and with the discovery of the distinctive fluorescent banding of chromosomes many more are shortly likely to be discovered. Further these will help establish the particular chromosomes on which linkage groups occur. Already, mainly from the analysis of abnormal chromosomal variation, it has been possible to assign some genes to their chromosomes. The 'uncoiler' locus is on chromosome 1 affecting the degree of coiling of part of an arm as seen in cytogenetic preparations; from the formal linkage studies it can be concluded that the Duffy blood-group system and congenital eye cataract are also on this chromosome. Studies of certain translocations have revealed that the locus controlling the α-polypeptide of the haptoglobin molecule is on chromosome 16, and there is evidence from experiments with cultures of hybrid human–mouse cells that the human gene determining the synthesis of the enzyme thymidine kinase is on chromosome 17.

Establishing linkages between genes on the X-chromosome is formally easier than those on autosomes, since linkage with sex indubitably fixes these genes on the same chromosome without necessity of testing for linkage between the genes themselves. Further there can be no crossing over in the male. Unfortunately apart from the variants of G6PD some of which reach high frequencies in some African, Asian, and Mediterranean populations and the Xg blood-group system, no loci on the X-chromosome carrying common alternative alleles (marker genes) and there are, therefore, few convenient regular reference points for determining cross-over values. Nevertheless it is now possible to draw up a tentative map of the relationship of genes on parts of the X-chromosome as follows.

(*Gene symbols:* Cd: deutan colour blindness; Cp: protan colour blindness; G6PD: glucose 6-phosphate dehydrogenase; Ha: haemophilia A; Ic: ichthyosis; Oa: ocular albinism; Xm: a serum protein antigen.)

It should be noted that this is not a definitive map and other arrangements are compatible with our present knowledge. It is also worth noting that it would not have been possible to identify from family analysis that the group of genes linked with the Xg locus and the group linked with the G6PD were both on the same chromosome, had they not been both clearly sex-linked.

# 9. Genes and their action

## Gene action

SO FAR, attention has been focused on what may be termed the mechanics of inheritance and little has been said about the way genes produce characters. In discussing the development of sex it was, however, intimated that the genotype and the phenotype are usually separated by a long process of differentiation. In fact, there is rarely a clear-cut relationship between the presence of a particular gene and the development of a particular character. Most characters result from the action of many genes acting together. Conversely, any one gene frequently determines a number of characters. Examples of this latter phenomenon, known as 'pleiotropism', have already been given. It was mentioned, for instance, that phenylketonurics not only excrete phenylpyruvic acid in their urine, but are also mentally defective. The manifestation of a particular gene may be yet more diverse. In the Laurence–Moon–Biedl syndrome, due essentially to a single gene in double dosage, obesity is associated with mental deficiency, polydactyly, and hypogenitalism. In arachnodactyly, which derives its name from the excessive length of the finger and toe bones, there are other skeletal abnormalities, and eye and heart defects. The developmental connection between these manifold effects of a single gene replacement is usually not completely known. However, all the features of hypogenitalism in the Laurence–Moon–Biedl syndrome are probably due to a single causative factor; a deficiency of gonadotrophins, and it is also known that other factors such as hypothalamic lesions which produce obesity, diminish the secretion of these hormones. A simply inherited pathological condition in the rat affects almost every skeletal and visceral system, but the whole constellation of characters has been shown to be due to faulty cartilage formation. This sort of situation suggests that the nearer one gets to the immediate action of genes, the more singular are the products, and there is wide belief that each gene is ultimately only responsible for the production of a particular protein, often an enzyme. This is the one gene/one protein hypothesis, and though it is preferably phrased today as the one gene/one polypeptide hypothesis, and even so, sometimes seems to require qualification, as, for example, in the synthesis of immunoglobulin molecules in mammals, much has been discovered, particularly from metabolic studies in bacteria and fungi, to support it. In man, the deficiency or absence of phenylalanine hydroxylase in phenylketonurics would seem to be the sole immediate effect of the responsible gene. All the other symptoms can certainly be explained in terms of it. This does not mean necessarily that the phenylketonuria gene in contrast to the normal allele produces nothing, but only that whatever is produced by it is incapable of transforming phenylalanine into tyrosine. Quite a small change in the chemical structure of an enzyme could have this effect. It may also be surmised that the principal reason why the replacement of the blood-group alleles by one another have such singleness of effect is because the blood-group substances are not far removed synthetically from the immediate products of gene action and because the blood-group substances themselves have only a small effect in determining other characters.

Since the prime action of a gene is to produce a polypeptide it is not surprising that most characters are dependent upon the action of many genes acting together. The development of any morphological system is determined by innumerable biochemical reactions and alterations in any one of these may, to varying degrees, change the course of morphogenesis. Thus, for instance, one does not inherit a gene for sightedness but rather a whole host of genes whose products interact in a complex way throughout life for the development and maintenance of a functional eye and brain. And if the system is disturbed either by genetic or environmental agencies then blindness may ensue. This in itself explains why there are so many genes causing blindness. Blindness, from the genetical as from the clinical point of view, is a heterogeneous character, since the genes which determine the lens are not likely to be the same as those that determine either the retina or the cornea; yet blindness can result from defects in all these as well as in many other structures.

Sometimes, genetics can be more discriminating than clinical medicine. Retinitis pigmentosa is a condition in which pigment migrates from the tapetum into the retina where it is visible with an ophthalmoscope. In consequence there is night blindness and a gradual contraction of the visual field which may progress so far as to cause total loss of sight. The severity is variable, but not in any clear-cut way. However, it seems that at least 3 distinct genes may produce the defect: 2 autosomal, one being dominant and one being recessive in effect, and an X-linked recessive. Only the autosomal recessive is clinically distinguishable since it also produces deafness in addition to retinitis pigmentosa. It is not known whether these genes are cumulative in effect or not, since they are rare in human populations and no known person has possessed more than one type, but either situation is possible.

## Multifactorial inheritance

Genes with a cumulative effect are very important in understanding the determination of characters such as stature, body-weight, body-build, and intelligence, which vary both in families and in populations quite differently from the blood-groups and pathological conditions so far considered where discrete classes of individuals can be recognized. There are not merely tall and short people but every grade of intermediate; the variation is quantitative rather than qualitative and any classes that may, for convenience, be recognized are largely arbitrary. These characters are studied by measurement on some continuous scale.

One very important feature of quantitatively varying characters is that their

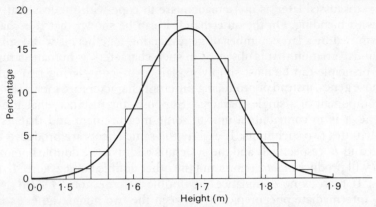

F I G. 9.1. Diagram showing the observed distribution of the heights of 117 males, exhibited in the form of a histogram together with a fitted 'normal' curve. (After Bailey, *Statistical methods in biology*, EUP, London, 1959.)

frequency distribution in a population conforms more or less to the 'normal' or Gaussian curve (Fig. 9.1). The mathematical properties of this symmetrical unimodal curve afford the basis for much of statistical science. The point on the abscissa from which a perpendicular divides the curve into two halves of equal area is the mean. Measures of the extent of scatter on either side of this mean are the variance, its square root, the standard deviation, and the co-efficient of variation, which is the variation expressed as a proportion of the magnitude of the dimension. If a distribution is not symmetrical, i.e. is not strictly normal, other averages, the median, and the mode, are different from the mean. The mode is the point on the abscissa from which a perpendicular bisects the apex of the curve, i.e. the most frequently occurring value. The median is the point which divides the horizontal extent of the scatter into two equal halves, i.e. the mid-point value. If samples of measurements of a character are taken from a population, and in biometry one is invariably dealing with samples, these will also be distributed more or less normally, unless the sample is very small, and the sample will have its own mean and standard deviation. This mean, however, is unlikely to be exactly the same as the true population mean; it will be affected by sampling error, and the smaller the sample the greater this error is likely to be. The degree of error is measured by the 'standard error of the mean'. Just how these various statistics are obtained can be found in any elementary statistical textbook.

For quite some time after this re-discovery of Mendel's laws it was generally felt that a particulate mode of inheritance could not explain the heritable basis of continuously varying characters and that some form of blending inheritance was involved. But inseparable mixture of the hereditary material necessarily reduces the variation in a population by a half in every generation. This obviously does not happen and it is now known that the origin of new variation, which is discussed later, is quite inadequate to cope with the loss that would occur with blending. On the other hand, it can be shown that if a character is determined by a large number of genes, acting together, it will display the continuous variation that is observed in such characters as human stature.

The principle can be most simply explained by considering two unlinked loci whose genes, instead of producing different characters are each responsible for a component of a single character. Suppose, for instance, that the effect of a gene $A$ is to contribute a unit to some measurement and that its allele $A'$ contributes two such units. If exactly the same effects are produced by the genes $B$ and $B'$ respectively and the system is additive the double homozygote $AABB$ will produce *in toto* 4 units and the other double homozygote $A'A'B'B'$ 8 units. If there is no dominance the double heterozygote $AA'BB'$ will be strictly intermediate phenotypically between the two homozygotes as it produces 6 units. Now consider an intercross of 2 heterozygotes, as in the following table, in which the number of units produced by the various genotypes are recorded. It will be seen that there are 5 phenotype classes and these occur in the ratio of 1 (4 units) : 4 (5 units) : 6 (6 units) : 4 (7 units) : 1 (8 units).

$$AA'BB' \times AA'BB'$$
$$6 \qquad\qquad 6$$

Gametes

| Gametes | $AB$ | $A'B$ | $AB'$ | $A'B'$ |
|---|---|---|---|---|
| | | Zygotes | | |
| $AB$ | $AABB$ 4 | $AA'BB$ 5 | $AABB'$ 5 | $AA'BB'$ 6 |
| $A'B$ | $AA'BB$ 5 | $A'A'BB$ 6 | $AA'BB'$ 6 | $A'A'BB'$ 7 |
| $AB'$ | $AABB'$ 5 | $AA'BB'$ 6 | $AAB'B'$ 6 | $AA'B'B'$ 7 |
| $A'B'$ | $AA'BB'$ 6 | $A'A'BB'$ 7 | $AA'B'B'$ 7 | $A'A'B'B'$ 8 |

In other words, the distribution of the variation of the measurement is symmetrical with the intermediate phenotypes more common than the extreme phenotypes. Something, in fact, resembling a normal curve is obtained. If the difference between the two extreme phenotypes, i.e. between 4 and 8 units of measurement, were determined by many pairs of genes instead of only 2, any one particular gene contributing only some fraction of a unit, the number of classes of intermediate phenotypes would obviously be greatly increased. This itself means that the differences between any class and those phenotypically adjacent to it must be correspondingly decreased.

It is apparent, then, that as the number of genes responsible for a particular variation increases, it becomes correspondingly difficult to recognize distinct classes and, if a very large number of genes are involved, the frequency distribution will be to all intents and purposes continuous. Further, such discontinuity that might be theoretically recognizable, will invariably be masked by interaction of the genotype with the external environment (p. 140). Factors like inequality of effect and dominance complicate the issue for they alter the shape of the frequency distribution, but they in no way invalidate the general principle that the inheritance of quantitatively varying characters can be explained in terms of particulate genes. Genes whose individual effects are small but act cumulatively in the determination of a single character are known as polygenes and the inheritance of such characters is said to be polygenic or multifactorial. Polygenes occur not only in the euchromatic sections of chromosomes (i.e. sections which stain lightly with chromosome dyes), where all the so-called 'major' genes are located, but also in the heterochromatic sections (i.e. heavily staining sections). This has been demonstrated in a number of ways, but a very striking one is the effect on some quantitative characters in *Drosophila* of an absent Y-chromosome. This chromosome is practically entirely heterochromatic. Genetic analyses of characters whose determination is multifactorial are much more complicated than those required for discovering the inheritance of differences due to one or a few major genes. Instead of being concerned with the frequency with which particular classes occur, information is obtained from the parameters of distributions of variation and the nature and degree of resemblance between relatives. One particular difficulty is the finding of scales on which gene action is additive, for there is no reason why a particular gene substitution should always have the same effect on the scale used for actually measuring a character. Some transformation to, for instance, logarithms or reciprocals is often needed. Nevertheless, despite this sort of difficulty, some quantitatively varying characters in plants and animals have been broken down into environmental and genetic components, and overall dominance, linkage, and minimal number of genes (i.e. effective factors) estimated, because with these organisms it is possible to make large-scale breeding tests with individuals whose general genetic constitution is known. Such tests are, of course, not possible with man, and the genetics of quantitatively varying human characters is, as yet, poorly understood. Skin colour in hybrid populations between Negroes and Europeans behaves as a quantitative character, and Stern has attempted to discover the number of loci involved by comparing the observed frequency distribution of skin colour in the American Negro with model distributions calculated for different numbers of gene pairs. The allele frequencies used in the model were based on the extent of the intermixture that has occurred between West African Negroes and Europeans in the American Negro. Necessarily a number of assumptions had to be made, such as equality and additiveness of effect, but it seems probable that about 3 to 4 gene pairs are involved in determining most of the difference in skin colour between African 'Blacks' and European 'Whites'. It is very likely that many more loci are involved in determining the variation of stature and similar anthropometric characters even within a single population.

Much can be learned of the inheritance of quantitative characters, and particularly of the extent to which differences in such characters are due to genetic rather than environmental causes by comparing the similarity of individuals within families. A parent passes on to its child a half of his or her chromosomes, so parent and child share half their genes in common. A grandparent and grandchild share only a quarter of their genes in common, since every child has four grandparents. Likewise, sibs on average will be similar in half the genes for which their parents are heterozygous because it is equally likely that a particular child will inherit the gene from a parent that has already been transmitted to its sib, as it is that it will inherit the other allele. By the same reasoning it is evident that an individual shares in common with an uncle or aunt a quarter of his or her genes, and with a first cousin only an eighth. In general terms, for each step away people are in relationship, the genes they share in common are reduced by a half. This, of course, means that if the genes responsible for some particular quantitatively varying character are additive in effect, with no dominance, on average half the genes in an individual make him like a parent or like a sib while his other half make him no more like any one of these relatives than a totally unrelated person. And not only will any particular individual tend to be 'half like' each of his parents and his sibs, but he will also tend to be a 'quarter like' his grandparents, aunts, and uncles and an 'eighth like' his cousins. To take a theoretical example: suppose human stature is entirely determined by heredity and the responsible genes are additive in effect and without dominance; if the mean height of a population is 1·70 m, and mates are chosen at random so far as stature is concerned, men who are 1·78 m tall will have sons whose mean height is 1·74 m, since the son will, on average, receive from his father a half of the genes which made the father 0·08 m taller than the population mean and the other half of the son's genes, on average, will be like those of the general population. Likewise, grandsons and nephews will average 1·72 m and great-grandsons and first cousins 1·715 m. In understanding this relationship it is a help to note that while there is a regression of sons on fathers, there is equally a regression of fathers on sons. Thus men who are 1·78 m tall will have fathers whose mean height is 1·74 m, since on average a half of the genes which made the sons 0·08 m taller than the population mean will have come from the fathers.

The effects of dominance depend upon the frequency of the genes concerned. In general terms this can easily be seen by considering a single locus at which there are two alleles, one dominant to the other. If the dominant gene is rare, and homozygotes are never formed, then the other two genotypes are phenotypically distinct and the likeness of relatives is the same as if there were no dominance. On the other hand, if the dominant gene is common, there may be no likeness between a child and its parents, for if both parents are heterozygous, they will be as different as any individual can be from a homozygous recessive child. The same situation will prevail between an individual and its grandparents, aunts, and uncles, etc. but there will tend to be some likeness between sibs, since if a child is a homozygous recessive, there is a quarter chance that another child born to the heterozygous parents will also be of this genotype. Thus, depending on gene frequencies, the phenotypic similarity between relatives can vary between the values given when there is no dominance, to a quarter for sibs and nil for other relatives. In general terms, the relationship between parent and offspring is $q/1 \times q$ and between sibs $1 + 3q/4(1 + q)$, where $q$ is the frequency of the recessive allele in the population.

The fact that quantitatively varying characters depend upon many loci, necessarily introduces the complications that at some loci there may be dominance, at others partial dominance, and at yet others no dominance at all, so that one can only think in terms of an overall dominance effect; and also that there will be linkage between the polygenes, and possibly non-additiveness of effect due to locus interaction, which cannot be scaled away. This is why studies of the genetic determination of quantitatively varying characters in man are still in their infancy.

## The gene complex

Locus interaction, even in relatively simply determined characters is well known in plants and animals. The purple flower colour in sweet peas depends upon the existence of particular genes at two loci. If either is absent the flowers are white. Such factors are said to be 'complementary' and the most probable biochemical explanation is that the product of one gene is needed for the action of the other. It may also happen, as in the plumage determination of White Leghorn fowls, that the expression of a gene at one locus prevents the expression of a gene at another locus. This is a sort of 'dominance' between loci and is known as 'epistasis'. Evidence is now accruing for similar types of locus interaction in man. As an example one can cite the interaction of the H, secretor, and Lewis loci, which control the biosynthetic pathways leading to the formation of ABH and Lewis blood-group substances and which particularly affect the specificities of these substances as found in the watery secretions of the body (cf. p. 252). One feature in this complex situation, is that individuals who are homozygote hh do not produce A or B blood group substances (in the ABO system) even though they possess A or B genes.

Another important type of locus interaction is known as 'position effect'. Here the expression of a gene is affected by its position on a chromosome, or by the nature of neighbouring genes. The Rhesus blood-group system (p. 261) affords a striking example, where individuals with the complexes $CDE/cDe$ have the same genes as individuals who are $CDe/cDE$, but the former produce a large amount of E antigen and little C and the latter produces a lot of c and little E. Thus when $C$ and $E$ are on the same chromosome the synthesis of C is inhibited and when $C$ and $E$ are on opposite chromosomes E synthesis is inhibited.

In more general ways there is also plenty of evidence for locus interaction in man. Quite often a gene which expresses itself in a definite way is not expressed at all in some individuals who possess it. Polydactyly is typically inherited as a dominant condition, but, occasionally, completely normal people have affected children. One of the explanations for this sort of situation is that the rest of the genotype acts in a way to suppress the action of the gene. Genes which may or may not find expression are said to show 'variable penetrance'. A similar phenomenon, known as 'variable expressivity', is the inconsistency in effect that a gene may have. In brachydactyly the fingers and toes are typically short and webbed, but one or more of these symptoms are frequently absent. This type of phenomenon indicates that the production of any character rests upon the action of many genes. The genotypes in a population have been conditioned by natural selection so that a particular gene replacement usually has a constant effect on the development of some normal character, but this does not mean that this gene is solely responsible for that character. It is therefore not surprising that deleterious genes, for which the genotype obviously has not been prepared, frequently have variable and multiple manifestation.

There is now every indication that what matters for the integrated development of the individual and, therefore, its evolutionary fitness is a co-adapted gene complex. It is easy to envisage how natural selection operates to produce this. Even when a gene whose overall effect is advantageous first arises, it is likely that some expressions will be deleterious and those individuals whose genotype does not buffer development from these undesired expressions, will have fewer offspring than those in whose genotype there happen to be means of suppressing some of these effects. Such suppressing mechanisms will be further improved by natural selection and the undesired effects, by which one means those that reduce either viability or fertility or both, can be ultimately eliminated completely. The genes causing this suppression of effect are just one group of the so-called 'modifying genes' which have been built into the genotype by selection to control the expression of other genes. Some of them seem to have now no other effect. In addition to those that suppress deleterious effects there are no doubt others that amplify advantageous expressions. Dominance itself can be evolved in this way. When a new gene arises, and is, therefore, rare, it will exist only in heterozygotes. If it is deleterious in effect, natural selection will operate in such a way as to suppress these effects through modifying genes. In other words, the gene will become recessive, and in becoming so, the normal allele is obviously automatically made dominant. Conversely, if the new gene confers advantage on its possessor, natural selection will operate to confer these advantages on those individuals who only possess it in single dosage and thus make it dominant. The fact that when a deleterious gene arises by mutation it is often recessive from the outset is not inconsistent with this view, for mutation, as will be seen, is a recurrent phenomenon, and a gene which arises now has probably arisen many times in the past, enabling a modifying system to be evolved which suppresses its effects in single dosage. Evidence in favour of this view has been obtained by hybridizing different populations of animals which possess the same dominant gene. When the dominance has been built up by different modifying systems in the two populations there is a complete breakdown of dominance relationships in the hybrid population.

## The nature of the gene

The genetic information is coded in the deoxyribonucleic acid (DNA) of the chromosomes. DNA is made up of a sequence of nucleotides with each nucleotide consisting of the sugar deoxyribose, phosphoric acid, and a nitrogenous base. The nitrogenous basis varies and may be one or other of two purines, adenine (A) and guanine (G), or one or other of two pyrimidines, thymine (T) and cytosine (C). The DNA of all higher organisms is composed of two strands of nucleotide sequences in which the strands are bonded together

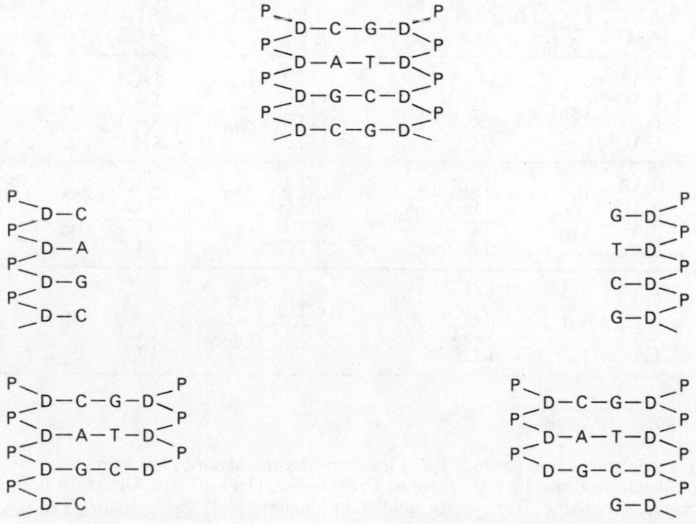

D = deoxyribose,     P = phosphoric acid,     C = cytosine,     G = guanine,
A = adenine,     T = thymine

FIG. 9.2. The replication of DNA.

by the bases, with adenine always bonding with thymine and guanine always bonding with cytosine. The bonded bases form, as it were, the steps of a ladder and the deoxyribose phosphoric acid molecules in sequence the sides. In fact as was first shown in the notable work of Watson and Crick, the strands are curved to form a 'double helix' and the structure of DNA is more comparable to a helical staircase than a ladder. In simplified form, and without the curvature the structure is shown in Fig. 9.2, which also shows how DNA has the capacity to replicate itself as is needed in the process of cell division. After the separation of the strands, two new strands are formed, each complementary to the original ones because one base precisely specifies the base with which it will pair.

TABLE 9.1

*The DNA code*

| | | Second base | | | | | | | |
|---|---|---|---|---|---|---|---|---|---|
| | | A | | G | | T | | C | |
| | A | AAA<br>AAG | Phe | AGA<br>AGG | Ser | ATA<br>ATG | Tyr | ACA<br>ACG | Cys | A<br>G |
| | | AAT<br>AAC | Leu | AGT<br>AGC | | ATT<br>ATC | Stop | ACT<br>ACC | Stop<br>Trp | T<br>C |
| | G | GAA<br>GAG | Leu | GGA<br>GGG | Pro | GTA<br>GTG | His | GCA<br>GCG | Arg | A<br>G |
| | | GAT<br>GAC | | GGT<br>GGC | | GTT<br>GTC | Gln | GCT<br>GCC | | T<br>C |
| First<br>base | T | TAA<br>TAG | Ile | TGA<br>TGG | Thr | TTA<br>TTG | Asn | TCA<br>TCG | Ser | A<br>G | Third<br>base |
| | | TAT<br>TAC | Met | TGT<br>TGC | | TTT<br>TTC | Lys | TCT<br>TCC | Arg | T<br>C |
| | C | CAA<br>CAG | Val | CGA<br>CGG | Ala | CTA<br>CTG | Asp | CCA<br>CCG | Gly | A<br>G |
| | | CAT<br>CAC | | CGT<br>CGC | | CTT<br>CTC | Glu | CCT<br>CCC | | T<br>C |

*Abbreviations for amino acids:*

Phe phenylalanine; Leu leucine; Ile isoleucine; Met methionine; Val valine; Ser serine; Pro proline; Thr threonine; Ala alanine; Tyr tyrosine; His histidine; Gln glutamine; Asn asparagine; Lys lysine; Asp aspartic acid; Glu glutamic acid; Cys cysteine; Trp tryptophane; Arg arginine; Gly glycine.

The genetic information in the DNA is conveyed from the cell nucleus to the cell cytoplasm by messenger ribonucleic acid (mRNA) (Fig. 9.3). RNA also consists of a series of nucleotides but in it the sugar is ribose and the pyrimidine uracil replaces the thymidine of DNA. In the course of the synthesis of the mRNA the DNA message is said to be transcribed: only one strand of the DNA is read, and the RNA possesses the complementary arrangement of bases to this strand, but with the adenine of the DNA transcribed as uracil. The mRNA becomes attached to the ribosomes in the cytoplasm, which themselves

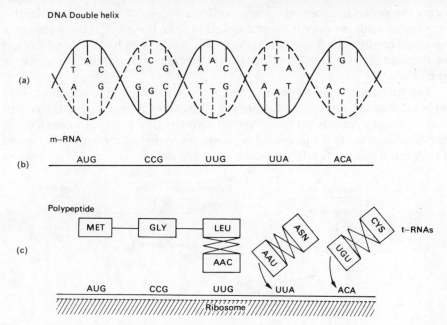

FIG. 9.3. The processes of protein synthesis: (a) the DNA code; (b) the m–RNA produced by that strand of DNA represented by a continuous line; (c) the formation of a polypeptide on a ribosome.

contain rRNA (ribosomal RNA), and from here directs the course of protein synthesis. The basic unit or 'word' in the message is a triplet of 3 nucleotides in which the 3 bases specify one of the 20 amino acids of which proteins are composed. These triplets, of which there are 64 possible combinations, are known as codons, and largely from the work of Nirenberg, the relationship between the codons and the amino acids most of them specify has been established. This is shown in Table 9.1. It will be noted that, whereas some amino acids are specified by only one codon (e.g. methionine by TAC in the DNA and AUG in the RNA), others are specified by 2 or more codons (e.g. phenyl-alanine by both AAA and AAG in the DNA). Because of the property of having more than one codon for a single amino acid the code is described as being degenerate or redundant. It will be noted that three codons ATT, ATC and especially ACT in the DNA (UAA, UAG, and UGA in the RNA) do not code for any amino acid. They would appear to act as stops in the message, separating the synthesis of one polypeptide chain from that of another.

Within the cell cytoplasm there is a third type of RNA known as transfer RNA (tRNA) or soluble RNA. Each molecule of this RNA is differentiated for a particular amino acid and carries the anti-codon to that specifying the same amino acid in the mRNA. Thus, for instance, some molecules have the anti-codon AAA and these carry the amino acid phenylalanine to those parts of the mRNA on the ribosomes with the code UUU. Others have UGU and bring the amino acid threonine to the mRNA codon ACA, and so on. In this way amino acids are assembled and linked to form polypeptides in a sequence specified by the mRNA and hence the DNA. Apart from having uracil instead of thymine the triplet bases in the tRNA, obviously, correspond to those on the DNA.

The first amino acid to be incorporated into a polypeptide appears always to be methionine. During the further synthesis of the polypeptide this terminal methionine may or may not be cleaved off, so many final proteins do not contain methionine in the first amino-acid position. Nevertheless the code TAC in the DNA and AUG in the mRNA can be regarded as the 'start' codon to contrast

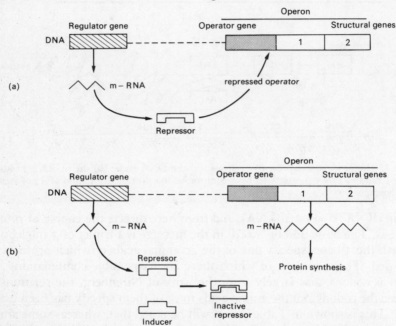

FIG. 9.4. The Jacob–Monod model of the control of protein synthesis.

with the 'stop' codons. It should, however, be noted that methione can also occur in the middle of a polypeptide and there are two types of tRNA, one for terminal methionine and one for internal methionine.

Although every nucleated cell of the adult organism typically possesses the full chromosome complement and genetic code inherited by the zygote, the cells become differentiated in their form and activity to perform the functions of the various tissues. In one type of tissue some genes are active and others not, whilst in other tissues different sets of genes dictate what polypeptides will be synthesized. There is some evidence that in most tissues only about 5 per cent of the genes are active, though in the brain this seems to rise to about 12 per cent. A model for explaining the control of gene activity and tissue differentiation has been put forward by Jacob and Monod, for which there is considerable experimental evidence, at least in micro-organisms (Fig. 9.4). This involves two types of gene: structural genes which code for the polypeptides synthesized on the ribosomes and controller genes which determine the activity of the structural ones. The latter are distinguished into 'operators' and 'regulators'. It is presumed that structural genes involved in coding for polypeptides concerned with the same metabolic process are frequently adjacent to one another (natural selection itself, as Sheppard first suggested, is likely to cause this) and that an operator gene controlling their activity is situated contiguous to one of a pair or more of these structural genes. This complex is known as an 'operon'. The regulator gene which is located some distance from the operon produces a repressor substance, now known to be a protein in at least some cases, which can react with the operator to switch it off and thus inactivate the structural genes. However, it may also react with certain small molecules ('inducers') which may be present in the intracellular milieu, and when this happens its configuration is so changed that it cannot act to repress the operator. The inducers are themselves metabolic products or 'food substances' and there is thus a feedback system which can lead to the switching on or off of the structural genes.

The exciting advances which have occurred in recent years in molecular genetics, and which have been very summarily described here, have revolutionized our understanding of the nature of the hereditary material and the way evolution and ontogenesis occurs, but for many purposes and especially in population genetics it is still convenient and meaningful to think in classical Mendelian terms.

# 10. Environmental interaction

THE total phenotype of an individual is not only dependent upon his overall genotype but also on the external environment in which he exists. Throughout life there is a constant interaction between these two sets of factors which, in the final analysis, are the only determinants of all the biological characteristics of the individual; and both are equally important. Sometimes, as in blood-group status, differences between individuals are entirely of genetic origin, since in all the environments consistent with life, a particular genotype has a constant expression, but though attention has been mainly directed to such conditions so that the principles of Mendelism could be described, they are exceptional, and even in these cases it is only the differences which are exclusively genetic; the characters still require an environment before they can develop. Likewise, when differences are entirely environmental in origin, there is an underlying genetic basis to the character concerned. Thus, for instance, a difference in the red blood-cell count (r.b.c.) of individuals is often solely due to the altitude at which they live, but the capacity of an individual to vary the concentration of his r.b.c. with atmospheric oxygen tension is genetic. These are the two extreme situations; more often, even the differences between individuals have both a genetic and environmental component. Differences in stature are inherited, but they are also environmentally determined, since growth is profoundly affected by nutritional state, disease experience and probably by climatic factors as well. In cases like this one is concerned with attempting to analyse what Dobzhansky has termed 'the norm of reaction' of the organism. He defines this concept as 'the entire range, the whole repertoire, of the variant paths of development that may occur in the carriers of a given genotype in all possible environments'.

The nature of the variation produced by environmental differences may often be similar to that produced by genetic factors. Abnormal environments can produce effects very similar to those produced by abnormal genes. For instance, rubella infections of mothers during the first three months of pregnancy sometimes produce deaf mutism and congenital cataract in the child, indistinguishable from the genetically determined varieties of these abnormalities. Such environmentally caused mimics of gene effects are known as 'phenocopies'. More important is the similarity in effect of polygenic determination and normal environmental variation.

It has been shown that polygenic determination produces a more-or-less symmetrical and unimodal frequency distribution of a character. Environmental variation produces the same type of effect, as can be seen from analyses of environmentally labile characters in genetically homogeneous experimental populations of plants and animals. The magnitude of this effect depends not only on the magnitude of the environmental variation, but also on the particular range over which it is varying and upon the genotypes with which it is interacting. Thus, for example, a temperature fluctuation around 70 °F (21 °C) does not produce the same phenotypic variability in the growth of mice as the same fluctuation around 90 °F (32 °C), and it seems often true that when two genetically homogeneous populations, one with individuals heterozygous at many loci and the other homozygous at these loci, are kept in the same environment the heterozygous one is less variable than the homozygous one.

A measure much used in studies of the roles played by hereditary and environmental factors in determining phenotypic variability is 'heritability'. Heritability is defined as that proportion of the observed variance of a character in a population which can be attributed to genetic causes. There are two types of heritability estimate: broad heritability which represents the overall contribution of genetic factors and narrow heritability which arises from only the additive components of the genetic variance, i.e. is due to the average effects of individual genes on a character irrespective of what other genes are present. Additional components of the total genetic variance arise from dominance and epistasis (inter-locus interaction), and only when these are negligible does a narrow heritability estimate correspond with a broad one.

The interpretation of heritability estimates is confounded by the possibilities of two major phenomena: genetic–environmental co-variation and genetic–environmental interaction. The first of these arises if particular genotypes tend to select particular parts of the environmental diversity to which a population is exposed. Variation arising from this cause is assigned by many estimation procedures into the genetic component although this is obviously misleading. On the other hand, genetic–environmental interaction, which arises from the differential response of different genotypes to the same environmental conditions, is frequently partitioned into the environmental component. The magnitudes of these phenomena may clearly be considerable especially for characters like behavioural traits in man, but they are often difficult to determine.

Another matter of importance in considering heritability estimates is to appreciate that they only relate to the particular population and the particular environment in which they were obtained. Qualitative and quantitative change in the genetic composition of the population or in the nature of environments, is likely to alter heritability.

A heritability estimate thus has no general significance and it is not permissible to extrapolate from the situation revealed by an analysis in one population to another. However, if a trait tends to show consistently high (or low) heritabilities in a number of different populations and environments it is not unreasonable to assume that it is environmentally stable (or labile) within the sort of ranges of environmental fluctuation in a single population.

Sometimes data are only relevant to within the smallest of population units—the family; in other types of data it is possible to sample the effects of genetic and environmental heterogeneity within and between the families constituting a single breeding population (i.e. between as well as within the families); but it is generally impossible to translate a situation found within a population into an explanation for differences between populations. In other words a trait may have a high heritability in each of two populations, but any difference between these populations could still be totally environmental in origin. Such a statement is not inconsistent with the above one that characteristics with high heritabilities in one population often show high heritabilities in others, since the environmental range within populations is often quantitatively if not qualitatively different from that between populations.

Among experimental plants and animals where large-scale breeding programmes can be undertaken it has been possible to analyse in some detail the magnitude and nature of heritabilities for many quantitatively varying traits in various genetic and environmental situations, by examination of the variances of groups of known genetic constitution and by measuring the response of a character to some regime of artificial selection. For obvious reasons it has not yet been possible to carry analyses of the so-called 'nature–nurture' problem so far in man, and most information has come from twin studies, supplemented by the examination of similarities between other types of relative and of adopted children with both their biological and foster kin.

Twins are of two types: they arise either from the fertilization of two separate ova, in which case they are said to be 'dizygotic' and will be no more genetically alike than ordinary sibs, or from the division of a single fertilized egg, in which case they are referred to as 'monozygotic' and will be genetically identical unless some somatic mutation (i.e. genetic change in non-gonadal cells) occurs after their separation. Differences between monozygotic twins will, therefore, be mainly environmental in origin, whilst differences between dizygotic twins will be caused by both environmental and genetic factors. Monozygotic twins, because of their complete genetic identity, will tend to react more uniformly to their environment than non-identical twins, but, in the main, such differences as occur in the variability of the two types of twins will be of genetic origin, when the heterogeneity of the environment surrounding different members of a pair is the same.

Not only is the genetic difference between relatives less than that between unrelated individuals, but environmentally caused variation will also tend to be less, since the conditions under which a family lives are more homogeneous than those prevailing in the population as a whole. Occasionally, however, members of a family are reared under very different environmental conditions, and when this happens to identical twins, one has the ideal opportunity of determining the contribution that environmental factors acting over a whole population are making to phenotypic differences in that population.

A common way of estimating the relative contributions made by environmental and genetic components to differences which can be considered qualitative, is to compare the concordance of identical and non-identical twins. Twins are said to be 'concordant' when they are alike for the character sidered, and 'discordant' when they differ. For instance, if both members of a pair develop some pathology, or if neither is affected, they are concordant; whereas if one member is affected and his twin is not, they are discordant. The concordance in monozygotic twins for such infectious diseases as measles is very high, but it is practically as high for dizygotic twins. High concordance in this case only means that if an individual is infected he is very likely to transmit the infection to his twin. On the other hand, the concordance between monozygotic twins for tuberculosis, and rickets, is considerably greater than the concordance in dizygotic twins, so although one of these diseases is basically infectious, and the other nutritional, there is strong genetic susceptibility.

For characters which vary quantitatively the differences between pairs of monozygotic (MZ) twins, expressed either as a correlation coefficient or as a mean within-pair variance, are compared with the differences between pairs of dizygotic (DZ) twins. The basic formula for estimating heritability is

$$\frac{\text{DZ variance} - \text{MZ variance}}{\text{DZ variance}}$$

When this ratio is one the within-family variation in the character concerned is entirely of genetic origin, and when it is o solely environmental. The most reliable way of determining the effect of environmental heterogeneity over a population is to compare the differences between monozygotic twins which have been reared together $(T)$ with those that have been reared apart $(A)$. If this comparison is expressed in the form

$$\frac{\text{variance } A - \text{variance } T}{\text{variance } A}$$

a value approaching 1 means that the character concerned is strongly determined by an environment which varies much more within the population as a whole, than it does within single families.

When these modes of analysis have been applied to such a character as body-weight it has been found that the environmental differences that occur within the compass of particular populations may contribute considerably to the phenotypic variation. Stature, however, seems to be very much less labile. The same methods have been applied to variations in behaviour and Table 10.1 shows some average estimates which have been obtained of the degree of similarity between twins and siblings for I.Q. in various European and North-American White populations. Interpretations of results such as these have, however, been a subject of some ongoing controversy, partly because of difficulties in measuring such complex traits as intelligence and personality but also because of limitations in the twin method, some of which become particularly serious in examining behavioural traits.

One difficulty common to all twin studies is the possibility of confusing monozygotic and dizygotic twins. The method of testing for zygosity involves comparing the similarity of twins in many genetically determined different characters. Identity or very close resemblance in all these characters is indicative of monozygosity, whilst a clear difference in only one is proof of dizygosity. The characters most useful for the purpose are those whose mode of inheritance is known, and which are based on loci having complete penetrance and uniform expressivity in all environments and at which alternative alleles are common in the population. Knowledge of the mode of inheritance enables one to determine the likelihood of a given identity being found in dizygotic twins. The blood-groups and similar traits are ideal, and if they are all considered along with such characters as finger-print patterns, which though not simply inherited are environmentally stable, then the likelihood of faulty diagnosis is very small. In the past, however, anthropometric measurements and characters such as eye colour and hair form had to be relied upon and errors were almost certainly common. If a correct diagnosis is of vital importance in some particular case, it is possible to distinguish the two types of twin by skin-grafting. Skin can only be successfully transferred between two individuals of the same genotype. It needs to be mentioned here that there is the possibility that twins may also arise by the fertilization with different sperm of an ovum that has previously divided or by the fertilization of the second polar body. It is also of importance that monozygotic twins are apparently sometimes mirror-images of each other and the possibilities of somatic mutation, early in development but after separation of the twins, cannot be ignored. Perhaps more important still, at least for behavioural traits, is that monozygotic twins, because of their complete identity of genotype, will react more uniformly to the environment than the genetically different dizygotic twins. They will for the same reason also tend to choose a greater identity in their environment. In other words, there are gene–environment interactions and gene–environment correlations whose magnitudes are almost impossible to estimate. It also needs to be remembered that all types of twin are different from singletons in that they share a common maternal environment and, to some extent at least, compete in this during pregnancy and early childhood. Twins are also subject to special kinds of parental treatment. The effect of being a member of a twin pair can be allowed for by comparing the degree of similarity between dizygotic twins with that between singleton sibs, but this needs information on the sibs when they were of the same age which is often difficult to obtain. Another dangerous source of error is the introduction of bias, which can readily occur if the twins for study are not collected in a systematic way. It is very easy to miss dizygotic twins which are discordant, particularly if one member of the pair has died. Finally, twins are far from common, only about 1 birth in 90 being a twin birth, and certainly as far as rare genetical abnormalities are concerned very few twins will be affected.

As Weinberg first pointed out, the numbers of monozygotic twins in a population can be obtained by subtracting from the total number of twins twice the number of unlike sexed twins, since dizygotic twins will be as often of dif-

TABLE 10.1

*Summary of observed similarities in intelligence in a series of studies*

| Relationships | Genetic correlation | Observed correlation coefficients | | | | | | | | | | |
|---|---|---|---|---|---|---|---|---|---|---|---|---|
| | | 0 | 0·1 | 0·2 | 0·3 | 0·4 | 0·5 | 0·6 | 0·7 | 0·8 | 0·9 | 1·0 |
| Unrelated persons reared together | 0·00 | | | ├─ | | | | | | | | |
| Foster parent and child | 0·00 | | ├─ | | | | | | | | | |
| Parent and child | 0·50 | | | ├────────────┼────────────┤ | | | | | | | | |
| Siblings reared apart | 0·50 | | | | ├────┼────┤ | | | | | | | |
| Siblings reared together | 0·50 | | | ├──────────┼──────────┤ | | | | | | | | |
| Dizygotic twins same sex | 0·50 | | | | ├──────┼──────────────┤ | | | | | | | |
| Monozygotic twins reared apart | 1·00 | | | | | | | ├───┼───┤ | | | | |
| Monozygotic twins reared together | 1·00 | | | | | | | | | ├───┼──┤ | | |

Horizontal lines represent the ranges in similarity in the different studies.
Vertical lines represent the mean values over the different studies.
Data based on the compilations made by Erlenmeyer-Kimling and Jarvik (1963).

ferent sex as of the same sex. It is found that about a quarter of all twins born are monozygotic.

It is interesting that twinning itself, particularly dizygotic twinning, is subject to environmental and genetic variation. The likelihood of having both monozygotic and dizygotic twins depends on the age of the mother. The monozygotic twinning rate is linearly related to maternal age whilst the dizygotic twinning rate reaches a maximum in mothers of about 37 years old. The latter rate is also dependent upon parity, i.e. the birth order of the children, being commoner among later births than earlier ones. Naturally, the effects of maternal age had to be removed before this parity effect could be found. The dizygotic twinning rate also fell in many European countries during the Second World War; this was probably due to the prevalent malnutrition. Mothers of dizygotic twins have an increased likelihood of another twin birth, and the sisters of mothers with twins have a greater tendency for twins than other women. There are also large racial differences in dizygotic twinning rates; such twins being more common in Negroes and less common in Japanese than in Europeans [p. 289].

Another quite different method of gaining insight into the ontogenetic effects of environmental factors is to examine migrants from one ecological situation to another. This approach was extensively applied by Boas in anthropometric studies of European migrants to North America and has recently been refined for the analysis of physiological variation. It is particularly useful in examining the physiological effects of living at different altitudes, since dramatic environmental changes occur in mountainous regions in relatively short geographical distances and often across populations between which there is so much exchange through migration that genetic differences could not arise. By comparing indigenous highlanders, recent lowland migrants to highlands, indigenous lowlanders, and recent highland migrants to lowlands it is possible to identify not only the immediate effects of altitude variation on development and physiology but also any genetic components to differences between the highland and lowland indigines when these have been isolated from one another. The main difficulty in this approach is that migrants may often not be representative samples, at least in some traits, of the populations from which they come.

Within the norm of reaction of an individual a response or set of responses to an environment may be either disadvantageous or advantageous. As an example of disadvantageous responses one can cite the effects of large doses of ionizing radiation. Individuals who did not show these effects would be more fit than those that do in environments where there is much radiation. Whilst such responses can in the broadest sense be considered to be genetically determined they have not been evolved. Indeed, if an increased radiation load becomes a permanent factor in some environments natural selection will operate to increase an individual's resistance to it, provided, of course, that all individuals are not destroyed first! The capacity of the individual to buffer his existence from environmental factors which are constantly tending to disintegrate it is known as 'homeostasis'. Since an individual's environment is constantly changing, the states of the homeostatic mechanisms will themselves change correspondingly in providing the desired buffer effect. If, then, the differences between individuals are due to differences in their environment demanding different homeostatic states, these differences are adaptive. The ability of the individual to respond adaptively to environmental change is conveniently distinguished from adaptations involving genetic change by referring to it as his 'adaptability'. As examples of man's adaptability, one can mention the variation of erythrocyte count with altitude, basal metabolic rate with temperature, and state of skin colour with intensity of solar radiation. Most of this adaptability resides in reversible physiological and behavioural mechanisms, but it seems that irreversible growth and developmental processes can be adaptable also.

# 11. Genetic structure of human populations: I. Mating systems

## The population

STUDY of the genetic structure of human populations is still in its infancy, but this branch of genetics is so important in understanding much in human biology that considerable attention must be given to the little that is as yet known. This will be dealt with in the framework of a few of the simpler principles of general population genetics.

In everyday language the term 'population' is usually used in some geographical or ecological context. One speaks of the population of a town, or a country, or a habitat. While such a population may well correspond to that recognized by the geneticist, he is, in the first place, more concerned with relationship than with locality. It is convenient, therefore, to distinguish populations in terms of the distribution of genes. This Dobzhansky has done by recognizing the Mendelian population, which he defines as 'a reproductive community of sexual and cross-fertilizing individuals which share in a common gene pool'. Like geographical populations in which, for instance, the population of a country is made up of the populations of many countries, so any particular Mendelian population may be compounded of others of smaller dimension. The largest Mendelian population is the species, since every individual potentially, if not actually, shares in all the genes present in the species, but different species, because they do not mate together, must draw upon different gene pools. There are frequently recognizable, within the species itself, different subspecies or races which are other Mendelian populations of subordinate rank, and these are themselves compounded of yet smaller groups. Different races are recognized because the individuals who comprise one race are genetically different from those that comprise another, but the first essential feature about populations generally is that from a breeding point of view they are, in varying degrees, isolated from one another. The isolating factors may be purely geographical, such as distance or other barriers to movement, but, so far as man is concerned, can equally well be social or religious, so that even the inhabitants of a restricted locality may often be arranged into a number of fairly separate groups or 'isolates'. The term isolate is usually confined to such small population units, but in principle it could be extended to larger groups, as long as from the breeding point of view they are fairly discrete. It is because mating circles often persist over many generations that different populations are frequently genetically different, since genes which, for reasons to be discussed later, become fixed in one group, tend to be confined to this group. In the past, at least, distance and other geographical features have been the most persistent barriers to the intermingling of populations and that is one of the reasons why broad geographical varieties of man occur.

## Random mating

One of the simplest types of mating system possible in populations of bisexual organisms is that in which any individual of one sex has an equal probability of mating with any individual of the opposite sex in the population. Such random mating is known as 'panmixis'. Strict panmictic units are not discrete in those human populations which are continuous over large areas; and even if in a group of people, homogeneous in origin and isolated from other groups, every individual has an equal opportunity of taking as a mate any member of the opposite sex, mate preference and social factors will prevent marriages being formed at random. Nevertheless, it is usually true that genes, such as those which determine the blood groups, which are rarely taken into account in mate selection, are distributed among the inhabitants of some fairly restricted locality as though mating were more or less at random.

The effect of random mating on the distribution of genes in a population is the foundation of population genetics. So that only this effect is considered, it will be assumed in the first place that there is no differential viability or fertility of genotypes, no mutation, and that the population is sufficiently large to obviate unrepresentative sampling of gametes. To understand the consequences of random mating it is convenient to envisage the formation of a new panmictic unit by the hybridization of a population which contains only one of a pair of genes, e.g. $A$ with another population which contains only its allele, e.g. $A'$. All the individuals in these 'ancestral' populations are obviously homozygous at the locus considered for the two genes respectively. In the hybrid population, however, there will not only be both homozygotes but also heterozygotes, and the question of import is in what frequency will these three genotypes occur if mating is random? The answer obviously depends upon the proportionate representation of the two ancestral populations compounded in the mixed one. Suppose the population which is homozygous $AA$ contributes a fraction $p$ of the parents of the hybrid population and the remaining fraction $q$ is contributed from the population which is homozygous $A'A'$, then, if males and females from each ancestral population are equally represented, the frequencies of the different sorts of mating will be $p^2 AA \times AA$, $2pq AA \times A'A'$, and $q^2 A'A' \times A'A'$, as can readily be seen from the following table.

| Frequency of matings | | Frequency of two types of male | |
| --- | --- | --- | --- |
| | | $pAA$ | $qA'A'$ |
| Frequency of two types of female | $pAA$ | $p^2 AA \times AA$ | $pq A'A' \times AA$ |
| | $qA'A'$ | $pq AA \times A'A'$ | $q^2 A'A' \times A'A'$ |

Matings between homozygous parents of one type can obviously only produce children of the same type, whilst matings between homozygotes of different type will produce only heterozygous children, so the frequencies of children produced from these matings will be $p^2AA$, $2pqAA'$, $q^2A'A'$.

| Frequency of types of mating | Frequency of types of children |
|---|---|
| $p^2AA \times AA$ | $p^2AA$ |
| $2pqAA \times A'A'$ | $2pqAA'$ |
| $q^2A'A' \times A'A'$ | $q^2A'A'$ |

These are the parents of the next generation, so instead of only 2 types of parent as in the initial matings, there will be 3 types. The consequences of this, however, are determined in exactly the same way as in the preceding generation; first the frequencies of the different types of mating are calculated and then the frequencies of the types of children from these matings.

| Frequency of different types of mating | | Frequency of three types of male | | |
|---|---|---|---|---|
| | | $p^2AA$ | $2pqAA'$ | $q^2A'A'$ |
| | $p^2AA$ | $p^4$ $AA \times AA$ | $2p^3q$ $AA \times AA'$ | $p^2q^2$ $AA \times A'A'$ |
| Frequency of three types of female | $2pqAA'$ | $2p^3q$ $AA' \times AA$ | $4p^2q^2$ $AA' \times AA'$ | $2pq^3$ $AA' \times A'A'$ |
| | $q^2A'A'$ | $p^2q^2$ $A'A' \times AA$ | $2pq^3$ $A'A' \times AA'$ | $q^4$ $A'A' \times A'A'$ |

In the above table 3 types of mating occur twice, so in considering the frequency with which children are produced reciprocal cross matings are added together.

| Types and frequency of mating | | Type and frequency of children | | |
|---|---|---|---|---|
| | | $AA$ | $AA'$ | $A'A'$ |
| $AA \times AA$ | $p^4$ | $p^4$ | | |
| $AA \times AA'$ | $4p^3q$ | $2p^3q$ | $2p^3q$ | |
| $AA \times A'A'$ | $2p^2q^2$ | | $2p^2q^2$ | |
| $AA' \times AA'$ | $4p^2q^2$ | $p^2q^2$ | $2p^2q^2$ | $p^2q^2$ |
| $AA' \times A'A'$ | $4pq^3$ | | $2pq^3$ | $2pq^3$ |
| $A'A' \times A'A'$ | $q^4$ | | | $q^4$ |
| Total frequency of different types of children | | $p^2(p^2+2pq+q^2)+2pq(p^2+2pq+q^2)+q^2(p^2+2pq+q^2)$ | | |

The total frequency of the children of the 3 types is obtained by adding together the contributions from the various matings to each of the columns. It will be seen that $(p^2+2pq+q^2)$ is common to each column and the 3 genotypes are, therefore, produced in the frequencies $p^2AA$, $2pqAA'$, $q^2A'A'$. These are the frequencies of the different types of parents. Thus, if only the effects of random mating are considered, the frequency with which the three genotypes occur in a population is the same from generation to generation; the equilibrium frequency is $p^2AA$, $2pqAA'$, $q^2AA'$; and following the mixture of populations this equilibrium is established in a single generation. These conclusions are all aspects of what is known as the Hardy–Weinberg law.

The fact that the genotype frequencies are constant from generation to generation must, of course, also mean that the frequency of the two genes remains the same. It will be recalled that the symbols $p$ and $q$ were used initially to represent the frequencies of the homozygotes $AA$ and $A'A'$ respectively among the parents of the new population. Since each of these individuals carries two genes of the same type, these symbols equally well represent the frequency of the genes $A$ and $A'$ in this population of parents. Now, whilst the frequencies of the genotypes changed in the first generation through the formation of a new genotype—the heterozygote $AA'$—the frequencies of the genes did not change, and they can therefore continue to be represented by $p$ and $q$ in every generation.

Gene frequencies are usually represented as decimals rather than as fractions or percentages. For example, if a quarter of the genes at a particular locus in a population are of the type $A$, this gene is said to have a frequency of 0·25. In this case, the allele $A'$ must obviously have a frequency of 0·75, if it is the only other allele in the population, since $p+q=1$.

It is often necessary to know the frequency of genes in a population. When the heterozygote is phenotypically distinguishable from both homozygotes, the frequency of two alleles can be counted directly. Thus, for instance, in the MN blood-group system every individual with only M-type blood possesses two $Ag^M$ genes whilst MN individuals have only one $Ag^M$ gene. The frequency of the $Ag^M$ gene in a population is therefore

$$\frac{2M+MN}{2T}$$

where $M$ and $MN$ represent the number of M and MN individuals respectively in the population and $T$ the total number of individuals. The frequency of $Ag^N$ can be calculated similarly, or by subtracting the $Ag^M$ frequency from 1. When the heterozygote is not distinguishable from one homozygote this procedure is obviously not possible. In such cases the gene frequencies have to be estimated indirectly. Consider the situation in PTC tasting; as has been shown, under random mating the three genotypes will be in the frequency $p^2TT:2pqTt:q^2tt$. Now $p^2+2pq+q^2$ is the expansion of $(p+q)^2$ and the frequency of the gene $T$, i.e. $p$ is the square root of the frequency of $TT$ individuals and the frequency of $t$, i.e. $q$, is the square root of the frequency of $tt$ individuals. The former are not distinguishable from the heterozygotes, but the latter are.

The square root of the frequency of non-tasters in a population is therefore the frequency of the non-taster gene and $p$ can be obtained by subtracting $q$ from $1$.

The principle can easily be extended from a pair of alleles to 3 or more. In the ABO system both A and B are dominant to O, but there is no dominance between A and B, i.e. the heterozygote $AB$ is recognizable while the heterozygotes $AO$ and $BO$ are not. When other alleles such as $A_2$ do not occur there are therefore only 4 distinct phenotypes. If $p$ represents the frequency of $A$, $q$ of $B$, and $r$ of $O$ with $p+q+r=1$ then, under a system of random mating the frequency $r$ is the square root of the frequency of individuals who are of O blood. $q$ can be calculated in the following way:

$$p^2 + 2pr + r^2 = f_A + f_O,$$

where $f_A$ and $f_O$ represent the frequency of A and O individuals respectively.

That is
$$(p+r)^2 = f_A + f_O$$
and so
$$p+r = \sqrt{(f_A + f_O)}.$$
But
$$p+q+r = 1,$$
therefore
$$1-q = \sqrt{(f_A + f_O)}$$
and
$$q = 1 - \sqrt{(f_A + f_O)}.$$

$p$ can similarly be shown to be equal to $1 - \sqrt{(f_B + f_O)}$. For use these formulae need to be slightly modified, but this explanation covers the essential principle.

Gene frequencies rather than phenotype or even genotype frequencies are usually used for expressing the differences between populations and need to be known in many genetic problems. They are particularly necessary in calculating the frequencies of unidentifiable heterozygotes, which is a matter of some importance when these are carriers for deleterious genes. As has been seen for a two-allele system the frequency of heterozygotes is $2pq$ under random mating. This means that the highest frequency of heterozygotes occurs when the two genes have equal frequency, i.e. $0.5$. At these frequencies 50 per cent of individuals will be heterozygotes. With a diminishing frequency of one of the genes there is a reduction not only in the homozygotes for this gene, but also in the heterozygotes.

A recessive condition may be very rare in the population and yet the frequency of carriers is comparatively high. Albinism, for instance, has an incidence of about $1/20\,000$. The frequency therefore of the albino gene $q$ is $\sqrt{(1/20\,000)} \simeq 0.00709$ and of the normal allele $p \simeq 0.99291$. The latter to all intents and purposes can be regarded as unity so $2pq = 2 \times 0.00709 = 0.01418$, which is approximately $1/70$.

## Inbreeding and outbreeding

Deviations from random mating can occur in two general directions. People who are related can marry either more frequently or less frequently than they would by chance. In the former case the mating system is one of inbreeding; in the latter, one of outbreeding.

A system, similar in effect to inbreeding, is positive assortative mating in which people who are phenotypically alike, and, therefore, tending to be genetically alike, marry each other more frequently than they would by chance. So far as man is concerned, it seems to be particularly marked for intelligence and stature; marriages between individuals similar in these characters being commoner than would be expected by chance. Negative assortative mating occurs when individuals who are unlike one another marry preferentially. There is evidence that red-haired people marry each other less frequently than is to be expected under random mating. The effects of negative assortative mating are in general terms similar to outbreeding but assortative mating, both positive and negative, obviously only affects the genetic systems controlling the traits for which the assortative mating occurs, whilst inbreeding and outbreeding, which can be thought of as assortative mating for ancestry, affect the whole genome.

The closest form of inbreeding, and one possible in many plants, is self-fertilization. It demonstrates in the simplest way the consequences of inbreeding. When a heterozygote $AA'$ fertilizes itself, a half of the progeny are heterozygotes, while the other half are homozygotes either $AA$ or $A'A'$. The selfing of these homozygotes, of course, produces only more homozygotes; but again a half of the progeny of the heterozygotes are homozygotes. This means that under self-fertilization the frequency of the heterozygotes in a population is constantly being reduced at the rate per generation of a half the heterozygote frequency in the previous generation. Ultimately, to all intents and purposes, no heterozygotes will occur and the population will be composed exclusively of the two types of homozygote. In this model only a single locus has been considered, but, of course, the trend to homozygosis will occur at the same rate at every locus, and eventually, if no other factors come into play, every individual produces offspring which are identical to it in all their genes. Another consequence is that a series of quite distinct lines is established. Starting with a double heterozygote $AaBb$, for instance, there are four such lines possible, namely $AABB, AAbb, aaBB$, and $aabb$. The rate of reduction in heterozygosity as a whole is independent of the number of gene pairs concerned, but the probable number of homozygous individuals and the number of individuals heterozygous at 1, 2, 3, etc., loci in any generation depends on the initial number of gene pairs and can be calculated by expanding the binomial $1+(2^r-1)^n$, where $r$ represents the generation concerned and $n$ the number of gene pairs.

It must be noted that in this model of the reduction in heterozygosis it is being assumed that every member of a generation reproduces and all its offspring are reared. If there is some non-random selection of parents then the rate at which complete homozygosity is approached depends obviously upon the genotype of the individuals chosen. To take an extreme example, if only one individual were taken as the parent of the next generation and this happened to be a homozygote, then obviously all subsequent generations from that time on would be homozygotes of the type chosen. On the other hand, if the chosen individual were heterozygous, no reduction in the frequency of heterozygotes would have occurred. One can at least say, however, for self-fertilization that no individual can ever be more heterozygous than its parent; it may be the same or less, but whatever homozygosity is gained is always retained.

This is not true of the next closest forms of inbreeding, brother–sister and parent–offspring, which are, therefore, mating systems that require a greater number of generations to eliminate heterozygotes. Thus, for instance, 6 generations of self-fertilization are more effective than seventeen generations of brother–sister matings in bringing about homozygosis. Only occasionally, as among the Ptolemies and the royal house of the Incas, do human societies permit such close inbreeding as brother–sister unions. Among the Ernadan of Malabar it is common for a man to take his eldest daughter as his second wife, but usually the closest forms of inbreeding permitted by human societies are between niece and uncle (or nephew and aunt) and between first cousins. Even the former is forbidden in many societies, and in the USA, for instance, over a third of the States forbid the latter. Continued cousin marriages will also tend to produce general homozygosis, but the rate at which heterozygotes are reduced in frequency is very considerably slower than with brother–sister or parent–offspring mating.

Marriages between related individuals, known as consanguineous marriages, are of considerable medical importance, since the likelihood of spouses having the same genes is obviously considerably greater if they are closely related than if they are unrelated. Relatedness, of course, is a state of infinite degree. In the evolutionary sense all people are related; at some stage in their history they had common ancestors. So far as some particular population is concerned, its past size, if all individuals were unrelated, would have to have been far greater than it actually could have been, since every individual has 2 parents, 4 grand-parents, 8 great-grandparents, and $2^n$ ancestors $n$ generations ago. Assuming that on average there have been 4 generations per 100 years, an individual would have $2^{40}$ or approximately a million million ancestors a thousand years ago, if there had been no consanguinity. It seems probable that the total population of the world in the tenth century did not exceed 200 million and it was very much smaller in yet earlier times! In considering degrees of relatedness it is therefore usual to recognize some hypothetical basal population in which it is assumed all individuals are unrelated.

It is also necessary to distinguish between genes which are 'alike in state' and genes which are 'identical by descent'. Two $Ag^M$ genes, for instance, are alike in state, they will replace one another with identity of genetic effect, but they may either have both originated from the replication of one gene in a pre-vious generation, in which case they can be said to be identical by descent or they may have no common origin or a common origin so distant that it can be neglected, in which case they are non-identical in terms of descent and can be referred to as 'independent'. Genes which are unlike in state must, of course, be independent in the absence of mutation.

The relationship between two individuals can be expressed genetically as the probability that at a particular locus each possesses a gene identical by descent. It was shown (p. 132) that this relationship, the so-called 'coefficient of relationship' between parent–child and between sibs is $\frac{1}{2}$. The coefficient between grandparent–grandchild and uncle/aunt–nephew/niece is $\frac{1}{4}$, and between first cousins $\frac{1}{8}$. So far as some deleterious recessive gene is concerned this means that even in a family in which no one is affected, the cousin of a carrier has, at least, a 1 in 8 chance of being a carrier also. The reason for giving a maximum value to the probability is because no account has been taken of this cousin being a carrier by virtue of independent genes. If the gene is rare this is a remote possibility. Nevertheless, the situation illustrates strikingly the increased likelihood of having an affected child if a carrier marries a cousin rather than an unrelated person, for the likelihood of marrying a heterozygote from the general population is $2pq$. It may be added that the probability of a cousin of an affected person being a carrier falls to at least $\frac{1}{4}$, since one knows with certainty that both parents of the affected individual must be heterozygotes and one of these is the uncle or aunt of the cousin in question.

In considering these cases, not only has no account been taken of independent genes, but also it has been assumed that the genotype of one of the cousin mates was known; but when this mate is a carrier this will usually not be so. It is therefore necessary to generalize the problem and ask: what is the chance of two non-affected cousins having an affected child for a recessive condition?

To answer this question one has to know the probability that an individual will have at a given locus two genes which are identical by descent. This is known as the coefficient of inbreeding, usually represented by $F$, and for the offspring of two completely unrelated parents is 0. In general form the inbreeding coefficient for an individual is $F = \frac{1}{2}^{n+n'+1} (1 + F_z)$, where $n$ and $n'$ are the number of steps in the lines of descent from the common ancestor to the *parents* of the individual concerned and $F_z$ is the coefficient of inbreeding of the common ancestor. If this ancestor can be considered as not inbred $F_z$ is 0 and the expression reduces to $F = \frac{1}{2}^{n+n'+1}$. The converse of the inbreeding coefficient, i.e. $1 - F$, is, of course, the probability that an individual will have at a given locus two independent genes.

In the case of first cousins, these relatives have, in their grandparents, two common ancestors. The possible lines of descent connecting them are represented in the diagram on p. 155.

Consider a gene present in the grandfather: the probability that it is transmitted to his son is a $\frac{1}{2}$, to his grandson $\frac{1}{4}$, and thus by this route to the offspring of the cousins $\frac{1}{8}$. But the same gene in the grandfather can also be transmitted to his daughter, and granddaughter to the cousins' offspring with the probability of $\frac{1}{8}$. Thus the probability of it meeting itself is $\frac{1}{8} \times \frac{1}{8} = \frac{1}{64}$. There are, however, 4 genes that can be transmitted in this way: the one exemplified, its allele in the grandfather and the corresponding 2 in the grandmother. There is thus a $4 \times \frac{1}{64} = \frac{1}{16}$ probability that a child of first-cousins will be homozygous for 2 genes identical by descent. Conversely there is a $\frac{15}{16}$ chance that no gene meets itself. The same result is obtained by applying the above general formula. Two steps (in this case generations) separate cousins from their grandparents in both possible lines of descent, so, if the grandparents themselves are not inbred, the coefficient of inbreeding of the offspring of cousins is

$$F \quad = \quad \tfrac{1}{2}^{2+2+1} \quad + \quad \tfrac{1}{2}^{2+2+1} \quad = \quad \tfrac{1}{16}.$$
$$\text{(male common ancestor)} \quad \text{(female common ancestor)}$$

For a recessive gene whose frequency in the population is $q$ the probability of a child with cousin parents obtaining two such genes which are identical by descent is $\frac{1}{16}q$. The probability of the gene not 'meeting itself' is $\frac{15}{16}q$, but in these cases it may come together with another of independent origin and the probability is $\frac{15}{16}q \times q$. The probability of the child being homozygous is the sum of these two probabilities, i.e. $\frac{1}{16}q + \frac{15}{16}q^2$, which equals $\frac{1}{16}q(1+15q)$. These ideas have been explained in terms of cousin marriages and recessive genes, because cousin marriages are the most frequent types of close relative matings in man, and because the paths of descent of recessive genes are particularly important in medical genetics, but the principles apply to all consanguineous matings and all genes. It is the laws of descent one is concerned with, not the nature or effect of genes.

The coefficient of inbreeding of a population can be represented as the mean of the coefficients of all the individuals who comprise it. Estimates of the level of inbreeding have been obtained for various groups, particularly small and isolated ones such as island populations and some religious sects. One of the highest levels found was among the Samaritans who have a mean coefficient of inbreeding of 0·0434, almost equivalent to the whole population being as

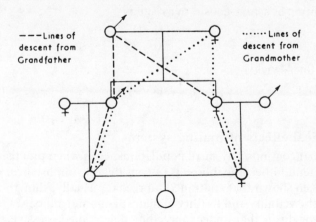

F ɪ ɢ. 11.1

inbred as the offspring of first cousins. Further it may be noted that coefficients of inbreeding tend to be minimal estimates, especially so when genealogical information is only available for a few generations, since often it is not possible to establish the extent to which common ancestors were themselves inbred.

While the offspring of consanguineous marriages are to some extent inbred, consanguineous marriages will, of course, occur in a randomly mating population. The frequency of cousin marriages in most western-European populations seems to be in the neighbourhood of 1 per cent or less. In certain populations, however, it is considerably higher as, for instance, in rural districts of northern Sweden, in Swiss alpine villages, and among Jewish communities in many German towns. Here it is not exceptional that 6 per cent of the marriages should be cousin marriages, and values as high as 12 per cent occur. It does not follow that in these populations cousin marriages are preferred, but rather that the populations are small. When the group from which a mate is chosen is small, the individuals composing the group will inevitably be more closely related than when the group is large. In particular, the frequency of first cousins is greater, and random mating will consequently lead to more consanguineous unions. In fact, when as in some small Swiss communities, the frequency of cousin marriages is relatively low, it may be surmised that they are being deliberately avoided and that mating is, therefore, not at random. The relationship between the frequency of cousin marriages and the size of isolates has afforded a method, devised by Dahlberg, of determining the latter.

If the average size of sibships in a population is $x$, an individual will have $(x-1)$ uncles or aunts on each parent's side, which *in toto* is $2(x-1)$. Since these uncles and aunts, on average, will have $x$ children the number of cousins will be $2(x-1)x$. But, a half of these cousins will be of opposite sex to the individual so the number of cousins from which a mate can be chosen is $x(x-1)$. Now, if the number of individuals in the isolate is $N$ there will be $N/2$ individuals of the opposite sex, which is the total number of available mates. Thus the probability $c$ of a first-cousin marriage is

$$c = \frac{x(x-1)}{N/2},$$

and solving for $N$ yields

$$N = \frac{2x(x-1)}{c}.$$

## The biological effects of mating systems

The fact that continuously small populations, even when practising random mating, will tend to become inbred is of considerable importance, since it has frequently been shown that continued inbreeding usually, though not invariably, lowers the viability and fertility of many plants and animals. One possible explanation for this is that under inbreeding deleterious recessive genes, most of which are concealed in random or outbreeding populations, are brought into a state of homozygosity. It is theoretically possible that none of these genes will be fixed in some line (p. 152), but if, as is usual, many loci are involved the likelihood is remote, particularly in a population which, by its very size, greatly limits the numbers of lines that can be established. It has also been suggested that 'inbreeding depression' is directly due to the loss of heterozygosity as such and that heterozygotes, because they have two different genes at a locus, have a greater biochemical versatility than homozygotes. There is much evidence in favour of this view; nevertheless, it is apparent that organisms can become adapted to homozygosity, since many naturally reproduce by self-fertilization without any ill consequences. This suggests that the particular nature of the genes and the ways they are integrated into a balanced genotype is the fundamental basis to the fitness of organisms.

Over short periods there may be a considerable advantage in self-fertilization, particularly in immobile forms such as plants. The combined effect of inbreeding with natural selection will tend to produce eventually a population in which all individuals are homozygous for the same genes. This means that it is possible for every individual to have the most desired phenotype for prevailing environmental conditions, but it also means that the capacity of the population to meet changing environmental demands is low. On the other hand, a population with great genetic variability has a much better chance of evolutionary persistence for, although the inevitable phenotypic variability means that fewer individuals have the most desired phenotype, the population is, in a sense, pre-adapted to environmental change. One might, therefore, expect that under constant environmental conditions a self-fertilizing species would compete successfully with one which is more outbreeding, but natural environments are always changing and most organisms do not practise self-fertilization. The great evolutionary advantage of bisexuality and cross-mating is that it affords a means by which a variety of genes can be combined in a variety of ways. In these quite general terms one can see why populations are genetically heterogeneous, and more specific situations leading to the same result will be considered later. It may particularly be expected that in a population more than one gene will be available for most polygene loci, since it is the extent of heterozygosity at these loci which essentially determines the distribution of the variation of quantitative characters (p. 130). Incidentally, this distribution is the ideal compromise between the demands for a single phenotype and for variability, and it is of consequence that changing environments are particularly likely to demand changes in those characters that vary quantitatively. The real point at issue now, however, is that in outbreeding organisms the majority of individuals will be heterozygous at many of their polygene loci, and it is these individuals, rather than the rare homozygous ones, which will most closely approach the desired phenotype. The homozygotes can be considered as inevitable by-products of the way quantitative characters are determined. Further, because heterozygotes are common natural selection can operate to build up in them efficient homeostatic mechanisms. It is, therefore, not surprising that the inbreeding of organisms that are genetically constructed in this way will at first produce forms poor in vigour, for they are forms that only rarely occur naturally and cannot have the appropriate phenotype.

The general population structure of the human species throughout most of its evolution has been one of small isolates existing discretely for long times but intermittently broken down by population expansion, migration, invasion, and intermixture. And the pattern of human evolution has to be seen in this context, with periods of differentiation in small populations interrupted by periods of gene flow. In recent times, however, the increased mobility that technological advance has given the individual, has widened his mating circle and isolates are breaking down, probably for ever, the world over. In many areas this has already progressed so far that anything like discrete units have vanished. But in environments unsuitable for a high population density and among closely knit social and religious groups, particularly when their technology is still primitive, the process has only just begun. As Darlington has indicated, the peoples of these small and long extant breeding isolates seem to suffer no obvious disadvantage from the inbreeding that must have occurred, and it is probable that they have become adapted at least to some extent, to homozygosity. Nevertheless, there is some evidence that the widespread increase in stature that has occurred in Europe throughout this century is, in part, due to the breakdown of isolates. It cannot be assumed that this sort of character is necessarily indicative of over-all fitness but it probably is. Among plants and animals that have suffered inbreeding depression, growth rate and adult body-size is typically diminished, and when such inbred forms are hybridized not only is vigour restored but growth is also greater. The increased viability and fertility that follows hybridization of different homozygotes is known as 'hybrid vigour' or 'heterosis'. Heterosis not only occurs when closely inbred forms are hybridized, but also when some different subspecies of plants and animals are crossed. So far as viability alone is concerned it may even occur on the hybridization of good species. This phenomenon obviously supports the view that mere heterozygosity confers survival value. In these cases, however, the vigour of the second generation seems to be not only less than that of the first-generation hybrids, but is also less than the parent subspecies. Second-generation hybrids between inbred lines are less vigorous than first-generation hybrids because as a whole they are less heterozygous, but they are still more fit than their inbred parents. Just how far this sort of situation prevails after human race-crossing it is as yet impossible to say. Hybridization between the major races has been fairly common in many places. Despite various types of restriction there are large mixed groups in South Africa and the USA; and in South America and in some of the Polynesian islands, particularly Hawaii, race-crossing has been widespread. Most unprejudiced observers have not found any real evidence for breakdowns in fitness, and on Pitcairn Island, where the mutineers of the *Bounty* took their Polynesian wives, there is some evidence that heterosis occurred.

# 12. Genetic structure of human populations: II. Changes in gene frequency

WHILST the breeding system practised within a population determines the frequency of the different genotypes, inbreeding tending to produce homozygosis, and outbreeding heterozygosis, it has no effect in itself on the frequency of genes. No genes are necessarily lost and none gained when a mating pattern changes. This is not to say that the breeding system is unimportant in evolution, but, since evolution means some degree of replacement of one set of genes by another, factors which change gene frequency are the basic evolutionary mechanisms. There are 4 such factors: hybridization, mutation, genetic drift, and natural selection. The first two introduce genes into a population, the last two determine what happens after they have been introduced.

## Hybridization

The change in frequency of a gene in a population following the introduction of individuals from another population obviously depends upon the number of immigrants and the frequency of the gene among them. If the frequency of two alleles, $A$ and $A'$, is $p_1$ and $q_1$ respectively, in the original population and $p_2$ and $q_2$ among the immigrants, and the new population is made up of a fraction $x$ of the original population and a fraction $y$ of immigrants, the frequency of $A$ becomes $xp_1 + yp_2$ and of $A'$, $xq_1 + yq_2$. In the case where the original population does not contain one of the alleles, if $q_1$ equals 0, for instance, then the frequency of $A'$ after intermixture is obviously $yq_2$. The effect of admixture on gene frequency can in this way be readily calculated; but the more usual sort of problem is to discover, in an already extant hybrid population, how much admixture has occurred. This can as easily be done if the frequency of some varying gene in both the parental populations and the hybrid one is known. The contribution of the original population to the hybrid population is $(q_k - q_2)/(q_1 - q_2)$, where $q_k$ is the frequency of the gene among the hybrids, $q_1$ the frequency of the gene in the original population, and $q_2$ its frequency among the immigrant group. The immigrant contribution is $(q_k - q_1)/(q_2 - q_1)$ or $1 - (q_k - q_2)/(q_1 - q_2)$. The values for $q_1$ and $q_2$, of course, have to be estimated from populations which are genetically like the founders of the hybrid population, but which themselves have not changed since the hybrid group was formed. Using such methods, it has been calculated that the amount of white admixture in the American Negro is about 25 per cent and in the Brazilian Negro about 40 per cent. Very rarely do two human populations, on being brought into contact, form a single new panmictic unit immediately. This is particularly true if the populations differ greatly in their physical features and social customs, when some sort of restriction is invariably imposed against random intermarriage. For a time, then, different groups may live together in the same locality yet remain in varying degrees genetically isolated from one another. Inevitably, however, there is always some intermixture which can be viewed as a process of gene flow from one population to the other. The rate of the introgression can be calculated from the equation

$$(1-m)^k = \frac{q_k - q_2}{q_1 - q_2}$$

where the right-hand side of the expression represents, as has been shown, the amount of admixture to date, and $k$ is the number of generations over which gene flow has occurred. The modal rate of gene flow $m$ is the fraction of genes in the mixed population which are introduced per generation from the population with the gene frequency $q_2$. Using this method, it has been calculated that the modal rate of gene flow from the white population into the Negro population in the USA is between 0·02 and 0·025 (i.e. between 2 per cent and 2·5 per cent) and in Brazil between 0·045 and 0·055.

If two genetically different populations are geographically some distance apart, but interconnected by a series of intermediate populations through which genes can flow there will tend to be a geographical gradient of gene frequency between the polar populations. This will only disappear when so much genetic interchange has taken place that they and all the intermediate populations are identical. Such gradients in gene frequency are known as 'genoclines', whilst the gradients in character variation they produce are known as 'phenoclines'. Clines are common in the pattern of human variation (see also p. 176). One of the best-known examples is the distribution of the blood-group B gene $B$ in Europe, which progressively diminishes in frequency from east to west. This cline is usually interpreted as indicating a gene flow from Asiatic peoples, largely effected by the repeated invasions from the east, to which Europe has been exposed.

## Mutation

Hybridization only forms a means by which genes already present in some populations within a species are introduced into other populations. It may result in genetic combinations which are entirely new, but the sole source of new genes is mutation. Mutation has been defined as 'the inception of a heritable variation', and in its widest sense can involve whole chromosomes as well as particular genes. The result of mutation is a mutant gene or chromosome, which can give rise to a mutant character. Gene mutation may occur at any time but is more likely to occur while a cell is dividing than while it is 'resting' and in gametogenesis is most likely to occur during meiosis. From the genetic point of view, it is mutation during the formation of the gametes that is important, but it is of some medical consequence that somatic mutation occurs. A mutant gene will reproduce itself with self-copying precision until it is affected by the next mutation.

Although the cause for gene or 'point' mutation is still far from clear, the unravelling of the genetic code has clarified its nature. Typically it involves the substitution of one base for another in the set of DNA triplets. Since the code is redundant some such substitutions will have no effect on protein synthesis, but often the change of one base will specify a different amino acid in a polypeptide sequence from that originally coded. Thus, for instance, if the cytosine in the triplet CTT is replaced by thymine to form TTT, the amino acid lysine instead of glutamic acid will be introduced at the corresponding place in the polypeptide being synthesized. This is the sort of change which has occurred in determining the $\beta$-chain of haemoglobin C as compared with the $\beta$-chain of normal adult haemoglobin (cf. p. 225). Sometimes, a base change will introduce a 'stop' in the reading of the code, as, for example, if adenine replaces cytosine in CTT to produce ATT. In this case there would be incomplete synthesis of the original polypeptide, only that portion prior to the stop being formed. There are also the possibilities of an 'insertion' of a totally new base, or the 'deletion' of an old one in the DNA sequence of triplets. Such events known as 'frameshifts' might cause changes of all the amino acids terminal to the mutation. For example, if there were an insertion of another cytosine prior to CTT (glutamic acid) AAA (phenylalanine) the code would read in triplets CCT (glycine) TAA (isoleucine)· A--.

Gene mutation is a reversible process; thus if gene $A$ mutates to $A'$ it is equally possible for $A'$ to mutate back to $A$. Put in molecular terms, if one base is replaced by another this does not preclude the possibility at a later stage of return to the original base sequence. It is often said that mutation is a random process, but this does not mean that there are unlimited ways in which a gene can change; only that whatever changes occur are unrelated to any environmental demands that are being made on an organism or its environmental experiences. Quite clearly, when the concern is with base changes in the DNA, the possibilities, though numerous, are finite, and the effects of change very much dependent upon the code in which the mutation occurs. It follows that usually a mutant gene will affect the development of the same character system as does the gene from which it arose; but it will affect it in a different way or to a different degree. For instance, a gene which determines eye colour may mutate from a state in which it produces brown eyes to one in which it produces blue; it is highly unlikely that it will mutate to one which determines blood-groups.

Chromosomal mutation may take two general forms; either there may be a change in the number of whole chromosomes, or a change within a single chromosome of the number and arrangements of genes. If the whole set of chromosomes is multiplied, a state of polyploidy is produced. Polyploidy arises as a result of failures in cell division during meiosis so that gametes with, for instance, the diploid number of chromosomes are produced. When such a gamete is fertilized by one carrying the normal haploid number a triploid zygote is formed; whilst if it is fertilized by another diploid gamete a tetraploid is produced. When only one or a few types of chromosomes are increased or decreased in number, rather than whole sets, the condition is known as 'hetero-ploidy' or 'polysomy'. A now-well-known example of a pathology arising from polysomy in man is Down's syndrome or mongolism. Individuals with this condition typically show retarded growth and development, abnormal dermato-glyphic pattersn, the presence of a well-developed epicanthic fold over the eye-lid which somewhat resembles that found normally in Mongoloid peoples, various pathologies including increased susceptibility to leukaemia, and gross mental retardation. The probability of having an affected child increases strikingly with maternal age from about 0·04 per cent in women under 30 to 3·15 per cent for women over 45. The condition is usually due to one of the Group-G chromosomes being present 3 times rather than twice in all the body cells as a result of chromosomal non-disjunction during meiosis or some other abnormality of early cell division. For a number of years the extra chromosome was identified as chromosome 21, and the condition is still referred to as 'trisomy 21', though it has recently been fairly certainly shown that the chromosome involved is number 22.

Gene number or arrangement can change in one of 4 ways. Part of a chromo-some may be lost, a condition known as deletion. As an example, the condition known as *cri du chat* can be given, which derives its name from the plaintive cry more or less continuously given by affected infants and involves severe men-tal and physical pathology. Affected individuals are heterozygous for a substan-tial loss of the short arm of chromosome 5.

The second type of change is in a sense the converse of deletion where a chromosome may be increased in length by the repetition of a segment, thereby forming a 'duplication'. Mechanisms are known whereby the full duplication and near complete duplication of at least a structural gene can occur. There is good evidence that the genes coding for the $\beta$- and $\delta$-chains of haemoglobin A and haemoglobin $A_2$ which are closely linked to one another arose by duplica-tion of one original DNA sequence, and duplication has also been important in the evolution of the various immunoglobin molecules and some of their respective parts. Duplication is clearly a process whereby the sum total of DNA can be increased; and it produces new genes which can be subject to mutational change and 'offered' for selection while old ones continue to perform original and necessary functions. It has probably played an extremely important role in evolutionary differentiation.

A third type of change involves the transference of a piece of a chromosome to a member of a non-homologous pair. This constitutes a 'translocation' and again a number of examples are now known in man. Thus part of a 21 chromo-some can become translocated on to another autosome, e.g. number 14. An individual possessing this is normal since he possesses the usual DNA comple-ment of one 14 chromosome, one 21 chromosome, and one 14.21 fusion chromo-some, but if during meiosis the 14.21 chromosome passes into the same gamete as the 21 chromosome and fertilization occurs with a normal gamete with a single 21 chromosome the zygote effectively has the 21 chromosome represented 3 times and shows Down's syndrome. Thus the basis for mongolism can be transmitted to offspring in a Mendelian fashion and not all mongols show a discrete extra-chromosome.

Finally, a segment of a chromosome may become turned round to produce an 'inversion'. Thus, for instance, the order of loci may change from $a$, $b$, $c$, $d$, $e$, $f$, $g$ to $a$, $b$, $c$, $f$, $e$, $d$, $g$. This type of chromosomal change is frequent in *Drosophila*, where it can readily be detected and is of great importance in determining the evolutionary fitness of the organism. It will almost certainly be shown to exist in man, but human chromosomes are too small for it to be easily detected.

Gene mutations occur with characteristic frequencies. For a single locus the general order of magnitude seems to be about 1 mutation per 100 000 germ cells, but there is considerable consistent variation from locus to locus. At every locus, however, mutation is an exceedingly rare phenomenon, but since there are at least between 5000 and 120 000 genes in man, and probably many more, mutation in the genotypes as a whole is by no means likely to be uncommon.

There are a number of factors that affect the mutation rate. It is known that there are more mutant genes in the sperm of young *Drosophila* males than in the sperm of old individuals and there is also an age effect in man on mutation to achondroplasic dwarfism: older couples having a greater likelihood of producing a mutant child than younger ones. Further, some totally sex-linked genes on the X-chromosome mutate more frequently in males than in females. Such a sex effect is easily recognized in sex-linked genes from the comparative frequency with which hemizygous sons and heterozygous daughters are produced by parents who do not possess the mutant gene. If a sex-linked gene mutates at the same rate in males as in females, one would expect this ratio to be 1 hemizygous son : 2 heterozygous daughters, since the third of the X-chromosomes of a population that occur in men are all transmitted to their daughters, whereas the two-thirds X-chromosomes in women are transmitted equally to their sons and daughters. If mutation only occurs in women a sex-linked mutant gene will as likely be transmitted to sons as to daughters, so the ratio of hemizygous sons : heterozygous daughters will be 1 : 1. On the other hand, if a sex-linked mutant gene arises only in the gametes of males it will first occur only in heterozygous state in daughters. From this type of analysis it has been estimated that some sex-linked mutations may possibly occur ten times more frequently in males than in females.

When adequate census figures are available, as they are in Denmark, the rate of mutation for a dominant trait with full penetrance can readily be obtained, since individuals who possess the mutant gene will express it as soon as it arises, and the mutation rate can be obtained from the frequency of children with the mutant character born to parents without it. In Copenhagen there were, among 94 075 births, 10 achondroplasic individuals. Two, however, of these were born to affected parents, so the frequency of new cases was 8 in 94 075. This reduces to approximately 1 in 12 000, and since every individual possesses 2 alleles the mutation rate of a normal gene to an achondroplasic allele is 1 in 24 000. This is a rather high figure, and there is some evidence that mutations at more than one locus may produce achondroplasia. It is also possible that sometimes achondroplasia is either recessive or a phenocopy. Nevertheless, the 'direct method' is the most reliable way of determining mutation rates for dominant traits. It obviously cannot be applied to recessive characters since, when mutation produces a gene which is recessive in effect, this gene will not express itself until it comes into combination with another of the same type. If the frequency of the gene is low, and it will be low if maintained in the population only by mutation, many generations may elapse before a homozygous recessive arises.

There is another way of determining mutation rates, known as the 'indirect method', which depends on a balance being established between the rate at which genes are gained in a population as a result of mutation and the rate at which they are lost as a result of natural selection. Most mutant genes are deleterious in their effect. This is not surprising when it is remembered that mutation is not environmentally orientated. The genotype is a highly integrated interacting system, and random changes in its constitution are most likely to disturb it adversely. Selection, therefore, operates to remove most mutant genes from the population, and the only reason they are present at all is because they are constantly being produced by mutation. Their frequency in a population will therefore be fixed when the rate of their production equals their rate of elimination. Equilibrium, of course, will only be reached if the mutation rate, and elimination rate, are constant over some time, but if both these factors are now likely to be changing they were probably more or less constant for long periods in the past.

Consider a rare dominant abnormality maintained in the population solely by mutation. If this abnormality has a frequency $x$ in a population of parents who number $N$, those parents who are affected will number $xN$. They will be heterozygous for the mutant gene so $xN$ of their genes will be mutant and $xN$ normal alleles. The non-affected parents will number $N-xN$ and will possess $2(N-xN)$ normal genes. The total number of normal alleles which can mutate is therefore $xN+2N-2xN=2N-xN=N(2-x)$. If the mutation rate is represented by $u$, the number of new mutant genes among the offspring of these parents is $uN(2-x)$. Since the frequency of the abnormality is very low, the effect of $x$ on this expression is very small and it can be neglected, so the number of mutant genes arising can be regarded as $2Nu$. The reproductive fitness $f$ of the mutant gene is defined as the frequency with which it is transmitted to the next generation compared with its wild-type allele. The frequency with which it is eliminated is therefore $(1-f)$. As already seen, the number of mutant genes in the population of parents is $Nx$, so the number of mutant genes which is lost in a full generation is $(1-f)Nx$.

In equilibrium, the number of mutant genes arising equals the number eliminated so $2Nu=(1-f)Nx$, whence $u=\frac{1}{2}(1-f)x$. For a recessive condition, $u$

must equal $(1-f)x$ at equilibrium, since two mutant genes are lost in every individual who is eliminated. For totally X-linked recessive traits $u = 1/3(1-f)x'$, where $x'$ represents the frequency of affected men, since the mutant gene will be mainly exposed to selection only in the males who carry a third of the population's X-chromosomes.

As an example of how this indirect method is applied, the case of achondroplasic dwarfism in Denmark may again be considered. As previously mentioned, among 94 075 births there were 10 achondroplasic individuals, so the frequency of the abnormality in the population ($x$) can be considered to be 10/94 075. An estimate of the fitness of the abnormal gene can be obtained by comparing the number of children born to dwarfs with the number of children born to their unaffected sibs. Since data were first collected in Denmark there are records of 108 dwarfs. In all they had 27 children, of which, incidentally, 10 were dwarf and 17 were unaffected. This does not differ significantly from the expected 1 : 1 ratio. The 457 unaffected sibs of the dwarfs had 582 children. The fitness of the mutant gene can, therefore, be considered to be $27/108 \times 457/582 = 0.196$ as, perhaps, can be more clearly seen by the following reasoning. On average 108 achondroplasia genes in one generation are represented by 13·5 (i.e. $\frac{1}{2} \times 27$) in the next, whilst 582 of the 914 ($2 \times 457$) normal alleles of the dwarfs' sibs are transmitted. The differential fitness must consequently be $13 \cdot 5/108 \times 914/582 = 0.196$. If, then, relative to the normal allele only 19·6 per cent of the mutant genes are transmitted from one generation to the next, 80·4 per cent are eliminated and $(1-f) = 0.804$. The estimate of mutation rate $u$ therefore equals

$$\tfrac{1}{2} \times 0.804 \times (10/94\,075) \doteqdot 0.000043,$$

i.e. 4·3 gametes in every 100 000 gametes carries a new mutant gene for achondroplasia and this, approximately, is 1 in 23 000. The agreement, therefore, between the direct and indirect methods is quite close. Other examples of mutation rates are $4 \times 10^{-5}$ for retininoblastoma, $3 \times 10^{-5}$ for haemophilia, and 0·8 to $1 \cdot 2 (\times 10^{-5})$ for epiloia, and it is probable that these represent some of the highest rates, since the relative commonness of the conditions makes them most suitable for investigation. However, mutation rates of the same general order of magnitude are found in plants and animals. It also seems that when mutation rates are expressed per generation all organisms have comparable values. Because of differences in generation time this inevitably means that there are great differences in the number of mutations occurring in unit time between different organisms.

Although mutation is not environmentally orientated, environmental factors, such as ionizing radiations and certain chemicals, increase the mutation rate. Ionizing radiations include X-rays, ultraviolet light, the $\alpha$-rays of radioactive substances, $\beta$-rays, and neutrons. Infrared radiation is also mutagenic in non-homeothermic animals, and mustard gas is frequently used in experimental studies as a chemical mutagen. The effectiveness of the various radiations in inducing mutation depends upon their penetrative power, but in terms of ionizing rates all are equally effective, and in the main they produce indiscriminantly all types of mutation, both genic and chromosomal. On the other hand, chemical mutagens do have some specificity with regard to the class of mutations produced and the loci at which mutation occurs.

The effects of radiation are also cumulative so that not all the radiation need be received at the same time. It has, however, recently been shown that chronic irradiation of, at least, the mouse gonad produces only about a quarter of the number of mutations produced by the same dosage applied acutely. Nevertheless, in many organisms it seems that within wide limits the number of mutations is directly proportional to the radiation dose received.

Although radiation effects are cumulative, the normal background radiation to which organisms are naturally exposed, i.e. about 90–150 mrad every year, is inadequate to account for spontaneous mutation rates, and it is of consequence that genes have been discovered which themselves increase the mutation rate. It is presumed that they place the rest of the genotype in a chemical environment which promotes instability. The important fact is that, since the spontaneous mutation is at least partly under genetic control, it is susceptible to natural selection.

In man exposure to high dosages of short-wave radiation produces radiation sickness. If a man receives about 600 R all at once he will develop within about 2 hours a feeling of nausea. There follows a period of no symptoms, but within a few days he will develop diarrhoea, vomiting, and an inflammation of the throat. This leads to fever and emaciation, and death occurs in about 2 weeks, when multiple haemorrhages, anaemia, and sepsis will be found. For those in an occupation with a radiation risk it has been calculated that the maximum allowable dosage is 0·3 R per week. This, however, takes little cognizance of the mutation risk, since it is believed that a dosage of about 80 R per generation would double the mutation rate, and, as already mentioned, from the genetic point of view the radiation received is cumulative in effect.

Mutant genes are most frequently recessive in effect. The reason for this is that they are usually deleterious, and, because mutation is recurrent, a population has been exposed to them many times in the past. Most genotypes have therefore become buffered to suppress their effects in single dosage (p. 134). Muller has estimated that, even in the most closely inbred populations, an individual homozygous for a recessive mutant gene, produced now as a result of increased radiation, is not likely to be born for some 600 years, and it may be several thousand years before such a homozygote is formed. The genetic hazards of radiation are, therefore, often not immediate, but the danger to future generations of the accumulation of deleterious genes in the population is not to be lightly dismissed.

The constant presence of deleterious mutant genes in a population, of which over the whole genome there must be many, has been regarded as a kind of load which the population must carry. In addition, however, to this mutational load another is envisaged arising from the segregation of homozygotes in poly-morphic systems (cf. p. 173) which have fitnesses lower than the heterozygote; as, for example, in the case of the locus governing normal and sickle-cell haemo-globin. The extent to which this segregational load, which with the mutational load makes up the so-called total 'genetic load', can in fact be regarded as a load is a matter of some dispute, and it is far from easy, especially in an organism like man to differentiate in practice between the mutational and segregational components. Estimates have been made, by those who consider the load con-cept useful, of the magnitude of the load in various human populations by com-paring the mortality rates among the offspring of consanguineous marriages, which, for reasons already given, are more likely to express the load, with those among the offspring of unrelated spouses. It would appear from these estimates that although different genetic loci contribute differentially to the genetic load in different human populations, its total magnitude is very much the same from one group to another.

The recurrency of mutation means that a gene is constantly being introduced into a population, but even when, as will occasionally happen, such a gene is not disadvantageous in its effect, the pressure of mutation will itself only cause an extremely slow increase in its frequency, since mutation is not only a very rare phenomenon but is also a reversible one. For a gene to spread, in any reasonable time, other factors must operate upon it.

## Genetic drift

One way in which gene frequencies may change relatively quickly is by chance or genetic drift. The possibilities of chance acting as an evolutionary factor have been mathematically developed by Wright, and drift is often referred to as the Wright effect.

As previously mentioned, a species is usually broken up from the breeding point of view, into many small more or less isolated units. The production of a generation of offspring by a generation of parents inevitably involves some sampling of the parents' gametes and the smaller the population the smaller the sample. In considering the Hardy–Weinberg law it was assumed that the gametes carrying one or other of two alleles $A$ and $A'$ were both produced in the frequency $p$ and $q$ and combined in zygotes in this proportion also. How-ever, if the sample of gametes from which a generation is formed is a small one the frequency of the two types may by chance deviate strikingly from the expected frequency. This can well be demonstrated by filling a bag with equal numbers of black and white beads and removing a handful. The beads can be considered as representing two alleles in a population with $p = 0.5$ and $q = 0.5$. It is highly unlikely that exactly half the beads in the sample will be black and the other half white, and the smaller the sample the more likely will be large deviations from this ratio. The procedure can be repeated by filling the bag again but this time with the two types of bead in the proportion with which they occurred in the sample, and taking another handful. This second sample may show yet further deviations from the 1 : 1 ratio in the same direction as in the first sample, or the direction may be reversed, but in any case if the procedure is continued long enough, and if the samples are small, eventually only one type of bead will occur in a sample. In genetic terms, one allele has been lost from the population and the other fixed. Once this has happened only mutation can restore the lost allele. Within small populations, then, it is possible for considerable fluctuations in gene frequency to occur and genes can be fixed or lost solely by chance.

The number of breeding individuals is not the only factor which determines the chance genetic stability of a population. Another is the variability in family size, since if a few matings by chance produce many offspring, and others only a few, there is likely to be less genetic heterogeneity among the offspring than if the same total number is produced by all the different marriages making equal contributions.

These two factors can be combined in an expression of what is known as the 'effective population size' $N$. This is defined mathematically as $N=(4N'-2)/2+\sigma_k^2$, where $N'$ is the number of individuals in a generation who are parents and $\sigma_k^2$ is the variance in the number of gametes contributed by the different parents to the next generation.

In the past human populations were more isolated and much smaller than most are today. The size of communities of Palaeolithic man is not accurately known, but all the evidence suggests that at their largest they comprised but a few hundred individuals, and this is certainly the case among present-day hunting and gathering societies such as the Australian Aborigine and the Bushman. Such populations contain not only representatives of 2 or 3 generations, but also some individuals who do not mate, and it may be expected that there are chance variations in family size. In fact, it seems probable that the effective size of human populations, throughout much of man's evolution, has not been much in excess of 100. And great increases in population size have little effect on the effective size, if such increases are followed by corresponding decreases.

Wright has shown that the rate of fixation of one or other alleles, solely by chance, is $L_T=L_0e^{-T/2N}$, where $L_0$ and $L_T$ are the numbers of unfixed genes in the initial and $T$ generation respectively, and e is the base of natural logarithms. If, therefore, in a population whose effective size is 100, there are a number of loci occupied by pairs of alleles in equal frequency chance will produce fixation at a half of these loci in 139 generations, and at a half of the remainder in another 139 generations, as can be seen from letting $L_T/L_0 = 0.5$ in the above expression and solving for $T(L_T/L_0=0.5=e^{-T/200})$.

While the population structure of the human species has been ideal for genetic drift to operate, it may still be asked whether drift has contributed substantially to the process of human differentiation. Throughout the foregoing argument it has been assumed that the 2 or more alleles at a locus were more or less of equal fitness. Just how often this is the case is a matter of considerable current debate. Some rather complex mathematical analyses and knowledge of the nature of protein variety within and between species has led some authorities to predict the existence of a large proportion of neutral genes. But the assumptions on which these predictions are made are certainly questionable and many still believe that in a highly co-adapted gene complex it is unlikely that the replacement of one allele by another will have a neutral effect on survival. A quite small selective advantage of one gene over another may be difficult to detect, particularly in man where the generation time is so long, but except in the smallest of populations it will prevent the genes from drifting wildly, and it is quite likely that the selective significance of replacing one allele by another in evolutionary terms is very great. It is probably true that the variation in some blood-group genes from village to village in remoter parts of the world are due to drift, particularly as it is possible that the selecting agent controlling these genes is an intermittent one. Drift is probably the cause for a small religious isolate of German origin in America differing in some gene frequencies from both the normal German and American values. Allowance for the stochastic or chance nature of many population phenomena has also increased the sophistication of our evolutionary thinking especially in the development of mathematical models for understanding the genetic dynamics in small human groups, but for many it still seems unlikely that drift has contributed substantially to the long-term evolution of man, or any other organism for that matter. In two circumstances, however, chance is an important factor in the genetics of populations. In the first place, an advantageous gene may arise many times by mutation, before it becomes established, because, being at first so rare it is easily lost by chance. It is highly likely that it will not even find itself in a zygote. Secondly, if a new territory is colonized by a small immigrant group, it is possible that among this group some gene will be by chance absent, or in such low frequency that it is easily lost. Unless mutation re-introduces it, all the descendants of this group will obviously also lack the gene, and the gene complex will become adapted to its absence. This is known as the 'founder-principle', and it is possible, though perhaps not very likely, that the absence of the B gene in most aboriginal American populations can be explained in this way.

## Selection

Though constant reference has been made in preceding sections to the process of natural selection it must now be discussed more systematically. Natural selection moulds the genotypes of organisms so that they produce phenotypes fitted to the environment in which organisms live. But natural selection does not operate directly on the genotypes; it acts through the phenotypes of individuals and their gametes. If an individual possesses some character which confers a greater viability or fertility on him compared with other individuals in the population, he will tend to have a greater number of offspring. In other words, he will be more fit in the prevailing environment, and the character can be said to be adaptive. When the character difference concerned is of genetic origin the genes responsible for it will be preferentially represented in the next generation, and will confer the advantage to the offspring in which they occur. In evolutionary terms, then, the interaction between genotype and phenotype is a reciprocating one and the consequence is that genes which produce advantageous effects will spread, replacing their less-fit alleles, and the relative proportions of the different phenotypes in the population will change. Conversely, as already seen (p. 164), if a gene arises which is deleterious in effect, it will tend to be eliminated by natural selection. The two situations are interdependent since, as one gene spreads because of an advantage, the allele it replaces by comparison is disadvantageous and is being lost. In other words, an effect which was once advantageous can become relatively disadvantageous, either because a new gene confers yet greater advantage in the same environment, or because the environment itself changes and is making different demands. In considering the relative fitness of genes it is very necessary to consider the environment this time in a selecting role (cf. p. 140) for a gene superior to one allele in one environment may be inferior to it in another. It is also important to note that selection, in the sense described, operates only through the differential reproductive fitness of individuals or their gametes. It should be noted, however, that a gene can be favoured even if it lowers the probability of survival of a specific individual possessor. This will happen when the reduction in the fitness of the individual is more than compensated for by the survival of his kin, who are likely to possess the same gene. Thus, for instance, a genetically determined character which leads to altruistic behaviour of a parent towards a child can be adaptive and the responsible genes can spread. Precisely, this will happen when the advantage to the child exceeds twice the disadvantage to the parent since parent and child share half their genes in common. Such selection, which is only an extension of classic Darwinian selection is termed 'kin selection'. However, it does constitute one category of the much debated issue of 'group selection'.

Considering group selection generally, it does seem that populations have genetic properties as populations, such as the Gaussian distribution of quantitatively varying traits which maintains genetic variability, which are likely to favour their evolutionary persistence. More troublesome to explain are apparent cases where the requirements of the population as a whole are in conflict with the selective pressures on individuals to maximize their reproductive success, as, for instance, in the regulation of population sizes so that environments are not over-exploited. If group selection for population regulation occurs at all, and many deny it, there is no known mechanism to explain it outside man. In the human situation, however, with man's unique capacity for non-biological inheritance, which means that all members of a group, and not only kin, can benefit from altruistic behaviour, the interests of individuals can be subordinated to the interests of the group. How often this occurs, however, is a matter of debate!

Genes both dominant and recessive in effect will spread if they are advantageous but, assuming they are of equal fitness, the rate of change is initially much faster for a dominant gene. This obviously follows from the fact that selection can operate on heterozygotes for the dominant gene, but only on homozygotes for the recessive one. When the gene first arises it will be rare in the population and most individuals who possess it will do so only in single dosage. On the other hand, but for the same reasons, if a dominant gene is deleterious in effect it will be eliminated more rapidly than a recessive one. Of course, when a dominant gene which has spread through a population is approaching fixation, the recessive gene it is replacing is in very low frequency and the rate at which it is lost is slowed down to the rate at which an advantageous recessive gene would increase in frequency when it is as rare. So the total time required for complete fixation of a dominant gene is the same as that required for a recessive one of equal adaptive value.

These rather general statements can be given greater precision by considering the change in genotype and gene frequencies, when a pair of alleles under Hardy–Weinberg equilibrium are exposed to selection through the differential fitness of genotypes. The simplest situation is that in which one homozygote always dies before reproductive age, but the other homozygote and the heterozygote have equal fitness, because one allele is truly dominant in all its effects. If, then, the alleles are $A$ and $a$ and they occur in a particular generation in the frequency $p$ and $q$ respectively, the three genotypes are produced in the frequency $p^2 AA$, $2pq Aa$, and $q^2 aa$. After selection has removed from the population all the homozygotes $aa$, the frequency of the homozygotes $AA$ is $p^2/(p^2+2pq)$, i.e. $(p/p+2q)$, and of the heterozygotes $Aa$ $2pq/(p^2+2pq)$, i.e. $2q/(p+2q)$ (i.e. their original frequency divided by the total of the new population).

Substitute $1-q$ for $p$ in $p/(p+2q)$ and the frequency can be expressed as $(1-q)/(1+q)$. Likewise, the frequency of $Aa$ can be expressed as $2q/(1+q)$. All the $a$ genes remaining in the population occur in the heterozygotes, a half of whose genes are of this type. Consequently the new frequency of the $a$ gene is $q/(1+q)$. The frequency of the other allele $A$ is $1-[q/(1+q)]$, which is $1/(1+q)$. Under random mating, therefore, the frequency of the three genotypes in the next generation is $(1/1+q)^2 AA$, $2(1/1+q)(q/1+q) Aa$, and $(q/1+q)^2 aa$.

The relationship between the frequency of gene $a$ from one generation to the next, i.e. $q$ to $q/(1+q)$, is a step in a harmonic series whose general term is $q_n = q_0/(1+nq_0)$, where $q_0$ is the initial frequency of the gene, $n$ is the number of generations of selection, and $q_n$ is the frequency of the gene after $n$ generations of selection.

Use of this formula clearly demonstrates the slow rate at which a recessive gene in low frequency is eliminated from a population even when its effects are as severe as they can be. It also demonstrates the inefficacy of the most severe eugenic measures to rid a population of some undesirable recessive trait. As an example, consider the effects of sterilizing before reproductive age all individuals who possess some rare recessive abnormality in each of 25 generations. If the initial frequency of the trait is $1/10\,000$, the frequency of the gene will be $1/100$, i.e. $0.01$. Substituting in the above formula one obtains

$$q_{25} = \frac{1/100}{1 + 25(1/100)} = \frac{1}{125}.$$

In other words, after 25 generations of such selection the frequency of the gene has been reduced to $\frac{4}{5}$ of its original frequency!

Rarely does a genotype have zero fitness and in the natural spread or loss of genes partial selection typically operates. The relative fitness of genotypes can be expressed as the fraction of an offspring each produces for every one offspring produced by the genotype with the greatest fitness. The extent by which the less-fit genotypes deviate from unit fitness is known as the 'selection coefficient' and represented by the symbol $s$. In the case just considered, where the recessive homozygote has zero fitness $s = 1$. When character differences are of neutral survival value $s = 0$, and the gene frequencies remain the same from generation to generation. The selection coefficient is, then, the complement of the fitness coefficient $f$, i.e. $s = (1-f)$, but in describing the indirect method of determining mutation rates (p. 164) attention was immediately focused on the fitness of the mutant gene rather than on the mutant genotype.

The effects of partial selection can again be seen in terms of a dominant gene being favoured over its recessive allele, with the heterozygote having the same fitness as the homozygote $AA$. This situation is presented in Table 12.1.

TABLE 12.1

| Genotypes | $AA$ | $Aa$ | $aa$ | Total |
|---|---|---|---|---|
| Frequency before selection | $p^2$ | $2pq$ | $q^2$ | $1$ |
| Relative fitness | $1$ | $1$ | $1-s$ | |
| Frequency after selection | $p^2$ | $2pq$ | $q^2(1-s)$ | $1-sq^2$ |

(The frequency of recessive homozygotes after selection can also, of course, be represented as $q^2 - sq^2$, which shows why the total after selection is $1 - sq^2$ since $p^2 + 2pq + q^2 = 1$.)

After selection the gene $a$ exists in the surviving homozygotes and in the heterozygotes, so its frequency is $pq + q^2(1-s)/(1-sq^2)$. If, again, $(1-q)$ is substituted for $p$ this expression becomes $(1-q)q + q^2(1-s)/(1-sq^2)$ and this simplifies to $q(1-sq)/(1-sq^2)$. The change in the frequency of gene $a$ from before to after selection $\Delta q$ is therefore the difference $q - q(1-sq)/(1-sq^2)$. It equals $q(1-sq^2) - q(1-sq)/(1-sq^2)$, which simplifies to $sq^2(1-q)/(1-sq^2)$. This decrement in the frequency of $a$ is, of course, an increment in the other allele $A$, so substituting $(1-p)$ for $q$ in the above expression one gets for the change in $p$, i.e. $\Delta p = s(1-p)^2 p/1 - s(1-p)^2$. If $q$ is $0.5$ in a population and $s = 0.1$ it will be found from the above equation that the decrement in the frequency of gene $a$ in the population in a single generation is $0.0128$, which is quite a considerable change, but if $q$ is initially small then the decrement is infinitesimal.

No genes are certainly known in man which as a result of being favoured by natural selection are now spreading through a population at the expense of a once common allele. This is not surprising in view of the length of a human generation and the difficulty of detecting even substantial advantageous effects. People do not seek medical advice if their fitness is greater than average! The phenomenon is certainly occurring in some plant and animal populations, and the power of selection in producing change is well demonstrated in the process of domestication and by laboratory experiments. One would strongly suspect that the frequency of some genes is changing in human populations as a result of selection particularly in populations which have undergone a recent radical environmental alteration, but no unequivocal cases have yet been discovered apart from those where medical treatment has improved the fitness of once highly deleterious genotypes. It is true that in many populations change is occurring, as for instance in stature and in head and palatal shape, but this is not necessarily due to selection, and much of it is probably not even of genetic origin. Analyses of the changes in these characters are complicated by the fact that, as in most human variation, the genetic determination is multifactorial, and the environment plays a direct role in controlling the development of the phenotype. That selection is operating even in societies with an advanced technology is suggested by estimates of Penrose that in Britain at least 15 per cent of conceptions miscarry early in pregnancy; 3 per cent of the remainder are stillborn, and neonatal deaths account for a further 2 per cent. Three per cent more fail to reach maturity, and of the survivors 20 per cent do not marry, and of those that do 10 per cent remain childless. Many of these 'reproductive' deaths are, of course, indiscriminate in their genetic effects, but there can be little doubt that differential fitness is also involved.

## Polymorphism

While a major gene is spreading through a population at the expense of an allele the character determined by the locus will exist in at least 2 and possibly 3 forms. This is an example of a polymorphic situation. Ford has defined polymorphism as 'the occurrence together in the same habitat of two or more discontinuous forms of a species in such proportions that the rarest of them cannot be maintained merely by recurrent mutation'. The definition is phrased to exclude: (1) differences between one population and another which is known as 'polytypism'; (2) continuous variation which, though it may often have a basically similar causation, is a directly contrasting form of phenotypic variation; (3) forms which are present solely as a consequence of mutation like achondroplasia and albinism.

The polymorphism occurring while gene replacement is in process is transient, since as soon as the favoured allele is fixed the population becomes monomorphic for the new character. Many characters, however, in a population are more or less permanently polymorphic. One of the most obvious examples of such 'balanced polymorphism' is sex. Others that occur in many human populations, affect the blood-group systems, secretor and taster status, haemoglobins red cell enzymes and serum proteins (see Chapters 16–18). Unless affected by hybridization the frequencies of the genes determining the variation in these characters remain more or less constant over long periods of time: the antiquity of some blood-group polymorphisms being strongly indicated by their presence in apes. It was at one time rather widely thought that genetic drift was responsible for such polymorphism, but as already mentioned it is unlikely that two genes will be so equivalent in fitness that drift can produce the variation observed. It is now widely accepted that balanced polymorphism always involves an equilibrium between opposed selective forces, as was first recognized by Fisher, Ford, and Haldane. Opposing selective forces may act in a variety of ways. The most important situation is that in which one allele of a pair is relatively advantageous in effect when in low frequency, but becomes relatively disadvantageous when in high frequency. And this will happen automatically if the heterozygote is more fit than either homozygote. This is apparent from the fact that if selection is favouring heterozygotes it must maintain both alleles in the population, but can best be considered in detail by attributing the selection coefficients $s_1$ and $s_2$ to the two homozygotes in Table 12.2.

TABLE 12.2

| Genotypes | $AA$ | $Aa$ | $aa$ | Total |
|---|---|---|---|---|
| Frequency before selection | $p^2$ | $2pq$ | $q^2$ | 1 |
| Relative fitness | $(1-s_1)$ | 1 | $(1-s_2)$ | |
| Frequency after selection | $p^2(1-s_1)$ | $2pq$ | $q^2(1-s_2)$ | $1-s_1p^2-s_2q^2$ |

The frequency of gene $a$ after selection is

$$\frac{pq+q^2(1-s_2)}{1-s_1p^2-s_2q^2}, \text{ which equals } \frac{q(1-s_2q)}{1-s_1p^2-s_2q^2}.$$

The change in its frequency as a result of selection is therefore $q-[q(1-s_2q)/(1-s_1p^2-s_2q^2)]$. The following steps in the simplification of this expression to

$$\Delta q = \frac{pq(s_2q-s_1p)}{1-s_1p^2-s_2q^2}$$

may prove helpful,

$$\Delta q = q - \frac{q(1-s_2q)}{1-s_1p^2-s_2q^2} = \frac{q(1-s_1p^2-s_2q^2-1+s^2q)}{1-s_1p^2-s_2q^2} = \frac{q(-s_1p^2+s_2q(1-q))}{1-s_1p^2-s_2q^2}$$

(substituting $p$ for $(1-q)$) $=\dfrac{pq(s_2q-s_1p)}{1-s_1p^2-s_2q^2}.$

It will be noted that if $s_2q$ is larger than $s_1p$ the expression is positive, and the gene $a$ has increased in frequency relative to its allele, whereas if $s_2q$ is smaller than $s_1p$ the gene has decreased in frequency. In whichever direction the frequency has changed it will continue to change until $s_2q=s_1p$, after which no further change in frequency can occur. The system then is in balanced equilibrium. The frequency of the gene at equilibrium can be obtained thus: $(s_2q=s_1p)=(s_2q=s_1(1-q))=(q=s_1/(s_1+s_2))$ and the frequency of the other allele $A$ at equilibrium is likewise $p=s_2/(s_1+s_2)$. It will be seen, therefore, that when heterozygotes are at an advantage the frequency at equilibrium of the genes in a two-allele system will be determined by the relative fitness of the homozygotes.

Only in very few cases, e.g. the abnormal haemoglobins, is there observational evidence that a heterozygote advantage is maintaining a polymorphism in human populations. Although selection is known to operate on the blood-groups and secretor and tasting status, the factors so far discovered are acting neither in the right direction nor often with the necessary intensity to maintain the polymorphism. Many of them operate only late in life, and differential mortality, of course, has an evolutionary effect only if it can affect net fertility. There are also complications when three-allele systems and other more involved genetic situations are considered. Nevertheless, it has been predicted that unless the responsible selecting agencies have been removed by technological and medical advance factors will be discovered which operate to maintain human polymorphisms through heterozygote advantage. One can feel fairly confident of this prediction, since it is likely that selection itself will confer a superior fitness on heterozygotes. As already seen genes have multiple effects and even a gene which in its overall effect is advantageous is likely to have some unfavourable effects. Selection will operate to make the advantageous effects dominant and the disadvantageous ones recessive (cf. p. 134). A heterozygote, therefore, formed by two genes whose disadvantageous effects are recessive will possess only advantageous characters. There is evidence, mainly from the levels of polymorphism found in enzyme systems and blood-groups, that about 16 per cent of all the structural gene loci in man are strictly polymorphic.

It is also now worth mentioning that it is quite possible that some apparently 'deleterious' recessive genes are present in a population, not merely as a consequence of recurrent mutation, but because individuals who are heterozygous for them have an advantage. If this is so then indirect methods of estimating the mutation rate (p. 164) are likely to be seriously awry.

Other situations, besides heterozygote advantage, can be envisaged in which there is an opposition of selective forces. A genotype, for instance, may be at a relative advantage when it is comparatively rare in a population but could come to have a disadvantage if it were common. In other words the nature of the selection on a gene may depend upon the frequency of that gene in the population. This is known as 'frequency-dependent selection'. Somewhat related to it is the situation in which the environment of a population is itself heterogeneous and different parts of it favour different genotypes. Genetic variability thus permits the more effective exploitation of the various ecological niches encompassed by the distribution of the population. This form of selection is known as diversifying selection or disruptive selection and has probably been very important in producing polymorphic variety in at least some organisms. How far it could operate in the case of a species like man with high individual mobility and behavioural plasticity is a matter of conjecture.

To summarize, it can be seen that while natural selection in the form of directional selection is the main if not the only force producing systematic genetic change in populations and is thus the paramount force in evolution, it also acts as a conservative influence to maintain the genetic *status quo* and an equilibrium level through 'normalizing selection' against undesirable mutant genes, through 'balancing selection' for heterozygotes, and through 'diversifying selection' in heterogeneous environments.

## Polytypism

Throughout the foregoing account of the evolutionary mechanism attention has been given principally to the way changes in gene frequency take place within one population, but the same factors of mutation and selection, with possible genetic drift sometimes playing a minor role, are responsible for the diversification of populations. Populations inhabiting different localities tend to be exposed to different selective forces. No two habitats are ever exactly identical over any length of time; and even if they were it is unlikely that exactly the same gene pool would be established, since the supply of new variation, if not different in nature, would inevitably come in a different order, and selection acts on what is available as it becomes available. Once differentiation has begun subsequent change is dependent upon that which has already occurred. It is not possible to escape from one form of adaptation if the only way involves passing through a stage in which individuals are less well adapted than at the present time, even though the advantage offered by an alternative state is greatly superior and the less-adaptive state was originally ancestral. If then populations are isolated from one another they will come to contain different genes and should the isolation persist long enough they will become distinct subspecies and ultimately different species, by which time, of course, they are reproductively isolated irrespective of their geographical position. Isolation need not be complete for some diversification to take place. What matters is the comparative force of selection pressure and gene flow. If selection is stronger in its differentiating effect than gene flow is in its unifying one divergence of populations will occur. A strong geographical gradient in a selective force can in fact produce a cline in gene frequency or character variation just as easily as centrifugal gene flow (p. 160). Nevertheless, diversification of populations will occur more rapidly if they are completely isolated from one another than if there is some gene exchange. But the phylal differentiation of a whole species will progress most rapidly when periods of isolation and diversification are interrupted by periods of hybridization. This type of reticulate evolution has characterized the origin of man and has maintained the essential unity of the human species.

Although genetic differences will inevitably be established in isolated populations, and the degree of difference is a function of the length of time they have been separated, it does not necessarily follow that two populations which are phenotypically or genetically similar have necessarily a recent common origin or that two very different populations have a remote common origin. If strong and opposite selective forces are acting populations will rapidly diverge. On the other hand, if populations are subject to similar selective forces they will become at least phenotypically similar, however different they have been in the past. This does not mean that they will inevitably be as genetically similar. It has been mentioned already that it is the phenotype on which selection acts and there are usually a number of possible genetic ways in which a single phenotype can be produced. It follows that when in a single population there is no phenotypic change it cannot be assumed that there has been no genetic change. The phenotypic variation may periodically be static; the genotypic probably never is. Phenotypic differences must, however, represent genetic ones if they are not merely caused by an environmental effect on the development of the individual. The biological significance of interpopulation differences are usually clearer to see than variability within a single population, since it is possible to obtain some idea of the selective forces operating from the correlation between the geographical variation in the character and the geographical distribution of environmental factors.

## Suggestions for further reading (Part II)

BAJEMA, C. J. (ed.) (1971). *Natural selection in human populations*. Wiley, New York.

BOYCE, A. J. (1976). *Chromosome variations in human evolution. Symposium of the Society for the Study of Human Biology*. Taylor and Francis, London.

CAVALLI-SFORZA, L. L. and BODMER, W. F. (1971). *The genetics of human populations*. Freeman, San Francisco.

CRAWFORD, M. H. and WORKMAN, P. L. (1973). *Methods and theories of anthropological genetics*. University of New Mexico Press.

CROW, J. F. and KIMURA, M. (1970). *An introduction to population genetics theory*. Harper and Row, New York.

DOBZHANSKY, TH. (1962). *Mankind evolving*. Yale University Press, New Haven, Connecticut.

—— (1970). *Genetics of the evolutionary process*. Columbia University Press.

HARRISON, G. A. and BOYCE, A. J. (1972). *The structure of human populations*. Oxford University Press, London.

LERNER, I. M. (1968). *Heredity, evolution and society*. Freeman, San Francisco.

LI, C. C. (1955). *Population genetics*. University of Chicago Press.

MATHER, K. and JINKS, J. L. (1971). *Biometrical genetics* (2nd edn). Chapman and Hall, London.

McKUSICK, V. A. (1969). *Human genetics* (2nd edn). Prentice-Hall, New Jersey.

MEDAWAR, P. B. (1960). *The future of man*. Methuen, London.

ROBERTS, J. A. F. (1973). *An introduction to medical genetics* (6th edn). Oxford University Press, London.

SCHULL, W. J. and NEEL, J. V. (1965). *The effects of inbreeding on Japanese children*. Harper and Row, New York.
SPUHLER, J. N. (1967). *Genetic diversity and human behavior*. Aldine, Chicago.
STERN, C. (1973). *Principles of human genetics* (3rd edn). Freeman, San Francisco.
STRICKBERGER, M. W. (1968). *Genetics*. Macmillan, New York.

# Part III: Biological variation in modern populations

N.A. BARNICOT

# 13. Introduction

THE preceding parts of this book have dealt with human palaeontology and with the principles of human genetics. We turn now to the diversity of the human species as it exists today. The differences of bodily size and form, colour, etc. between the inhabitants of major continental areas are familiar enough and have occupied the attention of anthropologists since the late eighteenth century, but in the last 50 years immunology and biochemistry have added numerous invisible variations that have great advantages for the study of populations. Although geographical differentiation forms a major part of our theme in this section it is not the whole of it. In large, complex societies we may expect to find biological differences between the various economic and other social elements that compose them. The study of such differences may be of considerable medical importance.

Human beings vary in numerous ways and live in a multiplicity of socially distinguishable groups scattered over much of the world. The labour of describing these variations would be futile unless it can lead to an understanding of how this regional differentiation came about and what is its biological significance today or in the past. Palaeontology and archaeology provided the most direct, tangible evidence of past events, and we might hope to build a coherent picture of the later phases of human evolution in this way; but in practice the material is often patchy and incomplete. Moreover, tissues other than bones and teeth are seldom preserved. Progress is therefore slow and limited in content. Archaeology can also tell us something about other variables of potential biological interest such as population size, age and sex structure, climatic conditions, and the way the people gained their livelihood.

Genetics lies at the heart of evolutionary problems because genes are the material link between generations and phylogenetic change depends on changes in the properties and frequencies of genes. The precision with which we can define the genotype depends largely on the kinds of characteristics we choose to study. We have not reached the ultimate refinement of being able to compare the structure of human genes by chemical analysis, but analysis of proteins, which are the close products of structural genes, brings us fairly near to this ideal. In the last 20 years or so many inherited variations of proteins have been discovered, using fairly simple biochemical techniques. It is not surprising that such biochemical traits have a strong appeal if we are aiming at a precise comparison of populations at the gene level and if we want to deploy the mathematical apparatus of evolutionary genetics in trying to interpret the results. We shall therefore devote a good deal of space to biochemical genetics in this section.

The inheritance of most human attributes, including susceptibility to various diseases, intelligence as measured by standard tests, and many other socially important properties cannot yet be analysed in such precise biochemical terms. Usually several or many genes are involved and variation may also be affected by the environment in which the individual develops. The body measurements and pigmentary variations of classical anthropology fall in this category. This certainly does not mean that such variations are of no interest to the human biologist, but it limits their value for evolutionary genetics because we cannot identify individually the genes we are dealing with.

## Biology and sociology

This section of the book deals with biological variation in man; but how do we define the domain of human biology? Men vary in bodily structure and in numerous biochemical and physiological traits. Without hesitation we assign such variations to the biologist to study by much the same methods as he uses in research on other animals. But they also speak different languages, conform to different laws, customs, and beliefs in the regulation of their social life and differ widely in the scope and style of their technology. Clearly these variations in socio-cultural behaviour can be just as important for survival as the proper functioning of the physical organism and should not be ignored in a comprehensive biology of man. This extraordinary elaboration of communication, technology, and social forms is unique to man. Its very complexity demands many special branches of study which the student of animal behaviour does not need and which we do not ordinarily think of as part of biology.

Cultural traits are transmitted by learning and social conditioning and not by the mechanisms of biological heredity. They can therefore change much more rapidly than can gene-coded traits controlled by natural selection. Nevertheless, the capacity to learn a language and to acquire the cultural heritage of a society certainly depends on properties of the brain, though we are still far from being able to give a detailed account of the neurological basis of learning and memory. Genes participate in the development and functioning of the cerebral machinery; this is dramatically demonstrated by the gross impairment of intellectual functions that can be caused by some mutations. However, the tissues that develop under the instructions of the genotype are not static but are endowed with the capacity to respond adaptively, within limits, to environmental change; this is conspicuously true of the higher cerebral mechanisms. The proper maturation of intellectual powers depends on exposure to a favourable social environment and *what* is learned depends on what a person is expected and encouraged to learn. In seeking to explain cultural diversity most authorities look to geographical and historical circumstances rather than to genetic variations affecting the nature and degree of cultural aptitude. If this view is correct, biology in the conventional sense has little to contribute to this aspect of socio-cultural anthropology.

In recent years ethological studies on animal behaviour, especially on non-human Primates, have stimulated a search for universal elements of behaviour that man may have inherited from his remote ancestors. But even if his present behaviour is in some ways circumscribed and channelled by such built-in preferences, it seems unlikely that this approach will go far in explaining the richness and diversity of human culture.

It certainly does not follow from what has been said above that human biologists can afford to ignore the social behaviour of man in their own researches. To start with a practical example; human communities are often heterogeneous and divided more or less clearly into social subgroups that may differ in wealth, occupation, religion, political status, language, ethnic origin, or some combination of these. Such subunits may also differ in genetical constitution, and in various facets of ecology such as dietary habits and exposure to disease. If a biologist is not aware of this heterogeneity his sampling of the population will very probably be biased and misleading and he may also miss the opportunity to make informative comparisons between the subgroups.

The pattern of mating determines the distribution of genes in the next generation. In man, as we have already remarked, mating is constrained by social as well as by geographical barriers. In some societies marriage or mating between different ethnic elements, such as Blacks and Whites, is prohibited by law, while in others marriage between persons of different religion is discouraged to varying degrees. Even where law or custom impose no restraints, people will often prefer to choose mates from their own social milieu and will have more opportunity to do so. Such behaviour impedes gene flow between groups. Societies also differ to some extent in the degree of relationship between mates that they tolerate or encourage. Consanguinity of mates increases the probability of gene replicates from a common ancestor finding their way into a zygote. It therefore affects the homozygosity of the population, though usually to only a small extent, and increases the incidence of rare recessive diseases. Social anthropologists have paid much attention to kinship, but their emphasis has been on socially prescribed rules and terminologies rather than on actual genetical relationships; this is a good example of the divergent interests and lack of communication between the social and biological sciences.

The problem of natural selection directs our attention to causes of differential mortality and fertility. Until quite recently transmissible diseases due to viruses, bacteria, and protozoa were major killers throughout the more densely populated regions of the world, and they still are in some impoverished areas. Work on animals has shown that genes can affect susceptibility to such diseases, and we have a certain amount of evidence that this is also the case in man. The prevalence of particular transmissible diseases is affected by many aspects of local culture, such as closeness of interpersonal contact and attitudes to hygiene and the disposal of excrement. Choice of habitat and modification of the environment by agricultural techniques may also affect exposure to disease and create favourable conditions for multiplication and dissemination of parasites. Historical records testify to the spread of disease by armies and by pilgrims and the decimation of American Indians and Pacific Islanders by infections introduced by European colonists are grim examples of the darker side of cultural contact. It is generally agreed that poor nutrition, especially in young children, increases the chance of death from infections. Local differences in the kinds of staple foodstuffs that are cultivated, in weaning practices and in taboos on particular items of diet may therefore be relevant.

In prosperous societies, in which the major causes of death are diseases which strike in the later phases of the reproductive span, differential fertility probably offers more scope for selection than does differential mortality. Although in some parts of the world infections may still have a significant influence on fertility, economic and religious factors affecting voluntary control of conception are certainly much more important in others. The biologist studying human reproduction can hardly ignore the complex problems of socio-cultural diversity.

## Races and populations

It is generally agreed that all living men belong to a single species, *Homo sapiens*; but mankind, like most other animal species, is not geographically uniform. There is no convincing evidence that this geographical differentiation is associated with any decrease of fertility between groups that could be attributed to genetical cases. Nor are there good grounds for believing that interpopulation hybrids are handicapped, except by circumstances arising from the ambiguous social position in which they may find themselves.

In the eighteenth century Blumenbach classified man into 4 major groups, but he was careful to point out that there are intergradations. Since then many more elaborate classifications have been published, based as a rule on a few early visible features such as skin colour, head shape, or hair form. Certain Asiatic peoples, for example, are classified as Mongoloids, and the group is characterized by such features as straight black hair, a flat face, and a fold of skin at the inner corner of the eye (epicanthic fold). However, in South East Asia and the Americas we find populations in which one or more of these diagnostic traits is uncommon or absent or is only slightly developed in the individual. Such peoples do not fit easily into a simple taxonomic scheme. Of course we can create additional groups to accommodate them, but, since all populations differ to some extent if they are examined thoroughly enough, it is not clear where this process of subdivision should stop. It is also worth noting that animal taxonomists aim to base their classifications on genetical differences or at least on differences that are not demonstrably affected by the action of local environment on individuals. There is evidence that stature and various other body-measurements in man are in fact susceptible to such environmental modification (p. 143).

Classifications of man into Mongoloids, Caucasoids, Negroids, etc. undoubtedly express certain genuine features of human variation but they do so in a crude and potentially misleading way. A mere list of diagnostic characters obscures the important fact that all populations are variable. Within any population individuals differ quite widely in stature and other traits that can be measured on a continuous scale. When we compare two populations we often find that the ranges of variation for such a character overlap, so that some individuals cannot be assigned with certainty to one or other on this criterion alone. Differences between populations can be conveniently summarized by comparing averages, though this simple statistic leaves out much of the information. Plotting a collection of population averages on a map helps us to appreciate the pattern of geographical distribution of a metrical trait, and we very often find gradients of change (clines) rather than sharp boundaries. We should remember, however, that there may also be physical differences between economic, religious, or other socially defined groups that live more or less intermingled in the same place; these differences are obviously difficult or impossible to represent on maps.

Population differences in discontinuous attributes, such as the presence or absence of a particular gene, have to be assessed by counting rather than by measuring. We may find that the gene occurs everywhere but varies regionally in *frequency* or it may be virtually absent in some places but more or less common in others. Again the assignment of individuals to a particular group is often a matter of probability and again we often find gradients when we plot gene frequencies on a map.

Classification into discrete categories is satisfactory if natural groups are in fact sharply distinguishable. This is evidently not the case in man. In view of the quantitative, statistical nature of population differences and the vagueness of geographical boundaries any precise definition of taxonomic groups is bound to be arbitrary.

For simplicity we have used single characters to illustrate the general nature of population differences; but if we are interested in population affinities it would be better to study many characters in order to avoid possible bias. This, in fact, is established practice among taxonomists in devising so-called *natural classifications*. If we have measured or counted large number of characters in a number of different populations we need some way of assessing the difference between them when all this information is taken into account. There are statistical methods for reducing such data to simple measurements of 'taxonomic distance' between population pairs and for assigning individuals to one or other population with minimal error. These multivariate methods are discussed on pp. 201. The inclusion of many characters complicates the problem of geographical representation; often the patterns for different characters do not coincide and boundaries may become even more nebulous.

In zoology the word 'race' is sometimes using in referring to subspecific groups and, although it has no official status, it is not disreputable. In the human context it has been so often misunderstood and abused that some authorities prefer to avoid it. If, for example, we speak of a German or a Jewish race we confuse biological and cultural differences. These are culturally defined groups, and if we call them races we tend to prejudge whether they are also genetically differentiated and if so in what ways and to what extent. Such misconceptions easily lead to racist doctrines that assert the purity and superiority of certain groups. No natural populations are pure in the sense of being genetically uniform, though some may have been less affected by recent inflow of genes than others. The question of superiority inevitably involves social and ethical valuations and in practice it is bound up with the desire of one group to dominate and exploit another.

In this part of the book we frequently use the word 'population', even at the risk of monotony. It is conveniently neutral since it refers to an aggregate of people and does not specify or imply how the group in question is distinguished from others. We are then free to define it in geographical, political, linguistic, genetical, or any other terms that may be appropriate to the work in hand. Geneticists are specially interested in groups that form a breeding unit, but only in cases of extreme geographical or social isolation are such groups easy to define. People living in a village, city, or country are more likely to mate with others from the same aggregate but some will mate with outsiders at varying distances from it. The boundaries of the mating unit are therefore diffuse. In practice biologists usually sample recognized and named social groups such as nations, tribes, or castes; the main requirement is that the nature of the sample should be defined in all relevant respects.

# 14. The size and shape of the body

## Anthropometry

THE need for exact measurements to supplement verbal descriptions of bodily size and form was already felt in the early nineteenth century when physical anthropology was becoming a distinct discipline, and until quite recently anthropometry has been the mainstay of the subject. It is true that the proportions of the body had interested artists long before this, but their aim was the definition of ideal types by numerical rules rather than accurate and systematic description of natural variation. It is not surprising that anthropologists, preoccupied with problems of evolutionary descent, have laid special emphasis on the measurement of the skeleton, for skeletal remains are the most direct evidence of the physique of earlier populations. This bias is reflected in the standard measurements used in comparing living peoples, many of which are essentially measures of skeletal dimensions. It was also felt that differences in individual environment were less likely to affect the bones than the soft tissues, and that skeletal characteristics being stable in this sense were therefore a better guide to genetic affinities; this, as we shall see, is a very doubtful assumption. From a wider biological standpoint soft-tissue measurements from which the amount of fat and muscle can be estimated are as important as skeletal ones, while in applied anthropometry, which deals with problems of fitting men into clothes, chairs, aeroplanes, etc., other measurements outside the usual anthropological repertoire may be required.

Both the living body and the skeleton are very complex forms. Given enough ingenuity and time, many of the finer points of shape can be expressed metrically, but for most purposes we use relatively few measurements chosen so as to represent only the major features.

In principle nothing would seem easier than to take linear or circumferential measurements with rulers, calipers, or tapes, but in practice meticulous attention to details of technique is needed to ensure reliable results. The terminal points on the body or bone, between which the measurement is to be taken, must be clearly described and attention must be paid to the posture of the subject since this may have a large effect on some dimensions. The accuracy of the instruments must also be checked periodically. In spite of many efforts to secure international agreement on points of anthropometric technique, it is only too often impossible to compare the data of different observers reliably because of uncertainties about their methods.

Statistical methods are as important in anthropometric research as are surface anatomy or osteology, for without them the laborious collection of measurements would yield little useful information. Because human populations are very variable we need statistical techniques to describe our findings in a compact form, and because we usually have to rely on restricted samples to characterize a whole group, we need them in order to take account of the element of chance in sampling. We can only refer briefly to some of the more important concepts and methods here, but the student is advised to consult the works cited in the bibliography for a fuller treatment.

## Stature

It is convenient to begin with stature because no measurement of the body is taken more often and because it serves to illustrate various principles which apply to metrical characters in general. Military service records provide us with a mass of data on the heights of young adult males in many countries and over a considerable period of time.

### Method of measurement

A fixed vertical scale with a crossbar which can be brought into contact with the top of the head is the normal equipment. The subject should stand erect, without shoes and with heels together, the line of vision directed horizontally. Any tendency to stoop can be corrected by the observer holding the subject's head behind the ears and exerting firm upward pressure.

Although stature is fairly simple to measure, it is anatomically complex since it includes the dimensions of the legs, pelvis, vertebral column, and skull, and the contribution of each of these to the total varies in different individuals and also, on average, in different populations. A man's height gives us some idea of his general size, but weight is a better measure of this since it depends also on transverse measurements. Obviously some people are tall and thin while others are both tall and broad. The relation between stature and weight, or between stature and one or more transverse diameters, can be used to assess such variation in body-build or physique (Part IV).

The empirical fact that body-weight in excess of the population average for a given height is associated with a lower expectation of life has made this relationship an important one in assessing life-insurance premiums.

The interrelations between stature and other body measurements can be conveniently summarized in the form of a correlation table (Table 14.1). If we take a number of different measurements on a large sample of subjects we can examine the data statistically to see whether there is a tendency for large values of one measurement, say stature, to be associated with large values of others (positive correlation) or conversely for large statures to be associated with small measurements in some other region (negative correlation). The correlation coefficient $r$, which can have values from $+1\cdot0$ to $-1\cdot0$, is a convenient measure of association. It is not surprising that leg length and trunk are highly correlated with stature because they are themselves the major components of height; the correlation in this case is said to be spurious. However, the correlation with arm length is also fairly high ($+0\cdot68$). The correlations with transverse

## TABLE 14.1

*Correlations between body measurements 2400 adult male RAF volunteers, ages 17–38 years. Averaged correlations for all ages*

| | Standing height | Sitting height | Arm length | Leg length | Thigh length | Abdomen girth | Hip girth | Shoulder girth | Weight |
|---|---|---|---|---|---|---|---|---|---|
| *Standing height* | — | 0·732 | 0·677 | 0·864 | 0·608 | 0·321 | 0·490 | 0·386 | 0·627 |
| *Sitting height* | 0·732 | — | 0·421 | 0·498 | 0·201 | 0·173 | 0·417 | 0·384 | 0·548 |
| *Arm length* | 0·677 | 0·421 | — | 0·683 | 0·447 | 0·266 | 0·483 | 0·363 | 0·466 |
| *Leg length* | 0·864 | 0·498 | 0·683 | — | 0·817 | 0·312 | 0·424 | 0·304 | 0·556 |
| *Thigh length* | 0·608 | 0·201 | 0·447 | 0·817 | — | 0·515 | 0·440 | 0·234 | 0·525 |
| *Abdomen girth* | 0·321 | 0·173 | 0·266 | 0·312 | 0·515 | — | 0·667 | 0·526 | 0·709 |
| *Hip girth* | 0·490 | 0·417 | 0·483 | 0·424 | 0·440 | 0·667 | — | 0·562 | 0·785 |
| *Shoulder girth* | 0·386 | 0·384 | 0·363 | 0·304 | 0·234 | 0·526 | 0·562 | — | 0·681 |
| *Weight* | 0·627 | 0·548 | 0·466 | 0·556 | 0·525 | 0·709 | 0·785 | 0·681 | — |

From Burt and Banks, *Ann. Eugen.*, 1947.

measurements are distinctly lower. Weight, as might be expected, shows fairly high positive correlations with all the other measurements.

### The statistical distribution of stature

The characteristics of a population with respect to a metrical character such as stature can be presented as a diagram of the distribution. Variation in stature is said to be continuous because people's heights can have any value within certain limits and do not fall into a definite number of distinct classes other than those imposed by the limited accuracy of measuring. In Fig. 14.1 the distribution of stature for a large sample of young Englishmen called up for military service in the Second World War is shown as a histogram. The heights have been grouped in intervals of 1 inch (1 inch=2·54 cm) and the number of men in each group is represented by the area of the corresponding rectangle. The distribution is bell-shaped with the most numerous or modal class near the centre and a more or less symmetrical diminution of numbers on either side of this peak. It resembles the Gaussian (sometimes called Normal) curve of errors quite closely. It is fortunate that the distributions of many metrical characters have an approximately Gaussian form since this distribution is fundamental in statistical theory and we can use the mathematical properties of the Gaussian curve in describing distributions and comparing them. In some cases, such as weight, the distribution of a body measurement is asymmetrical or skewed or in other instances the peak may be too flat (platycurty) or the tails too long (leptocurty). Skewed distributions can often be transformed to a more nearly Gaussian form by plotting logarithms of the measurements; this is true, for example, of measurements of body-fat by skin-fold calipers (see p. 311).

For many purposes the most convenient single measure of the stature of a population is the arithmetic mean or average. In the Gaussian curve this value is coincident with the mode, and also the median or central value. It is often important to measure the variability of the sample and at first sight it might

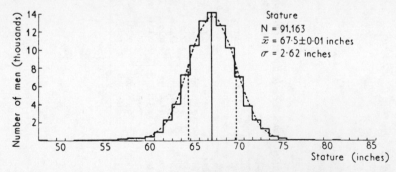

FIG. 14.1. Distribution of stature in young Englishmen called up for military service in 1939. The position of the mean ($\bar{x}$) is shown by a continuous line and of the standard deviation ($\alpha$) as broken lines. A Gaussian curve, calculated from the mean and standard deviation of the data is also shown. (Data from Martin, *Physique of young adult males*, HMSO, 1949.)

seem that the range or difference between the highest and lowest values would be suitable; but this would only utilize two measurements and ones which are likely to vary greatly by chance. The most useful statistic is the standard deviation. In the Gaussian curve vertical lines drawn to the standard deviations on either side of the mean divide the area of the distribution in such a way that about two-thirds (68 per cent) of the observations lie between them. We can say that the chance of getting a measurement outside these limits when sampling at random is about $\frac{1}{3}$ or about $\frac{1}{6}$ for each end of the distribution. Similarly, the chance of getting an observation at or beyond the limits of 2 standard deviations is only about 5 per cent.

Very often our aim in taking measurements is to characterize a whole population, but since for practical reasons we can generally only examine a small sample, our information about the distribution of the measurement in the entire group will be limited. If the sample is small (say less than 100), the histogram will probably appear irregular and we may not be able to tell whether the distribution is Gaussian. The smaller the sample the more likely it is that the mean and standard deviation calculated from it will deviate from the population values. We can, however, specify the accuracy of these estimates and it is usual when quoting a mean or standard deviation to give their standard error as a measure of reliability.

## Comparison of populations

Fig. 14.2 shows the distribution of stature in two populations. One of them, the Bambuti group of Pygmies from the Ituri forest region of Zaïre, is probably the shortest in the world, while the other, the Tutsi, a pastoral people from Ruanda-Urundi adjacent to Zaïre, is one of the tallest. The difference between the mean stature of the Pygmies (1·440 m) and that of the Tutsi (1·765 m) amounts to 0·325 m. Each population, however, shows considerable variability, and the ranges overlap slightly. This is an extreme example and we shall usually find that the difference between the means of two populations is very much less and the overlap of the distributions very much greater. Individuals in the regions of overlap cannot be assigned to one population or the other on the basis of their stature alone. If our samples are small or the populations very variable our estimates of the means will be correspondingly inaccurate and we must consider the possibility that any observed difference between them is due merely to chance in sampling rather than to any real distinction between the two populations. We must therefore assess statistically the probability that two samples, the means of which differ by this amount, could have been drawn by chance from a single population. This is a test of a so-called 'null hypothesis'. The appropriate methods, which can be found in standard texts, are to compare the difference in means with the standard error of the difference. If the samples are small, we must apply Student's $t$ test which is a more sensitive version.

The distribution of the stature of female Pygmies is also shown in Fig. 14.2. The mean value (1·37 m) is 4·9 per cent below the figure for the males. In all

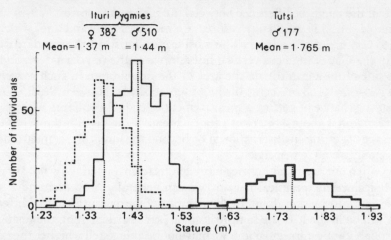

FIG. 14.2. Distribution of stature in male and female Ituri Pygmies (data from Gusinde, 1948) and male Tutsi (data by courtesy Dr. J. Hiernaux). The positions of the means are shown by a broken line.

populations women are on average shorter than men, the magnitude of the difference lying between about 5 per cent and 8 per cent.

## Geographical variations in stature

There is a great deal of information about stature variation throughout the world, but not infrequently it is based on samples which are either very small or were selected in a way which may render them unrepresentative of the general population. In many countries there are not only stature differences between localities but between socio-economic classes and between the inhabitants of rural and urban environments. In Martin's analysis of 1939 military call-up data the mean for men from rural areas was 1·72 m as compared with 1·71 m for highly urbanized districts. The differences between major regions of the UK were small, the averages ranging from 1·73 m for the Home Counties to 1·71 m for Lancashire. Trémolières found for French conscripts that regional variations were slight but there was a difference of rather more than an inch between upper and lower occupational grades. The undoubted increase in growth rates which has taken place in various prosperous countries in the last century has probably resulted in greater stature at maturity, and these secular changes must be remembered in comparing regional data from different periods.

On the whole the pattern of stature variation throughout the world shows no very striking regularities. Both tall and short peoples are to be found in most of the major regions. Relatively high averages (1·70–1·75 m) are centred in north-western regions of Europe such as Scandinavia but also in Albania, while in some parts of Spain and southern Italy the figures fall below 160 m. The Lapps, in common with various indigenous peoples stretching eastward across Siberia, are even shorter. In Africa we find extreme contrasts of stature, from the very tall Tutsi and Nilotic tribes such as the Nuer and Dinka to the diminutive Pygmies and Bushmen. In both the latter cases, however, there is considerable variation from one group to another. The Bushmen of the southern Kalahari, now greatly diminished in numbers, appear to have been the shortest (1·45–1·50 m), but farther north the average rises to 1·55 m or more. Among the shortest peoples of the world we may also mention the Andamanese, and certain aboriginal groups of central Malaya and of the Philippines, who are sometimes classified together as Negritos on account of their short stature and a number of other morphological similarities. In the New World, especially North America, there has been much relatively recent movement of tribes from their original homelands, and many have become extinct or much intermixed. It seems, however, that the tallest peoples (1·70 m or more) were in the Great Plains and the East Coast and also in Patagonia, while the shortest were in tropical central America and the northern parts of South America. This distribution of stature has been interpreted as an example of a cline with adaptive significance in relation to climate (Bergmann's rule). A substantial negative correlation between body-weight and mean annual temperature has been demonstrated for various regions of the world.

## Estimation of stature from long bones

It is useful in forensic work and in examining archaeological remains to be able to estimate the stature of an individual from the length of the arm and leg bones. In order to do this we need data on the relation between stature and, say, femur-length for a large random sample. If we then plot the two variables we find that the points do not lie exactly on a straight line (or some other regular curve) because of individual variability in the relationship. The statistical method of 'regression analysis', however, enables us to calculate the equation for a straight line, or if need be some other curve, which fits the set of points most closely. The criterion of fit is that the variability of the values about the line shall be minimal. The regression equation can then be used to calculate the most probable stature of an individual given the length of a particular bone. Trotter and Gleser, whose work was based on a large collection of American material, give the following linear equation for estimation of male stature (age 18–30 years) from the maximum length of the dried femur:

$$\text{stature (m)} = 2 \cdot 38 \times \text{femur-length (m)} + 0 \cdot 6141, \text{ S.E.} \pm 0 \cdot 0327 \text{ (m)}.$$

The estimate has a certain margin of error, indicated by the standard error $\pm 0 \cdot 0327$ m. In fact the stature would be estimated correctly within 0·06 m in 68 per cent of cases. The accuracy can be improved a little by including tibia-length together with femur-length, but the inclusion of the lengths of the arm bones makes little difference.

It should be emphasized that this and other estimates based on regression methods give the best predictions when applied to material derived from the population for which the equations were originally calculated. Different equations are needed for the two sexes, and the equations derived from European data may not provide as accurate prediction if they are applied to other populations. American Negroes, for example, have on average longer legs in relation to stature than do Europeans and also relatively longer distal limb segments. The use of regression equations based on a modern population to estimate the stature of fossil hominids of widely different structure is clearly a dubious procedure.

### The lengths of trunk and limbs

The most generally used measurement of trunk-length is the 'sitting height'. The subject is seated on a horizontal surface (e.g. a table top) and the measurement is taken from the vertex of the head to the sitting surface using a graduated rod with a movable cross-piece (anthropometer) or a fixed scale. Particular care must be taken to see that the back is stretched as straight as possible by applying upward pressure to the head or jaws; the thighs should be horizontal to avoid any tendency to lean backwards or forwards.

The difference between sitting height and stature is often taken as a convenient but arbitrary measure of lower-limb length, which is difficult to obtain directly because the greater trochanter of the femur is an ill-defined subcutaneous point. Obviously leg-length derived in this way is less than the anatomical length because the level of the acetabulum is some centimetres above the seat level.

There is some variation between populations in the average contribution of trunk-length to stature. In Australian Aborigines (Fig. 14.3) and in many Negro peoples of Africa the trunk is relatively short; the 'cormic index' or 'relative sitting height' $((SH/St) \times 100)$ lies between 45 and 50 per cent, whereas in some Chinese, Eskimo, and American Indian samples the value may be as high as 53 or 54 per cent.

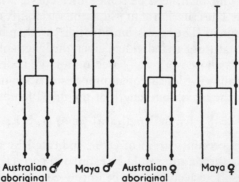

Australian ♂    Maya ♂    Australian ♀    Maya ♀
aboriginal              aboriginal

FIG. 14.3. Diagrams to show contrasting average body proportions of two populations. All measurements are as proportions of stature. The axial line represents sitting height. Bi-acromial width is drawn in at an arbitrary level, the same for each. The relative lengths of the upper limb segments are shown. The total length of the lower limb is taken to be stature minus sitting height. (Australian data from Abbie, 1957; Maya data from Steggerda, 1932.)

Measurement of the lower limb segments, especially the thigh, in the living subject is not entirely satisfactory, but the length of the dried bones can easily be measured. The usual apparatus is an osteometric board with a fixed upright face at one end against which the head of the bone can be pressed and a sliding upright which is applied to the other end of the bone. The length of the tibia in relation to femur-length (tibio-femoral index) tends to be high (85 per cent or more) in those populations with relatively long lower limbs.

The total length of the upper limb can be measured from the acromial point, the most lateral point on the margin of the acromion process of the scapula, to the tip of the longest (3rd) digit. The arm is held by the side of the body with hand pointing down, and with elbow, wrist, and finger joints fully extended. Arm-length measured in this way is longer than the anatomical length since the acromion lies above the head of the humerus. The length of the upper arm can be measured from the acromial point to the proximal margin of the head of the radius, which can be palpated at the elbow, and the length of the forearm from this radial point to the tip of the styloid process of the ulna at the wrist. In general the forearm tends to be long in relation to the humerus in those populations in which the distal (tibial) segment of the lower limb is also relatively long.

## Measurements of breadth

Three transverse diameters may be mentioned because they are fairly easy to measure. The width of the shoulders is taken as the distance between the two acromial points (biacromial breadth). This diameter changes if the shoulders are braced back and one should aim to control posture so as to get a maximal measurement; this is done by relaxing them downwards and somewhat forwards.

Two measurements are useful for the hip region. The bi-iliac or bicristal diameter is the distance between the tuberosities of the iliac bones, which lie close to the most lateral points on the iliac crests. The bispinal breadth is measured between the anterior superior spines of the ilia, which can be felt as fairly sharp prominences at the anterior ends of the iliac crests. Both measurements must be made with considerable pressure so as to compress covering fat as much as possible; even so they are somewhat inaccurate as measures of skeletal dimensions alone.

Circumferential measurements are sometimes taken with a tape at specified levels on the thorax, abdomen, or hips.

There are quite pronounced average differences between populations in the relations between transverse measurements and stature. The diagram in Fig. 14.3 shows the average proportions of males and females of a central Australian tribe compared with Maya Indians of Yucatan. The Australians, with their relatively narrow shoulders and hips, are said to be linear in build; the sex difference in hip proportions is less marked than in Europeans.

Anthropometry of the head

*The braincase*

No measurements in anthropology are more sanctified by usage than those of the length and breadth of the head. The 'cephalic index' (($B/L$) × 100), which is derived from these, was introduced by the Swedish anatomist Retzius over a century ago as a measure of skull shape and rapidly gained prestige as a means of classifying populations.

The maximum length, usually taken with spreading calipers, is measured from the glabella, the bony prominence between the eyebrows, and above the nasal depression, to the most posterior point on the occiput (opisthocranion). The maximum breadth, taken at right angles to the sagittal plane, is generally in the vicinity of the parietal eminences.

The statistical distribution of the cephalic index is continuous and approximately Gaussian in form. On average it is two units higher in the living subject than for the skull. It is a common practice to divide the range into three arbitrary groups, dolichocephalic (below 75), mesocephalic (75–80), and brachycephalic (above 80), and to compare the frequencies of these classes in different populations, but it is misleading to chop a continuous distribution into arbitrary categories in this way, and there is little to recommend it.

The index is only a crude measure of skull shape in the horizontal plane and skulls with the same index value may differ considerably in their overall form. It is hardly surprising that studies on the inheritance of this arbitrary character have yielded no clear results.

In Europe average values between 75 and 80 are found in the British Isles, parts of Scandinavia, and some regions of the Mediterranean zone. In west-central and central Europe the means are usually above 80 or even above 85 (Table 14.2). Most of the figures for Africa are below 75, but some central African peoples have values of 80 or more. Averages around 80 are found in many parts of China, Japan, Indonesia, and the East Indian islands, but in many peoples of New Guinea and other parts of Melanesia the indices are rather lower, while in Australian Aborigines particularly low values are found. The Greenland and Canadian Eskimos have mean indices around 75 in contrast to the more brachycephalic Alaskan ones. Archaeological finds from many different regions have shown a tendency for modern populations to be more brachycephalic than their predecessors. It should be emphasized that, as in the case of other body-measurements, all populations are very variable, the standard deviation of the index usually being about three points on either side of the mean.

*Cranial capacity*

In view of the low average cranial capacities of early Pleistocene hominids, this measurement is important in palaeontology, but it is doubtful whether the labour of measuring it in modern populations has been very rewarding. There

TABLE 14.2

*Mean cephalic index (C.I.) taken on living males in various populations*

| | Number measured | Mean C.I. | | Number measured | Mean C.I. |
|---|---|---|---|---|---|
| Montenegrins | 100 | 88·6 | Kikuyu (Kenya) | 384 | 76·0 |
| Albanians | 112 | 86·4 | Somalis | 244 | 74·3 |
| Norwegian Lapps | 254 | 85·0 | Moroccans | 5210 | 74·3 |
| Armenians | 234 | 83·5 | Koreans | 522 | 83·4 |
| Germans | 925 | 82·5 | Chukchi (Siberia) | 148 | 82·0 |
| Dutch | 4600 | 80·3 | E. Chinese | 359 | 81·7 |
| Norwegians (Troms) | 548 | 81·0 | Japanese | 6000 | 80·8 |
| Norwegians (Hedmark) | 988 | 77·7 | Ainu (Japan) | 95 | 77·3 |
| Scottish (N.E.) | 320 | 78·1 | Maya (Yucatan) | 133 | 85·8 |
| Portuguese | 11658 | 76·4 | Eskimos (S.W. Alaska) | 61 | 80·7 |
| Rwala Bedouin | 270 | 75·0 | Sioux (central USA) | 537 | 79·6 |
| Negritos (Philippines) | 147 | 82·7 | Otomis (S. Mexico) | 178 | 77·9 |
| Semang (Malaya) | 103 | 79·0 | Eskimos (E. Greenland) | 225 | 76·7 |
| Bengal Brahmins | 100 | 78·7 | Hawaiians | 203 | 84·0 |
| Nayar (Malabar) | 175 | 73·2 | Fijians | 133 | 81·5 |
| Baluba (Congo) | 367 | 81·6 | Maori | 421 | 77·7 |
| Ituri Pygmies | 386 | 76·5 | New Caledonians | 185 | 76·5 |
| Ibo (Nigeria) | 2603 | 76·4 | Australians (Arnhem Land) | 236 | 71·8 |

has been much disagreement about the technique to be used in estimating the capacity of skulls. A common method is to fill the cranial cavity with mustard seed and then measure the volume of seed. Estimates of the cranial capacities of living persons can also be obtained by formulae based on measurements of length, breadth, and height of the braincase.

The figure of 1450 cm$^3$ is often taken as an average for European males, and the figure for females is about 10 per cent lower. Somewhat higher means have been reported in some non-European peoples, e.g. Eskimos, while mean capacities somewhat below 1300 cm$^3$ for Australian Aborigines are among the lowest values.

Although increase of brain-size is a notable feature in earlier phases of hominid evolution, the significance of brain-volume in relation to mental functioning is by no means clear. Within a European population the range of cranial capacity is very wide and values of 400 cm$^3$ or more above or below the mean are compatible with normal or even outstanding intellectual ability. Individual differences in this measurement are partly a function of general body-size. It seems most unlikely that the average differences between modern populations have any relevance to the problem of variation in mentality.

The braincase height, which is needed in estimating volume from external dimensions, can be measured on the skull from the most anterior point on the foramen magnum in the midline (basion) to the bregma, the point of junction of sagittal and coronal sutures. Alternatively, the skull can be orientated in the Frankfort plane (bounded by lines drawn between the lowest points on the orbital margins and the uppermost points on the tympanic ring surrounding the auditory meatus) and a measurement of auricular height can be taken from the meatal point (porion) to the vertex. With special instruments a roughly comparable height measurement can be taken on the living subject.

*The face*

The length of the face is generally measured from the nasion at the root of the nose to the lowest point of the chin in the midline (total facial height). The nasion is really the junction between the upper margins of the nasal bones and the frontal in the midline but this suture is difficult to locate in the living person. A horizontal line tangential to the fold defining the top margin of the upper eyelid passes close to the nasion and provides a useful substitute. The upper facial height can be measured from nasion to the alveolar point, the lowest point on the bony wall between the central upper incisor teeth, or the lowest point on the gum in the living.

'Nasal height' is taken from nasion to the point of junction of the nasal septum with the upper lip, or on the skull to the midpoint of a line tangential to the lowest points of the pyriform aperture on either side of the nasal spine.

The most useful facial breadth measurements are the bizygomatic, between the most lateral points on the zygomatic arches in a plane at right angles to the sagittal, and the bigonial between the bony angles of the mandible. 'Nasal breadth' is taken as the distance between the most lateral points on the alae of the nostrils in the living and the maximum breadth of the pyriform aperture in the skull. The average nasal breadth index $((NB) \times 100/(NL))$ is as high as 104 in Ituri Pygmies and values above 90 are found in many African Negro peoples, in Melanesia, and in Australian Aborigines. The nose of Eskimos, on the contrary, particularly as measured on the skull, is unusually narrow. It has been shown that when American Negroes are grouped according to the proportions of European ancestry there is a corresponding proportional difference in the average nasal indices. In India the index shows a general but irregular correspondence with status in the caste hierarchy; it is lowest in Brahmins, higher in lower castes, and highest of all in some of the tribal peoples. It must be remembered, however, that measurements of the nose are liable to considerable errors.

## Muscle, fat, and bone

Although differences in the amount of fat and muscle have generally been ignored by anthropologists because they were felt to depend to a large extent on diet and exercise, they are certainly significant in nutritional and other branches of physiological research.

Methods of measuring total fat content by specific gravity and of determining the volume of the fluid spaces of the body can be applied in the laboratory but are not practicable for surveys on large samples. By comparing these estimates with those obtained by other methods it has been shown that fat content can be assessed from measurements of skin-fold thickness. Measurements taken with special calipers designed to give constant pressure can be made at various points, but the most informative for assessment of total fat are thicknesses measured midway down the upper arm over the triceps muscle and just below the angle of the scapula. A rough estimate of muscularity may be obtained from circumferential measurements of the forearm and calf after deductions for fat, and, if X-ray equipment is available, estimates of fat, muscle, and bone can be made from measurements of the widths of the shadows due to these component tissues in the calf. The radiographic diameter of the walls of the femoral shaft midway along its length are said to give a good estimate of skeletal weight; there are, however, variations in the compactness of the bone structure in shafts of similar dimensions.

So far we have very little comparative data on the body components, but there has been a good deal of work on European and American samples. In American servicemen (mean age 20·7 years) Newman estimated the mean quantity of body-fat at 7·4 per cent. The distribution of body-fat as percentage of weight is very markedly skewed with a long tail of high values extending to 25 per cent or more. At least in well-nourished European populations the proportion of body-fat increases with age.

## Anthropometry and the nature–nurture problem

It has often been tacitly assumed that population differences in skeletal dimensions are relatively little affected by the environment of the individual and must be attributed to genetic variation. No one supposes that the physique of an African Pygmy could be changed to that of a Tutsi or Nilotic Dinka by altering his environment during growth, but this is an extreme case and the possibility that some of the smaller differences which we commonly encounter in population comparisons are environmental in origin needs serious consideration.

The inheritance of anthropometric characters, in so far as they have been investigated, appears to depend on many genes and some of the characteristics of multifactorial inheritance have already been outlined in Part II. Resemblances between twins and between relatives, as measured by correlation techniques, are held to indicate that individual variation in stature is attributable to a large extent to genetic causes. There are, however, considerable difficulties in interpreting correlations from human material. Even if we accept an estimate of 'heritability' at its face value it must be remembered that it is valid only for the population for which it was determined. The relatively restricted range of environmental variation represented in western European samples may lead us to underestimate the potency of environment if we try to extrapolate the conclusion to the human species in general.

Various lines of evidence indicate that adult stature has in fact increased considerably during the last hundred years in a number of civilized countries. Well-marked differences in the average stature of social classes have also been observed in many European countries, and it seems much more likely that these are due to variations in environment, especially nutritional conditions, than

## TABLE 14.3

Body measurements of Japanese immigrants to Hawaii (B) compared with those of Hawaiian-born Japanese (C), and of Japanese in Japan (A)

| | (A) Male sedentes | | | (B) Male immigrants | | | | (C) Male Hawaiian-born | | | |
|---|---|---|---|---|---|---|---|---|---|---|---|
| | Number | Mean | ±S.E. | Number | Mean | ±S.E. | B–A | Number | Mean | ±S.E. | C–B |
| Age (years) | 172 | 35·55 | 0·64 | 178 | 40·60 | 0·55 | +5·05 | 188 | 26·15 | 0·26 | −14·45 |
| Weight (lb)† | 143 | 119·80 | 0·77 | 174 | 124·00 | 0·84 | +4·20 | 185 | 127·40 | 0·93 | +3·40 |
| Stature (cm) | 171 | 158·39 | 0·28 | 178 | 158·72 | 0·26 | +0·33 | 188 | 162·83 | 0·26 | +4·11 |
| Sitting height (cm) | 171 | 84·50 | 0·20 | 178 | 83·10 | 0·19 | −1·40 | 187 | 85·48 | 0·18 | +2·38 |
| Upper leg length (cm) | 170 | 35·78 | 0·17 | 177 | 37·52 | 0·15 | +1·74 | 186 | 37·72 | 0·16 | +0·20 |
| Lower leg-length (cm) | 171 | 31·71 | 0·10 | 178 | 32·65 | 0·10 | +0·94 | 188 | 33·93 | 0·10 | +1·28 |
| Biacromial (cm) | 171 | 39·53 | 0·10 | 178 | 40·28 | 0·09 | +0·75 | 187 | 41·35 | 0·09 | +1·07 |
| Head-length (mm) | 172 | 189·70 | 0·35 | 178 | 189·38 | 0·32 | −0·32 | 188 | 186·54 | 0·32 | −2·84 |
| Head breadth (mm) | 172 | 151·90 | 0·26 | 178 | 152·72 | 0·27 | +0·82 | 188 | 155·08 | 0·28 | +2·36 |
| Upper facial length (mm) | 172 | 72·66 | 0·23 | 178 | 81·40 | 0·25 | +8·74 | 187 | 81·62 | 0·25 | +0·22 |
| Nasal length (mm) | 172 | 47·88 | 0·19 | 176 | 50·24 | 0·20 | +2·36 | 188 | 50·22 | 0·18 | −0·02 |
| Nasal breadth (mm) | 172 | 36·50 | 0·14 | 176 | 35·80 | 0·15 | −0·70 | 188 | 34·56 | 0·14 | −1·24 |

† 1 lb = 0·45 kg.
(From Shapiro 1939.)

to ethnic stratification or differential migration, which have also been suggested as explanations. These topics are dealt with more fully in Part IV.

Another approach to the problem has been to compare the progeny of groups which have migrated to a new and generally more favourable environment with the parental group and also with their compatriots who remained in the original homeland. There have been several studies of this kind since the pioneer work of Boas in 1911 in which he showed that the progeny of Sicilians, Russian Jews, and others, reared in the USA, differed anthropometrically from the parent populations in Europe. The most ambitious study is that of Shapiro and Hulse on Japanese immigrants to Hawaii. The men migrated to become labourers in the plantations and later imported brides from their villages in Japan. After making due allowance for age differences it was found that the offspring reared in Hawaii were, on average, considerably different and generally larger in several body measurements than their parents (Table 14.3). The males, for example, were 4·1 cm taller, but a few measurements such as head length were actually lower. It was also shown that there were systematic differences in size and proportions between the first-generation immigrants and samples from the villages in Japan from which they came. Whatever the interpretation of this may be, it shows that comparisons of groups born and reared in the new country with those remaining at home can be misleading if they are taken to show exclusively the effects of maturation in a different environment. Lasker's work on Mexican immigrants to the USA indicated that, as might be expected, anthropometric changes were most pronounced in those who migrated while still immature, so that effects on growth are certainly involved. It is obvious that migration to a different country may involve changes in many environmental variables; it is not clear which are the most important in producing changes in bodily dimensions, but better nutrition and perhaps less illness due to infections and parasites may be the most significant.

## Multivariate methods

On p. 192 we compared the statures of Ituri Pygmies and the Tutsi Pygmies. The difference between the mean values gives us a measure of their dissimilarity in this respect and it can be visualized as a *distance* between the peaks of the distributions. Since it is based on samples the actual value is only an estimate of the true population difference, but its reliability can be assessed by its standard error.

Although a particular metrical character may have its own special interest and be worth studying in isolation, if we want to make a fair general comparison of two populations we feel that it ought to be based not on one but on many characters. To summarize the results we then need a measure of distance that takes account of many variates (characters). It is not easy to specify how these characters should be chosen, but the number should clearly be quite large so as to avoid giving undue weight to any one of them and they should not be highly correlated otherwise much of the information will be repetitive.† If we are interested in genetical differences, body-measurements are not ideal since they are apt to be affected by environment. We would do better to compare allele frequencies at a number of well-defined gene loci, such as those discussed in the chapters on biochemical variation (p. 221) and on blood-groups (p. 250). We have to assume that these loci, which happen to have been thoroughly explored because it is convenient to work on blood, are representative of the genome as a whole.

It is easy to make a geometrical representation of two or more populations that have been measured for two variates (Fig. 14.4). They lie in a plane and their positions are defined by their numerical values on the two axes ($x$ and

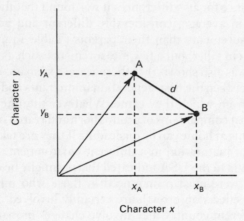

F I G. 14.4. Representation of two individuals A and B who have been measured with respect to two characters $x$ and $y$. $d$ is the 'distance' between them.

$y$). The distance $d$ between any pair can be calculated from Pythagoras's theorem. The representation can be extended to three dimensions, but becomes impossible with more. Nevertheless, the concept of distance and its mathematical treatment remains valid for a very large number of dimensions (characters).

One of the earliest and simplest measures of 'multivariate distance' is the coefficient of racial likeness (CRL or $C_H{}^2$) due to Karl Pearson. It is essentially the mean of the squared differences between a collection of average values for two populations. Since the various measurements are likely to differ widely in magnitude (e.g. stature and nasal height) it is convenient to reduce them to a common scale by expressing each in standard deviation units. In this standardized form the CRL for populations $j$ and $k$ can be written

$$\sum_{i=1}^{n} (\bar{x}_{ij}{}^2 - \bar{x}_{ik}{}^2)/n$$

† The word information is here used in a colloquial rather than a strictly mathematical sense.

where $\bar{x}_{ij}$ is the mean of character $i$ in population $j$, $n$ is the number of characters and $\sum$ indicates summation over all characters. A useful property of the CRL, as shown by Penrose, is that it can be partitioned into two uncorrelated components, size $C_Q^2$ and shape $C_Z^2$. As the name implies $C_Q^2$ measures difference in overall dimension while $C_Z^2$ is the variation between measurements when the size factor is removed. These statistics are easy to calculate and the results are usually found to agree quite closely with those obtained by more rigorous but lengthy procedures. Plotting size and shape values for a set of populations, as in Fig. 14.5, gives a useful picture of mutual resemblances and differences.

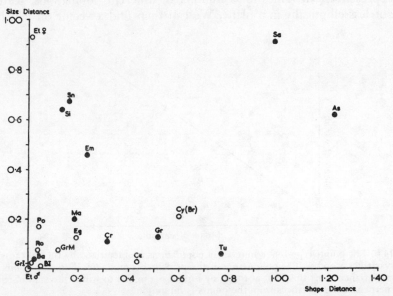

FIG. 14.5. Distance of certain Mediterranean peoples from Etruscan males. Size and shape statistics based on three skull measurements—length, breadth, and height. Po=Pompeian; Em=Emilian; Sa=Sardinian; Cr=Cretan; Ro=Roman; Sn=Siennese; Ma=Maltese; Gr= Greek; Si=Sicilian; Cy (Br)=Cypriot Bronze Age; GrM=Mycenean Greek; GrI=Iron Age Greek; Ce=Cephallenian; Tu=Turkish; Eg=Egyptian (26th–30th Dynasties); Ba=Basque; BI=Iron Age British; Et=Etruscan females; As=Ashanti. (From Barnicot and Brothwell, Medical biology and Etruscan origins, Churchill, 1959.)

The CRL was criticized because it ignores intercorrelations between measurements and therefore includes redundant information. The generalized distance $D^2$, of Mahalanobis, meets this objection by transforming the variates in such a way that intercorrelations are removed. The computations used to be laborious but this is no longer so now that electronic computers are widely available.

If we have data on a large number of populations and we have computed $D^2$, between each pair, we end up with a large table (matrix) of distance values, and it becomes difficult to visualize the pattern of population differences clearly. The points representing the populations are located in multi-dimensional space and we cannot plot them directly in two dimensions without distorting the distances and losing information. However, the method known as multidimensional scaling, due to Kruskal, is one method that has been used to overcome this difficulty. It may turn out that the scatter of points in multidimensional space can in fact be referred to two or three axes without excessive distortion. There are a number of related methods for finding such axes (vectors) and thus making it possible to represent the positions of the populations in one or more two-dimensional diagrams. 'Principal component analysis' is one such method. In the simplest case we can imagine a set of points which may represent mean values for a number of different populations, scattered more or less elliptically in a plane. We can then find a vector on which the

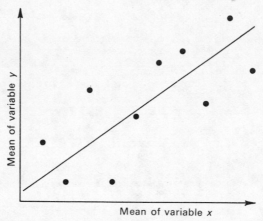

FIG. 14.6. The points represent a number of populations characterized by their mean values of the variables $x$ and $y$. The oblique line is the principal component. The data points have maximal variance along this line; at the same time it is the line to which the sum of squares of the perpendicular distances from the points is minimum.

projections of the points gives the maximal scatter (variance) in one dimension (Fig. 14.6). This vector is in fact the major axis of the ellipse. If the points are scattered in higher dimensional space we can proceed in the same way, finding first the vector that gives the greatest variance and then one at right angles, which will be uncorrelated with it, and so on until all the variation in the positions of the points is accounted for. It will often be found that the first two or three components account for most of the variance and suffice for a reasonably accurate representation of the data.

A somewhat different approach to multivariate comparisons is by using 'discriminant functions'. This statistic was devised by Fisher to cope with the problem of assigning an individual to one or other of two populations on the basis of multiple measurements (assuming, of course, that he actually belongs to one of them). The usual form of the discriminant function is a linear combination ($y = c_1 x_1 + c_2 x_2 \ldots c_n x_n$) of the measurements with weights $c$ so chosen that the chance of misclassification is minimized. The multiple measurements are

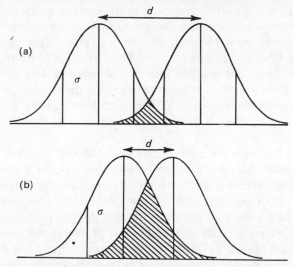

FIG. 14.7. (a) Two Gaussian distributions which overlap in the shaded area. $d$ is the distance between their means. (b) The distance $d$ is reduced, thus increasing the area of overlap and giving less efficient discrimination. $\sigma$ represents the standard deviation.

thus replaced by a single compound value. We can easily see that if we have only one measurement correct classification of an individual will depend on the extent of overlap between the two population distributions (Fig. 14.7) and this will in turn depend on the ratio between the difference $d$ of their means to their standard deviations $\sigma$. The discriminant function maximizes this ratio and thus makes the interpopulation distance as large as possible when the scatter of values around the means is also taken into account. The method can be generalized to deal with more than two populations so that we decide to which of a number of different populations an individual skull should be assigned; but in this case there is no unique solution. We can, however, calculate a sequence of functions that contribute successively less and less to efficient separation of the populations in multi-dimensional space. The distances between the populations obtained by multiple discrimination are not numerically equal to $D^2$ but are simply related to it by a scaling factor.

The estimation of multivariate distances from frequency data (e.g. gene frequencies) rather than continuous measurements raises a number of theoretical problems and several different procedures have been suggested. However, they all seem to give similar results in practice.

When we employ $D^2$ or discriminant functions the existence of separate groups is taken for granted. But we may sometimes have a situation in which we have characterized a collection of individuals by taking a large number of measurements (or by scoring the presence or absence of many characters) in each, and we want to arrange them systematically on the basis of their resemblances. There are several procedures for doing this. The results of such 'clustering' methods are often presented in the form of a tree or 'dendrogram' in which two individuals (or populations) are joined to a common branching point (node) if they resemble each other more closely than either resembles any other individual in the data (Fig. 17.8), p. 273. The problem of deciding whether a collection of items falls into two or more groups is not easy even if we are considering only one measurement: the distribution may show two or more obvious modes and we are then confident that we are dealing with more than one group; but if there is extensive overlap the decision becomes more difficult.

Multivariate methods are complicated in detail and we have only tried to present a very brief outline of some of the main concepts. It is worth emphasizing that, although statisticians can help us to extract the maximum amount of information from our data and to summarize it in a compact, quantitative form, it remains for the biologists to interpret the patterns that are revealed. In a sense multivariate methods simplify our problems because they replace an unwieldy mass of data by a few numerical values. But these derivatives are complex and it may be difficult to understand their meaning in biological terms. When we are comparing populations it is advisable to examine the individual characters and to make use of indices and other simple devices at the same time as we are applying these more sophisticated procedures. Like most other statistical methods, multivariate methods make certain simplifying assumptions about the properties of the data; e.g. the $D^2$ method assumes that the distribution of the combined measurements is normal (multivariate normality), and that variances and covariances are the same for all populations. These assumptions may not be justified for all biological data and misleading results can arise if the methods are applied mechanically without proper understanding.

# 15. Pigmentation and some other morphological characters

No normal variations are more immediately striking to the eye than those of pigmentation. Although the geographical distribution of skin, hair, and eye colour has been known in a general way for a long time, technical difficulties have hindered the collection of exact data. Genetical analysis has lagged behind for the same reason and also because the inheritance of pigmentary differences has usually proved to be complex. The pigments themselves are difficult to analyse chemically, and the biochemical approach has therefore made limited headway.

## Skin colour

The colour of the skin depends on two main factors; the blood in the smaller vessels of the dermis and the amount of the dark pigment, melanin, in the epidermis. In skin with little melanin the colour depends chiefly on the blood and varies according to the amount in the vessels and the state of oxygenation of the haemoglobin. In dark skin the contribution of the blood-supply to colour is masked to a greater or lesser extent by melanin.

The melanin is formed by specialized dendritic cells, the melanocytes, situated in the basal layer of the epidermis. These cells make granules of pigment about $0.5\,\mu m$ $(1\,\mu m = 1/1000\,mm)$ in diameter and pass them into epidermal cells by way of their processes. The number of melanocytes per unit area of skin varies somewhat in different regions of the body, but counts on Negroes and light-skinned people give essentially the same means for a given body region so that major population differences in skin colour do not appear to depend on variation in melanocyte numbers. In Negroes the granules are more numerous and larger; whereas in a light-skinned European only a few brownish granules can be seen in the basal layer of the epidermis, in a Negro this layer is densely black, and granules are also conspicuous in the Malphigian layer and in the stratum corneum.

Melanins are a widely distributed group of pigments, found in both plants and animals, which are formed by oxidation of phenolic compounds followed by polymerization of the products into highly insoluble dark complexes. In man and many other organisms melanin is formed from the amino acid tyrosine in a sequence of stages, some of which are catalysed by an enzyme tyrosinase. The indole-5,6-quinone produced in this way polymerizes to form the pigment. The resistance of melanins to degradation makes it difficult to study them analytically, but there is evidence that melanins made in the laboratory vary in structure according to the conditions under which they are formed. The melanin granules of the tissues contain protein and this makes the chemistry of the natural pigments even harder to work out.

*Methods of measurement*

Techniques for measuring pigmentation quantitatively are to be preferred both in surveys for comparing populations and also in genetical work where we need to compare members of a family. Direct chemical estimation of the pigment in the kind of way we use to determine the concentration of a substance in blood or urine, is not feasible, but a measurement of the contribution of melanin to skin colour can be obtained by reflectometry (reflectance spectrophotometry). The principle is to shine a beam of light on the skin and to compare the amount diffusely reflected from it with that reflected from a pure white standard under the same conditions. From a series of readings throughout the visible spectrum (400–750 nm), or if need be, the ultraviolet and infrared, a reflectance curve can be drawn representing the percentage of light reflected over the chosen range. Examples of reflectance curves from light and dark skin are shown in Fig. 15.1. The former rises fairly steeply from the blue to the

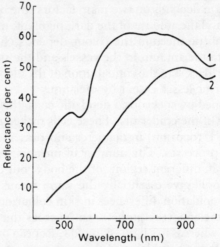

FIG. 15.1. Reflectance curves of fair European (1) and Negro (2) skin in the visible and near infrared range. Note the marked trough between 500 nm and 600 nm due to haemoglobin in (1) which is less pronounced in (2). The curves approach one another closely in the infrared. (From Barnicot, *Man*, 1957.)

red end of the spectrum and shows a pronounced trough in the green region owing to absorption of light by haemoglobin. In the latter this trough is hardly detectable and the curve is smooth and much more nearly horizontal, rising less steeply towards the red end. The large amount of melanin dominates the reflectance and the curve is similar to that obtained from a suspension of this pigment. Changes in blood-supply affect the reflectance at the red end relatively little and readings in this region give a convenient measure of the contribution of melanin.

Now that cheap, portable reflectometers are available this method should replace older and cruder techniques. The simplest but least accurate of these is to assign each subject to one of several arbitrary grades such as light, medium, or dark. Since no standards are used to define the groups, errors due to variations in the judgement of the observer are likely to occur and a meaningful comparison of the results of different observers cannot be made. To remedy this, standards made of various materials coloured to represent skin have been employed, but they are not very satisfactory because they do not resemble skin closely. Close attention to lighting is essential in order to minimize inaccuracy, and this may be difficult in field conditions, and even in the most favourable circumstances errors due to variation in the colour-matching capacity of different observers will remain.

Exposure to sunlight obviously increases the amount of melanin pigment in skin, and to minimize variation due to differences of environment readings are usually taken on some relatively unexposed but accessible area such as the inner side of the arm. Preliminary cleansing of the skin is a precaution not to be ignored.

## Inheritance of skin colour

Very little satisfactory work has been done on the genetics of skin colour. Reflectometric studies on matings between Africans and Europeans confirm the impression that clear segregation does not generally occur. More than one gene is involved, but opinions differ as to the most probable number. The statistical distribution of skin colour, as measured by reflectometry in a homogeneous population, is continuous, like the distribution of stature and other graded or metrical characters. The average measurements of melanin pigmentation in $F_1$ hybrids (mulattoes) from the above-mentioned crosses are close to the mid-value between the parental means, and the same is true of 'backcrosses' between mulattoes and members of the parental populations. It has been claimed that skin-colour differences in the progeny of matings between Australian Aborigines and Europeans can be attributed to segregation for a few genes only, but this needs confirmation by more precise methods. The belief that light-skinned parents with Negro ancestry may produce 'black' children seems to be exaggerated if not unwarranted. There is no evidence for recessive genes with a major darkening effect on pigmentation, and if the normal range is due to a number of genes with simple additive effects we should expect occasional cases in which a child was somewhat darker than either parent, but the difference would be slight. Much obviously depends on what we understand by black.

In some societies mating with respect to skin colour is clearly not random. In South Africa and in some States of America, unions between Negroes and Whites are prohibited by law. In Hindu society the higher strata in the complex system of endogamous castes are on the whole lighter-skinned, and marital restrictions work to maintain these differences. There may be a preference for light-skinned wives in some societies where the prestige of a white ruling group gives a value to less pigmented skins.

*Function of skin pigmentation; natural selection*

Radiation in the ultraviolet region, which is damaging to tissues, is strongly absorbed by melanin. Dark-skinned peoples are on the whole found in tropical regions and it has long been argued that this distribution is due to natural selection in favour of pigmented skin as a protection against strong sunlight. There are, of course, exceptions to the geographical rule; the American Indians are not notably different in skin colour throughout the continent, and the dark Tasmanians lived in a temperate climate. Such discrepancies are often discounted on the grounds that these peoples entered the habitat too recently for selection to have produced appreciable changes. The intensity of solar ultraviolet is not necessarily high in all tropical regions, e.g. tropical rain forests, and at least in certain seasons it may be high in the Arctic owing to reflections from snow. We lack satisfactory quantitative comparisons of the ultraviolet radiation load in various environments.

In very sunny regions such as South Africa, Australia, and parts of the southern USA, the incidence of cancer of the skin (epithelioma) of parts of the body habitually exposed to sunlight is considerably higher in light-skinned people than in the pigmented inhabitants of these regions. It is true that in Africans skin cancers of the lower limbs are not uncommon, but they appear to be a sequel to ulceration due to injuries. Tumours induced by solar radiation tend to occur fairly late in life and are not highly malignant; nevertheless, they might well have a significant effect on mortality if left untreated.

Vitamin D is formed from certain steroids near the skin surface under the influence of ultraviolet radiation, and it has been argued that depigmentation in northerly regions favours this beneficial effect of sunlight. The fact that rickets, a disease due to vitamin-D deficiency, used to be especially common in the immigrant Negro populations of northern cities is difficult to interpret in this context because their nutritional conditions are also likely to have been bad. Nor does it seem to be clear whether the vitamin is formed in layers of the skin which would be effectively shielded from ultraviolet by the pigment.

Black surfaces in general absorb visible light, the energy of which is thereby liberated as heat and dark-skinned people must experience an increased heat-intake for this reason. The extra load on the temperature-regulating mechanisms, even in strong sunlight, is probably small, but it might be a significant disadvantage when the subject is near the limits of tolerance.

It is widely accepted that at the temperatures prevailing at the skin surface radiation of heat from the skin is virtually independent of skin colour, though this has been disputed. If this is the case, dark skin is no advantage in cooling the body by radiant heat loss.

## Hair colour

The colour of hair is due to granular pigment contained in the keratinized cortical cells of the hair shaft. The granules are formed by melanocytes situated in the epithelium of the hair bulb adjacent to the dermal papilla.

Objective measurements of hair colour are easily obtained by examining small samples of hair by reflectometry. As the reflectance curve in Fig. 15.2 shows, even hair from highly depigmented albino subjects is far from white. With the exception of red shades, hair colours can be arranged in a continuous series from dark to light, representing in effect increasing dilutions of the same pigment, namely melanin. While we cannot exclude the possibility of variations

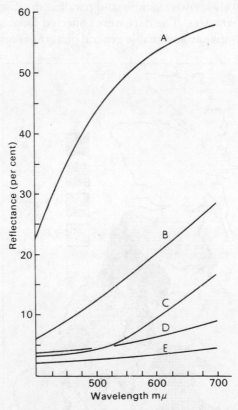

FIG. 15.2. Reflectance curves of human hair of various colours. (A) A European albino, (B) blonde European, (C) a European with strongly red hair; note upward deflection at about 520 nm, (D) brown-haired European, (E) African Negro. (From Barnicot, *Man*, 1957.)

in the chemical structure of the pigment, differences appear to be mainly quantitative; in the lighter shades of hair melanin granules are less numerous, smaller, and less completely impregnated with the melanin polymer than in darker ones. The reflectance curve for strongly red hair is distinctive in having a sharp upward deflection in the green region. The pigment is granular but very probably different in composition to melanin.

## Distribution

In most parts of the world hair colours are dark, and it is mainly in north-western Europe that the incidence of blonde and red shades is high. We should note, however, that even in dark-haired populations there may in fact be considerable variation in the actual amount of pigment in the hair, but it is not easy to detect differences by eye or even by reflectometry when the shade approaches black. Interesting regional variations in hair colour can be found within particular countries. The gradient of increasing blondeness from south to north in Italy is a well-known example and parallels the distribution of various other physical characters. The data were collected long ago by subjective methods but probably give an acceptable general picture of regional differences.

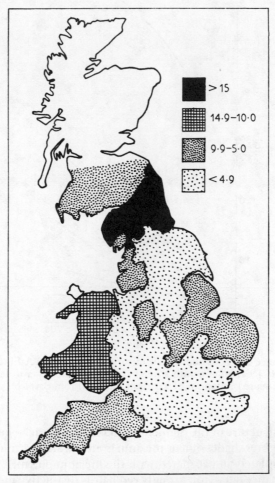

FIG. 15.3(a). Frequency of red hair in the UK expressed as the index of redness R. The statistics calculated from reflectance curves of hair samples from young soldiers. Note high frequencies in Wales and border countries. (From Sunderland, *Ann. Human Genet.*, 1956.)

In the UK red hair (measured by reflectometry) is more frequent in the north and west, and this distribution resembles that of blood-group O to some extent, though there is a discrepancy in East Anglia (Fig. 15.3).

Hair colour often changes during childhood. In parts of southern Europe, where the adult population is predominantly dark, lighter shades are quite frequent in young children, but in Chinese and Africans, on the other hand, the hair is darkly pigmented even in infancy. Blonde hair is by no means uncommon in young Australian aboriginal children.

### Inheritance

With the exception of red hair, the genetics of hair colour have been inadequately studied. Change of colour in the earlier and later phases of life compli-

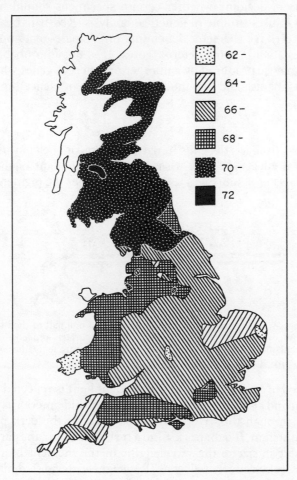

FIG. 15.3(b). Frequency of the gene *O* of the ABO system in the UK. (Based on Kopec, *The distribution of the blood-groups in the United Kingdom*, 1970.)

cates analysis. Variation in lightness and darkness due to melanin content probably depends on many genes which control the rate and extent of darkening.

The more extreme examples of red hair are certainly striking, but more detailed work on large population samples shows that this colour is not a sharply distinguishable category but merges into reddish-brown and reddish-blonde shades. Nevertheless, red hair colours can probably be regarded as a separate class, although they cannot be unambiguously distinguished by visual inspection or by reflectometry. The characteristic shape of the reflectance curve can be used to derive numerical indices of redness. Statistical methods can then be used to obtain the optimal sorting into red and non-red shades and this procedure is an improvement on subjective classification by eye. It is possible that chemical criteria may ultimately provide better means of discrimination. The difficulty of deciding whether certain specimens should be regarded as red naturally causes trouble in genetical analysis. Red hair behaves approximately as a recessive character depending on a single gene, but there seems to be manifestation in some heterozygotes. It is not improbable that similar phenotypes may be produced by a number of different genes which we cannot at present distinguish and that modifiers may also influence the expression of the character.

## Eye colour

The colour of the iris depends in part on granular melanin pigment and in part on optical effects. In dark irises there are abundant pigmented cells in the anterior layer of tissue (Fig. 15.4). In lighter types the pigment in this situa-

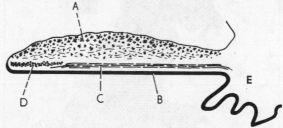

FIG. 15.4. Diagram of a transverse (i.e. radial) section of one half of the human iris. A, the anterior layer containing pigment cells, especially near the surface, and loose connective tissue. B, the posterior pigmented epithelium. C, the radial, dilator muscle. D, the circular constrictor muscle. E, the ciliary body.

tion is reduced in amount; some of the incident light is reflected from the residual pigment and also from the colourless but turbid anterior layer tissue, but some passes through this layer and is absorbed by the dark pigment of the posterior epithelium. If light passes into a turbid medium, the particles of which are comparable in size to the wavelengths of the incident beam, the shorter wavelengths are selectively reflected (Rayleigh scattering). This optical effect accounts for the predominance of blue in the light reflected from a depigmented anterior layer of the iris. A progressive decrease in the amount of pigment yields a graded series of colours from brown to green and finally to blue and grey. The iris is not, however, a uniformly coloured area; in the lighter types the tissue of the anterior layer is thinner in some regions than others, producing characteristic radial patterns and the melanin pigment is not evenly distributed, sometimes forming well-marked spots. It is not surprising, in view of these complexities, that eye colour is difficult to record accurately and difficult to analyse genetically.

Sets of glass eyes have been used as standards for matching eye colours, but the fact that the iris is a very small area, varying in extent with the degree of contraction of the pupil, and exhibiting a wide range of variation in detail, presents problems in recording that do not arise in the case of skin or hair colour.

It is often stated that dark eye colour is dominant to lighter shades, and while this may be true in a general way, clear segregation is only obtained if minor degrees of variation are ignored and colours are grouped in definite categories such as brown, mixed, and blue. The apparent simplicity is partly artificial, depending on the initial classification of phenotypes. It is probable that there are many genes involved, some exerting relatively large and some smaller effects either on the amount of pigment or on the pattern of tissue atrophy. It has sometimes, but not invariably, been found that in western European populations dark eyes are more frequent in females than in males, and it is claimed that sex-linked genes are involved. It should be noted that in some regions light eyes frequently occur in dark-haired individuals. Some genes appear to affect mainly the colour of the eyes, while others may have a more general effect on pigmentation.

The iris pigment restricts the entry of light into the eye to the pupil and helps to protect the retina against damaging ultraviolet radiation. It is by no means clear whether depigmentation within the range normally occurring in the population has any perceptible influence on visual functions, though the more extreme pigment deficiency of albinism is associated with avoidance of strong light (photophobia) and various visual defects.

## Finger- and palm-prints

On the palmar surfaces of the hands and plantar surfaces of the feet there are numerous fine epidermal ridges which form regular but complex patterns. Similar systems of 'dermatoglyphs' are found in other Primates besides man and also in some arboreal marsupials. Sweat ducts open at regular intervals along the ridges and when the skin contacts a smooth surface residual secretions leave an imprint of the pattern; but to get clear and permanent records suitable for detailed study the skin must be 'inked' with special compounds and pressed on a prepared paper. Francis Galton in 1892 was one of the first to classify finger-prints and to investigate their inheritance. Although most prints of the volar surface of the finger can be classified as one of the three types—arches,

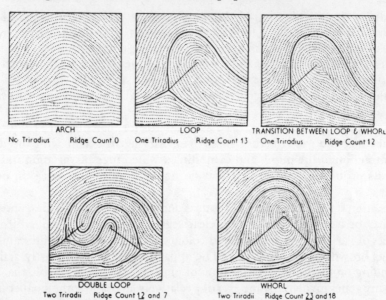

FIG. 15.5. The three main finger dermatoglyph types, arch, loop, and whorl, a transitional type between loop and whorl, and a more complex type, the double loop. The main lines which meet at a triradius are shown as continuous lines. A lighter line is drawn from triradius to core; the number of ridges crossed by this line is the ridge-count. (Drawn from original photographs by courtesy of Dr. Sarah Holt, Galton Laboratory.)

loops, or whorls, there is great individual variation in detail, so great indeed that no two people have identical patterns, not even monozygotic twins.

The three main volar pattern types are illustrated below (Fig. 15.5). The distinctions between them are not absolutely sharp for transitional forms can be found and complex types which cannot readily be fitted into the classification also occur. The arch is the simplest form with a parallel series of curved ridges passing transversely across the finger pad. In the case of a loop these adjacent systems of lines meet to form a Y-shaped point, known as a triradius or delta on either the ulnar or radial side; in a whorl there are two such triradii and the main lines which participate in them surround a central core.

In the British population (according to Scotland-Yard records) loops are the commonest pattern (70 per cent), whorls next (25 per cent), and arches the rarest (5 per cent). The scoring of finger-print patterns is complicated by the fact that they are often not the same on different fingers. In Europeans whorls are most frequent on the 1st and 4th digits (35 per cent) and least frequent on the 5th, while arches occur most often on the 2nd (11 per cent) and are rare on the 5th (1 per cent). Loops may be of the radial type with the opening directed to the radial side or they may have the reverse, ulnar, arrangement; radial loops are commoner on the right hand than on the left.

A count of the number of digital triradii on both hands is sometimes used as a measure of 'pattern intensity'. An arch typically lacks a triradius and therefore scores 0 (though in some in which the arch is much compressed laterally a triradius is formed at the centre); loops, with a single triradius score 1, and whorls 2. The range of pattern intensity can therefore vary from 0, where there are arches on all digits, to 20 where there are only whorls.

A measure of so-called 'pattern size' is obtained by ruling a line from each triradius to the core of the pattern and counting the number of ridges it crosses (Fig. 15.5). In this method arches again have a count of zero while whorls, with 2 triradii, have higher counts on average than loops.

Variation in the general shape of the pattern can be assessed by measuring the proportions of length and breadth by standard methods.

The major individual variations in finger-print patterns are largely under genetic control, but they have so far remained inexplicable on any simple scheme of inheritance. Holt's studies on the inheritance of the ridge-count, the distribution of which for a random population is continuous but non-Gaussian, showed a correlation close to $0 \cdot 5$ between sibs and between parents and children, with no evidence of dominance. The correlation between monozygotic twins was found to be $0 \cdot 95 \pm 0 \cdot 02$ as compared with $0 \cdot 46 \pm 0 \cdot 10$ for dizygotic twins. The non-Gaussian form of the ridge-count distribution may perhaps mean that much of the variation can be attributed to a small number of genes with major effects, but if so the metrical differences between genotypes overlap and are not distinguishable as separate modes in the distribution.

When we compare the dermatoglyphs of populations we can safely assume that the phenotypic differences reflect variations in the distributions of genes, but, as with metrical traits in general, we cannot analyse the results in terms of particular genes or specify their frequencies. The intricate nature of dermatoglyphs and the wealth of variation which they may show makes it difficult to summarize the facts in a concise, quantitative form. The usual method in population studies has been simply to compare the percentage of the three main pattern types and to give the index of pattern intensity in the way already described above. Some of the more extreme variations are shown in the diagram below (Fig. 15.6). In some Bushman populations, for example, arches are unusually common and pattern intensity corresponding low, whereas in Chinese and North American Indians whorls are very frequent and pattern intensity high.

The ridge patterns of the palm also show both individual and population differences. At least 5 triradii are usually discernible, four of them at the bases of digits 2–5 and the fifth near the centre at the junction of palm and wrist. The usual position of these triradii and of the lines which originate from them are shown below in a diagram (Fig. 15.7). Arches, loops, whorls, or more complicated patterns are found with varying frequency in the areas of the interdigital pads, on the thenar eminence overlying the first metacarpal and on the hypothenar area over the fifth. In Chinese and various other Mongoloid peoples the main lines are said to run more longitudinally than in Europeans, and the incidence of patterns in the first and third interdigital areas is relatively low.

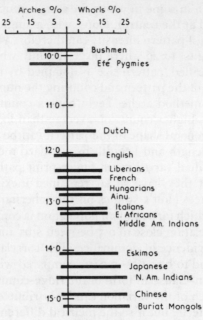

Arches %     Whorls %
25  15  5     5  15  25

10·0  Bushmen
      Efé Pygmies

11·0

      Dutch
12·0  English
      Liberians
      French
      Hungarians
      Ainu
13·0  Italians
      E. Africans
      Middle Am. Indians

14·0  Eskimos
      Japanese
      N. Am. Indians

15·0  Chinese
      Buriat Mongols

FIG. 15.6. The percentage of arches and whorls, horizontal scale, and the pattern intensity index for various human populations. (Modified from Cummins and Midlo, 1943.)

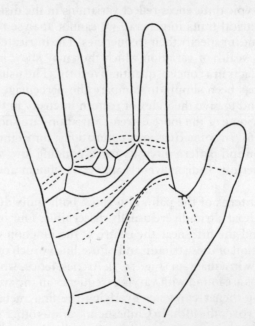

FIG. 15.7. The main lines and triradii of the palm. The palmar creases are shown as dotted lines.

In Bushmen, to give another example of contrasting morphology, hypothenar patterns are infrequent, but patterns in the second interdigital area are commoner than in most peoples.

We do not know what factors have brought about these regional differences in the frequencies of various finger- and palm-print patterns. The different phenotypes which are encountered in the normal population are not known to be associated with any physiological advantage or disadvantage which might provide a clue to selective influences. Variations in relation to disease have not on the whole received much attention, but in Down syndrome the palm- and finger-print patterns are markedly abnormal.

## Anatomical anomalies

Many variations in details of skeletal morphology in the musculature and in blood-vessel patterns have been described and some of them are known to vary in frequency in different populations. For the most part these anomalies are harmless, though some may on occasion give rise to disabilities. Studies on families have suggested a simple mode of inheritance for certain of these conditions, but these results are likely to be approximate because of the wide range of manifestation and the difficulty of scoring such characters accurately on the living subject.

Work on skeletal and dental variations in pure lines of mice has shown that phenotypically discrete variations, some of which resemble those in man, may nevertheless be genetically complex and that their incidence in various strains may depend not only on genetic differences but also on intra-uterine environment, diet, and probably other factors. Congenital absence of the third molar is not uncommon in Europeans, Eskimos, and Chinese, but infrequent in African Negroes. Absence of the homologous tooth has a fairly high incidence in some mouse strains, but here suppression of the tooth can be shown to be merely the extreme condition in a gradation of size reduction depending on multiple genes.

Variations in the vertebral column, including failure of fusion of the neural arches in certain regions (spina bifida), differences in the number of presacral vertebrae, the incidence of supernumerary ribs, and the form of the cervical spines, were studied in East African skeletons by Allbrook, who showed that their frequencies differed from those in various other populations.

Persistence of the metopic suture between the frontal bones (metopism) has a variable but irregular incidence; 5–10 per cent of west-European skulls show this anomaly but it is much less frequent in Australian Aborigines, Eskimos, and African Negroes. The occurrence of subsidiary ossicles (Wormian bones) along the lamboid suture is another cranial anomaly with a variable incidence.

The peroneus tertius muscle, the tendon of which can be felt running from the region of the lateral malleolus at the ankle to the base of the fifth metatarsal, may be reduced or absent. Family studies suggest that absence is inherited as a recessive trait but variations in the degree of reduction and differences in incidence between the sexes and between the two sides of the body complicate the analysis. Although figures for absence of the muscle should be treated with some reserve in view of these difficulties, the anomaly is evidently more frequent (about 15 per cent) in some African and American Indian peoples than in Europeans (6–8 per cent) or Japanese (3·5 per cent). There are also variations in the size of the palmaris longus muscle, the tendon of which lies superficially near the centre of the flexor surface of the wrist; the tendon cannot be detected in some 15–25 per cent of Europeans, but reduction is less frequent in Negroes and in Japanese.

# 16. Biochemical variation

## Introduction

THIS chapter is devoted mainly to variations of proteins because this branch of biochemistry has such important links with genetics. The reasons for this have already been discussed in several parts of the book, including the introduction to this section, and need not be repeated. The structures of the nucleic acids DNA and RNA are even more relevant but at present less accessible. The hybridization techniques mentioned on p. 46 are very useful for assessing divergence of the whole genome, but are not yet sensitive enough for studying subspecific differentiation in man.

The maxim that genetical information becomes clearer the closer one approaches the primary action of the gene applies in the biochemical sphere. For example, normal variations in the level of the blood-sugar are no doubt affected by gene-coded differences in the tissues that participate in its control; but, even if environmental factors can be standardized, these differences will be hard to analyse because the control mechanism has many components. On the other hand, there are many examples of simply inherited and severe metabolic disorders, such as phenylketonuria, galactosaemia, and the storage diseases in which lipids or carbohydrates accumulate in abnormal amounts in certain tissues. Biochemical studies have sharpened diagnosis and in many cases have pinpointed the step in a metabolic pathway that has gone wrong owing to mutational damage to a specific enzyme.

It may be helpful to recall certain general properties of proteins before embarking on specific examples of genetical variation. The proteins are an enormous class of macromolecules, varying in molecular weight from a few thousand to over a million, and varying greatly in their properties and functions. There are thousands of different enzymes, each catalysing a specific chemical reaction in the complex pathways of metabolism. There are proteins such as haemoglobin and transferrin concerned with the transport of particular substances such as oxygen or iron. There are the hormones, secreted by endocrine glands (into the bloodstream) that elicit particular responses in target tissues. Such proteins are water-soluble and in general have a more or less globular shape. There are also fibrous proteins in the form of long chains; some, like keratine of hair and skin, are closely bonded together and difficult to dissolve, while others such as collagen of the connective tissues and actin of muscle-fibres are more easily disrupted.

All proteins are built up of chains of amino acids firmly linked by peptide bonds. It is the sequence of different amino acids (the primary structure) of these chains that is coded by the genes. The polypeptide chains may be thrown into spirals at some parts of their length (secondary structure) and further folded in a specific pattern to form a globular unit. This 'tertiary structure' of the molecule is vital to its function. In many cases, the functional molecule consists of two or more identical or different subunits bonded together to form a larger structure (quaternary structure). The conformation of the molecule is often maintained by relatively weak bonds (hydrogen bonds and hydrophobic bonds) but in many cases firmer (covalent) bonds formed by sulphydryl (SH) groups contribute to stability. These various bonds are formed between the side chains of the amino-acid residues which project at regular intervals from the main (backbone) chain. The side chains vary in size and chemical properties. Some are water-repellent (hydrophobic) and, in the case of soluble proteins, are therefore directed towards the interior of the molecule, others are water-attracting (hydrophilic) and make contact with the aqueous medium at the surface. Some of these hydrophilic side chains are able to ionize and become positively or negatively charged. Changes of surface charge, due to substitution of a different amino acid as a result of a mutation, have made it possible to detect genetical variants by fairly simple methods (electrophoresis).

## Haemoglobin (Hb) variants

Haemoglobin (Hb) must be given pride of place among the proteins we are going to mention because a great deal is known about the structure and function of the molecule and because a large number of variants has been described. The first of these variants to be discovered, sickle-cell Hb, is specially interesting for population genetics as an example of a mutation held at high frequencies in some places by selective forces.

### Sickle-cell haemoglobin (Hb-S)

The beginning of the story was the recognition of a severe type of congenital anaemia in a West Indian in 1910. It was called sickle-cell anaemia (SCA) because blood-films showed that many of the red cells were distorted into an elongated, curved shape. Work on American Negro and African families established that this disease is simply inherited, the SCA cases being homozygous for an allele $Hb^S$. Most of these homozygotes die prematurely unless advanced medical care is available, so that most cases arise from a mating of two heterozygotes who both carry a sickle cell and a normal gene (genotype $Hb^A/Hb^S$). The blood of these heterozygotes looks normal when it is well oxygenated, but if oxygen is removed the cells assume the sickle form, reverting to the normal shape when oxygen is re-admitted. This heterozygous phenotype, known as 'sickle-cell trait' (SCT) is not usually harmful though it can cause trouble at high altitudes when there is oxygen deficiency. The kidney is also mildly deficient in ability to concentrate the urine, and this could be a disadvantage in dehydrating conditions.

An important advance was made by Pauling, Itano, Singer, and Wells in 1949 when they showed the SCT cells contain two types of haemoglobin that can be separated by electrophoresis. We have already mentioned that proteins have a surface charge; the magnitude and sign of this charge depends on the acidity (pH) of the medium. If an alkaline (pH 8·6) solution of normal haemoglobin is placed between electrodes and a voltage is applied, the red protein is seen to migrate towards the positive pole (anode). If this is done with SCT material a more slowly moving type, Hb-S, gradually separates from the normal haemoglobin, Hb-A. Solutions from SCA cases show no Hb-A, but only Hb-S, together with variable amounts of a foetal type of haemoglobin, Hb-F. In a normal new-born child most of the haemoglobin is Hb-F but it is gradually replaced by Hb-A in the first 6 months or so after birth. This transition is incomplete in SCA and certain other severe congenital anaemias. It is interesting that another mutant is also known that causes persistence of Hb-F into adult life. Heterozygotes for this gene occurs at frequencies around 1 per cent in West Africa, and it is found that the adult homozygote has only Hb-F but suffers no obvious disability.

The sickling phenomenon is evidently due to a mutation that makes the Hb much less soluble than normal when in the de-oxygenated state. It therefore precipitates in semi-crystalline sheaves that distort the red cell. Ingram went on to analyse Hb-S in more detail. He did this by first breaking the molecule into smaller fragments (peptides) by digestion with the enzyme trypsin. The mixture of peptides can be separated on filter-paper by applying electrophoresis in one direction followed by *chromatography* at right angles to this. Chromatography has been an immensely useful method for separating small

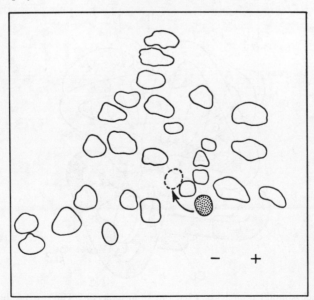

F IG. 16.1. Map of tryptic peptides of whole haemoglobin A. In the case of a digest of haemoglobin S the stippled dot is found to have moved to the position shown by the arrow. The direction of electrophoresis is horizontal and that of chromatography vertical. (Based on Baglioni 1961.)

amounts of biological substances. In one version of the method a strip of filter-paper bearing a spot of the material to be analysed is dipped into a suitable mixture of organic solvents. As the solvent creeps along the paper the more hydrophilic components adhere to the thin water layer on the cellulose and are retarded in relation to more hydrophobic constituents. Ingram was thus able to spread the mixture of Hb-S peptides out on paper and, after staining to show their positions, to compare the pattern of spots (finger-print) with that of Hb-A (Fig. 16.1). This revealed a change in position of one peptide and further analysis showed that it differed from normal in having valine (Val) instead of glutamic acid (Glu) at one position. This is the only difference between Hb-A and Hb-S and it can be accounted for by a change of one base in the corresponding base triplet of the gene (CTT or CTC to CAT or CAC). The amino-acid substitution explains the electrophoretic difference, since Glu is negatively charged while Val is neutral, but it is still not clear how this minute lesion makes Hb-S so insoluble when it is de-oxygenated.

Haemoglobin is a protein of moderate size with a molecular weight of 64 000 and is composed of 4 subunits. These are of two kinds, the $\alpha$- and the $\beta$-chains which differ at 57 per cent of their amino-acid sites but are folded in a closely similar way. The subunit compositions can thus be written $\alpha_2\beta_2$. A third type of chain, $\gamma$, is found in Hb-F ($\alpha_2\gamma_2$) and a fourth, $\delta$, in the minor component, Hb-A$_2$ ($\alpha_2\delta_2$) that is almost always present in normal adult red cells. These chain types arose by gene duplication followed by mutational divergence (see

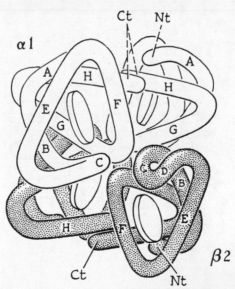

F I G. 16.2. Much-simplified model of a haemoglobin molecule. The two $\alpha$-subunits are light and the two $\beta$-subunits dark. A disc-shaped haeme group is contained in a pocket of each subunit. The helical regions, A–H, are labelled completely for one subunit only. Nt=N-terminal end, Ct=C-terminal end. The view is such as to show the proximity of the F–G and C regions where important $\alpha_1\ \beta_2$ contacts occur.

p. 162) and are thus coded by different gene loci, though the $\beta$, $\delta$, and $\gamma$ loci are closely linked. By convention the amino-acid residues of the chains are numbered starting from the end with a free amino ($NH_2$) group, the N- terminal end. The helical regions are denoted A–H starting again from this end. We can say then that Hb-S differs from Hb-A by having the change Glu$\rightarrow$Val at position 6 of the $\beta$-chain. The manner in which the chains are folded (Fig. 16.2) provides a pocket in which the flat haeme group is anchored by many bonds. The iron atom at the centre of the haeme group is the site of oxygen-binding. A great deal of work has been done, especially by Perutz at Cambridge (England), to discover what happens in the molecule when oxygen ($O_2$) is taken up and released. The process is far from simple; binding of $O_2$ moves a haeme group slightly and sets in train movements between the subunits which increase the $O_2$ affinities of the other haeme groups. These movements also affect the charge in certain regions of the molecule and its ability to bind carbon dioxide ($CO_2$). Quite recently it was discovered that a molecule of 2·3 diphosphoglycerate (2·3 DPG) can be bound at the entrance to the central hollow between the subunits and thus tends to stabilize the deoxy form. Changes in the concentration of this substance in the red cell provide an important mechanism of adjustment to $O_2$ deficiency.

Much has been learned about how haemoglobin works by studying the structure and properties of various mutants. Comparative work has also been important in showing that sites involved in vital functions, such as anchoring the haeme group or allowing movements at subunit contacts, are seldom changed in evolution.

## Other Hb variants

Following the discovery of Hb-S samples from many different populations were screened in the course of clinical work or to map the distribution of this gene. This led to the discovery of many other variants including a few that are quite common (5–30 per cent) in some parts of the world. About 80 $\beta$-chain variants and 50 $\alpha$-chain variants have been analysed and some half-dozen analysed variants of Hb-F and Hb-A$_2$ are also known. Most of these variants have a single amino-acid substitution that alters the surface charge. They seem as a rule to be harmless, at least in the heterozygous state; but, since the majority are rare, the homozygotes have usually not been seen. The preponderance of variants with changed surface charge is due to bias in the method of detection, namely, electrophoresis on paper or starch gels. Only about 25 per cent of the possible mutations would be expected to produce a charge change and the remainder are only likely to be detected if they produce clinical symptoms or obvious changes in the stability of the molecule *in vitro*.

Hb-C is a variant that migrates even more slowly than Hb-S at pH 8·6 (Fig. 16.3) because lysine (Lys) with a positive charge is substituted for Glu; the substitution is in fact at the same site in the $\beta$-chain as in Hb-S. This haemoglobin reaches quite high frequencies in a restricted area of West Africa. The

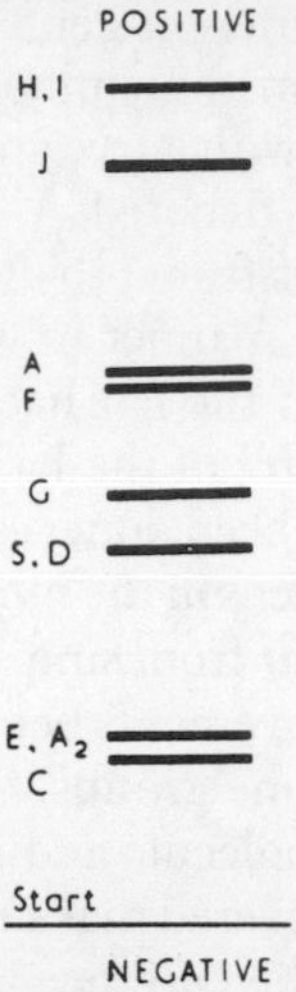

POSITIVE

H,I ━━━━

J ━━━━

A ━━━━
F ━━━━

G ━━━━
S,D ━━━━

E,A₂ ━━━━
C ━━━━

Start ━━━━━━━━

NEGATIVE

FIG. 16.3. The approximate relative positions of a number of different haemoglobins when separated by electrophoresis on paper. (Veronal buffer pH 8·6.)

homozygote ($Hb^C/Hb^C$) shows mild abnormalities of the blood film but suffers no great disadvantage.

Another slowly migrating variant, Hb-E, is common in Thailand and adjacent areas. The substitution is $\beta$26 Glu→ Lys. Again the homozygote is only mildly affected despite the fact that the substitution is in a subunit contact area and the $O_2$ affinity is somewhat lowered as a result.

Hb-D has been found in various parts of the world and reaches its highest frequencies (1–5 per cent) in Sikhs and Gujeratis. It has the same mobility as Hb-S but does not cause sickling. Later studies on Hb-D from various regions showed that it is heterogeneous, thus illustrating the limitations of simple electrophoretic screening of whole Hb for the identification of mutants. Hb-D Punjab ($\beta$ 121 Glu→ Gln) proved to be the same as half a dozen variants that were at first given different names. On the other hand, three other Hb-Ds have different compositions; Hb-D Ibadan is $\beta$87 Thr→ Lys, Hb-D Bushman is $\beta$16 Gly→Arg, and Hb-D Baltimore is $\alpha$68 Asn→Lys. Another group of haemoglobins, Hb-G, has also proved to be heterogeneous.

Among the more deleterious mutants we may mention the Hb-M group in which the patient has an abnormally high concentration of methaemoglobin, the brown derivative with the haeme iron in the oxidized (ferric) states. Since methaemoglobin cannot be reversibly oxygenated, the carriage of $O_2$ is decreased and a blue colour (cyanosis) is seen in affected infants. However, this defect is well compensated and compatible with a normal life, at least in western societies. In normal haemoglobin, histidines (His) at site 8 of the F-helix and site 7 on the E-helix interact with the haeme iron and tend to keep it in the reduced state. In four of the known Hb-Ms these histidines are replaced by tyrosine (Tyr) at $\alpha$F8, $\alpha$E7, $\beta$F8, and $\beta$E7 respectively.

There is also a group of mutants in which either the $\alpha$- or $\beta$-subunit is unstable because an uncharged residue in the interior is replaced by another of unsuitable size or chemical properties. In some of them (e.g. Hbs Torino, Bibba, and Sydney) bonding of the haeme group is weakened and it may fall out of the haeme pocket. The globin then undergoes structural collapse and precipitates in the cell, forming Heinz bodies. In Hb Genova proline (Pro), which is normally found near the ends of helices or in interhelical regions, is inserted in the B-helix and disrupts it. In Hb Wien a charged residue, aspartic acid (Asp), is substituted for an internal Tyr, producing marked instability and consequent anaemia even in the heteroxygote. Some variants, such as Hb Chesapeake, J Capetown, Yakkim, and Kempsey have raised $O_2$ affinity due to a substitution at a contact between $\alpha$- and $\beta$-subunits ($\alpha_1\beta_2$ contact) and a compensatory increase of red-cell count is observed.

In addition to damaging substitutions at a single site there are a few mutants in which one or more sites are deleted, probably due to crossing-over between slightly misaligned genes. In the Hbs Freiburg and Leiden one residue is missing and in Hb Gun Hill five residues are absent in a region of the $\beta$-chain that has important haeme bonds.

Another interesting variant is Hb Harlem, with two substitutions $\beta6$ Val$\rightarrow$ Glu as in Hb-S and $\beta73$ Asp$\rightarrow$ Asn, which occurs separately in an African variant, Hb Korle-bu. This suggests that Hb Harlem may have originated by a simple cross-over between these two alleles.

TABLE 16.1

| Haemoglobin variant | Site | Change | Effects |
|---|---|---|---|
| M Boston | $\alpha58$ (E7) | His$\rightarrow$Tyr | Haeme iron of the abnormal |
| M Iwate | $\alpha87$ (F8) | His$\rightarrow$Tyr | chain is stabilized in the |
| M Saskatoon | $\beta63$ (E7) | His$\rightarrow$Tyr | ferric state preventing its |
| M Hyde Park | $\beta92$ (F8) | His$\rightarrow$Tyr | combination with $O_2$. |
| Torino | $\alpha43$ (CD1) | Phe$\rightarrow$Val | Destroys a contact with haeme group. Unstable at 50 °C. Inclusion body anaemia. |
| Hammersmith | $\beta42$ (CD1) | Phe$\rightarrow$Ser | Haeme pocket accessible to water. Unstable at 50 °C. Inclusion body anaemia. |
| Sydney | $\beta67$ (E11) | Val$\rightarrow$Ala | Destroys a haeme contact. Unstable. Haemolytic anaemia. |
| E | $\beta26$ (B8) | Glu$\rightarrow$Lys | Weakens $\alpha_1\beta_1$ contact; lowered $O_2$ affinity. |
| Chesapeake | $\alpha92$ (FG4) | Arg$\rightarrow$Leu | Affects $\alpha_1\beta_2$ contact; raised |
| J Capetown | $\alpha92$ (FG4) | Arg$\rightarrow$Gln | $O_2$ affinity. |
| Yakima | $\beta99$ (G1) | Asp$\rightarrow$His | |
| Kempsey | $\beta99$ (G1) | Asp$\rightarrow$Asn | |
| Wien | $\beta130$ (H8) | Tyr$\rightarrow$Asp | Polar group replaces internal non-polar group. Unstable. Haemolytic anaemia. |
| Genova | $\beta28$ (B10) | Leu$\rightarrow$Pro | Proline disrupts B-helix. Haemolytic anaemia. |
| Gun Hill | $\beta92-96$ deleted | | Affects haeme contacts and contacts between subunits. Loss of haeme. Haemolytic anaemia. |

The Lepore group of deleterious variants are apparently due to cross-overs between different loci occupying adjacent positions on the chromosome (intercistronic cross-overs). Hb Lepore itself has a chain consisting of the first 87 residues of the $\delta$-chain and the last 31 of the $\beta$. There are other examples of such $\delta$–$\beta$ or $\beta$–$\delta$ fusions involving different positions on the two chains.

The properties of some of these deleterious mutants are summarized in Table 16.1. It will be evident from what has been said above that the effect of a mutation depends on the precise position of the resulting change in the three-dimensional structure of the molecule and the properties of the amino acid that is inserted or lost.

## Thalassemia

The Hb variants mentioned so far all have structural changes in the molecule. There is another group of inherited variations characterized by partial or complete failure of synthesis of one or other of the normal chains. The name 'thalassemia major' (Greek $\theta\alpha\lambda\alpha\sigma\sigma\alpha$, the sea) was given to a fatal type of congenital anaemia because it was commonly found in children of Mediterranean origin; it is also known as Cooley's anaemia. The blood-film shows many red cells of grossly abnormal size and shape and with a low mean Hb content. Compensatory growth of the bone marrow causes thickening of the skull vault and facial bones and growth is retarded. Electrophoresis shows Hb-A together with a variable amount (10–90 per cent) of Hb-F.

Cases of Cooley's anaemia are homozygous for a mutation $\beta^{thal}$, which is closely linked to the $\beta^{A}$ locus or possibly an allele. The heterozygous parents usually show a milder version of the disorder (thalassemia minor) but the blood-picture is very variable, ranging from normal to a condition similar to that in homozygotes. This variability is one reason for suspecting that there are at least two types of $\beta$ thalassemia, due to mutations that differ in severity of their effects. Reliable detection of heterozygotes in population surveys is not easy and requires several tests including red-cell counts and estimations of Hb level and red-cell fragility. An increase in the relative concentration of Hb-$A_2$ to about 5 per cent on average and, in many cases, a slight rise of Hb-F level are also useful diagnostic signs. The diagnosis is particularly difficult in populations with much anaemia due to iron deficency, an exception to the rule that the phenotypes of biochemical variations are easily distinguishable irrespective of environment.

Since $\beta$ thalassemia is quite common in certain regions where the structural variants, Hb-S, Hb-C, and Hb-E are also frequent, we can find heterozygotes carrying both types of mutation. The clinical and biochemical manifestations of sickle-cell thalassemia (genotypes $\beta^{thal}/\beta^{S}$) are very variable. Some cases are only mildly anaemic, others are as severely affected as sickle-cell anaemics. Depending on the degree of suppression of $\beta$-chain synthesis by the $\beta^{thal}$ gene the cells may contain mainly Hb-S or there may also be as much as 30 per cent of Hb-A. The symptoms of Hb-C thalassemia are also variable; in Negroes the condition is usually mild but Italian cases are often more severe. It has been suggested that this is because there are two different genes, denoted $\beta^{thal+}$ and $\beta^{thal\,o}$ respectively. Hb-E thalassemia is quite common in Thailand, and often gives rise to a condition similar to Cooley's analinia. It is clear that these deleterious interactions between $\beta$ thalassemia and structural variants must be taken into account in considering the action of natural selection on the frequencies of these genes (see p. 232).

It should be noted that Hb Lepore, which we mentioned earlier, produces a $\beta$-thalassemic condition because synthesis of the $\beta$–$\delta$ fusion product is abnormally slow.

As might be expected there are other types of thalassemia in which synthesis of the $\alpha$- rather than the $\beta$-chain is affected. The first form of $\alpha$ thalassemia to be recognized was Hb-H disease. This is an anaemic condition characterized by the presence of large amounts of a fast-migrating haemoglobin, Hb-H. This is not a variant of primary structure but a tetramer comprised of normal $\beta$-chains ($\beta 4$). It is somewhat unstable and staining with brilliant cresyl blue reveals many red cells with inclusions of precipitated Hb-H. Hb-H is produced because partial suppression of $\alpha$-chain synthesis leaves an excess of $\beta$-chains which then combine. If children who later develop Hb-H disease are examined at birth another fast-migrating haemoglobin, Hb Barts, is found in the cord blood. This is a tetramer of normal $\gamma$-chains ($\gamma 4$), a foetal version, as it were, of Hb-H.

It is commonly found that one of the parents of a case of Hb-H disease has mild thalassemic signs while the the other is virtually normal. The great difficulty of detecting the adult heterozygotes has been an obstacle in work on the genetics and population distribution of $\alpha$ thalassemias, but surveys of the amount of Hb Barts in the cord blood have yielded useful information. In parts of Thailand up to 30 per cent of infants have this Hb, but the concentration varies from 1 per cent to 90 per cent of the total haemoglobin and seems to fall into several distinct ranges. Very high concentration of Hb Barts is associated with a fatal oedematous condition (hydrops foetalis) of the newborn, while lower concentrations (around 30 per cent) are associated with Hb-H disease in later life. Putting together various lines of evidence it has been suggested that two different $\alpha$-thalassemia genes, $\alpha^{thal}_1$ and $\alpha^{thal}_2$ can be recognized. Homozygosity for $\alpha^{thal}_1$ leads to hydrops foetalis, while the heterozygote $\alpha^{thal}_1/\alpha^{thal}_2$ develops Hb-H disease. The heterozygote carrying one normal and one $\alpha^{thal}_1$ gene shows mild thalassemia as an adult while the heterozygote $\alpha^{thal}_2/\alpha^A$ can only be detected by the presence of 1–2 per cent of Hb Barts in the cord blood.

A very curious $\alpha$-chain variant which produces Hb-H disease when the gene is present together with an $\alpha$-thalassemia gene must also be mentioned. Hb Constant Spring has 31 additional residues attached to the C-terminal end of the $\alpha$-chain, perhaps due to a mutation of a chain-terminating codon. These abnormal $\alpha$-chains are either synthesized slowly or rapidly destroyed so that only very small amounts ( < 1 per cent) of the variant Hb are found in the blood and can easily be overlooked. It seems that this variant may be quite frequent in parts of the Far East.

The nature of the fundamental defect in the classical thalassemia mutations is still uncertain. In principle, it could be at the transcriptional level, leading to decreased production of mRNA, or it could affect one or other of the components involved in translating the messenger code into protein. Present evidence favours the first explanation but it is not clear whether there is a structural defect in the mRNA itself or whether we are dealing with a defective regulatory locus that controls the activity of the structural genes.

*The question of duplicate loci.* Interpretation of $\alpha$ thalassemias must take account of evidence that there are two $\alpha$ loci, at any rate in some populations. There are good reasons for believing that this locus is duplicated in certain other mammals, including the chimpanzee, and it is accepted that there are two human $\gamma$-chain loci and perhaps more. Schroeder has shown that Hb-F is a mixture of two types of molecule, one with glycine and the other with alanine at site 136 of the $\gamma$-chain.

It has been pointed out that heterozygotes for $\alpha$-chain structural variants generally have 25 per cent or less of the variant Hb, whereas heterozygotes for $\beta$-chain variants quite often have roughly equal amounts of Hb-A and the variant Hb. Duplication of the $\alpha$ but not the $\beta$ locus is a possible explanation but the evidence is not entirely consistent. More convincing are the observations on a Hungarian family segregating for two $\alpha$-chain variants. Some individuals had *both* these variants together with Hb-A indicating that three different $\alpha$ loci were present. On the other hand, homozygotes for the $\alpha$-chain variant Hb-J Tongariki, which was first discovered at moderate frequencies in a New Hebridean island, have no Hb-A. This is not compatible with the two locus theory unless we assume that the variant gene is closely linked to an $\alpha$-thalassemia locus that suppresses production of normal $\alpha$-chains completely.

## Population genetics and geographical distribution of Hb variants

More than 130 structural variants of Hb are known but only three of them, Hb-S, Hb-C, and Hb-E, are found in fairly large areas of the world at heterozygote frequencies of 10 per cent or higher. Many populations in the wet tropical belt of Africa have 20–30 per cent of the sickle-cell trait and comparably high values occur in a few Mediterranean localities and in various peoples of India (Fig. 16.4). In northern Europe and eastwards from India the gene is rare and it was almost certainly absent in the New World before the advent of African slaves. Hb-C is frequent in a somewhat restricted area of West Africa centring on Upper Volta and Northern Ghana, while Hb-E is remarkably common in Thailand and adjacent countries but fades out in Bengal and at the margins of Australasia.

A few other variants attain heterozygote frequencies around 5 per cent loc-

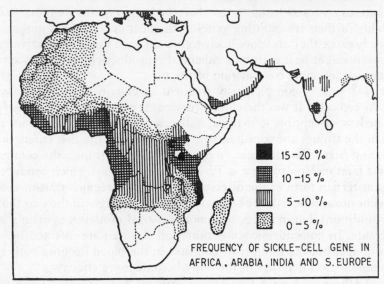

15 – 20 %
10 –15 %
5 –10 %
0 –5 %

FREQUENCY OF SICKLE-CELL GENE IN
AFRICA , ARABIA , INDIA AND S. EUROPE

FIG. 16.4. Frequency of the sickle-cell gene Hb$^S$ in various parts of the Old World. (After Allison, in *Genetical variation in human populations*, 1961.)

ally, e.g. Hb-D in the north-west of the Indian subcontinent, Hb-K in parts of West and North Africa, and Hb-O Indonesia in Celebes. The great majority of Hb variants are rare and do not reach a gene frequency of 1 per cent, which is sometimes taken as the arbitrary lower limit defining a polymorphism.

The incidence of genetical variants is sometimes given in terms of the frequency of the gene and sometimes of the heterozygote (trait frequency) and it is important not to confuse the two. The gene frequency is the more useful for theoretical work, but it is an inference from the phenotype and may therefore be uncertain unless relations between genotype and phenotype are entirely clear. It is worth noting that in simple cases, where one of a pair of alleles has a frequency of 10 per cent or less, the gene frequency is roughly half the heterozygote frequency since most of the variant genes are in the heterozygous state; but the error of neglecting the homozygotes increases as the gene frequency rises.

The high frequency of the gene Hb$^S$ in certain regions immediately poses a problem. Since sickle-cell homozygotes die prematurely, especially where medical facilities are lacking, Hb$^S$ genes are lost in each generation. One would therefore expect the gene frequency to fall to quite low levels in a period of several hundred years due to this negative selection. However, this loss of Hb$^S$ genes could be compensated if the heterozygotes are fitter than the normal homozygotes. In this case the Hb$^S$ frequency would reach an equilibrium level to which it would gradually return after a deviation caused, for instance, by an influx of Hb$^S$ or Hb$^A$ genes from outside the population. This type of equilibrium is said to be 'stable' and the polymorphism balanced. When we speak of the heterozygotes as being 'fitter' than the homozygotes we mean that the probability of their transmitting genes to the next generation is higher. This could be because they are more likely to live through the reproductive period of life, or it might be a matter of enhanced reproductive performance rather than survival, or some combination of the two.

The $Hb^S$ gene is conspicuously frequent in certain tropical regions and affects the red cells. It was therefore a reasonable guess that the heterozygotes might be less susceptible to malaria, a disease which is responsible for many deaths in the tropics and is caused by a protozoan parasite that enters the red cells during part of its life cycle. In many parts of the tropics the commonest and most fatal malaria parasite is *Plasmodium falciparum* which produces the malignant tertian form of the disease. In the wetter regions transmission by anopheline mosquitoes is more or less continuous throughout the year (holoendemic condition), but in places with more seasonal rainfall it is mainly in the wet periods. In holoendemic zones nearly all children are infected by about 2 years of age, but the number of parasites in the blood declines with age as the immunological defences of the body become more effective.

In 1954 Allison working on East African children, found that sicklers were less frequently infected with *P. falciparum* than were non-sicklers and that the number of parasites in a unit volume of blood was also lower on average. This result, which was confirmed by later studies, supports the idea that the sickle-cell trait confers some resistance to malaria in young children but it is inconclusive from the point of view of selection because it tells us nothing directly about differential mortality. In impoverished and disease-ridden countries it is often difficult to assign a precise cause of death in early childhood, though the sharp decline of deaths in this age range that often follows malaria eradication leaves little doubt that this disease is a major killer. There is, however, a particularly severe form of the disease in which the parasites invade the brain (cerebral malaria): deaths from cerebral malaria can be diagnosed with more confidence and it is significant that the frequency of sicklers among them is strikingly low.

If sicklers are less likely to die of malaria than non-sicklers then the proportion of sicklers in the population should be higher at older ages than it is in the first year of life. The magnitude of the expected change can be calculated from the relation $p_e/q_e = t/s$, where $p_e$ and $q_e$ are the equilibrium frequencies of $Hb^A$ and $Hb^S$ and $t$ and $s$ are the selective coefficents against the sickle cell and normal homozygotes respectively. If, for example, $Hb^S$ is in equilibrium at 15 per cent gene frequency and cases of sickle-cell anaemia are assumed to have zero fitness ($t=1\cdot0$) then the normals should be about 17 per cent less fit than the sicklers. Estimates of the relative fitness of sicklers and normals obtained in field studies accord reasonably well with expectation.

There is some evidence that sickler females may be more fertile than non-sickler females so that the fitness differential may not be wholly due to mortality in childhood. It is thought that invasion of the placenta by malaria parasites may sometimes cause stillbirth or neonatal death. These deaths would presumably be less frequent in births to sickler mothers if the trait confers some immunity during pregnancy.

The geographical distribution of $Hb^S$ is consistent with the malaria hypothesis in that the highest gene frequencies occur in regions where malignant tertian malaria is highly endemic, or has been so until quite recently. An exact correspondence is not to be expected because population movements may have changed the local gene frequency pattern and there has been too little time for equilibrium levels to be re-established. In East Africa the gene is infrequent or absent in Nilo-Hamitic pastoralists. This may be because they came from, and still inhabit, less malarious regions. It has also been suggested that the presence of cattle may divert the mosquitoes from biting humans. It may be that malaria only became a serious disease in the wet tropics when the rain forest was opened to agriculture and population densities increased. Possibly certain Liberian tribes have low sickling frequencies because they represent such an ancient forest population, but it is worth noting that sickling is frequent among the Efe Pygmies of the Ituri forest. In India the highest frequencies of $Hb^S$ are found in some of the tribal peoples, who are hunters and slash and burn agriculturalists, and also in certain lower Hindu castes that may be partly derived from them. Patches of high sickling, as in parts of Greece and certain Southern Arabian oases, may be correlated with locally intense malaria.

In general the $Hb^S$ frequencies in American Negroes are around 5 per cent which is about half that in many West-African populations; but there are some more or less isolated groups in which the gene frequency reaches 10 per cent. When slaves were taken from West Africa to the generally less malarious environment of the New World the selective advantage of the heterozygotes presumably declined or disappeared and the gene frequency would then have fallen due to selection against the homozygotes; but there are several uncertainties that complicate the interpretation of this situation. The initial gene frequencies are open to some doubt because the levels in West Africa are not uniform and slaves were exported from different regions to various parts of the Americas. In addition there has obviously been a good deal of intermixture with Europeans or American Indians and this would also lower $Hb^S$ frequencies. The extent of this intermixture no doubt varied in different places. In principle it can be estimated by studying a number of genes that have widely different frequencies in the parental populations but are not considered to be so strongly influenced by selection as $Hb^S$. The frequencies of the blood-group genes $R_0$ and $Fy^A$, for example, are very different in Africans and Europeans; but again the data are limited and there are some doubts about the relevant parental frequencies. It is also an oversimplification to suppose that the selective advantage of the $Hb^S$ heterozygotes was entirely abolished in the New World. Whether malaria of any kind was present in pre-Columbian times is disputed, but $P. falciparum$ is now well established in parts of Central and South America and it was present in the southern USA until quite recently.

The gene $Hb^C$ has a focus of high frequency (10–15 per cent) in a limited area of West Africa. It is not clear whether it confers protection against malaria or any other selective agent. Since the homozygous state for this gene is only mildly deleterious a small advantage of the heterozygote would suffice to maintain quite high equilibrium levels, but would be difficult to detect. However the situation is more complicated because $Hb^C$ occurs in regions where its allele $Hb^S$ is also frequent. The heterozygote $Hb^S/Hb^C$ is clearly at some disadvantage though it is not so severely affected as $Hb^S$ homozygotes. Whether the three alleles, $Hb^A$, $Hb^S$, and $Hb^C$ can co-exist at equilibrium or whether either $Hb^S$ or $Hb^C$ will be excluded depends on the relative fitnesses of the various genotypes and it is difficult to measure these fitnesses with the required accuracy. In those parts of West Africa where both $Hb^S$ and $Hb^C$ occur it is found that there is a negative correlation between their frequencies, $Hb^S$ being low where $Hb^C$ is high. It is possible that $Hb^C$ is spreading and ousting $Hb^S$ but this is by no means certain. We have already mentioned the diseases due to interaction between $\beta$ thalassemia and $\beta$-chain structural variants. Since $\beta$ thalassemia is known to occur in West Africa this is an additional, though perhaps minor, complication.

## Glucose 6-phosphate dehydrogenase (G6PD) variants

The mature red cell gets energy for its limited metabolic activities by anaerobic breakdown of glucose to lactate (Embden–Meyerhof glycolytic pathway). G6PD is active on a side loop (the hexosemonophosphate shunt, HMS) of this main path. It catalyses the conversion of glucose 6-phosphate to 6-phosphogluconate in the presence of the coenzyme NADP, which is reduced to NADPH in the process. NADPH is required to keep glutathione, a cysteine-containing tripeptide, in the reduced form (GSH), and this in turn appears to be important in stabilizing the red-cell membrane. Deficiencies of G6PD activity are often associated with a tendency for red cells to burst (haemolyse) when exposed to certain drugs and infective agents. In its active form the enzyme is a dimer of molecular weight 100 000, and the two subunits are thought to be identical and to be produced by a single gene locus (cistron).

It was noticed in the Korean War that many American Negro soldiers had episodes of haemolysis when given the antimalarial drug, primaquine. This primaquine-sensitivity was later traced to an inherited X-linked deficiency of G6PD activity. Electrophoretic screening of haemolysates, using specific stains to reveal the position of G6PD, shows that in many tropical African peoples two variants of the enzyme are remarkably frequent (about 20 per cent each). At pH 8·6 both migrate more rapidly towards the anode than the normal form [Gd(Bt)]. One of them, Gd(A+), has only slightly reduced activity in laboratory tests. The other, Gd(A−), has much lower activity (8–20 per cent of the normal level) and is associated with sensitivity to primaquine and various other drugs. It seems that the mutant enzyme decays unusually quickly in the mature red cell and it is mainly old cells that are deficient; activity in white cells and other tissues is normal.

A more severe type of G6PD deficiency, known as Gd-Mediterranean or Gd(B−), is frequent (15–20 per cent) in parts of Greece, Sardinia, the Middle East, and eastwards to India. The highest known frequency (50–60 per cent) is in a Jewish isolate that formerly lived in Kurdistan, but frequencies in European Jews are much lower. The activity of the enzyme in assays of haemolysates is less than 7 per cent of normal and activity in leucocytes is also reduced. The levels of enzyme activity in heterozygous females lie between those of hemizygous males and normal subjects, while female homozygotes are about as severely affected as the former. At least in some populations this type of G6PD deficiency is associated with increased susceptibility to jaundice in the newborn and to haemolysis after certain infections and after eating fava beans (*Vicia fava*). The disease known as 'favism' has been recognized in parts of the Mediterranean since classical times, and it can sometimes be fatal if modern treatment is not available. Susceptibility to favism seems to depend on other factors besides G6PD deficiency, but these are poorly understood.

With the example of haemoglobin in mind, it is perhaps not surprising that over 70 different variants of G6PD have been described. A battery of specialized laboratory methods is needed to identify them. These methods include electrophoretic comparisons, assays of activity with various substrates and at different ranges of pH, determination of affinity constants, and tests of heat stability. It should be remembered that activity tests *in vitro* are not necessarily a sure guide to the activity of the enzymes in the intact cells. The concentration of the enzyme in blood is low (1·0 mg/per 500 ml) and it is therefore difficult to get enough material to analyse the amino acid and sequences of variants; but there is evidence that Gd(A+) may differ from the normal enzyme [Gd(Bt)] by a single amino-acid substitution.

The majority of G6PD variants are rare and a considerable proportion of them show lowered activity. A thorough study in one region of Greece, where the overall frequency of severe deficiency was about 20 per cent, showed that Gd-Mediterranean accounted for 70 per cent of the cases but that 3 other variants causing severe deficiency, 3 causing mild deficiency, and 3 with normal activity were also present at low frequencies. G6PD deficiency is found in about 5 per cent of southern Chinese; it is due to at least three different variants the commonest of which is Gd Canton. Another variant, Gd Markham, seems to be fairly common in lowland areas of New Guinea. Although haemolysis due to G6PD deficiency is usually transient and elicited only by certain environmental agents, there are also several rare variants that are associated with chronic haemolysis (non-spherocytic haemolytic anaemias). Two points emerge clearly from work on this enzyme: G6PD deficiency is a very heterogeneous condition, and some of the variants causing it are characteristic of certain regions of the world.

Since the G6PD locus is X-linked, deficiencies are fully expressed in hemizygous males and the frequency of these gives an immediate estimate of the gene frequency. As we have seen, some of the common types of deficiency are deleterious to males in certain circumstances. We may ask how some populations have attained such high gene frequencies and whether these frequencies are at equilibrium. The gene-frequency dynamics of sex-linked recessives are complicated because we have to consider the relative fitnesses of 3 female and 2 male genotypes. Whether stable equilibrium at intermediate frequencies (i.e. between zero and 1·0) can be achieved depends critically on these fitness values and at present we can only estimate them very roughly for G6PD phenotypes. Balanced polymorphism is theoretically possible if there is heterozygous advantage in females or if the presence of the gene is advantageous in one sex but disadvantageous in the other; even so the differences of fitness must be within a certain range.

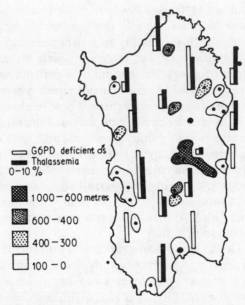

G6PD deficient ♂'s
Thalassemia
0–10 %

1 000 – 600 metres

600 – 400

400 – 300

100 – 0

FIG. 16.5. The frequencies of thalassemia and of G6PD deficient males in various regions of Sardinia, showing the correlation between the incidences of these conditions and altitude. The lower regions are the most malarious. The incidence of thalassemia is phenotype frequencies. (From Bernini, Carcassi, Latte, Motulsky, Romei, and Siniscalco, *Accad. Naz. Lincei*, 1960.

High frequencies of G6PD deficiency are usually found in areas that are, or were until recently, highly endemic for *P. falciparum* malaria. In East Africa and in Sardinia (Fig. 16.5), for example, the geographical correlation is impressive and suggests that the trait may have some protective value against this disease. In heterozygous females some red cells are G6PD deficient and some normal because one X-chromosome is inactivated at random. It is therefore possible to study the susceptibility of the two cell types to infection by *P. falciparum* in the same individual and it has been found that the deficient cells are less often invaded. Presumably both males and females are protected in this way although this advantage is offset to some extent in males and homozygous females by other, deleterious effects of the mutant allele.

## Variations of other red-cell enzymes

The list of enzymes that can be separated and specifically stained on starch gels is now long. We can only mention a few of them, choosing mainly ones that have been studied in a fair range of populations. Usually we find one or two variant alleles at polymorphic frequencies and rare alleles that come to light in large samples. No doubt technical refinements will reveal still more heterogeneity. Homozygous phenotypes may show single bands or a series of isozyme bands. Heterozygous patterns sometimes consist of simple additions of the bands produced by the two constituent alleles, but in some cases formation of hybrid molecules complicates the pattern.

### Red-cell acid phosphatase (AP)

This enzyme splits phosphate from various organic phosphates including phenolphthalein phosphate. Since phenolphthalein is an indicator dye that turns red in alkali this provides a simple method of locating sites of enzyme activity on the gel. Fig. 16.6 shows some of the commoner phenotypes, which can be accounted for by segregation of 3 alleles, formerly written $P^A$, $P^B$, and $P^C$. The phenotypes differ somewhat according to the buffer system that is used. However, recent evidence shows that 3 different loci may be involved in synthesis of this enzyme. These are now denoted as $ACP_1$, $ACP_2$, and $ACP_3$, and the common alleles become $ACP_1{}^A$, $ACP_1{}^B$, and $ACP_1{}^C$. It was thought at first that this acid phosphatase only occurs in red cells, but it can be detected in other tissues also if a suitable substrate is used; however, its physiological

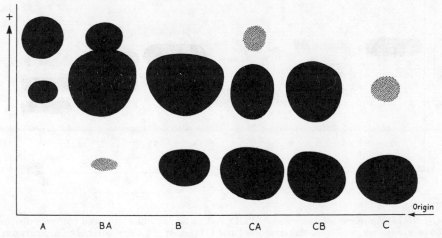

F IG. 16.6. Phenotypes of human red-cell acid phosphatase as seen when stained on starch gel. This represents the appearance when succinate buffer is used. (Based on Giblett, *Genetic markers in human blood*, 1969.)

role remains uncertain. The enzyme activity attributable to the products of the 3 alleles increases in the order $ACP_1$, $ACP_1$, $ACP_1$. Nevertheless, the distribution of activity for a random population sample is unimodal, because the activity range for each phenotype is wide and there is much overlapping; the underlying heterogeneity is thus concealed.

In general $ACP_1{}^B$ is the most frequent allele, ranging from about 60 per cent to 80 per cent, while $ACP_1{}^C$ is the least frequent. The latter is commonest in Europe (4–9 per cent) and less frequent in most other populations. The European range for $ACP_1{}^A$ is about 35–8 per cent, with rather higher values for some Lapp populations, but in Africa, as far as the evidence goes, frequencies of this allele are considerably lower. In New World Aborigines frequencies of $ACP_1{}^A$ seem to vary widely (25–67 per cent). A number of rare alleles have also been described.

### 6-phosphogluconate dehydrogenase (6PGD)

This enzyme follows G6PD in the HMS pathway, oxidizing 6-phosphogluconate to ribulose 5-phosphate and thereby generating NADPH. It seems that only one variant allele, $PGD^C$, is at all frequent anywhere. The phenotype patterns in white-cell extracts are quite simple (a in Fig. 16.7); the homozygotes for the normal alleles $PGD^A$ show a single band and the $PGD^C$ homozygotes have a single more cathodal band; heterozygotes, however, have an additional strong band of intermediate mobility attributed to recombination between molecular subunits. In human red cells, the $PGD^C$ homozygote and the $PGD^A$/$PGD^C$ heterozygote have more complex patterns (b in Fig. 16.7). The product

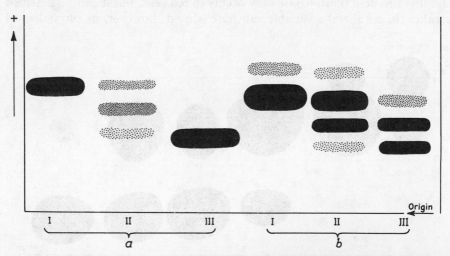

F I G. 16.7. Commoner phenotypes of 6PGD as seen in (a) white cells and (b) red cells. In the case of the white cells the homozygotes I and III consist of a single band. The heterozygote II has weaker bands corresponding to these in position but also a third intermediate band formed by recombination of subunits. The red-cell patterns are more complex. (Based on Giblett, *Genetic markers in human blood*, 1969.)

of the *PGD*^C allele has somewhat reduced activity in comparison with the normal enzymes and is less stable. Other rare alleles are known and some of these are associated with a more marked deficiency of activity.

The frequency of *PGD*^C varies around 3 per cent in Europe but appears to be rather higher in some African and Far East populations. Quite high frequencies have been reported in Bhutan (21 per cent) and amongst South African Bantu (15 per cent).

### Adenylate kinase (AK)

The enzyme is present in various tissues besides red cells and catalyses the conversion of adenosine triphosphate to adenosine diphosphate and monophosphate. In the standard starch-gel procedure the commonest phenotype (AK1) appears as a series of bands decreasing in strength towards the anode (Fig. 16.8). A variant allele, *AK*² produces a more cathodal type which is

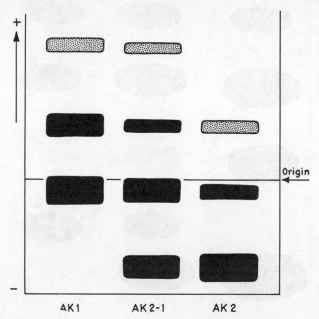

FIG. 16.8. The three commonest phenotypes of human adenylate kinase. The homozygote AK2 is rare. The heterozygote is composed of an addition of the bands present in AK1 and AK2. (From Giblett, *Genetic markers in human blood*, 1969.)

generally seen in heterozygous form (AK²⁻¹) because this allele is infrequent in most parts of the world. *AK*² frequencies are around 2–5 per cent in most European populations but in Africa and in many Asiatic populations this allele is less common. However, frequencies of about 10 per cent have been reported in several Indian populations. Naturally these relatively low frequency values of *AK*² have quite high standard errors if sample sizes are only a few hundred.

*Phosphoglucomutase (PGM)*

This enzyme, which catalyses the conversion of glucose 1-phosphate to glucose 6-phosphate, is also found in various tissues. It is produced by three loci which are not closely linked. The products of the loci $PGM_1$ and $PGM_2$ appear as two distinct sets of isozyme bands when haemolysates are examined by standard methods. The products of the third locus $PGM_3$ are not, as a rule, detectable in red cells but can be seen as a set of even more anodal bands in extracts of tissues such as placenta. A number of variant alleles at each of these three loci are known but only a few of them are common. Fig. 16.9 shows the phenotype patterns associated with the common $PGM_1$ alleles $PGM_1^1$ and $PGM_1^2$. The frequency of $PGM_1^1$ in England is 76 per cent and (if we exclude

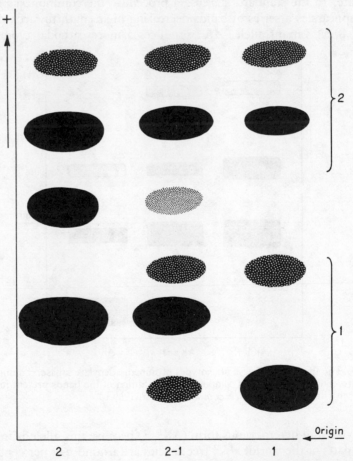

FIG. 16.9. Common phenotypes of human phosphoglucomutase. The pattern consists of a more cathodal set of bands produced by the $PGM_1$ gene and a more anodal set produced by the $PGM_2$ gene. In the diagram only variants at the $PGM_1$ locus are shown. The heterozygote pattern is seen to be an addition of the homozygous patterns 1 and 2. (Based on Giblett, *Genetic markers in human blood*, 1969.)

a few aberrant frequencies in small isolates) most values for other populations lie between 65 per cent and 85 per cent, with a tendency for high levels in African and American aborigines. The frequency of this allele in Lapps is sometimes low (45–79 per cent) but varies between Lapp groups. The rare variants $PGM_1{}^6$ and $PGM_1{}^7$ were found at frequencies of 1 per cent each in a Chinese sample. None of the four or more variant alleles of the $PGM_2$ locus seems to be common; $PGM_2{}^2$ has been detected at frequencies around 1 per cent in a number of African samples and was originally known as the Atkinson variant.

### Lactic dehydrogenase (LDH)

The enzyme is a tetramer formed of two types of subunit, A and B, which are products of different loci. The usual pattern in red-cell preparations is a series of 5 bands (Fig. 16.10). The most anodal band consists of 4 A subunits and the most cathodal band of 4 B subunits; the other 3 bands contain varying

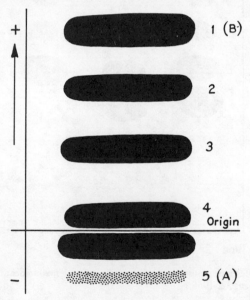

FIG. 16.10. The common pattern of lactic dehydrogenase in human blood-cells. There are 5 bands. The first of these is composed of 4 B-subunits and the fifth of 4 A-subunits. The 3 intermediate bands are products of subunit recombination. (Based on Giblett, *Genetic markers in human blood*, 1969.)

proportions of the 2 subunits (AAAB, AABB, ABBB). The relative strengths of the bands vary a good deal in different tissues. Electrophoretic variants of both the A and B subunits have been described but they do not seem to be common anywhere; 1–2 per cent of variant phentotypes have been reported in American Negro and Asiatic Indian samples but their distribution remains to be worked out in detail.

*Adenosine deaminase (ADA)*

The three commonest phenotypes of this enzyme are shown in Fig. 16.11. The frequency of the allele $ADA^2$ is about 5 per cent in much of Europe, but apparently rather high in Italians and Greeks and higher still (11–14 per cent) in various Jewish groups and in those Indian populations that have been tested. Again the Lapps, with $ADA^2$ frequencies of 10–16 per cent, diverge from most other Scandinavian peoples though this allele is also relatively common in Finns (10 per cent). A number of African populations have been found to have low $ADA^2$ frequencies (0–3 per cent), and the values for Greenland Eskimos and Japanese are also low (3 per cent).

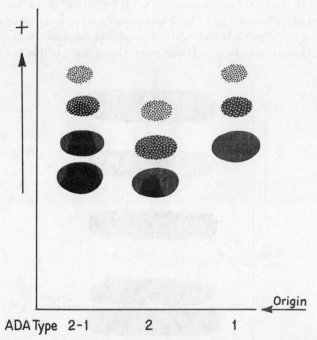

F I G. 16.11. The three commonest phenotypes of human adenosine deaminase. (From Spencer *et al.*, *Ann. Hum. Gen.* 32, 1968.)

*Other enzymes*

A few other enzymes can be mentioned briefly. Malate dehydrogenase (MDH) exists in soluble form and in mitochrondria. A few variants of the former have been found but seem to be rare everywhere; this is perhaps disappointing if one likes to see plenty of variation, but nonetheless interesting. Several variant alleles of phosphohexose isomerase (PHI) have been described, but again all of them seem to be quite rare; type 3–1 was found in 1 per cent of an Asiatic Indian sample and type 4–1 in 0·8 per cent of Japanese. The locus for phosphoglycerate kinase (PGK) is X-linked; the variant alleles $PGK^2$ and $PGK^4$ are moderately frequent (7 per cent and 5 per cent) in Micronesians and in New Guinea respectively but variants seem to be rare elsewhere. A variant allele, $GPT^2$, of glutamate–pyruvate transferase (GPT) is found in Africans. Placental alkaline phosphatase is produced by foetal tissue; three common alleles, $Pl^1$, $Pl^2$, $Pl^3$ (formerly $Pl^S$, $Pl^F$, $Pl^I$) are found. The frequency of $Pl^2$ ranges from about 26–9 per cent in Europe but it is much less frequent in Africans, Chinese, and Japanese (2–4 per cent). On the other hand, $Pl^3$ is common (21–4 per cent) in Chinese and Japanese and less frequent in Europeans (3–9 per cent) and Africans (4 per cent). This is a very variable enzyme and additional rare alleles have an overall frequency of 2·5 per cent in Europe. A number of rare variants of red-cell carbonic anhydrase, an enzyme that catalyses the released $CO_2$ from bicarbonate, have been described in various populations and a mutant of catalase, an enzyme that catalyses the breakdown of hydrogen peroxide, was found in Japanese. This mutation causes virtual absence of catalase activity.

## Serum protein variations

The serum, which is the fluid remaining after removing the fibrin from clotted plasma, contains a very complex mixture of proteins. Electrophoresis on paper separates them into a few crude fractions, the albumin and the $\alpha_1$, $\alpha_2$, $\beta$, and $\gamma$ globulins. The $\gamma$ globulins consists of antibody proteins (immunoglobulins) and inherited variations of these are discussed on pp. 273. Electrophoresis of serum on starch or acilamide gels gives better resolution of the various protein components because the fine pores of these media act as a sieve which separates them according to molecular size as well as electric charge.

### Haptoglobin (Hp)

Haptoglobin is an $\alpha_2$ globulin which has the property of binding free oxyhaemoglobin. The Hb–Hp complex can be detected by staining the gels for Hb with reagents such as o-tolidine/hydrogen peroxide. Three simply inherited phenotypes (Fig. 16.12) are found in virtually all populations, though in very varying frequencies. Type 1 is the homozygote for the allele $Hp^1$ and shows a single band. Type 2, the homozygote for the allele $Hp^2$, has a *series* of more cathodal bands and this seems odd if this gene codes for a single type of polypeptide chain in the orthodox manner. The heterozygote, 2–1, has a weak band at the Hp1 position together with a series of more cathodal bands that differ in position and relative strengths from those of type 2. It turns out that the $Hp^2$ allele does in fact code for a single kind of protein, but the molecules tend to stick together (polymerize) thus producing a series of polymers of increasing molecular weight. The haptoglobin molecule is composed of 2 light ($\alpha$) and 2 heavy ($\beta$) chains. The variations we have described are due to changes in the $\alpha$-chains, but a few rare variants of the $\beta$-chain have also been reported.

The Hp2 $\alpha$-chain is almost twice the molecular weight of the Hp1 $\alpha$-chain. Analysis of the amino-acid sequence shows that it in fact consists of 2 Hp1 chains joined end to end, with a piece missing at the junction. This suggests

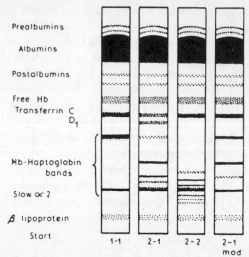

Prealbumins

Albumins

Postalbumins

Free Hb
Transferrin C
D₁

Hb-Haptoglobin
bands

Slow ∝ 2

β lipoprotein

Start

1-1    2-1    2-2    2-1
                     mod

FIG. 16.12. The pattern of haptcglobin, transferrin, and certain other protein bands as seen after electrophoresis of human serum in starch gel (tris-borate buffer system; horizontal method). Excess Hb has been added to the serum to saturate the haptoglobins. The three common haptoglobin types, 1–1, 2–1, and 2–2, and also a modified 2–1, are shown. In the type 2–1 specimen the transferrin variant TfD₁ is shown, running behind TfC. The globulin, much of which runs behind the starting-point, is not represented. (From Barnicot, 1961.)

that the $Hp^2$ gene was produced by a cross-over between two misaligned $Hp^1$ genes. In other Primates we find single-banded patterns resembling Hp1. It therefore seems that this cross-over must have happened in the hominid lineage and the fact the $Hp^2$ gene is found in man throughout the world suggests that it was already present in quite early human ancestors.

Another phenotype which looks like a type 2–1 with weak cathodal bands is fairly frequent (10 per cent) in Africans and is known as 2–1 modified (2–1M). In some tropical populations many individuals have no detectable Hp. This appears to be a transient state due to haemolysis from malaria or other causes; the Hb–Hp complex is removed from the blood and Hp is only gradually replaced by synthesis in the liver. However, cases of ahaptoglobinaemia with no apparent environmental cause are known and it seems that it can sometimes be an inherited condition.

If Hp1 phenotypes are examined in acid gels containing high concentrations of urea to break hydrogen bonds and mercaptoethanol to split sulphydryl bonds, the α-chains separate towards the anode and are found to vary in mobility. Populations are thus shown to be polymorphic for two types of Hp1 chain, determined by two alleles $Hp\alpha^{1F}$ and $Hp\alpha^{1S}$, and differing at a single amino-acid site. In western Europe the allele $Hp\alpha^{1S}$ is usually more frequent (20–5 per cent) and $Hp\alpha^{1F}$ (10–15 per cent) while in Chinese, Japanese, Eskimos, and Australian Aborigines $Hp\alpha^{1F}$ is rare. Nigerians, on the other hand, were found to have higher frequencies of $Hp\alpha^{1F}$ (47 per cent) than of

$Hp\alpha^{IS}$ (26 per cent). This variation of the $Hp\alpha$ chain is a good example of hidden diversity revealed by an appropriate modification of laboratory method.

Fig. 16.13 shows a world map of $Hp^1$ frequencies. High frequencies (60 per cent or more) are found in many tropical African peoples, in Central and South America, New Guinea, and Polynesia, while a zone of relatively low frequencies stretches from the Middle East to India and South East Asia, and includes Australia. It is still not clear whether the $Hp\alpha$ alleles are subject to selective pressures and, if so, how selection operates. Haemoglobin bound to Hp cannot pass the glomerular filter and this gives some protection against damage to kidney tubules and loss of iron; but it is uncertain whether the Hp phenotypes differ in protective efficiency, and there is no clear evidence that the heterozygotes have an advantage over the homozygotes in this respect. Haemolysis due to malaria and other diseases is common in Africa, where $Hp\alpha^1$ frequencies tend to be high, but is equally prevalent in parts of Asia where the frequencies of this allele are conspicuously low.

## Transferrin (Tf)

Transferrin (molecular weight 70 000) is a $\beta$ globulin that transports iron from sites of red-cell destruction and from the intestine to the bone marrow, where Hb is synthesized. Each molecule can bind 2 atoms of iron, but it is uncertain whether the molecule is composed of 2 subunits.

About 20 inherited variants have been distinguished by differences of electrophoretic mobility. These variations probably depend on a series of alleles but, since most of the variants are rare, families segregating for two of them are seldom found. The commonest type, TfC, appear as a single band on gels while heterozygotes for one of the slow (D) variants or one of the fast (B) variants have an additional band. Transferrin bands can be identified specifically by adding radioactive iron ($^{59}Fe$) to the serum and, after electrophoresis, placing the cut gel surface on a photographic plate. When the plate is developed, after a suitable time of exposure, areas that were in contact with radio-labelled Tf show up as dark bands.

A slow (cathodal) variant, $TfD_1$, is quite common in African populations (gene frequency 1–5 per cent) and also in Australia, New Guinea, and adjacent islands. In some Australian aboriginal groups the gene frequency is as high as 20 per cent. Peptide analysis (finger-printing) shows that African and Australian $TfD_I$ have the same amino-acid substitution. Whether the same mutation occurred independently in these two regions and then increased in frequency due to selection or drift in each or whether both received it from some remote common ancestor is uncertain. Another variant, $TfD_{chi}$, with an electrophoretic mobility very much like that of $TfD_I$ was first described in Chinese and has been found in various populations of South East and East Asia, in the Veddahs of Ceylon, in some Indian tribes, and also in a number of American-Indian populations. Most of the B variants are infrequent, but Navajo Indians of the south-western USA were found to have 8 per cent of $TfB_{0-I}$. Experiments have

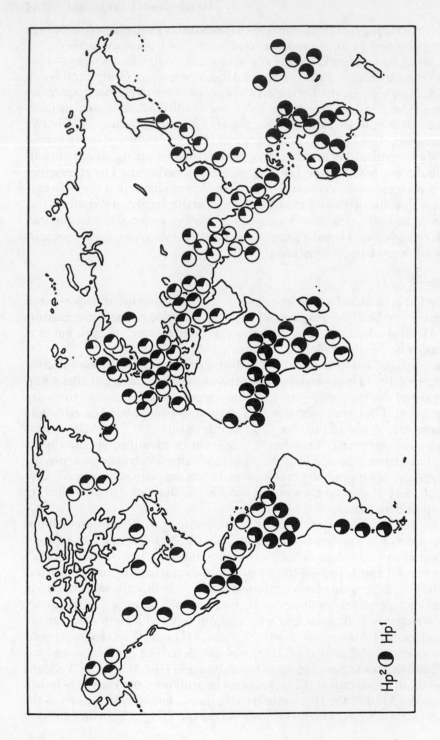

FIG. 16.13. World distribution of the frequencies of the haptoglobin genes Hp¹ and Hp².
(From Walter and Steegmüller, *Human Heredity*, 19, 1969.

Hp² ◗ Hp¹

so far failed to reveal any differences between the commoner types of Tf in their iron-transporting properties.

*Serum albumin (Al)*

To those who like to see a lot of polymorphism, albumin once seemed to be a rather boring protein that seldom varied. Then it was discovered that a fast (anodal) variant, was remarkably frequent (gene frequency 9–14 per cent) in Naskapi and Montagnais Indians of Labrador. What appears to be the same allele ($Al^{\text{Naskapi}}$, now re-named $Al^{\text{Algonkin}}$) is found at lower frequencies in various other Algonkian-speaking tribes such as the Cree, Objibwa, and Blackfoot, in Athabascan peoples, Sioux, Tlingit, and in Alaskan but not Greenland Eskimos. Though the distribution of this gene is mainly in northern USA and Canada it also occurs in the Navajo and Apache of the south west who are linguistically related to the Athabascans. The Apache and Navajo and other south-western tribes, such as the Zuni and Pima, also have quite high frequencies of another albumin variant, which was discovered in Mexican Indians and is called albumin Mexico.

More than a dozen rare albumin variants have been reported from various parts of the world including Malaysia, India, Africa, Europe, and New Guinea.

*$\alpha_1$ antitrypsin (Pi system)*

This protein inhibits trypsin and certain other proteolytic enzymes. Its physiological role may be to block the proteolytic enzymes released from white cells at sites of inflammation. In acidic starch gels the protein separates as a series of bands anodal to the albumin. In a large sample of Norwegians 4 alleles were present at appreciable frequencies, $Pi^m$ (95 per cent), $Pi^s$ (2·3 per cent), $Pi^z$ (2·0 per cent), and $Pi^f$ (1·3 per cent), and 2 other rare alleles were also found. Little is known at present about the world distribution of these alleles, but in Lapps, Finns, and some Asiatic samples $Pi^s$ was not found. Homozygotes for $Pi^s$ show a marked deficiency of antitryptic activity and it is also lowered to a lesser extent in the $Pi^z/Pi^m$ heterozygotes and in subjects carrying the $Pi^s$ allele. $Pi^z$ homozygotes are unusually susceptible to chronic obstructive lung disease, tending to develop it in their late 30s on average, and it may be that susceptibility is also increased in heterozygotes. These deleterious effects presumably imply some selection against these genes, but the age of onset is fairly late in the reproductive span and this would diminish the selective pressure.

*The C3 component of complement*

Complement was the name given long ago to a factor in fresh serum that is needed for the destruction of foreign cells that have been coated with antibody. It turns out to be a very complex system of 11 proteins that interact in sequence when the first in the series becomes attached to antibody molecules that have combined with the invading antigen. Polymorphism of one of the complement components, C3, can be detected by electrophoresis of serum at high voltage in agarose gels. Two common alleles, $C3^1$ and $C3^2$, and about 10 rare alleles are known. $C3^1$ has a frequency of 15–25 per cent in most European populations that have been tested. So far these genetical variations have not been found to affect complement activity.

## The Gc (group-specific) component

This protein can be seen as a series of two or more faint bands just cathodal to albumin on starch, or better acrilamide gels run at alkaline pH. However identification depends ultimately on reaction with a specific anti-Gc antibody. Immunoelectrophoresis is commonly used to detect genetical variants; the serum sample is first crudely fractioned by electrophoresis in a thin layer of agar. A slit is then cut in the agar parallel to the direction of protein migration and filled with antibody. An arc of precipitated protein appears where antigen (Gc) and antibody meet by diffusion (Fig. 16.14). Three phenotypic patterns,

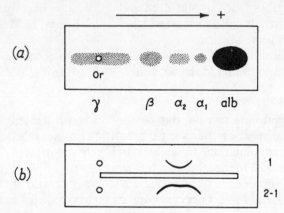

FIG. 16.14. Micro-immunoelectrophoresis. (a) A microscope slide has been coated with a thin layer of buffered agar. Serum is placed in a small hole cut in the agar near one end (Or). The slide is then connected to buffer tanks and a voltage is applied. Separation of the serum proteins into albumin and four globulin fractions is achieved. This slide has been stained to show the positions of the protein fractions. (b) Serum to be examined for Gc is placed in the two holes. After electrophoresis agar is cut from the central line to form a slot which is filled with anti-Gc serum. Precipitation in the form of arcs occurs where antigen and antibody meet by diffusion in suitable concentration. The slide shows a homozygous (type 1) with a single arc and a heterozygote (types 2–1) with two overlapping arcs.

due to 2 common alleles, $Gc^1$ and $Gc^2$, are found in all populations. $Gc^2$ frequencies vary around 25 per cent in Europe but are lower (about 10 per cent) in Lapps, Africans, and Australian Aborigines. There is considerable variability in American Indians, the Navajo having only 2 per cent of $Gc^2$ and the Xavante of Brazil 69 per cent. Another allele $Gc^{\text{Chippewa}}$ was discovered in certain North American Indians and yet another, $Gc^{\text{Aborigine}}$ in Australia and New Guinea. The latter is not distinguishable by present methods from an allele that occurs in Africans. It is interesting that the Gc locus is closely linked to that for serum albumin, and it has been suggested that it may have been derived from the latter by gene duplication. It has been claimed very recently that the Gc protein may be involved in the transport of vitamin D, and it may be that this will lead to an understanding of the action of selection on this system.

*Serum pseudocholinesterase*

If alkaline starch-gel preparations of human serum are treated with a mixture of $\alpha$-naphthylacetate and a suitable diazo dye, a series of 4 coloured bands develops. They are isozymes of pseudocholinesterase, an enzyme which hydrolyses certain organic esters and is present in various tissues, but not in red cells. It is distinct from acetylcholinesterase which is active in splitting the neurotransmitter substance acetylcholine at neuromuscular junctions and which also occurs in red cells. It was noticed that some individuals develop prolonged paralysis and breathing difficulties when given the muscle-relaxant suxamethonium (succinyl dicholine) prior to surgery. Careful studies, using various substrates and enzyme inhibitors, showed that these individuals are usually homozygous for a rare pseudocholinesterase allele $E_I^a$ which reduces the activity of the enzyme. Heterozygotes for this and the normal allele $E_I^u$ show intermediate activity levels. The frequency of $E_I^a$ is about 1·5 per cent in various European populations but considerably lower in Africans, East Asiatics, American Indians, and Australian Aborigines. A third allele, $E_I^f$, can be distinguished by its effect in lowering the sensitivity of the enzyme to inhibition by fluoride, and there is a rare allele, $E_I^s$, which, in the homozygous state, is associated with virtual absence of enzyme activity.

# 17. The blood-groups

## Introduction

BLOOD-group variations depend on differences in the structure of certain complex carbohydrate constituents of the red-cell membrane; at least this is true of the ABH and Lewis blood-groups on which most of the chemical work has been done. It is therefore somewhat artificial to deal with blood-groups separately from other biochemical variations, but it is convenient because the tests used to detect them are largely immunological (serological) and because the chemistry of most of them is not known.

The blood-group substances are 'antigens', i.e. they elicit the formation of specific antibodies when introduced into an individual who does not have the particular antigen in question. Many antigens are proteins, but other examples of carbohydrate antigens are known in bacteria. The antibodies are proteins (immunoglobulins) that are released into the blood plasma by special antibody-synthesizing cells. Specific antibodies that will detect blood-group variations are usually discovered by testing serum from pregnant women (who may have been immunized by the foetus) or from people who have received many blood-transfusions. However, some occur 'spontaneously' in persons of particular blood-group constitution and a few (e.g. anti-M and anti-N) have been produced by immunizing rabbits with human red cells.

The principle technique used to detect blood-group variations of red cells is 'agglutination'. When washed red cells are mixed with serum containing the specific antibody they become coated with antibody protein and clump together. However, some blood-group antibodies combine with the cells but do not agglutinate them; they are said to be 'incomplete'. Even so agglutination can be produced by doing the reaction in a protein-rich medium, by pre-treating the cells with certain proteolytic enzymes, or by adding antibody that combines with human $\gamma$ globulin. The last-named procedure (Coombs test) depends on the fact that the incomplete antibodies are themselves $\gamma$ globulins. The anti-$\gamma$ globulin therefore combines with them and links the cells into clumps.

It is a curious fact that some useful blood-grouping reagents can also be obtained by extracting the seeds of certain leguminous plants. These 'lectins' are themselves globulins. A valuable anti-H is got from seeds of gorse (*Ulex europaeus*), an anti-A from *Dolichos biflorus*, and an anti-N from *Vicia graminea*.

Blood-group variations obey Mendelian rules of inheritance with gratifying precision. They are therefore very valuable in paternity testing, in distinguishing monozygotic from dizygotic twins, and in work on genetical linkage. Since many blood-group variations have high, but variable, frequencies in different populations, they are also valuable in anthropology. Moreover, most of them are detectable at birth and do not change thereafter except in a few rare diseases. It seemed at first that the rule 'one antigen, one gene' was a valid principle, but advances in molecular genetics and the discovery of certain odd blood-group phenomena have exposed its limitations. Structural genes are known to be segments of DNA that code for the amino-acid sequences of protein poly-peptide chains. The carbohydrate antigens detected in blood-grouping cannot therefore be direct gene products. The genes are believed to affect the enzymes (glycosyltransferases) that build up these carbohydrate chains. Furthermore, genes contain numerous base sites each of which can undergo mutation. It is possible that a mutation affecting an enzyme could lead to a change in more than one antigenic specificity of the blood-group substance. We shall mention below several examples in which a group of antigenic specificities are inherited together. This situation can be formally explained by postulating a series of very closely linked genes; but if linkage is so close that cross-overs are virtually never observed this postulate is merely a convenience and throws no real light on gene structure. Serology is a sensitive and powerful tool, but less illuminat-ing than chemistry from this point of view. It is unfortunate that very little is known about the physiological significance of the blood-group substances since knowledge of their functions might guide our search for selective agents acting on them. This ignorance may soon be dispelled by the intensive work now being done on cell membranes.

In 1968 Race and Sanger in their classic book listed 14 different blood-group systems, i.e. blood-group specificities or groups of specificities that appear to be controlled by independent gene loci. In addition there are a fair number of blood-group antigens that hardly ever vary (public antigens) and some that have been found in only one or a few families (private antigens).

## The $A_1A_2BO$ system

This system was the first to be discovered; in 1900 Landsteiner showed that the serum of some individuals agglutinated the washed red cells of certain other individuals. This discovery laid the foundation of safe blood-transfusion and also gave geneticists and anthropologists a set of simply inherited variations that are quite frequent in most populations, are easy to detect, and are virtually unaffected in expression by the sex, postnatal age, and environment of the in-dividual. It was not in fact until 1924 that Bernstein established the mode of inheritance of the ABO blood-groups. Table 17.1 shows the essence of the mat-ter. Red cells can carry either A or B antigens or both or neither, so we have 4 phenotypes, groups A, B, AB, and O. Inheritance depends on 3 alleles $A$, $B$, and $O$[†] which segregate to form 6 genotypes, $AA$, $AO$, $BB$, $BO$, $AB$, $OO$. The presence of the A antigen can be detected by mixing the cells with serum containing anti-A, whereupon they agglutinate; the B antigen is similarly

---

† In the first edition of this book we used the symbols $G^A$, $G^B$, and $G^O$, suggested by E. B. Ford, but this notation has not gained in popularity and we have therefore reverted to the less satisfactory, but com-moner, device of using roman type for phenotypes and italic for genes and genotypes.

detected with anti-B. No true anti-O is known, and we are therefore unable to distinguish homozygous A or B from heterozygous A or B (*AO* and *BO*) by serological tests. It also follows from this that we cannot determine the gene frequencies of a population simply by counting genes. We have to use indirect methods, making the assumption that the sample is in Hardy–Weinberg equilibrium for these alleles.

Anti-A occurs regularly in the serum of people who lack this antigen and anti-B in those who lack antigen B. It appears that these naturally occurring antibodies are formed in response to A-like and B-like antigens of bacteria and other organisms that invade the alimentary canal soon after birth.

TABLE 17.1
*Genetics and serology of ABO groups*

| Phenotypes | Genotypes | Cell antigens | Antibodies in serum |
|---|---|---|---|
| Group A | *AA* and *AO* | A | anti-B |
| Group B | *BB* and *BO* | B | anti-A |
| Group O | *OO* | — | anti-A and anti-B |
| Group AB | *AB* | A and B | neither |

Group A can be subdivided into Groups $A_1$ and $A_2$. $A_2$ cells react weakly with ordinary anti-A but we have no specific anti-$A_2$ to identify this variation. However, some $A_2$ and $A_2$B people produce a specific anti-$A_1$ which can be used to subtype A cells. Nevertheless, we cannot distinguish serologically between the genotypes $A_1A_2$ and $A_1A_1$ or $A_1O$, or between $A_2A_2$ and $A_2O$. Various other quantitative variations of group A such as A-intermediate (A-int), which seem to be relatively frequent in Africans, have been described.

## The secretor factor and the chemistry of ABH and Lewis antigens

In western Europe about 75 per cent of group A, B, and AB subjects also have A and/or B antigens in their saliva and other mucous secretions. Secretion of these antigens in water-soluble form is inherited as a dominant trait depending on a gene *Se* which segregates independently from the *ABO* locus. In some populations, such as American Indians and Australian Aborigines this gene is even more frequent and non-secretors (*se/se*) correspondingly rare.

Group-O secretors can be distinguished because they secrete an antigen known as H, which combines with the anti-H lectin obtained from gorse seeds. The H antigen is not specific to group O but is produced by other ABO phenotypes also, though in lesser amounts. It is a precursor substance which is converted to A or B antigen if the *A* or *B* genes are present and its formation depends on a gene *H* which is inherited independently from the *ABO* genes. There is thus an interaction between the *H* and *ABO* loci, the former producing a substance which can be acted upon by the products of the latter. Rare families are known in which some members have no ABH antigens either in their red cells or in their secretions (Bombay phenotype). Such individuals are apparently homozygous for $h$, a rare allele of $H$, and are therefore unable to form H antigen.

The Lewis antigens $Le^a$ and $Le^b$ were first described as red-cell antigens determined by a locus $Le$ inherited independently from the $ABO$ locus. It was then noticed that people with Le(a−b+) cells are usually secretors of ABH and those with Le (a+b−) cells are usually ABH non-secretors. Nevertheless, Le (a−b+) individuals have both $Le^a$ and $Le^b$ in their secretions. It seems that the Lewis antigens are primarily water-soluble antigens that become attached to red cells only if their concentration in the plasma is high enough. Production of $Le^a$ depends on a gene $Le$ and if this gene is present $Le^a$ is secreted whatever the ABH secretor type of the individual. $Le^b$ specificity, however, depends on the presence of genes $H$ and $Se$ in addition to $Le$.

These rather complex relations between the genotypes at the $H$, $Se$, and $Le$ loci and the antigens found on red cells and in secretions are summarized in Table 17.2.

TABLE 17.2

*Relations between antigens on red cells and in mucous secretions and genotypes at the $H$, $Se$ and $Le$ loci*

| Genotypes | | | Antigens on cells ABH $Le^a$ $Le^b$ | Antigens in mucous secretions ABH $Le^a$ $Le^b$ |
|---|---|---|---|---|
| H-locus | Secretor locus | Lewis locus | | |
| HH or Hh | SeSe Sese | LeLe Lele | + − + | + + + |
| HH or Hh | sese | LeLe Lele | + + − | − + − |
| hh | SeSe SeSe | LeLe Lele } Bombay types | − + − | − + − |
| hh | sese | lele } | − − − | − − − |
| HH or Hh | sese | lele | + − − | − − − |
| HH or Hh | SeSe Sese | lele | + − − | + − − |

They become easier to understand in the light of chemical work on the ABH and Lewis antigens. Most of this work has been done on the water-soluble forms since these are easier to handle than the lipid-associated antigens of the red-cell membrane. The water-soluble antigens are big molecules composed largely (80–90 per cent) of carbohydrate. The carbohydrate is in the form of chains built up of several different types of sugar united and attached at one end to a polypeptide core. Largely due to the work of Morgan and Watkins, it has been established that ABH and Lewis specificites depend on the pattern of carbohydrate residues at the free ends of the chains (Fig. 17.1). The various

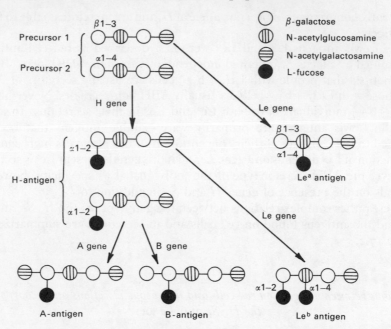

FIG. 17.1. Structure and synthetic interrelations of the A, B, H, and Le blood-group antigens. Specificity depends on the structure of the terminal ends of the carbohydrate chains and only these are shown. The arrows indicate the actions of particular genes. (Based on data in Watkins, *Science*, *N.Y.*, **152**, 1966.)

genes involved are thought to code for enzymes (transferases) that catalyse the linking of particular sugar residues, but the structure of these enzymes is not yet known. There are two closely similar precursor substances, both of which can be converted to H antigen if the genes *H* is present. However, production of a fucosyl transferase that can form water-soluble H antigen depends in some way on the presence of the gene *Se*. The *A* and *B* genes code for transferases that add respectively either *N*-acetylgalactosamine or galactose to the termination of the H-chain. If the gene *Le* is present fucose is added to the penultimate residue of precursor 1 to form *Le*a antigen and *Le*b is formed by a corresponding transformation of H antigen.

## Geographical distribution of the $A_1A_2BO$ blood-groups

More is known about the distribution of this system than any other because it was the first to be discovered and because strong antisera for the relatively simple grouping techniques are easy to obtain. In medically advanced countries large numbers of people are ABO grouped by the blood-transfusion services so that relatively small regional variations in frequency may be detectable, for example in the UK (see Fig. 15.3 (b)).

The broad pattern of the gene frequencies of the alleles *O*, *B*, and *A* throughout the world are shown as contour maps in Figs 17.2, 17.3, and 17.4. Since

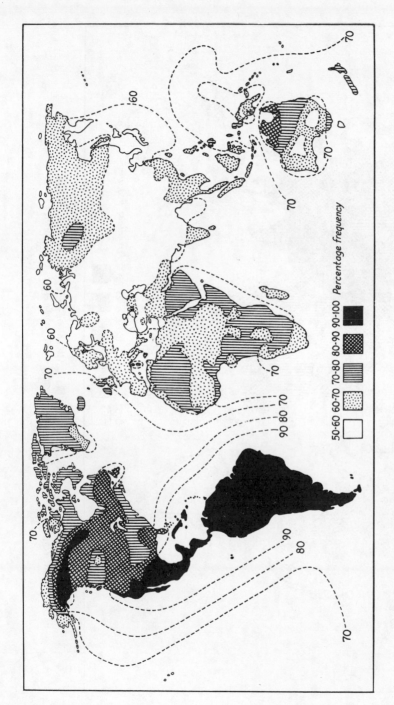

FIG. 17.2. The frequency of the gene *O* of the ABO blood-group system. (Redrawn from Mourant, Kopec, and Sobczak, *The distribution of human blood groups* (2nd edn.), 1976.)

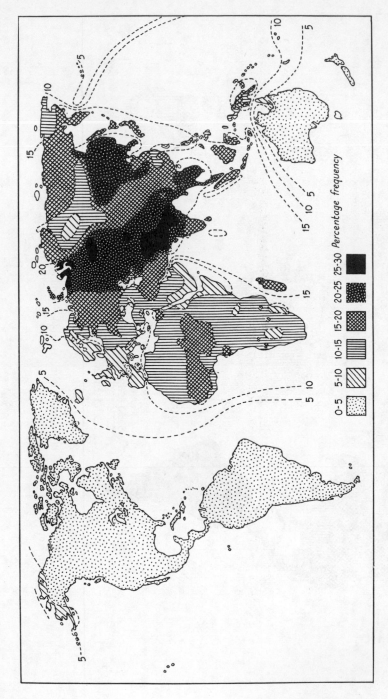

FIG. 17.3. The frequency of the gene *B* of the ABO blood-group system. (Redrawn from Mourant, Kopec and Sobczak, *The distribution of human blood groups* (2nd edn.), 1976.)

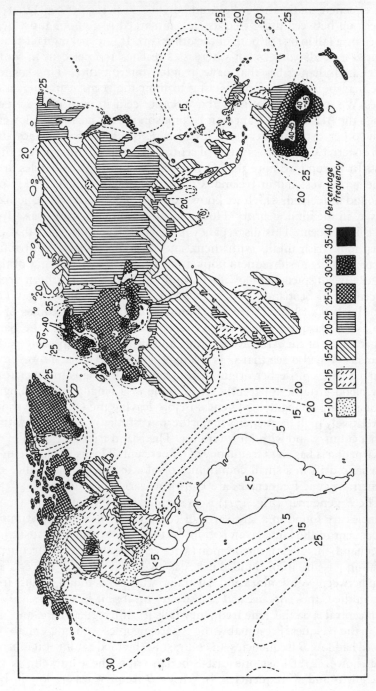

FIG. 17.4. The frequency of the gene *A* of the ABO blood-group system. (Redrawn from Mourant, Kopec and Sobczak, *The distribution of human blood groups* (2nd edn.), 1976.)

the frequencies of the three alleles add up to 1.0 (or 100 per cent) there is some correlation between these frequencies; a marked rise in one must be accompanied by a fall in one or both of the other two. It is a striking fact that neither $A$ nor $B$ exceeds 50 per cent whereas $O$ reaches 100 per cent in some South American Indian tribes that have avoided intermixture. This suggests that there may be selective forces acting to limit the relative frequence of these alleles. We see in fact that $O$ is above 80 per cent in most of the New World though the Alaskan and Canadian Eskimos in the far north have lower values. At the other extreme there is a broad zone of low $O$ frequencies stretching from eastern Europe across much of central Asia and reaching part of the Pacific coast. In Europe we note that $O$ frequencies in the British Isles are higher in the north-west and in Ireland. Comparably high frequencies (75 per cent) are found in Iceland, which we know from written records was colonized from Norway in the ninth century. However, no region of Norway has a frequency above 66 per cent. This discrepancy is probably due to the fact that the Norsemen took Irish thralls with them, and these presumably contributed disproportionately to subsequent population growth. The frequency of the secretor gene is conspicuously low in Iceland (36 per cent), northern Ireland (45 per cent), and Scotland (46 per cent) in comparison with Norway (53–9 per cent). Pockets of high $O$ are also found in certain other peoples of Europe, such as the Basques, whose language is of obscure affinities, the Sardinians, Berber tribes of the Atlas Mountains, and people living in some parts of the Caucasus. We also see that $O$ is relatively high in Arabia; however, Arabic-speaking tribes of Berber origin differ from the Arabians in other features of their blood-groups, apparently an example of a language spreading without much accompanying flow of genes. Before leaving the $O$ map we should note the relatively high frequencies in northern Australia as compared with the rest of that country and with New Guinea. The island tribe, the Tiwi of the Gulf of Carpentaria has an $O$ frequency of 95 per cent. This is no doubt an instance of genetic drift in a small community or of a founder effect; other examples of aberrant gene frequencies are known in various islands of this region.

The $B$ gene map (Fig. 17.3) is to some extent the inverse of $O$; high frequencies are found in a large area of central east Asia with maximum of 25–30 per cent in the Himalayan region. In the New World and Australia, on the other hand, this allele is uncommon (5 per cent) or absent. The frequency tends to fall in passing from South East Asia to Indonesia, and there is a marked drop between New Guinea and Australia, where $B$ is found, in low frequency, only in the Cape-York area. $B$ is also rare or absent in Polynesia. Westwards from central Asia the gene frequency falls in an irregular cline and is notably low in the Basques. Presumably the Asiatic peoples who first entered the New World had low $B$ frequencies, in contrast to the modern inhabitants of eastern Asia; however, at least one east-Siberian tribe, the Chuckchi, is known to have low $B$ and $A$ frequencies. In Africa $B$ frequencies are low in Bushmen, but much higher in Hottentots.

Turning to the $A$ map (Fig. 17.4) we see that frequencies are quite high in Europe, with some unusually high patches, notably in Lappland and Armenia. In the New World the $A$ pattern is to some extent the inverse of $O$. The gene is rare or absent in South and Central America, but much more frequent in North America, reaching 25 per cent or more in certain tribes such as the Blackfoot and Blood Indians. $A$ is also frequent among Eskimos stretching from Alaska to Greenland. Again in Australia there is a resemblance of $O$ and $A$ patterns because the more southerly tribes, with low $O$ have conspicuously high $A$ frequencies, reaching 40 per cent or more in some cases.

The subgroup $A_2$ has a much more restricted distribution than $A_1$. The frequency of this gene is around 10 per cent in much of Europe and Africa, but falls to 5 per cent or less in India and South East Asia. In other parts of the world it is rare or absent. The $A_2$ gene is conspicuously frequent (25–37 per cent) in the Lapps, though varying in different Lappish groups; it is also relatively frequent in the Finns. This is one of several examples of deviant gene frequencies in the Lapps, a peoples whose origins still remain obscure.

It is also interesting to consider not only the local frequencies of an allele but where it occurs in greatest abundance. This means that population sizes have to be taken into account. Some Australian tribes have very high $A$ frequencies but these genes contribute a negligible fraction of $A$ in the world because these tribes are small. McArthur and Penrose worked out the average frequencies for various regions and found that for the world as a whole they were $O = 62·5$ per cent, $A = 21·5$ per cent, and $B = 16·2$ per cent. They suggested that these average values would provide a useful standard against which the deviations of local populations could be assessed.

## The ABO groups and natural selection

The fact that the great majority of the world's populations are polymorphic for 2 and usually 3 $ABO$ alleles suggests that this variation has persisted during the many millenia of human dispersal when populations were small and liable to lose alleles by drift; however, we do not know how far gene flow between human groups may have hindered this process in these early times.

Antigens that closely resemble human ABH antigens occur in the great apes, which are also polymorphic for 2 or 3 alleles. It is therefore conceivable that the ABO polymorphism was already present much earlier, when the hominid and pongid lines diverged.

The recognition that the presence of a blood-group antigen in the foetus that was not present in the mother could lead to serious disease of the newborn in the case of the Rhesus system (p. 261) revived and stimulated a search for similar effects in the ABO blood-groups. In fact comparable damage to the newborn due to ABO incompatibility does occur but it is rare. The possibility remains, however, that immunological damage might take place at a much earlier stage of pregnancy and would pass unnoticed without special investigation. In general, apart from small chance fluctuations, we expect the $ABO$ gene frequencies in a large sample of newborn children to be the same as in their parents. We can therefore look to see if there is a significant deficiency of certain phenotypes in the progeny of particular ABO matings. Some studies (usually on mother and child only) have shown remarkably large deficiencies in the births of children born to O mothers, but other investigations have not confirmed this. It must be remembered, of course, that very large samples, in the region of 15–20 thousand subjects, may be needed to give convincing evidence of selection in the 1–5 per cent range, a selective pressure which could nevertheless have substantial evolutionary effects. Selection by mother-foetus incompatibility necessarily involves the elimination of heterozygous progeny so that the gene-frequency equilibrium would not be stable unless there were some compensating mechanism such as heterozygous advantage in later life.

Another line of thought is that a person's ABO group may confer some protection against certain diseases. With this in mind the ABO frequencies of large samples of patients suffering from particular diseases were compared with those of the control populations from which they were drawn. A significant excess of group A was found in those with gastric cancer and of O in those with duodenal ulcers (Table 17.3). Similar but less impressive results were obtained for several other diseases. Such associations of blood-group and disease might not necessarily indicate a causal relationship. If the population were heterogeneous in origin, it could happen that there was a subgroup with high O which was particularly susceptible to duodenal ulcers for some quite different reason. However, the magnitude of some of these effects and the fact that consistent results have been obtained in several widely separated places makes this explanation by social stratification unlikely. The mechanism by which the blood-groups produce these effects on disease susceptibility are still obscure; in the case of diseases of the gastro-intestinal tract the antigens are present in the mucous secretions, at least in the case of secretors. Since diseases such as duodenal ulcer tend to occur late in reproductive life the selective effect on ABO groups must be small.

Antigens that resemble human ABO antigens are found on the surfaces of various bacteria. It therefore seems probable that a group-A person, for example, would be handicapped in forming antibodies against organisms with A-like antigens. It has indeed been claimed that group-A subjects are more susceptible to smallpox (judging mainly by vaccination reactions), but these results have not been confirmed, and it is doubtful whether the smallpox virus carries the A antigen except when it has been cultivated in A-positive chick embryos. The area of relatively low O and high B in Asia coincides roughly with the reservoir of plague-bearing rodents. The plague bacterium, *Pasteurella pestis*, has an H-like antigen, and it argued that group-O subjects might be particularly susceptible. There is some evidence, based on experimental infections with common-cold virus, that ABO phenotypes may influence susceptibility.

We see then that there are many indications of selective action on the ABO groups, but the evidence is often ambiguous and no clear picture of how the polymorphism is maintained has yet emerged.

TABLE 17.3

*Frequencies of blood groups O and A in duodenal ulcer patients and in control series*

| Centre | Size of sample | | Group O frequency (per cent) | | Group A frequency (per cent) | |
|---|---|---|---|---|---|---|
| | Ulcer | Controls | Ulcer | Controls | Ulcer | Controls |
| London | 946 | 10 000 | 56·6 | 45·8 | 32·9 | 42·2 |
| Liverpool | 1059 | 15 377 | 59·6 | 48·9 | 29·0 | 39·1 |
| Glasgow | 1642 | 5898 | 57·7 | 53·9 | 31·5 | 32·3 |
| Copenhagen | 680 | 14 304 | 50·3 | 40·6 | 38·4 | 44·0 |
| Vienna | 1160 | 10 000 | 41·0 | 36·3 | 41·3 | 44·2 |
| Iowa | 1301 | 6313 | 53·7 | 45·8 | 36·3 | 41·6 |

(Adapted from Fraser Roberts, *Brit. med. Bull.*, 1959.)

## The Rhesus (Rh) system

In 1940 Landsteiner and Wiener found that antisera obtained by immunizing rabbits with rhesus-monkey red cells agglutinated the cells of about 85 per cent of white Americans. Two phenotypes, Rh-positive and Rh-negative, could thus be distinguished, the former behaving as a dominant trait. Inheritance could be attributed to two alleles *Rh* and *rh*, which segregated to produce two dominant types, *Rh/Rh* and *Rh/rh*, and a recessive, rhesus-negative type, *rh/rh*. Subsequently antisera were discovered in the blood of pregnant women or in multiple transfused subjects that gave essentially the same results. We now regard these latter antisera, derived from humans, as detecting an antigen D which is different from, but related to, the antigen in rhesus monkeys. The Rh-positive genotypes can thus be rewritten *D/D* and *D/d*, with *d/d* as the Rh-negative type.

The medical limelight was thrown on the Rhesus groups, when, as a result of work by Levine and Stetson in 1939, it was realized that they were connected with a severe disease of the newborn child. It emerged that this only occurred if the mother was Rh-negative (*d/d*) and the father Rh-positive (*D/D* or *D/d*). In a certain proportion of such matings the foetus is heterozygous (*D/d*) and thus carries the antigen D which the mother lacks. Disruption of the placenta at parturition allows some of these D-positive foetal cells to enter the maternal bloodstream and immunize her to the D antigen. In subsequent pregnancies anti-D antibody may cross the placental barrier and damage the red cells of the foetus, which is therefore born with a severe anaemia (haemolytic disease of the newborn, HDN). If the father is heterozygous (*D/d*) the risk is reduced because one half of the progeny on average will be *d/d* and lack the D antigen.

Taking the frequency of Rh-negatives in this country to be approximately 16 per cent gives a $d$ frequency of 40 per cent and about 9 per cent of random matings should be at risk for this disease. However, the incidence of HDN is only $\frac{1}{150}-\frac{1}{200}$, so that there must be other factors that reduce the risk. One of these is the ABO groups of the parents. If these are also incompatible, foetal cells entering the mother will be destroyed by her ABO antibodies and will have no chance to produce anti-D immunization.

Until quite recently prompt blood-transfusion was the standard method of saving the lives of children with HDN. Then in 1965 Clarke and his colleagues realized that foetal D-positive cells that had got into the mother's blood could be destroyed by giving suitable doses of anti-D. This method has been very successful in preventing maternal immunization.

## The Rh system and natural selection

We have already mentioned immunological selection against heterozygous foetuses in relation to the ABO system. In the case of Rh it is $D/d$ genotypes that are eliminated by this mechanism. Selection against heterozygotes only yields a balanced equilibrium if the frequencies of the two alleles are exactly 50 per cent; otherwise the less frequent allele is gradually eliminated. In all populations, except the Basques, the frequency of $d$ is below 50 per cent, and it may be that the polymorphism is transient and $d$ is declining. If so we have to explain how it achieved such high frequencies locally in the first place. It has been suggested that the Basques are a remnant of a prehistoric western European population in which the $d$ frequency was very high and which later mixed with eastern peoples with very high $D$ frequencies. However, it is possible that the equilibrium is actually stabilized, perhaps by some unknown advantage of $D/d$ heterozygotes in later life.

## Further complexities of the Rh system

We have so far spoken of the Rh system as if it consisted solely of the antigens D and d, which are in fact the most important ones medically. However, intensive work on human sera soon showed that there are additional associated antigens. In 1943, noticing certain regularities in the serological results, Fisher put forward a scheme to explain the genetics of the system. He postulated 3 very closely linked gene loci, each of which could be occupied by one of a pair of alleles, $D$ or $d$, $C$ or $c$, and $E$ or $e$. This would allow 8 types of gene triplet, or haplotypes (p. 277) on a chromosome as shown below:

| Fisher–Race notation | CDE | CDe | cDE | cDe | cde | Cde | cdE | CdE |
|---|---|---|---|---|---|---|---|---|
| Wiener notation | $R_z$ | $R_1$ | $R_2$ | $R_0$ | $r$ | $r'$ | $r''$ | $r_y$. |

Fisher thought that each gene produced its particular antigen and the corresponding 6 antisera would ultimately be discovered. This prediction was fulfilled except that anti-d has never been found and may not exist. Fisher also noticed that $CDe(R_1)$, $cDE(R_2)$, $cDe(R_2)$, and $cde(r)$ are the commonest types, and suggested that the rarer ones could have been produced by very rare cross-overs between them. Indeed, unless cross-overs do occur we have no genetical way of distinguishing the hypothetical triplets from single genes. Wiener in fact did not accept Fisher's concept and preferred to envisage a set of 8 alleles with complex antigen-determining properties. His notation, which is conveniently simple, is given above alongside the Fisher–Race symbols. No doubt the chemical structure of the antigens, which is still unknown, will resolve these controversies.

The reader will realize that since each gene-triplet is located on a single chromosome a person's genotype may, for example, be $CDe/cde$ ($R_1/r$) or $cDE/cDe$ $R_2/R_0$, containing 6 genes. Tests with the 5 available antisera do not necessarily give unambiguous genotypes since they do not tell us how the 6 genes are arranged as a pair of haplotypes, except in certain cases such as $(c+)$, $(C-)$, $(D-)$, $(e+)$, $(E-)$, which must be the homozygote $cde/cde$. In individual cases the genotype can usually be resolved from family data but in population material the presence of some of the rarer haplotypes may be in doubt.

## TABLE 17.4

*Frequencies of variants at the Rh locus in various populations*

| | No. tested | CDE $(R_z)$ | CDe $(R_1)$ | cDe $(R_2)$ | cde $(R_0)$ | Cde $(r')$ | CdE $(r_y)$ | cdE $(r'')$ | cde $(r)$ |
|---|---|---|---|---|---|---|---|---|---|
| English | 1798 | 0·27 | 41·43 | 14·50 | 2·62 | 1·19 | 0·00 | 0·97 | 39·03 |
| Italians (Milan) | 772 | 0·35 | 47·56 | 10·77 | 1·63 | 0·67 | 0·33 | 0·69 | 38·00 |
| Basques | 383 | 0·00 | 37·56 | 7·07 | 0·50 | 1·47 | 0·00 | 0·25 | 53·15 |
| Sardinians | 107 | — | 66·84 | 8·84 | 2·12 | 0·00 | — | 0·00 | 22·19 |
| Norwegian Lapps | 183 | 0·00 | 52·46 | 18·37 | 10·34 | 0·00 | 0·00 | 0·00 | 18·83 |
| N.W. Pakistanis | 253 | 0·63 | 66·69 | 7·78 | 0·00 | 0·50 | 0·00 | 0·00 | 24·40 |
| S. Chinese | 250 | 0·49 | 75·91 | 19·51 | 4·09 | 0·00 | 0·00 | 0·00 | 0·00 |
| Australians | 234 | 2·08 | 56·42 | 20·09 | 8·54 | 12·87 | 0·00 | 0·00 | 0·00 |
| New Caledonians | 147 | 0·00 | 80·27 | 12·71 | 7·02 | 0·00 | 0·00 | 0·00 | 0·00 |
| Blood Indians | 241 | 4·06 | 47·81 | 38·84 | 0·00 | 0·00 | 0·00 | 3·42 | 9·87 |
| Chippewa Indians | 161 | 2·04 | 33·67 | 53·03 | 0·00 | 0·00 | 0·00 | 3·22 | 8·03 |
| S.W. Nigerians | 145 | 0·00 | 9·51 | 8·28 | 61·91† | 1·87 | 0·00 | 0·00 | 18·43 |
| S. African Bantu | 644 | 0·00 | 2·81 | 4·27 | 73·95† | 7·07 | 0·00 | 0·00 | 11·84 |
| Bushmen | 232 | — | 9·04 | 1·96 | 89·00† | 0·00 | — | 0·00 | 0·00 |

† Including $cD^ue$.

Research on the Rh factor has revealed many curious serological phenomena not all of which are fully understood. We can mention only a few, especially those that affect population studies. Certain D antigens react weakly with some anti-D antisera and are designated $D^u$; moreover the reaction strength varies suggesting a series of different $D^u$ antigens. $D^u$ is common in Africa and may be mistaken for D-negative by the unwary.

An antiserum anti-V was discovered which gave positive reactions with the cells of less than 1 per cent of white Americans, Orientals, and American Indians but reacted with those of 40 per cent of West Africans. The interpretation of anti-V seems to be that it reacts with cells that have both c and an allele of e, $e^s$, on the same chromosome. Other antisera of this kind such as anti-ce, and anti-Ce have been discovered.

Rare individuals have been found who appear to have only the D antigen ($-$D$-$) and some which give no reactions for any of the Rh antigens (Rh null). In at least one of the latter cases the parents were positive for Rh antigens and these must have been supressed in the child.

## Geography of the Rh groups

The Rh system with its 8 haplotypes and variety of alleles at each locus gives great scope for variation as we see from Table 17.4 in which the frequencies in a selected range of populations are given. $CDe(R_1)$, for example, ranges from less than 5 per cent in some African populations to over 90 per cent in many tribes of New Guinea. There is a tendency for this haplotype to be more frequent in the Mediterranean zone than elsewhere in Europe and for $cde(r)$ to be correspondingly low. This trend, which is marked in the Sardinians, continues into northern India and in the Far East $cde(r)$ is rare. An allele of the gene C, $C^w$, is unusually frequent in Lapps, Finns, and Latvians. $cDE(R_2)$ is conspicuously frequent in American Indians and it is fairly high in Polynesia and South East Asia. $cDe(R_0)$ is remarkable because the frequencies in Africa greatly exceed those in any other region. Frequencies of over 90 per cent have been recorded in peoples as physically contrasted as certain Nilotic tribes and the Bushmen. As we approach the Middle East, $R_0$ frequencies fall but are still 50–60 per cent in Ethiopia, 15–20 per cent in some tribes of the Yemen, and 10–16 per cent in the area south of the Caspian Sea. Moderately high $R_0$ frequencies have also been found in a few other scattered peoples such as Negritos of Malaya, and some tribes of northern Australia.

Among the rarer haplotypes we find that $CDE(R_z)$ is relatively high among some of the so-called Veddoid tribes of India, and in some Australian tribes, though not among the Veddah themselves. The rare type $cdE(r'')$ is surprisingly frequent among the Ainu of northern Japan.

We have mentioned the 'compound' antigen V($ce^s$). Like cDe high frequencies of this antigen are characteristic of Africa, where gene frequencies range from 20–30 per cent, falling to 5–10 per cent in Arabia.

## The MNS system

The MN blood-groups were discovered in 1927 by Landsteiner and Levine as a result of immunizing rabbits with human red cells. Rabbit antisera are still in general use for work on this system, but various purification procedures are necessary and it is not easy to prepare antisera which are both strong and specific for the required antigen. The inheritance is very simple; 3 phenotypes M, MN, and N can be recognized corresponding to the 3 genotypes $MM$, $MN$, and $NN$ (or $Ag^M Ag^M$, $Ag^M Ag^N$ and $Ag^N Ag^N$ cf. p. 99).

The $M$ map of the world (Fig. 17.5) shows some major regional contrasts,

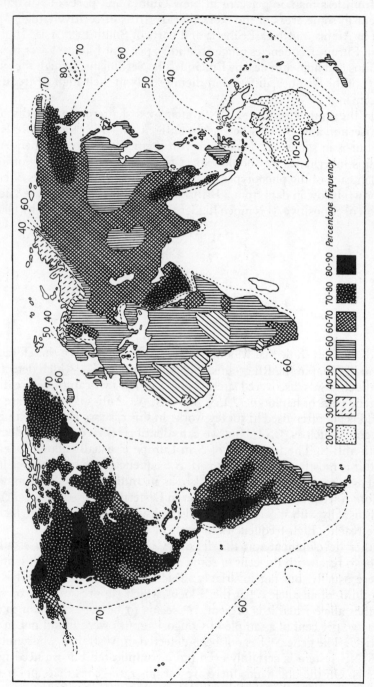

FIG. 17.5. The frequency of the gene M of the MN blood-group system. (Redrawn from Mourant, Kopec, and Sobczak, *The distribution of human blood groups* (2nd edn.), 1976.)

ranging from less than 20 per cent in New Guinea and parts of Australia to 90 per cent in some areas of the New World. Areas of relatively high $M$ are also seen in Arabia, north east Siberia and parts of South East Asia. In much of western Europe frequencies range around 50 per cent but are lower in some Lapp groups and higher in nearby Finland. The Sardinians, though they show the high $O$ of the Basques, differ from them greatly in their high $M$ frequency (75 per cent).

In 1947 the simplicity of the MN system was shattered by the discovery of an antiserum, anti-S. This detects an antigen which is clearly different to M or N but is in some way associated with them. If S were independent of MN groups inheritance we should expect to find the same proportion of S-positives in each of the phenotypes M, MN, and N within the limits of error; but as shown below in data from a British sample this is not the case and the proportion of S-positive M is much higher than would be expected by chance.

|  |  | M+MN | N |  |
|---|---|---|---|---|
| anti-S | + obs | 93 | 15 | 108 |
|  | exp | 82 | 26 |  |
|  | − obs | 52 | 30 | 82 |
|  | exp | 63 | 19 |  |
|  |  | 145 | 45 | 190 |

Studies of families show that M and S segregate as a pair. We therefore have a situation like that in the Rh groups. The antiserum anti-s, which detects the allelic antigen s, was discovered later. Using 4 antisera we can therefore distinguish 4 gene pairs or haplotypes, $MS$, $Ms$, $NS$, $Ns$. Anti-s is a fairly rare antiserum and is not often used in survey work; in this case we cannot distinguish heterozygotes, such as $MSMs$ but we can identify $MsMs$ because it does not react with anti-S. The frequency of $S$ in Europe is usually about 30–35 per cent, and it is mostly associated with $M$. $S$ frequencies are even higher in the Middle East (40 per cent) and here, also, as in India, $MS$ is the commonest association. $S$ frequencies are much lower in Eastern Asia (5–20 per cent), and here $M$ is usually with $s$. $S$ is virtually absent in Australia despite the fact that this gene reaches high frequencies in parts of New Guinea.

A further development was the discovery of anti-U. This antiserum was found not to react with the cells of some American Negroes and these individuals were usually, but not invariably, negative for both S and s. It is now usual to think of an allele $S^u$ at the S locus which suppresses the expression of the other allele when it is present. $S^u$ seems to be very common in parts of Africa; 36 per cent of a sample of Congo Pygmies were found not to react with anti-U. The gene $S^u$ has not been detected in Australian Aborigines.

The MNS system is certainly even more complicated but we need not go into details. On the one hand, there are various rare genes that appear to be alleles of $M$, $N$, or $S$ and on the other there are additional specificities associated with the system as MN is with Ss. One of these, Henshaw, was detected by rabbit antisera to a Nigerian subject. It appears to be widespread in Africa, but not frequent (5 per cent or less), and, at least in West Africa, is associated with NS.

### The P system

Although the elucidation of this system since Landsteiner discovered it has been an interesting example of serological detective work, we shall say little about it on the grounds that technical difficulties have often made survey work unreliable. At first two phenotypes P(+) and P(−) could be distinguished using the single antiserum, anti-P. Many years later it was discovered that the antiserum to a very common antigen, Tj$^a$, could agglutinate both P(+) and P(−) cells but not those of the very rare phenotype Tj(a−). It appeared that the situation was analogous to $A_1A_2O$ in the ABO system, and P(+) and P(−) were renamed $P_1$ and $P_2$ respectively. Anti-Tj$^a$(PP$_1$) therefore behaves like anti-A and agglutinates both $A_1$ and $A_2$ cells, while the original anti-P behaves like anti-$A_1$ and agglutinates only $P_1$ cells. The phenotype Tj(a−) is regarded as the homozygote for a very rare allele $p$ of the P system.

There are certainly large regional variations in the frequencies of the $P$ genes. $P_2$ is around 50 per cent in Europe, though somewhat lower in Finland, but in West Africa it is less than 5 per cent and at the other extreme about 75–80 per cent in China and Japan.

### The Lutheran (Lu) system

The first Lutheran antibodies to be discovered gave positive reaction with about 4 per cent of English subjects. Later the antithetical antibody that reacts with Lu$^a$-negative cells was found. Using both antisera we can therefore detect three phenotypes Lu(a+b−), Lu(a+b+), and Lu(a−b+) corresponding to the 3 genotypes $Lu^aLu^a$, $Lu^aLu^b$, and $Lu^bLu^b$. The very rare type Lu(a−b−) has been observed and in some cases seems to be due to an independent locus that can block the formation of Lu substances.

The gene $Lu^a$ is found in Europe and also in Africa but always at low frequencies. It occurs in still lower frequencies in Burma, is rare in India, and virtually absent in Australasia. The low frequencies encountered in Amerinds may be the result of introduction in post-Columbian times.

### The Kell system

The antigen K, rather like Lu$^a$, is nowhere very frequent and is rare or absent outside Europe and the Middle East. The highest known frequencies (10 per cent) are in Arabia, falling to 5 per cent or less in western Europe. The gene is uncommon in Africa and India and virtually absent in the Far East and in Australia and the New World. The antiserum that detects the antigen k produced by the allelic gene is known. Incompatibility for K and k is sometimes responsible for haemolytic disease of the newborn.

Further study of the Kell system has shown that, like Rh and MNS, it is an association of loci or antigen-producing sites. About 2 per cent of white Americans were shown to be positive for an antigen $Kp^a$ which segregates with k. $Kp^a$ seems to be very rare in American Negroes. However, they commonly carry an antigen Sutter, $Js^a$, and this has also been shown to be associated with the Kell system. The system therefore comprises the allelic pairs $Kk$, $Kp^aKp^b$, and $Js^a$, $Js^b$ but only half of the expected eight haplotypes have been found because $K$ and $Kp^a$ are almost exclusive to Whites and $Js^a$ to Negroes, and intermixtures are too recent for all the possible recombinations to have been formed by crossing-over.

$Js^a$ has a frequency of about 9 per cent in American Negroes and seems to be much more frequent in Africa and immediately adjacent regions than anywhere else.

## The Duffy system

The first of the Duffy antigens, $Fy^a$, was discovered in 1950, and a year later antiserum that would detect the allelic product $Fy^b$ was found. Segregation of the pair of alleles produces the 3 phenotypes Fy(a+b−), Fy(a+b+), and Fy(a−b+). It was therefore a surprise when it was found that about 70 per cent of American Negroes react to neither antiserum and are Fy(a−b−). It is not clear whether the gene $Fy$ produces an antigen to which no antibody has yet been found or whether it supresses the formation of antigen by its partner.

$Fy$ probably makes a greater distinction between European (Caucasoids) and Africans than any other gene yet discovered. In a sample of Western Pygmies the $Fy$ frequency was 100 per cent and values in the 90 per cent range have been reported in several Central African tribes. In the Beja, south of the Red Sea, we find 78 per cent, in Arabia 50 per cent, and 15–50 per cent in Kurds of northern Iran and Iraq. In western Europeans, however, the frequency is a mere 3 per cent or less. Outside Europe and the Middle East $Fy$ is probably infrequent, but the data are scanty.

The gene $Fy^a$ (Fig. 17.6) also shows wide frequency variations. It reaches 100 per cent in some Australian Aborigines and is also high in American Indians and in Asiatic Indians. In western Europe the frequencies fall to 35–45 per cent, but are higher in Lapps (54–82 per cent). It is interesting to note than in Africa 5–10 per cent of $Fy^a$ has been found in Bushmen.

## The Diego system

The antigen Diego was first detected in a Venezuelan family and for a time ranked as a so-called 'private' antigen with a very restricted, familial distribution. About 30 per cent of Diego-positives were then found in certain South American Indian tribes. Some of the distribution data for this gene are given in Table 17.5. Somewhat lower frequencies occur in North American Indians and lower still in Chinese and Japanese. The antigen has been detected in Bor-

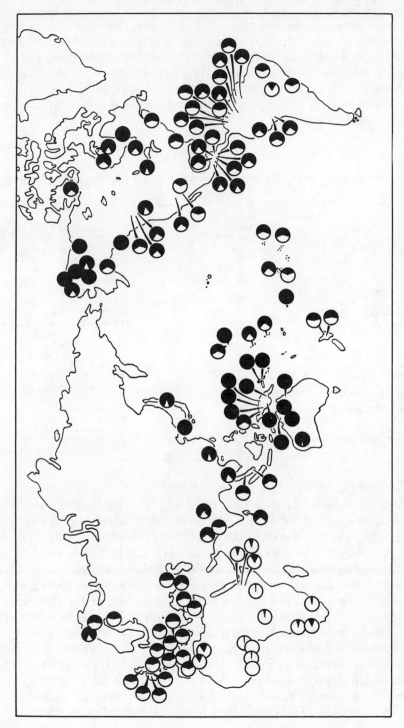

FIG. 17.6. World distribution of the Duffy gene $Fy^a$. The map does not include all published values. (From Barnicot, *Proc. XIth Int. Cong. Gen.*, reprinted *Genetics Today*, 1963.)

neo, but it has not so far been found in Melanesia, Polynesia, or Australia, nor in Europe or Africa. Its area of distribution seems, therefore, to be among those oriental populations which are broadly classified as Mongoloids, but its frequency distribution does not correspond closely to those of the various morphological criteria on which this grouping is based; indeed, it reaches its highest frequencies in certain peoples among whom Mongoloid characteristics are rather inconspicuous.

TABLE 17.5

*Frequencies (per cent) of Diego-positive (Di(a+)) phenotype in various populations*

| Population | Number tested | Percentage Di(a+) | Author |
|---|---|---|---|
| Caingangs, Brazil | 48 | 45·8 | Junqueira *et al.* (1956) |
| Carajas, Brazil | 36 | 36·1 | Junqueira *et al.* (1956) |
| Caribs, Venezuela | 121 | 35·5 | Layrisse *et al.* (1955) |
| Maya Indians | 363 | 17·6 | Matson, Swanson (1959) |
| Guahibos, Venezuela | 76 | 14·5 | Layrisse, Arends (1956) |
| Japanese | 65 | 12·3 | Layrisse, Arends (1956) |
| Chippewa Indians | 148 | 10·8 | Lewis *et al.* (1956) |
| Koreans | 277 | 6·1 | Chong Duk Wou *et al.* (1960) |
| Guajiros, Venezuela | 152 | 5·3 | Layrisse *et al.* (1955) |
| Apache Indians | 73 | 4·1 | Gershowitz (1959) |
| Alaskan Eskimos | 241 | 0·8 | Corcoran *et al.* (1959) |
| Eskimos | 156 | 0·0 | Lewis *et al.* (1956) |
| Norwegian Lapps | 433 | 0·0 | Kornstadt (1960) |
| Polynesians | 80 | 0·0 | Simmons (1957) |
| New Britain | 74 | 0·0 | Simmons (1957) |
| Australian Aborigines | 162 | 0·0 | Simmons (1957) |
| USA Whites | 1000 | 0·0 | Levine *et al.* (1956) |
| Asiatic Indians | 75 | 0·0 | Gershowitz (1959) |
| Africans (Liberia, Ivory Coast) | 775 | 0·0 | Gershowitz (1959) |
| Bushmen | 114 | 0·0 | Weiner and Zoutendyk (1959) |

## The Xg antigen

In 1962 an antigen, $Xg^a$, was discovered which is clearly determined by a gene, $Xg^a$, on the X-chromosome. Moreover, the frequency of $Xg^a$ in Europeans is high, 68 per cent as estimated from the prevalence of Xg(a+) males. About 90 per cent of females also carry this gene, and of these about 45 per cent are heterozygous and therefore useful for linkage studies.

Unfortunately the value of $Xg^a$ for linkage research has turned out to be limited because the locus appears to be near the end of the short arm of the X-chromosome and thus far distant from most of its other loci. However, this disappointment has perhaps been compensated by the great value of $Xg^a$ in the investigation of the various X-chromosome aberrations in which either the number or structure of this chromosome is abnormal (see p. 111). Thus in cases of Klinefelter's syndrome (XXY) it may be possible, using $Xg^a$ as a marker, to tell whether the extra chromosome came from the mother or the father and therefore in which parent a meiotic abnormality occurred.

Some population variations in the frequency of Xg$^a$ are shown below in Table 17.6.

TABLE 17.6

*Population frequencies of Xg$^a$*

| Population | N | Xg$^a$ (per cent) |
|---|---|---|
| New Guinea | 263 | 85 |
| Australian Aborigines | 352 | 79 |
| Navajo American Indians | 308 | 77 |
| Sardinians | 322 | 76 |
| Israelis | 201 | 68 |
| N. Europeans | 5388 | 66 |
| Indians, Bombay | 100 | 65 |
| Chinese, mainland | 171 | 60 |
| Chinese, Taiwan | 178 | 53 |
| New York Negroes & Jamaicans | 219 | 55 |
| Taiwan Aborigines | 164 | 38 |

(From Simmons, *Nature, Lond.* **227**, 1363, 1970.)

It is a curious fact that an antigen indistinguishable from Xg$^a$ has been found in gibbons (*Hylobates lar lar*), though not in pongids or in a few monkey species that were tested. The antigen is also X- linked in the gibbon as far as can be determined from small samples.

## Building phylogenetic trees

The main aims of collecting gene frequency data on the populations of the world is to work out their evolutionary relationships and try to understand the processes that brought about the existing pattern. We expect populations that have separated recently to retain many common features of gene frequency patterns, but if they remain reproductively isolated for long periods we expect, in general, progressive divergence due to various evolutionary forces. Evolution is conveniently pictured as a tree with the tips of surviving branches representing existing populations. In the case of subspecific evolution gene flow is still possible between populations and may slow divergence; in the extreme case two populations may intermix completely, thus forming a loop on the tree. There is also the possibility (in evolution in general) that remotely related populations may come to be more alike, at least in certain respects, due to adaptation to similar environments.

In the last 10 years, electronic computers have made it possible to reconstruct the *most probable* tree that would give rise to an observed pattern of gene frequencies. We can give only a superficial account of this work here, and we insert it at this point simply because the pioneers, Cavalli-Sforza and Edwards, chose to use data on human blood-group frequencies.

Fig. 17.7 shows 4 populations whose positions in a plane are defined by their frequencies for 2 genes. Considering the origin of this pattern by a process of divergence in time, the arrangement shown seems intuitively the most likely.

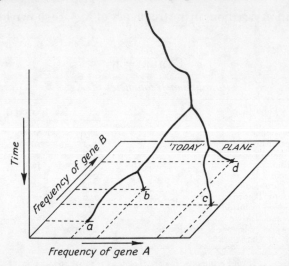

FIG. 17.7. A hypothetical tree of evolutionary descent connecting four populations a, b, c, d that have been characterized by their frequencies for two genes *A* and *B*. (From Cavalii-Sforza, *et al.*, *Cold Spring Harb. Symp. quant. Biol.*, 1964.)

However, we want to use data on as many loci and alleles as possible so that the populations must then be regarded as points in multi-dimensional space (p. 201).

The simplest and mathematically most attractive model of gene-frequency divergence is one due solely to random genetic drift; but this produces divergence of populations that are already separated and does not produce fission. In general, we have little evidence about the time and causes of such splits so in this model we assume that they occur at random.

Even with this relatively simple model the number of possible trees grows very rapidly with the number of populations. It seems that the identification of the most probable, or group of most probable, trees by orthodox mathematical methods meets with difficulties and the authors resorted to plausible approximations. One of these is that the most probable tree will be close to the one that involves the minimal length of evolutionary paths.

Fig. 17.8 shows a tree for 15 human populations based on the same 5 blood-group loci for each (ABO, Rh, MNS, Fy, Di). The vertical scale is not time but number of gene substitutions which if drift alone were operating would depend on (effective) population size and time since separation.

Clearly this model is greatly simplified and many biologists will surely feel that selection played an important, though not necessarily exclusive, part in the geographical differentiation of man. A very important feature of drift is that it acts on all loci and (after correction for gene-frequency differences) produces a steady increase of gene-frequency variance. Selection, on the other hand, will tend to act differently on different loci, changing the frequencies

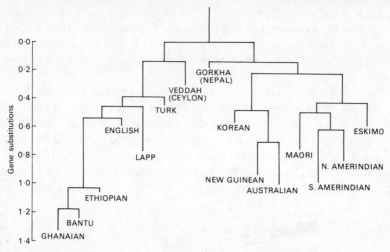

F I G. 17.8. Most probable tree of relationships between 15 populations based on the gene frequencies for 5 blood-group systems. The scale is in terms of number of genes substituted over the given span of time. (From Cavalli-Sforza *et al.*, *Cold Spring Harb. Symp. quant. biol.*, 1964.)

of some genes rapidly and stabilizing others. If an estimate can be made of expected gene-frequency variance due to drift, discrepancies in the values for particular loci may indicate whether they have been under selection. As the authors point out, the power of drift to produce gene-frequency differentiation is quite considerable. They estimated that the variance that they found in their exploratory model could have occurred in a period of half a million years even if (effective) population sizes were as high as 10 000.

## The Gm and Inv groups

### Immunoglobulins (Ig)

The Gm and Inv factors are serologically detectable variations of certain antibody proteins (immunoglobulins) of the serum. The immunoglobulins are a physiologically very important but highly complex class of proteins. We must therefore say something about their structure and functions, but our account can only be a sketch of a vast subject.

In the course of postnatal life antibodies are formed to a great variety of micro-organisms, foreign proteins, and complex carbohydrates that gain entry to the tissues. It is a remarkable property of antibodies that they combine more or less specifically with the antigen that elicited their formation. This is presumably because the antigen-binding part of the Ig molecule fits closely to certain regions (antigenic determinants) of the antigen surface. It is known that this antigen-binding region is extremely variable in amino-acid sequence, and this is not unexpected if many different antigens have to bound. It is accepted that this variability is coded by genes, but it is uncertain how much of the genetic information is transmitted by gametes and how much is generated somatically in the individual. According to the prevailing 'clonal theory' the antigen does not act as a template moulding the antibody to fit it, but its presence somehow stimulates multiplication of pre-existing cells coded to produce the appropriate antibody.

A schematic representation of an Ig molecule is shown below in Fig. 17.9. It is Y-shaped and is composed of two identical halves each of which contains a heavy (H) chain with a light (L) chain attached to it in the arm of the Y. The two halves and also the H and L chains are held together mainly by disulphide bonds. The highly variable parts of the L and H chains (labelled V in the diagram) form the N-terminal halves of the arms of the Y. Each Ig molecule therefore has two identical combining sites and there is electron microscopical

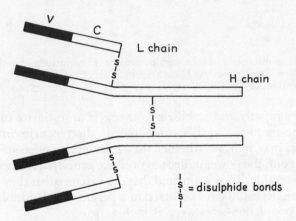

FIG. 17.9. Diagram of an immunoglobulin molecule. Each half consists of a light (L) chain and a heavy (H) chain. The two halves are held together by disulphide bonds. Disulphide bonds also connect the L and H chains of each half. The black areas indicate regions of the L and H chains that are variable in amino-acid composition and the white areas indicate the constant regions.

evidence showing that this bivalency results in the formation of aggregates of antigens and antibody molecules. The remaining (constant or C) regions of the L and H chains are much less variable in sequence. Nevertheless, several structurally distinct classes and subclasses of these chains can be distinguished and there is additional polymorphic variation of restricted regions of certain chain types giving rise to the Gm and Inv specificities. In man and higher vertebrates in general there are 2 types of L chains ($\kappa$ and $\lambda$), and 5 classes of H chains ($\gamma, \alpha, \eta, \delta, \varepsilon$). The latter characterize 5 classes of Ig molecule (IgG, IgA, IgM, IgD, IgE) which differ in their immunological properties. IgG, which is the most abundant type in normal serum, is able to pass the placental barrier and much of the Ig of new born children is maternal IgG. The IgM molecule (molecular weight 900 000) is composed of 5 subunits, each roughly the same size as the single molecule of the other classes, and it is generally the first type

## TABLE 17.7

### Some properties of Ig classes

| Class | IgG | IgA | IgM | IgD | IgE |
|---|---|---|---|---|---|
| Chains | $(\kappa$ or $\lambda)_2\gamma_2$ | $(\kappa$ or $\lambda)_2\alpha_2$ | $((\kappa$ or $\lambda)_2\mu_2)^5$ | $(\kappa$ or $\lambda)_2\delta_2$ | $(\kappa$ or $\lambda)_2\varepsilon_2$ |
| Molecular weight | 150 000 | 152 000 or 385 000 | 900 000 | 175 000 | 190 000 |
| Carbohydrate content (per cent) | 2·5 | 5–10 | 5–10 | | 11·5 |
| Mean adult serum concentration (mg/ml) | 12·0 | 1·8 | 1·0 | 0·03 | 0·0003 |
| Functional characteristics | Complement fixation; placental transfer | In external secretions | Complement fixation; early response; high agglutinating efficiency | | Associated with certain types of allergy |

of antibody to be formed in response to an antigenic challenge. IgA is mainly found in mucous surfaces and in their secretions. Some of the properties of these chains are summarized in Table 17.7. Although the chains are represented as straight in the diagram they are in reality folded in certain regions and the folds are stabilized by intrachain disulphide bonds.

The Gm specificities, now some 20 in number, are due to variation in the H chains of IgG only. Four subclasses of IgG heavy chains can be recognized ($\gamma$G1, $\gamma$G2, $\gamma$G3, $\gamma$G4). Some of the Gm specificities are associated with $\gamma$G1, others with $\gamma$G3, one or two with $\gamma$G2 and none as yet with $\gamma$G4 as shown in Table 17.8.

TABLE 17.8

*Associations of certain Gm factors with IgG H-chain subclasses*

| IgG H-chain subclass | Gm factors |
| --- | --- |
| $\gamma$G1 | 1, 2, 3, 4, 17 |
| $\gamma$G2 | 23 |
| $\gamma$G3 | 5, 6, 11, 13, 14, 21 |
| $\gamma$G4 | None known |

In a few instances the amino-acid substitutions underlying Gm specificities have been established. Thus molecules positive for Gm(1), the first Gm factor to be discovered by Grubb in 1956, have Asn and Leu at two nearby H-chain sites, whereas Gm(1)-negative molecules have Glu and Met. The Inv specificities are on the $\kappa$ L chains and it is known that in Inv(3) positives Val is substituted for Leu at site 191. A few other polymorphic variations of Ig chains may be briefly mentioned; Isf is located on H chains of IgG, Oz on the $\theta\ \lambda$ chains, and Am on the H chains of IgA.

It is evident that the Ig proteins of normal serum are enormously heterogeneous in structure and it is virtually impossible to separate pure fractions in amounts sufficient for chemical analysis. However, certain rare tumours of the bone marrow (myelomas) produce large amounts of homogeneous Ig, and free L chains are excreted as Bence–Jones protein in the urine. It is thought that these tumours are formed by multiplication of a single antibody-producing plasma cell. A single plasma cell can produce only one class and subclass of Ig at a given time; furthermore if the patient is heterozygous for Gm factors, only those coded by one of the two alleles are found on the H chains it produces. This 'allelic exclusion' is reminiscent of the inactivation of one X-chromosome in females.

We have seen in discussing haemoglobins that structurally different chains such as $\alpha$, $\beta$, and $\gamma$ are coded for by different gene loci (cistrons). This must also be true for the various classes and subclasses of Ig L and H chains. Moreover, according to one view, there are also separate V and C genes coding respectively for variable and constant regions; a single cell would need to use 4 genes ($V_L$, $V_H$, $C_L$, and $C_H$) to produce an Ig molecule.

If we study the inheritance of single Gm factors such as Gm(1) we find that Gm(1) positive and negative types segregate as expected for traits determined by a pair of codominant alleles. But if we test for several different factors we find that some of them are transmitted together in groups, a phenomenon we have already met in discussing Rh and MNS blood groups. In Europe, for example, the patterns Gm (1,17,21), Gm (1,2,17,21), and Gm (3,5,13,14) are common and are inherited as units. We know that factors 1,2,3, and 17 are on $\gamma$G1, whereas 5,13,14, and 21 are on $\gamma$G3 and must therefore be produced by different loci. These loci are presumably very closely linked since other combinations of factors that could be produced by intercistronic cross-overs are seldom found in a given population. Cases of such cross-overs in families have been claimed, and it is possible that some of the combinations present in different populations have been produced in this way. Since the combinations of Gm factors are evidently transmitted by segments of DNA containing more than one cistron it is convenient to speak of them as 'haplotypes'. The term indicates a set of factors regularly transmitted together by the haploid chromosome set of a gamete.

*Detection of Gm and Inv factors*

The usual testing method is haemagglutination inhibition. Red cells are first coated with incomplete Rh antibod (see p. 261) carrying the Gm factor to be detected. These coated cells can be agglutinated if an antibody specific for this factor is added. Suitable antisera can be obtained from rheumatoid arthritis patients and from some normal people. If the serum under test is included in the mixture of antiserum and coated cells it will compete for antibody if it carries the same Gm factor as that present on the coated cells and agglutination will be prevented. In the case of a few Gm factors antibodies that precipitate the IgG protein directly have been produced by immunizing rabbits or monkeys with appropriate H chains but the classical method is still the more sensitive.

*Distribution of Gm and Inv factors*

Two systems of notation for these factors are still in common use, and this does not help to clarify a somewhat complicated subject; the relations between them are shown in Table 17.9.

The number of populations that have been tested for as many as 9 Gm factors is still not very large but the data assembled in Table 17.10 serves to show that there are some striking differences between the indigenous people of major geographical areas and in some cases between populations living in the same area. Certain haplotypes are frequent in some populations but rare or virtually absent in others. Gm (3,5,13,14), for example, is common in Europeans (Caucasoids) but is infrequent or absent elsewhere unless there has been recent admixture with Europeans. There are 4 haplotypes that attain high frequencies in African Negroes or populations largely derived from them. It is interesting

TABLE 17.9

*Relation between original symbols and WHO symbols for Gm and Inv factors*

| Number | Original name |
|--------|---------------|
| *Gm* 1 | a |
| 2 | x |
| 3 | $b^w = b^2$ |
| 4 | f |
| 5 | $b = b^1$ |
| 6 | $c = c^5$ |
| 7 | r |
| 8 | e |
| 9 | p |
| 10 | $\alpha$ |
| 11 | $\beta$    $b^0$ |
| 12 | $\ddot{\gamma}$ |
| 13 | $b^3$ |
| 14 | $b^4$ |
| 15 | s |
| 16 | t |
| 17 | z |
| 18 | Rouen 2 |
| 19 | Rouen 3 |
| 20 | 20 |
| 21 | g |
| 22 | y |
| 23 | n |
|  | $b^5$ |
|  | $c^3$ |
| *Inv* 1 | 1 |
| 2 | a |
| 3 | b |

that about 10 per cent of Gm (1,5,13,14,17) an African haplotype is found in Kurdish Jews of Iraq and about 2 per cent in Ashkenazi Jews. It will be noticed that the Bushmen have a deviant pattern, including one haplotype, Gm (1,5,17), that is peculiar to them and to peoples with whom they have mixed (Fig. 17.10). They also have another haplotype, Gm (1,13,17) that is found in eastern Asiatic peoples, but is not otherwise characteristic of Africans.

It is evident from Table 17.10 that testing for many factors increases the power of Gm studies for distinguishing between populations. For example, Gm (1,5) occurs in many parts of the world, but, when additional factors are examined, it is seen to include 4 different haplotypes in Africa and a different combination again in eastern Asia and Oceania. It is an interesting fact that Gm(1) and Gm(5) segregate independently in Europeans.

Table 17.10 gives a broad view of regional contrasts in Gm haplotypes, but conspicuous frequency variations have also been reported in more restricted areas. A clinal increase in Gm(1) in passing northwards in Europe was noted some years ago. In work on Australian Aborigines it was found that certain tribes of northern Queensland have appreciable frequencies of Gm(1,5,13,14), which is absent in tribes of the central and western deserts. This, and certain other Gm data, are consistent with gene flow to Australia across the Torres

# TABLE 17.10

## Common Gm haplotypes in various populations tested for 9 factors

| | A | B | C | D | E | F | G | H | I | J | K | Haplotypes |
|---|---|---|---|---|---|---|---|---|---|---|---|---|
| European (Caucasoids) | + | + | + | | | | | | | | | A (1,17,21) |
| Mongoloids | + | + | | | | | | + | + | | | B (1,2,17,21) |
| Ainu | +++ | +++ | | | | | | + | + | | | C (3,5,13,14) |
| New Guinea | +++ | +++ | | | | | | | | | | D (1,5,13,14,17) |
| Australian | | | | + | + | | + | | | + | | E (1,5,14,17) |
| Africans (Negroids) | | | | + | | + | | + | | | | F (1,5,6,17) |
| Bushmen | + | | | + | | | | | | | + | G (1,5,6,14,17) |
| | | | | | | | | | | | | H (1,13,17) |
| | | | | | | | | | | | | I (1,3,5,13,14) |
| | | | | | | | | | | | | J (2,17,21) |
| | | | | | | | | | | | | K (1,5,17) |

(After Steinberg, 1973).

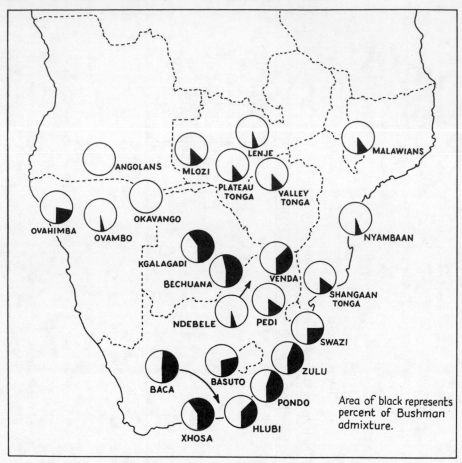

F IG. 17.10. Map of southern Africa showing the estimated percentage of Bushmen admixture in various tribes as determined by the frequency of the Gm1,13 haplotype. (From Jenkins et al., *Am. J. phys. Anthrop.*, **32**, 1970.)

Straits. In New Guinea itself there is a good deal of local variation in haplotype frequencies. In the Markham Valley area the frequencies of certain Gm haplotypes are correlated with the linguistic division between Melanesian- and non-Austronesian-speaking tribes and this evidence tends to support the view that the former came from South East Asia. The frequency of Gm(1,13) has been used to chart Bushman–Hottentot admixture among the South African Bantu (Fig. 17.9).

Steinberg, who has been associated with much of the anthropological work on Gm factors, estimated the amount of Caucasoid and Khoisan (Bushman–Hottentot) admixture in Sidamo tribes of south-western Ethiopia and found 40 per cent and 12 per cent respectively. He also studied the Ainu of Hokkaido,

Japan, who have one haplotype Gm(2,17,21) peculiar to themselves, and he concluded that his sample of Ainu had about 30 per cent of Japanese admixture.

If the impression that Gm haplotype frequencies show greater contrasts between various populations than do other genetic markers is substantiated by further work, we must ask why these contrasts have been maintained in the face of gene flow and recombination tending to disrupt linkage associations. Strong regional selective forces would be an obvious, but at present speculative answer. The suggestion that certain haplotypes are associated with antibodies that are effective against particular diseases is attractive but unproved.

Three Inv factors, Inv(1), (2), and (3), are known. Inv(1) and Inv(2) are closely associated in inheritance and Inv(3) is almost antithetical to them. Most of the population work has been done using anti-Inv(1) or anti-Inv(2) sera. Inv(1,2) has been found at appreciable frequency in all populations examined. The frequency is relatively low ($<$ 20 per cent) in Europe and the Middle East but higher elsewhere, reaching a maximum of 94 per cent in certain Venezuelan American Indian tribes.

## The histocompatibility (HL-A) system

It is well known that skin and other tissues grafted from an individual to another usually evoke an immunological reaction leading to destruction of the graft. This graft-rejection is in general less severe if host and donor are closely related. Inherited differences in the HL-A antigens of the tissues are an important factor in these incompatibilities and the system has been intensively studied with a view to improving graft-tolerance by matching the antigens of donor and recipient. The HL-A antigens are detectable in most tissues but not on red blood-cells; it is nevertheless convenient to mention them in this chapter.

Antisera to HL-A antigens are usually obtained from pregnant women who have become immunized by the foetus; however, unlike some of the blood-group antibodies they do not damage the unborn child. The antigens are detected by a cytotoxicity test. Lymphocytes from the person to be tested are mixed with a specific anti-HL-A antiserum in the presence of complement (p. 247). If the cells carry the corresponding antigen they are damaged and can be distinguished from normal cells by staining with certain dyes.

The HL-A antigens are determined by two different but closely linked loci, LA and 4. At least 14 different LA-locus antigens and 17 4-locus antigens are known in Europeans and they appear to depend on a series of alleles at each locus. Due to the close linkage of the loci certain pairs of antigens such as 1(LA) and 8(4) and 11(LA) and 5(4) are inherited together in a given population. We can refer to such combinations as HL-A haplotypes in the same way as we speak of Gm haplotypes (p. 277). In the course of time crossing-over would be expected to break up these associations until, at equilibrium, they are no longer discernible in a population. The fact that they have persisted suggests that there may be selective forces favouring certain combinations of alleles.

## Table 17.11

| | N | LA locus | | | | | | 4-locus | | | | |
|---|---|---|---|---|---|---|---|---|---|---|---|---|
| | | 1 | 2 | 3 | 9 | 10 | 11 | 5 | 7 | 8 | 12 | 13 |
| England | 100 | 18 | 29 | 14 | 8 | 3 | 7 | 4 | 17 | 13 | 18 | 13 |
| Germany | 442 | 14 | 26 | 16 | 9 | 6 | 5 | 7 | 15 | 10 | 12 | 4 |
| France | 152 | 12 | 32 | 13 | 12 | 7 | 5 | 7 | 12 | 5 | 21 | 3 |
| Iceland | 116 | 11 | 34 | 18 | 12 | 7 | 6 | 2 | 23 | 8 | 13 | 1 |
| Basque | 142 | 9 | 28 | 8 | 13 | 9 | 7 | 11 | 11 | 9 | 24 | 2 |
| Sardinia | 200 | 3 | 32 | 3 | 11 | 9 | 10 | 8 | 2 | 3 | 3 | 0 |
| Skolt Lapps | 178 | 1 | 28 | 37 | 16 | 7 | 8 | 9 | 23 | 2 | 1 | 1 |
| Arabs | 181 | 16 | 20 | 14 | 10 | 6 | 7 | 20 | 3 | 4 | 5 | 2 |
| Punjab | 150 | 15 | 11 | 7 | 10 | 6 | 15 | 19 | 4 | 13 | 9 | 2 |
| India (various) | 153 | 11 | 17 | 10 | 18 | 2 | 14 | 12 | 10 | 3 | 13 | 3 |
| Malays | 137 | 3 | 15 | 2 | 40 | 1 | 16 | 6 | 5 | 0 | 3 | 8 |
| New Guinea (E. Highlands) | 214 | 0 | 0 | 0 | 76 | 3 | 4 | 0 | 0 | 0 | 0 | 5 |
| Australians (Walbiri) | 177 | 0 | 13 | 0 | 31 | 43 | 10 | 0 | 0 | 0 | 0 | 21 |
| Japanese | 127 | 0 | 27 | 1 | 37 | 14 | 4 | 18 | 5 | 0 | 8 | 1 |
| Chinese (Canton) | 166 | 1 | 31 | 1 | 17 | 5 | 28 | 6 | 1 | 0 | 1 | 12 |
| Ainu | 127 | 0 | 29 | 1 | 31 | 17 | 3 | 11 | 1 | 0 | 5 | 0 |
| Tibetans | 138 | 9 | 29 | 4 | 33 | 6 | 16 | 21 | 6 | 0 | 2 | 1 |
| Papago | 105 | 0 | 51 | 6 | 37 | 0 | 0 | 5 | 0 | 0 | 1 | 0 |
| Guatemala | 131 | 0 | 51 | 0 | 22 | 0 | 0 | 5 | 1 | 0 | 1 | 0 |
| Quechua (Peru) | 111 | 1 | 59 | 1 | 22 | 0 | 1 | 3 | 0 | 0 | 1 | 0 |
| Greenland (Eskimos) | 177 | 1 | 16 | 0 | 65 | 0 | 2 | 17 | 1 | 0 | 2 | 0 |
| Canadian (Eskimos) | 336 | 0 | 28 | 0 | 63 | 0 | 0 | 15 | 0 | 0 | 0 | 0 |
| Zambians | 172 | 2 | 14 | 5 | 11 | 5 | 0 | 1 | 10 | 2 | 19 | 1 |
| Shi (Zaire) | 114 | 7 | 26 | 4 | 13 | 9 | 2 | 17 | 12 | 1 | 16 | 1 |
| Kung Bushmen | 84 | 5 | 17 | 8 | 14 | 7 | 0 | 9 | 4 | 4 | 6 | 2 |

The frequencies of some HL-A alleles show considerable geographical variation. Table 17.11 gives some examples for a limited number of these alleles. Although most of the samples are quite small, and the standard errors of the allele frequencies correspondingly large, certain trends are apparent. Frequencies in Europe are fairly uniform but a few populations, such as Lapps, Sardinians, and Basques, show deviations as they do for various other genes. Some alleles, such as 1,3,7,8, and 12, are much less common in eastern Asiatic, Australasian, and American Indian populations than they are in Europe. On the other hand, 9 is conspicuously frequent in New-World Aborigines, especially Eskimos. In general, African frequencies are less divergent from European values, though some antigens are now known that appear to be characteristic of this region. It should be noted that there is a good deal of variation between tribes in Australia and in New Guinea; such local variation is always troublesome when one tries to present the data in a compact form. The HL-A system, with its numerous polymorphic alleles, is outstandingly useful for the study of population affinities.

At present we know little about the nature of selective forces acting on the HL-A system but we have a few hints and some interesting speculations. Divergent frequencies of particular alleles have been found in samples of patients suffering from certain uncommon diseases such as Hodgkin's disease (lymphatic leukaemia) and lupus erythematosus. There is also evidence of loci closely linked to HL-A that influence the effectiveness of immunological response to certain viruses.

# 18. Miscellaneous variations

## Taste-deficiency for phenylthiourea

A CHANCE observation by Fox in 1931 showed that some people are unable to taste the synthetic compound phenylthiourea (phenylthiocarbamide or PTC) which others describe as very bitter like quinine. It was later shown that the ability to taste this substance is inherited as a simple Mendelian dominant. The simplest form of test is to give people crystals of PTC, or paper impregnated with it. A better method is to get the subject to taste a series of dilutions of the substance in water and this test shows that tasters vary considerably in sensitivity. The diagnosis of a taster or non-taster is, however, essentially subjective, depending on the subject's description of his sensations. The test can be further improved by Harris and Kalmus's procedure in which the subject is asked to pick out the PTC solutions from a number of samples, half of which are water. By repeating the test with increasing concentrations of PTC the threshold concentration at which the substance is first detected can be determined, and the distribution of thresholds in a population can then be plotted as a histogram (Fig. 18.1). A bimodal distribution is obtained, one mode for the tasters and one for the non-tasters, but there is usually some overlap so that a few subjects are difficult to classify. The test can be further refined by correcting for the slightly greater sensitivity of females, the decline of taste acuity with age, and for general taste sensitivity to bitter materials by control tests with brucine. Inability to taste PTC is inherited as a recessive trait, but there is some evidence that the threshold is higher in the heterozygous tasters ($Tt$) than in the homozygotes ($TT$).

## Distribution

A limited number of populations have been tested by the sorting technique and some results are shown below (Table 18.1). The frequency of the non-taster phenotype in north-western Europe is 35–40 per cent, but appreciably lower in Mediterranean samples. In Africans, Chinese, Japanese, American Indians, and also in the Lapps it is very much less frequent.

## Selective influences

Many other compounds chemically related to PTC show taste bimodality, though PTC itself gives the widest separation of the two phenotypes. It appears that the following configuration is essential:

$$\begin{array}{c} \text{---C---N} \\ \parallel \\ \text{S} \end{array}$$

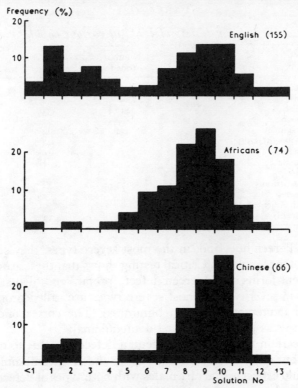

F IG. 18.1. The distributions of taste-thresholds for PTC in three populations. The solution numbers represent serial dilutions by one-half of a 0·13 per cent solution of PTC. The tests were made by the sorting technique. The form of the non-taster distribution, occupying the region from solution 5 to less than 1 is clearly shown in the case of the English sample. (From Barnicot, *Ann. Eugen.*, 1950.)

The corresponding urea derivatives in which oxygen (O) is substituted for sulphur (S) are inactive in this respect.

The fact that certain thioureas, notably thiouracil, are used clinically for the suppression of thyroid activity led to the idea that the polymorphism for the taster gene might be in some way connected with thyroid function. Taste-testing of patients with various thyroid diseases has shown that the taster frequency in samples with certain types of goitre is divergent.

Observations on the reactions of chimpanzees to PTC solutions suggest that taste-deficiency may also occur in these apes. If this is so, it has been argued, the polymorphism may be one which has been maintained, presumably by heterosis, since a remote stage of human evolution.

### Colour blindness

Defective colour vision of the kind known as 'red–green colour blindness' is a familiar example of human X-linked inheritance. Affected people tend to

TABLE 18.1

*Frequency of non-tasters of PTC in various populations*

| | Number tested | Non-tasters (per cent) |
|---|---|---|
| Hindus | 489 | 33·7 |
| Danish | 251 | 32·7 |
| English | 441 | 31·5 |
| Spanish | 203 | 25·6 |
| Portuguese | 454 | 24·0 |
| Negritos (Malaya) | 50 | 18·0 |
| Malays | 237 | 16·0 |
| Japanese | 295 | 7·1 |
| Lapps | 140 | 6·4 |
| West Africans | 74 | 2·7 |
| Chinese | 50 | 2·0 |
| South American Indians (Brazil) | 163 | 1·2 |

confuse red and green hues and, in the most severe types, they seem to have no perception of these colours. Critical testing shows that there are two physiologically different forms of red–green defect, 'protan' and 'deutan', and each of them varies in severity. The most severe types are called protanopia (red blindness) and deuteranopia (green blindness). The corresponding milder defects are known as protanomaly and deuteranomaly.

It is almost certain that protan and deutan defects are due to mutations at two different, but quite closely linked, loci on the X-chromosome. If this is the case we would expect to find rare males with both types of defect. We would also expect to find occasional families in which a woman with normal colour vision has protan, deutan, and normal sons; this situation could arise if the mother were heterozygous at both loci and produced a normal chromosome by crossing-over. Both these situations have been reported, though the diagnosis of mixed defects is not easy. Differences in the severity of red–green defects are thought to be due to two or more allelic variants at each locus.

The mode of action of the colour-defect mutations is obscure; it is difficult to get material for detailed biochemical work on the human retina. However, some elegant optical experiments on living subjects suggest that protanopes lack the red-sensitive pigment in the cone receptors; their sensitivity to light in the red range is in fact very low. Deuteranopes, on the other hand, have normal light sensitivity in both the red and green ranges, and it may be that the defect is at some higher level of neural organization. We must also mention that there are autosomally inherited defects of colour perception in the blue–yellow region ('tritan' defects), but they are rare. Cone monochromatism, in which perception of colour is entirely lacking, is even rarer. The approximate frequencies of these various deficiencies in western European populations are shown in Table 18.2. It will be noted that deuteranomaly is the commonest type. The frequencies are considerably higher in males than in females as expected for X-linked recessive traits. The frequency in males gives a direct estimate of the gene frequency $q$, and, at equilibrium, the frequency of affected females (homozygotes) is expected to be $q^2$.

A thorough investigation of colour-vision defects involves measuring sensitivity to light and ability to make colour matches and discriminate between hues throughout the spectrum. This requires plenty of time and quite elaborate apparatus. Simpler and quicker methods are therefore needed for screening large samples of populations. Colour-confusion charts, such as the well-known Ishihara set, are generally used, though they tend to miss some of the milder defects. The subject is asked to name a series of coloured numerals on a coloured background or to trace a wavy line if he is illiterate. Both numerals and background are composed of coloured dots, mostly in shades of red or green, and these are chosen so that colour-blind subjects either fail to see the figure or see only parts of it and so mistake it for another numeral. The tests are designed for use in diffuse daylight and can give false results in other illumination.

The Nagel anomaloscope is a useful instrument for detecting the less severe defects and it has been adapted for work in the field. Normal subjects can match a spectral yellow with a mixture of monochromatic red and green. In fact they can match any coloured light by mixing not more than three coloured lights, usually suitably chosen red, green, and blue. They are therefore known as 'trichromats'. Protanopes and deuteranopes match all colours with only two colours and are called 'dichromats'. In using the anomaloscope the subject looks through an eyepiece at a circular field one half of which is illuminated with a spectral yellow. By turning calibrated knobs he can add red or green to the other half-field until a match is obtained. The proportion of red and green chosen by normal people varies little but dichromats are much more erratic. Protanomalous subjects require more red and deuteranomalous subjects more green than normal. Red and green perception is evidently weak rather than absent and they are therefore referred to as 'anomalous trichromats'. The inter-

TABLE 18.2

*Frequencies of various types of colour-vision defects in Europeans*

| Type of defect | Frequency in population (per cent) | |
|---|---|---|
| | Male | Female |
| Monochromatism | Very rare | Very rare |
| Dichromatism | 2·105 | 0·06 |
| Protanopia | 1·0 | 0·02 |
| Deuteranopia | 1·1 | 0·01 |
| Tritanopia | 0·005 | 0·003 |
| Anomalous trichromatism | 5·9 | 0·40 |
| Protanomaly | 1·0 | 0·02 |
| Deuteranomaly | 4·9 | 0·38 |
| Tritanomaly | Fairly rare | Fairly rare |
| Colour-vision defects | (approx.) 8·0 | (approx.) 0·46 |

(Modified from Wright, 1953.)

pretation of anomaloscope results may need special care when studying unsophisticated populations who are unfamiliar with such gadgets and unaccustomed to making precise colour matches.

Table 18.3 shows the frequencies of red–green defects as a whole in male samples from selected populations tested by rapid methods. Values for Europe are around 7–8 per cent; they are somewhat lower in various peoples of eastern Asia. In India, as far as we can tell from relatively small samples, there is a good deal of variation between the caste groups of some regions and between certain tribal and Hindu populations. Values for sub-Saharan Africa, the New World, and Australasia are relatively low (1–3 per cent). It has been suggested that colour blindness in males is selectively disadvantageous in hunting–gathering peoples and that with the coming of agriculture and civilized life this negative selection was relaxed. However, the data on hunter–gatherers are meagre, and it is questionable whether mutation pressure could have produced such a large increase of gene frequency in a period of less than 10 000 years.

Few populations have been studied with the anomaloscope and there is therefore little information about the relative frequencies of different types of defect throughout the world. Deuteranomaly seems to be the most variable type, ranging from about 5 per cent in Europeans to 1–2 per cent in Uganda, New Guinea, and Thailand (Adam 1970); but if selection has been relaxed one might have expected the frequencies of the more severe defects to be most affected.

TABLE 18.3

*Frequency of red–green colour blindness in males of various populations*

| Population | Sample size | Colour-blind males (per cent) | Author |
|---|---|---|---|
| Arabs (Druse) | 337 | 10·0 | Kalmus (1961) |
| Norwegians | 9047 | 8·0 | Waaler (1927) |
| Swiss | 2000 | 8·0 | Von Planta (1928) |
| Germans | 6863 | 7·7 | Schmidt (1936) |
| Belgians | 9540 | 7·4 | De Laet (1935) |
| British | 16 180 | 6·6 | Grieve (1946) |
| Iranians | 947 | 4·5 | Plattner (1959) |
| Andra Pradesh (India) | 292 | 7·5 | Dronamraju (1961) |
| Chinese (Peiping) | 1164 | 6·9 | Chang (1932) |
| Chinese (all) | 36 301 | 5·0 | Chun (1958) |
| Tibetans | 241 | 5·0 | Tiwari (1969) |
| Japanese | 259 000 | 4·0 | Sato (1935) |
| Mexicans | 571 | 2·3 | Garth (1933) |
| Navajo Indians | 535 | 1·1 | Garth (1933) |
| Eskimos | 297 | 2·5 | Skeller (1954) |
| Tswana | 407 | 3·0 | Squires (1942) |
| Hutu | 1000 | 2·9 | Hiernaux (1953) |
| Tutsi | 1000 | 2·5 | Hiernaux (1953) |
| Zairians | 929 | 1·7 | Appelman (1953) |
| Australian Aborigines | 4455 | 1·9 | Mann (1956) |
| Fiji Islanders | 608 | 0·8 | Geddes (1946) |

**Twinning rates**

Medical records provide a large amount of data on twin births so that population differences can be demonstrated in spite of the fact that the incidence of twinning is quite low. Dizygotic twinning rates vary considerably, but monozygotic rates are remarkably uniform. The likelihood of a dizygotic twin birth increases both with maternal age and also parity and a more informative comparison is obtained if these factors are taken into account. Care must be taken to avoid biased estimates of frequency due to the method of sampling; the preferential selection of twin pregnancies for hospital attention may, for example, result in an overestimate if these figures are taken to represent a region. The diagnosis of individual cases as monozygotic or dizygotic may require elaborate tests, especially blood grouping, but an acceptable estimate of the proportions of the two types in population data may be calculated by Weinberg's method. We may argue that pairs of unlike sex are necessarily dizygotic, and if the sex ratio is unity, we may therefore expect an equal number of like-sexed dizygotics; subtraction of the number of unlike-sexed twin pairs from the total of like-sexed pairs then gives an approximate value for the number of monozygotic pairs.

TABLE 18.4

*Twinning rates per 1000 maternities in various populations*

| Population | Dizygotic | Monozygotic |
|---|---|---|
| Negroes, Nigeria | 39·9 | 5·0 |
| Negroes, Rhodesia | 26·6 | 2·3 |
| Negroes, Zaire | 18·7 | 3·1 |
| Negroes, Jamaica | 13·4 | 3·8 |
| Negroes, USA | 11·8 | 3·9 |
| Greece (1931–8) | 10·9 | 2·9 |
| England and Wales (1946–55) | 8·9 | 3·6 |
| Sweden (1946–55) | 8·6 | 3·2 |
| Italy (1949–55) | 8·6 | 3·7 |
| France (1946–51) | 7·1 | 3·7 |
| Spain (1952–3) | 5·9 | 3·2 |
| Japan (1926–31) | 2·7 | 3·8 |

(From Bulmer, *Ann. Hum. Genet.*, 1960.)

Table 18.4, taken from Bulmer's study, shows that there are distinct differences in dizygotic rates within Europe. Considerably higher rates are reported in various African populations and to a lesser degree in Jamaica and in American Negroes. The African and Jamaican figures are not age- and parity-standardized, but if they were, the estimates would probably be somewhat higher. The dizygotic rates for Japan, on the other hand, are considerably lower than the European values.

There is a definite tendency for dizygotic twinning to be concentrated in families, but no simple mode of inheritance has been established. At least provisionally the geographical variation in standardized dizygotic twinning rates may be taken to reflect genetical differences.

## Distribution of rare inherited conditions

Many of the serological and biochemical variants which we have discussed are common, at least in certain populations, and this makes it easy to compare regional frequencies by examining quite small samples. It is more difficult to get reliable frequency estimates for rare conditions, but it is, nevertheless, evident that some of them are by no means uniformly distributed and they present some interesting problems in population genetics. Inherited diseases causing serious disability are likely to come to medical attention despite their rarity and even rare benign variations may be detectable in mass screening of blood or urine samples for other purposes. Although many populations are too remote from highly developed medical services for reliable data to be collected, geographical variations in the incidence of inherited disease may sometimes be inferred from experience with immigrants to better-equipped countries. In systematic attempts to determine the frequencies of rare conditions in the general population, methods of ascertainment must be carefully considered so as to avoid false estimates due to biased sampling.

Cases of rare recessive disorders are often found to be concentrated in restricted localities in which the small size and isolation of the community inevitably raises the incidence of consanguineous unions. If an isolate is descended from a small number of ancestors amongst whom a given gene happened to be present, the local gene frequency may be much higher than in the population as a whole. Homozygosis due to inbreeding exposes a recessive gene with deleterious effects to more stringent selection and a small advantage of the heterozygote which might otherwise suffice to maintain equilibrium at a low frequency might be inadequate to prevent its local extinction under these conditions. Changes due to chance in the transmission of genes also becomes significant if the population is very small.

The infantile type of amaurotic idiocy is a severe neurological disorder inherited recessively, which leads to premature death. Its incidence in certain European countries is estimated at $1/10\,000$, but a high proportion of the affected cases are found to be Jews. The very rare and apparently harmless anomaly known as l-xyloketosuria, in which an unusual sugar is excreted in the urine, is also found mainly in Jewish subjects, most of them derived from a certain region of Russia. Another form of inherited mental defect, phenylketonuria, on the other hand, is certainly very uncommon in Jews. It has been found in many parts of Europe, with some suggestion of regional frequency differences, but is much rarer in American Negroes and very probably in African populations and also in Japan. A rare inherited deficiency in the enzyme catalase in the red cells is so far known only in Japanese. The depigmentation of albinos, who are homozygous for a recessive gene, makes them especially easy to detect in pigmented populations and they have been recorded in most parts of the world. Defects in eyesight generally bring them to medical attention in places where facilities are sufficiently advanced. The frequency of cases of albinism has been estimated at 1/10 000 to 1/20 000 in some European countries, but in West Africa it is probable that it is three to five times as high and even higher incidences (1/200) have been reported in certain Indian tribes of Panama who live in relatively small village communities on islands.

Recent concern regarding the genetical effects of atomic radiations has emphasized the need for more exact knowledge about the incidence of the less common inherited abnormalities including those lumped together under the heading of congenital malformations. This group includes, among others, deformities such as hare-lip, club-foot, congenital hip dislocation, polydactylies, and central nervous defects such as anencephaly and spina bifida. The rates of occurrence of congenital malformations as a whole seem to be similar, namely 1–1.5 per cent in European populations, American Negroes, and Japanese, but there is evidence that these populations differ in the incidence of particular defects. The reasons for such differences must undoubtedly be complex; though there is a tendency for certain malformations to be concentrated in families, no clear genetic basis has been established for most of them. Some types which are grouped together because they resemble one another phenotypically are no doubt genetically heterogeneous. Differences in population incidence may reflect not only differing gene frequencies, but also the effects of environment on the manifestation of genes and on the liability to produce phenocopies.

The distribution in Europe of anencephaly, a severe congenital defect in which the brain is grossly underdeveloped, has been summarized by Penrose, who showed that the frequency varies from 1·0 per cent to 0·32 per cent in Ireland and certain western regions of the UK, falls to about a tenth of this in much of western continental Europe, and is even lower in certain regions of south-eastern France. Searle examined records for various ethnic groups in Malaya and found frequencies varying from zero in the Hakka group of Chinese, to 0·65 per cent in Sikhs. The cause of anencephaly are still largely obscure, but a consideration of population distributions along with other evidence suggests that both environmental and genetical factors are involved.

## Lactose tolerance

Newborn mammals have an enzyme, lactase, in the small intestine that splits lactose, the characteristic sugar of milk, into one molecule each of glucose and galactose. By the time of weaning this enzyme has decreased greatly in amount. In many human children this is also the case by about 4 years of age. Humans are peculiar mammals in that they learned (probably about 10 000 years ago) to use the milk of cows and certain other domesticated ungulates as food, and in some cultures fresh milk is an important item in the adult diet. It has been noticed that many individuals from various Asiatic and African populations develop colic and diarrhoea if they consume much milk. These symptoms are due to fermentation of undigested lactose in the large intestine. On the other hand, this intolerance of lactose is much less frequent in western Europeans and also in certain pastoralists such as the Tutsi and Fulani of Africa, who drink much fresh milk. A convenient quantitative test for lactose-intolerance is to give 2·0 g lactose per kg body-weight up to a maximum of 50–100 g and then to follow the rise of blood glucose at intervals. Subjects are considered to be lactose-intolerant if the rise is less than 20 mg per 100 ml, though not all of them develop intestinal symptoms as a result of the test. Since cow's milk contains 4·5–5·0 per cent of lactose the test dose is equivalent to drinking some 3 l of milk and is therefore quite high.

It appears that in Chinese, Japanese, Thai, and Eskimos and in the Ibo, Yoruba, Ganda, and Bushmen of Africa 80 per cent or more of the population are lactose-intolerant, whereas in the Tutsi, Fulani, and various western European peoples the figure is between 5 per cent and 25 per cent.

The question arises whether lactose-tolerance is due to *induced* persistence of relatively high levels of lactase in the adult as a result of prolonged consumption of milk or whether it is an inherited trait. Family studies in Nigeria, Israel, and elsewhere suggest that tolerance may be inherited as a simple dominant condition but it is not known how the gene acts; the analogy with hereditary persistence of foetal haemoglobin comes to mind. Presumably the mutation conferred a selective advantage in populations that adopted fresh milk as a major food. However, the situation is not entirely straightforward; there is evidence that adults who have little or no lactase, as judged by the above test or by enzyme assays of intestinal biopsies, can be trained to tolerate quite high intakes of lactose without ill effects. Since this adaptation is not accompanied by a rise of their lactase levels it is presumably due to a change in the intestinal flora. It should also be noted that in some cultures milk is consumed in a fermented state, and in this form it is no menace since most of the lactose has already been broken down by bacteria.

## Wet and dry ear wax

In western European populations 90 per cent or more of individuals have yellow, sticky ear wax (cerumen), but a few have a greyish, dry type, containing less lipid. This curious variation depends on a pair of alleles and the dry type is the homozygous recessive. The wet type is uncommon in northern Chinese (4·2 per cent) and Koreans (7·6 per cent) but more frequent in southern Chinese (21–42 per cent). A good deal of work has been done on Central and North American Indians and the frequency of the wet type has been found to vary greatly, from 36·7 per cent in Navajo Indians to 93·3 per cent in the Tzetzal Maya (Table 18.5). Very little is known about this trait in Africans, but it appears that the wet type may be at least as frequent as it is in Europeans. The functional significance of this dimorphism is obscure.

TABLE 18.5

*Frequency of wet type of ear wax in various populations*

| Population | Number of sample | Frequency of wet type of ear wax (per cent) |
|---|---|---|
| Germans | 514 | 91·6 |
| Caucasoids | 368 | 98·7 |
| Negroes | 51 | 100·0 |
| †Tzetzal Maya | 296 | 93·3 |
| †Choctaw | 432 | 79·2 |
| Ainu | 30 | 86·7 |
| Melanesians | 732 | 72·2 |
| Formosan Aborigines | 1420 | 71·4 |
| †Chilcotin | 261 | 66·7 |
| †Nootka | 244 | 63·6 |
| †Sioux | 147 | 63·3 |
| Micronesians | 458 | 62·9 |
| Aleuts | 140 | 51·4 |
| †Papago | 437 | 50·3 |
| Chinese | 169 | 41·5 |
| Ryukyu Islands | 898 | 37·5 |
| †Navajo | 183 | 36·7 |
| Southern Chinese | 463 | 21·2 |
| Koreans | 381 | 7·6 |
| Northern Chinese | 216 | 4·2 |

†American Indians

(Data from Matsunaga, *Ann. Hum. Genet.* 1962, and Petrakis, *Nature, Lond.* 1969.)

## Inactivation of isoniazid

We have already mentioned two inherited biochemical variations that were brought to light by treatment with drugs in the course of medical practice; the Negro type of G6PD deficiency by primaquine and a deficient type of serum pseudocholinesterase by suxamethonium. Here is another example.

The drug isoniazid was introduced in 1952 for treatment of tuberculosis. It was noticed that there were wide individual variations in the rate of its excretion in the urine and this led to more systematic testing. If a standard dose is administered and the concentration in the plasma is estimated after 6 hours, a histogram of concentration for a random sample shows two distributions with some overlap. Family studies showed that slow inactivation behaves as a simple recessive trait.

From the limited amount of comparative data (Table 18.6) it appears that among Europeans about 50 per cent are slow inactivators giving a frequency of (70–80 per cent) for this allele. It is possible that in Africans the figure is even higher. However, in various populations of South East and East Asia frequencies are distinctly lower (30–60 per cent), and this was also the case in samples of Eskimos and North American Indians.

TABLE 18.6

*Isoniazid inactivation*

|  | Sample size | Slow allele-(per cent) |
|---|---|---|
| American Whites | 122 | 73·0 |
| American Negroes | 41 | 76·5 |
| Sudanese | 102 | 79·8 |
| Indian, Madras | 321 | 78·1 |
| Burmese | 121 | 61·2 |
| Thais | 108 | 54·2 |
| Chinese | 60 | 52·1 |
| Japanese | 209 | 28·9 |
| Ainu | 86 | 30.8 |
| Canadian Eskimos | 216 | 22·4 |
| N. American Indians (Sioux) | 15 | 45·8 |

## Human chromosome polymorphism

Satisfactory study of the human karyotype first became possible about 20 years ago, and it soon became apparent that some chromosomes showed consistent variations that were not associated with clinical abnormality. The most striking of these variations was in the length of the Y-chromosome which might be as large as a member of the G(13–15) group or as small as a short acrocentric. The usual staining methods showed the chromosomes as essentially homogeneous in structure but in 1970 distinct transverse banding was detected by observing quinacrine stained (Q-stained) chromosomes in ultraviolet light. The distal region of the long arm of the Y was strongly fluorescent and variations in length of this chromosome depend on the amount of this Q-staining heterochromatin, which may, in some cases, be virtually absent. Not much comparative work on populations has been done but it appears that a long Y is relatively common among Japanese and a very short one in Australian Aborigines. Q-staining also shows strongly fluorescent bands in the centromere region of chromosomes 3 and in the short arms and satellites of the D and G groups. Polymorphic variations in the size of these bands has also been observed. Methods have also been devised that stain mainly heterochromatin around the centromere (C-banding); particularly large C-bands are seen in chromosomes 1, 9, and 16, and these also show polymorphic variation. Whether these differences in the amount of heterochromatin fall into distinct categories or form a graded series is not entirely clear. The exploitation of these recent discoveries for population comparisons lies in the future.

## Mental attributes

For centuries travellers have been intrigued, amazed, or disgusted by the behaviour of alien societies compared with their own. It is tempting but rash to ascribe such differences, which may in some instances coincide with striking physical distinctions, to genetically determined variations in mental functioning. The great changes which can result from transfer to a new cultural milieu at a sufficiently early age should warn us against superficial conclusions. On the other hand, it is clear that genetical variation can, indeed, have a profound effect on mentality, as we can see from the many examples of inherited mental disorders. The genetics of intelligence within the normal range as measured by standard tests have been studied by the various methods appropriate to multifactorial inheritance. Correlations between relatives and between members of monozygotic and dizygotic twin pairs, and comparisons of monozygotic twins raised together and apart, lead to the conclusion that genetic differences account for a considerable proportion of the normal range of variation between individuals. These results, however, apply only to the relatively homogeneous western European population on which the studies were made and they do not tell us what part environment may play in determining differences between widely dissimilar cultures. It is not unreasonable to expect that genes affecting cerebral or other functions related to mental performance may vary in frequency geographically, but we must first ask whether we can hope to establish the existence of such 'innate' differences with the methods available to us.

The belief that certain peoples are inherently limited in intellectual capacity has a long history, and where partisan feelings run high scientific objectivity is apt to suffer.

To overcome the pitfalls of subjective judgement in rating intellectual level or temperament, psychologists have devised numerous standard tests. We cannot enter into the details of these; some are designed to test memory, general knowledge and social awareness, verbal facility or ability to solve problems, while others are aimed at detecting emotional dispositions. Such tests when applied to people brought up in a western European manner have proved useful in assessing suitability for various occupations or as aids to psychiatric diagnosis, but serious difficulties arise when they are used to rate subjects from widely different backgrounds.

The limitations of tests requiring familiarity with a particular language are obvious enough, but even when they are translated they may prove useless because they involve knowledge and concepts which are peculiar to our own type of society. Non-verbal tests in which the subject is asked to detect relationships between abstract designs, to arrange coloured blocks, to draw a man, to trace a path through a maze, etc., have been devised to overcome this trouble and it has been claimed that they avoid the influences of culture. Experience with such tests on Africans, American Indians, Australian Aborigines, and others, throws grave doubts on this assumption. Low scores are just as likely to be due to inexperience in manipulating bricks or other toys, in interpreting conventionalized drawings, or in discriminating colours as to any defect in innate mental powers. It is doubtful whether a 'culture-free' test can be devised, and, indeed, the idea that it could be is probably absurd.

The tests might give information more relevant to our problem if we could compare groups of different ethnic origin brought up in identical conditions. A great deal of work has been done on American Negroes with this in mind.

The results, summarized as the average intelligence quotient, or I.Q., of the group, have often shown scores in the region of 80 for Negroes as compared with 100 for Whites. There are, however, great variations between individuals in both populations, as with many other metrical characters, and considerable overlap of the distributions. The Negro scores are higher in those groups brought up in more favourable conditions and may in fact exceed those of Whites from an inferior environment. Although some workers are convinced that there are genuine differences in average intellectual level between Whites and Negroes, which cannot be accounted for by environment, others have questioned this conclusion. Negroes in the USA remain a more or less segregated group with a generally inferior status, and it is doubtful whether in these circumstances equality of environment should ever be assumed in interpreting test results.

We can infer from the comparative work that has been done that non-European peoples in the existing state of cultural diversity are often unsuited to the kind of tasks that Europeans find important; but this is hardly surprising. To what extent, if they so desire, they might equal or surpass European standards when given suitable education and encouragement is still largely a matter to be settled by trial.

## Suggestions for further reading (Part III)

### General

BUETTNER-JANUSCH, J. (1973). *Physical anthropology—a perspective*. Wiley, New York.
BURNET, A. M. (1973). *Genes, dreams and realities*. Penguin, Harmondsworth.
CAVALLI-SFORZA, L. L. and BODMER, W. (1971). *The genetics of human populations*. Freeman, New York.
EBLING, J. (ed.) (1975). *Racial variation in man*. Institute of Biology, Blackwells, Oxford.
HALDANE, J. B. S. (1956). The argument from animals to men: an examination of its value in anthropology. Huxley Mem. Lecture. *J. R. anthrop. Inst.* 86, 1.
HARRISON, G. A. (ed.) (1961). *Genetical variation in human populations*. Pergamon, Oxford.
—— PEEL, J. (1969). *Biosocial aspects of race*. Blackwells, Oxford.
HULSE, F. (1971). *The human species*. Random House, London.
GARN, S. (ed.) (1968). *Readings on race*. Thomas, Springfield, Illinois.
ROBERTS, D. F. and HARRISON, G. A. (eds) (1959). *Natural selection in human populations*. Pergamon, Oxford.
—— SUNDERLAND, E. (eds) (1973). *Genetic variation in Britain*. Taylor & Francis, London.
YOUNG, J. Z. (1971). *An Introduction to the study of man*. Clarendon Press, Oxford.

### Anthropometry

BARNICOT, N. A. and BROTHWELL, D. R. (1959). 'The evaluation of metrical data in the comparison of ancient and modern bones', *CIBA Symposium on medical biology and Etruscan origins*, p. 131. Churchill, London.
SHAPIRO, H. L. (1939). *Migration and environment*. Oxford University Press, London.
TREVOR, J. C. (1953). Race crossing in man: the analysis of metrical characters. *Eugenics Lab. Mem. XXXVI. Galton Laboratory, London*. Cambridge University Press.
WEINER, J. S. and LOURIE, J. A. (1969). *Human biology—a guide to field methods*. IBP Handbook no. 9, Blackwell, Oxford.

*Statistics*

CAVALLI-SFORZA, L. L., BARRAI, I., and EDWARDS, A. W. F. (1964). Analysis of human evolution under random genetic drift. *Cold Spring Harb. Symp. quant. Biol.*, **29**, 9–20.

HILL, A. B. (1971). *Principles of medical statistics*. Oxford University Press, London.

MORONEY, M. J. (1969). *Facts from figures*. Penguin, Harmondsworth.

SNEATH, P. H. and SOKAL, R. R. (1973). *Numerical taxonomy*, Chapter 5. Freeman, New York.

SNEDECOR, G. W. and COCHRAN, W. G. (1967). *Statistical methods* (6th edn). Iowa State University Press.

VAN DER GEER, J. P. (1971). *Introduction to multivariate analysis for the social sciences*. Freeman, New York.

WEINER, J. S. and HUIZINGA, J. H. (eds) (1972). *The assessment of population affinities in man*. Oxford University Press, London.

*Biochemical variation*

ALLISON, A. C. (1965). Population genetics of abnormal haemoglobins and G6PD. In *Abnormal haemoglobins in Africa* (ed. J. H. Jonxis). Blackwells, Oxford.

BODMER, W. F. (1972). Evolutionary significance of the HL-A system, *Nature, Lond.* **237**, 139.

GIBLETT, E. R. (1969). *Genetic markers in human blood*. Blackwells, Oxford.

GRUBB, R. (1970). The genetic markers of human immunoglobulins. *Molecular biology, Biochemistry and Biophysics*, Vol. 8. Chapman and Hall, London.

HARRIS, H. (1969). *Human biochemical genetics*. Cambridge University Press.

LEHMAN, H. and HUNTSMAN, R. G. (1974). *Man's haemoglobins*. North-Holland, Amsterdam.

LEHMAN, H. and CARRELL, R. W. (1969). Variation in the structure of human haemoglobin. *Br. med. Bull.* **25**, 14–23.

LIVINGSTONE, F. B. (1967). *Abnormal haemoglobins in human populations*. Aldine, Chicago.

*Blood-groups*

FRASER ROBERTS, J. A. (1959). Some associations between blood groups and disease, *Br. med. Bull.* **15**, 129.

KOPEC, A. C. (1970). *The distribution of the blood groups in the United Kingdom*. Oxford University Press, London.

MOURANT, A. E. (1959). '*Blood groups*', *genetical variation in human populations* (ed. G. A. Harrison), p. 1. Pergamon, Oxford.

—— KOPEC, A. C., and SOBCZAK, K. (1958). *The ABO blood groups. Comprehensive tables and maps of world distribution*. Blackwell Scientific Publications, Oxford.

—— (1976). *The distribution of the human blood groups*. Oxford University Press.

RACE, R. R. and SANGER, R. (1968). *Blood groups in man*. Blackwells, Oxford.

ROBINSON, M. G., TOLCHIN, T., and HALPERN, C. (1971). *Enteric bacterial agents and the ABO blood groups. Am. J. Human Genet.* **23**, 135–45.

SHEPPARD, P. M. (1959). Blood groups and natural selection. *Br. med. Bull.* **15**, 134.

VOGEL, F. (1970). ABO blood groups and disease. *Am. J. Human Genet.* **22**, 464.

WEINER, A. S. (1970). Blood groups and disease. *Am. J. Human Genet.* **22**, 4.

*Special senses*

KALMUS, H. (1965). Diagnosis and Genetics of Defective Colour Vision, Pergamon, Oxford.

KRETCHMER, N. (1972). Lactose and lactase. *Sci. Am.*, Oct. 1972.

WRIGHT, W. D. (1953). Defective colour vision. *Br. med. Bull.* **9**, 36.

Biological variation in modern populations

CUMMINS, H. and MIDLO, C. (1962). *Fingerprints, palms and soles*. Dover, New York.
HOLT, S. B. (1968). *The Genetics of dermal ridges*. Thomas, Springfield, Illinois.
PENROSE, L. S. (1969). Dermatoglyphics. *Sci. Am.*, December.

BARNICOT, N. A. (1957). Human pigmentation. *Man*, no. 144.
HARRISON, G. A. (1961). Pigmentation. In *Genetical variation in human populations* (ed. G. A. Harrison), p. 99. Pergamon, Oxford.

ADAM, A. (1973). Genetic diseases among Jews. *Israel. J. med. Sci.* 9, 1383.
CARTER, C. O. (1969). Genetics of common disorders. *Br. med. Bull.* 25, 52.

BODMER, W. F. and CAVALLI-SFORZA, L. L. (1970). Intelligence and Race. *Sci. Am.*, October 1970.
BUTCHER, H. J. (1968). *Human intelligence*. Methuen, London.
JENSEN, A. R., KAGAN, J. S., HUNT, J. McV, CROW, J. F., *et al.* (1969). Environment, heredity and intelligence. *Harvard Educational Review Reprint Series* No. 2.
PENROSE, L. S. (1972). *The genetics of mental defect* (4th edn). Sidgwick and Jackson, London.
VERNON, P. E. (1969). *Intelligence and cultural environment*. Methuen, London.

# Part IV: Human growth and constitution

J. M. TANNER

# 19. The human growth curve

THE study of growth is important in elucidating the mechanisms of evolution, for the evolution of morphological characters necessarily comes about through alterations in the inherited pattern of growth and development. Growth also occupies an important place in the study of individual differences in form and function in man, for many of these also arise through differential rates of growth of particular parts of the body relative to others.

In Fig. 19.1 is shown the growth curve in height of a single boy, measured every 6 months from birth to 18 years. Above is plotted the height attained at successive ages; below, the increments in height from one age to the next. If we think of growth as a form of motion, then the upper curve is one of distance travelled, the lower curve one of velocity. The velocity or rate of growth naturally reflects the child's state at any particular time better than does the height attained, which depends largely on how much the child has grown in all the preceding years. The blood and tissue concentrations of those biochemical substances whose amounts change with age are thus more likely to run parallel to the velocity than to the distance curve. In some circumstances acceleration rather than velocity may best reflect physiological events; it is probable, for example, that the great increase in secretion from the endocrine glands at adolescence is manifested most clearly in acceleration of growth (see Fig. 20.3, p. 324).

The record of Fig. 19.1 is the oldest published study of the growth of a child; it was made during the years 1759–77 by Count Philibert de Montbeillard upon his son, and was published by his friend Buffon in a supplement to the *Histoire Naturelle*. It shows clearly that in general the velocity of growth in height decreases from birth onwards, but that this decrease is interrupted shortly before the end of the growth period. At this time, from 13 to 15 years of age in this particular boy, there is a marked acceleration of growth, called the adolescent growth spurt, which will be discussed in the next chapter. A slight increase in velocity is sometimes said to occur between about 6 years and 8 years, providing a second wave on the general velocity curve, known as the juvenile or mid-growth spurt. Though Fig. 19.1 seems to show evidence of it, examination of many other individual records from 3 to 13 years of age fails to reveal this juvenile growth spurt in the great majority; if it occurs at all, it is only in a minority of children.

## Prenatal growth

The general velocity curve of growth in height begins a considerable time before birth. Fig. 19.2 shows the distance and velocity curves for body length in the prenatal period and first 2 postnatal years. The peak velocity of

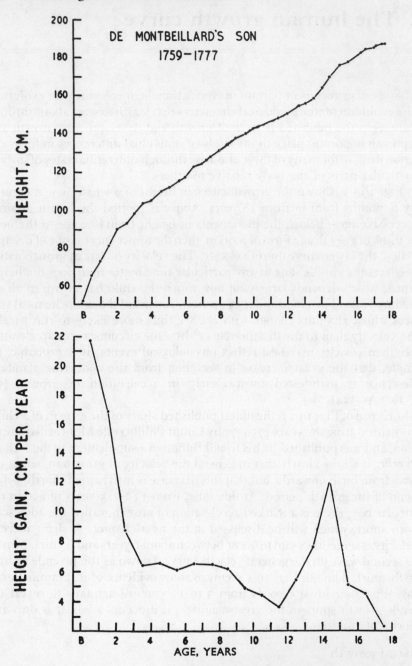

FIG. 19.1. Growth in height of de Montbeillard's son from birth to 18 years, 1759–77. *Above*, distance curve, height attained at each age; *below*, velocity curve, increments in height from year to year. (From Tanner 1962.)

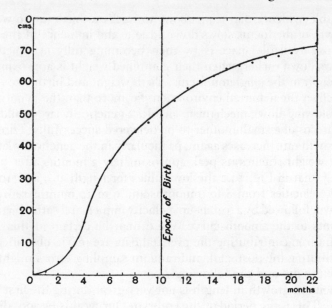

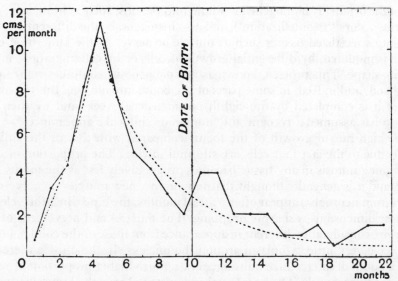

FIG. 19.2. Distance (*above*) and velocity (*below*) curves for growth in body length in prenatal and early postnatal period. (From Thompson 1942.)

length is reached at about 4 months postmenstrual age. (Age in the foetal period is usually reckoned from the first day of the last menstrual period, an average of 2 weeks prior to actual fertilization, but as a rule the only locatable landmark.)

Growth in weight in the foetus follows the same general pattern, except that the peak velocity is reached later, usually at the 34th postmenstrual week. There is considerable evidence that from about 36 weeks to birth (at 40 weeks), the rate of growth of the foetus slows down, due to the influence of the maternal uterus, whose available space is by then becoming fully occupied. Twins' growth slows down earlier, when their combined weight is approximately the 36-week weight of the singleton foetus. Birth weight and birth size in general therefore reflect the maternal environment far more than the genotype of the child. The slowing-down mechanism enables a genetically large child developing in the uterus of a small mother to be delivered successfully. Directly after birth the growth rate increases again, particularly in the genetically large children, and in weight reaches its peak approximately 2 months after birth.

It is likely that in Fig. 19.2 the low values for length at 9 and 10 months, and the low velocities from 8 to 9 months and 9 to 10 months represent this slowing down, followed by a 'catch-up' velocity immediately after birth, returning the points to the smooth curve. We cannot be certain of this, however, since the children contributing the prenatal data are inevitably different from those contributing the postnatal, and random sampling errors might possibly account for the dip and the following rise.

The velocity of growth in length is not very great during the first 2 months of foetal life. This is the period of the embryo. During this period, differentiation of the originally homogeneous whole into regions, such as head, arm, and so forth, occurs ('regionalization'), and also histogenesis, the differentiation of cells into specialized tissues such as muscle or nerve. At the same time each region is moulded, by differential growth of cells or by cell migration, into a definite shape. This process, known as morphogenesis, continues right up to adulthood, and indeed, in some parts of the body, into old age. But the major part of it is completed by the eighth postmenstrual week, and by then the embryo has assumed a recognizably human or child-like appearance.

The high rate of growth of the foetus compared with that of the child is largely due to the fact that cells are still multiplying. The proportion of cells undergoing mitosis in any tissue becomes progressively less as the foetus gets older, and it is generally thought that few, if any, new muscle- or nerve-cells (apart from neuroglia) appear after 6 foetal months, the time when the velocity in linear dimensions is sharply dropping. The muscle- and nerve-cells of the foetus are considerably different in appearance from those of the child or adult. Both have very little cytoplasm around the nucleus. In the muscle there is a great amount of intercellular substance and a much higher proportion of water than in mature muscle. The later foetal and postnatal growth of muscle consists of building up the cytoplasm of the muscle-cells; salts are incorporated and proteins formed. The cells become bigger, the intercellular substance largely disappears, and the concentration of water decreases. This process continues quite actively up to about 3 years of age and slowly thereafter; at adolescence it briefly speeds up again, particularly in boys, more substances being incorporated into the fibres under the influence of androgenic hormones. During the same period increase of the absolute amount of DNA occurs, indicating that further nuclei are appearing (since DNA is confined to the nuclei of cells, where it occurs in nearly constant concentration). Thus fibres come to have increasing numbers of nuclei associated with them throughout the whole growing period. In the nervous system cytoplasm is added, nucleoprotein bodies appear, and axons and dendrites grow.

Thus, postnatal growth is, for at least some tissues, a period of development and enlargement of existing cells rather than the formation of new ones. Adipose tissue is an exception to this rule; the number of fat cells continues to increase till about the beginning of puberty; the rate of increase, however, gets continuously less. Even in this tissue, however, the quantitatively more important change during postnatal growth is an increase in the size of each cell.

## Fitting growth curves

Growth is in general an exceedingly regular process. Contrary to opinions still sometimes held, it does not proceed in fits and starts. The more carefully the measurements are taken—for example, with precautions to minimize the decrease in height that occurs during the day for postural reasons—the more regular does the succession of points in the graph become. Fig. 19.3 demonstrates the fit of a smooth mathematical curve to a series of measurements all taken on a child by the same observer every 6 months from age $3\frac{1}{2}$ to 10 years.

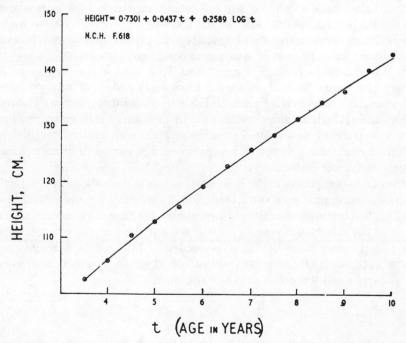

FIG. 19.3. Curve of form $y = a + bt + c \ln t$ fitted to stature measurements taken every 6 months by Whitehouse on a girl from age $3\frac{1}{2}$ to 10 years. Harpenden Growth Study. (From Israelsohn in Tanner 1960.)

In a series of children followed this way deviations from the fitted curves were seldom more than 6 mm, and were distributed equally above and below the curve at all ages. Many children, however, show a regular seasonal variation, adding a 6-month rhythm about the general height curve, with an increased rate in the spring and a decreased rate in the autumn. This seasonal effect is large enough to make growth rates over periods of less than a full year unreliable for medical purposes; the average child in the UK grows about 3 times as fast in his fastest quarter of the year as in his slowest quarter.

Many attempts have been made at finding mathematical curves which fit human and animal growth data. Most have ended in disillusion or fantasy; disillusion because fresh data failed to conform to them, or fantasy, because the system held eventually so many parameters and was so complicated that it became quite impossible to interpret biologically. What is needed is a curve or curves with relatively few constants, each capable of being interpreted in a biologically meaningful manner. The fit to empirical data must, of course, be adequate, within the limits of measurement error. Part of the difficulty in reaching this goal is that most of the measurements to which curves are fitted are themselves biologically complex. Stature, for example, consists of leg length and trunk length and head height, all of which have considerably different growth curves. Even with relatively homogeneous measurements such as tibia length or calf-muscle width, it is still not clear what purely biological assumptions should be made as the basis for the form of the curve. The assumption that all cells are continuously dividing leads to an exponential formulation such that the increment is proportional to the measurement ($dy/dt = ky$, or $y = e^{a+bt}$), where $y$ is the measurement at age $t$ and $k$, $a$, and $b$ are constants. The contrary assumption that all cells are continuously adding or incorporating a given amount of non-dividing material leads to constant increment. The more complex and realistic assumptions that the proportion of cells either multiplying or incorporating new tissue decreases steadily with age and that the rate at which they do these things varies from one age period to another lead to a variety of further formulations.

However, fitting a curve to the individual values is the only way of extracting the maximum information about an individual's growth from the measurement data. This fact becomes increasingly inescapable as research progresses on such matters as the effects of illness on growth rate, or the genetics of growth patterns. Clearly more than one curve is needed to fit the postnatal age range. It seems at present that two curves will suffice, at least for many measurements such as height and weight. A curve of the form

$$y = a + bt + c \log t$$

appears to fit well from a few months after birth to the beginning of adolescence at around age 10 years. This is the curve shown in Fig. 19.3. The adolescent growth spurt is fitted well by the logistic curve, an S-shaped symmetrical exponential, of the form

$$y = P + (K/1 + e^{a-bt}),$$

where $P$ is the lowest asymptote and $K$ the total adolescent gain. A similar, alternative curve is the Gompertz, a skewed exponential. Fig. 19.4 shows a Gompertz curve fitted to measurements of stature during puberty in a girl.

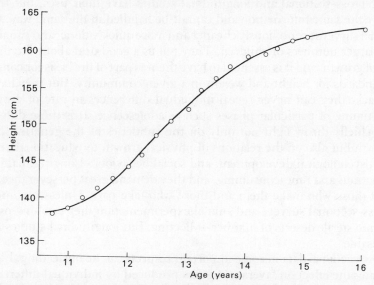

F IG. 19.4. Curve growth of a girl measured at 3-monthly intervals during puberty by White-house. Solid line is the fitted Gompertz curve. (From Tanner 1963.)

## Longitudinal and cross-sectional data

Such curves have to be fitted to data on single individuals: yearly averages derived from different children each measured once only in a mass-survey type of study do not, in general, give the same curve. The two sorts of investigation are distinguished as 'longitudinal' and 'cross-sectional'. In a cross-sectional study each child is measured once only, and all the children at age 8, for example, are different from all those at age 7. In a longitudinal study, on the other hand, each child is measured at each age and therefore all the children at age 8 are the same as those at age 7. A study may be longitudinal over any number of years. There are short-term longitudinal studies extending over a couple of years and full birth-to-maturity studies in which children may be examined once, twice, or more times every year from birth till 20 years. In practice it is always impossible to measure exactly the same group of children every year for a prolonged period; inevitably some children leave the study and others, if desired, join it. A study in which this happens is called a 'mixed longitudinal' study, and special statistical techniques are needed to get the maximum information out of its data. In the past this has not been generally understood, with the truly appalling result that three-quarters and more of the useful information of mixed studies has been lost. One particular type of mixed study is that in which a number of relatively short-term longitudinal groups are overlapped; thus one might have groups of ages 0–6, 5–11, 10–16, and 15–20 years to cover the whole age range. However, problems arise at the 'joins' unless the sampling has been remarkably good.

Both cross-sectional and longitudinal studies have their uses, but they do not give the same information and cannot be handled in the same way. Cross-sectional surveys are obviously cheaper and more quickly done, and can include much larger numbers of children. They tell us a good deal about the distance curve of growth, and it is essential to have them as part of the basis for constructing standards for height and weight in a given community. But they have one drawback: they can never reveal individual differences in rate of growth or in the timing of particular phases such as adolescence. It is these differences which chiefly throw light not only on the subtleties of the genetical control of growth but also on the relations of physical growth to educational achievement, psychological development, and social behaviour. Longitudinal studies are laborious and time-consuming, and they demand great perseverance on the part of those who make them and those who take part. Unless accompanied by cross-sectional surveys and animal experimentation they can sink over the years into sterile deserts of number-collecting. But longitudinal studies are indispensable.

Cross-sectional data in some important respects can be misleading. Fig. 19.5 illustrates the effect on 'average' figures produced by individual differences in the time at which the adolescent spurt begins. The left half of Fig. 19.5 shows a series of individual velocity curves from 6 years to 18 years, each individual

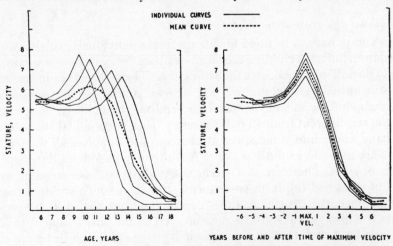

FIG. 19.5. Relation between individual and mean velocities during the adolescent spurt. *Left*, the height curves are plotted against chronological age; *right*, they are plotted according to their time of maximum velocity. (From Tanner 1962.)

starting his spurt at a different time. The average of these curves, obtained simply by treating the values cross-sectionally and adding them up at age 6, 6, 7, etc. years, and dividing by 5, is shown by the heavy interrupted line. It is obvious that the line in no way characterizes the 'average' velocity curve; on the contrary, it is a travesty of it. It smooths out the adolescent spurt, spreading it along the time axis. Averages at each age computed from cross-sectional studies inevitably do this and resemble the interrupted line; they fail to make clear the speed and intensity of the individual spurt. In the right half of Fig. 19.5 the same curves have been arranged so that their points of maximum velocity coincide; here the average curve characterizes the group quite nicely. In passing from one diagram to the other the time scale has been altered, so that in the right side the curves are plotted, not against chronological age, but against a measure which arranges the children according to how far they have progressed along their course of development; in other words, according to their true developmental or physiological status. We shall return to consider this point at length in Chapter 21.

It is just this sort of problem that curve-fitting to individual data deals with so well. Suppose we have two children with adolescent spurts identical in form and intensity but beginning at different times. If our fitted mathematical curve is well chosen, one or more of its parameters will characterize the slope of the spurt, another its peak intensity, and so on. These parameters will be equal for the two children because they are unrelated to time. A further parameter of the growth curve will refer to the time at which the spurt starts, and in this the children will differ, with values characterizing their chronological advancement or retardation.

In comparing different groups of children by means of curve-fitting one important point has to be borne in mind. To obtain the average value of a parameter $a$ of the growth curve for a group of children it is necessary to ascertain the values of each individual's parameter $a$ and then average these, if the equation of the curve is at all a complex one. A different and, for most applications, erroneous average will be obtained if the equation is fitted to the mean values of the *measurements* of the group at each age. The former, correct, curve for the group, is called the 'mean-constant curve'; it cannot generally be reached by any route except fitting the curve to each individual's measurements.

## Growth curves of different tissues and different parts of the body

Most skeletal and muscular dimensions follow approximately the growth curve described for height. So also do the dimensions of organs such as the liver, spleen, and kidneys. But there are other tissues which have curves sufficiently different to need description. These are the brain and skull, the reproductive organs, the lymphoid tissue, and the subcutaneous fat.

In Fig. 19.6 these differences are shown in diagram form, using the size attained by various tissues as a percentage of the birth-to-maturity increment. Height and the majority of body measurements follow the 'general' curve. The

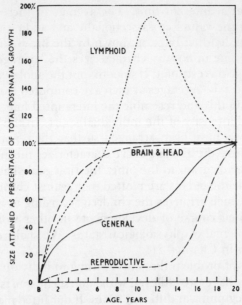

FIG. 19.6. Growth curves of different parts and tissues of the body, showing the four chief types. All the curves are of size attained and plotted as percentage of total gain from birth to maturity (20 years) so that size at age 20 years is 100 on the vertical scale. *Lymphoid type:* thymus, lymph nodes, intestinal lymph masses. *Brain and head type:* brain and its parts, dura, spinal cord, optic apparatus, head dimensions. *General type:* body as a whole, external dimensions (except head), respiratory and digestive organs, kidneys, aortic and pulmonary trunks, musculature, blood volume. *Reproductive type:* testis, ovary, epididymis, prostate, seminal vesicles, Fallopian tubes. (From Tanner 1962.)

reproductive organs, internal and external, follow a curve which is perhaps not very different in principle, though strikingly so in effect. Their prepubescent growth is slow and their growth at adolescence very rapid; they are less sensitive than the skeleton to one set of hormones and more sensitive to another.

The brain, together with the skull covering it and the eyes and ears, develops earlier than any other part of the body (see Chapter 22 for details). It thus has a characteristic postnatal growth curve. At birth it is already 25 per cent of its adult weight; at age 5 years, 90 per cent, and age 10 years about 95 per cent. Thus if the brain has any adolescent spurt at all it is a very small one. A small but definite spurt occurs in head length and breadth, but all or most of this is due to thickening of the skull bones and the scalp together with development of the air sinuses. The face follows a curve midway between that of the top portion of the skull and the remainder of the skeleton. It is nearer its mature dimensions at birth—later than is body-length, but has still a considerable adolescent spurt, which is greatest in the mandible. Thus the head as a whole is more advanced than the remainder of the body, and the top part of it, that is, the eyes and brain, are more advanced than the lower portion, that is, the face and jaw.

The lymphoid tissue, of tonsils, adenoids, appendix, intestine, and spleen, has quite another growth curve (Fig. 19.6). It reaches its maximum amount before adolescence, and then, probably under the direct influence of the sex hormones, declines to its adult value.

The subcutaneous fat layer has also a curve of its own, and a somewhat complicated one. Its width can be measured either by X-rays or by specially designed calipers applied to a fold of fat pinched up from the underlying muscle. The distance and velocity curves of skin folds taken on the back of the arm over the triceps muscle, and under the angle of the scapula, are shown in Figs 19.7 (a) and (b). Subcutaneous fat begins to be laid down in the foetus at about 34 weeks and increases from then until birth, and from birth until about 9 months (in the average child; the peak may be reached as early as 6 months in some and as late as a year or 15 months in others). From 9 months, when the velocity is thus zero, the subcutaneous fat decreases, that is, has a negative velocity, until age 6 years to 8 years, when it begins to increase once again.

It must be noted that we have discussed the width of the fat layer; a decrease in this width does not necessarily imply a decrease in the cross-sectional area of fat. The fat is a ring around a musculo-skeletal centre which is itself increasing at all ages; if the cross-sectional fat area stayed constant the width of the ring would be reduced simply by enlargement of the musculo-skeletal core.

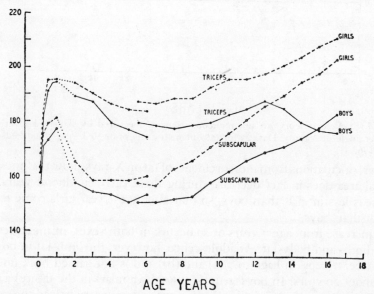

AGE  YEARS

FIG. 19.7(a). Distance curve of subcutaneous tissue measured by Harpenden skinfold calipers over triceps and under scapula. Logarithmic transformation units. Data: *0–1 year*, pure longitudinal, 74 boys and 65 girls Brussels Child Study; *2–7 years* London Child Study Centre with pure longitudinal core 4–6 of 59 boys and 57 girls and actual mean increments subtracted or added to get means at 2,3, and 7; *5–16 years* London County Council, cross-sectional, 1000 to 1600 of each sex at each year of age from 5 to 14, 500 at 15, 250 at 16. (From Tanner 1962.)

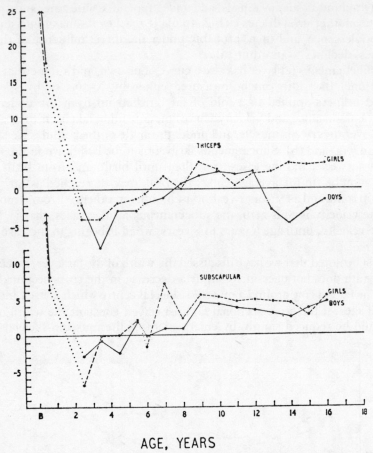

## AGE, YEARS

FIG. 19.7 (b). Velocity curve of subcutaneous tissue as measured by skin-folds over triceps and under angle of scapula. Data as for (a) but with gains prior to 1 year smoothed. (From Tanner 1962.)

However, calculations from measurements of fat on X-rays show that the cross-sectional area does in fact decrease during these early childhood years. The decrease is less in girls than boys, so that after age 1 year girls come to have more fat than boys.

The increase from age 7 years or so occurs in both sexes, in measurements of both limb- and body-fat. At adolescence, however, the limb-fat in boys decreases (see 'triceps' in Figs 19.7 (a) and (b)) and is not gained back until the age of about 20 years. In boys' trunk-fat ('subscapular' in the figure) a much smaller loss, if any at all, occurs; there is only a temporary halt to the gradual increase. In girls there is a slight halting of the limb-fat increase, but no loss; and the trunk-fat shows nothing but a steady rise until the age of discretion is reached.

Because body-weight represents a mixture of these various tissues its curve of growth is often less informative than those of its component parts. In general, however, individual velocity curves of weight follow a similar course to the height curve. Though to some extent useful in following the health of a child, weight has the severe limitation that an increase may signify growth in bone and muscle, or merely an increase in fat. Similarly, failure to gain weight in the older child may signify little except a better attention to diet and exercise, whereas failure to gain height or muscle would call for immediate investigation.

## Organization and disorganization of the growth process

We have seen that growth of a single dimension is a very regular process, and also that different tissues and different areas of the body grow at different rates. These differential growth velocities are responsible for the appearance of the characteristic human shape in embryogenesis, and for the change of shape from that of the baby to that of the adult in postnatal development. Clearly they are highly organized, in the sense that the initiation of one process must depend on the achievement of a particular stage in one or, more likely, several others. How this organization works, or rather in what terms we can best describe it, is one of the most fundamental problems of growth.

Differences in the velocity of growth of particular parts produce many of the foetal, childhood, and adult differences in morphology seen between different species or genera. Man is distinct from apes in having longer legs relative to body or arms; and this comes about by his greater relative velocity of leg growth from early foetal life onwards. Again, the joint between the head and the vertebral column is situated further forward in man than in other Primates. At birth, however, this distinction is not present; all Anthropoidea have joints in about the same relative position. But the postnatal growth of the head in monkeys and apes is greater in front of the occipital condyles than behind them, and so the joint shifts backwards. In man the growth rates of pre- and post-condylar parts of the head are more nearly equal, and the position of the joint remains unchanged. Differential growth rates are very often the mechanism of morphological evolution.

CANALIZATION

Despite the importance of the problem, we know as yet very little about how these intricate growth patterns are organized. It is evident that there are regulative forces holding the processes of development in predetermined channels, for in the long and complex process which intervenes between the primary chemical action of the genes and the finished adult form there are many opportunities for slight deviations, slight discrepancies between chemical reactants, to occur and to get progressively multiplied. When a single egg divides to give identical twins, for example, it is unlikely that exactly equal amounts of cytoplasm go to each half. When the chemical substances produced by the genes go out to organize the cytoplasm it is unlikely, therefore, that exactly the same concentration of chemical reactants will be formed in the two organisms. During subsequent development these differences could become enormously magnified. Yet uniovular twins do, in fact, greatly resemble each other, to the degree where only precise measurements can distinguish them. Their similarity, not their difference, requires an explanation.

It is thought, in fact, that the processes of differentiation and growth are self-stabilizing or, to take another analogy, 'target-seeking'. Now that we are beginning to understand more about the dynamics of complex systems consisting of many interacting substances, we realize that the capacity to reach a similar final form by varying pathways is not such an exceptional property, nor one confined to living things. Many complex systems, particularly those (called 'open') which have a continuous interaction with other surrounding systems, even if composed of quite simple lifeless substances, show such internal regulation as a property consequent on their organization.

The power to stabilize and return to a predetermined growth curve after being pushed, so to speak, off trajectory persists throughout the whole period of growth and is seen in the response of young animals to illness or starvation. This property is called by Waddington 'canalization' or 'homeorhesis' (homeostasis being the maintenance of a static situation and homeorhesis the maintenance of a flowing or developing one). The unusually large velocity occurring during the process has been named 'catch-up' growth by Prader, Tanner, and von Harnack. An example is given in Fig. 19.8 (b); a similar catch-up occurs when, for example, a state of hypothyroidism is corrected or a cortisol-producing (hence growth-inhibiting) tumour is removed. The velocity

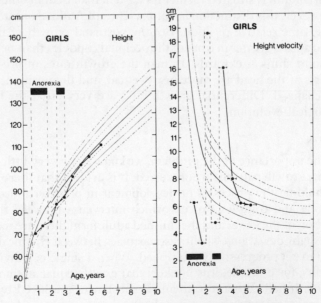

FIG. 19.8. Height and height velocity of girl with two periods of reduced food intake, each followed by catch-up growth. Redrawn from Prader *et al. J. Pediat.* 1963.

during the initial period of catch-up may reach three times the normal for age. The allied term 'compensatory growth' is sometimes used by nutritionists to describe a similar phenomenon; however, that term was first applied to the quite different phenomenon of the replacement growth of organs or parts. Thus when one kidney is removed the other hypertrophies and is said to be showing compensatory growth. Catch-up may be complete or incomplete; if the stress has been severe, and particularly if it has been applied early in the animal's life, then even though a catch-up velocity may be established for a while it may be insufficient to return the animal completely to its normal distance curve of growth. The mechanism of this regulation is almost totally obscure.

*Growth gradients*

One way in which the organization of growth shows itself is through the presence of maturity 'gradients'. One such is illustrated in Fig. 19.9. Taking the simpler, right-hand panel first, the percentage of the adult value at each age is plotted for foot length, calf length, and thigh length in boys. At all ages the foot is nearer its adult status than the calf, and the calf nearer than the thigh. A maturity gradient is said to exist in the leg, running from advanced maturity distally to delayed maturity proximally. In the left-hand panel of Fig. 19.9 the same gradient is illustrated in the upper limb, together with the fact that girls are more advanced to maturity at all ages than boys (see Chapter 20) without this affecting in any way the distal–proximal gradient.

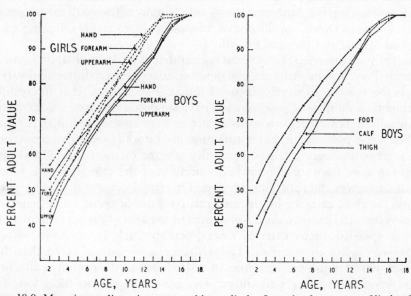

F ɪ G. 19.9. Maturity gradients in upper and lower limbs. Length of segments of limbs plotted as percentage of adult value. Note hand nearer adult value than forearm, and forearm nearer than upper arm at all ages, independent of sex difference in maturity. Mixed longitudinal data. (From Tanner 1962.)

Many other gradients exist, some covering small areas only and operating for short periods, others covering whole systems and operating throughout the whole of growth. The head, for example, is at all ages in advance of the trunk, and the trunk in advance of the limbs. Within the trunk, however, this cephalo-caudal gradient fails to be manifested; it is replaced by more complicated, smaller-area gradients. Gradients in the brain, clearly of the utmost importance for educational theory and practice, are described in Chapter 22.

The multitude of chemical reactions going on during differentiation and growth demands the greatest precision in the way one type of growth is linked to another. Thus for normal acuity of vision to occur the growth of the lens of the eye has to be harmonized closely with the growth in depth of the eyeball. It is small wonder that the success of this co-ordination varies, and that most people are just a little long-sighted or short-sighted. Again, it would seem that many features of the face and skull are individually governed by genes which do not much influence other, nearby features. But in general the parts of the face fuse to constitute an acceptable whole, and this is because the final growth stages are plastic, and in fitting together, for example, upper and lower jaws forces of mutual regulation come into play which do not reflect the original genetic curves of the discrete parts.

These regulative forces do not always succeed. If the original genetic forces begin by being too unbalanced, normal development cannot occur. For example, if one of the chromosomes is reduplicated so that an abnormal number and distribution of genes occurs in the fertilized egg, abnormalities occur which usually lead to abortion, but sometimes—as in trisomy of the small chromosome 21, giving rise to Down's syndrome or 'mongolism'—to viable offspring with abnormal mental and physical growth.

Short of such disorders, however, it is clear that many individual differences in morphology, and probably in function too, arise through differential variations in the velocity of development of different structures. It is interesting that recently a number of psychologists have supposed that some of the many individual differences in personality structure may arise in a similar fashion. Further, some psychological abnormalities, or culturally excessive deviations from average (analogous to an inconvenient degree of short-sightedness) are thought to arise from insufficient harmonization of the velocities with which various structures and functions develop. This could occur either for genetic reasons, the child carrying by chance a relatively disharmonic set of genes, or for environmental reasons, the development of one area of the personality having been speeded up by external forces, perhaps early in childhood, while another was relatively retarded. Though there is no certain proof that this occurs in man, a number of examples of disharmonious development affecting behaviour in animals are well known. Oedipus behaviour in the goose, for example, can be produced at will by mating a wild-strain gander and a domesti-cated goose. The domestic goose carries genes for early sexual maturation and in some of the young male offspring sexual maturity occurs before the mother-following response has disappeared. The young bird in consequence insists on copulating with its mother. Since the wild father's sexual activity arises only later in the spring he remains insensible to the drama.

## Sensitive periods

Sensitive or critical periods are extreme examples of this linking of differential growth events. By 'sensitive period' is meant a certain stage of limited duration during which a particular influence from another area of the developing organism or from the environment evokes a particular response. The response may be beneficial, indeed essential, to normal development, or it may be pathological. An example of a normal sensitive period is given by the differentiation of the rat hypothalamus into male or female discussed below. During the first 5 days after birth the rat hypothalamus must receive the stimulus of testosterone if it is to become fixed as male; before this period testosterone has no effect and after the 5 days have passed the same is true. As in most sensitive periods the sensitivity is quantitative, rising gradually to a peak and then falling again.

A second example is furnished by the classical work of Hubel and Wiesel and their followers, who showed that a kitten must receive light during the first few weeks after its eyes have opened for the cells of the central nervous system subserving light reception to develop. When the 3 weeks have passed, the animal can no longer become sighted whatever its experience of light. Animals are born into 'expected' environments, where the events that have to occur in each sensitive period normally, of course, do so.

## Post-adolescent growth

Growth of the skeleton does not entirely cease at the end of the adolescent period. In man, unlike some other mammals such as the rat, the epiphyses of the long bones close completely and cannot afterwards be stimulated to grow again. But the vertebral column continues to grow from age 20 to 30 years by apposition of bones to the tops and bottoms of the vertebral bodies. Thus height increases by a small amount, on average 3–5 mm, during these years. From the age of 30 to 45 or 50 years it remains stationary, and then begins to decline. The timing suggests that androgenic hormones may be of importance in maintaining this growth, as they are in stimulating the vertebral column growth at adolescence (see Chapter 20). For practical purposes, however, it is useful to have an age at which one may say that growth in stature has virtually ceased, that is, after which only some 2 per cent is added. Longitudinal records indicate that an average figure for this is currently about 17·5 years for boys and 16·0 years for girls, with a normal variation for different individuals of about 2 years either side of these averages.

Most head and face measurements continue to increase after adolescence steadily, though very slowly, to at least age 60 years. The increase from 20 to 60 years amounts to between 2 per cent and 4 per cent of the 20-year-old value.

## The human growth curve as a Primate characteristic

The characteristic form of the human growth curve is shared by apes and monkeys. It is apparently a distinctive Primate characteristic, for neither rodents nor cattle have curves resembling it.

There are as yet very few longitudinal series of linear measurements on species other than man, so that we have to use curves for body-weight rather than length in comparing species. In Fig. 19.10 the weight velocity curve for the mouse is shown. There is little interval between weaning and puberty, and no visible adolescent spurt because there is no period of low velocity between birth and maturity. In terms of the maturation of its organs the mouse is born earlier in development than man. The peak velocity of its weight curve occurs at a time corresponding closely, by this organ maturation calendar, with birth in man, which is when the first peak of man's weight velocity occurs. The curve for the rat is similar to that of the mouse, except that the rat is born still earlier; the guinea-pig, born more mature, has its peak velocity actually at birth.

In the chimpanzee, on the other hand, shown in Fig. 19.11, the curve is quite different, and resembles entirely that of man. The first peak velocity of weight must be shortly before or at birth, but this is followed by a gradual decrease of velocity during the long interval between weaning and puberty. At puberty a considerable adolescent spurt occurs, particularly in the male. The rhesus monkey has a similar curve, though with less time intervening between weaning

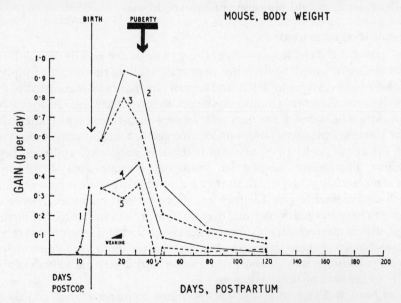

FIG. 19.10. Weight velocity curve for the mouse. *Curve 1*, sexes combined, cross-sectional. *Curves 2 and 3*, males (18) and females (18), pure longitudinal, large strain bred by MacArthur. *Curves 4 and 5*, small MacArthur strain. Time of puberty from Engle and Rosasco, giving first oestrus in albinos at 37 days, standard deviation 5 days. (From Tanner 1962.)

CHIMPANZEE, BODY WEIGHT

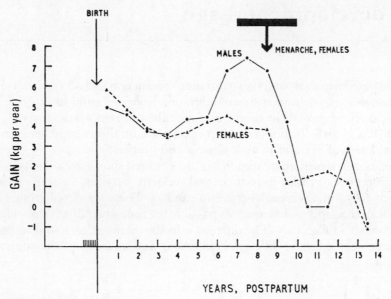

F I G. 19.11. Weight–velocity curve for the chimpanzee. Menarche average 8·8 years, range 7·0 to 10·8 years. (From Tanner 1962.)

and puberty. The magnitude of the adolescent spurt, and in particular the degree of sex dimorphism occurring at it, varies from species to species.

It seems, therefore, that the prolongation of the time between weaning and puberty, often with the acquisition of an adolescent growth spurt, is an evolutionary step taken by the Primates. The essential change seems to be a postponement of the time of puberty, for other mammals continue to grow for a good deal longer, relatively speaking, after sexual maturity has been reached. The immediate cause of the postponement appears to be traceable to a mechanism in the hypothalamus, for it is the brain which initiates the events of the adolescent spurt. The increased time necessary for the maturing of the Primate brain has been sandwiched in between weaning and puberty, and the maturation of the hypothalamus has been put back until maturation of the associative areas of the cortex is well advanced.

This process has been carried successively farther in monkeys, apes, and man. For at least some of the evolutionary reasons for it are not far to seek. It is probably advantageous for learning, and especially learning to co-operate in group or family life, to take place while the individual remains relatively docile and before he comes into sexual competition with adult males. The actual existence of groups containing numbers of these tractable but moderately able individuals may itself be advantageous.

# 20. The adolescent growth spurt and developmental age

THE adolescent growth spurt is a constant phenomenon and occurs in all children, though it varies in intensity and duration from one child to another. The peak velocity of growth in height averages about 10 cm a year in boys, and slightly less in girls. In boys the spurt takes place on the average between $12\frac{1}{2}$ and $15\frac{1}{2}$ years of age and in girls some 2 years earlier.

The sex difference can be seen in Fig. 20.1, which shows the velocity curves for a group of boys who have their peak velocity between 14 and 15, and a group of girls with their peak between 12 and 13. These restricted groups have been taken so as to avoid as much as possible the time-spreading error referred to previously in Fig. 19.5. The difference in size between men and women is to a large degree due to differences in timing and intensity of the adolescent

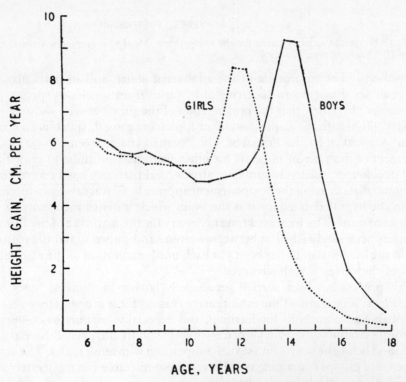

FIG. 20.1. Adolescent spurt in height growth for girls and boys. The curves are from subjects who have their peak velocities during the modal years 12–13 for girls, and 14–15 for boys. Actual mean increments, each plotted at centre of its $\frac{1}{2}$-year period. (From Tanner 1962.)

spurt; before it boys and girls differ only by some 2 per cent in height; after it by an average of about 8 per cent. The difference partly comes about because of the later occurrence of the male spurt, allowing an extra period for growth, even at the slow pre-pubertal velocity; and partly because of the greater intensity of the spurt itself.

Practically all skeletal and muscular dimensions take part in the spurt, though not to an equal degree. Most of the spurt in height is due to trunk growth rather than growth of the legs. The muscles appear to have their spurt about 3 months after the height peak; and the weight peak velocity occurs about 6 months after the height peak.

The heart has a spurt in size no less than the other muscles, and other organs accelerate their growth also. Probably even the eye, the most advanced of any organ in maturity and thus the one with least growth still to undergo, has a slight spurt, to judge from the particularly rapid change towards myopia (short-sightedness) which occurs about this age. The degree of myopia increases continuously from age 6 or earlier till maturity, but this accelerated rate of change at puberty would be most simply accounted for by a fractionally greater spurt in axial than in vertical diameters.

It is not clear whether a spurt occurs in brain-growth. In the bones of the face there is a spurt, though a relatively slight one. Individual variability is sufficient so that in some children no detectable spurt occurs at all in some head and face measurements, including those of the pituitary fossa. In the average child, however, the jaw becomes longer in relation to the front part of the face, and also thicker and more projecting. The profile becomes straighter, the incisors of both jaws more upright, and the nose more projecting. All these changes are greater in boys than in girls.

### Sex differences

Many of the sex differences of body size and shape seen in adults are the result of differential growth patterns at adolescence. The greater general size of the male has already been discussed. The greater relative width of shoulders in the male and hips in the female is largely due to specific stimulation of cartilage cells, by androgens in the first instance and oestrogens in the second. The greater growth of the male muscles also results from androgen stimulation, as do some other physiological differences mentioned below.

Not all sex differences develop in this way. The greater length of the male legs relative to the trunk comes about as a consequence of the longer pre-pubescent period of male growth, since the legs are growing faster than the trunk during this particular time. Other sex differences begin still earlier. The male forearm is longer, relative to the upper arm or the height, than the female forearm; and this difference is already established at birth, and increases gradually throughout the whole growing period. It is probably caused by the laying down in early foetal life of slightly more tissue in this area in the male, or of slightly more active tissue. It occurs in some other Primates, as well as in man.

A similar mechanism may be responsible for the sex difference in relative lengths of second and fourth fingers. The second finger is longer than the fourth more frequently in females than in males and this difference is also established before birth. The most striking of all the pre-puberty sex differences, however, is the earlier maturation of the female, discussed in the next chapter (see p. 333).

## Development of the reproductive system

The adolescent spurt in skeletal and muscular dimensions is closely related to the rapid development of the reproductive system which takes place at this time. In Fig. 20.2(b) the events of adolescence in the male are outlined diagrammatically. The solid areas marked 'penis' and 'testis' represent the period of

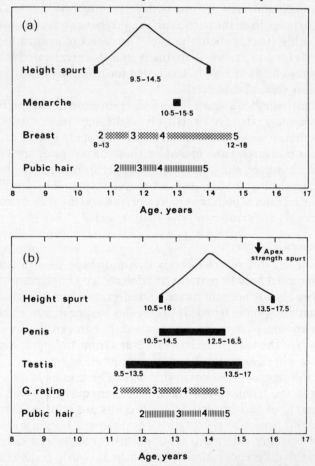

FIG. 20.2. Diagram of sequence of events at adolescence in girls (a) and boys (b). An average child is represented; the range of ages within which each event charted may begin and end is given by the figures placed below its start and finish. (From Marshall and Tanner, *Archs Dis. Childh.*, **45**, 1970.)

accelerated growth of these organs, and the horizontal lines and rating numbers marked 'pubic hair' stand for its advent and development. The sequences and timings represent in each case the average value. To give an idea of the individual departures from this, figures for the range of ages at which the spurts for height, penis, and testis growth begin and end are inserted under the first and last points of the curves or bars. The acceleration of penis growth, for example, begins on average at about age $12\frac{1}{2}$ years, but sometimes occurs as early as $10\frac{1}{2}$ years and sometimes as late as 14 years. There are thus a few boys who do not begin their spurts in height or penis development until the earliest maturers have entirely completed theirs. At age 13 and 14 there is an enormous variability in development amongst any group of boys, who range practically all the way from complete maturity to absolute pre-adolescence. The fact raises difficult social and educational problems and is itself a contributory factor to the psychological maladjustment sometimes seen in adolescence (see Chapter 22).

The *sequence* of events is much less variable than the age at which they take place. The first sign of puberty in boys is an accelerated growth in testes and scrotum. Slight growth of pubic hair may start at about the same time, but proceeds slowly until about the time the height and penis simultaneously accelerate, when it also grows faster. This is usually about a year after the first testicular acceleration. The testicular growth is mainly due to increase in size of the seminal tubules; the androgen-producing Leydig cells appear to develop more or less simultaneously.

Axillary hair usually first appears about 2 years after the beginning of pubic hair growth, though there is sufficient individual variability so that in a very few children axillary hair actually precedes pubic hair in appearance. Circumanal hair, which arises independently of the spread of pubic hair down the perineum, appears shortly before axillary hair. In boys facial hair begins at about the same time as axillary hair. An increase in length and pigmentation occurs first in the hair at the corners of the upper lip, then spreads medially. Hair next appears on the upper part of the cheeks and in the midline just below the lower lip, and finally along the sides and lower border of the chin. The remainder of the body-hair appears from about the time of first axillary hair development until a considerable period after puberty. The ultimate amount of body-hair an individual develops seems to depend largely on heredity, though whether because of the kinds and amounts of hormones secreted or because of the reactivity of the end-organs is not known.

The enlargement of the larynx in boys occurs at about the time the penis growth is nearing completion. The voice change is a gradual one and is often not complete until adolescence is practically over. In boys at adolescence there are frequently some changes seen in the breast; the areola enlarges in diameter and darkens. In some boys—about a third of most groups studied—there is a distinct enlargement with projection of the areola and the presence of firm subareolar mammary tissue. This occurs about midway through adolescence

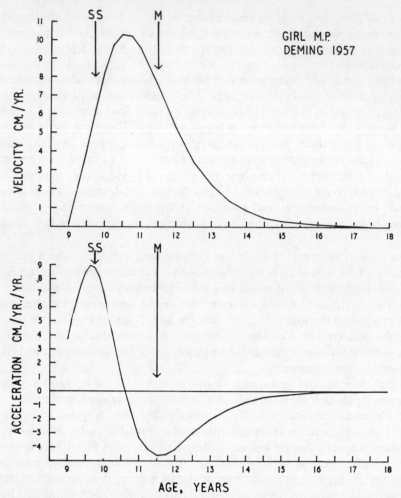

F IG. 20.3. Velocity (*above*) and acceleration (*below*) curves of growth in stature of girl from age 9 years to 18 years. Calculated from data using first and second derivatives of fitted Gompertz curve. SS represents the first appearance of breast development and M the menarche. (From Israelsohn in Tanner 1960.)

and lasts from a year to 18 months, after which in the majority of boys the mound and tissue disappear spontaneously.

A designation of how far a child has progressed through adolescence is frequently needed in clinical, anthropological, and educational work, and standards for rating the development of pubic hair, genitalia, and the breasts will be found in texts on adolescent development.

A diagram of the events of adolescence in girls is given in Fig. 20.2 (a). As in boys, there is a large variation in the time at which the spurt begins, though the sequence of events is fairly constant. The appearance of the breast-bud is as a rule the first sign of puberty, though the appearance of pubic hair may sometimes precede it. The uterus and vagina develop simultaneously with the breast. Menarche (the first menstrual period) occurs almost invariably after the peak of the height spurt has been passed. In Fig. 20.3 is shown a Gompertz curve fitted to the growth in height of an individual girl, differentiated to give curves of velocity (above) and acceleration (below). The form of the acceleration curve is interesting and shows the gradual increasing acceleration, the change to sharp deceleration, and gradual reduction of the deceleration. The points marked SS and M stand for the first appearance of breast-bud and menarche respectively. It is striking how the one coincides with maximum acceleration and the other with maximum deceleration.

Menarche marks a definitive and probably mature stage of uterine development, but it does not usually signify the attainment of full reproductive function. The early menstrual cycles frequently occur without an ovum being shed; during the first year or more after menarche there is a period of relative infertility, characteristic of apes and monkeys as well as the human.

## Changes in physiological function and motor development

Considerable changes in physiological function occur at the same time as the adolescent growth spurt. They are much more marked in boys than girls and serve to confer on the male his greater strength and physical endurance. Before adolescence boys are on average a little stronger than girls, there being more muscularly built or mesomorphic boys than girls in the population even then; but the difference is quite small. After adolescence boys are much stronger, chiefly by virtue of having larger muscles, and perhaps also by being able to develop more force per gram of muscle present. They have larger hearts and lungs relative to their size, a greater capacity for carrying oxygen in the blood, and a greater power for neutralizing the chemical products of muscular exercise. In short, the male becomes at adolescence more adapted for the tasks of hunting, fighting, and manipulating all sorts of heavy objects, as is necessary in some forms of food-gathering.

In Fig. 20.4 are plotted (as distance curves) data for two strength tests taken from a group of boys and girls followed longitudinally through adolescence. Arm-pull refers to the movement of pulling apart clasped hands held up in front of the chest, the hands each holding a dynamometer handle; arm-thrust refers to the reverse movement, of pushing the hands together. Each individual test represents the best of three trials made in competition with a classmate of similar ability and against the individual's own figure of 6 months before. Only with such precautions can reliable maximal values be obtained. There is a considerable spurt in the boys from about 13 to 16 years. Little spurt can be seen in the girls' data, though figures for hand-grip taken from the same group show a slight acceleration at about 12 to $13\frac{1}{2}$ years.

The male increase in the number of red blood cells at puberty, and consequently in the amount of haemoglobin in the blood, is shown in Fig. 20.5.

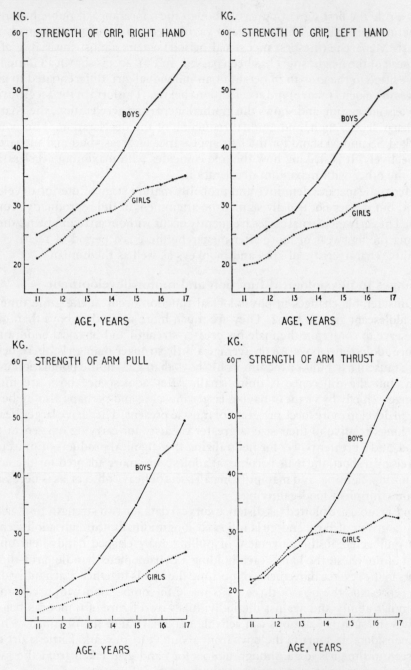

FIG. 20.4. Strength of hand-grip, arm-pull, and arm-thrust from age 11 years to 17 years. Mixed longitudinal data, 65–93 boys and 66–93 girls in each group, from Jones (1949). *Motor Performance and Growth.* Univ. Calif. Press.

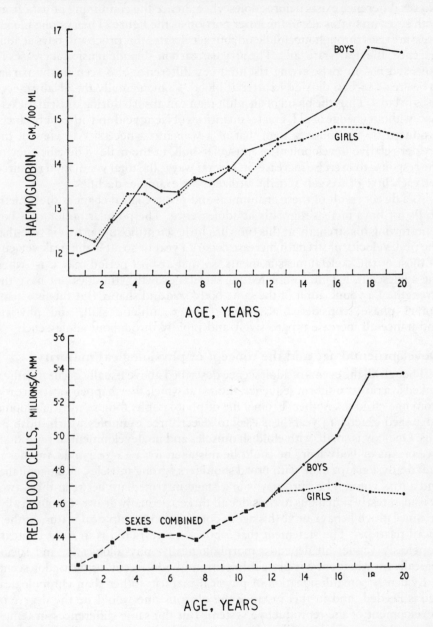

F IG. 20.5. Change in blood haemoglobin (measured by Van Slyke manometric $O_2$ capacity) and number of circulating red blood-corpuscles during childhood, showing the development of the sex difference at adolescence. Distance curves. Mixed longitudinal data reported cross-sectionally, from Mugrage and Andresen (1936, 1938). *Amer. J. Dis. Child.* (From Tanner 1962.)

No sex difference exists before adolescence; hence the combining of data from both sexes up to this age in the lower portion of the figure. The systolic blood-pressure rises throughout childhood, but accelerates this process in boys at adolescence; the heart-rate falls. The alveolar carbon-dioxide tension increases in boys and not in girls, giving rise to a sex difference also seen in the partial pressure of carbon dioxide in arterial blood. Coincidentally the alkali reserve rises in boys. Thus the blood of an adult man can absorb during muscular exercise, without change of pH, greater quantities of lactic acid and other substances produced by the muscles than that of a woman—a necessity in view of the greater relative development of muscular bulk in the male. The efficiency of the response to exercise increases in several ways; the total ventilation required for each litre of oxygen actually utilized, for example, declines.

As a direct result of these anatomical and physiological changes the athletic ability of boys increases greatly at adolescence. The popular notion of a boy 'outgrowing his strength' at this time has little scientific support. It is true that the peak velocity of strength increase occurs a year or so after the peak velocity of most of the skeletal measurements, so that a short period may exist when the adolescent, having completed his skeletal growth, still does not have the strength of a young adult of the same body-size and shape. But this is a temporary phase; considered absolutely, power, athletic skill, and physical endurance all increase progressively and rapidly throughout adolescence.

## Developmental age and the concept of physiological maturity

Though all the events of adolescence described above usually occur together, linked in a rather uniform sequence, the *age* at which they happen varies greatly from one child to another. From a file of photographs of normally developing boys aged exactly 14 years it is easy to select three examples which illustrate this. One boy is small, with childish muscles and no development of reproductive organs or body-hair; he could be mistaken for a 12-year-old. Another is practically a grown man, with broad shoulders, strong muscles, adult genitalia, and a bass voice. The third boy is in a stage intermediate between these two. It is manifestly ridiculous to consider all three as equally grown-up physically, or, since much behaviour at this age is conditioned by physical status, in their social relations. The statement that a boy is 14 years old is in most contexts hopelessly vague; all depends, morphologically, physiologically, and sociologically on whether he is pre-adolescent, mid-adolescent, or post-adolescent.

Evidently some designation of physical maturity other than chronological age is needed, and in this instance the obvious one would be the degree of development of the reproductive system. But the same differences in tempo of growth, as its first describer, Franz Boas, called it, occur at all ages, though less spectacularly than at adolescence. Thus we need a measure of developmental age or physiological maturity applicable throughout the whole period of growth. Three possible measures exist at present; skeletal maturity, dental maturity, and shape age.

*Skeletal maturity*

The most commonly used indicator of physiological maturity is the degree of development of the skeleton as shown by radiography. Each bone begins as a primary centre of ossification, passes through various stages of enlargement and shaping of the ossified area, acquires in some cases one or more epiphyses, that is, other centres where ossification begins independently of the main centre, and finally reaches adult form when these epiphyses fuse with the main body of the bone. All these changes can be seen easily in a radiograph, which distinguishes the ossified area—whose calcium content renders it opaque to the X-rays—from the areas of cartilage where ossification has not yet begun. The sequence of changes of shape through which each of the bone centres and epiphyses pass is constant from one person to another and skeletal maturity, or bone age, as it is often called, is judged both from the number of centres present and the stage of development of each.

In theory any or all parts of the skeleton could be used to give an assessment of skeletal maturity, but in practice the hand and wrist is the most convenient area and the one generally used. A radiograph of the hand is easily done without any radiation being delivered to other parts of the body, it requires only a minute dose of X-rays, and it demands only the minimum of X-ray equipment, such as a dental or a portable machine. Finally, the hand is an area where a large number of bones and epiphyses are developing. The left hand is used, placed flat on an X-ray film with the palm down and the tube placed 76 cm above the knuckle of the middle finger.

The figure for skeletal maturity is derived by comparing the given radiograph with a set of standards. There are two ways in which this may be done. In the older 'atlas' method one matches the given radiograph successively with standards representing age 5, age 6, and so on, and sees with which age standard it most nearly coincides. The more recently developed method is to establish a series of standard stages through which each bone passes, and to match each bone of the given radiograph with these stages. Each bone is thus given a score, corresponding to the stage reached, and the whole radiograph scores a total of so many maturity points. This score is then compared with the range of scores the standard group at the same age and a percentile status is then given to the child in skeletal maturity, that is, the percentage of normal children with lower scores at that age, perhaps 80 per cent, is read off. (The child would be in this case at the 80th percentile.) A skeletal age may also be assigned, this being simply the age at which the given score lies at the fiftieth percentile.

*Dental maturity*

Dental maturity can be obtained by counting the number of teeth erupted and relating this to standard figures in much the same way as skeletal maturity. The deciduous dentition erupts from about 6 months to 2 years and can be used as a measure of physiological maturity during this period. The permanent or second dentition provides a measure from about 6 years to 13 years. From 2 to 6 years and from 13 years onwards little information is obtainable from the teeth by simple counting, but recently new measures of dental maturity have been suggested which use the stages of calcification of teeth as seen in jaw X-rays in just the same way as the skeletal maturity assessment uses the stages of wrist ossification.

## Shape age

As the child grows older his shape changes because of the differential growth velocities described in Chapter 19. In principle, the degree of shape change achieved could be made a measure, and a practically very convenient one, of developmental maturity. But a difficulty enters here which does not arise in the skeletal and dental measures. The shape change is useful only if its measure is completely independent of the final shape reached (as skeletal and dental ages are, the final state being identical in everybody). This is the trouble which besets the 'height age' and 'weight age' once much used by paediatricians, and also the mental age or I.Q., used by psychologists. The height age of a given child is the age at which the average child achieves the height of the given one. Suppose the given child is tall for his age; this may be *either* because he is advanced developmentally (which is what we are trying to measure) *or* because he is simply going to be a taller-than-average adult and is already exhibiting the fact.

For shape age to be effective, therefore, a combination of body measurements must be found which would change with age, but independently of final size and shape. This is a mathematically complex and difficult proposition, but not an impossible one. Shape age is at present a research problem, not a practical method for use.

## Relations between different measures of maturity

The data of Fig. 20.2 must not be allowed to obscure the fact that children vary a great deal, both in the rapidity with which they pass through the various stages of puberty and also in the closeness with which the various events including skeletal maturity are linked together. At one extreme one may find a perfectly healthy girl who has not menstruated although she has reached adult status in breasts and pubic hair and is 2 years past her peak velocity of height. Her bone age, however, will be retarded like her menarche, for skeletal maturity and menarche are quite closely related. The standard deviation of chronological age at menarche is approximately 1 year; the S.D. of bone age at menarche, however, is only 0·7 years; thus the normal limits in the UK currently are 11·0–15·0 years in terms of chronological age but 11·5–14·5 in terms of bone age. Bone age is not related to the age at which breasts first develop and only slightly to the age of pubic hair appearance. Pubic hair and breasts develop their sequences with considerable independence as do genital growth and pubic hair in boys. Differences between individuals in the extent to which maturational events are tightly or loosely linked together presumably reflect differences in the organization of the hypothalamic–hypophysial system.

As Fig. 20.6 shows, children tend to be consistently advanced or retarded during their whole growth period, or at any rate after about age 3 years. In the figure three groups of girls are plotted separately; those with an early, those with a middling, and those with a late menarche. The early menarche girls are skeletally advanced not only at adolescence but at all ages back to 7 years; the late menarche girls have a skeletal age which is consistently retarded. The points M1, M2, and M3 represent the average age of menarche in each group.

At all ages from 6 to 13 children who are advanced skeletally have on average more erupted teeth than those who are skeletally retarded. Likewise, those who have an early adolescence erupt their teeth earlier, as illustrated in Fig. 20.7. But the relationship of dental to skeletal maturity is not a very close one, as

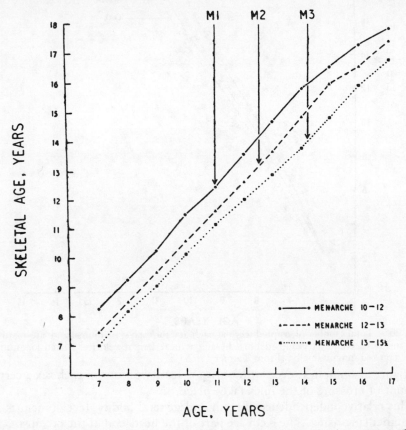

F IG. 20.6. Relation of skeletal maturity and age at menarche. Skeletal development ages (Todd Standards) for early-, average-, and late-menarche groups of girls, from age 7 to maturity. M1, M2, M3, average time of menarche for each group. Mixed longitudinal data. (From Tanner 1962.)

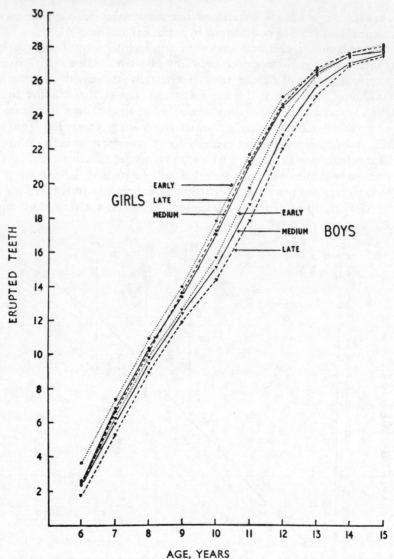

FIG. 20.7. Total number of erupted teeth at each age for early-, medium-, and late-maturing girls and boys. Maturity groups defined by age at peak height velocity. Mixed longitudinal data, reported longitudinally. (From Tanner 1962.)

the figure also implies: even with only 3 maturity groups in each sex a certain amount of crossing of the lines takes place.

This relative independence of teeth and general bodily development is not altogether surprising. The teeth are part of the head-end of the organism, and we have already seen in Chapter 19 how the growth of the head is advanced over the rest of the body and how for this reason its curve differs somewhat from the general growth curve.

Evidently there is some general factor of bodily maturity throughout growth, creating a tendency for a child to be advanced or retarded as a whole; in his skeletal ossification, in the percentage attained of his eventual size, in his permanent dentition, doubtless in his physiological reactions, probably also in his intelligence test score, as described below, and perhaps in other psychological reactions also. Set under this general tendency are groups of more limited maturities, which vary independently of it and of each other. The teeth constitute two of these limited areas (primary and secondary dentition being largely independent of each other); the ossification centres another; probably the brain at least one more. Some of the mechanisms behind these relations can be dimly seen; in children who lack adequate thyroid gland secretion, for example, tooth eruption, skeletal development, and brain organization are all retarded; whereas in children with precocious puberty, whether due to a brain disorder or a disease of the adrenal gland, there is advancement of skeletal and genital maturity without any corresponding effect upon the teeth or, as far as we can tell, upon the progression of organization in the brain.

The percentage of adult height attained at a given age is quite closely related to skeletal maturity from about age 7 years onwards. Regression equations are available for predicting the adult height of a child from height, chronological age, and bone age. In the case of girls some improvement can be made by including information as to whether or not menarche has occurred, and in both sexes a further allowance can be made for parents' height.

*Sex difference in developmental age*

Girls are on the average ahead of boys in skeletal maturity from birth to adulthood, and also in dental maturity during the whole of the permanent dentition eruption (though not, curiously, in primary dentition). It would seem, therefore, that the sex difference lies in the general maturity factor (as well as in various more detailed specific factors), which prompts the question as to whether it may not exist in intelligence tests and social responses also.

The skeletal age difference begins during foetal life, the male retardation being ultimately traceable to the Y-chromosome. Children with the abnormal chromosome constitution XXY (Klinefelter's syndrome) have a skeletal maturity indistinguishable from the normal XY male, and children with the chromosome constitution XO (Turner's syndrome) have skeletal maturities closely approximating to the normal XX, at least up till puberty. In what manner these genes work we cannot say. Possibly the slowing up of male maturation may begin as early as the differentiation of testis or ovary in the second intra-uterine month and represent some basic difference in developmental timing. More probably it may be due to the secretion shortly after this time of sex-specific hormones by the foetal gonads or adrenals. The curious feature here is that all male-specific hormones so far known produce advancement rather than retardation of bone maturity.

At birth, boys are about 4 weeks behind girls in skeletal age, and from then till adulthood they remain about 80 per cent of the skeletal age of girls of the same chronological age. It is for this reason that girls reach adolescence and their final mature size some 2 years before boys. The percentage difference in dental age is not so great, the boys being about 95 per cent of the dental age of girls of the same chronological age.

This sex difference in maturity is not confined to man; it occurs in apes, monkeys, and rats, and may well be characteristic of all or most mammals. Its full biological significance is not at present obvious.

*Physical maturation, mental ability, and emotional development*

There is considerable evidence that intellectual and emotional advancement is to some extent linked to advancement in skeletal maturity. This may be most simply construed, at least so far as intellectual development goes, as evidence that the brain is affected by the general factor of developmental tempo, in the same manner as the teeth. Thus those advanced in physical development do better in mental tests than those retarded in physical development. This subject is further discussed in Chapter 22.

There is little doubt that being an early or late maturer has considerable repercussions on emotional development and social behaviour, particularly at adolescence. These problems are also discussed in Chapter 22. Clearly the occurrence of tempo differences in human development has profound implications for educational theory and practice.

# 21. Hormonal, genetic, and environmental factors controlling growth

THE endocrine glands are of great importance in the control of growth and development, being one of the chief agents for translating the instructions of the genes into the reality of the adult form, at the pace and with the result permitted by the available environment.

## Prenatal period

Genes on the Y-chromosome cause the previously undifferentiated gonad to become a recognizable testis at the ninth week of foetal age, reckoned post-menstrually (or seventh week post-fertilization). Whether this is the result of hormonal action is at present uncertain. At the eleventh postmenstrual week Leydig cells appear in the testis and by the twelfth week they secrete testosterone or an allied substance, probably under the influence of chorionic gonadotrophin, which reaches a peak in the mother's urine at this time (where its presence is used as the standard test for pregnancy). The testicular hormone causes the previously undifferentiated external genitalia to form a penis and scrotum.

In the female, it seems that differentiation of the ovary and external genitalia proceeds more passively. In the absence of the Y-chromosome, nothing happens at the ninth week and at about the tenth postmenstrual week the gonad turns into an ovary. The external genitalia become female at around the fourteenth week, apparently without hormonal intervention.

There is another aspect of this sexual differentiation, so far studied only in animals, but of much importance in man in principle and perhaps in practice too. In the rat the Leydig-cell secretion acts on the brain as well as on the external genitalia. In all mammals investigated, endocrinological and to a large extent behavioural maleness is dependent on the structure of the hypothalamus. If a female rat pituitary is grafted into an adult male whose own pituitary has been removed, then, when vascular connections with the hypothalamus have been established, the pituitary will secrete gonadotrophic hormones in a male, not a female cycle. The converse is also true.

In the rat, differentiation of the hypothalamus is caused by testosterone secreted by the Leydig cells during the first 2 or 3 days after birth. This is a true sensitive period. Testosterone given a few days before birth will not cause brain differentiation, nor will testosterone given later than 5 days after birth to a rat whose testes were removed at birth. The message has to reach the hypothalamus at exactly the right time. A single injection of female sex hormone on the fifth day after birth will stop the proper male differentiation, and a single injection of testosterone into a female on the fifth day will produce the 'androgen-sterilized female', a rat without female reproductive cycles when it becomes adult. It is known that some areas of the brain selectively take up testosterone. These must include areas concerned in sexual behaviour as well as in control of gonadotrophin releaser. Female rats given testosterone neonatally do not show any female sexual behaviour when adult, even though ovariectomized and given oestrogen–progesterone replacement therapy so that their sex-hormone state is that of a normal female. If ovariectomized and given testosterone, however, they behave as males.

It is already clear that the rat is not an exception among mammals in this respect. To what extent and with what timing an analogous situation holds in man is not yet known. Birth in the rat corresponds probably to about the sixteenth to eighteenth postmenstrual week in man, though since man seems to develop Leydig cells relatively earlier than other mammals investigated, perhaps we should think in terms of about the fourteenth to sixteenth week. In fact, this would correspond well with foetal testosterone secretion. Whether this work has significance for human sexual behaviour patterns is not at present known.

The prenatal role of other endocrine glands is somewhat uncertain. Maternal oestrogen passes across the placenta and causes the uterus of newborn girls to be temporarily enlarged at birth. Thyroid hormone is necessary for the normal development of the brain, and is secreted by the foetal gland. The adrenal gland has a special zone which is well developed at birth and regresses soon afterwards; its significance and its cause, however, are still matters of debate.

## Postnatal period

The most important hormone controlling growth from birth up to adolescence is somatotrophin or growth hormone. This is a polypeptide secreted by the pituitary and showing a greater degree of species (or rather order) specificity than other pituitary hormones. Thus, only human or monkey hormone has a growth-stimulating effect in man.

Though growth hormone is present in the foetus it is not necessary for foetal growth. From birth onwards, however, it is essential for a normal rate of growth to occur. By the age of 2 children with isolated growth-hormone deficiency are recognizably smaller than normal (though in fact they seldom are recognized till age 5 or later when they go to school, or when younger siblings come to surpass them in height).

Growth hormone does not itself act on the cartilage; it causes growth by stimulating the liver to produce an intermediary hormone called somatomedin. This is also a peptide but of smaller size than growth hormone. The administration of growth hormone to a person who lacks it causes growth of muscle with increased incorporation of amino acids into tissues to form protein. It also causes diminution of the amount of adipose tissue, shifting the metabolic balance from the laying down of fat to the laying down of protein. Thus children who lack the hormone are fat as well as small.

The secretion of growth hormone, like that of other pituitary hormones, is controlled by the hypothalamus. At the time of writing the existence of an inhibiting hypothalamic hormone (somatostatin, a 14-amino-acid peptide) has been established but the existence of a hypothalamic releasing hormone is uncertain.

Growth hormone is secreted in pulses, not continuously, throughout the 24 hours of the day. Exercise, anxiety, and sleep regularly cause secretion but other factors are uncertain. Much is still unclear about its regulation and indeed about its function in adults. Because it is released in pulses it is difficult to establish 24-hour secretion rates for growth hormone, and it is not yet clear what if any changes in rate take place during childhood. What is tolerably clear is that shortness and tallness within the normal range are not caused by differences in growth hormone secretion. Conceivably they may be due to differences in amounts of somatomedin but much more probably in amounts or characteristics of receptors in the cartilage cells.

Thyroid hormone plays a vital role throughout the whole of growth. The activity of the thyroid decreases gradually from birth to adolescence, at which time it probably increases or at least falls less rapidly for a year or so. So far as rate of growth in size is concerned, the action of the thyroid is permissive and not controlling. In hypothyroidism growth is delayed; skeletal maturity, dental maturity, and growth of the brain are all affected.

Though clearly the normal mechanism controlling the rate of skeletal maturation must be hormonal, the balance of hormones is not yet clear. Lack of thyroid hormone and lack of growth hormone both cause retardation; sex hormones and adrenal androgens cause advance. Small quantities of sex hormones and adrenal androgens circulate in the blood before adolescence, but what part variations in their amount play in controlling tempo of growth is quite unknown.

## Adolescence

At adolescence a relatively new phase of growth occurs in which hormones from the gonads and the adrenal combine with growth hormone to produce the adolescent spurt. It seems that a full spurt is dependent on both sets of hormones being present; boys with growth hormone deficiency have a spurt only reaching about half the normal peak velocity.

Two out of the three major groups of hormones produced by the adrenal circulate in the blood at relatively unchanged levels from birth onwards; these are cortisol and aldosterone, the latter being the hormone which maintains within acceptable limits the concentrations of electrolytes in the tissue fluid.

The third group of adrenal hormones, the androgens, appears in quantity only at adolescence. These androgens, together with growth hormone, are thought to be responsible for the whole of the female adolescent growth spurt and that portion of the male spurt not attributable to testosterone secreted by the testes. There is little doubt that testosterone is the major cause of the increase in size and strength of the male muscles at adolescence, and the increase in number of red blood-cells. Whether there is a sex difference in the amounts or varieties of adrenal androgen secretion at adolescence is not yet clear.

No complete theory of the sequence of endocrine events at puberty exists yet, though many parts of the complicated puzzle are recognizable. The sequence is initiated by events in the hypothalamus. Before puberty the pituitary contains gonadotrophins, or can manufacture them, but does not release them to the general circulation because it is not stimulated by the hypothalamus to do so. Gonadotrophin release is caused by a releasing substance, luteinizing hormone releasing hormone (LHRH) an octapeptide which is synthesized in certain hypothalamic cells and reaches the pituitary via the hypophysial-portal system of blood-vessels. It is the hypothalamus that carries the information as to maturity, not the pituitary. At the 'correct' stage of bodily maturity the hypothalamus matures in some way and LHRH is released.

The way in which this happens has a general importance for the clarification of developmental mechanisms. In pre-pubertal childhood there is a feedback system already established and in operation, whereby the very low levels of circulating testosterone (in boys) and oestrogen (in girls) inhibits the hypothalamic neurons which secrete LHRH. Thus gonadotrophin level is also kept extremely low, though detectable. Then at puberty something happens to decrease the sensitivity of the hypothalamic neurons to the sex steroid. The circulating level is insufficient to inhibit LHRH and the sequence LHRH→gonadotrophins→oestrogen (in girls) is set in continuous increase until the oestrogen level becomes so high that it does again inhibit LHRH release. This new blood concentration is sufficient to cause breast growth and the other changes of puberty. Just what causes the decrease in sensitivity in the hypothalamus, however, remains a mystery. Clearly we are dealing with some sort of internal clock but one dependent on the passage of numerous prior events in the organism and not simply dependent on chronological nor even wholly on developmental time.

The reason for the increase of adrenal androgens at puberty is less clear. Since cortisol continues to be secreted at pre-adolescent rates it is unlikely that adrenocorticotrophic hormone secretion is increased at puberty. Probably the adrenal androgen-secreting cells are specifically sensitized so that the same amount of adrenocorticotrophin produces more androgens. Oestrogen has been shown to sensitize some animal adrenals in this way. Testosterone does not appear to sensitize the male adrenals, so how the mechanism works in the male is unknown.

Much else remains obscure. The cause of the pre-adolescent increase in fat is unknown, though its timing seems to coincide with increasing gonadotrophin release. The identity of the adrenal androgen causing growth of the pubic and axillary hair in women is still a matter of debate. Though we are beginning to understand the delicate linkage of the hormonal events of adolescence, detailed knowledge will have to wait upon longitudinal studies conducted with the more sensitive chemical and biological methods that have recently become available.

## The interaction of heredity and environment in controlling growth rate

Many factors that affect the rate of development are known. Some are hereditary in origin and act by hastening or retarding physiological maturation from an early age. Others, such as dietary restriction, season of the year, or severe psychological stress, originate in the environment and simply affect the rate of growth at the time they are acting. Others again, such as socio-economic class, reflect a complicated mixture of hereditary and environmental influences.

The height, weight, or body-build of a child or an adult always represents the resultant of both the genetical and environmental forces, together with their interaction. It is a long way from the possession of certain genes to the acquisition of a height of 2 m. In modern genetics it is a truism that any particular gene depends for its expression firstly on the internal environment created by all the other genes, and secondly on the external environment. Furthermore, the interaction of genes and environment may not be additive. That is to say, bettering the nutrition by a fixed amount may not produce a 10 per cent increase in height in all persons irrespective of their genetical constitutions; instead a 12 per cent rise may occur in the genetically tall and an 8 per cent rise in the genetically short. This type of interaction is called 'multiplicative'. In general a particular environment may prove highly suitable for a child with certain genes and highly unsuitable for a child with others. Thus it is very difficult to specify quantitatively the relative importance of heredity and environment in controlling growth and physique under any given circumstances; the particular circumstances must always be made clear. In general the nearer optimal the environment the more the genes have a chance to show their potential actions, but this is an overall statement only and undoubtedly many more subtle and specific interactions occur, especially in growth and differentiation.

Genetic factors, however, are clearly of immense importance. The fundamental plan of growth is laid down very early, in the comparative safety of the uterus. An immature limb bone removed from a foetal or newborn mouse and implanted under the skin of the back of an adult mouse of the same inbred strain (which therefore produces no antibodies to it) will continue to develop until it closely resembles a normal adult bone. Furthermore, the cartilage scaffolding of the bone, removed at the stage preceding actual bone formation, will do the same. Thus the structure of the adult bone in all its essentials is implicit in the cartilage model of months before. The later action of the bone's environment, represented by the muscles pulling on it and the joints connecting it to other bones, seems to be limited to the making of finishing touches.

### Genetics of growth

The genetical control of growth rate is manifested most simply in the inheritance of age at menarche. Identical twin sisters reach menarche an average of

2 months apart; non-identical twin sisters an average of 10 months apart. The correlation coefficient between age at menarche of mother and daughter is about 0·4, only slightly lower than similar correlations for height. These are indications that a very high proportion of the variability of age at menarche in populations living under European conditions is due to genetical causes. The inheritance of age at menarche is probably transmitted as much by the father

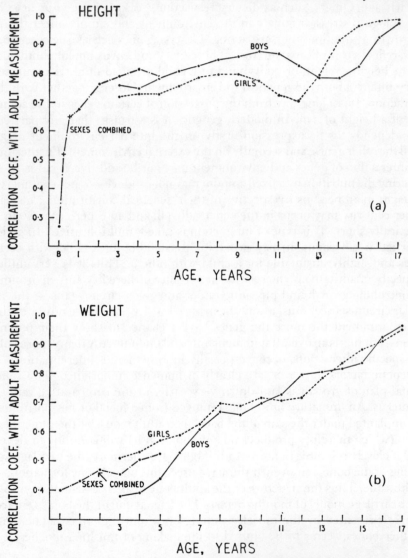

FIG. 21.1. Correlations between adult height and weight and heights and weights of same individuals as children. Sexes-combined lines (0–5) from 124 individuals of a study in Aberdeen with + points from Bayley. Boys' and girls' lines (3–17) from 66 boys and 70 girls of California Guidance Study. All data pure longitudinal. (From Tanner 1962.)

as by the mother, and is due not to a single gene but to many genes each of small effect. This is the same pattern of inheritance as that shown by height and other body measurements.

This genetical control operates throughout the whole period of growth; skeletal maturity shows a close correspondence at all ages in identical twins. The time of eruption of the teeth, both deciduous and permanent, and also the sequence in which they calcify and erupt, is largely determined by heredity. Genes controlling growth range all the way from those affecting rate of growth of the whole body, probably through endocrine mechanisms, to those bringing about a highly localized growth gradient causing one tooth to erupt before another, or one ossification centre in the wrist to appear before another.

Not all genes are active at birth. Some express themselves only in the physiological surroundings provided by the later years of growth; their effect is said to be 'age-limited'. This is the probable explanation of the curve described by the correlations between measurements of a child at successive ages and his measurements as an adult, which have been obtained by long-term longitudinal studies (see Fig. 21.1). The correlation of length at birth with adult height is very low, since birth length reflects uterine conditions and not the child's genotype. The child's genes increasingly make themselves felt and the correlation rises steeply during the first 3 years; but after this only a small rise occurs until adolescence. It seems likely that the magnitude as well as the time of the spurt is genetically controlled, perhaps by genes causing the secretion of large or small amounts of androgenic hormones. Such genes may produce no effect until the moment when androgen secretion begins. Certainly there is a considerable degree of independence between growth before and growth at adolescence.

*Race and ecological conditions*

There are racial differences in rate and pattern of growth, leading to the differences seen in adult build. Some of these are clearly genetically determined, while others depend perhaps on climatic differences and certainly on nutritional ones. We must suppose that in each of the major populations of the world the growth of its members was gradually adjusted, by means of selection, to the environmental conditions in which they evolved. We should be able to see the remnants of this process in modern populations—the remnants only, because relatively recent migrations have much altered the distributions of peoples, so that many no longer live in the areas in which they evolved. There is, in fact, a quite close positive relation between the linearity of peoples, as judged by their adult weight for height, and the average annual temperature of where they live. Differences in size must be sharply differentiated from differences in shape, for the former are relatively easily affected by malnutrition and the latter are not. A European who is starved throughout childhood ends up a small adult, but he does not come to have the relatively short legs and long body of the Japanese or the long legs and short body of the African. His skeletal

shape is little if at all affected, though he will be lacking in fat and, if the malnutrition has been severe and prolonged enough, lacking also in muscle.

Height-for-age curves of the best-documented groups of European, African
(in the sense of origin), and Asian peoples each in comparable and well-off
circumstances, thus under similar, presumed near-optimal, nutritional conditions, show little if any difference between Negroes and Europeans; but the
well-off Chinese are shorter and clearly are finishing their growth earlier, which
may account for their shortness of limb. In contrast for two groups of genetically similar populations under very different environmental circumstances, the
gross restriction of growth in the malnourished is plain to see.

Contrary to popular belief, climate has little direct effect on rate of growth.
The average age of menarche in relatively well-nourished Nigerian schoolgirls
has been reported as 14·3 years, and that of Eskimo girls as 14·4 years. Burmese
and Assamese girls living under excellent nutritional and medical circumstances but with a hot-weather temperature of 45°C have an average age of
menarche of about 13·2 years, a figure practically identical with the average
in Europe at the same time. Nutritional effects on menarche (see below) are
so marked that they overwhelm possible climatic ones, which, if existent at
all, are relatively minor.

Some differences in shape between populations seem mostly to be due to
genetic causes. Children between 6 and 11 years in American Indian tribes
in Arizona are heavier for their height than the local White children, despite
being in worse economic circumstances. One could conceivably explain this
by a differential effect of malnutrition, the diet causing a stunting of growth
in length but an excess of growth in breadth of bone and muscle. But data
on African Negroes, and particularly Nilotics, shows that they, by contrast,
are lighter at all ages for their height than are Whites. Either the character
of the malnutrition is totally different in the two areas, or, far more probably,
genetic differences are involved.

Certainly genetic differences are the cause of the Negroes, in West Africa,
East Africa, and the USA, being ahead of the White in skeletal maturity at
birth and for the first year or two. This is associated with advancement in motor
behaviour, and earlier passing of the milestones such as sitting-up and crawling.
The advancement, at least in Africa, disappears by about the third year, either
partially or wholly because of inadequate nutrition. Well-off Negro girls in the
USA remain in advance of Whites throughout the whole growth period. The
permanent teeth also erupt earlier in Negroes than Whites, by an average of
a year. The teeth-buds are laid down early in life and their growth is more
resistant to malnutrition and disease than is the skeleton, probably because it
is less affected by hormonal alterations.

*Season of year*

In most data from industrialized countries in temperate areas a well-marked seasonal effect on growth velocity can be seen. Growth in height is on average fastest in spring and growth in weight fastest in the autumn. The average velocity of height from March to May is about twice that from September to October in most of the older western European data.

Individual children differ surprisingly, however, both in the time when their seasonal trend reaches its peak, and in the degree to which they show a seasonal trend at all: in a considerable number little evidence of any seasonal effect is seen. These differences may reflect individual variation in endocrine reactivity.

*Nutrition*

Malnutrition delays growth, as is shown from the effects of famine associated with war. In Fig. 21.2 the heights and weights of schoolchildren in Stuttgart are plotted at each year of age from 1911 to 1953. There is a uniform increase at all ages in both measurements from 1920 to 1940 (see secular trend discussion below) but in the latter years of the Second World War this trend is sharply reversed.

Children have great recuperative powers, provided the adverse conditions are not carried too far or continued too long. During a short period of malnutrition the organism slows up its growth and waits for better times. When they arrive growth takes place unusually fast until the genetically determined growth curve is reached or approached once more, and subsequently followed. During this 'catch-up' phase weight and height and skeletal development seem to catch up at approximately the same rate. In cattle, alternation of periods of good feeding and underfeeding may alter the final shape and tissue composition according to the timing of the periods, the fastest-growing tissues suffering most during malnutrition. There is little evidence that anything similar occurs in malnutrition in man.

Girls appear to be better buffered than boys against the effects of malnutrition or illness. They are less easily thrown off their growth curves, perhaps because the two X-chromosomes provide better regulatory forces than one X- and the small Y-chromosome.

*Psychological disturbance*

That adverse psychological conditions might cause a degree of retardation in growth is a thought that comes readily to mind. In recent years it has been clearly established that in certain children under emotional stress the growth hormone secretion is inhibited and they come closely to resemble cases of idiopathic growth-hormone deficiency. However, when taken out of the stressful conditions they begin to secrete growth hormone again and have the usual rapid catch-up growth. They are relatively uncommon cases, although Neligan in Newcastle estimated their incidence in that population as about 3 times that of idiopathic growth-hormone deficiency.

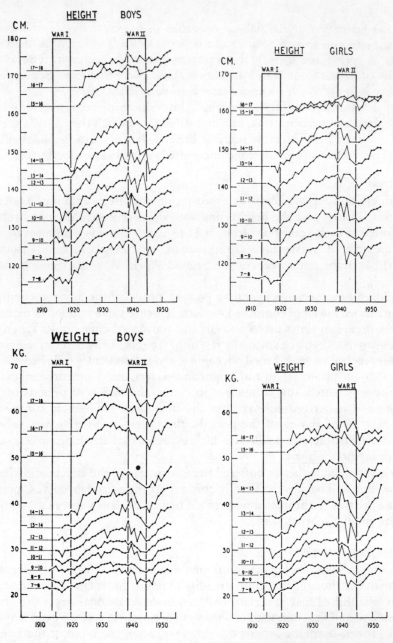

F IG. 21.2. Effect of malnutrition on growth in height and weight. Heights and weights of Stuttgart schoolchildren (7–8 years to 14–15 years, Volkschule; 15–16 years upwards, Oberschule) from 1911 to 1953. Lines connect points for children of same age, and express secular trend and effect of war conditions. (From Tanner 1962.)

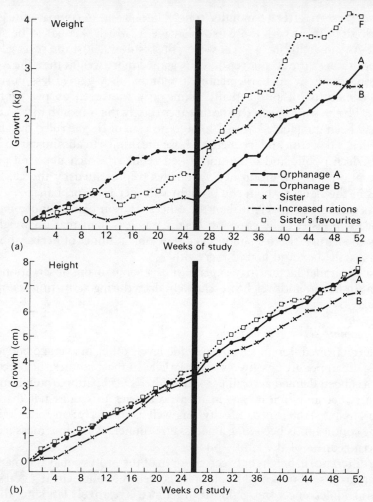

FIG. 21.3. Influence of sister-in-charge S on growth in weight (a) and height (b) of orphanage children. Orphanage B diet supplemented at time indicated by vertical bar, but sister simultaneously transferred to B from A. Note magnitude of growth follows presence or absence of sister, not amount of rations. The curves (F) with squares are for 8 favourites of sister, transferred with her to B from A. (From Tanner 1962.)

A similar thing may happen under less extreme circumstances and account for smaller variations in individuals' growth, though good evidence on this is naturally hard to come by. However, one experimental investigation by Widdowson, is clearly (one might almost say providentially) controlled.

In studying the effect of increased rations on orphanage children living on the poor diet available in Germany in 1948 Widdowson had the rare opportunity of observing the change brought about by replacement of one sister-in-charge by another. The design of the experiment was to give orphanage B a food supplement after a 6 months' control period and to compare the growth of the children there with those in orphanage A, which was not to be supplemented. As shown in Fig. 21.3, however, the result was just the reverse of that expected; though the B children actually gained more weight than the A children during the first, unsupplemented, 6 months, they gained less during the second 6 months, despite actually taking in a measured 20 per cent more calories. The reason appeared to be that at precisely the 6-month mark a certain sister had been transferred from A to become head of B. She ruled the children of B with a rod of iron and frequently chose mealtimes to administer to individual children public and often unjustified rebukes, which upset all present. An exception was the group of 8 favourites (represented by the curve with squares in the figure) whom she brought with her from orphanage A. These 8 always gained more weight than the others, and on being supplemented in B gained still faster. The effect on height was less than that on weight, but of the same nature. 'Better', quotes Widdowson, 'a dinner of herbs where love is than a stalled ox and hatred therewith'.

Possibly similar factors may explain in part some of the observations made on gains in height and weight in schoolchildren during term-time as opposed to holidays.

## Socio-economic class: size of family

Children from different socio-economic levels differ in average body-size at all ages, the upper groups always being larger. In most studies socio-economic status has been defined according to the father's occupation, though in recent years it is becoming clear that in many countries this does not distinguish people's living standards or life-style as well as formerly; an index reflecting housing conditions is becoming a necessary adjunct, as is some measure of the child-centredness of the family budget.

The difference in height between children of the professional and managerial classes and those of unskilled labourers is currently about 2 cm at 3 years, rising to 5 cm at adolescence. In weight the difference is relatively less since the lower socio-economic class children have a greater weight for height.

In Fig. 21.4 the heights of a national sample of 7-year-old children from all over Great Britain (those born in one week of 1958) are plotted in relation to socio-economic class and numbers of children in the family. The tendency of the better-off children to be taller is visible in families of all sizes.

The greater part of the height difference is due to earlier maturation of the well-off classes, though some is due to their being larger as adults. There seems to be a difference in age at menarche of 2 to 3 months between daughters of the managerial class and those of unskilled workmen; permanent tooth eruption occurs earlier in the more favoured groups by about the same margin, when all the teeth are averaged.

The causes of this socio-economic differential are probably multiple. Nutrition is almost certainly one, and with it all the habits of regular meals, sleep, exercise, and general organization that distinguish, from this point of view, a good home from a bad one. Home conditions are more related to the growth differences than are the economic conditions of the families, and home conditions reflect to a considerable degree the intelligence and personality of the parents. Minor illnesses such as measles, influenza, and even antibiotic-treated middle-ear infection or pneumonia cause no discernible retardation of growth in the great majority of well-nourished children, but they may have some effect on relatively ill-cared-for ones. Possibly the greater incidence of such illnesses in the worse-off and more socially disorganized families contributes to their reduction in growth rate, though this has not yet been certainly established. The socio-economic size differential has been getting somewhat less during

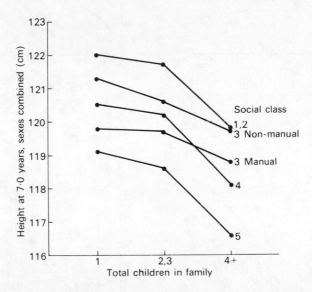

F IG. 21.4. Differences in height of 7-year-old children according to occupation of father ('social class') and number of siblings in family. Sexes pooled. (From Goldstein, *Hum. Biol.* 43, 1971.)

the last 50 years, as social conditions have improved. It still persists, however, being seemingly dependent now more upon home conditions and parents' education than upon simple income.

It is perhaps not altogether surprising therefore that more intelligent children (at least by tests of ability) are at all ages taller than less intelligent children from the same occupational background. This association probably represents a complex mixture of environmental and genetical effects, the one reinforcing the other. There is evidence that the height differential between social classes in the adult population is kept in being by a system of social mobility which, perhaps rather curiously, produces an average movement of tall persons upward and short persons downwards.

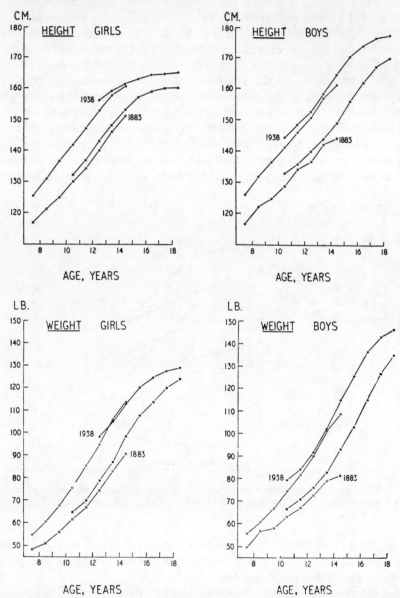

FIG. 21.5. Secular trend in growth of height in Swedish children 1883–1968. (From Ljung,,B., Bergsten-Brucefors, A. and Lindgren, G. *Ann. hum. Biol.* **1**, 245, 1974.)

## Secular trend

During the last 100 years there has been a very striking tendency for children to become progressively larger at all ages. The magnitude of this trend is considerable and quite dwarfs the differences between socio-economic classes. In

Fig. 21.5 are plotted the heights and weights of Swedish schoolchildren measured in 1883, 1938, and 1965–71. At all ages from 7 years onwards the 1938 children are larger than their 1883 counterparts and the 1965–71 children a little taller still.

British, Scandinavian, German, Polish, and North American data all give secular trends of very similar magnitude. The average gain between 1880 and 1950 is about 1 cm in height and 0·5 kg in weight per decade at ages 5–7 years, it increases to about 2·5 cm and 7 kg per decade during adolescence and decreases to a figure of about 1 cm per decade for the fully grown adult. The rather scanty pre-school-age data indicate that the trend starts at birth and relative to absolute size is probably actually greater between 2 years and 5 years than subsequently. It seems that this trend is still continuing in most European countries and is especially marked in Japan. However, in the most well-off section of the community it has apparently stopped; these children are perhaps fulfilling their genetic height potential. It is not clear when the present trend started, though an astonishing series of Norwegian growth data stretching back to 1741 indicate that little gain in adult height took place from 1760 to 1830, a gain of about 0·3 cm per decade took place from 1830 to 1875, and a gain of about 0·6 cm per decade from 1875 to the present day. Danish data stretching back to 1815 show a similar lack of gain till about 1845. In Fig. 21.6 figures for the growth of boys in England are plotted from 1833 to the present. The secular trend has overridden the social-class differences and, though these still

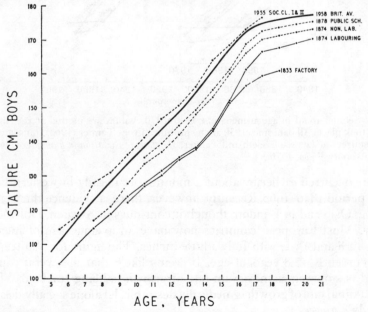

FIG. 21.6. Height of English boys, 1833–1958, to show secular trend. 1833 factory boys; 1874 labouring and non-labouring classes; 1878 public school (upper classes); 1955 social class I and II from Birmingham Survey; 1958 British average. (From Tanner 1962.)

exist, the average boy of today is taller at all ages than the upper-class boy of 1878.

This trend in children's size is due both to earlier maturation, culminating in final adult height being reached earlier now than formerly, and also to this adult height having itself increased. The secular trend at completion of stature is about 1 cm per decade or approximately 2·5 cm per generation in most European data.

The acceleration of growth is shown in the marked secular trend of the age of menarche, shown in Fig. 21.7. The trend is remarkably similar in all the series of data, and over the whole period for which records are available.

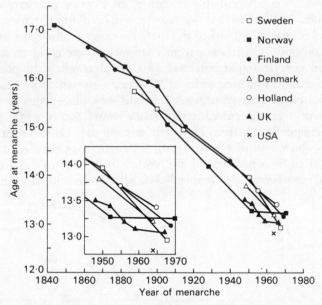

FIG. 21.7. Secular trend in age at menarche 1840–1970. Values are plotted at year in which menarche took place. All data since 1930 are by probits. (From Tanner (1962), plus later additions: for sources of data see Eveleth and Tanner, *Worldwide variation in human growth*. Cambridge University Press, 1976.)

Menarche occurred earlier by about 4 months per decade in western Europe over the period 1830–1960. Recently, however, there is evidence the trend has stopped in Oslo and in London, though it continues in Sweden, Holland, and Hungary. Most European countries now have an average age of menarche between 12·8 and 13·2, with Italy a little earlier. The figure for Whites in the USA is currently 12·8 years of age. It seems likely that in several countries the trend is stopping as maximum rate of growth is being reached. Whether such a maximal rate of growth is medically desirable, let alone socially desirable, is anybody's guess.

Nobody knows for certain why the secular trend occurred. Better nutrition and generally improved environmental circumstances are usually given the credit, and with considerable reason. But the increase is by no means confined to the less-well-off classes, and if nutrition is the cause then it must be a change in the balance of the diet or of the intake of certain essential factors, and not just an increase in calories. It has been suggested that the trend of adult stature may be genetical in origin and caused by the progressive breaking down of genetical isolates, that is, of the tendency for marriages to be contracted between members of the same village community. An increasing degree of out-marriage has certainly been occurring ever since the introduction of the bicycle. But for this to cause an increase in height demands that the many genes governing height act so that on average the children of a tall and a short parent would not be exactly halfway between the parents in height, but a little taller. To date there is no really solid evidence that height genes do fulfil this condition though a little presumptive evidence that they may. The idea that taller people now survive to have more offspring than formerly, perhaps due to the suppression of bacterial infections, is entirely unable to account for the speed of the trend, even if it were true, which is improbable.

There is evidence that a considerable retardation in puberty occurred in Europe with the advent of industrialization, and that the present trend began when the standard of living started to rise. However this may be, the secular trend both in earlier maturation and in greater size is one of the most considerable phenomena of human biology at present, and has, into the bargain, a host of medical, educational, and sociological effects.

# 22. Physical and psychological development

CLEARLY the study of growth and development qualifies as one of the two or three basic sciences on which educational theory and practice must ultimately rest. Early educators had close links with human biology, and some of the pioneers were themselves doctors or anthropologists. But during the first half of this century educators paid little attention to the facts of physical growth, perhaps because the rapid rise of educational psychology temporarily filled the whole horizon. This state of affairs has now clearly ended, and teachers increasingly demand expert and comprehensive data from human biology on the growth of the brain, the occurrence of critical periods and of stages of growth, the relation of intelligence-test results to rate of maturation, the effects of early or late physical maturation upon emotional stability, the secular trend, and so forth.

Many of the answers are all too sketchy, for the study of growth and development has been a neglected field. But we do have a considerable array of facts and a number of principles derived from them which are of importance in education. Chief amongst these are the questions of growth gradients in the brain; individual variability in tempo of growth, particularly at adolescence; and the relation between tempo of intellectual and physical development.

## Growth of the brain

From early foetal life onwards the brain, in terms of its gross weight, is nearer to its adult value than any other organ of the body, except perhaps the eye. In this sense it develops earlier than the rest of the body (see Fig. 19.6, p. 310). At birth it is about 25 per cent of its adult weight, at 6 months nearly 50 per cent, at $2\frac{1}{2}$ years about 75 per cent, at 5 years 90 per cent, and at 10 years 95 per cent. This contrasts with the weight of the whole body, which at birth is about 5 per cent of the young adult weight and at 10 years about 50 per cent.

Different parts of the brain grow at different rates, and reach their maximum velocities at different times. Fig. 22.1 illustrates this for the prenatal period in the same manner as Fig. 19.9 (p. 315) which showed the growth gradients in upper and lower limbs. In Fig. 22.1 the percentages of the value at birth are plotted for the weights of the cerebrum (including the corpus callosum, basal ganglia, and diencephalon, with the thalamus and hypothalamus), the cerebellum, the midbrain, the pons and medulla, and the spinal cord. The midbrain and the spinal cord are the most advanced at all ages from 3 foetal months to birth, and the pons and medulla are next. The cerebrum is less advanced, but still much ahead of the cerebellum. Though data on the postnatal growth

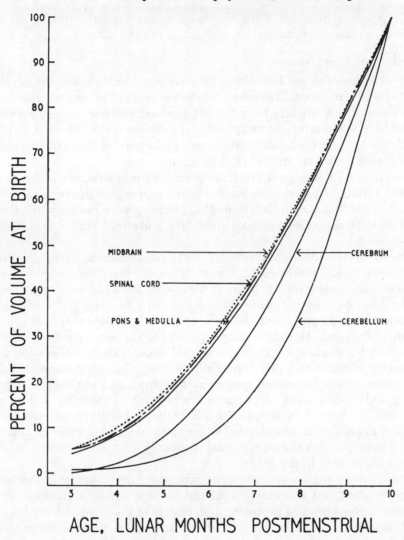

AGE, LUNAR MONTHS POSTMENSTRUAL

F i g. 22.1. Percentage of their volume at birth reached at earlier months by parts of the brain and spinal cord. Cerebrum includes hemispheres, corpus stratium, and diencephalon. (From Tanner 1961.)

of these parts are mostly lacking it is clear that these relationships would be essentially unchanged if the plots were made in terms of percentage of adult value; that is, no counter-gradients appear, so far as is known, during the post-natal period.

The maximum velocity of growth is reached first by the spinal cord, mid-brain, and pons at about 2 postmenstrual months, then by the cerebral hemi-spheres at about 3 postmenstrual months, and finally by the cerebellum at about

6 postmenstrual months. Thus the brain shows regular growth maturity gradients in just the same way as other parts of the body.

### Cerebral cortex development

As yet we know all too little about the growth of the brain and the development of its organization. Anatomical studies of brain structure are immensely laborious and few workers have had the courage, persistence, and technical support needed to carry out morphological analyses of the brains of children at different ages. Physiological studies, such as the pattern of electroencephalogram change with age, are still in their infancy.

Most of our knowledge of the development of brain structure is due to the devoted studies of Conel, who has published analyses of the cerebral cortex at birth, 3 months, 6 months, 15 months, 2 years, 4 years, and 6 years. Before birth our information is scanty and qualitative, and after 6 years it is practically non-existent.

The cerebral cortex is identifiable at about 8 postmenstrual weeks; thereafter it increases in width and by about 26 weeks it has developed the typical structure of 6 somewhat indeterminate layers of nerve-cells with a layer of fibres on the inside. The layers do not mature simultaneously; the cells of the fifth layer are most advanced up to birth, followed in order by those of the sixth, third, fourth, and second. All the nerve-cells present in the adult are thought to be formed during the first 15–18 postmenstrual weeks, except perhaps for some in the cerebellum, which may appear a little later. Thereafter axons and dendrites grow, nucleoproprotein appears in the cytoplasm and the cells increase in size, and axons acquire varying amounts of myelin as sheaths; but no new nerve cells are formed. Neuroglia, the cells of the supporting connective tissue, continue to appear for considerably longer; after the early period of development they outnumber the neurons, and eventually contribute some 90 per cent of the cells present in the brain.

From these changes a series of criteria for maturation of parts of the cortex can be obtained, just as criteria for skeletal maturity can be obtained from the changes in appearance of the ossification centres of the hand and wrist. Conel uses nine criteria, amongst which are the number of neurons per unit tissue, size of neurons, condition of Nissl substance and neurofibrils, length of axons, and degree of myelination.

Two clear gradients of development occur, the first concerning the order in which general areas of the brain develop and the second the order in which bodily localizations advance within the areas. The leading part of the cortex is the primary motor area of the pre-central gyrus (see Fig. 22.2); next comes the primary sensory area of the post-central gyrus; then the primary visual area in the occipital lobe; then the primary auditory area in the temporal lobe. All the association areas lag behind their primary stations. Gradually development spreads out, as it were, from the primary areas; thus in the frontal lobe the parts immediately in front of the motor cortex develop next and the tip

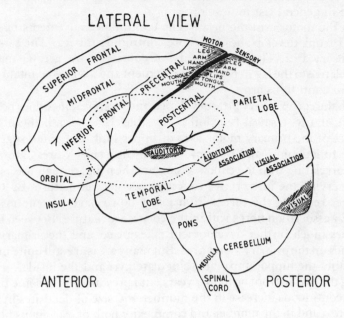

LATERAL VIEW

SUPERIOR FRONTAL

MIDFRONTAL

PRECENTRAL

INFERIOR FRONTAL

MOTOR

LEG
ARM
HAND
LIPS
TONGUE
MOUTH

SENSORY

LEG
ARM
HAND
LIPS
TONGUE
MOUTH

POSTCENTRAL

PARIETAL LOBE

ORBITAL

INSULA

AUDITORY

AUDITORY ASSOCIATION

VISUAL ASSOCIATION

VISUAL

TEMPORAL LOBE

PONS

CEREBELLUM

MEDULLA

SPINAL CORD

ANTERIOR

POSTERIOR

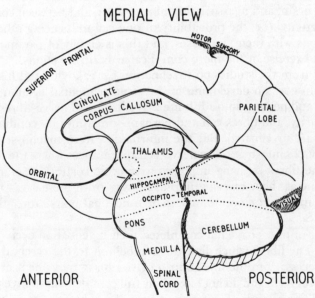

MEDIAL VIEW

MOTOR SENSORY

SUPERIOR FRONTAL

CINGULATE

CORPUS CALLOSUM

PARIETAL LOBE

THALAMUS

ORBITAL

HIPPOCAMPAL

OCCIPITO - TEMPORAL

VISUAL

PONS

CEREBELLUM

MEDULLA

SPINAL CORD

ANTERIOR

POSTERIOR

FIG. 22.2. Lateral and medial views of the brain, to show divisions of cerebral cortex and areas of localization of function. (*a*) Lateral view of cortex; (*b*) medial view of cortex and subcortial structures. (From Tanner 1961.)

of the lobe last. The gyri on the medial surface of the hemisphere and in the insula are in general last to develop.

Within the motor area the nerve-cells controlling movements of the arms and upper trunk develop ahead of those controlling the leg. The same is true in the sensory area. This corresponds, of course, to the greater maturity of the arm relative to the leg in bodily development and also to the infant's greater capacity to control his arms.

At birth the cortex is very little developed and its appearance does not suggest that much, if any, cortical function is possible. By 1 month the histological appearance of the primary motor area of upper limb and trunk suggests that it may be functioning, and by 3 months all the primary areas are relatively mature, correlating with the child's vision and hearing, though the association areas subserving the interpretive functions are not yet mature. By 6 months some fibres reaching the cortex from lower down have become myelinated, though few association fibres within the cortex are mature. Between 6 months and 2 years much further development takes place, and the primary sensory area catches up the primary motor area. But many areas are still quite immature, most notably the hippocampal and cingulate gyri and the insula.

During the period from birth to 4 years, and presumably for some time after, there is a continuous increase in the number and size of dendrites in all layers of the cortex, and in the number and complexity both of exogenous fibres from lower in the brain, and in association fibres within and between cortical areas. The 'connectivity' (i.e. the probability of one cell influencing others through its connections with them) increases, and this is clearly of paramount importance to the exercise of the more complicated brain functions.

It is clear from the studies on myelination by Yakovlev and his colleagues that the brain goes on developing in the same sequential fashion at least till adolescence and perhaps into adult life. Myelination of nerve-fibres is only one sign of maturity, and fibres can and perhaps sometimes do conduct impulses before they are myelinated. But the information from myelin studies agrees well with Conel's information on nerve-cell appearances where the two overlap. As a rule the fibres carrying impulses to specific cortical areas myelinate at the same time as those carrying impulses away from these areas to the periphery: thus maturation occurs in arcs or functional units rather than in geographical areas.

A number of tracts have not completed their myelination even 3 or 4 years after birth. The fibres which link the cerebellum to the cerebral cortex and which are necessary to the fine control of voluntary movement only begin to myelinate after birth and do not have their full complement of myelin till about age 4 years. The reticular formation, a part of the brain especially developed in Primates and man and concerned with the maintenance of attention and consciousness, continues to myelinate at least until puberty and perhaps beyond. Myelination is similarly prolonged in parts of the forebrain near the midline. Yakovlev suggests that this is related to the protracted development of behavioural patterns concerned with metabolic, visceral, and hormonal activities during reproductive life.

Throughout brain growth from early foetal life the appearance of function is closely related to maturation in structure. Fibres of the sound-receiving system (the 'acoustic analyser') begin to myelinate as early as the sixth foetal month, but they complete the process very gradually, continuing until the fourth year. In contrast, the fibres of the light-receiving system or 'optic analyser' begin to myelinate only just before birth, but then complete the process very rapidly. Yakovlev points out that in foetal life the sounds of the functioning of maternal viscera are the chief sensory stimuli, apart from anti-gravity sensation. They are evidently not perceived at a cortical level; but at a subcortical one the analyser is working. After birth, however, visual stimuli rapidly come to predominate, for man is primarily a visual animal. These signals are very soon admitted to the cortex; the cortical end of the optic analyser myelinates in the first few months after birth' The cortical end of the acoustic analyser, on the other hand, myelinates slowly, in a tempo probably linked with the development of language.

There is clearly no reason to suppose that the link between maturation of structure and appearance of function suddenly ceases at age 6 or 10 or 13 years. On the contrary, there is every reason to believe that the higher intellectual abilities also appear only when maturation of certain structures or cell assemblies, widespread in location throughout the cortex, is complete. Dendrites, even millions of them, occupy little space, and very considerable increases in connectivity could occur within the limits of a total weight increase of a few per cent. The stages of mental functioning described by Piaget and others have many of the characteristics of developing brain or body structures and the emergence of one stage after another is very likely dependent on (i.e. limited by) progressive maturation and organization of the cortex.

To what extent environmental stimulation can influence brain maturation or organization is not clear. Cajal and Hebb supposed that use of a cell actually increases its connectivity, but there is little experimental evidence yet to support this view.

Many aspects of brain function seem quite unaffected by variations in environmental input within the range of what we consider normal environments. Thus children born before the normal 40 weeks' gestation period develop in most neurological aspects quite in parallel with children of the same post-fertilization age growing in the uterus. Pre-term babies become able to stand and walk no sooner by being exposed to the stimuli of the outside environment longer. This is not to say that maturation of the brain is not affected by any outside conditions. Certain states, such as severe malnutrition or the presence of toxic substances, can affect normal growth. To what extent the sort of undernutrition encountered in some areas of underdeveloped countries can retard or prevent brain maturation is a much disputed and at present unresolved issue. Much confusion has been caused by experimenters who failed to realize that starvation of a rat immediately after birth corresponded, auxologically speaking, to starvation of the human mid-term foetus and not to the human infant. Most of the rat work showing permanent effects of such starvation relates only to children born small for gestational age due to disease of the placenta. A classic follow-up study of children severely starved in Holland in 1944–5 while they were foetuses, newborns, etc. has recently been made by Susser and Stein (Stein, Susser, Saenger, and Marolla 1975). All the male children were measured as to height and mental ability on entry to the Dutch army aged 18. In neither measurement did they differ from 18-year-olds who were not starved. The evidence at present is that the great potential for catch-up ensures full restoration of height and probably mental development even after an episode of severe malnutrition, provided that in the rehabilitation period conditions are good. Often this last proviso is not met in developing countries. Susser and Stein sum up the present state of knowledge in this area admirably when they write 'We believe we must accept that poor *prenatal* nutrition cannot be considered a factor in the social distribution of mental competence among surviving adults in industrial societies. This is not to exclude it as a possible factor in combination with poor *postnatal* nutrition, especially in preindustrial societies' (1975).

## Effects of the tempo of growth

Individual differences in tempo of growth have been described in Chapter 20, and it was pointed out there that they had important social and educational effects, particularly at adolescence. These can be conveniently discussed first in relation to intellectual, and secondly in relation to emotional, development.

### Intellectual ability

There is good evidence that, in the European and North American school systems, children who are physically advanced towards maturity score on average slightly higher in most tests of mental ability than children of the same age who are physically less mature. The difference is not great, but it is consistent and it occurs at all ages that have been studied, going back as far as $6\frac{1}{2}$ years. Thus in age-linked examinations physically fast-maturing children have a significantly better chance than slow-maturing children.

It is also true that physically large children score higher in I.Q. tests than small ones, at all ages from 6 years on. In a random sample of all Scottish 11-year-old children, comprising 6940 pupils, the correlation between height and score in the Moray House Group Test was $0.25 \pm 0.01$, allowing for the effect of age difference from 11·0 to 11·9 years. An approximate conversion of these test scores to Terman–Merrill I.Q. leads to an average increase of 0·67 points for each centimetre of stature. A similar correlation has been found in London children. The effects can be very significant for individual children. In 10-year-old girls there was a 9-point difference in I.Q. between those whose height was above the 75th percentile and those whose height was below the 15th. This is two-thirds of the standard deviation of the test score.

It was usually thought that both the relationships between test score and height would disappear in adulthood. If the correlations represented only the effects of co-advancement both of mental ability and physical growth, this might be expected to happen. There is indeed no difference in height between early- and late-maturing boys when both have finished growing. But it is now clear that, curiously, at least part of the height–I.Q. correlation persists in adults. It is not clear in what proportion genetical and environmental factors are responsible for this; differential social mobility is probably the main factor involved.

*Emotional development*

There is little doubt that being an early or late maturer has repercussions on behaviour, and in some children these repercussions may be considerable. The world of the small boy is one where physical prowess brings prestige as well as success, and where the body is very much an instrument of the person. Boys who are advanced in their development, not only at puberty, but before as well, are more likely than others to be the leaders. Indeed, this is reinforced by the fact that muscular powerful boys on average mature earlier than others and have an early adolescent growth spurt. Conversely, it is the unathletic, lanky boy, unable perhaps to hold his own in the pre-adolescent rough and tumble, who on average has a late adolescence.

At a much deeper level the late developer at adolescence sometimes begins to have doubts about whether he will ever develop his body properly and whether he will be as well endowed sexually as those others he has seen developing around him. Much of the anxiety about sex is, of course, at an unconscious level, and much proceeds from sources that are considerably more complex and deep-rooted than these. Yet even here the events—or lack of events—of adolescence may act as a trigger to reverberate fears accumulated deep in the mind during the early years of life.

The early maturers perhaps appear to have things all their own way. It is indeed true that most studies of the later personalities of children whose growth history is known do show the early maturers as more stable, more sociable, less neurotic, and more successful in society, at least in the USA (though this may be because on average they are less linear in build and more muscular). But the early maturers have their difficulties also. Though some glory in their new possessions, others are embarrassed by them. The girl whose breasts are beginning to develop may slouch instead of standing erect when asked to recite in front of a class; and the adolescent boy may have similar embarrassments. The early maturer, too, has a longer period of frustration of his sex drive and his drive towards independence and the establishment of vocational orientation, factors which all writers on adolescence agree are major elements in the disorientation that some young men and women experience at this time.

Such are some of the social problems brought about by the great variability in tempo of growth. Practically all this variability is biological in origin; there are no social steps by which we can significantly reduce it. It therefore behoves us to fit our educational system, in theory and in practice, to these biological facts, matching the biological variability with an equal degree of social flexibility.

# 23. Analysis and classification of physique

## Introduction

THE study of human constitution is an attempt to answer the question 'In what ways do men consistently differ from one another, and how do these differences come to exist?' 'Consistently' is used here in its ordinary sense; it is those aspects of structure, function, or behaviour which do not change much in a single individual from day to day, or even from year to year, that are referred to as constitutional traits.

In any group of people studied the total variability of a character observed repeatedly over a period of time can be divided into the between-individual variability and the within-individual variability, by which latter is meant the changes which occur with time in a single individual. These sources of variability can be distinguished and estimated separately by refinements of the statistical technique of analysis of variance, provided the experiment has been correctly designed. It is those traits for which between-individual variation is high in relation to within-individual variation that are the concern of constitutional study. Characteristics which alter in immediate response to the environment are the ones excluded from consideration. Traits showing only the individually consistent and steady changes characteristic of growth, maturation, and senescence, may be just as much constitutionally controlled as those which do not change at all. Also it must be remembered that manner of reacting to environmental change may be a constitutional characteristic. In some physiological traits, resting values show greater within-individual variation than values taken under maximal stress; for example, an individual's resting heart-rate may be more variable and less constitutionally controlled than his heart-rate upon maximal exertion, where constitutional factors assume greater importance. Perhaps similar considerations hold for some psychological traits. An individual's constitution embraces characteristics of morphology, physiology, and psychology; the historical trisection has no theoretical place in constitutional study, though in the techniques of investigation it necessarily serves as the present-day framework.

No explicit distinction between heredity and environment enters into the definition of constitution, because the study of constitutional differences is older than the science of genetics. Obviously genetical factors are of prime importance in this field. Yet many constitutional traits have a very complex genetical background, and some, it is reasonable to suppose, may be due more to the ineradicable effects of early experience than to genetical influences. Thus the study of constitution covers a wider field than human genetics in the strict sense. Nowadays, however, genetics embraces more and more the study of epigenesis, that is, the development of adult characteristics through the many interactions of growth, and in this way constitutional and genetical studies are becoming increasingly indistinguishable.

In medicine, the chief branch of applied human biology, constitutional diseases are assuming more and more importance as the bacterial disorders are successfully brought under control. The aim here was memorably stated in 1881 by Beneke, a pathologist who was amongst the first to apply really scientific methods in constitutional work. 'The different constitutions', he wrote, 'and the different resistances conditioned by them form only the soil in which certain diseases develop when the individual is subjected to certain stresses. The importance of this point of view for general hygiene and therapy goes without saying. It is in our power to lead the different constitutions happily through the dangers of life if we recognize them correctly and if we understand rightly their physiological differences.' This we are still far from doing.

In morphological features the within-individual changes are relatively small; stature changes little from week to week, and not very much from year to year, except in the periods of childhood and senescence. Some physiological characters, such as blood-groups or the ability to taste PTC (phenyl thiocarbamide), change even less, and these are the characteristics classically used in human genetics. But most physiological characteristics change more, even the stable ones such as excretion of ketosteroids or creatinine, or basal body temperature. Behavioural characters are still harder to pin down to constancy, though certain aspects of reacting to cirumstances, and certain traits of character and temperament persist throughout life and seem clearly to be constitutional in the sense given above. Morphology offers the clearest and simplest hunting ground in constitutional research at present, even if not fundamentally the most important. Accordingly, in this section constitutional differences in physique, or body-build, will claim most of our attention; physiological differences linked with them will be described in Chapter 24 and behavioural patterns, also alleged to be related to physique, will be discussed there also (see p. 377).

There are great differences in bodily form amongst humans, and these differences occur in all degrees of detail, from the general size and shape of the individual to the curve of the eyelid or the form of the particular finger. These variations are certainly not recent in origin; they represent a form of quantitative balanced polymorphism, if we may somewhat stretch the meaning of that word. Other animals show a similar polymorphism in build, though whether to a greater or lesser degree than man it is impossible to say, since our main knowledge comes from artificially maintained and hence not comparable stocks.

Presumably the same forces that maintain single locus polymorphisms such as the blood-groups, also maintain the quantitative polymorphism of build. Different builds have presumably different advantages in different circumstances and at different times. Selection may favour first one build then another. There is evidence, for example, that the long, thin build of the Nilotic Negro has arisen through the very definite advantage such a build confers in maintaining physiological function in a hot environment (see section on ecology). As in the case of the blood-groups, certain diseases select against one build more than against others; tuberculosis, for example, caused more deaths in long, thin people than in short, stocky ones (see below), and coronary heart disease nowadays causes more deaths in fat and muscular people than in lean, bony ones. Sometimes it may be the build that is selected for or against as such (as in the case of Nilotes); more usually perhaps it is physiological characteristics associated with build which are selected. Clearly there are considerable physiological differences between persons of differing builds; but as yet we know almost nothing about them.

The sex difference in physique is the most striking example of this quantitative balanced polymorphism. Even before puberty there are differences, not, probably, between boys and girls of the same physique (or somatotype, see below), but between the incidence of different physiques, or somatotypes, in either sex. The more muscular physiques occur in smaller numbers amongst the girls. (In Sheldon's system (see p. 365), it may be that before puberty a girl 4-4-2 differs very little from a boy 4-4-2, but there are few girl 4-4-2s, and no girl 2-7-1s, born.) The advantage of the mechanism is obvious; it reconciles the demand for a wide variety of physiques in the population, on the one hand, and for specialization of physique for various tasks on the other. Primate reproduction requires a relatively less mobile female who for considerable periods cannot be relied upon in fighting and in rapid changes of territory. Selection might thus produce an equilibrium such that the predominance of the more highly mobile and powerful physiques appeared in the males and the predominance of less mobile but in other ways more advantageous physiques in the females. The process could not go too far without a loss of physical variability occurring. The chromosomal and embryological mechanisms of the equilibrium are not known; there is some slight evidence, however, from the study of XXY and XO individuals that genes on the X chromosome may somehow inhibit the development of large muscles. Individuals with the karyotype XYY have a tendency to be tall, but seem not to be more muscular than other people.

## The classification of physique by external body form

There have been numerous attempts to classify the varieties of physique in ways which will relate to physiological function, habitual behaviour, or susceptibility to disease. It is, of course, perfectly easy to take a series of anthropometric measurements on an individual and compare each of these figures with the range of values exhibited by a standard group of the same age and sex. The given individual can then be described as being at the 70th percentile for height, 75th for sitting height, 65th for weight, 80th for head breadth, 50th for calf circumference, and so on. (Since most anthropometric measurements are distributed in a Gaussian, or Normal, curve, with the exception of measurements by caliper or X-ray of subcutaneous fat thickness, which are log-Normally distributed, the individual can alternatively be said to be $+0.5$ standard deviations above the mean for height etc.)

One difficulty with such a description is its inefficiency. Practically all body measurements are positively correlated one with another, so that the amount of new information becomes less in each subsequent measurement. When height and leg-length have been measured, arm-length is practically known and its measurement tells us very little. Thus a careful selection of measurements has to be made with some particular end in view. This may be to define a few basic components of physique which are uncorrelated (see below), or to estimate the amounts of different tissues, such as fat, muscle, and bone, in the body.

The second difficulty about this simple description is that it fails to communicate much information about body shape, even if the information does in fact lie locked in the figures. This is a real difficulty in many circumstances, particularly in medical work. One wants to be able to describe a person's physique so that one's audience can form a mental picture of his size, shape, and composition. This is very hard to do from a recital of a multitude of measurements, though it is not altogether impossible with practice.

The human body varies in a thousand ways, even in externals alone, and each classification of physique must necessarily be based on the selection of some characters and the ignoring of others. Classifications stand or fall by the way in which they link up with other areas of human biology and illuminate problems of growth, evolution, physiology, disease, or behaviour. Judged on this criterion there are 4 classifications by external form which merit description. Three are associated with those of the names of their originators: Viola, an Italian physician; Kretschmer, a German psychiatrist; Sheldon, an American psychologist; and the fourth results from the application of the statistical technique known as factor analysis to multiple anthropometric measurements.

## Viola

Viola's classification, dating from the beginning of this century and now largely fallen into disuse, was the first to be based on a comprehensive system of body measurements. For general purposes, ten measurements were used. These were combined together in a rather empirical way (modern biometry being at that time in its infancy) to give four indexes. In each of the indexes the position of the individual relative to the standard group of the same age and sex was recorded and the person classified as 'longitype', 'brachitype', 'normotype', or 'mixed-type'. The longitypes had long limbs relative to their trunk volume, a large thorax relative to their abdomen, and large transverse diameters relative to antero-posterior ones. Brachitypes were the reverse, normotypes in between, and mixed types those whose four indexes failed to agree amongst themselves, one placing the individual in one category and another elsewhere (mixed-types were thus what we would call 'dysplastics' nowadays).

An enormous amount of work was done using this system, and several

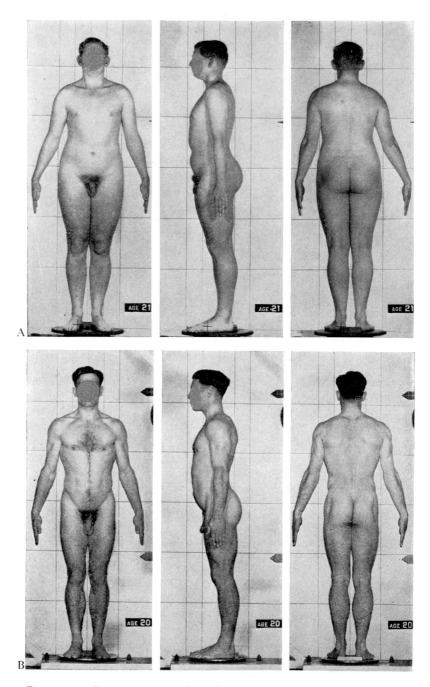

PLATE II. Persons representing the extremes of the three Sheldon somatotype components, together with a person of average physique.

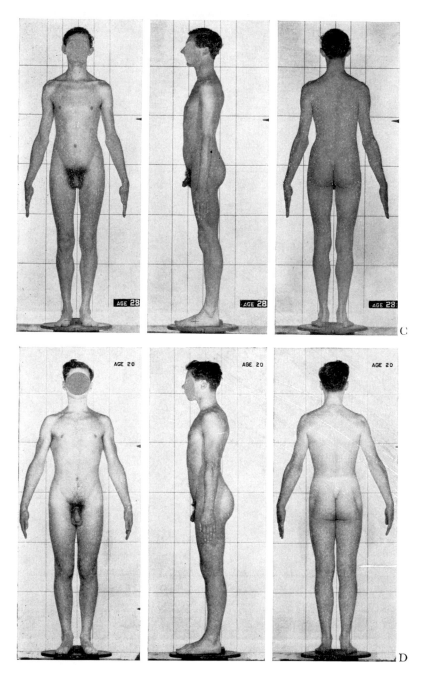

A, extreme in endomorphy, somatotype 6–3–2; B, extreme in mesomorphy, somatotype $1\frac{1}{2}$–7–2; C, extreme in ectomorphy, somatotype $1\frac{1}{2}$–2–$6\frac{1}{2}$; D, average physique, somatotype 3–4–4.

hundred papers published covering morphological analyses, differential susceptibility to disease, and, to a lesser extent, physiological and psychological relations. Viola's work has been unjustly neglected, and some parts of it have still considerable value.

## Kretschmer

Kretschmer's system is better known because it was translated into English and made its way into the psychiatric textbooks. It was much less objective than Viola's, however, relying entirely on anthroposcopic inspection. Kretschmer described and illustrated three types, the 'pyknic', and 'leptosome', and the 'athletic'. The pyknic was broad, round and fat, sturdy and stocky; the leptosome long, thin, and linear; and the athletic heavily muscled with large thorax and shoulders and narrow hips.

This system is now entirely outmoded, for it suffered from a fatal error (partly, but only partly, shared by Viola's). It supposed people were really classifiable into separate discrete types, with only a few unfortunates left out in the cold in between. This assumption—widespread up to about 1930—involved the later practitioners of the system in hopeless difficulty, for honest classifiers simply had to admit that most people fell in between the established, and obviously fairly extreme, types.

## Sheldon

Though Sheldon's system has some relation to Kretschmer's, being a three-way rather than a two-way classification, it starts from the outset with the idea, now universally accepted, that there are no discrete 'types' but only continuously distributed 'components' of physique. 'The concept of types' Sheldon wrote in 1940, 'has been useful in the study of personality, but, like the poles supporting a clothes-line, it provides only end suspension for distributive classifications. As the line becomes filled, the notion of types recedes and finally vanishes altogether, perhaps submerged under a smooth distribution. The path of progress is from the notion of dichotomies to the concept of variation along dimensional axes.'

Sheldon's choice of three components sprang from his initial observational technique. He began by taking nude standardized photographs showing front, side, and rear views of some 4000 college students. Disregarding the attribute of largeness or general body size, which his classification ignores, he sorted for extremes of body shape, and he found three. These are illustrated in Plate II. Each extreme represented the end of the distribution of a component. Every individual was then assigned a place in each component. This was done anthroposcopically, using a rating scale of 1 to 7 with equal-sized intervals between the numerals (i.e. the man rated 3 for one particular component appears to be as much more so than one rated 2, as the 2 is more than the 1). Thus the first extreme example was rated 7-1-1, the second extreme 1-7-1, the third 1-1-7: the components were named 'endomorphy', 'mesomorphy', and 'ectomorphy', respectively, on a theory, not generally accepted, of their genesis from embryonic germ layers. The whole system is known as 'somato-typing'—a word strictly reserved for this system and not to be used as syno-mynous with any effort at classifying physique. The set of three numerals is a person's 'somatotype'.

The components are best described by reference to their extreme manifesta-tions. The extreme in endomorphy (7-1-1) approaches the spherical as nearly as is humanly possible; he has a round head, a large fat abdomen predominating over his thorax, and weak, floppy, penguin-like arms and legs, with much fat in the upper arm and thigh, but slender wrists and ankles. Relative to his general size he has a large liver, spleen, and, it is said, gut; large lungs and a heart shaped differently from those of the other extreme physiques. He has a great deal of subcutaneous fat and might be simply called a fat man were it not that his whole body, including his thoracic and pelvic skeleton, is greater in the antero-posterior than in transverse direction. When starved, he becomes, in Sheldon's phrase, simply a starved endomorph, not somebody high in ecto-morphy or mesomorphy. It seems that fatness is related to this build more or less inevitably, and it is thought that the amount of weight put on as a person gets older is fairly directly related to his rating in endomorphy. Though the tide can be delayed by dieting and exercise it continually threatens, in a way that it fails to do in persons high in ectomorphy. It may be that persons high in endomorphy have more fat cells than persons low in this component, just as those high in mesomorphy have, presumably, more muscle-cells. But little is known about the quantitative human histology either of fat or muscle cells, and this is hypothesis, not fact.

The extreme in mesomorphy is the classical Hercules. In him muscle and bone predominate. He has a cubical, massive head, broad shoulders and chest, and heavily muscled arms and legs, with the distal segments strong in relation to the proximal. Relative to his size his heart muscle is large. He has a minimal amount of subcutaneous fat and the antero-posterior diameters of his body are small.

The extreme in ectomorphy is the linear man; he has a thin, peaked face with a receding chin and high forehead, a thin, narrow chest and abdomen, a narrow heart, and spindly arms and legs. He has neither much muscle nor much subcutaneous fat, but, relative to his size, a large skin area and a large nervous system.

Naturally the vast majority of people are not extremes like these, but have a moderate amount of each component. Thus the common somatotypes are the 3-4-4, 4-3-3, or 3-5-2. A method of plotting somatotypes on a plane diagram is shown at p. 382 (Fig. 24.1).

All parts of the body may not agree in the extent to which they show these characteristics, and the difference between the somatotypes of different regions is called 'dysplasia'. Dysplasia is in theory probably of great importance, but in practice in Sheldon's system it is hard to assess consistently since its assessment is made by assigning regional somatotypes to head, arms, legs, trunk, and thorax separately, and this involves more error than somatotyping the whole body.

Somatotyping is carried out anthroposcopically, by inspection of photographs, which for this purpose have to be well made, with the subject standing in a rigidly standardized pose, rotated on a turntable between pictures, and placed a long distance from the camera to avoid the nearer parts of his body appearing significantly larger on the photograph than parts farther away. The technique has been much developed, and pictures are now taken from which bodily dimensions can be accurately measured with specially devised calipers, a technique known as photogrammetric anthropometry.

In somatotyping, however, such measurements are not used. (In Sheldon's original publication, tables of photographic measurements are given and a system for reaching the somatotype through their application is described, but this system does not work and has never, in fact, been used.) The somatotype is assigned by inspection of the photograph, but its comparison, if necessary, with photographs of known somatotypes, and by reference to tables of height/$\sqrt[3]{}$ weight for each somatotype at each age, published in Sheldon's *Atlas*. Though this sounds, and is, a subjective procedure, trained somatotypers, who nowadays use half-unit ratings to give thirteen instead of seven points for each component, agree with each other to half a unit in 90 per cent of ratings. In only 10 per cent of cases should there be a difference of a whole unit, and very seldom a difference of more than that. The technique is not a difficult one to acquire, though like others, it needs a month or two of training, and spells of practice from time to time.

A number of criticisms can be levelled at somatotyping as a system. First amongst them is that the components are not independent; they are oblique, not orthogonal, in the language of multivariate analysis. They are negatively intercorrelated so that a high rating in one precludes to some extent high ratings in the others. Thus there are 2-3-5s, 3-3-5s, and 4-3-5s, but no 1-3-5s, 5-3-5s, 6-3-5 or 7-3-5s. Also there are 6-4-1s and 4-4-4s, but no 7-7-1s, 5-5-5s, 3-3-3s, or 1-1-1s. The lack of independence makes for biometrical difficulties in handling somatotype correlations with other variables, and, more seriously, creates difficulties in thinking, for it is remarkably hard not to think of the components as if they were independent or orthogonal. Orthogonal components are certainly more convenient; however, if the somatotype components truly have their roots in physiological and genetical mechanisms then the decision between oblique and orthogonal components depends on the biological, not the statistical, situation. It may be that embryological development does in fact produce variation of this negatively interrelated sort. Recent data on the amounts of fat, muscle, and bone in various parts of the body, discussed below, seem mercifully to indicate, however, that at least these tissues develop along quite independent directions.

The independence of widths of bone and muscle (see below) is a more serious criticism of the concept of mesomorphy as at present defined, since it includes both wide bones and large muscles. However, it is the size of the muscles that is chiefly used in the assessment, and dropping the bone width from the description would make little difference in practice.

The subjectivity of somatotyping is naturally a source of criticism, although in one way it is a strength and not a weakness. Sheldon defines the somatotype as the best guess the investigator can make at the subject's 'morphogenotype'. The somatotype, by definition, remains constant throughout life; the appearance of the body changes, and so do the body's measurements, but not the somatotype. Hence different measurement criteria have to be used for somatotyping at different ages. Again, the effects of disease, or the muscular hypertrophy caused by weight-training, change body contours but not the somatotype. Hence the somatotyper confronted with a picture has to take into account, so far as he is able, age, disease, and muscular exercise. This is not always as hard as it sounds; to an experienced eye the effects of weight-lifting are usually obvious enough, and a weight loss of more than 4 kg or 5 kg is usually revealed by wrinkles and folds in the skin clearly visible in the photograph. The eye can see and make allowances where the caliper is blind.

Though the assignment of a somatotype is theoretically best done only after following a subject for several years, in practice the physique shown in a state of normal nutrition at age 20–25 years is usually taken as the basis of the definitive estimate. Children at present cannot be somatotyped with any certainty, since the necessary longitudinal studies demonstrating what each child turns into at age 20 are not generally available. When sufficient pictures and measurements have been accumulated, however, it should be possible to predict a child's somatotype at least by age 5, and probably by age 3, with the proviso that a minor degree of inaccuracy may be introduced by the relative independence of changes at adolescence. Somatotyping women also raises difficulties at present since no published atlas exists; the same general criteria apply as in somatotyping men, however, and this leads to an excess of high endomorphs in women as compared with men, and a total lack of degrees 6 and 7 in mesomorphy. There have been a number of variations of somatotyping suggested since Sheldon's work first appeared, but none has much to recommend it. Parnell promulgated a system dependent on body measurements only, designed to approximate the somatotype. It does this less effectively, however, than the standard multiple regressions of somatotype on body measurements given by Damon and his colleagues. Heath and Carter have suggested a variant in which ratings above 7 are admitted, with the object of relating the components more linearly to measurements such as height, weight, skinfolds, and limb bone widths. The advantages of these methods are not obvious; the Sheldon system as conceived in 1940 and illustrated in the 1954 atlas is coherent; whatever its theoretical background it is intensely practical and communicates its information very readily. To know that a man is a large 3-2-5 is sufficient to recognize him at once amongst a hundred others.

*Factor analysis of physique*

The factor analysis classification results from the purely quantitative, mea-
suremental approach to human physique—an approach not opposed to but
complementary with that of photographs and subjective assessments. Factor
analysis is a branch of multivariate statistical technique used for reducing a
large number of measurements, all of which are intercorrelated, to a smaller
number of factors, which account for most of the variability defined by the
original measurements. The factors may be themselves intercorrelated, or
'oblique', or they may be independent or 'orthogonal', the choice being made
by the investigator. The starting-point is a table of correlation coefficients for
a group of, say, a dozen or more body measurements. The finish is a series
of, say, three orthogonal factors A, B, and C which together perhaps account
for some 80 per cent of the variability of the dozen measurements. Factor analysis enables one to escape from the otherwise well-deserved charge, in physical
anthropology, of measuring the same thing over and over again.

There are several alternative techniques of factor analysis, but the application
of the one most used gives rise to a general factor of gross size, followed by
several group factors, which can be themselves subdivided into smaller groups.
The results of analysing various tables of correlations are quite consistent and
define the series of factors outlined in Table 23.1. The true situation is probably
not so simple as this implies, and additionally should include factors for head
and hand and feet size and shape.

Factors are essentially statistics, just like standard deviations. They cannot
*a priori* be equated with genetical or physiological mechanisms. But in the
analysis of shape they will probably only be useful if it turns out that they
do represent fairly directly physiological mechanisms, and link up straightfor-
wardly with the facts of growth. It seems quite hopeful that they may do so,

TABLE 23.1

*Summary of factor-analysis classification of physique in terms of
orthogonal subdivided group factors*

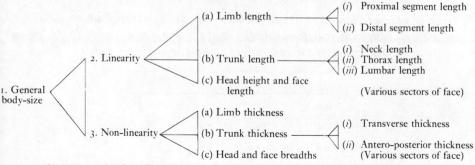

Slightly modified from Tanner (1953). Growth and constitution. In *Anthropology today*
(ed. A. L. Kroeber). Chicago University Press.

at least if the original measurements to be factored are chosen with biological considerations clearly in mind. The multivariate statistical approach to the classification and understanding of physical differences is capable of much further development. One of the hopeful lines which this development is taking is described in the next chapter.

## The analysis of physique by tissue components

The classifications of physique described above are all based on external body-form. An alternative approach is to classify by means of quantitative differences in tissue structure; e.g., by the relative amounts of fat, muscle, and bone possessed by different individuals. The two approaches are neither independent nor mutually exclusive. Some aspects of external form, for example overall size, may be practically independent of structure. But shape and structure are inevitably somewhat related; a fat man, try as he may, cannot be anything but rounded; a heavily muscled man cannot appear fragile and linear. For each separate tissue shape and structure are more independent; a man with a given percentage of bone may have long limbs and a short trunk or vice versa.

The total amount of fat and water in the body can now be estimated by chemical and physical means with an accuracy of about $\pm 15$ per cent and the amount of muscle approximated in favourable circumstances by the estimation of the radioactive potassium $^{40}$K content. Such methods, however, only lead to statements about the over-all amount of a certain constituent of the body. They cannot tell us where the fat, for example, is, nor how, except in quantity, it is contributing to the external bodily contours.

A bridge between the two approaches has been made by the use of X-rays for measuring the widths of fat, muscle, and bone in the limbs and by the introduction of a special caliper for measuring the thickness of subcutaneous body fat. This is done by pinching up a fold of skin and fat away from the underlying muscle and applying the caliper to this skin-fold. At certain sites in the body this can be done readily and accurately.

### TABLE 23.2

*Average intercorrelations of measurements by X-ray of widths of subcutaneous fat, muscle, and bone (humerus, femur, tibia) in upper arm, thigh, and calf. 166 young women (upper rows) and 125 young men (lower rows)*

|        | Fat    | Muscle | Bone  |
|--------|--------|--------|-------|
| Fat    | 0·66   | —      | —     |
|        | 0·75   | —      | —     |
| Muscle | 0·09   | 0·43   | —     |
|        | 0·08   | 0·49   | —     |
| Bone   | 0·09   | 0·13   | 0·37  |
|        | −0·07  | 0·09   | 0·48  |

(From Tanner, Healy, and Whitehouse, unpublished.)

The sites most simply X-rayed are the upper arm, calf, and thigh. The dose of X-rays is extremely small and delivered at low kilovoltage; leaded clothing is used to shield the gonads completely. In the radiographs of the upper arm the widths of the subcutaneous fat, the muscle, and the humerus are measured halfway between the acromion and the top of the radius. In the thigh, the widths of fat, muscle, and femur are taken at a point one-third of the leg-length up from the bottom of the femoral condyles. In the calf the widths of fat, muscle, and tibia (fibula omitted) are taken at the maximum total diameter.

When these X-ray measurements are intercorrelated a clear pattern emerges (Table 23.2) (analysis of calculated cross-sectional limb areas yields identical results). The three measurements of each tissue correlate positively one with another, but are virtually independent of measurements of the other tissues. Thus muscle width in the calf correlates with muscle width in the arm and thigh, but not with bone or fat width in the calf or elsewhere. In Table 23.2 the average of the three fat–fat, three muscle–muscle, three bone–bone, and corresponding cross-correlations are given. The within-tissue correleations, shown in the diagonal, are high for fat and moderate for muscle and bone; the between-tissue correlations, including those between muscle and bone, are virtually zero. There are, therefore, three orthogonal tissue-component factors, representing fat, muscle, and limb-bone width respectively. Further measurements show that these limb-bone widths represent width of medullary cavity irrespective of width of cortical bone, which relates somewhat to the amount of muscle but not at all to the width of the marrow cavity.

This type of analysis can be pushed further by including other measurements of the skeleton taken by ordinary anthropometric methods, of fat taken by the skinfold caliper, and of external body contours measured by photogrammetry. Correlations can be calculated (using the logarithms of the fat measurements, since these are distributed log-normally) and the matrix factor-analysed. As more measurements are added the situation becomes naturally somewhat more complex, but the three prime orthogonal components persist. In Table 23.3 an analysis of this sort is shown. The columns of figures represent the saturations of each measurement in the factors; these saturations vary from 0 to 1, and are interpreted in a similar fashion to correlation coefficients.

*Fat*

All measurements of subcutaneous fat correlate very highly with each other; thus a fat factor is defined. In Table 23.3 this is factor (I), with very high saturations in arm, calf, and thigh fat, and low saturations in the other measurements. Other data show that in women there is a subsidiary factor for fat on the trunk versus fat on the limbs. Though there is no certain evidence in these data of its presence in men the differential growth curves of triceps and subscapular fat at adolescence in the male (see p. 311) make its presence very likely. Systematic regional variations, that is, fat arms versus fat legs or fat chest versus fat abdomen, do not seem to occur. But a good deal of purely local variation

## TABLE 23.3

Factor analysis (maximum likelihood) of measurements on 166 young women (left-hand columns) and 125 young men (right-hand columns). Saturation of measurements in first five rotated orthogonal components

| | I | | II | | III | | IV | | V | |
|---|---|---|---|---|---|---|---|---|---|---|
| **Fat width:** | | | | | | | | | | |
| arm | 0·81 | 0·92 | 0·09 | 0·05 | 0·09 | 0·10 | 0·01 | 0·02 | −0·09 | −0·11 |
| calf | 0·83 | 0·82 | −0·01 | 0·03 | 0·03 | −0·7 | −0·15 | 0·00 | −0·02 | 0·11 |
| thigh | 0·86 | 0·87 | 0·01 | −0·05 | −0·10 | −0·06 | 0·01 | −0·02 | 0·08 | 0·03 |
| **Muscle width:** | | | | | | | | | | |
| arm | 0·13 | 0·04 | 0·52 | 0·70 | 0·06 | −0·04 | 0·15 | 0·10 | 0·05 | 0·02 |
| calf | 0·06 | 0·10 | 0·65 | 0·67 | −0·01 | 0·10 | 0·11 | −0·22 | −0·12 | 0·05 |
| thigh | −0·04 | 0·07 | 0·72 | 0·84 | 0·10 | 0·30 | 0·12 | 0·26 | 0·01 | 0·07 |
| **Bone width:** | | | | | | | | | | |
| arm | −0·05 | −0·08 | 0·12 | 0·09 | 0·28 | 0·28 | 0·51 | 0·56 | −0·01 | −0·03 |
| calf | 0·05 | 0·12 | 0·03 | −0·09 | 0·45 | 0·37 | 0·51 | 0·75 | 0·06 | −0·03 |
| thigh | 0·10 | −0·06 | −0·11 | −0·01 | 0·47 | 0·37 | 0·51 | 0·57 | 0·06 | 0·04 |
| Sitting height | −0·34 | −0·10 | 0·21 | 0·17 | 0·69 | 0·72 | 0·00 | 0·11 | −0·23 | 0·02 |
| Leg-length (subischial) | −0·05 | 0·02 | 0·03 | −0·28 | 0·66 | 0·77 | 0·21 | −0·10 | 0·48 | 0·55 |
| Biacromial diameter | 0·17 | 0·02 | 0·26 | −0·16 | 0·63 | 0·75 | 0·07 | 0·07 | 0·22 | 0·11 |
| Bi-iliac diameter | 0·02 | 0·04 | 0·18 | −0·07 | 0·46 | 0·54 | 0·29 | 0·03 | −0·17 | 0·03 |
| Bicondylar humerus | 0·17 | 0·03 | 0·35 | 0·23 | 0·49 | 0·55 | 0·41 | 0·24 | −0·00 | −0·12 |
| Bicondylar femur | 0·40 | 0·31 | 0·36 | 0·30 | 0·53 | 0·53 | 0·28 | 0·22 | −0·14 | −0·02 |
| Percentage of total variance accounted for | 16·4 | 16·2 | 11·0 | 13·0 | 17·2 | 20·1 | 8·2 | 9·7 | 2·8 | 2·4 |
| **Average saturations:** | | | | | | | | | | |
| fat | 0·83 | 0·87 | 0·03 | 0·01 | 0·01 | −0·01 | −0·04 | 0·00 | −0·01 | 0·01 |
| muscle | 0·05 | 0·07 | 0·63 | 0·74 | 0·05 | 0·09 | 0·13 | 0·05 | −0·02 | 0·05 |
| all skeletal measurements | 0·03 | 0·01 | 0·01 | 0·02 | 0·52 | 0·54 | 0·31 | 0·27 | 0·03 | 0·5 |
| limb-bone breadth | 0·02 | −0·09 | 0·16 | 0·00 | 0·40 | 0·34 | 0·57 | 0·63 | 0·04 | −0·01 |
| leg-length | −0·05 | 0·02 | 0·03 | −0·28 | (0·66) | 0·77) | 0·21 | −0·10 | 0·48 | 0·55 |

(From Tanner, Healy, and Whitehouse, unpublished.)

remains, this meaning that one person may have a particularly large fat layer over the calves, another a particularly large layer over the upper arms, and so on. Such single-measurement factors are known as 'specifics'. It is the trunk-versus-limbs factor and the specific local factors which give the characteristic shape of fat covering to an individual, whether fat or lean. We may suppose that these 'fat-shape' factors reflect the numbers of fat-cells present at the various sites and that the over-all fat factor represents the degree to which all these cells are filled with fat. There is evidence that the amount of internal abdominal fat is closely correlated with the amount of subcutaneous fat in young adults. In older age-groups it is possible that the relationship is less close. Probably, for all this, the fat factor represents fairly well the percentage of fat in the body. It can be simply estimated by measuring the two skin-folds whose growth curves were presented in Figs. 19.6 and 19.7, (1) over the triceps muscle at the back of the upper arm, and (2) beneath the angle of the left scapula, taking the log transforms of each and adding them.

In the factor analysis of Table 22.3 it will be seen that of the skeletal measurements only sitting height and bicondylar femur breadth (width of knee) have consistent saturations in the fat factor (I). The knee-width saturation comes about for purely technical reasons; some fat is unavoidably included in the measurement itself. But the negative saturation of sitting height definitely implies that in these young adults the capacity for becoming fat is greater in short-bodied individuals than in long-bodied ones. The embryological and physiological reasons for this are not known. Adherents of somatotyping say that the degree of endomorphy can be gauged from the skeletal shape, at least in theory and with some difficulty; and they adduce in fact, a short trunk and large antero-posterior skeletal diameters as indicators of this component. Possibly endomorphy, as they conceive it, measures the number of fat-cells; and fatness the amount of fat per cell.

## Muscle

The correlations between muscle widths in different parts of the body are not as high as those between fat measurements, but are still very appreciable. The muscle factor (Table 23.3, component II) can be reasonably estimated by simply adding the three muscle widths in the limb X-rays. Photogrammetry makes it clear that this is a factor measuring muscle all over the body, including the trunk and back. There is little evidence of important regional factors, such as arm muscle versus leg muscle, but large specifics certainly exist.

## Skeleton

The skeleton is far and away more complicated. If we describe it in terms of orthogonal factors, however, the result shown in Table 23.3 (factors III, IV, and V) is at least reasonable. One of the great difficulties with factor analysis is that it does not lead to a unique solution; it is possible, even maintaining orthogonality, to find other components which would equally well describe the original correlations between measurements. One must be guided by biological considerations; and to provide components different from the fat and muscle ones would be absurd, but the skeletal configuration is more subjective and more debatable.

In Table 23.3 the skeleton is described by way of a skeletal frame size factor (III), in which all skeletal measurements saturate; a limb-bone width factor (IV), which represents the widths of the shafts of the long bones; and a limb-length factor (V), which represents the length of limbs as opposed to trunk.

Further analyses show that the limb-bone width is unrelated to the width of the vertebral bodies, so that slenderness of limb bones is independent of slenderness of spine. Furthermore, trunk length may be split into several surprisingly independent components; head and neck length, thorax length (top of sternum to umbilicus), and pelvic length (umbilicus to ischial tuberosities). Measured this way, thorax and pelvic lengths are entirely independent. Bi-iliac diameter is similarly largely independent of other skeletal measurements. There is evidently a 'rear-end' or 'hindquarter' factor in human physique, both in males and females. A similar factor has been described in cows. The neck length, on the other hand, is little related to thorax length, but more so to limb length. Long arms, long legs, and a long neck go together. The size of the hands and feet, related one to the other, are largely independent of all the factors so far considered, and so also is head-size and the shape of the individual features of the face.

The cause of these patterns into which body measurements fall must be sought in differential growth rates. Many components similar to those in man are found in animals, and experimental work using inbred strains is helping to elucidate their genesis. An example of the sort of explanation that must be looked for may be given from Table 23.3. In men there is a negative saturation of leg-length in the muscle component ($-0.28$). We know that muscular males are in general early maturers (see above) and that early maturers have a shorter period during which the legs are growing faster than the trunk, so that they will end up relatively short-legged.

The first, simple results of tissue-component analysis are summed up in the diagrams of Fig. 23.1. We can postulate a set of orthogonal or independent factors so that we reconstruct the major elements of an individual's physique (shorn of head, hands, feet, and various interesting soft parts) in terms of scores in:

(a) skeletal frame size (Fig. 23.1 (A));
(b) limb-bone width (Fig. 23.1 (B), where figure has larger than average limb-bone width);
(c) limb-bone length (Fig. 23.1 (C), where figure has larger than average limb-bone length also);
(d) muscle width (Fig. 23.1 (D));
(e) fat thickness (Fig. 23.1 (E)).

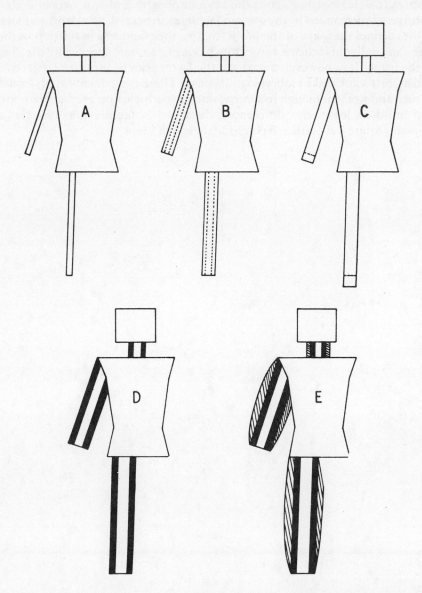

FIG. 23.1. Diagram of shape successively defined by 5 orthogonal factors ((A), (B), and (C) skeletal size and shape, (D) and (E) soft tissue). (A) Individual defined by a score in skeletal frame-size factor (other skeletal factors all having average values.) (B) Individual now given a higher-than-average score in limb-bone width factor. (C) Individual additionally given a higher-than-average score in limb-bone length factor. (D) Individual additionally given a score in muscle factor. (E) Individual additionally given a score in fat factor. (From Tanner, Healy, and Whitehouse, unpublished.)

Factors (b)+(c) together define the amount of extra limb size over and above that average demanded by the score in factor (a), general skeletal size; and factor (b)/(c) defines the shape of the limbs, that is, their linearity in relation to their size. Naturally this scheme leaves much out of account; specifically the shape of the trunk. It is, however, a start; all the factors can be measured objectively and at least some make embryological sense. These components apply equally to men and women, though in some women score higher on average than men, and in others lower. Sex differences, discussed in the previous chapters on growth require yet further factors for their definition.

# 24. Physique and its relation to function, disease, and behaviour

## Function

REMARKABLY little is yet known about relationships between body-build and physiological function. It seems fairly certain that such relationships must exist, at least in endocrine function and in metabolism. It is unlikely, for example, that persons high in the muscular component of physique have exactly the same amount of certain endocrine secretions as those low in it, or that persons at the opposite ends of the scale of endomorphy have metabolisms which are indistinguishable. It seems unlikely, also, that differences in the structure and the habitual function of the central nervous system are entirely independent of differences in body-build; but this is as yet a completely unexplored field.

The older literature on constitution contains a good many allegations about relationships between endocrine function and physique. There is even one system of classification, by 'biotypes', which is based upon these alleged relationships. Nearly all these suggestions are quite lacking in scientific support, and founded on the flimsiest clinical analysis. Physique may indeed relate to endocrine activity, or it may relate to amounts of the tissue receptors which translate the endocrine message into information regulating the cells themselves. Only very recently have tests of endocrine secretion reached a point where habitual individual differences may be characterized; tests of amount of receptor substance are in their infancy.

Only physiological functions which are relatively stable from week to week or year to year can be expected to relate to build, and so the first search must be for measurable functions characterized by a low within-individual variability and a high between-individual one. By using a suitable statistical design involving measuring the individuals twice or more over a period of time, it is possible to separate the stable and the fluctuating components and to calculate the relation between the stable values for each individual and various indexes of his build.

The results of one such study are shown in Table 24.1. Urinary 17-ketosteroid and 17-ketogenic steroid excretions are measures of two quite different aspects of adrenal function. The 17-ketosteroids represent the end-products of adrenal androgen secretion, together with those of testosterone from the testis. The 17-ketogenic steroids are the end-products of adrenal corticoid secretion, that is, of the hormones controlling, amongst other things, carbohydrate metabolism. Both groups of substances are excreted in relatively constant amounts from week to week by young individuals living under ordinary circumstances. Creatinine is a substance known to be derived wholly or mostly from the muscle in the body, and is also excreted at a relatively constant rate.

TABLE 24.1

*Correlation coefficients between stable ('between-person') values of daily urinary excretions of chemical substances and widths of fat, muscle, and bone in the limbs, and height and weight*

|  | Fat | Muscle | Bone | Height | Weight |
|---|---|---|---|---|---|
| 17-ketosteroids | 0·10 | 0·39† | 0·23 | 0·05 | 0·31‡ |
| 17-ketogenic steroids | −0·12 | 0·10 | 0·49† | 0·29‡ | 0·30‡ |
| Creatinine | 0·16 | 0·77‡ | 0·26 | 0·17 | 0·76‡ |

† Significant at 5 per cent.        ‡ Significant at 1 per cent.

(From Tanner, Healy, Whitehouse, and Edgson 1959.)

The 17-ketosteroid excretion is significantly related to the amount of muscle in the body, the multiple correlation with muscle width and body surface (to give an approximate measure of total muscle bulk) being 0·56. The 17-ketogenic excretion in this data, rather surprisingly, is related to the width of the shafts of the bones, or more precisely to the width of the marrow cavities. It is also related, much more than is 17-ketosteroid excretion, to the overall size of the body. Creatinine excretion, as anticipated, relates closely to muscle bulk.

These results are still a long way from revealing differences in rates of secretion of hormones by the adrenal itself, for the amounts of steroids excreted in the urine are influenced by tissue utilization, liver conjugation, and the amount of each individual steroid cleared from the blood by the kidney. But we can be confident that ultimately research along these general lines will reveal the true manner in which the emergence and maintenance of each physique is dependent on hormonal agents and their receptors.

There are few confirmed data on other relationships. A persistent tradition has it that linear, ectomorphic individuals have higher habitual rates of thyroid secretion than others, but no studies with modern methods have been reported. A number of studies have shown that systolic and diastolic blood-pressure, as measured by the cuff method, are higher in broadly built persons than in linear ones; but there is some doubt as to whether this represents merely the effect of a large arm-circumference producing a systematic measuring error, or whether it would also occur in intra-arterial measurements. Blood-volume has been shown to be higher, relative to body-weight, in persons high in mesomorphy and lower in those, either ectomorphs or endomorphs, who are low in mesomorphy. It is said that the reaction time is less the higher the degree of ectomorphy, but this requires confirmation.

### Disease
There is no question that persons of particular builds are more susceptible to certain diseases. In the case of at least one disease, pulmonary tuberculosis,

it has been shown by studies of physique made before the disease started that the build differences are not caused by the disease, but genuinely precede it.

Pulmonary tuberculosis is a disease of ectomorphic builds, or at least of persons with a low weight for their height. In one longitudinal study it has been shown that the initial infection with the tubercle bacillus occurs irrespective of physique, but that a spread of the germ to cause clinical disease several years later occurs much more frequently in tall people of relatively low weight than in others, despite all living under similar circumstances. Evidently the linear builds supply a more favourable soil, though in what way we do not know. One difficulty in this and in other disease studies is that investigators have often been content to characterize build simply by height and weight, thus failing to differentiate fat from muscle and heavy from light bones. Consequently all chance of a physiological analysis of the situation is lost.

Coronary thrombosis is also certainly related to physique, the incidence being higher in persons of high weight for height. The details of this are still not clear, but it seems that both above-average fat and above-average muscle contribute to the susceptibility. In principle, either or both of these relations may be of physiological or of sociological origin. It may be that mesomorphic men put themselves more than others into positions where they are at increased risk of developing coronary thrombosis, perhaps because of increased stress. There is some data to indicate that a special susceptibility may characterize mesomorphic men who fail to exercise their muscles, while not affecting less muscled but equally lazy persons. A physiological mechanism for such a differential susceptibility might reside in utilization of androgenic hormones in exercise, or something similar.

Diabetes is another disease related to build. Clinically, two forms are distinguished. One appears early in life and requires much insulin for its control; the other appears in middle age and requires little insulin. The physiological background of the two forms is believed to differ; the build of the patients certainly does. Sufferers from the late-onset form are more endomorphic than sufferers from the early-onset form. In the old Italian literature most cancers are said to occur more frequently in the brachitype than the longitype; and more modern studies by Damon and his colleagues tend to bear this out, at least for breast cancer.

Amongst mental disorders there is a marked affinity with build. Schizophrenics are usually high in ectomorphy; manic-depressives low in ectomorphy and high in both other Sheldon components; paranoids are high in mesomorphy. All these results have been repeatedly confirmed by various techniques and can be regarded as proven; but again no mechanisms are known. It has been said that neurotic breakdowns occur most frequently in those of more than ordinary degrees of dysplasia, but this needs further confirmation. It is also believed that the type of symptoms shown in neurotic breakdown is associated with build; hysterical and depressed patients tend to be high in mesomorphy and endomorphy, anxious patients high in ectomorphy.

Thus many empirical relationships have been described, but few causal physiological or sociological analyses performed. It seems most likely that in many of these cases physique acts as an expression of the gene complex affecting the penetrance or expressivity of more specific genes predisposing to particular disorders. The field is one wide open to research.

## Behaviour

Practically all those who have concerned themselves with human physique have been interested also in the relation between body-build and behaviour. The older authors took such a relation for granted and felt no need for justifying statistics. More recently, research has been concentrated on finding out what elements of behaviour remain more or less consistent and unaltered throughout life, whether these are related to physical differences, and, if so, to what differences and how closely.

Intellectual capacity in the sense of ability to score highly on I.Q. tests remains relatively constant, but is very slightly, if at all, related to build. The relationship with build is greater for temperament, by which is meant the deepest layer of personality, wherein lie habits of behaviour ranging from such traits as 'indiscriminate amiability' right down into obviously physique-conditioned aptitudes, such as love of physical adventure and relaxation in posture. Kretschmer described originally two types of temperament, the 'cyclothyme' and the 'schizothyme', which corresponded more or less to Jung's 'extravert' and 'introvert'; he related these closely to the types of build, the cyclothyme being pyknic, the schizothyme leptosomic. Later he also ascribed a particular temperament to the athletic.

Sheldon carried the same work much further and used, for his description of temperament, components rather than types, in precisely the same way as he had for physique. He began by rating some 30 subjects on 50 traits chosen

TABLE 24.2

*A selection of traits from Sheldon's scale of temperament*

| Trait no. | Viscerotonia | Somatotonia | Cerebrotonia |
|---|---|---|---|
| 1 | Relaxation in posture and movement | Assertiveness of posture and movement | Restraint in posture and movement, tightness |
| 2 | Love of physical comfort | Love of physical adventure | Inhibited social address |
| 3 | Greed for affection and approval | Psychological callousness | Secretiveness of feeling, emotional restraint |
| 4 | Smooth, easy communication of feeling; extraversion of viscerotonia | Horizontal mental cleavage; extraversion of somatotonia | Vertical mental cleavage; introversion |
| 5 | Relaxation and sociophilia under alcohol | Assertiveness and aggression under alcohol | Resistance to alcohol and to other depressant drugs |
| 6 | Need of people when troubled | Need of action when troubled | Need of solitude when troubled |
| 7 | Orientation toward childhood and family relationships | Orientation toward goals and activities of youth | Orientation toward later periods of life |

to define the persistent aspects of behaviour as obtained from a 50-hour clinical history. The traits fell into 3 clusters, and from this start, by adding other traits gradually, Sheldon produced 3 components of temperament, each defined by 20 traits. Each trait is rated on a 7-point scale, and the average of the 20 ratings gives the score in each component. A selection of traits is given in Table 24.2. The temperamental components are called 'viscerotonia', 'somatotonia', and 'cerebrotonia', and, when the scores in these of 200 subjects were related to their somatotype components, Sheldon found correlations of the order of 0·8 between viscerotonia and endomorphy, somatotonia and mesomorphy, and cerebrotonia and ectomorphy.

This is a somewhat closer, or at any rate more precise, relation than has previously been described, and the study has been criticized, though more on the grounds of incredulity than of conflicting evidence. The chief problems calling for attention seem to be two. First is the extent to which different raters of Sheldon's temperamental traits agree when each has acquired the necessary prolonged life-history of the subject, and the extent to which the ratings of a subject differ at different times in his life. The genetical background of the temperamental components also needs to be examined. Scales constructed on traits of this sort are always liable to petrify what is really plastic. Second, the work needs confirmation, with particular efforts to avoid any possible 'halo' effect, that is, with the somatotyper and the psychologist separate, and the psychologist working either from another man's notes or from a recording of another man's interviews, so that he never sees the subject's physique at all. One such study has been done, and, though it covered only a portion of the field, relating dominant cerebrotonia to dominant ectomorphy, in this portion it confirmed Sheldon's findings.

There are two theories as to how the relationships between physique and temperament may come about. One ascribes them to the actions of pleiotropic or of closely linked genes, the other to early conditioning. The first maintains that genes concerned in body shape also have effects on the brain and endocrine structure and that these dictate temperament: alternatively, it maintains that there exist separate but closely linked genes for each. The other view is, for example, that the highly mesomorphic child, on mixing with other children, finds by chance that he can knock down the others and continues thereafter to do so because of his success and because it comes to be expected of him. The two theories are not, of course, mutually exclusive; probably conditioning supports and reinforces an originally genetic tendency.

Persons of different physique do, on average, choose different careers, and this must reflect at least to some degree a temperamental inclination to lead one sort of life rather than another. In Fig. 24.1 are shown the somatotype distributions of a sample, believed relatively representative, of Oxford University undergraduates; an entire entering class of officer cadets at the Royal Military Academy, Sandhurst; and a class of student teachers of physical education at Loughborough Training College, an institution specializing in the

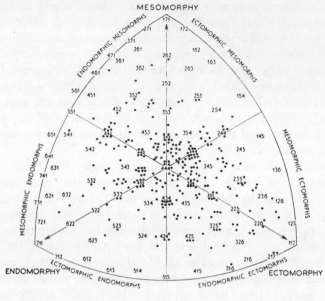

FIG. 24.1(a)

FIG. 24.1. Somatotype distribution of samples of (a) Oxford University students, (b) officer cadets of Royal Military Academy, Sandhurst, and (c) student teachers of physical education at Loughborough Training College.

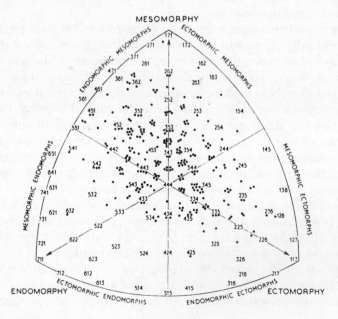

FIG. 24.1(b)

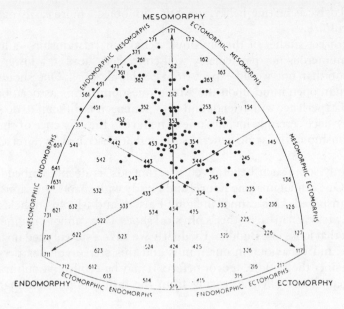

FIG. 24.1(c)

training of physical educators. The cadets are significantly more mesomorphic than the Oxford students and the physical educationists are still more mesomorphic than the cadets. (The method of representing somatotype distributions on a plane surface is visually useful, but tests of significance have to be applied, of course, to the figures themselves.)

This is a simple, and perhaps expected, result. One scarcely enters physical education unless good at games, or the regular army without some proclivity for rough and tumble. But more subtle choices of career have also been described: men on the research side in a factory, at all wage levels, were more linear than those on production; long-distance transport drivers and aircraft pilots were more mesomorphic than the general population; students at Harvard University enrolled in the faculties comprising natural and social sciences were more 'masculine' in body-build than those in arts, letters, and philosophy; students of engineering, medicine, and dentistry were more mesomorphic and less ectomorphic than students of physics and chemistry; youths convicted of delinquent behaviour were decidedly more mesomorphic than the average.

All these results point in a rather consistent direction. The fact that both army officers and juvenile delinquents are comparable in being above average in mesomorphy should occasion no surprise. For both careers some of the expectations are the same—power, risk, action, crisis; it is the *object* towards which this energy is directed which is different. It may well be that somatotonic energy and drive is an inborn characteristic of the same nature as the instinctual responses described by the ethologists. Somatotonia may be as much an instinctual drive as mating behaviour, but with objects more easily manipulated by the culture.

Most direct studies of the physique–behaviour relationship—and they are neither numerous nor particularly well conceived—lead to a lower degree of association than one would expect from Sheldon's work. One should perhaps maintain an open mind upon the whole question of this association, though in face of experience with friends and with patients it is difficult to do so. Everyday experience certainly inclines one to believe in the existence of some degree of relationship of the same general sort as that described by Kretschmer and Sheldon.

Certainly some such belief, even if erroneous, is deeply embedded in our culture. One cannot imagine Laurel and Hardy with shapes the same but behaviour transposed. One cannot imagine Falstaff and Mephistopheles, Scrooge and Pickwick each in each other's physical shoes. One cannot imagine a portrait of Christ that looks like Buddha. Evidently we have a stereotyped image linking physique and behaviour in our minds and this stereotype has persisted unchanged since the Middle Ages or before. It may be a collective cultural fantasy; but it seems more likely to spring from the firm ground of human biology.

## Suggestions for further reading (Part IV)

*Growth*

FALKNER, F. (1966) (ed.). *Human development.* Saunders, Philadelphia.

GOSS, R. J. (1973) (ed.). *Regulation of organ and tissue growth.* Academic Press, London.

LE GROS CLARK, W. E. and MEDAWAR, P. B. (1945) (ed.). *Essays on growth and form presented to D'Arcy Wentworth Thompson.* Clarendon Press, Oxford.

MARSHALL, W. A. and TANNER, J. M. (1974). Puberty. In *Scientific foundation of paediatrics* (ed. J. A. Davies and J. Dobbing). Heinemann, London.

STEIN, Z., SUSSER, M., SAENGER, C. and MAROLLA, F. (1975). *Famine and human development.* Oxford University Press.

TANNER, J. M. (1960) (ed.). *Human growth.* Symposium of the Society for the Study of Human Biology No. 3. Pergamon Press, Oxford.

——(1961). *Education and physical growth: the implications for educational practice of the facts and principles derived from the study of children's physical growth.* University of London Press.

——(1962). *Growth at adolescence: with a general consideration of the effects of hereditary and environmental factors upon growth and maturation from birth to maturity* (2nd ed.) Blackwell Scientific Publications, Oxford.

——(1963). Regulation of growth in size in mammals. *Nature, Lond.* **199**, 845.

——(1972). Human growth hormone. *Nature, Lond.* **237**, 431–7.

——(1977). Physical growth and development. In *Textbook of paediatrics* (eds J. O. Forfar and G. C. Arneil). (2nd ed.) Edinburgh and London, Churchill and Livingstone.

——INHELDER, B. (1956–60). (ed.). *Discussions on child development,* Vols I–IV. A consideration of the biological, psychological, and cultural approaches to the understanding of human development and behaviour. Tavistock Publications, London.

THOMPSON, D'ARCY WENTWORTH (1942). *Growth and form* (revised edn.). Cambridge University Press.

WADDINGTON, C. H. (1957). *The strategy of the genes*. Allen & Unwin, London.

*Physique*

BROZEK, J. (1965). (ed.). *Human body composition. Symposia of the Society for the Study of Human Biology*, Vol. 7. Pergamon, London.

DAMON, A., BLEIBTIEN, H. K., ELLIOT, O. and GILES, E. (1962). Predicting somatotype from body measurements. *Am. J. phys. Anthrop.* **20**, 461–73.

HEATH, B. H. and CARTER, L. (1967). A modified somatotype method. *Am. J. phys. Anthrop.* **27**, 57–74.

PETERSEN, G. (1967). *Atlas for somatotyping children*. Royal Vangorcum, Assen Netherlands.

SCHREIDER, E. (1960). *La biométrie*. Presses Universitaires, Paris.

SHELDON, W. H., DUPERTUIS, C. W. and MCDERMOTT, E. (1954). *Atlas of men*. Harpers, New York.

——HARTL, E. M. and MCDERMOTT, E. (1949). *The varieties of delinquent youth*. Harpers, New York.

——STEVENS, S. S. (1942). *The varieties of temperament*. Harpers, New York.

——TUCKER, W. B. (1940). *The varieties of human physique*. Harpers, New York.

TANNER, J. M. (1956). Physique, character and disease: a contemporary appraisal. *Lancet* **2**, 635–7.

——(1963). The regulation of human growth. *Child devel.* **34**, 817.

——(1964). *The physique of the olympic athlete*. George Allen and Unwin, London.

——HEALY, M. J. R., WHITEHOUSE, R. H. and EDGSON, A. C. (1959). The relation of body build to the excretion of 17-ketosteroids and 17-ketogenic steroids in healthy young men. *J. Endocr.* **19**, 87–101.

VIOLA, G. (1935). Critères d'appréciation de la valeur physique, morphologique et fonctionelle des individus. *Biotypologie* **3**, 93.

——(1936). Il mio metodo di valutazione della costituzione individuale. *Endocrinol. Patol. costit.* **12**, 387.

# Part V: Human ecology

J. S. WEINER

# 25. Introduction

THE integrity, persistence, and, when it occurs, expansion of human groups rest on a continuous action on, and interaction with, the environment—a continuous exchange of material and energy, out of which the group fashions the necessary materials and conditions of its existence. Ecology in the broadest sense denotes the dynamic interrelation of the community with its total environment. The adjustments necessary for successful existence in a particular habitat are termed 'adaptations'. Adaptability is a property of each of the individuals making up the group as well as of the group as a whole. Ecological interactions are to be understood (a) as biological processes affecting the functioning, growth, and form of the group's members, and (b) as non-biological processes taking the form of cultural, technical, and social responses. Adaptation involves a two-way process—changes in bodily and social activities are necessary for dealing with the demands of the environment while the environment itself, its inanimate and its living components, is changed to meet the demands of the organism. The 'environment' represents the totality of the surroundings in which the community finds itself, and includes physical and living elements, that is, the geology, topography, and climate of the terrain and its communications; the vegetational cover and the insect, animal, and bird life. Even in the simplest societies the environment goes beyond the immediate habitat since movement or trade will greatly widen the communities' contacts. The natural environment may be partly or largely replaced by a domesticated or industrialized environment of shelters, gardens, and farmlands or even by complete urbanization.

Human groups vary greatly in size and organization. The simplest relatively isolated self-sufficient group would correspond to the animal 'deme' or natural population, larger entities range from deme-complexes organized in tribes and tribal associations, to national and supranational entities.

The organization–environmental complex is often referred to as an 'ecosystem'. The ecosystem is a fundamental biological entity since it is the 'going concern', the actual, living community satisfying its needs in dynamic relation to the habitat. It is the scene of the 'struggle for existence', efficiency of adapta-- tion being the measure of success and 'natural selection' the long-term biological process at work. By 'human ecology' we mean the study of a total ecosystem viewed specifically from the point of view of the human component within the whole system. The human species is basically a widespread network of populations exploiting a wide variety of habitats. Human populations are thus polytypic both in their population characters and in their ecological relationships. The functional human group in a defined ecosystem could be regarded as constituting the zoologist's deme. In the ecological context the 'race' concept is of little or no applicability in so far as many populations drawn from a variety of ecosystems can be and have been consigned to a race category on the basis of the common or frequent possession of a few bodily features. On the other hand, a similar ecosystem, e.g. in a desert biome, may be exploited by groups or demes who are to some extent genetically distinct. Differences between human groups arise from differences in their total ecological relationships and these differences are only partially genetic.

## Ecological adaptive processes

There are two main channels of organism–environmental interaction. One concerns the strictly biological changes induced in the human body by the stresses or demands of the environment or in the course of acting on the environment. We may here distinguish the responses and activities of the individual man, women, and child, from those that concern the group as a whole. It has been suggested that for individual reactions the term 'autecology' and for the group the term 'synecology' should be used. Individual responses are, in the first place, physiological. The body can adapt, acclimatize, or become immune to a wide variety of external factors—nutritional, climatic, pathological—by virtue of a general somatic property of physiological adaptability. This is a species property—all members of *Homo sapiens* can exhibit this flexibility of response. It should be appreciated that this 'physiological plasticity' is an evolutionary product of the species, comparable to such crucial properties as the generalized human limb structure or the highly developed conceptual activity of the human brain.

Secondly, there are biological responses specific to particular individuals and determined by particular genotypes. Traits of this kind may be entirely peculiar to a few individuals; or they may confer special advantages on particular populations (e.g. narrowness of nose in cold or excessively dry conditions). The emergence by natural selection of such adaptive characters must have played an important part in the survival of the first hominids in their primitive habitats. But many regionally or racially distinguished characters are difficult to demonstrate as possessing survival value.

The purpose or significance of adaptation may be said to be the maintenance of biological *homeostasis*, defined by Cannon as 'the totality of steady states maintained in an organism'. Homeostasis involves two interwoven processes— steady balance and self-regulation. In the physiological sense it refers to the preservation of that constancy of internal cellular conditions necessary for the life of the body. In the growing organism, 'developmental homeostasis' is the restriction to a determined channel of growth. As far as we know 'homeostatic' steady states are attained within the same limits in all races, e.g. body temperature, blood H-ion concentration, sugar content, or osmotic pressure, though the exact level, within this range, may be set at values depending on particular 'load' factors of activity or of the environment. Any serious threat to the 'homeostatic level' calls into play compensatory processes tending to neutralize such a threat and to stabilize internal characters within the normal range. The body thus exhibits physiologically both 'inertia' and 'adaptability'.

The compensatory processes respond up to the limits of their capacity, as for example the heart output during exercise or the buffering power of the blood. When these limits are exceeded the body begins to undergo pathological changes. It is this adaptive capacity which is enhanced both in sensitivity and in magnitude by such processes as acclimatization, training, habituation, drug induction, and immunization. It seems likely that individual variation in adaptive capacity reflects differences of genetic endowment.

By virtue of its genetic constitution, the human group likewise, as a group, displays homeostatic properties. There is a strong tendency to stability in the range of bodily features with a clustering of the majority round a mean value. This distribution arises (Chapter 9) inevitably from the fact that many additive genes are involved. The mean represents the greatest degree of heterozygosity, while the extremes represent a greater degree of homozygosity. The mean value is on the whole the most favourable, the extremes the less favourable expression of the phenotypes. Elimination of the less fit (in the interest of group adaptability) does not, however, deprive the group of genetic variability, for the more favoured heterozygotes continue to supply this (Chapter 11). There is thus a genetic homeostasis maintaining both the optimum and the range, and providing the material for a shift to the appropriate genotypes should circumstances change. The group is therefore adaptable genetically while maintaining a genetic inertia. The genetic variation inseparable from all breeding populations carries another adaptive significance. It enables a population to adapt and exploit a large range of environments and living conditions (see also p. 131 for a discussion on the biological significance of polygenes).

In addition to biological processes making for homeostasis there are those social and technical activities which allow the group to come to terms with or to dominate the environment. We must remember that non-biological means—organization, division of labour, social customs, etc.—still serve biological purposes. Often the social institutions are not recognizably or directly concerned with the satisfaction of biological needs, but they play this role none the less. We can trace this in the institutional arrangements for the production and distribution of food (as Audrey Richards has done), for constructing shelters in the planning of the work schedules, in measures for caring for offspring, and so on. Examples abound. Thus amongst the New Guinea Tsembaga religious rituals play a demonstrable role in redistributing land and pig surpluses so assuring the supply of pork and protein for the group as a whole (Rappaport). Moore suggests that the ritual of shoulder-blade divination among certain North American Indian tribes served to randomize the choice of caribou-hunting sites and so to outwit the caribou; Aschmann believes that the sexual licence permitted during a particular seasonal ceremonial amongst the Baja of the Central Desert of California resulted in a seasonal pattern of reproduction related to the seasonal fluctuation in the food supply. In New

Guinea the dispersal of settlements has been seen as a protection against the spread of disease. There is, of course, nothing like a simple correspondence between institutional forms and biological needs—'biologism' is inadequate as a basis for strictly *social* analysis. Social organization has its own aims, functions, and values and these characters transcend the purely biological. Socially defined activities are conceived in social terms such as status, duties, and kinship obligations, i.e. in terms of social structure. Nevertheless, the limiting role of the environment is always discernible even on social organization as it is on material culture (Graham Clarke), and on biological structure and function.

TABLE 25.1
*Habitats classified*

I. *Equatorial forests*
Dense rain forest, evergreens, tall and canopied, wet, will not burn, difficult to clear.

II. *Tropical forest and scrub*
Less dense, semi-deciduous forest which can be cleared; scrub forest with grass or brush floor and some small thorny trees, merges with equatorial forest and with grassland.

III. *Tropical grasslands (savannahs)*
Great stretches of grassland with scattered trees or patches of forest or parkland. Abundant animal life.

IV. *Deserts and dry lands*
Vegetation scanty, plants are (a) water-storing succulants and/or thorny cacti or aloes; (b) annuals, dominant; (c) perennials with long roots. Surface water scarce, little shade, animal life scarce, climate ameliorated in oases and nearby river systems.

V. *Temperate forests*
The natural broad-leaf deciduous forest merging into coniferous forest and moorland with evergreen heaths on western European seaboard. Now largely cleared. Abundant animal life.

VI. *Mediterranean scrub*
The *maquis*—evergreen rather than deciduous (oaks and chestnuts) small trees and shrubs, plants deep-rooted and xerophytic, grassland in patches. Animals not abundant.

VII. *Temperate grasslands*
Steppes of short grass; prairies of long grass. The prairies and chernozem, well-watered and water-retaining.

VIII. *Boreal lands*
Coniferous forest mostly of spruce, fir, larch, rarely birch, beech, poplar; lakes, rivers, and swamps. Abundant animal life, e.g. moose, caribou, puma in America, tiger in Siberia.

IX. *Polar lands and tundra*
Tundra begins at edge of boreal forest as scrub of dwarf willows, ash, alder, then becomes carpeted tundra of sedges, mosses, lichens; then desert tundra with isolated patches of grass tundra, flowers blossoming in spring. Animals abundant; fish, sea mammals; many Arctic species, e.g. foxes, hares, bears.

X. *Mountain habitats*
Depend on locality and altitude and orientation in relation to light and shade, e.g. at equator succession of tropical forest, mixed forest, conifers, alpine meadows.

(From Preston James, and Coon and Chappell.)

# TABLE 25.2

## *Habitats—geographical distribution (some examples)*

| Habitats | Africa | Asia | Europe | America | Australasia |
|---|---|---|---|---|---|
| I. Equatorial forests | Congo basin<br>Cameroun | India<br>South East Asia<br>Indonesia | | Amazon | New Guinea<br>Melanesia |
| II. Tropical forests and scrub | Angola<br>Uganda<br>Southern Sudan | India<br>Southern China | | Yucatan<br>Gran Chaco | Polynesia<br>Cairns regions |
| III. Tropical grasslands (savannahs) | Sudan<br>Tanzania | Indonesian grasslands | | Pampas<br>Llanos | Northern Australia |
| IV. Deserts and dry lands | Sahara<br>Kalahari<br>Namib | Arabian<br>Indian<br>Turkestan | | Californian<br>Atacama<br>Paraguay | Central Australia |
| V. Temperate forests | | China south of Great Wall and north of forest belt | Between Mediterranean and Boreal east of grasslands<br>Gulf Stream coasts | East of Mississippi<br>St. Lawrence Valley<br>North-west coast of North America<br>Chile | Australia<br>Tasmania<br>New Zealand |
| VI. Mediterranean scrub | South shore of Mediterranean Sea<br>Cape Peninsula | Palestine<br>Lebanon<br>South coast of Black sea | Crimea<br>Northern shore of Mediterranean | California to Vancouver<br>Middle Chile | Perth region<br>Adelaide region |
| VII. Temperate grasslands | High veld, Transvaal<br>Strip south of Atlas Mountains | Turkestan<br>Manchuria<br>Mongolia | Eastern Russian steppe<br>Chernozem belt | Prairies<br>Pampas<br>Patagonia | |
| VIII. Boreal | | Siberia | Lapland | Northern Canada<br>Alaska<br>Extreme South America<br>Greenland | New Zealand mountains |
| IX. Tundra | | Siberia | Lapland | | Antarctica |
| X. Mountains | Ethiopia<br>Basutoland | Tibet<br>Hindu Kush | Swiss and Austrian Alps | Mexico<br>Peru<br>Chile | New Zealand in South Island |

### The variety of man-modified ecosystems

To appreciate the variety of ecosystems exploited by man we need only consider the range offered by different combinations of habitat and economy. In order to do this, classifications of both habitats and economic groups are needed which will include the ecosystems or pre-literate and prehistoric man as well as of more advanced societies. A simple classification of habitats should indicate the chief climatic, vegetational, faunal, and topographical characters, and a classification of economic or social groups should sufficiently indicate the mode of livelihood and the complexity of the community. Elaborate classifications of habitats, economies, or ecosystems are not really called for since their variation is immense. The ecologist finds it essential always 'to make analyses of each active society' (Forde).

Habitats may be roughly classified (Table 25.1) into 10 groups (Following Preston James), of which all but one depend broadly on geographical latitude, the exception being that determined by altitude. The ecological 'stresses' vary in these different habitats, largely through different combinations of climatic, nutritional disease, and other factors. In Table 25.1 are given the main biotic features of these 10 groups of habitats and in Table 25.2 their occurrence in different continents is shown (Europe and Asia should perhaps be regarded as one continental land mass).

As shown in Table 25.3, the largest populations today are found in two very contrasting habitats—in tropical forest and scrub lands and in temperate mixed forest lands. The relative density of populations is shown in the third column of the table. Very likely the hominids originated in tropical grasslands or scrub lands, so that modern man has successfully extended his area of occupation to achieve high densities in habitats as different as tropical forest lands (with twice the overall average density), Mediterranean scrub lands (4 times the average), and the temperate mixed forest lands (6 times). Mountain habitats have also been settled in fair density.

TABLE 25.3

*Population distribution*

| Habitats | Area percentage of total land area | Population percentage of total present world population | Relative density |
|---|---|---|---|
| Dry lands and deserts | 18 | 4 | 0·2 |
| Tropical forest lands ⎰ Tropical scrub lands ⎱ | 15 | 28 | 1·9 |
| Tropical grasslands (savannah) ⎰ Temperate grasslands (continental) ⎱ | 21 | 12 | 0·6 |
| Temperate mixed forest lands | 7 | 39 | 5·6 |
| Mediterranean scrub lands | 1 | 4 | 4·0 |
| Boreal lands (cold temperate) | 10 | 1 | 0·1 |
| Polar lands and tundras | 16 | (<1) | 0·01 |
| Mountain habitats | 12 | 12 | 1·00 |

The type of economy may be roughly classified according to the major productive technique used (Table 25.4). This serves to indicate the volume of production and type of labour organization as well as the social complexity of the community. Too much emphasis should not be placed upon any classification in terms of technology, however, since productive methods are seldom mutually exclusive and social structure may vary greatly amongst groups using the same production technique.

TABLE 25.4

*Types of economy*

---

*Food-gatherers* live by collecting their food—small game, insects, roots, fruits, honey. Their material culture (clothing, shelters, domestic utensils, etc.) is crude or scanty. The only domestic animal is the dog.

*Higher hunters* live by trapping and hunting, in addition to gathering. They often have good dwellings and know something of pottery and weaving. The populations of the Palaeolithic and Mesolithic stages of culture fall within these first two categories.

*Herdsmen and pastoralists* live mainly by keeping herds of cattle; they may also have flocks of sheep and goats. They often have substantial houses. Hunting or tilling is quite subsidiary.

*Nomads* are herdsmen who move in a regular seasonal cycle to tribal grazing lands.

*Simple cultivators* practise a simple garden agriculture, but rely also on gathering and hunting; a little domestication of pigs or poultry may be added. The societies in the Neolithic cultural stage would be classified in this category.

*Advanced cultivators* rely on agriculture as their main means of subsistence. They appreciate the significance of soil fertility and the importance of crop rotation. In post-Neolithic time water conservation and irrigation began to be practised.

---

It is obvious (Tables 25.5, 25.6, and 25.7) that race is no barrier to the occupation of a wide range of habitats or the practice of different economies. In particular habitats one and the same racial group has established a succession of economies often of increasing complexity.

For a given technology some habitats are obviously more favourable than others; indeed, some environments entirely preclude the development of certain economies. On the whole, however, the habitat has not exercised great restrictions on the emergence of economies of all stages. Most habitats can be exploited in very different ways. The resulting ecosystems will, of course, vary greatly, particularly in their population densities. Given the technology of advanced cultivators, settlements of high density are possible in nearly every type of habitat.

The intrusion of human communities into natural ecosystems may lead to a situation of stable or of dynamic equilibrium. In the first case the human group maintains its essential biological characteristics more or less unchanged over long periods of time—its population size, density, and composition, its energy and nutrient balances, its general standard of living. The social structure and technology will reflect this conservetism. Approximations to ecological stability are attainable in different habitats, with different economies, and at high or low population densities. Dynamic ecological equilibria which charac-

## TABLE 25.5

### The relation of habitats and racial groups

| | Negroid | Caucasoid | Mongoloid | Australo-Veddoid |
|---|---|---|---|---|
| I. Deserts | Bushmen | Middle-eastern peoples | Mongols (Gobi) Atacama Indians Southern Mongoloids Malays American Indians | Australian Aborigines |
| II. Equatorial forests | Pygmies | Indo–Dravidians | American Indians (South America) | 'Murrian' Veddas |
| III. Tropical forest and scrub | Bemba Angolan Bantu | Indo–Dravidians | American Indians (South America) | Veddoids of India |
| IV. Tropical grasslands | Nilotic Hausa | Spanish Americans | American Indians | Australian Aborigines |
| V. Temperate forests | | North and Central Europeans | North American Indians North-western Mongols (China) | Polynesians Tasmanians |
| VI. Mediterranean scrub | Hottentot | Mediterranean groups | | |
| VII. Temperate grasslands | Bantu (Sotho) | European groups | North American Indians American Indians Mongols (Manchuria) | |
| VIII. Boreal | Lapps | Lapps | Ostiaks Samoyeds | Ainu |
| IX. Tundra | Lapps | Lapps | Eskimos Chuckchi | |
| X. Mountains | Bantu | Armenoid and Alpine groups | Mongoloids of Tibet, Persia, and Bolivia | New Guinea Highlanders |

The table gives examples to show that peoples of all races are capable of enduring a wide range of habitats.

## TABLE 25.6

### The relation of economies and race

| | Negroid | Caucasoid | Mongoloid | Australo-Veddoid |
|---|---|---|---|---|
| 1. Food-gatherers | Bushmen<br>Veddas | 'Mesolithic' communities | Fuegians<br>Californians<br>Eskimos<br>American Indians | Australians |
| 2. (Higher) hunters and fishers | Pygmies<br>Melanesians<br>West Africans | (Ainu)<br>Predmost | | |
| 3. Pastoralists | Bantu<br>Masai<br>Hottentots | Lapps<br>Iron-Age Nordics | Southern Manchurians | |
| 4. Nomads | (Nilotes)<br>Sahara Negroids | Bedouins<br>Tuareg | Mongols<br>Turkestan<br>Chuckchi | |
| 5. Simple cultivators | Bantu<br>New Guinea<br>West Africans | Indo-Dravidians | Southern Mongols<br>Malays | Melanesians |
| 6. Advanced cultivators | | Mediterranean peoples | Hopi Maya<br>Indonesians<br>Northern Mongols | Polynesians |

The table gives examples to show that peoples of all races have, to a large extent, developed economies of all categories.

## TABLE 25·7

### *Habitats, economies, and peoples (some examples)*

| | Food-gatherers | Hunters | Pastoralists | Nomads | Simple cultivators | Advanced cultivators |
|---|---|---|---|---|---|---|
| I. Equatorial forests | Siamang | Pygmies Melanesians | | | Amazon New Guinea Indo-Dravidian South American Indians | Indonesia Java Bantu |
| II. Tropical forest and scrub | Grand Chaco Indians | Bantu peoples | Bemba | | | |
| III. Tropical grasslands (savannahs) | Australians | Hadza (East Africa) | Nilotes | Nilotes | North American Indians | Hamites |
| IV. Drylands and deserts | Bushmen Australians | | | Bedouins Tuaregs | Oases dwellers | Oases (riverine) |
| V. Temperate forests | Australians Mesolithic European | Tasmanians Predmost | Iron-Age Europeans | | Chinese | Peasant Chinese |
| VI. Mediterranean scrub | Strand lopers | Californian Indians | Balkans | Berbers | Neolithic Iron-Age Maori | Medieval Europe |
| VII. Temperate grasslands | Paleolithic European | North American Indians | Mongols | Buriats Mongols | Siouan Indians | Pawnee Indians |
| VIII. Boreal | Fuegians | Samoyeds | | Lapps | | |
| IX. Tundra | | Eskimos | | Lapps | | |

terize many expanding and developing communities require that the constantly increasing needs for food, water, raw material, waste disposal are met by increasing activity and energy output and intensified explitation of both the biotic and abiotic environment. This kind of equilibrium (or approximation to it) is particularly characteristic of human communities in the era of industrialization. There are of course periods in the history of communities where ecological balance cannot be maintained with far-reaching social and biological consequences. In an ecological analysis the aim is to understand the biological properties of the community and its constituent families and individuals in terms of equilibrium processes and interchanges—the energy flow, the transport of food and water, the transmission of pathogens—through the total ecosystem.

Ecological 'success' may be thought of in terms of 'standards of living'. Such standards may be biological, medical, or demographic. The population size and its maintenance, the mortality, longevity, or nutritional status are examples of overall indices of 'fitness' or adjustment. Depopulation is perhaps the most telling index of maladjustment. It is seen, for example, in the failure of an immigrant group to establish itself. The analysis of the 'efficiency' and 'capacity' of an ecosystem require detailed surveys of specific societies. Limitations may be discovered in any of the organism–environmental relationships. These limitations may, for instance, be climatic in the direct or indirect sense (e.g. lack of building material); they may be attributable to nutritional shortcomings or to particular diseases. The limits may arise only secondarily from defects in social organization as perhaps in the organizing of work over the yearly cycle or in the storage of food. Obviously some habitats are far less favourable than others. For example, the tropical habitats of Africa and South America have always presented a combination of great difficulties—poor soil, climatic and nutritional stresses and debilitating diseases. The beginnings of the first complex societies and of civilization in the 'Fertile Crescent' were the outcome of the peculiarly advantageous conditions existing simultaneously in the ancient river valleys—abundant water supply, a propitious climate, easy riverine communications, and the protection afforded by the surrounding arid lands.

# 26. Nutritional ecology

LET us examine the ecosystem as a system for the exchange of material and energy, i.e. from the nutritional aspect.

**Energy**

The maintenance in every adult of an overall balance between calories expended and calories taken in so as to resist large changes in body-weight is a 'homeostatic' character and depends on regulatory centres in the central nervous system.

Energy must be obtained from the dietary to maintain the resting and basal metabolism of the body, for muscular activities, for growth and reproduction, and to maintain bodily warmth. Energy needs can be quite exactly stated for these different items, and a balance-sheet drawn up of the calorie cost of supplying the biological needs of the family or of the entire group. The calorie cost of the various items needs a brief comment.

1. Joules for basal and resting metabolism provide the energy expended by the individual at rest, sitting and sleeping, during pregnancy and lactation, and during growth. For the adult a rough value for sleep and inactivity can be put at 300 kJ per hour. This value depends on body-size. For pregnancy and lactation, say, 400 kJ per hour; for a child, depending on age, 150–250 kJ per hour.

2. Joules for food-getting activities are treated separately to show what proportion of all the calories consumed has to be expended on the actual work needed to provide the total energy supply. The cost depends on the nature of the work. It may vary from, say, 450 kJ per hour for ordinary walking or light work, as in fetching water or collecting greenstuffs, up to 1600–2000 kJ per hour, for heavy work, but at this level the work itself can be sustained for a few hours only of the working day. Not many of the tasks of simple societies have been assessed for their energy costs. Here are some examples (based on Passmore and Durnin—1955).

| Activity | kJ/h |
|---|---|
| Log-carrying | 840 |
| Planting groundnuts | 920 |
| Hoeing | 1050–1470 |
| Weeding | 1340 |
| Clearing bush | 1700 |
| Tree-felling | 2000 |

In western Europe the heaviest industrial work requires in an 8-hour shift for men 10 000 kJ or 1250 kJ per hour, and for women about 6700 kJ or 838 kJ per hour. We can adopt two average 'levels', say 8400 kJ for a day's hard work and a lower one of 5000 kJ for a lighter day's work.

3. The total cost of activities other than those directly involved in the continuous labour of food-getting is not easy to specify. In simple agricultural communities these include domestic tasks, collecting firewood, preparation of food, repairing of kit, building shelters and furniture, making clothing and utensils. Such activities can hardly be less than resting metabolism plus 50 per cent, say 460–500 kJ. Some tasks, e.g. pounding rice, cost 1250 kJ per hour and a woman may spend as much as 2 hours per day on pounding maize or cassava (Platt 1946). Many recreations, dances, and other ceremonies are as strenuous as moderate or even hard work and allowance should strictly be made for these. Extra energy will be needed for the additional activity (and shivering) induced by cold—a rough increment on the basal value of, say, 30 per cent would be appropriate.

The total daily needs can be calculated for a hypothetical family consisting of the parents, two small children, and one nearly grown child, the two elder children taking part in food-getting. Maximum and minimum values are given for energy cost (Table 26.1).

TABLE 26.1

*Energy needs for a hypothetical family*

|  | Basal and resting | | | Food-getting | | | Other activities | | Total kJ | |
|---|---|---|---|---|---|---|---|---|---|---|
|  | Hours | J | | Hours | J | | Hours | J | | |
|  |  | (min.) | (max.) |  | (min.) | (max.) |  |  | (min.) | (max.) |
| Father | 8 | 2 350 | 2 560 | 8 | 5 040 | 9 200 | 8 | 3 790 | 11 180 | 15 600 |
| Mother | 8 | 2 350 | 3 700 | 6 | 3 780 | 5 020 | 10 | 3 790 | 9 920 | 12 530 |
| Child 1 | 10 | 2 520 | 2 770 | 6 | 2 520 | 3 150 | 8 | 3 070 | 8 070 | 8 950 |
| Child 2 | 11 | 2 310 | 2 520 | 4 | 1 680 | 1 850 | 9 | 3 030 | 7 020 | 7 400 |
| Youngest child | 12 | 2 100 | 2 180 | 0 | — | — | 12 | 3 530 | 5 630 | 5 710 |
| Total | — | 11 630 | 13 730 | — | 12 920 | 19 220 | — | 17 170 | 41 820 | 50 190 |

Kilojoules needed per head per day:  8 364, say  8 500 minimum.
10 038, say 10 000 maximum.

The resting energy intake is influenced by a number of constitutional factors, namely age, sex, and body-size. These last two introduce a genetic factor into energy requirements. Basal metabolism for a given age is expressed in terms of surface area calculated from the well-known DuBois height–weight formula

$$A = W^{0.425} \times H^{0.725} \times 71.84,$$

where $A$=surface area in cm², $W$=weight in kg, and $H$=height in cm. The size factor also affects the cost of activity, e.g. walking at 3 m.p.h. has an energy cost, independent of age and sex, given by kJ per min=$0.197 \times$ weight$+4.284$.

The average need per *head* per day in all human communities can be said to range from about 8500 kJ as a lower and 12 750 kJ as an upper value. These limits take into account such factors as body-size, climate, and severity of work.

Ecosystems vary much more, however, in the proportionate cost of producing the necessary energy. In the theoretical example, in Table 26.1, it is apparent that of every 40 kJ needed by the family per day for all purposes 10 (with light and consequently more efficient work) or 15 (with heavy work) go into the direct activity of food production. This 'productive' or 'extractive' ratio of 30 or 40 per cent would seem to be characteristic of subsistence economies. This is no doubt a considerable advance on subhuman Primates (such as great apes) confined as they are to incessant food-collecting where the ratio would be nearer 70 per cent. In the most efficient agriculture the lightest work, say, 6700 kJ per day, might suffice for the needs of 20 or more individuals, i.e. for every 40 kJ used only about 1·2 kJ (3 per cent) is needed in primary food production. For a given economy a change of habitat may alter the 'productive ratio' by a factor of perhaps 50 per cent, whereas in a particular habitat a change of technique may alter it by 1000 per cent or more.

A similar but crude index useful in the field situation is to calculate the index of subsistence effort as the ratio $W/C$, where $W$=number of man-days of work and $C$=number of man-days of consumption. For a baboon troop this index approximates to unity—continuous foraging. For the !Kung Bushmen the value is about 25 per cent. In some simple communities (e.g. in New Guinea) the efficiency of supplying the energy is much higher when extractive ratios are as low as 10 per cent.

The simple classification presented in Table 25.7, which illustrates 50 different combinations of habitat and economy, makes obvious that the sources of food and energy are very diverse. The great physiological flexibility man shows in utilizing these varied sources arises simply from (a) the ability of the human body to ingest and metabolize the three energy-yielding substances, fat, carbohydrate, and protein, in a great variety of combinations, and (b) the ability to accept each of these substances from a great variety of foodstuffs.

The metabolic flexibility of human populations is easily illustrated as in Table 26.2, which shows the average daily intake per head in four contrasting economies.

These are four examples of widely differing dietary combinations giving the requisite energy in contrasting ecosystems. Not only do the proportions of these energy-yielding foods vary greatly; each may be obtained from many different sources and these depend in turn on the habitat and food-getting techniques. The main sources of carbohydrate are cereals, starchy roots, fruits, and sugar; of fats—fats and oils, and animal foods; of protein—animal products (including fish and milk), pulses, and nuts.

In European countries the intake of energy in fat expressed as a percentage of total intake ranges from about 21 per cent in the Mediterranean area to about 31 per cent in western Europe and USA. The value (Table 26.2) for the Eskimo diet is about 47 per cent, for the Kikuyu under 10 per cent. Protein, on the other hand, tends to assume a more constant proportional value in different diets—protein energy values vary within the rather narrow range of 9–12 per cent.

TABLE 26.2

*Average daily intake, per head, of fat, carbohydrate, and protein*

|  | British | | Kikuyu | | Eskimos | | Barbados Islanders | |
|---|---|---|---|---|---|---|---|---|
|  | (g) | (kJ) | (g) | (kJ) | (g) | (kJ) | (g) | (kJ) |
| Fat (38 kJ g$^{-1}$) | 110 | 4 150 | 22 | 832 | 162 | 6 120 | 63 | 2 380 |
| Carbohydrate (17 kJ g$^{-1}$) | 400 | 6 730 | 390 | 6 500 | 59 | 990 | 416 | 7 000 |
| Protein (17 kJ g$^{-1}$) . | 100 | 1 680 | 100 | 1 680 | 377 | 5 870 | 45 | 756 |
| Total | — | 12 560 | — | 9 012 | — | 12 980 | — | 10 136 |

Only in regard to one or two nutrients is there so far evidence to suggest that the utilization of particular dietaries by different human groups is associated with specific genetic qualities. The most-cited example refers to the traditional Eskimo diet, the higher fat content of which is repulsive to Europeans and which cannot be metabolized without some degree of incomplete oxidation. This is attended by the accumulation of ketone bodies in blood and urine. From this 'ketosis' the Eskimos are said to be free. Even supposing the Eskimo are genetically more efficient at absorbing and metabolizing this diet (and for this there is no evidence as yet), the superiority can be only one of degree. In experiments some European subjects have shown ability to become accustomed to high-protein and high-fat diets. It can be accepted that populations can change their diets, if not so readily psychologically, yet without physiological difficulty. This is one of the most far-reaching adaptive properties of *Homo sapiens*.

## Energy balance

Obviously a group that maintains its population size and numbers constant in a given area over a period of years or generations must be successful in balancing its energy expenditure against its intake of energy. But the attainment of balance may in fact be far from easy to regulate and may often be a precarious one. Food-gathering and simple agricultural groups are sensitive to water shortage and other features of their food supply, as will be noted in examples given later (p. 417, p. 470).

To assess the efficiency with which a community obtains its energy supplies and balances its energy output the extractive ratio and the level of energy flow need both to be considered. A low extractive ratio which gives a high energy yield is clearly an efficient combination particularly if the community obtains a surplus of calories above requirements available for storage or trade. A high extractive ratio could lead to the same result but at much greater cost. But in simple societies there is often a combination of low extractive ratio and a low energy yield, a situation not easy to interpret without further investigation. In this case the group may be content with a low level of activity; they work no harder than necessary. It may in fact have reached the 'subsistence optimum'—further work yielding in the particular ecological circumstances only a marginally greater return.

## Metabolic nutrients

Protein, fat, and carbohydrate are used in the body for purposes additional to their energy yield; they fulfil particular metabolic functions. The constituent amino acids of the ingested protein are required for tissue growth and repair as well as for the synthesis of many special proteins. Fat is needed as body insulation and for fuel storage, while carbohydrate is the primary substance in all energy-yielding reactions. The blood-sugar is therefore maintained steady within relatively narrow limits.

That these requirements can be met by widely differing combinations of carbohydrate, fat, and protein (Table 26.2) illustrates once again the physiological flexibility of metabolic processes. There is interchangeability amongst the nutrients in that both protein and fat can serve as sources for carbohydrate and their intake to some extent spares the body the task of manufacturing this fuel. While high intake of carbohydrate can maintain fat stores and so compensate for lowish fat intake it is probable that a minimal quantity of fat, especially unsaturated varieties, must be supplied. Foodstuffs supplying protein of animal origin carry a higher biological value than those of vegetable origin as they contain much more of the essential amino acids. It is possibly by combining animal and vegetable protein to supply protein adequate in amount and quality. This, therefore, permits quite considerable flexibility of diet in different habitats. As protein inadequacy is one of the great dietary hazards, particularly of simple societies, a minimal intake of animal protein is essential. The best estimate that can be made for protein needs (g per day) is 30–50 g at age 4 years, 50–80 at age 12 years, 50–90 for adult males, 40–70 for adult females, and 55–90 g during the last half of pregnancy and for lactation. The replacement needed of nitrogen lost in the sweat in hot climates is small—less than 10 per cent. There seem to be no racial differences in protein metabolism. It is likely that the reported nitrogen intake of New Guinea highlanders has been inaccurately estimated or that present standards are too high rather than that some special genotype is present. Nevertheless, protein deficiency, as evidence by the incidence of kwashiorkor after weaning, is widespread. The intake of protein in these cases is below 30 g per day. Although the amount of fluid falls, the milk of mothers on poor diets still has a high protein content. This represents a partial safeguard for the child kept on unduly prolonged breast-feeding, a practice which is so widespread in simpler societies. Indeed the long taboo on postpartum sexual intercourse to protect the nursing infant is found much more commonly in societies with a low protein availability.

An example to illustrate the difficulties of deciding between the action of environmental and genetic factors is provided by the finding of a high $\gamma$-globulin level in many dark-skinned peoples (e.g. West Africans, Australian Aborigines, Navajo Indians). This has been considered to be of genetic origin, but infections, especially malaria, have also been held responsible. Low levels of serum albumin appear to be of dietary origin.

The marked variability between individuals in the excretion of the amino acid D-phenylalanine and $\beta$-amino-isobutyric acid, as we have seen, has a genetic basis. Variations between different population groups in the excretion of $\beta$-amino-isobutyric acid cannot, however, be regarded as indicating peculiarities of intermediary metabolism for it seems that kidney function is mainly involved in bringing about this polymorphism.

## Minerals and water

The most important items under this heading are iron, salt, iodine, calcium, and water, substances in the supply of which habitats vary enormously. Physiologically there is simply a steady balance between bodily intake and loss. A sudden increased bodily demand, if not immediately satisfied from outside sources, will result in a calling on bodily reserves to meet the 'negative balance'. The loss from the bodily stores is made up when sufficient supply is again available, leading to a temporary 'positive balance'. Thus in different habitats this balance will be found now at a high, now at a low, level of intake

### Water

The proportion of water in the body varies quite widely between individuals largely because of differences in the fat content. If body-weight fluctuations due to energy imbalance are minimized (by a close equivalence of energy input and output) the daily body-water change is maintained within 1 per cent of body-weight. This close balance reflects the efficacy of the thirst mechanism and of the kidney in regulating intake and output within homeostatic limits. There is no good evidence that desert dwellers, the nomadic Bedouin, possess any special property of water regulation, such as a greater concentrating power of the kidney.

Maintenance of an equilibrium between water supply and water needs for all purposes, including washing and waste disposal, is a paramount ecological requirement for all societies. The dependence of population size on water availability is discussed later. Although some shortage of drinking water can be tolerated by the excretion of a more concentrated urine, the margin that this provides, about 500 ml a day, can only be regarded as an emergency adaptation.

### Calcium

Wide limits of intake can be tolerated by establishing a simple balance between intake and output. It appears that, on diets poor in calcium, the growing child or adult can increase the proportion of calcium absorbed from the intestine and so go some way to re-establishing balance as well as meeting (in the child) demands of growth. Although the process is not understood, this helps to explain the resistance to relatively low-calcium diets. Another factor which makes for improved utilization of calcium is the exposure to the ultraviolet light in solar radiation. The absorption of ultraviolet light in the superficial layers of the skin in some way promotes the conversion in the subcutaneous tissues of a substance allied to ergosterol to the closely related vitamin-D compounds. The exclusion of ultraviolet light from the deeper layers of darkly pigmented skin has been thought to conduce to rickets and osteomalacia (as in women secluded in purdah): light skin may carry some advantage in latitudes of reduced sunshine.

Calcium intake is probably low in many countries, for few foods except milk and cheese contain much of the mineral. On diets very low in calcium people are often small in stature and in bone length; tooth development may be poor, and it is likely that children will not be growing at optimal rates. When extra calcium is given these children retain it. Calcium deficiency has been reported in peasant communities on a high-carbohydrate diet, poor in meat and milk, e.g. amongst the poorer inhabitants of Sri Lanka and Newfoundlanders.

The view that low calcium intake has brought about the existence of small-statured racial groups has been advocated, but with little supporting evidence. The analogy is drawn with the occurrence of small breeds of sheep in calcium-poor areas (Marett). There are, of course, people of short stature whose calcium supply and intake is more than adequate, e.g. Eskimos and Laplanders. Whether peoples of shorter stature are specially resistant to calcium deficiency is not known.

### Iron

Daily needs are small and fairly easily met, but the breast-fed infant is liable to deficiency. Equilibrium between intake and output is easily established and temporary shortages can be made good from iron stores. A higher intake is required where there is anaemia due, for example, to infestation with parasites, particularly malaria and hookworm, two serious hazards of many tropical habitats. Profuse sweating also increases iron loss. Some anaemias are due, not to environmentally induced deficiency of iron, but to genetic defects, e.g. thalassaemia and sickle-cell anaemia, and the effects can be crippling or fatal. The genes responsible reach fairly high frequencies in some communities since in the heterozygote the anaemia is far less severe and, indeed, the heterozygote enjoys some compensating advantage (p. 230). Dietary iron in populations liable to anaemia must be supplied at higher levels.

Iron is available in a wide variety of foodstuffs and consequently geographical limitations are not serious. The risk of deficiency on a mixed diet with adequate meat and vegetables is small but diets in many habitats, for some periods during the year, may well be inadequate for the needs of pregnant and nursing mothers, and growing children.

### Salt

Man cannot exist without a minimal daily intake of sodium chloride. The loss from the body will also be increased by sweating in hot climates. But the intake does not need to be much higher in these climates than in temperate conditions, since in the course of acclimatization equilibrium can be re-established at moderate levels of intake. This comes about through a compensatory reduction of salt loss in the urine and the sweat. Newcomers to hot climates feel the lack for varying periods, but after acclimatization these, like indigenous people, will often be found to be subsisting on quite moderate amounts (8–10 g daily).

The fact is that both low and high levels of intake can be tolerated. Eskimos who do not eat much vegetable matter are said not to have any special craving for salt. Where the water is brackish the level of salt intake is high, as amongst some Bedouin. Salt is used in many communities as a preservative and it is by the habitual use of large amounts that a 'craving' for salt can be established.

There is no evidence that the need for salt or the ability to adjust to changes in supply varies in any way from one population to another. Leschi claims that in tropical Africans the blood-sodium level is somewhat lower than in Europeans. This would not be necessarily a racial character since it is known that Europeans in the tropics likewise exhibit a somewhat reduced plasma level. It probably represents a physiological accompaniment of acclimatization.

Salt is not universally found (the sea, saline springs, and saline earths are the main sources), and this has meant that the search for it has helped to prevent the social isolation of groups, e.g. salt caravans still traverse the Sahara; purchase and bartering are widespread and salt expeditions, even warlike, are known.

*Iodine*

A minute daily intake of iodine is essential for normal growth and function. There are habitats where this element is seriously deficient in the soil, water, and plants. The world's goitrogenic areas are related, not to climate but to present and past volcanic regions. There is only a limited adaptability to iodine insufficiency. To some extent overactivity of the thyroid gland (with production of the characteristic goitre or neck swelling) will compensate by a more intensive utilization of the available iodine, but failure results in serious stunting and other effects on skeletal growth. There is no reason to regard any Pygmy population as a race of thyroid-deficient dwarfs, though iodine deficiency is present in the Ulele district of Zaïre. These pygmy cretins have an impairment of thyroid uptake of iodine, a defect absent in normal Pygmies. But no genetic element is involved in the cretinism. No racial group is immune to the effects of lack of iodine. Peoples of the Punjab, Hottentots, and Bantu of South Africa, Eskimos, Europeans, all are liable to iodine deficiency; this may be primary because of local insufficiency or due to various goitrogenic factors in the diet which interfere with iodine utilization.

## Vitamins

The body cannot manufacture vitamins; like the essential amino acids they must be supplied in the diet. Accordingly the diet must be sufficiently varied over the year to ensure that the dozen or so vitamins, even in the necessary small amounts, are present. The body does contain some reserves of vitamins or their precursors so that in times of insufficiency these can be drawn upon. The effects of vitamin deficiency may take some time (weeks or months) to develop. Vitamin-deficiency diseases affect peoples of all races; the clinical picture will vary only with the diet provided by a given habitat and the co-existence of several types of vitamin and other deficiency. On diets poor in animal food vitamins A and D may be in deficient supply, but fresh vegetables are good sources so that a varied diet can to a large extent provide an adequate supply. This is true also of the vitamins of the B group and vitamin C. Thus adequate vitamin intake is possible in many different habitats. It is only when the diet is monotonously high in cereals with low fat and protein content that vitamin deficiencies appear. For example, a high maize diet will conduce to nicotinic-acid deficiency and therefore to pellagra. With the adoption of white flour or polished rice, deficiency diseases due to lack of thiamine and riboflavin make their appearance. If the diet is poor in animal fat and fresh vegetables, vitamin-D deficiency will occur much more readily where ultraviolet light is reduced by cloudy moisture-laden atmospheres and by wearing heavy clothing. Dark-skinned people (p. 449) will be at greater risk. There is evidence that rickets made its appearance amongst children of Indian immigrants in the UK in the early 1970s.

## Distribution of nutritional diseases

The world distribution of nutritional deficiency diseases (Fig. 26.1) has been mapped by the American Geographical Society. The close relationship of pro-tein and vitamin deficiency, and the resulting diseases, to the areas poor in cattle, sheep, and pig production and in fishing is obvious. These also are the areas of high carbohydrate intake. (Maps of the American Geographical Society are available to illustrate the world distribution of carbohydrates, protein, and other foodstuffs.) In a survey of 21 countries carried out between 1955 and 1962, the chief nutritional problems were found to be protein malnutrition or kwashiokor, calorie under-nutrition and marasmus, iodine deficiency, nutritional anaemias, avitaminosis A, thiamine deficiency (beri-beri), aribofla-vinosis, vitamin-C deficiency, and niacin deficiency (pellagra).

## The dietary and its adequacy in different types of habitat

The great variety of human ecosystems is matched by a corresponding diversity of food sources. The nutritional situation can only be ascertained by close analysis of each community. Nevertheless, a number of general statements about types of dietary can be made. In nutritional terms an important dis-tinction can usefully be drawn between 3 groups: hunting (including fishing) and pastoral societies; peasant cultivators, where cereal grain is the staple crop; communities subsisting on mixed crop and animal husbandry. The composi-tion of the diet in these 3 groups may be categorized roughly. The first may be termed the 'high-protein' dietary group, the second the 'low-protein-high-

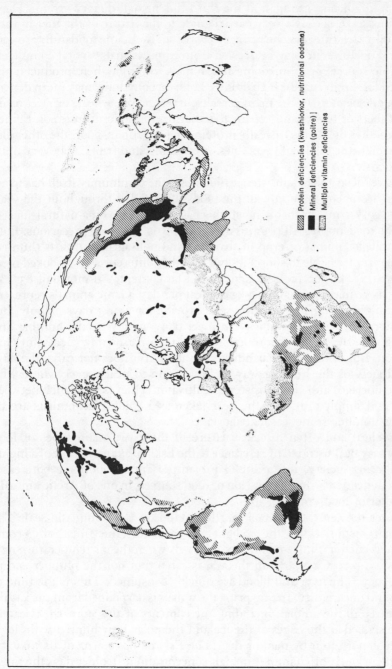

Fig. 26.1. World distribution of nutritional deficiency diseases. (From the American Geographical Society, *Atlas of diseases*, Plate 9.)

Protein deficiencies (kwashiorkor, nutritional oedema)

Mineral deficiencies (goitre)]

Multiple vitamin deficiencies

carbohydrate' dietary group, and the third the 'mixed' dietary group. These distinctions serve as only a very partial guide to the nature of the diet in each case. Within each category the primary sources of the staple foodstuffs are very variable. 'High protein' may be derived from game animals—not a completely dependable source, or from domestic animals, or from their products; the associated fat supply may be high or low. 'High carbohydrate' may mean dependence on one or more of the main cereal sources, maize, wheat, or rice, or on starchy tubers or tubers and cereals together or, in modern times, on refined sugar. Whether the diet is basically protein-rich or protein-poor, the other elements, namely the intake of vegetables, greenstuffs, and fruits, may vary quite independently.

Primitive dietaries are subsistence dietaries—the community itself has to act on the environment to supply all the foodstuffs needed throughout the year. In many ecosystems, probably most, there is dependence on a natural succession in the foodsupply. All primitive foodsupply is therefore precarious. Both agriculturalists (animal or crop husbandry) and non-agriculturalists (hunters and gatherers) are liable to shortages but in rather different ways. Cooked meat yields 850–1250 kJ per 100 g, depending on fat content. An intake of 8371 kJ per half day requires then about 1 kg of meat per day. Game animals represent food in a highly compact form and may provide for 2 or 3 days' supply, but hardly more, for several families. To meet daily energy needs, hunting and gathering dietaries are therefore less reliable than reasonably successful crop cultivation. But primitive husbandry, even though it does not carry the day-to-day anxiety of the hunting way of life, is cursed nearly everywhere with seasonal shortages and the subsistence cultivator achieves a balance between demand and supply only over the year taken as a whole. Pastoralists are by no means immune from seasonal shortages.

The cyclical and often insecure nature of these two main types of food economy may be illustrated by reference to the Eskimo as an example of a highly skilled hunting society, and to the Gambian peasant economy. In both cases there is a dependence on a succession of food sources, in one of Arctic animals, in the other of food crops.

In winter the central Eskimos (north of Hudson Bay) hunt the seal. The hunter waits on the ice-floe, the daylight hours are short, thick mists often come down, succeeded not infrequently by blizzards when the air temperature may be as low as $-35\,°C$. Nearly all the seal is eaten, but not the blubber except in emergency. The liver and blood are quickly consumed. This is the time of shortage and uncertainty. In the spring the walrus is harpooned from the kayak; again, nearly all the animal, including the contents of the stomach, is eaten. Seals are stalked at the edges of the ice and the polar bear hunted with dogs. The liver is not eaten by man or dog. The Eskimo has learnt of its toxicity, the result curiously of vitamin A in high concentration. In older days the musk ox was yet another food animal. There is in this season an abundance of food and large amounts of blubber are stored in pits. In summer the vegetation sprouts and inland the caribou are ambushed on their annual migration. The caribou live on mosses and lichens and the sour, fermented contents of the caribou paunch are eaten. Other land animals are hunted—wolves, hares, ducks, and geese—and there is also fishing for salmon. At this season the Eskimo ceases to be a strict carnivore, berries (cranberry, blueberry) and various roots, and young leaves of the dwarf willow, are included in the diet.

The outcome of this diet is shown in Table 26.3.

The striking features of this hunters' diet are the high protein and fat and low-carbohydrate content; the supply of iron, vitamin A, D, B complex, and C at more than adequate levels, and the vitamin D is also sufficient especially if allowance is made for bones eaten. It is obvious, however, that on this dietary large quantities of meat must be eaten daily or at a single sitting. Sinclair quotes figures testifying to the extraordinary ability of Eskimo and Yakuts to consume 10 kg, or even more, at a single meal. When the food supply becomes difficult to maintain in winter, when fog may prevent hunting, there may be starvation; when the game can be caught regularly an all-round adequate diet can be provided.

The Eskimo does not suffer from rickets, scurvy, or other vitamin deficiencies, and protein-deficiency diseases are absolutely unknown. Iodine deficiency has been reported and a few goitrogenic areas have been described.

## Foods of early man

The carnivorous diet of the Eskimo, while exceptional perhaps in the small use of vegetable food, illustrates the essentials of hunting dietaries, including that of Palaeolithic and Mesolithic man, except in one particular. Cannibalism is believed to have been practised by *H. erectus* in China, by Neanderthal, and by some late Palaeolithic groups of *H. sapiens*. It is not unknown amongst contemporary or recent food-gatherers and simple hunters and horticulturalists (see p. 421).

In general, it is true to say that the dietary of the successful hunter, utilizing all the resources of the environment available to him, will result in a satisfactory nutritional intake so long as the gross calorie supply can also be maintained. That this state of affairs must have obtained in pre-agricultural economies of prehistory seems very likely.

Peking man, it can be inferred, had available and ate (judging from broken and burnt bones) now-extinct species of bison, horse, rhinoceros, flat-antlered deer, brown bear, big-horned sheep, mammoth, camel, ostrich, antelope, water buffalo, wild boar, hyena, and others. Most of these are known with certainty to have been successfully hunted by other hunting communities, both extinct and recent. The charred fragments at Chou-ku-tien include as well remains of fox, large cats, macaques, and baboon. The ashes of the firewood reveal the existence at that time of *Celtis sinensis*—a dwarf species of hackberry—now growing 10 m high, and of *C. occidentalis* bearing fruit about 2 cm long of which

## TABLE 26.3

### Nutritional value of the adult Eskimo daily diet in 1855

| Foodstuff | Weight of edible portion (g) | Energy intake (kJ) | Total protein (g) | Animal protein (g) | Carbohydrate (g) | Fat (g) | Iron (mg) | Calcium (mg) | Phosphorus (mg) | Vitamin A (i.u.) | Carotenoids (µg) | Vitamin D (i.u.) | Thiamine (mg) | Nicotinic acid (mg) | Riboflavin (mg) | Ascorbic acid (mg) |
|---|---|---|---|---|---|---|---|---|---|---|---|---|---|---|---|---|
| Sea flesh | 860 | 7 100 | 163 | 163 | 26 | 103 | 23·2 | 95 | 1 686 | 7 740 | 0 | 0 | 0·95 | 42·1 | 1·2 | 69 |
| Other flesh | 225 | 1 855 | 43 | 43 | 7 | 27 | 6·1 | 25 | 441 | 2 025 | 0 | 0 | 0·25 | 11·0 | 0·32 | 18 |
| Capelin (salmon) | 620 | 2 710 | 105 | 105 | 0 | 19 | 6·2 | 155 | 1 500 | 508 | 0 | 6 144 | 1·30 | 4·61 | 0·87 | 56 |
| Other fish | 370 | 1 862 | 61 | 61 | 0 | 11 | 3·3 | 67 | 699 | 56 | 0 | 0 | 0·15 | 8·5 | 0·18 | 7 |
| Eggs | 5 | 34 | 1 | 1 | 0 | 1 | 0·1 | 3 | 10 | 35 | 30 | 3 | 0·01 | 0 | 0·02 | 0 |
| Berries | 50 | 60 | 0 | 0 | 3 | 0 | 0·6 | 30 | 22 | 0 | 27 | 0 | 0·02 | 0·2 | 0·02 | 45 |
| Bread | 27 | 269 | 2 | 0 | 13 | 0 | 0·3 | 6 | 20 | 0 | 0 | 0 | 0·02 | 0·2 | 0·01 | 0 |
| Barley and peas | 6 | 60 | 0 | 0 | 2 | 0 | 0·4 | 11 | 19 | 0 | 0 | 0 | 0·03 | 0·1 | 0·02 | 0 |
| Sugar | 6 | 100 | 0 | 0 | 6 | 0 | 0 | 0 | 0 | 0 | 0 | 0 | 0 | 0 | 0 | 0 |
| Coffee | 6·5 | 80 | 1 | 0 | 2 | 1 | 0·3 | 9 | 10 | 0 | 0 | 0 | 0·06 | 0·6 | 0 | 0 |
| Total | — | 14 130 | 377 | 373 | 59 | 162 | 40·5 | 401 | 4 407 | 10 364 | 57 | 6 147 | 2·78 | 108·8 | 2·64 | 195 |
| Oxford Nutrition Survey Standard | — | 12 600 | 72 | 36 | 432 | 102 | 10 | 750 | 1 000 | 833 | 3 000 | 200 | 1·2 | 12 | 1·8 | 30 |
| Proportion of standard met (per cent) | — | 112 | 524 | 1 036 | 14 | 159 | 405 | 54 | 441 | 1 244 | 2 | 3 074 | 232 | 907 | 147 | 650 |

(After Sinclair 1953.)

the juice is sweet (sucrose and hexoses) and a very good source of vitamin C. *Pithecanthropus pekinensis* is said to have eaten a pea-sized variety.

With Neanderthal man at Krapina, evidence of fire is again present, and of bone-breaking for marrow. Likely food-animals include horse, pig, otter, bear, and rhinoceros. It seems generally accepted that at Krapina, as at Peking, cannibalism was practised. At Gibraltar many of the now extinct great auk birds were caught and large amounts of mussels and limpets were consumed. That Neanderthal man could exploit the varied resources of the habitat seems obvious enough and makes one doubt whether his extinction, considering his fairly wide geographical range, and the food sources available, could be attributable to nutritional causes, e.g. vitamin-D deficiency has been suggested.

The hunting activities of men of the Aurignacian culture are known both from their material remains and the cave art. The Gravettians left vast heaps of bones of mammoth and rhinoceros, showing that they had evolved effective hunting methods. At Soutre there are the remains of an enormous number of horses; at Vistonice and Predmost heaps of mammoth bones were found, mostly of young animals which were killed by stampeding them over a cliff; mammoth thigh bones were broken for the marrow. In the Capsian (North African blade and burin tool culture) the food-animals were large-horn buffalo, elephant, rhinoceros, and zebra, which were eaten along with ostrich eggs and land snails. The spears and harpoons of the Magdalenian culture provide evidence of extensive hunting of reindeer and of fishing. The intensity of exploitation of ecological niches in the transition from collecting to agriculture is well illustrated in Mesoamerica.

## A peasant society—Gambia

Let us turn to cultivators, taking as example a Gambian peasant community. The succession of crops recorded by frequency of use is shown in Fig. 26.2. The cereals (findi, maize, rice, bulrush millet, and sorghum) succeed each other as staples through the year. Findi, an early crop with grain the size of grass seed, is eaten soon after harvesting in July. Rice, the most popular staple, is eaten alone as long as the stocks last. When the rice is exhausted, some time in April, millet and sorghum form the staple. In the preparation of these cereals the chaff and much of the bran are removed by pounding in a mortar. Rice is eaten whole, but the other cereals are reduced to flour, the extraction rate of which varies from 70 per cent to 85 per cent. Eggs and milk are very uncommon. The dietary thus consists predominantly of carbohydrate with small amounts of meat and dried fish, and with groundnuts, beans, and various green leaves and fruits in season.

The outcome in nutritional terms is shown in Table 26.4 and this is compared with dietaries of other peasant communities and of the UK. The contrast between the Gambian diet and that of the Eskimo (Table 26.3) is obvious. Protein deficiency is the most serious consequence and kwashiorkor and liver cirrhosis are frequently found. The nitrogen balance is at a very low level, the

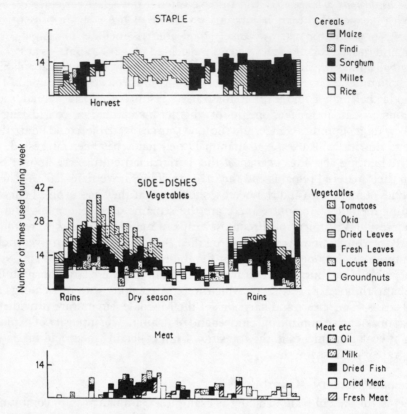

FIG. 26.2. Frequency of use of different foods in an African peasant economy. Each column represents one week and its height shows the number of times that kind of food was used during that week. (Chart supplied by M. W. Grant, M.R.C. Applied Nutrition Unit, London School of Hygiene.)

total urinary loss being about half that of American children. The liability of maize-eating populations to vitamin-B deficiencies, to cheilosis and pellagra, and of rice-eating populations to beri-beri, cheilosis, and stomatitis is well known. Iron and calcium are also often deficient, but on the whole calcification of teeth and bones is surprisingly good, probably because of the more efficient absorption of the available calcium. The weakness of the dietary is clearly revealed at and after weaning. Before then, and despite the poor diet of the mother, the milk remains adequate and its protein content unaffected, but prolongation of breast-feeding for 3 or 4 years brings about a progressive quantitative inadequacy. This is not necessarily rectified at weaning, for the diet now will consist almost entirely of carbohydrate gruels and pastes. On this almost exclusively carbohydrate food the infant continues to suffer a chronic lack of protein.

## TABLE 26.4

### Nutrient contents of dietaries

| | Values recommended as an immediate objective for populations of developing territories | Nutrients available per head per day | | | Nyasaland survey, 1938-9 | | | |
| --- | --- | --- | --- | --- | --- | --- | --- | --- |
| | | UK 1944 | Barbados 1944 | Gambian village 1945 | Hill village | Foothill village | Lake-shore village | Urban area |
| | i | ii | iii | iv | v | vi | vii | viii |
| Energy (kJ) | 10 500 | 12 250 | 10 100 | 8 518 | 7 580 | 8 610 | 7 300 | 6 950 |
| Protein (g) | 60 | 87 | 45 | 56 | 50 | 59 | 26 | 54 |
| Fat (g) | — | 117 | 63 | 25 | 15 | 16 | 9 | 11 |
| Carbohydrate (g) | — | 381 | 416 | 396 | 357 | 400 | 387 | 334 |
| Alcohol (mg) | — | — | — | — | 2·5 | 8·6 | 1·4 | 0·8 |
| Calcium (mg) | 800 | 1037 | 254 | 219 | 280 | 476 | 1065 | 702 |
| Iron (mg) | 20 | 16 | 12 | 26 | 25 | 34 | 21 | 24 |
| Vitamin A (i.u.) (as $\beta$-carotene) | 5 000 | 3773 | 5 215 | 3 536 | 7 757 | 10 220 | 6 020 | 6 914 |
| Vitamin B$_1$ (aneurin, thiamine) (mg) | 1·6 | 2·0 | 0·8 | 1·8 | 0·8 | 1·2 | 0·7 | 0·8 |
| Riboflavin (mg) | 1·8 | 2·1 | 0·8 | 0·5 | 0·5 | 0·7 | 0·5 | 0·6 |
| Nicotinic acid (mg) | 12 | 19·7 | 7·0 | 14·5 | 9·0 | 11·5 | 9·6 | 7·0 |
| Vitamin C (ascorbic acid) (mg) | 30 | 123 | 69 | 28 | 86 | 98 | 120 | 73 |

(After Platt, Trans. Roy. Soc. trop. Med. Hyg., 40, 379, 1947.)

The dietary difficulties of the primitive cultivator, as already mentioned, become especially evident during the 'hungry season' when adults lose weight, children's growth slows down, and clinical signs of malnutrition become apparent. The balance between calories expended and the calories available has been quantitatively analysed for the Gambian economy by Fox and is summarized in the diagram (Fig. 26.3).

From about March until May, the villagers had little or no work to do. . . . Body weight remained stationary. Energy intake at a relatively low level was balanced by available energy supply. . . . In May the farmers began to clear the land in preparation for the start of the rains and energy expenditure began to rise. In June the heavy

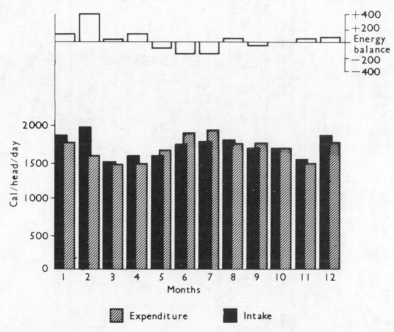

FIG. 26.3. Schematic representation of energy intake, available energy, and energy expenditure for the villagers during one year. To convert energy in Calories to kilojoules multiply by 4.2. (Adapted from Fox, R. H., A London University Ph.D. thesis, 1953, by Dr T. P. Eddy, London School of Hygiene and Tropical Medicine.)

work started in earnest and both energy intake and expenditure increased. At this time owing to food shortage, expenditure exceeded intake and body tissue was drawn on (per kg of weight lost represents about 20 927 kJ calories). In September and October the energy expended on crop production was less but energy intake had also declined and was still in short supply. The fall in body weight continued. In November the energy expended was near its lowest level, little work was done. With food supplies beginning to improve, intake of energy began to exceed energy expenditure. Body weights stopped falling and began to rise, a rise which continued throughout December, January and February as work on the crops came to an end at a time when abundant food from the newly harvested crops was available.

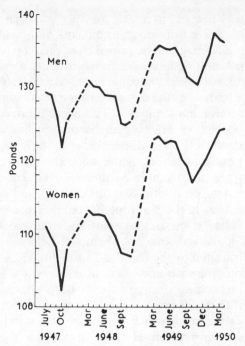

F IG. 26.4. Body-weight changes in the course of the agricultural cycle. (From Fox, R. H., *A study of energy expenditure of Africans engaged in various rural activities*, London University Ph.D. thesis, 1953.)

Notice that in the period between early July and late October, a period of some 6 months, the energy deficit had to be made up by using tissue stores (Fig. 26.4). Only by utilizing this store does the community achieve an overall equilibrium between food energy demand and supply.

The primitive herdsman is also liable to be afflicted by seasonal shortage. In the Sudan (e.g. the Butana) the short wet season is followed by a long dry one during which grazing and cultivation both become difficult if not impossible. There is, therefore, a seasonal deficiency of animal protein, riboflavin, and vitamins A and C. Soon after the beginning of the rains, milk and green food become plentiful, and somewhat later there is a sufficiency of grain since many of the herdsmen grow an annual crop.

The strength and weaknesses of the dietaries made available by different forms of ecosystem are manifest. The vulnerability of the hunting diet lies not in its composition so much as simply in quantity resulting from its precariousness of supply. A severe failure may mean an all-round failure in both food energy and aliments. By contrast the cultivators' diet is more secure as regards overall energy supply. But the seasonal shortage and the high dependence on carbohydrate make the dietary qualitatively often inadequate. Improvement may ensue from the guaranteed water-supply of irrigation schemes, but the dependence on a very few staple cereals may become even more pronounced with consequent ill-effects from protein, mineral, and vitamin deficiency.

There are clearly advantages to be gained from mixed types of farming, and it seems that much Neolithic farming approximated to a mixed economy and was nutritionally of reasonable adequacy. In central Europe the so-called 'Danubian' culture represents the earliest farming population at a date around 4000 B.C. It lasted several thousand years. The agricultural technique was based on some kind of wooden hoe. The crop husbandry was based on several crops: barley, one-grained wheat (Einkorn), emmer, or in some regions bread wheat, as well as beans, peas, and lentils. Some stock animals were kept, but on a small scale—sheep, pigs, and oxen. In Neolithic A of Greece, the peasants culti-vated barley, wheat, figs, pears, and kept cattle, sheep, and goats. Hunting still went on, e.g. of red deer. In the Neolithic Fayum they grew wheat and barley, killed game, fished, had domesticated animals, cattle, and sheep for meat.

The advantages of a mixed economy, characteristic of much Neolithic farm-ing, is strikingly illustrated by the way the Yaruro Indians of the south central Venezuela plains combine slash-and-burn cultivation with food-gathering, pig-herding, hunting, and fishing, changing their food-producing activities to con-form to the season. In the dry season there is a marked increase of gathering, particularly of roots and seeds which appear to store starches, whereas fruits appear mainly in the rainy season. Hunting increases in the dry season when animals are more highly concentrated in and near the rivers and streams. Fish-ing also increases in the dry season as the waters become shallower and less grass choked and clearer of mud. The dry season precludes growing some crops, such as pineapples and millet, and reduces the output of sugar cane and cova.

A mixed economy was probably more usual in regions not artificially irrigated before iron tools made possible an almost complete dependence on the intensive cultivation of a few crops.

## Physical and racial differences in relation to nutrition

Anthropologists have often been ready to ascribe differences of physique and bodily dimensions, as well as of cranial or facial size and form to long-standing racial or genetic factors, when environmental and, in particular, nutritional effects might well explain such differences. Twin studies (p. 142) reveal the extent to which differences in height or in weight, and therefore changes corre-lated with these, may arise from non-genetic causes. Studies of the effects of migration (p. 145) point in the same direction, as do comparisons between raci-ally similar groups under dissimilar environmental conditions. The effects of economic status and particularly of nutrition on growth have been fully dealt with in Chapter 21.

For the most part it is only by inference that diet can be established as the probable cause of physical differences. When the bodily size of one group is found to be larger than that of another group of similar genetic constitution living in the same general locality and the diet of the former is superior, there can be little doubt dietetic factors are involved. In comparisons of the physique or growth of peoples of different races nutritional factors may well prove more important than genetic differences.

Hiernaux provides a well-analysed example. Two genetically similar groups of the Hutu people of Ruanda subsisting on very different diets exhibited a marked contrast in their mean bodily measurements. These turned out to be those which twin studies have shown to be environmentally sensitive. Bodily dimensions with a strong heritable component showed correspondingly less difference between the two groups.

In India the greater stature, stronger constitution, and superior physical resistance of the Sikhs of northern India, as compared to the Madrassi of the south, seem directly related to the high protein of the Sikh diet derived from meat, milk, and milk derivatives as compared to the vegetarian diet of the Madrassi. McCarrison fed rats on these two types of diet; those on the Sikh diet weighed an average of 255 g compared to 155 g on the other. Of the two genetically similar populations of Hutu in Ruanda, studied by Hiernaux, those living in the more fertile and healthier regions were on average 7 kg heavier and had greater thigh- and chest-measurements.

In the studies of Boyd Orr and Gilks in East Africa, on the Kikuyu and the Masai tribes of Kenya, we are faced with the operation probably of both genetic and nutritional factors. The Kikuyu are farmers, living on a diet of cereals, tubers, and legumes; the Masai, on the other hand, are cattle-raisers, whose diet includes meat, milk, and ox-blood which they take from the animals. These two human groups, living side by side in the same natural environment and the same climate, differed markedly in their physical measurements. The Masai men were 7·5 cm taller and 10·25 kg heavier than their Kikuyu counterparts. This difference in Boyd Orr and Gilks's opinion is a direct result of their fundamentally different diets. The Masai, through an abundant use of food of animal origin, enjoy a diet balanced in proteins, while the Kikuyu live under conditions of permanent protein hunger.

De Castro observed something similar in the north-east of Brazil. In the littoral regions and in the dry backland area far from the coast, a tall type predominates, while throughout the intervening jungle zone a short type predominates and average height is lower there than it is in the other two areas. Along the coast the diet is high in proteins because the inhabitants live by fishing. In the backland also the protein intake is high, since it is a cattle-raising region with abundant production and consumption of meat, milk, and cheese. But in the jungle zone, where sugar-cane monoculture established itself and drove out all other food-producing activities, the diet is very poor, being based on cassava or manioc flour, the protein content of which is extremely low. These dietary differences, particularly of protein, would explain the differences in body-size between three human groups living within a fairly restricted geographical area.

From detailed nutritional surveys Nicholls concluded that the differences in weight and height of Sri Lankan communities were not dependent on race but on economic and social status. The boys of the upper classes, for instance, were 12·5 cm taller and weighed 9 kg more than those of the lower classes, at the age of 15. Indeed, the two social classes are farther apart than were the Masai and the Kikuyu. The rate of growth in all classes of boys increased rapidly between the ages of 5 and 8 years, more markedly in the boys of high social status; the poorer boys lost ground especially between 11 and 14 years and thereafter some compensation occurred in adolescence.

From Puerto Rico comes another example. Here Thieme has shown that Negroes of a better economic class are taller not only than their poorer fellow Africans but also than poorer Europeans.

While improved nutrition must be held responsible for relatively large effects on body-size, many characters of physique and body proportion remain unaffected. This is true, for example, of Negro limb proportions. Japanese children grow much more on Californian diets but still retain the sitting-height: stature ratio characteristic of native-born Japanese.

To explain with some precision the differences in body-size existing over a smaller or larger area in terms of genetic and environmental factors is not at all easy. Partly this is because these factors interact, partly because of the complexity of the genetic determination of stature and other dimensions, and partly because climatic or disease factors may in some cases be more important than nutritional. (Further discussion of this topic will be found in Part IV of this book.)

## Social aspects of nutrition

The main emphasis so far has been on the biology of nutrition. But the obtaining of food is a social process. It involves in the first place parental responsibilities even in the simplest conceivable society, since the young are for many years quite dependent. Audrey Richards writes that 'as a biological process nutrition determines more widely than any other function the nature of social groupings and the forms their activity takes.' Whether social anthropologists generally would support Richards's view cannot be examined here, but there can be no doubt that many aspects of the sociology of nutrition have an immediate biological significance. Of these, consideration should be given to:

(1) the community's knowledge of the habitat;
(2) the community's knowledge of food values as evidenced in preparation, storage, and distribution;
(3) the limitations, social and technological, on satisfying food requirements.

Close examination shows that most primitive communities possess a detailed knowledge of the food resources of their habitat and a lively awareness of what is inedible or poisonous. Australian Aborigines are ecologically expert. They have names for each type of botanical association and for every tree or plant. They can describe the food harvest at each season of the year. The knowledge of game by hunters is seen in the mimicry indulged in, for instance, by Bushmen in dances or as depicted in cave paintings. Honey-hunting is portrayed in the Palaeolithic caves of Arana (Spain). The dietary of many primitive groups contains many items entirely strange, if not repulsive, to the urbanized observer. What might otherwise be thought of as a diet devoid of, say, fat or protein or essential nutrients, turns out to be nutritionally rather better when account is taken of these items: e.g. the Bushmen dietary includes grubs, caterpillars, frogs, snakes, lizards, locusts, ants, and termites.

Bodenheimer cites many other examples drawn from all types of ecosystem. He shows that insects particularly constitute an important item. In Australia moths, beetles, and ants play as important a part in nutrition as in totemism. In Africa the swarms of tiny gnats over Lake Tanganyika are collected off the ground, a flour is made from them and used for cake-making. Termites offer certain peoples, e.g. in West Africa, substantial important sources of protein, fat, and calories.

Some 400 species of poisonous plants are recognized. A striking example of the knowledge possessed by pre-literate people of undesirable and poisonous substances is afforded by the detoxication by Amazon Indians of manioc tubers of their hydrogen cyanide content. This is done by soaking the sliced tubers and allowing them to ferment so that the cyanide is converted to harmless substances. The pulp is eventually dried and powdered.

In addition to the use of 'strange' foods, many practices in the preparation of food for consumption turn out on closer examination to be of real value in enhancing or preserving the nutritional value. In Africa, leaves of the baobab tree are dried in the shade and not in the sun, before being crushed to make soup. This treatment avoids loss of vitamins. Many fermented foods, e.g. Kaffir beer or pulque (Mexico), have high antiscorbutic and mineral value. In the preparation of tortilla, or 'daily bread', of Mexico the maize is soaked in a 1 per cent lime suspension. The calcium content is increased some 20-fold compared with that of the original maize. In Asia the soybean has its nutritive value increased by germination (bean sprouts) and fermentation (soy sauce). Cookery has as one of its effects the destruction of various micro-organisms and so greatly extends the available foodsupply. Use of glazed and washable pots must also have had a beneficial effect.

In contrast to such sound nutritional practices there are traditional beliefs about particular foods which may adversely affect the diet. For example, in some countries fresh cows' milk and fish are regarded as unsuitable for young people. In some rice-eating countries the reverence for rice as absolutely essential for full health is so great that it is introduced in the diet of the infant within a few days of birth, so producing digestive upset. Many examples of such beliefs and taboos could be given. Clan taboos on particular fooods are widespread amongst tribal peoples.

Here we must make a reference to cannibalism. One makes a distinction between the cases in which the object is that of making a meal and that in which it is purely ceremonial, when only a small portion of the body is eaten. The total number of recorded cases of cannibalism is in fact small in comparison with the numbers of peoples on whose dealings in war-like matters we have information. Of 70 instances of real cannibalism 20 per cent occur among hunters (mostly in the Australasian group) and 50 per cent in the simpler agriculturalists. It is almost unknown among pastoral peoples. Human sacrifice is likewise almost confined to agricultural peoples. It has been argued (Garn and Block) that a 'moderate' degree of cannibalism could have provided a critically important quantity of protein for some precariously nourished New Guinea tribes. An admitted cannibal group like the New Guinean Miyanmins of the Sepik headwaters, numbering about 100 people and liable to protein shortage, could have obtained 10 per cent of their protein requirement by consuming the equivalent of 15 60-kg adults per year! In the last Miyanmin raid against the Atbalmin people in 1956, 16 people, of whom 11 were adults, were butchered and eaten. It would be going beyond the available evidence to suggest that cannibalism anywhere provided a sizeable or continuous source of protein.

Weaning methods have many repercussions on the health, survival, and, indeed, differential selection within the population. Infants of western civilization pass by degree from a regime of breast milk to a mixed diet using carefully prepared items, amongst which cows' milk is prominent. The western practice ensures as safe a transition as can be devised. In pre-literate communities suckling and weaning are surrounded by all kinds of ritual and magical ideas and the treatment of the infant at this critical time affords a striking contrast with European practice. The African infant often passes abruptly to a diet composed of the ordinary foods of the family. In some cases the change is not quite so sudden. From a very early period, the child may be given 'adult' food in small and softened portions, e.g. porridge among the Tallensi, or sour milk and a pap of Kaffir corn by the Xhosa, or pre-masticated food and vegetable gruels in Alor.

The widespread practice of prolonged breast-feeding means that the growing infant cannot obtain the requisite protein because his needs increase and the breast milk falls in volume, even though the composition of the milk may remain fairly constant. 'After a grossly inadequate intake of breast milk over many months', one author writes, of north-east Africa, 'the infant is marasmic and anaemic and ready to succumb to the diarrhoea set up by unsuitable foods at weaning.' The transition to a predominantly carbohydrate diet, often of staples such as cassava or millet, with low protein value, is a potent cause of the serious condition of kwashiorkor. The weaned infant may be left to the inadequate care of an elder brother or sister while the mother joins the rest of the tribe in cultivating the land. The preparation of porridge entails hours of grinding if fine flour is to be produced; the mother may often be too tired or unwilling to spend the necessary time, so that the infants are fed on an incomplete and gritty flour—a potent cause of diarrhoea.

Inefficiency or mismanagement of productive resources is a pervasive reason for inadequate dietary. In some African areas cattle are mainly a sign of wealth and family possessions and attention is given to them more as producers of milk than of meat. Many peasant communities suffer large wastage of food after harvest through faulty storage or because of complete lack of storage facilities. Loss due to rats, insects, and fungi may amount to as much as one-third of the cereals and pulses harvested.

In the agricultural cycle various factors act as brakes on production. The Gambian economy already described serves as an illustration of the fixity of the ecological balance and of the difficulties in the way of a decisive shift to higher productivity, with less hard work and a surplus. The rain falls between June and October and is very uneven. The crops must be planted quickly after the rains begin and before the soil gets baked and dry and early enough to mature before the rains end. On days when rainfall is particularly heavy no agricultural work is possible. Thus the rainfall limits the number of days available within that season. A further loss of days is occasioned by religious beliefs against working on certain days. The male farmer in June and July works as hard as possible—the total energy expenditure per day reaches 14 230 kJ or more and so reaches a maximum of energy output. But this is the period of food shortage and the population suffers loss of body-weight and this in turn hastens the onset of fatigue. There is yet another adverse factor; in July the combined effect of solar and soil radiation, of air temperature, and humidity yielding mean corrected effective temperatures (see Chapter 27) of 27°C, places further limitation on the work of ridging, hoeing, and planting. These same handicaps attend attempts to cultivate a larger area; even the extra work entailed in walking to and from still more distant lands would materially increase energy cost and, at the same time, reduce working time.

The actual nutritional intake in seemingly simple societies may not be at all easy to assess. The most suitable method is by direct survey of family consumption. The catering arrangements may be quite complex and individuals may shift around to different huts for different meals. These may be determined by kinship duties and reciprocal hospitality; Zulu men traditionally ate first, then the women, and finally the children; the warriors would thus maintain their strength by ensuring their needs and getting the best food. To allow for variations in intake, the survey must sample a complete cycle of days of activity and rest; this is not necessarily a 7-day period—it may often be 10 days. Seasonal variation is large and must be allowed for. Moreover, festivities and ceremonies may be very important dietetically, as providing the occasion for the intake of extra amounts of high-protein and vitamin foods.

# 27. Climatic adaptation

EVERY habitat imposes a particular climatic regime on man, his domestic animals, and crops. These regimes vary widely, and it is only because man can make appropriate adjustments that he has come to occupy habitats more diverse than those of any other mammalian species (except perhaps the rat). Like all living organisms, the human body is sensitive to many of the elements that go to make up the climate of a place. This sensitivity and responsiveness arise from the need to maintain homeostasis. Under conditions of extreme heat or cold the heat regulatory system acts to maintain the body temperature steady within relatively narrow limits (homeothermy). For life at high altitudes it is the respiratory system which keeps the pressure of oxygen and carbon dioxide of the body-fluids adjusted within stable limits. In addition to the stresses imposed by thermal factors and by the low barometric pressure of high altitudes, other environmental hazards are provided by excess of short-wave radiation (ultraviolet light and ionizing radiation).

## The thermal environment

Climate and weather are terms used to denote the state of the atmosphere. The climate is the seasonal average of the weather conditions experienced in a locality. A full description of the atmospheric properties making up the weather and the climate and recorded at regular intervals over a period of time would include the air temperature, humidity, speed and direction of the wind, amount and type of cloud, hours of sunshine and total radiant heat received, rainfall, snow, dust, and other special features. The climate enveloping man is really made up of a series of climatic 'shells'—the microclimate of clothing, of domestic and working enclosures, and the geographical macroclimate. The climatic factors of primary physiological significance are those which exert a direct influence on the rate of heat exchange between the body surface (nude or clothed) and the surroundings. If any thermal environment is to be completely specified account must be taken of the air temperature, the air humidity, the wind speed, and the mean radiant temperature of the surroundings. Indoors these surroundings are the walls, fires, and other surfaces which radiate towards the subject. Out of doors, radiation is received from the sun, the sky, and the terrain. Together all these thermal elements determine the rate of heat that the body can lose to the exterior. There are, of course, situations where environmental heat adds to the 'internal' bodily heat derived from general metabolism and muscular activity.

To the extent to which homeothermy tends to be disturbed so there are effects on the body's efficiency. The adaptive relations which the human body enters into with the thermal environment are again (cf. Chapter 26) of three sorts:

1. Physiological adjustments in the heat regulatory, metabolic, and circulatory systems make it possible to work and survive in a wide variety of environments. The ability to make these adjustments is a highly developed property of the human species as a whole. They are both short- and long-term.

2. There are a number of somewhat specialized physiological and anatomical adaptive responses based on particular genotypes.

3. Cultural and social adjustments are involved in the provision of shelter, clothing, warmth, and ventilation. These cultural responses to biological needs are, like nutritional requirements, 'institutionalized' in Malinowski's sense, but have not been so clearly analysed. The effectiveness of these cultural responses can be judged by biological criteria.

The efficient adaptation of the human body to climatic change is necessary for (a) the attainment of bodily comfort, (b) the performance of physical work without undue fatigue, (c) the performance of skilled work calling for alertness and dexterity with a minimum of errors, and (d) the attainment of normal growth and development.

As a measure of the human capacity to endure climatic stress consider the extreme conditions of human occupancy. At the village of Verkhoyansk in eastern Siberia almost on the Polar circle, where some of the coldest temperatures ever have been recorded, the coldest month, January, has a mean which is $35°C$ below the mean for the year ($-18°C$). At the oasis of Insalah in the Algerian Sahara, the hottest month, July, ($38°C$) is some $12°C$ above the annual mean. Human communities are found successfully surviving summer extremes as great as $55°C$ ($-17$ to $38°C$) and as much in the winter season, $-16°C$ up to $+28°C$.

By contrast the deep body temperature fluctuates within a range of relatively small amplitude compared to the extremes of high and low environmental temperatures to which the body may be subject. The body temperature has a diurnal range of about $2°C$ and is highest in the early evening and lowest at about 4 a.m. In tropical countries the cycle is shifted upwards by about $0·2°C$. This shift takes place irrespective of race; Europeans (in India or Singapore) have body temperatures of the same values as indigenous peoples. In men habituated to Antarctic cold the diurnal cycle is shifted about $0·2°C$ down from temperate values.

The body can tolerate no great departure beyond the excursions of the diurnal cycle, and the existence of this narrow band of fluctuation in the face of different conditions (daily, seasonal, and geographical) betokens a sensitive system of internal regulation. This is provided primarily by a 'thermostatic' mechanism in the brain (hypothalamus) which is sensitive to a rise or fall in body temperature when heat is added to, or removed from, the body in amounts which threaten the normal level. Within a certain range of heat and cold stress (e.g. air temperatures between 27 °C and 32 °C approximately) the internal (rectal) body temperature of the nude subject is maintained close to 37 °C without undue change in skin temperature (within the limits of 30·5 °C and 33 °C approximately), so that feelings of thermal comfort are not much disturbed; under greater degrees of stress some heating or cooling of the periphery with associated discomfort can be tolerated in the interests of a steady internal temperature and of physical and mental efficiency. The limits to which climatic adjustment can be made must be looked at in terms of these two biological desiderata—the maintenance of comfort and the overriding maintenance of heat balance.

The basic relation underlying homeothermy is simply

$$\text{heat gain}-\text{heat loss}=\pm\text{heat storage,}$$

or, more specifically, $M\pm C\pm R-E=\pm S$,

where $M$=rate of heat produced by metabolism and work, $C$=rate of heat gain or loss by convection, $R$=rate of heat gain or loss by radiation, $E$=rate of heat loss by evaporation of skin moisture, $S$=net heat exchange. $S$ can be kept relatively constant while the other variables change over a wide range. The changes in $S$ represent additions to, or losses from, the total heat content of the body so that the overall change in heat content is largely damped. In this lies the flexibility of response to extremes of heat and cold. When this equilibrium is threatened (i.e. when storage or withdrawal of heat becomes excessive) a number of immediate counter-adjustments are made; over and above these are long-term processes which make for further improvement and these are referred to as 'acclimatization'. These physiological responses have all been demonstrated in men of different races.

### Responses to heat

The immediate physiological response to overheating is a compensatory increase in heat dissipation from the body. This occurs firstly through the circulatory system and, secondarily, by sweating. The circulatory adjustment takes the form of an increased flow of blood through the skin, the increase being made possible by an opening up (vasodilatation) of the skin vessels and, when necessary, by an increase in heart output accompanied by an increased pulse rate. The increased amount of heat brought to the surface is dissipated to the surroundings by increased convection and radiation; the increased dissipation is a consequence of the rise in skin temperature. The rate of heat loss by convection per unit surface area is proportional to the gradient between skin and outside air temperature (and to the square-root of the speed of air movement). The rate of radiation per unit surface radiation area is proportional (approximately) to the difference between the mean skin temperature and the mean temperature of the surroundings. Human skin, irrespective of colour, acts as a complete 'black-body' radiator. If these processes cannot maintain heat balance, and body temperature rises, sweating begins. The rate of heat loss by evaporation of sweat depends on the difference between the vapour pressure at the skin surface and that of the air, on the extent of the wetted surface area, and on air movement. The rise in skin temperature means an increased vapour pressure at the skin surface. The loss by latent heat of vaporization can be increased greatly since the number of sweat glands stimulated and the output of fluid of each gland can be increased progressively. A maximum water loss of about 1 l per hour, equivalent to 2500 kJ heat loss per hour can be achieved.

Although the total number of sweat glands varies in different individuals, there is no evidence of any striking differences in this as between different racial groups, as Table 27.1 indicates:

TABLE 27.1

*Total number of glands of adult males*

(means in millions $\pm$ S.D.)

| | | | |
|---|---|---|---|
| Hindu | (6) | $1{\cdot}51\pm0{\cdot}19$ | (Knip) |
| Indian | (19) | $1{\cdot}69\pm0{\cdot}16$ | (Weiner) |
| Dutch | (9) | $1{\cdot}47\pm0{\cdot}29$ | (Knip) |
| British | (2) | $1{\cdot}66\pm0{\cdot}19$ | (Weiner) |
| European in West Africa | (21) | $1{\cdot}75$ | (Thomson) |
| West African | (26) | $1{\cdot}66$ | (Thomson) |
| Bush Negro Surinam | (8) | $1{\cdot}69\pm0{\cdot}14$ | (Knip) |

The methods used by Thomson are not quite comparable to those of the other investigators. The density of glands has been found to be fairly similar and to have a very similar distribution (Table 27.2) in all groups and in decreasing order in the upper limb—dorsum of hand, forearm, upper arm; in the lower limb—foot, leg, thigh; and over the trunk—abdomen and thorax.

TABLE 27.2

*Number of sweat glands per square centimetre (adult males)*

| | | Trunk | Hand | Forearm | Arm | Foot | Leg | Thigh |
|---|---|---|---|---|---|---|---|---|
| European | (29) | 69 | 206 | 98 | 85 | 132 | 87 | 59 |
| Dutch | (9) | 75 | 145 | 86 | 80 | 119 | 66 | 52 |
| Indian | (19) | 89 | 209 | 97 | 91 | 152 | 91 | 62 |
| Hindu | (6) | 87 | 170 | 121 | 93 | 119 | 81 | 60 |
| West African | (26) | 94 | 240 | 109 | 119 | 175 | 78 | 85 |

The flexibility of physiological response is clearly demonstrated by considering the way homeothermy is maintained in situations which impose a high heat load and which recur in a variety of habitats (Table 27.6) as, for example, (1) a hot, humid, and still-air condition, (2) a combination of hot, dry conditions with moderate air movement and high solar radiation, (3) a cool, dry condition with solar radiation, (4) hard work in moderate temperatures. (For a detailed analysis of these situations the student is referred to textbooks of human physiology and monographs given in the list.)

### Acclimatization to heat

On continued or repeated exposure to heat a striking improvement in adaptation to heat stress takes place. In particular there is a marked improvement in the ability to carry out work. In laboratory experiments the subjects were able to work for four hours on the fifth day of exposure, whereas they gave up after less than an hour on the first day. Accompanying this, the circulatory performance is much improved and the initially high pulse rate, and heart output, are substantially reduced. The heat regulatory system becomes much more efficient. The body temperature, which rises rapidly to high levels on the early exposures, rises more slowly or attains a 'plateau' with continued exposure to the heat. The skin temperature also rises less with acclimatization. All these changes of rapid acclimatization which are elicited under artificial conditions (hot and humid or hot and dry) can also be shown to occur as a result of life in hot climates, equatorial or desert. The main cause of this improvement is that the sweat glands become more sensitive to thermal stimulation, they respond faster, and their output increases. This means that the area from which evaporation takes place is 'wetted' much more rapidly and evenly and the amount of heat lost by evaporation is increased, as it has to be if the rise in body temperature and in heat storage are to be minimized.

The complex of changes that make up physiological acclimatization to heat has been demonstrated in peoples of different races living in hot climates—in Nigerians, among Chinese, Indians, and Malayans living in Malaya, among Kalahari Bushmen and South African Bantu, as well as in Europeans in the tropics or in hot deserts.

That people of different races should possess this acclimatizing ability is not surprising when we recall that the hominid genera evolved under equatorial conditions favouring the development of these properties. Physiological acclimatization enables man today to carry out his active form of life under a wide variety of hot conditions and makes it possible for one species *Homo sapiens* to occupy very different kinds of tropical and equatorial habitats. This is evident from the distribution of population in relation to habitat shown in Tables 25.3 and 25.5. Genetic selection of various bodily characters for life in diverse climates has been superimposed on this physiological plasticity.

### Responses to cooling

The immediate responses to cooling are directed to reducing the heat loss $(C+R)$ as well as to increasing the heat production $(M)$ and so maintaining homeothermy. At an air temperature of about 31 °C—the 'critical' temperature—a nude subject at rest must increase his metabolic rate to prevent a fall of deep body temperature. This level of critical temperature is characteristic of tropical animals generally. To combat heat loss the insulation value at the body surface can be increased. Reflex vasoconstriction greatly reduces the thermal conductance of the skin, but the maximum effect is rapidly reached so that below the critical temperature skin temperature falls continually as air temperature is lowered. To survive in the cold man must provide extra insulation and so reduce the critical temperature. The insulation provided by thick layers of subcutaneous fat or by fur, so highly efficient in Arctic animals, can be obtained by man by the use of animal skins or other clothing material. Added insulation of 1 clo (an insulation roughly equivalent to a 0·6 cm still-air layer) will extend the critical temperature down to 20 °C and 2 clo to 10 °C, but below this a progressive increase in metabolic heat is also required to withstand exposures of several hours. Eskimo clothing of caribou fur in a thickness of 3·75–7·5 cm has a value of 7–12 clo. This goes far to meet all requirements; when sleeping 10–12 clo is needed and 4 clo while active at −40 °C. Eskimo dwellings are kept at 21 °C during the day, 10 °C during the night. Eskimos spend roughly 1–4 hours per day outdoors in winter, 5–9 hours in summer. Only the face and occasionally the hands are exposed to chilling.

Differences in thickness of subcutaneous fat-layer are significant; the level to which skin temperatures fall on exposure to cold is highly correlated with skin-fold thickness and fatter subjects show longer endurance on immersion in cold water.

Heat production in the cold is increased involuntarily by shivering and voluntarily by muscular activity. Shivering can provide up to about 3 times the resting heat production. It is induced by a fall of skin temperature with a consequent reflex stimulation, by cold receptors, of a hypothalamic centre. Large amounts of heat can be produced by voluntary exercise and this is limited only by physical fitness and availability of food. To maintain body temperature with the temperature of the air at freezing-point and using treble thickness of normal clothing would require about twice resting metabolism. Eskimos have learned to run for long periods behind their sledges at a rate sufficient to keep them warm but not to exhaust them, and their fitness measured by standard tests is high compared to Canadian Whites (Shepherd).

The local reaction to cold of the hands is important. There is first an intense vasoconstriction followed after about 5 minutes by a vasodilatation and a cyclical continuation of these vasomotor changes. This local vasodilatation serves the function of preventing the tissue temperature dropping to frostbite levels.

## Acclimatization to cold

There are clear indications that acclimatization, that is, increased tolerance to cold, gradually develops. For example, newcomers to Arctic regions will wear all their available clothing at the outset; yet as winter comes on and air temperatures fall no further protection is sought. Men on expeditions often wear less at work, or while asleep, during the winter than at the beginning. It has been observed that members of an expedition who spent the greater part of their time indoors suffered frostbite at low temperatures in the wind in under $1\frac{1}{2}$ minutes, whereas an outdoor group resisted this for nearly 10 minutes. At the same time well-adapted individuals have a keener appreciation of their lower limb and face temperatures and will take the necessary action to prevent frostbite (Irving). There is also evidence pointing to improvement in the processes concerned in maintaining thermal equilibrium. The basal metabolic rate is somewhat increased as compared to values in tropical regimes. Eskimos show a larger increase (varying from $+7$ per cent to $+30$ per cent) than Europeans ($+8$ per cent) living in comparable cool conditions. How far the raised metabolism depends on cold exposure directly, or on altered endocrine function, or on peculiarities of the diet, remains rather uncertain. The total food energy intake in the Arctic is high relative to that in the tropics but fluctuates widely, depending on indoor conditions as well as on work. Some authorities believe that a higher protein intake and specific dynamic action account for the increased metabolic heat production. It seems, however, that fat is equally or perhaps more important than protein in exerting a protective effect against cold. Many Arctic explorers and others living in the north report that fat becomes positively desired. United States members of an Antarctic expedition who had an abhorrence of fat at home would eat fat in great quantity. Thus, the two processes common in the animal kingdom for enhancing adaptation to cold are also operative in man—increase in heat production and increase in fat insulation layers, though man depends, of course, on artificial insulation as well.

With acclimatization increased heat production reduces the extent of fall of the rectal temperature in conditions of severe exposure, and by allowing skin temperatures to rise secondarily, would account for improvement in subjective comfort. Such changes in body temperature have been reported.

Quite clear evidence of 'local' acclimatization has been forthcoming (Fig. 27.1). Subjects in a cold room, exposed 2 hours a day, 5 days a week for 5 weeks at $-15\,°C$ and wearing heavy clothing but no gloves, showed reduced tactile discrimination, but this gradually returned. Outdoor groups scored much higher on tests of tactile discrimination than did indoor, sheltered groups. The ability of fishermen of Nova Scotia to tolerate immersion of their hands in ice-cold water has long been known.

The outdoor group of experimental subjects were found to have higher skin temperatures, particularly so after severe exposure to cold. This would point to a greater resting finger and hand blood-flow in the habituated group.

There is evidence, therefore, that cold acclimatization or increased tolerance can be acquired. Changes of the same kind are demonstrable in indigenous peoples. Thus central Australian Aborigines sleep naked with little apparent discomfort at air temperatures of about $0\,°C$ and radiant temperatures of $-45\,°C$. The investigators under the same conditions were unable to sleep because of shivering and the discomfort of low skin temperatures. The Aborigines were able to endure greater fall of skin temperature than the Europeans.

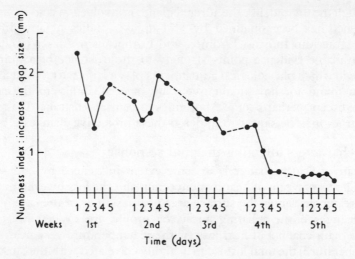

FIG. 27.1. Day-by-day trends in $V$-test numbness index during cold-acclimatization exposure, winter tests ($N=14$). (From Mackworth, *Proc. R. Soc. B*, **143**, 392–407, 1955.)

Like the Australian Aborigines the Bushmen of the Kalahari sleep in extremely cold conditions with the protection of a single covering and a small fire. A high degree of cold tolerance (reported also by Darwin of the Tierra del Fuegians) can to a large extent be acquired by Europeans. Norwegian students who lived in the open for 6 weeks with minimal protection were at first unable to sleep but later were able to do so in spite of shivering.

Eskimos are stated to have a far greater tolerance to cold in the hands than white men. Laboratory evidence comes from a comparison of finger temperatures following immersion in water near freezing-point using Eskimo, Indian, Negro, and European subjects. The greater propensity of Negroes to frostbite was attested by experience in the Korean war. In tests of sensori-motor function Eskimos and Indian young men in the North-West Territory of Canada were definitely superior to a comparable group of European workers with only 6 weeks' residence.

The ability of acclimatized men, and particularly the Eskimo, to use the hands efficiently at low temperatures (Fig. 27.1), is associated with an increased blood-flow. The following results when blood-flow was measured with fore-arms immersed in water at 24 °C are representative (Brown and Page, *J. app. Physiol.*, **5**, 221, 1952).

| | Number | Observations | Blood-flow (cm³ per 100 cm³ per min) | Skin temperature (°C) |
|---|---|---|---|---|
| Control subjects | 5 | 122 | $4·7\pm0·19$ | 32·8 |
| Eskimo | 6 | 148 | $8·6\pm0·43$ | 33·8 |

Although the thyroid, like the adrenal gland, is involved in cold adjustments, no evidence has been obtained by $^{131}$I-uptake studies of any differences between American Indians, Eskimos, and Europeans in Alaska (Rodahl).

The available evidence points strongly to the existence of acquired cold tolerance in which physiological adjustments play a large part. No racial group has been found to show qualitatively any special ability to develop cold tolerance except perhaps some Aborigines of central Australia. It is possible that Negroes may be slower to undergo these protective changes.

## Bodily characters affecting thermal response

The rate of heat exchange is to some extent influenced by body-size and shape. The loss or gain of heat by convection and the loss by evaporation will be the greater the larger the surface area of the skin or in the case of radiant heat exchanges, of the radiating surface or 'profile' area. When sweating provides the main channel of heat loss (with air temperature very near or above skin temperature) the total lost is fairly highly correlated with the surface area, but the actual correlation value ($+0.8$) makes clear the existence of quite considerable individual variability in sweat capacity so that physique is not the only factor involved.

The amount of heat produced by a working subject is highly correlated with his body-weight and this is the case for many types of physical work. Hence the heat produced per kilogramme weight tends to be the same for large or small individuals. This heat output will, however, not be a constant amount per unit surface area, for the smaller the subject the greater the surface area available per kilogram of body-weight. This follows from the fact that while the body-weight increases as the cube, the surface area increases only as the square; also for a given body-weight physique which approaches a linear (ectomorphic) rather than a spherical (endomorphic) shape will have a relatively greater surface area. Larger men have a larger ratio of weight to surface area. Thus per unit of heat produced the smaller individuals have a larger dissipating surface available for convection or evaporation. Consequently the heat loss will be (or needs to be) smaller per unit area and this has been confirmed by direct observation as illustrated in Fig. 27.2.

Body-shape affects heat loss in another way. Both convective and evaporative coefficients (i.e. the heat loss per unit area and per unit temperature or vapour pressure gradient respectively) approach constant values for large surfaces but increase rapidly as the diameter of the limbs is reduced below a diameter of about 10 cm. At a diameter of, say, 7 cm the coefficient of evaporative heat loss will be nearly twice as great as at 15 cm.

These anatomical properties make it unnecessary for the smaller individual to sweat as much per unit area as the larger, and the total water requirement by the smaller individual is both relatively and absolutely less. The heavier subject, putting out more sweat per unit area, will need to have harder-working sweat glands (for it is likely the glands are not present in greater density). Thus

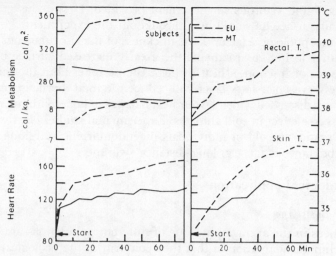

F IG. 27.2(a). Records of body temperature, metabolism, and heart-rate of the subjects during experiment 1. EU=heavy subject, MT=light subject.

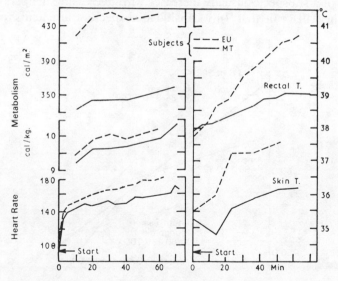

F IG. 27.2(b). Records of body temperature, metabolism, and heart-rate of the subjects during experiment 2. EU was exhausted and stopped after 63 minutes of the walk.

in hot environments individuals of smaller and of linear build would appear to possess some biological advantage. Robinson's heavy subject (Fig. 27.2) in contrast to his light subject, could not achieve heat balance when the work rate was high at a chamber temperature of 32 °C and relative humidity 70 per cent and only reached thermal equilibrium when the humidity was reduced to 44 per cent and vigorous air movement provided. Despite his greater heat loss per unit surface he stored heat throughout the experiment.

A third morphological factor is the thickness of the subcutaneous fat layer. It is true that in hot environments the greatly increased surface blood-flow carries the major fraction of heat through the periphery but the thickness of the relatively avascular fatty layer will reduce the total thermal conductance.

The factors discussed which favour heat balance in hot environments should have a converse effect in cold climates. Experimental studies clearly show the greater tolerance to cold of individuals of endomorphic physique and with greater subcutaneous fat, e.g. long-distance swimmers.

## Anthropological applications

### Body-size and shape

Differences in the average physique of different populations are of significance in climatic adaptation in that they conform to the ecological 'rules' of Bergmann (1847) and Allen (1877) applicable to animal populations in general. The Bergmann rule states that 'Within a polytypic warm-blooded species, the body-size of a subspecies usually increases with decreasing temperature of its habitat', the Allen rule that 'In warm-blooded species there tends to be an in-

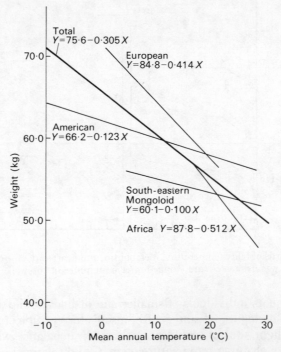

FIG. 27.3. Total regression of weight upon mean temperature and some of its component intravarietal regressions. (After Roberts, *Am. J. phys. Anthrop.* 11, 533–58, 1953.)

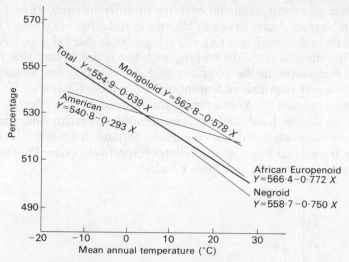

FIG. 27.4. Total regression of relative sitting height upon mean temperature with some of its component regressions. (After Roberts, *The geographical distribution of the physical characters of Man*, D. Phil. thesis, University of Oxford.)

crease in the relative size of protruding organs such as the ears and tail with increasing temperature of the habitat'. These rules are applicable to a large majority of warm-blooded species (J. Huxley).

That human body-size and shape tend to follow these rules has been demonstrated in several studies. The mean body-weight of populations in hot regions is demonstrably lower (in all continents) than that in temperate and cooler climates (Fig. 27.3).

Roberts has also shown that the ratio of sitting height to total height becomes less as mean annual temperature increases, i.e. the lower limbs tend to be longer in hotter climates (Fig. 27.4). The tendency towards 'attenuation' of limbs in hotter climates is seen also in the upper limbs, since the ratio of span to height is greater. The dimensions of the trunk also become less in hotter climates. These findings can be combined, as Schreider has done, to show that the body-weight/surface-area ratio declines from temperate to hotter climates, as indicated in Table 27.3. It should be noted that the correlations between body shape or size and mean temperature account for about 50 or 60 per cent of the total inter-population variance; clearly other factors, particularly population movements, also influence the variation in physique.

## TABLE 27.3

### *Ratio of body-weight (kg) to surface area (m²)*

| Frenchmen | 38 | Somalis | 35 |
|-----------|----|---------|-----|
| Albanians | 37 | Mexicans | 35 |
| Arabs | 36 | Andamanese | 32 |

The data on subcutaneous fat covering of different populations is meagre. American Negroes clearly have a smaller mean and range of skin-fold thickness than American Whites (Fig. 27.5), and it is probable that Eskimos have thicker fat covering than Negroes. In keeping with this is the finding that the endomorphic component in the physique of Kikuyu and other Africans in hot climates is lower than that of Europeans or Japanese (Danby).

Striking examples of Allen's 'rule' are afforded by the contrast between Eskimos, on the one hand, and the linear central Australian Aborigines or the even more attenuated Nilotes (see Plate III) on the other. It could be plausibly argued that Pygmies and Nilotes respectively exemplify the extreme operation of Bergmann's and Allen's 'rules'.

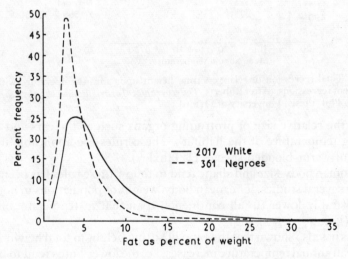

FIG. 27.5. Body-fat of Whites and American Negroes. (*Note:* body-fat has been derived from measurements of skin-fold thickness.) (From Newman, *Human Biol.*, 28, 1956.)

*Growth and development*

Because of the differences in adult physique it is to be expected that growth patterns should show some relationship to climatic variation. The fact that linearity of physique tends to be more prevalent in people living in hotter regions fits in with the finding that the growth period is prolonged and maturation somewhat delayed in warm regions. A linear build, e.g. a relatively greater height per unit body-weight, is attained by a delayed skeletal (and physiological) maturation (Bayley). The evidence drawn from tropical peoples on these points is scanty and findings are complicated by other factors such as nutrition, disease, social class, etc. African children (who are noticeably more linear than Europeans of the same age) from a number of regions exhibit.a delay in skeletal age, the difference being about a year at adolescence.

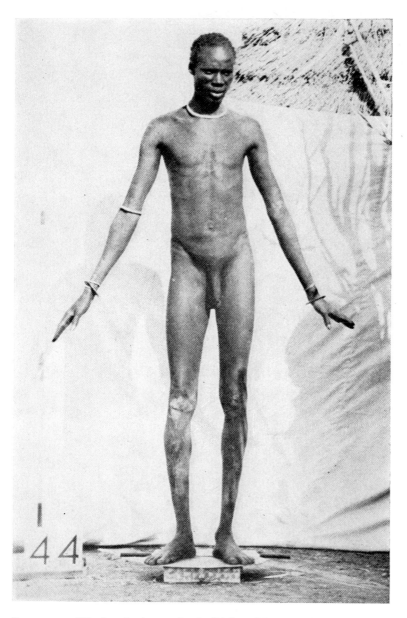

PLATE III. Nilotic physique—Ageir Dinka. (Photograph by D. F. B. Roberts.)

*The Mongoloid face*

The attractive but not experimentally proven hypothesis has been advanced by Coon, Garn, and Birdsell that the Mongoloid face exhibits features specially adapted to life in extreme cold. These include the reduction of brow-ridges and with them the frontal sinuses, flattening and widening of orbital and malar regions to permit more fat padding and the reduction of nasal prominence. North American Indians and Eskimos are said to show a very much smaller liability to cold injury despite long periods of explosure to cold.

*Nose-shape*

There is a high correlation between the shape of the nasal aperture (expressed as the nasal index) and climatic variables.

TABLE 27.4

*Nasal index and climate*

| Nasal index (146 groups living) correlated with | Correlation coefficient | Standard error |
|---|---|---|
| Dry-bulb temperature† | 0·63 | 0·050 |
| Relative humidity† | 0.42 | 0.068 |
| Dry-bulb temperature and relative humidity† | 0·72 | 0·040 |
| Wet-bulb temperature‡ | 0·77 | 0·034 |
| Vapour pressure of the air‡ | 0·82 | 0·027 |

† Thomson and Buxton.    ‡ Weiner.

The suggestion from these figures is that the nose-shape may functionally be more concerned with moistening the inspired air (since the vapour pressure governs moisture exchanges between the respiratory surface and the air) rather than with heat exchange. This would explain why relatively narrow noses are found in both hot and cold deserts—both regions of excessive dryness. It is known that the vitality and activity of the cilia of the respiratory epithelium are reduced far more by drying than by heating or cooling. Under normal conditions the mucus secretion moves at speeds of up to $10$ mm min$^{-1}$ in the direction of the pharynx by the action of the cilia and so soot and bacteria are cleared out of the respiratory tract. There is a clear correlation between this rate and the relative humidity of the inspired air. Low humidity can actively stop the normal mucus flow. This sensitivity to drying of the respiratory tract may explain the relatively high incidence of nasal, sinus, or respiratory infections which has been reported in Eskimos (Bertelsen), whereas the rarity of such ailments in African Negroes, New Orleans coloured people, or Malayan Aborigines has been attributed to their possession of larger and wider nasal passages, so rendering blockage and subsequent infection less likely.

## Genetic and non-genetic factors in climatic adjustments

In the above discussion some evidence in favour of the functional advantages of certain body characters has been adduced, and at the same time their regional occurrence in indigenous peoples indicated. Superficially this would imply that regional selection has proceeded on Darwinian lines and that climatic differences are in many cases ascribable to genetic differences. Twin studies indicate that variations in body-shape, size, fat deposition, growth pattern, skeletal, and physiological maturation are all determined by genetic constitution to a larger extent than by purely environmental factors. Certain of the population differences rest undoubtedly on distinctive genotypes or multifactorial recombinations, e.g. nose-shape or the ratio of limb-length to trunk-length since such characters remain unaffected on change of environment. The situation is, however, more complicated, for it appears that the action of climate on body-weight and growth rate of non-indigenous individuals is somewhat similar to that seen in established indigenous peoples. Europeans in the tropics possess body-weights lower on the average than those in colder environments (Roberts 1953). There is a marked seasonal effect on body-weight and growth *(idem)*. In animals it is well known that even in the first generation body conformation undergoes changes in the directions indicated by the Bergmann and Allen rules. In other words, exposure to high temperature during the growth period can result in morphological (and physiological) changes which confer higher resistance to heat stress (Harrison). The capacity to make immediate responses, like the tendency to suntan, may perhaps have lent themselves to relatively rapid selection (cf. Waddington's assimilation principle) so that the appropriate growth patterns have become genetically established in some populations. It is perhaps not so surprising, then, that in all continents the Bergmann and Allen relation of body-build to climate should be found irrespective of race (Roberts); in some cases these may rest on genotypic differences but not necessarily so.

For adaptation to heat in a wide variety of habitats we have seen that the rapid physiological changes of acclimatization are available; at the same time it would seem that advantageous morphological features have also appeared, presumably through natural selection. It is thus possible to account for the observation that while tropical peoples readily adjust to additional heat stress by further acclimatization and increased sweat-gland activity, their sweat loss

### TABLE 27.5

*Comparison of Asians and Europeans exposed to similar hot conditions*

| | Mean weight (kg) | Energy cost per (kgh⁻¹) | Energy cost (total body-wt+h⁻¹) | Mean surface area (m²) | Heat produced (kJm⁻²h⁻¹) | Heat loss by evaporation (kJm⁻²h⁻¹) | Total sweat loss (gh⁻¹) |
|---|---|---|---|---|---|---|---|
| Asian group | 55 | 4 | 220 | 1·6 | 575 | 694 | 440 |
| European group | 80 | 4 | 320 | 2·0 | 673 | 820 | 650 |

is lower than that of fully acclimatized Europeans. Their much lower body-weight and linear build make it possible, as we have seen, for their heat output during work in a hot environment to be balanced by a smaller sweat loss per unit surface area. Table 27.5 (Weiner and Lee) illustrates this point.

The fact that each major racial group, 'Europenoid', 'Mongoloid', 'Negroid', and 'Australoid' occupies a wide range of climates is to be ascribed in part to the widespread phenomenon of physiological acclimatization, partly to the existence of Bergmann and Allen body-size differences and other physical 'racial' differences and partly to technological adjustments to climatic conditions.

It is as well to illustrate by some examples (see also Table 25.5) the extent of climatic adaptation of human racial groups. The Amerindian is in this respect perhaps the most striking. On the American continent the American Indian varieties include the Athabascan Indians near Great Bear Lake, who live in as severe a climate as the Eskimo; the peoples of Tierra de Fuego, who have a poorer material culture and whose climate is cold, damp and stormy, and the Indians of the Maya region in Yucatan or Guatemala, who live in a hot, wet climate. The Australian Aborigines, like the Fuegians, endure cold with a minimum of protection. In winter at night in central Australia the Anwatjera and Ilpirra tribesmen, and those at Alice Springs, experience temperatures of $-2\,^{\circ}$C to $-10\,^{\circ}$C. These same natives may even in winter experience very high temperatures during the day—a hot, dry environment with air temperatures of $30\text{--}35\,^{\circ}$C. Aborigines in the hot humid parts of Australia experience dry-bulb temperatures of $28\text{--}32\,^{\circ}$C and relative humidity of 70–80 per cent. There are Negroes who live in the cold uplands of Basutoland, Ethiopia, Kenya and others in jungle and hot, humid terrain. Mongoloids include not only the circumpolar peoples but also the central Asiatic peoples habituated to great diurnal swings and the Chinese of South East Asia in hot, humid climates. The present climatic range of Europeans is also very wide. In hot habitats we should note the immigrant European populations living in the Amazon basin, the Italians of northern Australia, the Kotas and other Europenoids of India, and the Mediterranean desert peoples of North Africa and Persia. Laplanders are Europeans living in extremely cold conditions.

## Limits of biological tolerance

There are limits to climatic adaptation and these can be sufficiently specified in terms of comfort, efficiency, and health, and examined in relation to different habitats. A knowledge of these limits is important if appropriate technological adjustments are to be made.

### Comfort limits

The relation between subjective impressions of warmth and the environment is usually expressed in terms of the American Effective Temperature (E.T.) Scale (Fig. 27.6), which enables one to specify the combined effect of the wet-

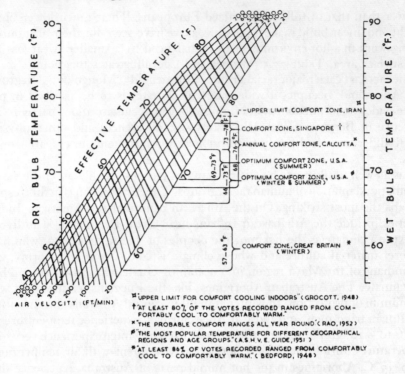

TO ASCERTAIN THE EFFECTIVE TEMPERATURE A STRAIGHT LINE IS DRAWN THROUGH THE
POINTS ON THE VERTICAL SCALES WHICH REPRESENT THE OBSERVED DRY AND WET
BULB TEMPERATURES AND THE POINT AT WHICH THE LINE CUTS THE LINE ON THE GRID
CORRESPONDING WITH THE OBSERVED AIR VELOCITY INDICATES THE EFFECTIVE TEMPERATURE.

FIG. 27.6. Comfort zones for different parts of the world. (From Ellis, Hunterian Lecture, *Ann. R. Coll. Surg.* 13 (Fig. 6, 1953).

bulb temperature, dry-bulb (or indoor globe temperature), and the air movement as a single temperature index. The upper limit of comfort is in winter, in the UK is 63 °F (17 °C) E.T., and in the USA is 71 °F (22 °C); owing to acclimatization, the limit in summer is raised to 71 °F (22 °C) and 75 °F (24 °C) respectively; these are for people wearing light clothing and doing sedentary work; for an individual stripped to the waist the upper limit of the zone of comfort and thermal neutrality begins at about 80 °F (27 °C) E.T. Over 80 per cent of Europeans in Singapore were reasonably comfortable between 73 °F (23 °C) and 78 °C (26 °C) E.T. A high proportion of native-born White Australians can tolerate 80 °F (27 °C) E.T. without undue discomfort. Results on Indians and Iranians confirm these higher comfort limits for tropical regions. Fig. 27.6 shows the comfort zones for different parts of the world (Ellis). The effects of warm climates on women seem to be little different.

Many habitats have a seasonable or daily period with effective temperatures above these comfort limits (Table 27.6). That these places are found tolerable

## TABLE 27.6

### Characteristic thermal conditions in different habitats and climatic zones

| Habitat | Zone | Climatic provinces | Hot dry | Hot humid | Warm dry | Warm humid | Cool dry | Cool humid | Cold dry | Cold humid | Some examples |
|---|---|---|---|---|---|---|---|---|---|---|---|
| I. Desert and dry lands | Hot | Tropical desert | 29 | — | 17 | — | 10 | — | — | — | Sahara, Atacama, Australia |
| | Cold | Cold, dry desert | 25 | — | 20 | — | 10 | — | 6 | — | Gobi |
| II. Tropical forests | Hot | Equatorial | — | 28 | — | 21 | — | — | — | — | Zaïre, Malaya, Amazon Basin |
| | Hot | Equatorial and monsoonal | — | 28 | — | 22 | — | — | — | — | E. India, Tanzania |
| | Hot | Tropical marine | — | 28 | — | 17 | — | — | — | — | Brazil coast, Mozambique, IndoChina |
| | Hot | Tropical marine and monsoonal | — | 27 | 20 | 17 | — | — | — | — | Queensland coast |
| III. Tropical scrub | Hot | Tropical continental | 28 | 23 | 20 | — | 17 | — | — | — | Interior of Africa and S. America |
| | Hot | Tropical, continental, and monsoonal | 24 | 22 | 20 | 17 | 12 | — | — | — | India, Australia (not tropical) |
| IV. Tropical grassland | Hot | Tropical continental-plateaux | 28 | 22 | 16 | — | 10 | — | — | — | Peru, S. Africa |
| V. Temperate forests | Warm | Warm temperate | 25 | 27 | 20 | 20 | 10 | — | — | — | N. and S. Wales, Argentine |
| | Cool | Cool marine | — | 26 | — | 20 | 10 | 12 | — | — | UK, Germany, New Zealand |
| VI. Mediterranean scrub | Warm | Warm temperate | 28 | 27 | 16 | — | 10 | — | — | — | California, Mediterranean |
| VII. Temperate grassland | Cool | Cool continental | 25 | 20 | — | 17 | — | 12 | 4 | — | Prairie, Pampas, Chernozem |
| VIII. Boreal lands | Cold | Cold marine | — | 22 | — | 17 | — | 12 | 3 | 3 | Alaska |
| | Cold | Cold continental | — | — | — | 17 | 12 | 12 | 3 | — | Siberia, Canada, west of Winnipeg |
| IX. Polar lands | Cold | Arctic tundra | — | — | 25 | — | 12 | 10 | 2 | — | Greenland |

(Values are based on monthly averages and in terms of effective temperature in °C) and, indeed, are well populated, is made possible by appropriate ventilation, housing, and clothing, and also because acclimatization enables work to be done at temperatures higher than the upper limit of comfort. No doubt the possession of body-build appropriate to these climates must play a part in the successful exploitation of what would seem to be extremely trying conditions.

## Limits for physical work

Remarkably high effective temperatures can be sustained in special circumstances by men doing hard physical work. The special circumstances are that these men should be physically fit, well trained for the work, young, and highly acclimatized. In laboratory experiments Europeans have worked at levels of 1050 kJ per hour (i.e. at levels appropriate to moderately hard industrial work) for 4–5 hours at a time, 5 or 6 days a week over a period of 6 months, at effective temperatures of 32 or 33 °C. South and West African mine-labourers are capable of the same feat. At these levels the subjects maintain a high rectal temperature at a steady level, and the sweat output is of the order of $3\frac{1}{2}$–4 l per 4 hours. Above these levels even these fit men will give up with circulatory collapse.

There is thus a large gap between the acceptable resting comfort limit of about 26 °C E.T. and the maximum possible of, say, 32 °C E.T. for hard work. That these high limits are exceptional must be recognized, though at the same time they indicate the astonishing adaptability of the human organism to severe heat stress.

For work of moderate intensity to be undertaken over years of working life, it seems that an upper limit in the region of 26 °C to 28 °C E.T. should be acceptable.

## Limits for skilled work

A variety of investigations using different types of skilled tasks (tests of vigilance, wireless telegraphy, pursuit meters, tracking tasks) give much the same temperature level at which deterioration begins and mistakes begin to increase rapidly. At an effective temperature of 27 °C performance is not greatly affected, but between readings of 28·5 °C and 31 °C E.T. the accuracy falls of. The critical value given by different investigators is between 28·5 °C and 29·5 °C E.T. In a study of deterioration of wireless operators Mackworth found that skilled operators have somewhat greater resistance to thermal stress than less skilled.

The value of 28·5 °C E.T., while well above the comfort zone, applies to all forms of work, physical or mental, as about the basic for most subjects (including acclimatized subjects). At this temperature sleep is also disturbed.

At low temperatures the performance of manual tasks requiring dexterity is closely related to the skin temperature. Acclimatization to cold makes possible improvement in accuracy and discrimination (Fig. 27.1) and this in turn is related to an improvement in local hand circulation (p. 430). It will be recalled that acclimatized Europeans resemble Eskimos in this respect. Accidents (in industry) are 34 per cent higher at temperatures below 13 °C as compared to the rate at about 18 °C. Similarly, skilled work (tracking performance) using the bare hands, deteriorates below this air temperature even when wearing heavy protective clothing.

*Health hazards*

In hot climates a number of disabilities are caused directly by the climate (though far more serious are those diseases, bacterial or parasitic, which are favoured by the heat and humidity). At effective temperatures above 27 °C, vague 'fatigue' may be experienced and this discomfort as well as prickly heat and sunburn may be important factors in discouraging some immigrants from life in the tropics. Nevertheless, prickly heat has been reported in indigenous peoples, including Negritos in Malaya and Arabs in Aden, but it is not known whether the incidence is less in these people. Heat stroke is an uncommon malady, but Africans and Europeans are both prone to it. A combination of circumstances is necessary for its occurrence including pre-existing fever, lack of acclimatization, water shortage, and hard work. In heat-waves, older over-weight people with poor circulation and over-clothed infants are those at risk. As protection against heat illness improved performance of the heat regulatory system through acclimatization, as well as the morphological features already described, appear to be the important biological factors. Selection against obese individuals or those poorly endowed with sweat glands or with glands liable to damage (e.g. by sunburn) would undoubtedly be intense. Albinos may well be in this last class. Small-sized and lighter built individuals would appear to be at advantage against the risks of water shortage, as well as of heat stress.

The hazards of cold, particularly of frostbite, affect people without the requisite facilities of clothing and shelter and without the experience of the dangers. It is likely that some individuals are especially cold-sensitive and perhaps acclimatize poorly.

## Climates of the world

The distribution and seasonal progression, over the world's surface, of heat and cold, of sun and cloud, of wind and calm, rain and drought, are determined by the interaction of a number of planetary factors—latitude, distance from the sea, relation of land to wind, the surface relief, and altitude. Complicated as this interaction is at any one place or time, the major single factor responsible for the existence of the greater climatic zones is, of course, latitude. The oldest and simplest division of the world's climate—into hot, warm, cool, and cold zones—arises from the latitudinal effect of the sun's transit. These zones roughly occupy latitudes 0–30 (hot), 30–45 (warm), 45–60 (cool), and beyond 60 (cold).

Each large zone contains within itself a multiplicity of subtypes (or climatic provinces) for the latitudinal effect is profoundly modified in detail by factors such as altitude, proximity to the sea, and the particular exposure to the winds. These further subdivisions which climatologists (for details, see Miller 1946) specify on the basis of variations in the extent and timing of temperature change and rainfall correspond therefore to topographical entities. The 'provinces' within each zone represent different combinations of air temperature, air humidity (or vapour pressure), solar radiation, air movement, the combinations changing diurnally and seasonally. It is these different combinations which yield the overall physiological and subjective effects characteristic of the zone. One can give a rough mean annual effective temperature rating to cover each zone—thus, hot climates 27–21 °C, warm climates 21–16 °C, cool 15–7 °C, and cold, below 5 °C. But these figures, being mean values of an integrated index— as explained above—disguise the profound differences (and overlap) between zones and within each zone.

When we come to survey and compare the twenty or so different climatic 'provinces' of the world, we shall find the task more manageable if we regard each as built up of a number of recurrent characteristic complexes, these coming into prominence according to season and time of day.

Table 27.6 sums up, in a necessarily rough fashion, the varieties of climatic experience to which man is exposed in the major 'provinces' related to the main habitats. It is clear that almost everywhere there is some measure of daily and/ or seasonal contrast and that even in those habitats (Table 25.3) containing large populations the range of conditions may be large and is often extreme. In only one region in particular is there a relatively restricted set of climatic conditions—in the equatorial monsoonal lands, but this is, nevertheless, a region of high agricultural productivity and large populations. The facts show how naïve it is to assume *a priori* that there is one 'ideal' climate and, moreover, that this one is necessarily confined to a narrow range around the 20 °C iso- therm.

Table 27.6 reveals how common are the climatic episodes which are severe enough to call forth physiological and cultural adjustment. One may single out as peculiarly trying conditions which restrict physical work, make error of judgement likely, and demand extensive physiological adjustments in (1) the 'equatorial' combination of still air, high wet-bulb and dry-bulb temperatures, and intense radiation, (2) the 'scorching' combination conducive to convective overheating by wind at temperatures above that of the skin, intensified by solar heat, (3) the great chill of freezing conditions (despite still air) when cloud or darkness exclude radiant heat, made worse by damp, and (4) the severe combi- nation of great cold and wind, even when the air is dry. One or more of these extremes (and conditions which approach them) are seen, in Table 27.6, to offer a challenge to human life and efficiency in practically every climatic region. It is true that in the milder regions—the Mediterranean in the warm temperate zone and the marine in the cool temperate—great heat or cold is by comparison with other regimes not so common or so prolonged. Even so there is no exemp- tion anywhere from the rigour of climate at some time or other. The challenge of climate is indeed one which faces the human species as a whole. It must have done so from the time of man's origin in a habitat which must itself have been sufficiently rigorous and varied to have favoured the evolution of a heat-regulatory mechanism of great flexibility.

## Cultural aspects of climatic adaptation

The spread of man over so many contrasting habitats would not have been possible if biological adaptation was not supplemented by technological measures. Man began in the early Pleistocene in tropical surroundings and moved into northern latitudes at first only during warm interglacial or inter-stadial periods. He remained in a cool periglacial region for the first time probably only at the beginning of the fourth glaciation. The loess-steppe of Europe provided ample food for grazing animals, and many hunting and occupation sites have been discovered. By this time the use of fire was well established and both the tools and timber were available for constructing shelters. That serviceable clothing was made is amply documented in the Upper Palaeolithic by the bone awls used for joining pieces of skin and the occurrence of flint scrapers for preparing the skin. No doubt the shelters were often no better than those of today's Bushmen or Fuegians and biological acclimatization played a large part. But the ability of simple societies to construct remarkably efficient habitations is borne out by the practices of many circumpolar peoples today.

The history and technology of housing, heating, cooling, and clothing are large subjects, and only a few comments can be made here. Housing to meet the requirements of extreme cold demands a sufficiently high insulation of walls, roof, and floor to make the best use of space and warming appliances and at the same time to provide efficient ventilation (without draughts) both for the occupants and for fuel burning. The traditional winter habitations of the central Eskimo and those of Alaska and Greenland, though based on frame-works of different materials, display a remarkable mastery of these principles. Others, e.g. the Reindeer Chukchee, do not reach so high a standard probably because of the need to make their houses portable. If these really warm indoor temperatures are not always attained, much moisture condenses, clothing remains damp, and the covers of the house become mildewed.

The heating principles in use among circumpolar peoples illustrate in detail their mastery of environmental stress. (Their detailed knowledge of the habits and morphology of their game animals is another example of their ecological expertise.) The Eskimo house with deep entrance pit and low, domed roof enables cold air to be admitted at the bottom of the dwelling, heating up as it enters and reaching the occupants at a suitable temperature. Above the level of occupation there is little space for warm air to collect away from the occupants. The outward flow is controlled by manipulating the exits in the roof.

A second Eskimo principle is to jam a lot of people into a small space, with minimum ventilation and letting body heat warm up the room. This is the practice of the inland Eskimos when they have no fuel; it enables them to keep alive under conditions so unfavourable that they would probably perish otherwise. The same principle is used, to some extent at least, in the fur sleeping box or inner room of the Chukchee. Here lamps heat the space at supper time, but body heat is relied on after people have gone to bed. It is confined first by a blanket of caribou fur, and second by the walls of the fur sleeping room.

The striking thing about sleeping arrangements among all these peoples is the absence of sleeping bags. The tendency is rather to warm the sleeping space, by one means or another, and to sleep naked under fur blankets. The reason, perhaps, is that this solves the problem of the accumulation of insensible perspiration in the bedding, so troublesome to Arctic explorers. Another instance of Eskimo mastery of the Arctic environment lies in their awareness of the inadvisability during winter of building their huts in any depression in the land surface, for example a river bed, in which cold, heavy air is likely to be trapped.

Compared to circumpolar peoples the shelters available to many other peoples are often much less elaborate. The Yaghans (Fuegians) in their cold, wet conditions, or Australian Aborigines and Bushmen in the cold nights of the deserts, make do with one or two blankets or skins and with quite simple shelters constructed of a framework of sticks bent over and fastened together and covered with skins, grass, or bark. The Ainu traditionally lived in simple houses with small hearths. The state of cold-tolerance or adaptedness reflects the efficiency of the shelters. The Ainu and Australian Aborigines appear to be in a much more developed state of cold-resistance than Eskimo or Lapps or even Kalahari Bushmen, whose use of fuel, windbreak, and skin cloak and often blankets is effective in achieving, near the skin, an air temperature in the thermoneutral range (Wyndham).

Man's technological understanding of hot climates had also undergone much development even before the historical period. Appropriate building methods to deal with the complex factors of hot dry or hot humid conditions were long ago developed. Such methods can nowadays be related to physiological principles and standards of comfort and efficiency (for details, see Lee 1951). These involve in all hot climates (a) an awareness of the need to reduce human heat production as evidenced in labour-saving devices and convenient arrangements for housing and storage, (b) measures to reduce heat gain by radiation and promote heat loss by radiation, e.g. by the provision of external shade, by awnings, screening of windows, eaves on roofs and projections, and by reducing ground reflectivity. In hot, dry countries use is often made of insulation against solar radiation by a thick-walled construction ('capacity' type of insulation) with ventilation of roof spaces and controlled ventilation by doors and windows. In hot, humid countries an open construction is called for. Maximum wall-openings to catch the breeze and supply cross ventilation day and night are features of traditional housing. (For further details of housing in hot climates as practised by various communities, the reader is referred to works by Lee (1951) and Wulsin (1949).)

Clothing, including footwear and handwear, may be examined, like housing, in terms of heat exchanges in different climates, both hot and cold. This has been done in some detail by Siple. Wulsin relates these principles to the clothing adopted by peoples in various habitats.

## Short-wave radiation

Of particular importance to human life is the environmental solar radiation in the ultraviolet range, the radioactivity in the form of cosmic rays and the emissions by radioactive elements in the earth's outer layers and in the air. Though man has had a long geological period in which to develop adequate adjustment to ultraviolet radiation and to natural levels of radioactivity, he is now faced with a great new ecological hazard in the release and accumulation of artificial radioactivity.

### Ultraviolet light

Sunburn and suntan are produced by the absorption of ultraviolet radiation at wavelengths shorter than $0.32\,\mu$m. The absorption which specifically induces erythema increases rapidly at $0.3\,\mu$m and reaches its maximum at $0.28\,\mu$m.

The world distribution of ultraviolet radiation is not known exactly, but a strong latitudinal effect can be assumed. Absorption by ozone which excludes nearly all wavelengths shorter than $0.285\,\mu$m, explains most of the variation of ultraviolet light with season, time of day, and latitude. For example, when the sun moves from zenith to 60° from zenith, the intensity may be cut down by more than half. Seasonal movement of the sun explains why in the north temperate zone erythemal radiation may be more intense in early May than in the summer, or why, at the time of the summer solstice with the sun over the Tropic of Cancer, places on the equator and at latitude 47° get the same degree of sunlight. Although absorption by ozone will mean that little ultraviolet light is received directly from the sun when it is more than 45° from zenith, there is still a high proportion of erythemal radiation coming by reflection from the sky. Shorter wavelengths are scattered much more by gas molecules of the atmosphere than are the longer ones (hence the blueness of the sky) and so sky radiation is richer in ultraviolet than in visible radiation. Dust and smoke also absorb ultraviolet radiation and this is important in the neighbourhood of industrial cities.

*Sunburn and suntan.* The changes underlying sunburn are complex; the key event appears to be the damage sustained by epidermal cells. There is a release of substances which dilate the small blood-vessels; oedema and other signs of inflammation follow. Adaptation occurs in that the erythema threshold is raised as the sunburn subsides and suntan develops. Even after a mild degree of sunburn this raised threshold may remain for about two months. The protective effect which develops seems to involve two processes—thickening of the stratum corneum and melanization. The decrease in epidermal penetration to ultraviolet radiation brought about by corneal thickening is demonstrable in vitiliginous and in albino skin, which do not tan, but which do increase their erythemal threshold. Melanization must also play a part in normal skin for the effect of tanning is to induce an increase in pigment formation (after about 24 hours) and a migration of melanin pigment from the basal cell towards the surface. It has been shown that the presence of pigment in the corneum affects the amount of ultraviolet absorption. Once formed the pigment persists in the epidermis for many months and even years. Under the influence of waves longer than 0·32 μm a 'secondary' darkening occurs in skin previously sunburned and retaining traces of sunburn.

The damage to the skin by sunburn would appear to involve the sweat glands, and during the erythematic period an individual's heat-regulatory ability would be disturbed (Thomson). The pigmented skin is immune to such damage.

The activation in the skin by ultraviolet light of antirachitic substances allied to vitamin D has already been mentioned.

*Skin cancer and ultraviolet light.* Evidence of the role of sunlight in causing cancer of the skin includes the following: (a) in White populations cutaneous cancer (basal-cell and squamous-cell cancer) predominates on the face (95 per cent) and on the other principal exposed site, the back of the hand, (b) it is more prevalent in outdoor than indoor workers, (c) the incidence is greatest in regions of the world receiving most sunlight. There is (Fig. 27.7) a decrease

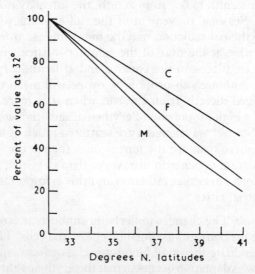

FIG. 27.7. Variation with latitude of the carcinogenic radiation; and incidence of cutaneous cancer. C, estimated maximum variation of annual carcinogenic radiation with latitude. F, variation of skin cancer in white females in the USA with latitude. M, variation of skin cancer in white males in the USA with latitude. (From Blum, *Carcinogenesis by ultra-violet light*, Princeton University Press, 1959.)

in incidence in American Whites with increasing latitude. Squamous-cell carcinoma increases much more with decreasing latitude than does basal-cell carcinoma. The same applies to the incidence of melanoma, which becomes more common among white-skinned people as the tropics are approached. Skin cancer is about 20 times more frequent in Queensland than in England.

*Anthropological considerations.* Using the reflectance values for a large number of populations it has been shown that a high correlation (over 0·9) exists between skin colour and latitude (Roberts and Kahlon) and to a small degree with mean annual temperature. These findings support the theory that geographical variation in the intensity of skin melanin is closely related to the intensity of ultraviolet radiation. The Sudanese regions of Africa are exposed to the most intense solar radiation and here is found the heaviest pigmentation. Other hot-desert and savannah peoples, such as the Australian Aborigines, who do not possess clothing or have acquired it only recently, tend also to be very dark-skinned. Where less heavily pigmented peoples are living under comparable conditions, there is usually evidence that they are relatively recent immigrants, as, for example, in the hot deserts of the New World.

The clouded western seaboards of continents in temperate latitudes have the least sunlight. In the Arctic the open dust-free skies of summer and reflection from snow and ice expose the individual to strong ultraviolet radiation. As already mentioned, Arctic peoples tend to be darker than temperate ones.

The threshold for sunburn is much higher in Negroes than in Whites. That this is not merely a matter of a greater thickening of the corneum (as claimed by Blum) is shown by Thomson's experiments. Sheets of strata corneum obtained by blistering from Negroes were slightly if at all thicker than those from Europeans; the greater opacity of the Negro corneum with its darker melanin colouring pigment to an ultraviolet source could be readily demonstrated.

Cancer of the skin is very rare in Negroes in the USA and in South Africa. When cancer of the skin does occur in Negroes it is to be found as often on unexposed as exposed skin, contrary to the finding in Europeans. The incidence of epithelioma in the Cape-coloured (White–Khoi-khoi hybrids) is much less than that of the European. In the Argentine nearly all cases of skin cancer occur amongst immigrants, very rarely in Indians or Negroes. Melanomas are also rarer in Negroes than in Europeans.

Thus, the geographical relation between ultraviolet light and skin colour would appear to be determined by the protective effect of dark pigmentation; darker-skinned varieties are on the whole found in regions of higher ultraviolet light intensity. Even in tropical zones there seems to be a difference between jungle-shaded and non-shaded peoples, e.g. African Pygmies are lighter coloured on the whole than the surrounding Bantu.

The selective significance of basal-cell carcinomas is not easy to assess since they rarely cause severe debility and typically only develop later in life. The melanomas are much more rapidly fatal and a high proportion occur in the reproductive period. The late development of basal-cell carcinomas, however, is no doubt partly due to the protection usually afforded by tanning and clothing and in any case can only be said to characterize the disease in temperate and sub-tropical zones. If naked Europeans were exposed to strong ultraviolet radiation, it seems likely that selection would strongly favour the darker individuals through their lower susceptibility to skin cancer. Nor must the immediate burning effect of solar radiation be neglected. Under natural conditions severe sunburn will be extremely disabling.

While the development of heavy pigmentation in regions of strong insolation can be explained in terms of protection offered against the carcinogenic and burning effects of ultraviolet radiation, the unpigmented state that occurs particularly in peoples of European origin cannot be explained directly in the same terms. Unless this is an ancestral condition which now is without biological significance—an unlikely situation—there must be some positive advantage in being light-skinned in regions of low ultraviolet incidence. The nature of this advantage is not certainly known, but it is evident that ultraviolet radiation will have its greatest antirhachitic activity when there is maximum penetration of the epidermis. Absence of melanin facilitates the penetration and in regions of low sunlight this factor could be critical (Coon, Garn, and Birdsell 1950).

The suntanning which is acquired by lighter-skinned individuals as a protective character may be regarded as a phenocopy of genetically determined darker colour of peoples in tropical and equatorial countries. Dark pigmentation may well have arisen independently more than once, namely in the dark Europeanoid peoples of south India and Arabia, among Oceanic Negroes, and in Africa, since these peoples are in many genetic characters rather distantly related.

### Ionizing radiation

Background radioactivity is that resulting from natural sources (i.e. sources not under man's control). These comprise cosmic rays, naturally occurring materials such as radium and thorium in the earth's crust and potassium in earth and water, and carbon-14 and tritium water-vapour in the air. Each person receives on the average a total whole body 'natural' dose over a 30-year period of about 3–5 R. At high altitudes, because of the greater incidence of cosmic rays, the value rises to about 5·5 R. Some areas, for geological reasons, provide a much higher natural background, e.g. Kerala State in southern India and some areas in Brazil. Under modern conditions artificially produced radiation adds to the radiation exposure. In westernized countries medical X-rays contribute to the total received by the gonads over a 30-year period (in the USA about 3 R on the average); another source is the luminous dials of watches. But the world at large faces a continuous increase in radioactivity unless the testing of atomic weapons and the consequent radioactive fall-out are controlled. Radioactive products enter the body by inhalation and ingestion; some, like strontium-90 and caesium-137, are readily absorbed from the intestinal tract. The radioactive dust as it settles is subject to meteorological conditions; rain in some cases will wash it away into areas with fewer exposed persons. People inside houses will be considerably more protected than those outside; so that inhabitants of tropical countries would be at a disadvantage. If atom and hydrogen bomb explosions were to continue at the high rates of 1953 and 1955, it would represent a 30-year gonadal dose of nearly 1 R.

The important and serious biological consequences of ionizing radiations arise from their mutagenic action on the genes of the reproductive cells; these mutations may involve microscopically visible changes in the chromosomes or may be submicroscopic. Each species has its own natural store of mutant genes and although the 'spontaneous mutation rate' is not known with certainty for many species, it ranges probably from 1 mutation in $10^5$ to 1 in $10^6$ germ cells per generation (cf. p. 163). But only a very small fraction of this spontaneous mutation can be attributed to the background radiation.

The mutations induced by radiation, like the spontaneous mutations, are both dominant and recessive in their effects, the latter being much the more frequent. Visible dominant mutations, which are exceedingly rare, will show in all the children of irradiated parents. X-ray-induced recessive mutations will show only in individuals who have received the same mutated gene from both parents. In a species like man, in which incest rules operate, many generations would be needed for these induced recessives to show their effect, though in some instances this would occur somewhat sooner in that some induced mutations would meet the same genes already present by spontaneous origin in the population. Moreover, sex-linked recessive mutations would show in every male who had received from his mother an X-chromosome carrying the mutation.

Among recessive mutations the most numerous are those which have little or no visible effect but which reduce fertility and longevity, and those 'lethals' which kill the developing organism. It follows that no immediate increase in obvious genetic malformation is to be expected in the children of survivors of nuclear bomb explosions (as in Japan). Dominant lethals kill the embryo at an early stage and abortions would be early and go unnoticed.

The real danger comes from the recessive lethal gene which may spread to many individuals through many generations before it comes into the open in an individual in the homozygous conditions. Mankind, like other species, has attained, through natural selection, a rate of elimination of both recessive and dominant harmful genes essential for its survival and fitness. Harmful dominant genes are eliminated rapidly; they disappear by the embryonic or early death of the recipient. The recessive lethal will eventually be eliminated (in double dose) though after a long time.

Artificial radiation adds, and could do so on an increasing scale, to the load of naturally occurring harmful genes. The American National Research Council believes that about 2 per cent of all live births in the USA have tangible defects of genetic origin which appear before sexual maturity; those comprise certain mental defects, congenital malformations, neuromuscular cutaneous, skeletal, endocrine, and defects in vision, hearing, the gastro-intestinal and genito-urinary tracts. Present genetic evidence indicates that the frequency of submicroscopic mutations increases linearly with the radiation dosage. The 'doubling dose' which would lead to a doubling of deleterious mutant genes has been variously estimated as 'more than 5 R and less than 150 R', perhaps 30–80 R, but 3 times the natural background value, i.e. about 10 R, has been regarded as the most likely value. The National Research Council calculated that this would mean that for all the children to be born to the present alive population of the USA, in the first generation alone, 200 000 (or 10 per cent) of the new instances of tangible inherited defect would occur in the first genera-tion. The present dosage of artificial ionization is more or less of the order of 5 R over a generation. A dose of even 10 R would produce 50 000 cases of inherited disability in the first generation and about 500 000 per generation ultimately. These figures, of course, do not measure all the genetic damage, as we have seen, but they show the scale of medical and social dangers of this new ecological hazard.

Selection, acting upon mutation, eliminates unfavourable genes and con-serves those with survival value. Nevertheless, as a means of supplying advanta-geous mutations radiation has nothing to commend it. Mutations, radiation-induced or spontaneous, occur at random, and before useful mutations appear large numbers of inferior mutants must be suffered and eliminated. Moreover, in modern communities it is unlikely that 'good' mutations could be fixed as in animal breeding or under natural conditions.

In nature, good mutations can spread through a species because their carriers leave more offspring than the average, and bad ones are eliminated through the death or infertility of their carriers. Neither process is likely to be effective in other species, in which family size is kept low, superior mutants are not likely to have larger families than the average and physically and mentally weak mutants are generally eliminated by natural selection (Auerbach).

## The effects of altitude

Some 10 million people live permanently at heights between 3600 m and 4000 m. Life at high altitudes imposes a complex ecological stress—that of low barometric pressure (which acts by lowering the oxygen and carbon-dioxide pressure in the inspired air), the low moisture content of the air, and cold. In addition the terrain is difficult and high levels of muscular activity are often required.

### Lowered barometric pressure

Oxygen constitutes about 21 per cent of the atmosphere by volume; hence the pressure of oxygen is roughly one-fifth of the total barometric pressure. At the 'sea-level' pressures of 150 mmHg (about 20 kP) oxygen diffuses across the lung membranes to the blood at a rate sufficient for all needs. As the oxygen pressure falls with increasing altitude the rate of transfer decreases proportionately; at levels in the vicinity of 2400–3000 m and above demands for oxygen during physical work become increasingly difficult to meet and beyond about 4000 m the rate of oxygen transfer is insufficient to satisfy efficiently the needs of even the sedentary man. To the first exposures to such conditions the body displays a rather limited compensatory response and breakdown may easily be produced. However, secondary processes of physiological acclimatization make possible work and permanent residence at surprisingly high levels. There is cultivated land in Tibet at altitudes of 2700–4500 m and in the Andes permanent settlements at 5200 m, and daily work visits (for mining) at 5800 m. The area above 4000 m is predominantly pastoral with some agriculture, below this the reverse obtains (Baker).

*Responses*

The immediate response to lack of oxygen (anoxia) is an increase in the volume of air respired per minute. This is brought about by more rapid and by deeper respirations. This response has only a limited result in improving the oxygen supply. Oxygen transport is aided by the fact that oxygen dissociates more easily at low oxygen pressures (i.e. per unit difference of pressure on the steep part of the dissociation curve). The increased breathing leads to the 'washing out' of carbon dioxide from the air passages and consequently from the blood. This loss of carbon dioxide changes the homeostatically controlled acid-base balance of the body to a more alkaline level—an 'alkalosis'. In mountain sickness, anoxia and alkalosis both play a part. The anoxia shows itself in tiredness, headache, loss of attention, and a feeling akin to 'drunken confidence'; as the alkalosis develops there is nausea, vomiting, and dizziness. In the early stages of exposure respiration is poorly controlled and tends to 'hunt' (Cheyne–Stokes breathing). Any exertion is accompanied by an abnormal increase in pulse-rate. Elevation of resting heart-rate and cardiac output under the influence of hypoxia return with acclimatization to sea-level values.

With continued exposure a considerable tolerance can be developed. The acclimatization processes involve a persistent hyperpnoea, though permanent residents ventilate less than acclimatized visitors. This brings about a smaller gradient of oxygen pressure between the atmosphere and lung alveoli resulting in a gain in the arterial oxygen tension. The carbon-dioxide pressure in the alveolar air, though low, is higher than without the increased ventilation. The alkalosis must be counteracted and this is done by the kidney, which excretes a more alkaline urine, so eliminating the excess of base and keeping the blood pH reaction at normal levels.

At the same time red blood-cells are formed in increased numbers, the red-cell count and the cellular haemoglobin concentration rise, so that the oxygen-carrying capacity of the blood is increased. There is a linear relation between haemoglobin concentration and barometric pressure up to 3500 m, with a steeper rise thereafter. This response together with respiratory adjustments enables native residents to achieve an arterial oxygen content above that of pressure at sea-level. There is probably also an increased ability of tissues to work at low oxygen tensions.

In native residents the pulmonary arterial pressure is higher than in visitors and is associated with right ventricular hypertrophy. Some workers believe that this has adaptive value in that the perfusion of pulmonary areas is improved and blood gas exchange facilitated. Natives when working can attain higher cardiac outputs than acclimatized visitors; blood lactate levels and oxygen debt after submaximal exercise are lower.

At 4500 m acclimatization takes place in some 10 days. In the long run morphological changes ensue—the thorax enlarges with the increased respiration and the vital capacity is demonstrably larger.

In most high-altitude regions winter temperatures are very low; in Tibet at 5000 m values down to $-33\,^{\circ}C$ are found and summer temperatures rise only to about 13 °C. Clothing, shelter, and heating arrangements are generally effective in protecting against cold, though some degree of physiological acclimatization is detectable.

*Populations at high altitude*

Some slight adaptive changes are detectable even at 2000 m and have been found in peoples in the Caucasus, Pyrenees, and even the High Veld of South Africa. A variety of racial groups therefore exhibit these physiological phenomena. These include the Tibetans, living up to 4500 m, the inhabitants of Kashmir at 3000 m, those of the high uplands at 2500 m, and of the Andes at 5500 m. At these altitudes the acclimatization processes are well in evidence, for example in Peru the native inhabitants may have red-cell counts 30 per cent above the sea-level value.

While the responses described are secondary acquisitions, it is quite conceivable that some characteristics could under selection have been fixed genetically. The llama, the vicuna, and Bolivian goose, all native to high altitudes, have high values for red-cell count and increased affinity of the haemoglobin for $O_2$ and these characters are retained by first-generation llamas born at sea-level. Monde argues that selection among the Spanish invaders of the Andes eliminated the majority who were infertile and that pure Spaniards established themselves only after some generations. But convincing evidence of genotypes adaptive for altitude stress in man has yet to be produced.

## Work capacity

The survival of mankind has depended very largely on the individual's ability to perform the muscular work inseparable from hunting, load-carrying, forest clearing, hoeing, digging, etc. Man possesses a highly flexible, homeostatically controlled, energy-producing system capable of coping both with continuous hard work and with peak outbursts at high intensity. This system depends essentially on the rapid usage of high-energy phosphate bands and their replenishment both during and after activity by a supply of oxygen and its utilization at appropriate rates (see standard textbooks of physiology).

One method of assessing an individual's capacity for muscular work is to measure his ability to transfer and utilize oxygen from lungs to muscle. For comparative purposes the maximum rate of oxygen usage can be determined during an individual's maximum rate of working. This measurement—the maximum aerobic power or $V_{O_2max}$—has now been obtained on a fairly considerable number of populations and various factors which influence the observed variance have been examined.

$V_{O_2max}$ is fairly high correlated with body size, particularly body-weight and lean body-mass; and since most tests of $V_{O_2max}$ have been made on the stationary bicycle ergometer there is a close correlation also with lower-limb volume

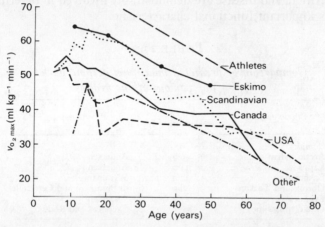

F IG. 27.8. The maximum oxygen intake per kilogram body weight in relation to age and geographic region. Data collected from the literature by Shephard.

and muscle mass. Accordingly, for intra- and interpopulation comparisons allowance for body-size or muscularity must be made. It can be seen from Fig. 27.8 that there is a marked decline in maximum aerobic power with age. This is in some measure due to the reduction in the level of habitual activity, that is in the state of 'training'. Like other characteristics of major adaptive significance (e.g. heat or altitude tolerance), work capacity can be improved by daily repetition or by progressive intensification of muscular effort. The degree of improvement in $V_{O_2max}$ is of the order of 20 per cent.

Communities or occupational groups who habitually perform heavy work show a higher mean $V_{O_2max}$ than those who engage in light or sedentary tastes, e.g. Yoruba heavy workers (55·5) compared to light workers (45·9). From Table 27.7 there appears a clear tendency for simple subsistence peoples to show a higher $V_{O_2max}$ than the 'urbanized' groups. A large and well controlled study of the Canadian Eskimo (Rode and Shepherd) has demonstrated that Eskimo boys and men actively engaged in hunting have both a level of energy expenditure (i.e. habitual activity) and an aerobic power much in excess of that of Canadian urban Whites. It should be noted that some European communities (e.g. Swedes—mean $V_{O_2\text{max}}$ 52·0) show a conspicuously high level of fitness.

The question of the contribution made by heritability to the work capacity variance, is raised (a) by the fact that changes in $V_{O_2\text{max}}$ due to training can only account for a proportion of the total variance of an adult male population, and (b) the fact that athletes are clearly a highly selected group. Twin studies have shown that the genetical component may account for over 80 per cent of the variance. But the range of environmental variation in such studies is much less than in ordinary populations and this will tend to increase the heritable component. Since $V_{O_2\text{max}}$ depends on the individual's body-size and muscularity it is apparent that both genetic and non-genetic factors including training, nutrition, and disease are demonstrably involved in determining the range of this important functional characteristic.

TABLE 27.7

*Comparison of predicted maximum aerobic power*
*($V_{O_2\text{max}}$) of various ethnic groups*

| Ethnic group | $V_{O_2\text{max}}$ (ml kg$^{-1}$min$^{-1}$) | Authors |
|---|---|---|
| *'Simple'* | | |
| Arctic Indian | 49·6 | Andersen et al |
| Lapps | 54·0 | Andersen et al. |
| Bushman | 47·9 | Wyndham |
| Dorobo and Turkana | 46·0 | di Prampero and Cerretelli |
| Pygmies | 47·4 | Andersen |
| Canadian Eskimos | 56·5 | Shepherd and Rode |
| *'Urbanized'* | | |
| Bantu | 44·6 | Wyndham et al. |
| American | 43·5 | Taylor et al. |
| British | 41·0 | Davies et al. |
| Canadian | 44·5 | Shepherd et al. |
| Czechoslovakian | 40·6 | Skranc |
| German | 40·5 | Konig et al. |
| Italian | 45·0 | di Prampero and Cerretelli |
| Norwegian | 44·0 | Hermansen and Andersen |
| South African | 45·6 | Wyndham et al. |
| Japanese | 45·0 | Ikai and Shindo |

(Modified from Davies *et al. J. appl. Physiol. 33*, 726, 1972.)

# 28. Disease

THE ecological aspects of disease reveal themselves clearly in three ways. (1) The physical environment represents a direct and immediate source of injury and ill health. There is consequently a clear geographical distribution in the pathological effects of climatic extremes (e.g. heat stroke), of high altitude (mountain sickness), and ultraviolet light (e.g. rodent ulcer). Air pollution by smoke and associated substances has in recent years become an important environmental hazard in many countries. (2) The biotic component of the environment harbours injurious agents in the form of pathogenic organisms—viruses, bacteria, protozoa, fungi, as well as poisonous plants and insects and dangerous animals. (3) There are nutritional disorders arising from the failure to utilize food sources, animal and vegetable (and also mineral) correctly.

Over and above these environmentally produced diseases, there is a large group of illnesses that make their overt appearance as a result of some maladjustment of growth, function, or control within the organism, but their effects and full consequences are realized in relation to the external environment, particularly in social relationships. Genetic defect may mean an inability of the individual to support himself, while psychological disorder manifests itself in an inability fully to understand and respond to external events and demands.

The ecology of disease is a large and intricate subject but in general the distribution and incidence of disease are to be understood by the population biologist in terms of the interaction between environmental and biological, including genetic, factors. The principles of adaptation, biological and technological, need always to be borne in mind.

## Infectious disease

As a result of his hunting and trapping activities, as well as other measures such as deforestation and swamp drainage, man has disposed of his larger competitors for space and food, in many cases to the point of needless extermination of many species. But the dangers and diseases that spring from man's contact with other living organisms represent phases of ecological conflict which have not as yet entirely been resolved in man's favour. Man still contends with smaller creatures, such as rodents, insects, fungi, and micro-organisms. Some of these are parasitic on his food and shelter, others are directly parasitic or injurious to his body.

The geographical background is the biggest single factor governing the type and abundance of parasites and pathogens. Micro-organisms may be waterborne, airborne, or carried by insects, other animals or other men. The relation between host and organism may often take a complex course depending on the number of stages and factors involved—vector, intermediate host, and one or more reservoirs. Analysis of the locality will often reveal that ecological relationships are strongly influenced by physical features such as wind, rainwater, drainage, temperature, and humidity. The pathogen itself may have a limited environmental tolerance. The vector usually requires particular conditions for breeding, e.g. ticks or fleas may need a dry climate. Again, the carrier may have a restricted habitat, e.g. tree-living squirrels in the Malayan rain forest. The breeding possibilities of the female *Anopheles* is controlled by pool formation and hence by the rainfall, the structure of the soil, and its water-retaining properties. The tsetse fly, vector of African sleeping sickness, requires a relatively dense vegetational cover.

The geographical distribution of many diseases is thus simply that of their intermediate hosts and vectors. Schistosomiasis is common in riverine populations in warm climates as the bladderworm needs a particular snail for one stage of its development. Rickettsial diseases, e.g. Rocky Mountain spotted fever, are linked with ticks found chiefly in North America, Bengal, and North Africa; the Asiatic form, scrub typhus, carried by mites, occurs in Japan, Formosa, and Oceania; the typhus group of Europe and central Asia is linked with fleas and lice. Brucellosis is geographically related to the use of milk and milk products, that is, to cattle herds as the main reservoir.

A microbial disease with a fairly simple relationship to climate is yaws—80 per cent of the yaws areas lie within the mean annual 27 °C isotherm, the remainder between 21 °C and 27 °C, and the disease is particularly rife where the annual rainfall is 125–175 mm. In what way high humidity and temperature favour the survival and transmission of the treponeme is not clear. Hookworm infection requires a temperature between 25 °C and 30 °C and a precipitation of 150 mm or more. The disease occurs therefore mostly between the 40th parallels north and south.

Because the ecological relations are so complex, only a relatively few kinds of parasites characterize any given locality out of the thousands of varieties which parasitize man as a species. Thus the particular ecological relations of most micro-organisimal disease will be unravelled only by quite specific regional analysis. Audy gives an example: Somaliland has a dry climate and much of the country is semi-desert and thorn scrub. Hence cataract and eye infections are causally associated with the flying sand and sun-glare as well as the flies which breed freely because of the dry climate. The climate also favours the existence of soft ticks carrying relapsing fever. There is moderate incidence of Madura foot, the fungal spores being inoculated into the skin by the thorns. The intense dryness and frequent sandstorms encourage infected sore throats (which the Somalis have come to treat by snipping off the uvula!). Sand, dryness, and glare are the prime physical factors that can be identified in this ecological complex. Another example may be drawn from the Arctic. Here, despite the great number and variety of mosquitoes and other arthropods of the Arctic region, none is known to transmit infectious disease, but throughout the North American Arctic, dogs, which still provide the chief means of winter transport, act as a main reservoir of human disease including salmonellae, meat and fish tape-worm, and rabies. The seasonal incidence of these diseases is due simply to the fact that the insanitary disposal of waste in the vicinity of dwellings is rendered innocuous in the frozen state but the preserved pathogens are released with the spring thaw.

The character of man's settlements and type of housing may introduce factors favourable to the spread of particular diseases. Thus both in cold climates (among Eskimos) and hot, dry countries where nomadism prevails, there is crowding of people in small living quarters, for warmth in one case, or because of the need to carry as little as possible in the other. In both cases the overcrowding is conducive to the spread of respiratory infections notably pneumonia and tuberculosis. The small Melanesian house in the New Hebrides is not only air-tight but also ghost-tight! In the Yemen schistosomiasis is spread through the communal use of ritual ablution pools.

Human settlement may require clearance and deforestation and this in turn may provide conditions favourable for the propagation of infectious disease. Thus deforestation of the hills of Sri Lanka led to more frequent pool formation during dry spells and hence to mosquito-breeding. In Malaysia certain rats capable of carrying tick disease are very rare in the natural forest but after deforestation they occur in great numbers. Irrigation systems are highly conducive to the spreading of bilharzia in Africa, China, and Japan.

The great plague and cholera epidemics were in the main social phenomena arising from improvements in transport and the contacts between dense populations. These epidemics were carried along the routes of caravans, ships, and railroads at increasing speeds. The pilgrimage to Mecca was at one time a prime cause of new cholera epidemics.

### Biological responses

Resistance to infectious disease—like resistance to other stresses—may involve one or both of two factors. These may be genetic factors making for natural resistance or there may be an 'active' immunity acquired only as a result of contact with the disease agent. (The passive immunity acquired when circulating antibodies are transferred to the baby's circulation from the mother, disappears a few months after birth.) The capacity to develop immune reactions may be regarded as a physiological attribute, possessed by the human species as a whole and a product of evolutionary selection. As Burnet says, 'in a world full of micro-organisms capable of infecting living tissues, it is a positive necessity for survival that most experiences of infection by any given microbe should be followed first by recovery and secondly by a persisting insusceptibility to an attack of the same disease'. Indeed, as he points out, the type of immunity characteristic of human beings reflects the habitat of man's arboreal ancestry in tropical jungles, for in such environments it seems likely that the major type of pathogen would be those protozoa and viruses spread by insect (and especially mosquito) vectors and the immune reactions involved are essentially those to deal with infection by viruses of the yellow-fever type.

Whenever the body is invaded by a pathogenic organism the defence process gets underway; this takes the form essentially of the production of modified protein (in highest concentration in the blood) called antibodies, since they possess the property of penetrating or adhering to, and acting on the pathogen and so preventing its activity and multiplication. The antibodies so formed are specific and persistent; since they remain in the bloodstream and tissues in significant amounts, re-entry of the pathogen is countered immediately and more effectively. Immune antibodies against a wide variety of pathogens can be formed by virtue of the innumerable modifications which can be made to the molecular pattern of the basic protein (the serum protein $\gamma$ globulin) to allow of a specific 'recognition' of, and interreaction with, particular invading pathogens.

Airborne infections (e.g. influenza, common cold, measles, or smallpox) die out completely in moderately small communities because there is insufficient frequency and variety of contacts between individuals. Such infections cannot have become adapted to and established in human communities until man became urbanized.

At any one time different populations may be at different stages of resistance according to the pathogens to which they happen to have been exposed. A disease which has reached a certain state of balance and is mildly endemic in one people may spread in serious epidemic waves through populations which do not have this acquired immunity.

Resistance to disease through acquired immunity falls into a category analogous to that of physiological acclimatization to extremes of heat or cold or altitude. These are all the result of exposure to particular environmental stresses; in all cases the adaptability is a property common to the species as a whole, while the individual capacity to develop these responses must have some genetic determinant of which, however, very little is known.

A question for the medical anthropologist is whether there are any examples of differences in susceptibility or resistance to infectious disease between different groups which result, not from acquired immunity, but from gene-controlled characters regardless of whether or not recent contact with disease has occurred.

It has been postulated (Haldane) that infectious disease might well have been the most effective agent of natural selection of man in favouring the survival and reproduction of those individuals possessing genes making for resistance. Most chronic or degenerative diseases (e.g. arterosclerosis) would not be expected to act as selective agents as they kill after reproduction has ceased, unless they are in some way also associated with decreased fertility. That genetic resistance to infectious (and some other) diseases exists is not in doubt, though in only a few cases, so far, has the responsible gene (and its metabolic role in disease protection) been identified.

*Malaria*

This is by far the best-analysed example of a disease against which certain genes confer a measure of resistance. There is evidence that three red-blood-cell polymorphisms of man, the sickling trait, thalassemia, and glucose 6-phosphate dehydrogenase (G6PD) deficiency, owe their present population frequencies to selection by falciparum malaria (the nature of these balanced polymorphisms has already been discussed in Chapter 16). The geographical distribution of these characteristics in relation to regions of high malarial incidence is striking. Figs. 28.1 and 28.2 show the world distribution of falciparum malaria before 1930, the distribution of the sickle-cell trait (Hb-S) and also of G6PD deficiency and thalassemia. It can be seen that in Africa there is a fairly good correlation between the frequency of sickling and enzyme deficiency; though not the same individuals were necessarily affected. In various populations children possessing sickling trait or those with the enzyme deficiency have been found to harbour significantly fewer malarial parasites. The protection against malaria increases the survival of sickle-cell heterozygotes between birth and reproductive age and may also increase the fertility of women heterozygous for the sickle-cell gene (Allison 1960). From this and other evidence Motulsky concludes that malaria has acted as a common selective agent favouring independent mutations both for sickling and G6PD deficiency. One of the most striking and unexplained differences in susceptibility to malaria infection is the lack of sensitivity to *P. vivax* by West-African Negroes.

On archaeological evidence, a relationship between the distribution of the thalassemia gene and malaria has been claimed to exist in the eastern Mediterranean area. The bony evidence of thalassemia—porotic hyperostosis—seems to have been in evidence among Neolithic farmers occupying and clearing areas which facilitated the spread of the mosquito. In the preceding hunting period, when drier ground was occupied, the hyperostosis was not present (Angel 1940).

There is fairly strong suggestive evidence (Motulsky 1958) that genetic resistance factors play a role in a number of other important diseases (e.g. tuberculosis, measles, and poliomyelitis), though in none of these has the genotype conferring increased or decreased susceptibility been specifically identified. One line of evidence is based on the decreased mortality which follows several generations of exposure during a period when remedial or hygienic measures were little or not at all in operation. There is often a noticeable familial incidence, even though conditions of exposure are similar for different families. Some populations may be much more resistant than others, despite similar rates of infection. It is by no means easy to separate the action of acquired immunity in these circumstances from that of genetically determined host resistance, but animal experiments show clearly that by artificial selection it is possible to establish strains resistant or susceptible to a number of diseases including some closely related to those of man, e.g. tuberculosis in rabbits, poliomyelitis in

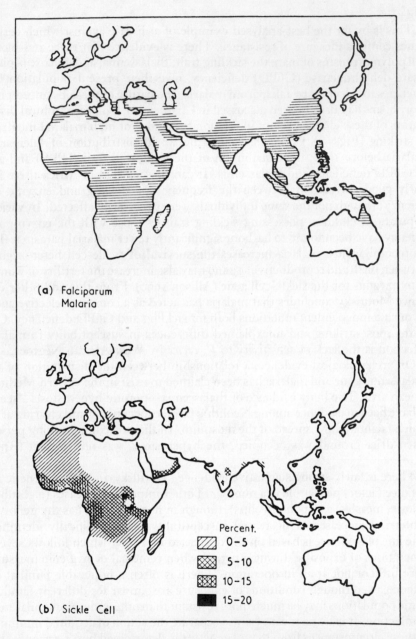

(a) Falciparum
Malaria

(b) Sickle Cell

Percent.
▨ 0–5
▨ 5–10
▨ 10–15
■ 15–20

F IG. 28.1(a). Distribution of falciparum malaria. (After Boyd, Malariology, a comprehensive study, Saunders, Philadelphia, 1949.)

F IG. 28.1(b). Distribution of sickle cell in the Old World. (From Allison, *Genetical variation in human populations*, Pergamon, Oxford, 1961.)

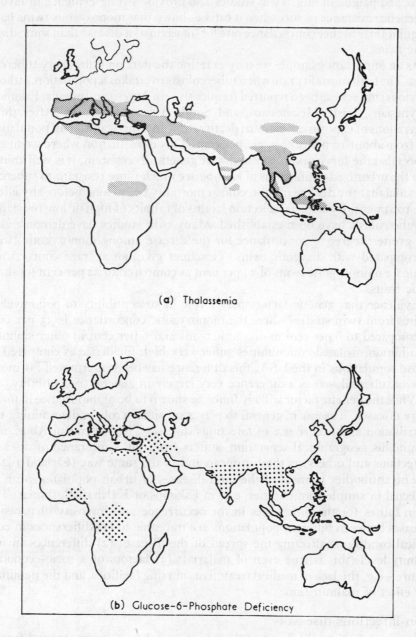

FIG. 28.2(a). Distribution of thalassemia. (See Chernoff, *Blood*, 14, 1959.)
FIG. 28.2(b). Distribution of glucose 6-phosphate dehydrogenase deficiency. (From Motulsky, *Hum Biol.*, 32, 1960.)

mice, and plague in rats. Twin studies also provide strong evidence in favour of genetic resistance factors when it can be shown that monozygous twins have a significantly higher concordance rate for (or against) a disease than some dizygotic twins.

As an important example we may examine the data on pulmonary tuberculosis. The high mortality rate when tuberculosis overtakes a population without previous contact has been reported frequently—in American Indians, Eskimos, Polynesians, Irish, Melanesians, and South African Bushmen. After three generations of exposure the annual death rate of an American Indian population fell from about 10 per cent to 0·2 per cent. This is a situation where we might expect that the survivors are those who are genetically resistant. It is well known that the urbanized populations of Europe are much more resistant to tuberculosis and that the decline in tuberculosis mortality began long before any effective treatment. By artificial selection strains of rabbits of high or low resistance to tuberculosis have been established. Many twin studies have demonstrated the greater degree of concordance for the disease among monozygotic twins as compared with dizygotic twins. Verschuer gives an average concordance value for monozygotic twins of 53 per cent as compared to 22 per cent for dizygotic twins.

Evidence that genetic factors play a role in susceptibility to poliomyelitis comes from twin studies where the monozygotic concordance is 35 per cent as compared to 6 per cent in dizygotic twins and 6 per cent in other siblings. In addition, isolated communities suffer very high incidence as compared to dense populations in the USA; this difference has been interpreted (as in the case of tuberculosis) as a difference very largely in genetic susceptibility.

While the genetic factor will no doubt be shown to be of importance in many more diseases, it seems in general to play a subsidiary role in determining the distribution and occurrence of infectious disease. The Australian Aborigine, despite his geographical separation, suffers from the same range of diseases (infectious and others) as the European and in the same way (Cleland 1928).

The antibodies of most of the viral diseases of urban populations can be detected in simple communities, e.g. in Eskimos or Kalahari Bushmen. The main causes for the differences in the occurrence and intensity of parasitic diseases between different populations are traceable to (1) differences in ecological conditions affecting the spread of the disease; (2) differences in immunity level (this is true even of malaria); (3) factors of a socio-economic nature—e.g. the lack of medical treatment, nursing facilities, and the debilitating effect of malnutrition.

## Non-infectious diseases

In non-infectious disease, too, the whole complex of environmental factors and biological responses (inborn and acquired) must always be considered when trying to account for regional variation. The fact that Negroes are more susceptible to frostbite than are Eskimos or North American Indians may well be attributable to both lack of acclimatization and to some genetic susceptibility. The malformation of the central nervous system, spina bifida and anencephaly, whose exact aetiology is not known, have been shown from family and ethnic studies by Carter to involve genetic factors: social class, birth order, and maternal age effects as well as secular seasonal variation indicate that environmental factors are also important in their causation.

The geographical aspect of cancer has received much attention in the hope that a study of local conditions associated with high or low incidences may give a clue to aetiology, but on the whole this approach has raised at least as many problems as it has solved. Cancer of one kind or another has been reported in all human populations, but there are remarkable variations in the incidence of particular neoplasms. It is not easy to make reliable estimates of the population frequencies, especially in places with rudimentary medical services, and even in advanced countries improvements in diagnosis and in the efficiency of screening and reporting may necessitate revision of the figures from time to time. Even so, many population differences cannot be dismissed as sampling artifacts. The risk of many types of tumour increases greatly with age so that crude cancer rates for the two sexes provide a poor comparison of susceptibility if the age structure of the populations is different.

Higginson and Oettlé made a survey of cancer in Bantu peoples of the Transvaal and compared the observed incidences of various types of tumour with the incidences to be expected in American Whites, American Negroes, and Danish populations of corresponding age distribution (Table 28.1). They found cancer of the stomach, colon, and rectum to be much less common in Bantu

TABLE 28.1

*Number of cases of cancer in Bantu of Johannesburg (1953–5), and expected numbers in three other populations when standardized for age*

| Site of cancer | Bantu (observed) | American White | American Negro | Danes |
|---|---|---|---|---|
| *Males* | | | | |
| Buccal and lip | 2 | 21·3 | 2·0 | 24·3 |
| Tongue | 8 | 12·9 | 9·3 | — |
| Oesophagus | 53 | 20·9 | 36·5 | 12·2 |
| Stomach | 41 | 89·0 | 128·4 | 119·4 |
| Colon | 7 | 75·7 | 54·1 | 43·6 |
| Rectum | 5 | 67·8 | 45·7 | 61·0 |
| Liver | 114 | 13·8 | 25·7 | 1·4 |
| Lung (bronchus) | 40 | 103·0 | 104·3 | 51·1 |
| Penis | 8 | 3·9 | 11·4 | 3·6 |
| Skin | 14 | 212·7 | 18·2 | 49·5 |
| *Females* | | | | |
| Cervix uteri | 198 | 119·1 | 266·6 | 122·1 |
| Corpus uteri | 1 | 27·9 | 25·5 | 23·2 |
| Breast | 50 | 221·9 | 170·7 | 131·8 |

(From Higginson and Oettlé, *J. natn. Cancer Inst.* 24, 589, 1960.)

males and the rates for cancer of the breast and body of the uterus to be much lower in Bantu females than in the control groups. On the other hand, cancer of the liver (hepatoma), and to a lesser extent of the oesophagus, were much more frequent in the Bantu males. In some respects the rates for Bantu and American Negroes were very different, but both had a low incidence of cancer of the mouth, lip, and skin, attributable in part to their pigmentation, and a high rate of cancer of the cervix uteri as compared with either of the White groups. It will also be noticed that there are marked differences between the American Whites and the Danes in the frequencies of gastric, hepatic, and mammary cancers.

Many more examples of population variations in cancer incidence could be given. In some cases it is plausible to indict a specific environmental factor. The high rate of bucco-pharyngeal cancers in parts of India is said to be associated with tobacco-chewing, and cancer of exposed skin areas in white men in very sunny regions is attributable to solar ultraviolet radiation. Primary cancer of the liver, common in the African, seems to be a late sequel of the widely prevalent liver cirrhosis, and this in turn is bound up with the consumption from infancy of a diet chronically low in animal protein and overweighted with carbohydrate. Striking 'racial' differences in the incidence of coronary disease on analysis are found to be associated with diets high in fat. The differences in fat consumption of European and Bantu in South Africa, reflecting economic status, are paralleled by the liability to coronary disease, highest amongst Europeans and lowest in the Bantu.

Interestingly enough, the low fat–low calorie diet of many Negro populations, while disadvantageous in certain respects, would seem to have favoured an extremely low incidence of diabetes mellitus. That this is not a 'racial' difference follows from the observation that, as food habits change, Negroes (e.g. in the USA) suffer as much as Europeans, while Europeans forced on to a low fat–low calorie diet by exigencies of war (as in Sweden and Britain) experienced a fall in incidence of this disease. The nature of the diet thus determines the expression or course of the disease, for it has recently been claimed that a predisposition to diabetes is inherited as a simple autosomal recessive gene with a frequency in the USA between 20 per cent and 25 per cent (Steinberg and Wilder). That a hereditary liability to diabetes exists can also be inferred from the observation that people with the disease are more likely to have diabetic relatives than people without the disease, and it occurs more often in twin pairs if they are identical. Indeed these degrees of kinship are reflected in the height of the blood-glucose 'tolerance' response following oral administration of glucose.

Many diseases and malformations are known to have a simple gene basis; the afflicted individual is usually homozygous for the recessive gene, though genes with dominance are also involved in some conditions. Nearly all such 'genetic' diseases are very rare. A number, however, occur in particularly high frequencies in certain populations. Thalassemia and sickle-cell anaemia are associated with the presence of genes for particular haemoglobin variants (see Chapter 16). Haemolytic disease of the newborn, due to Rhesus incompatibility (p. 261), is characteristic of European but not of most Mongoloid or American Indian populations, since they are devoid of Rh-negative individuals. The incidence of duodenal ulcer seems in part accountable by the frequency of the O group, and people with group A are more prone to cancer of the stomach than those of other blood-groups.

The comparison of populations in contrasted environments has also played a part in research on cardiovascular disease. Chronically raised blood-pressure is recognized as a predisposing factor to coronary thrombosis and cerebral haemorrhage. Many cases of hypertension fall into the category of 'essential hypertension' for which no definite pathological explanation can be found. In countries with a high standard of living the statistical distribution of systolic blood-pressure in a given age group is continuous but non-Gaussian in form, with an extended tail of high values (positive skewing). The mean systolic and diastolic pressures in the population increase with age especially in males in the range over 50 years. Some workers believe that cases of essential hypertension (sometimes arbitrarily defined by pressure of 150/100 or more) do not constitute a distinct category but are simply the more extreme variants in a distribution with a single mode; the continuous form of distribution is due, so they believe, to the combined actions of many genes and multiple environmental factors. Others hold that the hypertensives are in fact a distinct group depending, as some think, on a comparatively simple genetic difference. On this view the essential bimodality of the distribution is obscured by extensive overlapping with normals. Essential hypertension (Pickering and Fraser Roberts) affects the people who happen to inherit the tendency to high blood-pressures at the extreme end of the scale. Genetic differences are therefore involved both in the incidence of hypertension in different populations and in the variation in the mean and range of the blood-pressure. The multifactorial nature of blood-pressure distribution must also include environmental factors. For example, American Negroes have higher blood-pressures (which increase with age) than African Negroes; urbanized Bantu have higher pressures than non-urbanized.

Even within a given region or ethnic group there may be very marked heterogeneity in mean blood-pressure at a given age and also in the incidence of deaths due to hypertension. In Japan both variables have their highest incidence in the north-eastern regions (with the exception of the island of Hokkaido), and it is thought that varying levels of indoor and outdoor temperature together with dietary differences are important causal factors. Among Australian Aborigines relatively low systolic pressures were found in tribes in the central desert living a nomadic hunting life, but rather higher values in those with more European contact as amongst the Queensland tribes. It seems that numerous factors including nutrition, exercise, environmental temperature, and psychogenic stress may underlie geographical variations in blood-pressure and liability to hypertensive disease.

The deviation in blood-pressure between elderly monozygotic twins is hardly less than that between elderly siblings and dizygotic twins; this points to a strong environmental effect on blood-pressure in the elderly. But what environmental factors are involved is a matter of controversy; differences in amount of exercise taken or diet—particularly in fat, salt, or protein—or psychological factors have all been invoked. Pickering estimates that inheritance is roughly equivalent to environment in producing hypertension. The fact that natural selection has failed to eliminate high blood-pressure as a cause of death in many populations is presumably because it kills in the post-reproductive age span.

## Toxic chemicals and pollutants

Ingestion of toxic chemicals as contaminants of food or drink or as excessive doses of drugs is by no means a hazard only of this present era of chemical synthesis. Pre-literate peoples, as part of their ecological knowledge, are well aware of the dangers of particular plants, roots, or berries. They use various preparations for medicinal purposes with circumspection. Many hunter groups understand how to prepare and handle the poisons with which their arrows or spears are tipped. But modern man faces vastly more hazards than pre-literate man in the form of toxic substances, particularly those derived from industrial processes, which are ingested, inhaled, or absorbed through the skin.

Bodily changes in response to toxic agents show the usual wide range within populations. We have therefore to consider the interaction of environmental and biological factors in accounting for variation in tolerance or susceptibility. Biological factors in turn can either be acquired or reflect differences in genetic endowment.

Many toxic compounds undergo inactivation through conversion to inactive metabolites by liver enzymes, or they are excreted by the kidneys, or both processes occur. These can be regarded as primary adaptive responses. Metabolism and elimination of pollutants depend on the particular physio-chemical properties involved. Some pollutants can be excreted unchanged if they are not readily diffusible or are not lipid-soluble. The de-toxicating liver enzymes are quite distinct from the enzymes of normal intermediate metabolism; they must have been evolved (suggests Brodie) to permit the organism to dispose of lipid-soluble substances ingested in the food, such as hydrocarbons, alkaloids, terpenes, and steroids. These enzymes are highly non-specific, and before the industrial era could have dealt with many harmful materials found in nature. The rate of metabolic de-toxication varies greatly between individuals, and there is a genetic basis for this, since monovular twins have identical rates of drug metabolism, whereas for binovular twins the rates may be as different as between any other members of the population.

Enzyme induction is the property responsible for enhanced resistance to toxic substances. Some environmental chemicals can stimulate or increase their own metabolic disposal. Like all 'training' phenomena this enzymic induction sets in after a period of administration of the substance, usually after several days; following its withdrawal the induction passes off within 2 or 3 weeks. Induction involves an enhanced activity as well as increased synthesis of metabolizing enzymes, mainly hepatic. Induction can be prevented by inhibiting protein synthesis, e.g. by administering actinomycin D.

Environmental toxicants which induce enzymic enhancement include chlorinated hydrocarbons (the DDT group), alcohol, tobacco, and many drugs. Phenobarbitone, after 2 weeks of administration, undergoes a reduction in persistence, as measured by its half-life, from 13 hours to 5 hours. This drug stimulates the liver enzyme glucoronyl transferase. There is, of course, a limit in induction capacity, and it is likely that genetic factors determine the extent of the induction response (Lawrence). The population variation in drug tolerance thus reflects both variation in exposure as between different individuals and the degree of enzymic induction.

# 29. Population stability

EVERY community, as we have seen, is called on to make a variety of adjustments to the stresses and challenges issuing from the physical and organic components of the environment. An important resultant of these ecological interactions is the population size; life statistics constitute a significant measure of the effectiveness of the ecological control exerted deliberately or otherwise by the community.

## Population density and size

The great diversity of human ecosystems is reflected in a correspondingly great range of population size. The rough relation between the type or stage of the economy and population density is indicated in Table 29.1.

Within each economic group clearly many factors are at work. In general the population density in a given environment will depend on the following factors:

(1) the variables of the environment in terms of climate, soil, and topographya;
(2) the variables afforded by the local animal and vegetational resources;
(3) the variables in technology which determine the 'extractive efficiency'.

With simple societies of relatively uniform cultural organization over a given area, the operation of a fairly direct environmental determinism on population level is discernible. In Australia, as analysed by Birdsell (1953), it is the mean annual rainfall which yields a simple relationship to population density, with an overall correlation of $+0.8$ for all population sizes. Where population size is in the region of 500 persons, the equation of density 'prediction' takes the form $Y = 7112.8 X^{-1.5845}$ (where $Y$ is the size of the tribal territory and $X$ is the mean annual rainfall).

It does not follow that regions which seem environmentally similar will necessarily show similar densities even for peoples of about the same level of extractive efficiency, and in these cases it is differences in local biota and food chains which exert the major effect in bringing about density differences. The Bushmen of the Kalahari Desert and the Shoshoni of the Great Basin have quite different densities from the Australians for the same rainfall conditions. The fact that Indians of middle Baja California with even lower rainfall but much higher extractive efficiency show a density 50 times the Australian is attributable to the local wealth of starchy plant food (in the form of half a dozen species of agave). As we pass from simple hunting and collecting cultures to more complex societies, social and technological variables obviously play a progressively more important role in determining population characteristics, since

TABLE 29.1

*Population density*

| Category | Square miles per head | Heads per square mile |
|---|---|---|
| 1. *Food-gatherers* | 200 to 0·5 | up to 2 |
| Upper Paleolithic man (Britain) | 200 | — |
| Australian Aborigines | 25 | — |
| Tierra del Fuego Islanders | 8 | — |
| Andaman Islanders | 0·5 | — |
| 2. *Higher hunters and fishers* | 200 to 0·05 | up to 20 |
| Eskimos and Indians (N.W. Territories) | 200 | — |
| Eskimos (Alaska) | 30 | — |
| Mesolithic man (Britain) | 10 | — |
| Pampas Indians | 2 | — |
| British Columbians | 0·05 | — |
| 3. *Early cultivators* | 0·05 to 1 | ½ up to 50 |
| Neolithic man (Britain) | | 2 |
| 4. *Pastoralists and nomads* | — | 10–100 |
| 5. *Advanced cultivators* | — | 10–150 |
| Iron Age man (Britain) | | 10 |
| Middle Age man (Britain) | | 50 |
| Swidden farmers | — | 20–150 |

more efficient use can be made of the resources of the environment and its limitations overcome.

For most of human history the technology remained at the simplest level of food-gathering, hunting, and subsistence horticulture. Consequently world population remained for a long time very low and its growth was very slow; occupation by *Homo sapiens* of cooler regions probably only began in the last stages of the Pleistocene and Australia and America were only occupied some 12 000–15 000 years ago. Acceleration of population growth began with agriculture and the urban life which it made possible some 8000 years ago; only in the very recent past has industrialization brought about the present phase of prodigious expansion. Roughly speaking it would appear that in the stage of food-gathering and hunting corresponding to that of Palaeolithic and Meso-lithic culture, the density was well below 1 head per square mile; in the cultivat-ing stage corresponding to the Neolithic it rises by a factor of about 10; in the metal-using and early stages of civilization by a further factor of 10. In the first stages total world population has been estimated as of the order of 5 million, reaching 20–40 million in the first urban period. It took *Homo sapiens* some 20 000 years to reach a figure of about 200 million (at the time of the early Roman Empire). A further 1500 years (to A.D. 1600) sufficed to bring it to 500 million, and 200 years more to double this (1000 million in 1800). Today, over 100 years later, the figure is of the order of 3000 million and more.

At all times there has existed a great unevenness in the distribution of the world's population. Even today 50 per cent of the population is contained in about 5 per cent of the occupied area (see Table 25.3) while 80 per cent of the area has a density of only 9 per square mile. At all times, since urbanization began, there have existed communities of small size in many different habitats alongside large and dense population aggregates.

## Population control

Human populations display various patterns of population dynamics—of increase, of stability, and of depopulation. Since the simplest human societies seem to approach stability of numbers the principles of the 'natural control' system of animal populations, as formulated by animal ecologists (Elton, Nicholson, and Solomon) are worth consideration in the human context. The salient features of this 'natural' control system are as follows.

1. An approach to stability in numbers means in reality the existence of fluctuations or oscillations within a definite range.

2. The stable level of density is imposed by the capacity of the system (as we have seen in the case of Australian aboriginal populations).

3. Processes making for limitation of fluctuations arise from within the ecosystem of a fixed capacity. These control processes are known as 'density-dependent' processes.

4. External and abnormal events may drastically upset the equilibrium but are not concerned in bringing about stability.

5. Any given ecosystem possesses an 'optimum' (Elton 1941, p. 118) around which control processes tend to act, though the optimum is not always achieved.

These principles may be applied to human societies, though only with caution because of their obvious peculiarities. First, the agencies of human population control are not only biological but cultural, and while the latter often operate quite deliberately, in traditional societies they may be so subtly woven into institutionalized behaviour as to act as impersonally as biological forces. Secondly, the capacity of the system becomes progressively more capable of expansion, and in the recent period this has allowed a continuous increase in numbers without approach to equilibrium.

Density-dependent control processes fall into two categories—the 'concurrent' and the 'inverse'. The 'concurrent' processes act in the same sense as the change in population density. As the density increases the agencies making for limitation become increasingly effective; conversely, as density falls these controls progressively relax. These processes show themselves, as density increases, in the intensification of competition for supply factors, for food, water, fuel, and raw materials, for space and shelter; also, as density increases, there may be deterioration and contamination of the environment, leading to a more frequent outbreak of disease and its quicker spread by direct contact and by pollution of air and food, water, and utensils. As numbers fall the intensity of action of all these limiting agencies falls concurrently.

Opposed to these processes are the 'inverse' density-dependent factors. With these the intensity of limiting action weakens as density increases, and rises as the density decreases. As the population grows it may become more effective in its exploitation of the environment, particularly in its food-getting activities. There may be better co-operation in hunting or fishing, in land-clearing and irrigation, building of shelters, and so on. The more populous community can make better arrangements for mutual protection and offensive action against other groups and animals. One may well add that the store of genetic variability is increased. As density decreases these advantages will become less in evidence and the sparse community will be more exposed to competition from without, and will be able to draw less on close-knit co-operative measures.

In the animal kingdom these natural control processes, acting in opposed directions, appear to be capable of confining population change within the narrow limits compatible with continued survival in a given ecosystem. Evidence in favour of relatively stable human ecosystems in non-industrialized societies comes from the following sources.

1. The highly conservative nature of the technology in a given habitat over long periods of time is revealed in the archaeological record (Childe and G. Clark). The Stone Ages (or Stages) exhibit such unchanging cultures as to justify Childe's remark 'in so far as the adjustment achieved (to the environment) is successful, the community will tend to become conservative'. Indeed, the abruptness of change in the archaeological record often points to the incursion of new and culturally distinct invaders.

2. The ethnographic evidence illustrates the conservatism of contemporary simple societies (Forde); e.g. amongst the Australian Aranda sacred ceremonies and traditions were subject to the most scrupulous scrutiny and transgressors were severely punished. Economic activities are carried out to strict rules, and the routine of the working day can often be seen, in detail, to represent the outcome of long trial and error. The strict observance of territorial limits in tribal society points strongly to a stable population, since resources will remain substantially unchanged.

3. Simple food-producing economies are almost completely dependent on local resources. The close balance achieved over the year between food production and needs has already been described in some detail in the case of peasant communities. Population stability is imposed by the inflexibility of the ecosystem. Collecting and hunting may use up nearly all the available work energy allowance of 6278–8371 kJ per head per day since this is the cost of moving about continuously. One can calculate that a population density of about one head per square mile is to be expected in these ecosystems. The change to agriculture will at first allow a denser population, but does not at the outset necessarily mean that a significant social surplus can be accumulated. It may take

as much energy to obtain food from 1·2 ha per year per person as from the 200 ha of the hunting economy. The density of the horticultural population can therefore reach an equilibrium as high as 100 persons per square mile or more.

4. Direct evidence on population changes in simple societies is scanty. Indeed, the appropriate survival statistics are often inadequate even for advanced literate societies. Figures for crude birth- and death-rates are not sufficient for the calculation of replacement. The most relevant information is that on the rate of production of daughters by mothers. An approximate approach to this is afforded by an estimate of 'total fertility' (C. Clark 1958). This is defined as the number of children born to an average woman by the end of her reproductive life. In circumstances favourable to reproduction (every woman marrying young, surplus males waiting to re-marry widows) and assuming the onset of infertility 20 years after marriage, the total fertility should be about 8. This implies the birth of a child for every $2\frac{1}{2}$ years of married life and allows for some miscarriages and some temporary sterility during marriage. In conditions of high mortality with few surviving to the age of 40 years, a total fertility of 6–8 will only just suffice to maintain the population (C. Clark). In simple societies the total fertility is frequently below 6 (Table 29.2). If such communities maintain themselves for long periods it follows that mortality is not so high as to require a replacement rate based on a total fertility of 6–8 and that effective

TABLE 29.2

*Total fertility (number of children born per mother)*

| | |
|---|---|
| *Food-gatherers and single hunters* | |
| Australians: Western | 4–6 |
|            Central | 5 |
| Tierra del Fuego Islanders | 4 |
| *Hunters* | |
| Eskimos: Greenland | 3–4 |
| North American Indians: Nootka | 3 |
|                      Chinook | 3 |
|                      Omaha | 4–6 |
| *Simple agriculturalists* | |
| Orang Kibu of Sumatra | 4 |
| Ainus | 3–4 |
| *Advanced agriculturalists* | |
| Bantu | nearly 6 |
| Nigerians | 4·3 |
| Indians | probably 6–8 |
| Chinese | probably 6–8 |
| *Peoples of developing regions* (Population Council 1965) | |
| (Africa, South West and South East Asia) | 5·1–7·0 |
| *Peoples of developed regions* (Population Council 1965) | |
| North America | 3·7 |
| Central, Northern, and Western Europe | 2·7 |
| USSR | 2·9 |

(From Carr-Saunders 1922.)

restriction on birth is taking place. This appears to be the usual state of affairs in food-gathering, hunting, and simple horticultural societies (see below). Of the 4 or 5 actually born only about 2 or 3 reach maturity and the existence of this small family size has been abundantly documented (Carr-Saunders). In denser agricultural communities, however, higher mortality would seem to have prevailed, and in these the evidence suggests a total fertility of a higher order, population stability requiring a total fertility of 6–8.

*Control processes*

In societies of limited resources and conservative technique, the strength of human fecundity is such that resources would in the long run inevitably be overwhelmed. If, in fact, steadiness of numbers is achieved control processes operating to maintain stability should be identifiable.

The Malthusian view is that these curbs are inevitably starvation, epidemics, and war. Malthus postulated that, whereas the population grew at a geometric rate, food resources increased only arithmetically. Malthus advocated 'moral restraint', i.e. postponement of marriage until it was too late to have large families.

Some population theorists (e.g. Hawley 1950), however, are completely Malthusian in their analysis of population dynamics of simple societies. According to Hawley population size

tends to vary directly with fluctuation in the available supply of subsistence materials. ... In these circumstances population problems must be resolved within the local area, since isolation limits the opportunity of securing assistance from without. ... A simple technology exposes a population to the effects of radical environmental fluctuations. It has but a nominal protection against variations in climate such as drought, flood and shortening of the growing season, invasions by pests and predators on the food supply, and other untoward events in the habitat. The local physical and biotic environment is thus for the group with a stable organisation a highly variable factor. ...

The adjustment of population size to changes in the supply of sustenance materials occurs automatically, for the most part, through variations in the death rate. Mortality rises steeply in years of adversity and falls just as abruptly in periods of plenty. Although data on vital phenomena in isolated groups are very fragmentary, the death rate for a given population seems to range about an average annual figure of approximately 40 per 1000. Rates of more than 100 per 1000 have been known to occur, as have also rates of less than 25 per 1000. In general, however, isolated populations live close to the brink of catastrophe at all times. That is indicated by their high average death rates and life expectancies of about 30 years or less. The margin of safety is sometimes so small that a decline of but a few inches in the annual rainfall or the loss of a few days from the normal growing season is sufficient to produce widespread suffering and loss of life.

The conclusion would appear to be that in these conditions there must be a high turnover both in the birth-rate and the death-rate.

Population pressure on resources tends to be maintained by a continuously high rate of reproduction. The women of an isolated group are almost constantly pregnant, though both the prenatal and postnatal losses are so great that relatively few progeny reach adulthood. Nevertheless, the wellspring of life is such that there is always a potential population ready to absorb whatever margin of excess food a good crop year may produce. Unless its numbers have been too thoroughly decimated, a group therefore may quickly recover the losses suffered during a period of shortage. . . . [Hawley]

The view that most demographers take of the population characters of simple societies is that (like many animal societies) stability of numbers is in fact aimed at and more or less achieved.

There is, I think, ample evidence to show that in the long centuries of so-called tribal society men acquired a vague but adequate appreciation of the relation between their terrain, their customary food standards, and the size of their population. Droughts, dessications and inundations they could not, of course, entirely foresee; but they allowed, where they could, for the inevitable 'hungry seasons'. They tended to limit the growth of numbers by such crude but effective checks as abortion, infanticide, perpetual widowhood, and taboos upon cohabitation over certain seasons. Accidents, pests and disease took their occasional toll. But, in general, licensed infanticide, abortion and taboo provided an all too human means of controlling the growth of population. [Le Gros Clark, *The Malthusian heritage*, p. 17.]

Elimination by mortality in primitive society must often represent a true density-dependent regulatory process, brought about, directly or indirectly, from overpopulation tendencies. It is the suckling and the infant who are particularly vulnerable to the effects of overcrowding and insanitary living conditions. They are apt to be neglected when the women are called upon to work, and they are obviously more sensitive, especially at the weaning period, to the consequences of such neglect than are older children. The lack of nursing care, owing to the incessant demand for labour, also acts as an inverse density-dependent factor, and indeed, when the able-bodied fall ill the food-getting activities suffer. Thus the aged and infirm become competitors for rather than suppliers of food and suffer the results of deprivation.

Population growth must thus be understood as a balance between the three demographic processes—fertility, mortality, and migration (for a good discussion see Nag 1973). The evidence for small-scale migration as in the local fission of a simple agricultural community and of large-scale displacement—both to be distinguished from slash-and-burn movement—is well documented.

As argued by Carr-Saunders, population growth, if it is not to overwhelm the resources of the community, necessarily requires deliberate and social practices of control, and this control (taken with that exerted by natural causes) will be exercised so as to maintain an 'optimum' density, i.e. at a standard of living (or survival at a given standard) appropriate to the technology and resources of the particular community.

The 'optimum' theory can be regarded as illustrating for human ecosystems the processes of 'natural' regulation operating through opposing density-dependent control factors. On the one hand, there is the tendency of population growth to raise real income of services and commodities per head; on the other, there is a tendency to diminishing returns in that 'with a given volume of natural resources and [capital] equipment and a given state of technique, any increase in the numbers of the working population means that the amount of other factors of production [e.g. land] becomes smaller and output per head will tend to fall.' The resultant of these opposing forces will be that 'at any given time ... knowledge and circumstances remaining the same, there is what may be called a point of maximum return, when the amount of labour is such that both an increase and decrease in it would diminish proportionate returns.'

Technical improvement will allow a new 'optimum' to be attained but effective action may require a choice between alternatives, perhaps with a period when over-population is not avoided. A good example is that of wet-rice cultivation. Extension and development of an already-existing irrigation system may be more profitable than to construct new waterways. In the long run no further progress may be possible and quite new solutions must be sought. This idea of steady numbers in simple societies kept near an optimum, but threatened by the pressure of fecundity implies the existence of social measures of control and represent a very different situation from the passive Malthusian condition. An example of such 'social' regulation is provided by the exigencies of Australian and other food-gathering communities, where the nomadic search for food and water and the mother's difficulty in carrying more than one child over long distances and keeping up with the group, means that the newborn are on occasion killed or abandoned. In an agricultural economy the size of population is not haphazard and tends to be governed by the work-load peaks which come in the planting and harvesting seasons. There must be enough workers to complete these activities in a short space of time. Throughout the remainder of the year there is often underemployment and, when food supplies dwindle (see

TABLE 29.3

*Population regulatory measures (number of instances in tribes)*

($+$ = recorded instances; $-$ = no recorded instances)

|  | Infanticide | Abortion | Restriction on intercourse |
|---|---|---|---|
| *Food-collectors and hunters* | | | |
| Australian tribesmen | + | + | − |
| Tasmanians | + | + | − |
| Bushmen | + | − | − |
| American Indians | + | + | + |
| Eskimos | + | + | − |
| *Agriculturalists* | | | |
| American Indians | + | + | + |
| Africans | + | + | + |
| Oceanians | + | + | + |

above), over-population. Nevertheless, the population density is such as to allow an overall equilibrium for the year.

Some of the evidence of deliberate regulatory measures, collected by Carr-Saunders, is summarized in Table 29.3.

Many less drastic measures are in vogue in simpler communities, e.g. postponement of marriage by various institutionalized procedures. Interestingly enough, consummation of marriage below the age of 17 years tends in the long run to reduce rather than increase total fertility, according to the Indian evidence (C. Clark). There is also evidence that fertility is not fully attained for a year or so after menstruation (Montagu). Prolonged lactation can postpone conception for up to a year. In some societies there is also abstinence from sexual intercourse during the post-partum period. *Coitus interruptus* has been and continues to be widely practised, and abstinence and the rhythm method were responsible for the initial reductions of fertility in western societies, a reduction now mainly sustained by mechanical and chemical contraceptives.

It is possible that the intensity of social control needed may often be less than Carr-Saunders indicated, since, apart from the high infantile mortality rate, there may well be biological factors making for some degree of infertility. Chronic illness may be such a factor—malaria, hookworm, and venereal disease. A poor diet, and especially the seasonal hunger period, may perhaps act in reducing the viability of the unborn.

Instances of surprisingly low fertility rates have also been reported, the low fertility owing apparently little if anything to deliberate interference and, indeed, appearing not as a uniformly low level but affecting strongly a proportion of the females. The reason for this may lie in venereal disease, but it is not necessarily so. It has been suggested (Goodhart 1956) that a true genetic selection for low fertility has taken place in the long-established simpler societies and that a balance between high and low fertility lines exists; a woman with few offspring is not at a disadvantage in a food-gathering or hunting group. This balance would change in favour of the high fertility lines where conditions of high mortality prevail as in dense peasant communities where spread of disease becomes serious and where the demands of agriculture require large working families. The hypothesis of 'genetic' control rather than 'environmental' (Malthusian) or social (as in the 'optimum' theory) requires more evidence.

Increasing numbers are often thought of as the normal feature of human society whereas in fact numbers throughout human history as a whole have been stationary. In accordance with the 'optimum' theory, when social organization becomes elaborate and skill increases, the desirable number frequently changes, becoming much larger as has been the case in the modern period. 'In the past the solution [to the human population problem] has been unconsciously or semi-consciously achieved; it has now come within the power of mankind—deliberately to decide what the best solution may be!' (Carr-Saunders).

*Ecological indexes*

The welfare or standard of living of a human community consistent with its survival depends on the way in which the community attains its equilibrium in its particular ecological setting. Equilibrium may be purchased at the cost of a high overall mortality or a high liability to particular disease, of unremitting work, of much minor ill health, or of physical discomfort. One could therefore employ many different criteria, demographic, nutritional, the state of bodily fitness, the energy, or the money income available per head of population. Two demographic indexes deserve special mention in the anthropological context— infantile mortality and longevity.

*Infantile mortality*

As an index of ecological control the infantile mortality rate (death-rate in the first year of life per 1000 live births) is especially significant since it reflects many of the community's hazards and inefficiencies—malnutrition, overcrowding, insanitation, ignorance. It is a particularly sensitive index, since reduction in the infantile death-rate does not necessarily follow the decline of deaths at older ages. In the UK at the end of the nineteenth century the rate was still high (150 per 1000 live births), but mortality in late childhood and middle age had decreased steadily throughout the century. Dietary and socio-economic standards are clearly reflected in the infant mortality rate as shown in Table 29.4. In simple societies the rate is invariably high and, as

TABLE 29.4

*Vital statistics (1938) (approximate)*

| | Percentage of energy intake in potatoes and cereals | Average expectation of life in years | | Infant mortality rate per 1000 live births |
|---|---|---|---|---|
| | | Males | Females | |
| Australia | | 63·5 | 67·1 | 38 |
| New Zealand | | 65·0 | 67·9 | 50 |
| USA (Whites) | 30–39 | 60·6 | 64·5 | 51 |
| Canada | | 59·0 | 60·7 | 63 |
| UK | | 60·2 | 64·4 | 55 |
| Norway | | 61·0 | 63·8 | 37 |
| Germany | 40–49 | 59·9 | 62·8 | 60 |
| Netherlands | | 65·1 | 66·4 | 37 |
| Hungary | | 48·3 | 51·3 | 131 |
| Czechoslovakia | 50–59 | 51·9 | 55·2 | 121 |
| Belgium | | 56·0 | 59·8 | 73 |
| France | | 54·3 | 59·0 | 66 |
| Bulgaria | | 45·9 | 46·6 | 144 |
| Poland | 70–79 | 48·2 | 51·4 | 140 |
| Japan | | 46·9 | 49·6 | 114 |
| India | 80–89 | 26·9 | 26·6 | 167 |

already mentioned, this may serve as an important agency of control of population levels in ecosystems of limited capacity.

*Expectation of life*

Estimates of the age of death have been made for human communities of the Upper Pleistocene and later prehistoric times by means of (1) the state of tooth eruption, (2) the stage of ossification of the small wrist bones, (3) the degree of union of the epiphyses, and (4) the degree of closure of the cranial sutures. It is possible to group skeletal remains into 4 or 5 age-categories: childhood (0–12/13 years), youth or adolescence (12/13–21 years), adults (21–40 years), mature or middle-aged (40–59 years), and aged (60+ years). Approximate as these estimates are they show that for most of the period of man's existence the age at death was very much earlier than it has become in recent times in conditions of western civilization. Survival beyond the age of 40 years was the lot of not more than about 10 per cent of the population, and about only half lived beyond the age of 20. According to Vallois, only one of some 40 known Neanderthal individuals passed the age of 50 years, of some 76 Upper Palaeolithic Eurasiatic *Homo sapiens* only 2 did so, of 65 Mesolithic individuals also only 2; amongst 94 Silesian Neolithic skeletons, only 4 were over 50 years old. Mortality of this order seems characteristic also of food-gathering, hunting, and horticultural communities of recent and present times. For the Indian Knoll people, a pre-agricultural tribe of the Indian settled community of Pecos, deaths before the age of 21 years are 57 per cent. The figure is of the same order for Early Greek times. Sub-adult deaths seem generally high amongst the Plains Indians (Mohave 43 per cent, Dakota 65 per cent, Seminole 44 per cent). The few figures available for Africa are similar.

Exceptions to this high mortality are on record: e.g. about 20 per cent of Guanche skulls are reported as over 50 years and in Melanesia (New Ireland) over 75 per cent of those born survived until marriage.

A very gradual increase in longevity during early civilization is suggested in a study by Angel (1940) of a series of Greek skulls which cover a long period of time. The increasing average age at death, as indicated in this survey, may well be related to advances in living conditions and in nutrition which are indicated in the archaeological record. In addition, the emergence of medical skills early in Greek history must have contributed to the advance in longevity over that of prehistoric times.

Longevity in Roman Egypt about 2000 years ago was studied by Karl Pearson from the ages at death recorded on mummy cases. From these data he drew a curve of expectation of life according to age, which yielded a figure of about 22 years as the expectation at birth.

The longevity in antiquity was probably somewhere between 20 and 30 years. In the Middle Ages a value of 35 years has been computed for thirteenth-century Englishmen.

There was apparently little change in average length of life during the five centuries following the period covered by Russell's study. A life-table by the astronomer Halley, based upon records for Breslau during 1687–91, gave 33·5 years as the average length of life. A figure of 35·5 years was found by Wigglesworth from death records in Massachusetts and New Hampshire for a period before 1789. The rising standard of living which was beginning to make itself felt then evidently had a beneficial effect upon longevity. According to life-tables constructed by the statistician William Farr for England and Wales, covering the period 1838–54, the average length of life had increased to 40·9 years. As medical and sanitary science developed in the remaining years of the century, the average length of human life rose to 49·2 years in the period 1900–2. In 1945 the average length of life in the USA was 65·8 years, having increased 16 years in less than 5 decades. At the present time longevity has nearly stabilized in western countries at just under 70 years.

Nevertheless, in the modern era, great differences in infantile mortality and life expectation remain. That these are to a large extent related to socio-economic circumstances is borne out in Table 29.4. The standard of living (in 1938) may be judged by the percentage of total energy contributed by carbohydrate. In general the countries with high-protein and mixed dietary are much better off in terms of these ecological indexes.

*Ecology today*

Ecology today means world ecology—world interchange—and problems of a kind not easily confined to, or resolved within, a small area. The problems are those of population pressure, the conservation of material and energy, a fairer distribution of material and energy, the disposal of radioactive and other wastes, the planning of travel on a world scale, the understanding of 'race' and the elimination of war, and of other forms of waste.

## References and suggestions for further reading

ALLISON, A. C. (1960). Abnormal haemoglobins and erythrocyte enzyme-deficiency traits. In *Genetical variations in human populations* (ed. G. A. Harrison). Pergamon, Oxford.

ANGEL, J. L. (1940). The length of life in ancient Greece. *J. Gerontol.* **2**, 18–24.

BAKER, P., and WEINER, J. S. (eds.) (1966). *The biology of human adaptability*. Clarendon Press, Oxford.

BARNICOT, N. A. (1959). Climatic factors in the evolution of human populations. *Cold Spring Harb. Symp. quant. Biol.* **24**, 115–29.

BIRDSELL, J. B. (1953). Some environmental and cultural factors influencing the structuring of Australian aboriginal populations. *Amer. Naturalist.* **87**, 171.

BLUM, H. F. (1945). The physiological effects of sunlight on man. *Physiol. Rev.* **25**, 483.

BRASS, W. (ed.) (1971). *Biological aspects of demography*. Symposium No. 10. Society for the Study of Human Biology. Taylor and Francis, London.

CANNON, W. B. (1932). *The wisdom of the body*. W. W. Norton, New York.

CARR-SAUNDERS, A. M. (1922). *The population problem: a study in human evolution*. Clarendon Press, Oxford.

CLARK, C. (1958). World population. *Nature, Lond.* **181**, 1235.

CLARK, G. (1947). *Archaeology and society*. (2nd ed) Methuen, London.

# 482 Human ecology

CLEGG, E. J., HARRISON, G. A., and BAKER, P. T. (1970). The impact of high altitudes on human population. *Human Biol.* **42**, 486–578.

CLELAND, J. B. (1928). Disease amongst the Australian aborigines. *J. trop. Med. Hyg.* **31**, 53–327.

COON, S. C., GARN, S. M., and BIRDSELL, J. B. (1950). *Races, a study of the problems of race formation in man.* Thomas, Springfield, Illinois.

DAMON, A. (ed.) (1975). *Physiological anthropology.* Oxford University Press, New York and London.

DAVENPORT, C. B. (1945). The dietaries of primitive peoples. *Amer. J. phys. Anthrop.* **47**, 60–82.

EDHOLM, O. G. (1967). *The biology of work.* Weidenfeld and Nicolson, London.

ELTON, C. (1949). *Animal ecology.* Sidgwick and Jackson, London.

FORDE, C. D. (1949). *Habitat, economy and society.* Methuen, London.

FOX, R. H. (1953). *A study of energy expenditure of Africans engaged in various rural activities.* Ph.D. thesis, University of London.

GARLICK, J. P., and KEAY, R. W. J. (eds.) (1975). *Human ecology in the tropics.* Symposium No. 16. Society for the Study of Human Biology. Taylor and Francis, London.

GARN, S. M. (1961). *Human races.* Thomas, Springfield, Illinois.

GOODHART, C. B. (1956). World population growth and its regulation by natural means. *Nature, Lond.* **178**, 561–5.

HARRISON, G. A., and WALSH, R. J. (eds.) (1974). A discussion on human adaptability in a tropical ecosystem. An I.B.P. investigation of two New Guinea communities. *Phil. Trans. Roy. Soc. B.* **268**, 221–400.

HAWLEY, A. H. (1950). *Human ecology: a theory of community structure.* The Ronald Press, New York.

JAMES, PRESTON E. (1959). A geography of man. (2nd ed). Ginn, London.

KATZ, S. H. (ed.) (1947). *Biological anthropology,* readings from *Scientific American,* W. H. Freeman.

LEE, D. H. K. (1951). Thoughts on housing for the humid tropics. *Geog. Rev.* **41**, 124–47.

MILLER, AUSTIN A. (1946). *Climatology* (4th ed). Methuen, London.

MONI, N. (1973). Anthropology and population. *Pop. Studies.* **27**, 59–68.

MONTAGU, ASHLEY M. F. (1946). *Adolescent sterility.* Thomas, Springfield, Illinois.

MOTULSKY, A. G. (1958). Metabolic polymorphisms and the role of infectious diseases in human evolution. *Human Biol.* **30**, 43–72.

NEWBURGH, L. H. (ed.) (1949). *Physiology of heat regulation and the science of clothing.* Saunders, Philadelphia.

NICHOLSON, A. J. (1933). The balance of animal populations. *J. Anim. Ecol.* **2**, 132–78.

PASSMORE, R., and DURNIN, J. V. G. (1955). Human energy expenditure. *Physiol. Rev. 35*, 801–39.

PLATT, B. S. (1946). The colonial nutrition problem. *Proc. Nutr. Soc.* **5**, 1–17.

PUGH, L. G. C. E. (1965). High altitudes. Chapter 9 in *The physiology of human survival.* (eds. O. G. Edholm and A. L. Bacharach). Academic Press, London.

RICHARDS, A. I. (1932). *Hunger and work in a savage tribe.* George Routledge, London.

ROBERTS, D. F. (1953). Body weight, race and climate. *Amer. J. phys. Anthrop.* **11**, 533–58.

ROBINSON, S. (1942). The effect of body size upon energy exchanges in work. *Amer. J. Physiol.* **136**, 363.

SCHREIDER, E. (1951). Race, constitution, thermolyse. *Revue scient. Paris.* **89**, 110–19.

SEARS, P. B. (1959). The ecology of man. *Smithsonian Report for 1958,* pp. 375–98.

SINCLAIR, H. M. (1953). The diet of Canadian Indians and Eskimos. *Proc. Nutr. Soc.* **12**, 69.

SOLOMON, M. E. (1949). The natural control of animal populations. *J. Anim. Ecol.* **18**, 1–35.

WEINER, J. S. (1973). *The natural history of man.* Anchor Books, Doubleday.

WEINER, J. S. (ed.) (1976). *Physiological variability and its genetic basis.* Symposium No. ???
Society for the Study of Human Biology. Taylor and Francis, London.

WULSIN, F. R. (1949). Adaptations to climate among non-European peoples. In *Physiology
of heat regulation and the science of clothing.* (ed. L. H. Newburgh). Saunders, Philadelphia.

WYNDHAM, C. H. *et al.* (1964). Heat reactions of Caucasians and Bantu in South Africa.
*J. Appl. Physiology. 19,* 598–606.

YOUNG, J. Z. (1971). *An introduction to the study of man.* Clarendon Press, Oxford.

# Author Index

# Subject Index